CRUCIBLE OF POWER

CRUCIBLE OF POWER

A History of American Foreign Relations from 1945

HOWARD JONES

ROWMAN & LITTLEFIELD PUBLISHERS, INC.
Lanham • Boulder • New York • Toronto • Plymouth, UK

ROWMAN & LITTLEFIELD PUBLISHERS, INC.

Published in the United States of America
by Rowman & Littlefield Publishers, Inc.
A wholly owned subsidiary of The Rowman & Littlefield Publishing Group, Inc.
4501 Forbes Boulevard, Suite 200, Lanham, Maryland 20706
www.rowmanlittlefield.com

Estover Road
Plymouth PL6 7PY
United Kingdom

British Library Cataloguing in Publication Information Available

Library of Congress Cataloging-in-Publication Data

Jones, Howard, 1940–
    Crucible of power : a history of American foreign relations from 1945 /
Howard Jones.
        p. cm.
    Includes bibliographical references and index.
    ISBN-13: 978-0-7425-6453-4 (cloth : alk. paper)
    ISBN-10: 0-7425-6453-3 (cloth : alk. paper)
    ISBN-13: 978-0-7425-6454-1 (pbk. : alk. paper)
    ISBN-10: 0-7425-6454-1 (pbk. : alk. paper)
    eISBN-13: 978-0-7425-6455-8
    eISBN-10: 0-7425-6455-X
    1. United States—Foreign relations—1945–1989. 2. United States—
Foreign relations—1989- 3. United States—Foreign relations—
1945–1989—Decision making. 4. United States—Foreign relations—
1989—Decision making. I. Title. II. Title: History of American foreign
relations from 1945.

    E744.J6693 2008
    327.73009'04—dc22   2008036872

Printed in the United States of America

∞™ The paper used in this publication meets the minimum requirements of
American National Standard for Information Sciences—Permanence of Paper
for Printed Library Materials, ANSI/NISO Z39.48-1992.

In Memory of Howie

CONTENTS

LIST OF MAPS

ACKNOWLEDGMENTS

This book, like most publications, has benefited from the contributions of others. At this press, Niels Aaboe, Asa Johnson, and Lynn Weber were enormously helpful in the editorial process. Superb suggestions have come from both undergraduate and graduate students here at the University of Alabama as well as from numerous friends in the profession along with the anonymous readers of the manuscript. In particular, I wish to thank Carol Jackson Adams, John Belohlavek, Kinley Brauer, Susan Brewer, Becky Bruce, Douglas Brinkley, Paul C. Clark, Robert A. Divine, Robert H. Ferrell, Ryan Floyd, Andy Fry, Mark Gilderhus, Paul Grass, Mary Ann Heiss, Peter Hill, Jonathon Hooks, Richard Immerman, Tim Johnson, Tim Maga, Pete Maslowski, Stephen McCullough, Forrest and Ellen McDonald, Teresa Peebles, Charity Rakestraw, Donald A. Rakestraw, Ron Robel, Stephen Schwab, Guy Swanson, Justin Turner, Hamilton Walters, Randall B. Woods, and David Zimov for their encouragement along with many useful comments. For helping me through the countless trials and tribulations of securing the illustrations, I thank Scott Keller and Nancy Smelley. No one can write a book without the gift of time. For affording me that precious commodity, I express sincere gratitude to Kay Branyon, Loretta Colvin, Julie P. Moore, Nancy (again), and Fay Wheat.

On a more personal level, I wish to express appreciation to the most important people in my life—my family. Only these loved ones understand the time and solitude required in research and writing, and only they were willing to put up with my short temper and abrasive behavior as I attempted to make sense out of my many meaningless sentences and hopelessly tangled paragraphs. To my parents (in memory), to my spouse, best friend, and closest confidante, Mary Ann, to my daughters Deborah and Shari, to Howie, whose brief life provided lasting memories, and to the lights of my life—my grandchildren, Timothy, Ashley, and Lauren—I extend heartfelt gratitude for your patience and, most important, your love.

PREFACE

From 1945 to the present, the United States continued its quest for security by seeking to preserve its world power status against the steady rise of other nations following World War II. Presidential administrations were fairly consistent in their strategy of containing the spread of communism, although some pursued more aggressive policies than others. John F. Kennedy approved an attempt to overthrow the Fidel Castro regime in Cuba by the abortive Bay of Pigs invasion in April 1961. Soon afterward, the Cold War reached its hottest level in the Cuban missile crisis of October 1962, when Soviet leader Nikita Khrushchev sought to test the young president's mettle after the Bay of Pigs debacle and helped bring the two nations to the brink of nuclear war. In the meantime, the U.S. intervention in Vietnam grew into America's longest war, a contest understandable only within the context of the longstanding Cold War with the Soviet Union.

The Cold War ended with the Soviet collapse in 1989, but international relations soon intensified again with the onset of regional conflicts that threatened to draw in other nations. When the Berlin Wall came down, Americans claimed a victory of capitalism over communism but soon confronted a series of regional struggles in the Middle East that meshed with the 9/11 terrorist attacks on the United States in 2001, the George W. Bush administration's decision to wage a preemptive war with Iraq, another in Afghanistan, and the Global War on Terrorism. The U.S. invasion of Iraq in March 2003 led to the demise of Iraqi leader Saddam Hussein but left a power vacuum in the Middle East that Iran has sought to fill. The result is another Cold War, this one between the United States and Iran, now banded with Syria and two U.S.-labeled Islamic terrorist groups, Hamas and Hezbollah, all seeking to rid the region of Western and Israeli influence.

History, according to more than a few of its students, demonstrates the complexities of intervention, the inability of governments to shape historical events, and the necessity of cultivating and maintaining allies. The following narrative will examine whether America's postwar leaders have shown an understanding of history in formulating the nation's foreign policies.

CHAPTER 1

Cold War and Containment in Europe and the Near East, 1945–1950

Prospectus for Trouble

Even though the United States emerged from World War II as the unquestioned leader of the world, its new global stature did not automatically ensure peace and security either at home or abroad. With power came the responsibility for maintaining peace, and with global power came that same responsibility on a global scale—or so the new Harry S. Truman administration seemed to think. The wartime struggle for self-determination had combined with the collapse of the old colonial system and the widespread social, political, and economic dislocation resulting from the greatest war in history to cause internal turmoil in numerous countries and massive international disorder. The widespread havoc provided a predictable invitation to totalitarian exploitation and hence an obstacle to postwar trade, stability, and peace. The war had bequeathed a global system dangerously divided between two vastly different cultures, economies, and political ideologies—those of the United States and the Soviet Union. Contrary to the aftermath of World War I, however, the United States intended to take the lead in stimulating its own economy and establishing world order through multilateral trade, the principle of self-determination, and a vast network of foreign aid programs and military alliances.

The bipolar power structure of the postwar world soon contributed to Americans' belief that nearly every international problem emanated from the Soviet Union. Distrust between the superpowers received impetus from the clashing ideologies of capitalism and communism. Each nation constructed exaggerated images of the other's military strength until each rival perceived the other as omnipresent and omnipotent (especially when both nations had atomic bomb capabilities). Perceptions became realities as opposing ideologies took on moral and spiritual overtones, leaving no room for compromise.

In this increasingly tense atmosphere, it is doubtful that any leaders of state could have convinced their counterparts that a push for security did not necessarily entail imperialist aggression. Some members of the Truman administration were aware of the Soviets' traditional drive westward and admitted to their postwar need for security along borders fronting Poland and much of the rest of Eastern Europe. But few were willing to retreat on the idealistic promises of the Atlantic Charter and Yalta Declaration because, in short, the establishment of such ideals translated into

1

President Harry S. Truman
Among the foreign policy decisions of his administration were the Truman Doctrine, the Marshall Plan, the Berlin airlift, NATO, Point Four, and the Korean War. *(Library of Congress, Washington, D.C.)*

realistic contributions to the security of the United States. At the same time, Soviet leader Joseph Stalin was more a realist concerned about personal and national security than he was an ideologue committed to worldwide Communist revolution, and he refused to endanger his homeland in the name of self-determination. The Soviet Union had undergone numerous invasions along its sprawling western frontier. Because "friendly neighbors" (i.e., Communist governments) were unlikely to emerge from democratic elections, he exploited local Communist movements when it was to his advantage. In two instances, however, Stalin permitted elections—in Czechoslovakia and Hungary—but only out of uncertainty about what the United States would do regarding Eastern Europe. When the White House showed no inclination to guarantee the Yalta Declaration, the chances for more elections came to an end. By 1947, the intensification of these and other conflicting interests had taken on the appellation of the "Cold War."

Fear of Soviet Communist aggression stimulated U.S. political and military intervention in postwar Europe and the Near East. Somehow the United States had to help restore economic, political, and military order in Europe, even if these objectives entailed a break with its long-standing opposition to political and military involvement on the continent. The advent of the atomic bomb had dictated actions and counteractions short of outright war, but it had also created a mind-bending paradox: the United States possessed the most powerful weapon in the world, yet the sheer destructive power of that very bomb prohibited its use except in matters directly threatening the United States.

And therein lay the problem, according to White House advisers: the Soviets were not equipped for full-scale aggression in the immediate postwar period and consequently engaged in indirect tactics that a *New York Times* correspondent called "a new kind of war." Although possessing extensive ground forces in

Eastern Europe and Germany, the Soviets lacked a strong navy and air force, did not have atomic weapons, and were reeling from crippling economic and population losses in the war. The Soviets, therefore, resorted to any means short of all-out war in achieving postwar objectives. Infiltration of a country through subversive methods and the use of its people as proxies became the hallmarks of Soviet expansion, whether for security or aggression. The primary goal was to safeguard Soviet borders, a move the West interpreted as territorial aggressions similar to those of the 1930s. The Soviets, hurt so badly by World War II, undoubtedly wanted security above all else, even though Americans believed that Stalin's support of the Communist-led Lublin government in Poland constituted the first step in a well-organized plan of conquest. The Communists sought imperial expansion, according to Americans long reared in anti-Soviet feeling and fearful of the conspiratorial and revolutionary nature of Communist ideology. President Truman noted in 1947 that "there isn't any difference in totalitarian states. I don't care what you call them, Nazi, Communist, or Fascist."

Postwar tension mounted most immediately in Eastern Europe, but the center point of East–West rivalry was always Germany. Like the period following World War I, Germany had lost on the battlefield but paradoxically loomed as the most powerful country in Europe in terms of human and material resources. The Soviets, of course, remained determined to strip Germany of all power, and joining them were the French, who likewise feared another resurgence of their longtime hated neighbor. The British, however, recognized the importance of maintaining a formidable (though controlled) German presence on the continent to counter the Soviets, and they found a ready ally in the United States. Germany, located at the very crossroads of East and West in Europe, became both the symbolic and the real hot spot of the Cold War.

The rapid postwar demobilization of U.S. military forces proved a vital determinant in the nation's foreign policy. Overseas troops received orders to return home soon after the fighting ended in Europe, leaving a power vacuum that Washington's policymakers feared the Soviets would fill. Americans believed that wars ended when the firing ceased, not realizing that power balances often shift as the victors tie up the loose ends of a conflict. But Americans in 1945 were in no mood for further overseas commitments. The Great Depression followed by war had sapped their willingness to sacrifice, and foreign affairs no longer had priority. The nation sought demobilization and reconversion of the economy to peacetime production. The military was severely weakened by a policy that granted the hurried discharge of soldiers through a point system based on length of service because it meant that battle-seasoned veterans went home first. In an address at the Pentagon in 1950, General George C. Marshall recalled the military problems facing the nation during the Cold War 1940s:

> I remember, when I was Secretary of State, I was being pressed constantly, particularly when in Moscow, by radio message after radio message to give the Russians hell. . . . When I got back, I was getting the same appeal in relation to the Far East and China. At that time, my facilities for giving them hell—and I am a soldier and know something about the ability to give hell—was 1½ divisions over the entire United States. That is quite a proposition when you deal with somebody with over 260.

For several reasons, the Truman administration feared that Americans, as during the late 1920s, would reject a leadership role in international affairs after World War II. Such an inner-directed policy at first appeared feasible. President Franklin D. Roosevelt had left the foundations of a United Nations organization to keep the peace, and the United States held military predominance in the world, primarily because of the bomb. Prosperity born of war would surely combine with superior economic resources to enable the country to surge far ahead of others. Moreover, to some observers at least, the Soviets seemed to have changed. General Dwight D. Eisenhower had noted after visiting Moscow that "nothing guides Russian policy so much as a desire for friendship with the United States." Yet, ironically, diplomats possessed little leverage because of the sheer destructive magnitude of the bomb. What events could so directly threaten U.S. security to justify use of the bomb? Soviet–American tension was unavoidable because of differing ideologies, cultures, and definitions of security, but leaders of both nations realized that tension must never lead to war. A fine line wound its way between toughness and aggression, between security and expansion. These perilous times demanded careful leadership because the international climate of distrust made any words susceptible to misinterpretation and any events open to misperception.

The postwar world situation almost inevitably led the United States into adopting a form of economic diplomacy that gradually became military in thrust. As in the 1920s and 1930s, U.S. leaders argued that international trade was vital to the maintenance of world peace, the spread of democratic institutions, and the prevention of another postwar depression through the growth of capitalism. Truman made his position clear when he declared that "the three—peace, freedom, and world trade—are inseparable." Americans would prosper, of course, from an economically open world, but such a system would benefit others too. Yet the chief snag was that war-devastated Europeans lacked the means to buy U.S. goods. The path to peace therefore seemed to lie in an ambitious foreign aid program. By 1950, however, U.S. involvement in European and Near Eastern affairs above the Mediterranean Sea had become so military in nature that almost every action widened the division between East and West and thereby intensified the Cold War.

Onset of the Cold War

The first real sign of impending Soviet–American postwar difficulties arose at a late 1945 series of Council of Foreign Ministers' meetings. From September through October, the ministers met in London to draw up peace treaties with Italy and the other former Axis states of Romania, Bulgaria, Hungary, and Finland. Despite an agenda that related only to European matters, Soviet Foreign Commissar Vyacheslav Molotov repeatedly protested against the independent postwar occupation of Japan by the United States (discussed in the next chapter). He also wanted Italy to award the Soviet Union some territory in the Mediterranean and $100 million in reparations. American Secretary of State James F. Byrnes joined the British in opposing Soviet advances into the Mediterranean and in arguing that Italy's war-ravaged economy could not permit huge reparations. He also rejected any peace terms with Romania and Bulgaria that did not require the establishment of democratic governments. Molotov refused to give such assurances, defending his stance by pointing to the dominance of Britain in Greece and the United States in Japan. At one point during the proceedings, Molotov asked Byrnes if he had "an atomic bomb in his side pocket." The South Carolinian wittily replied, "You don't know Southerners. We carry our artillery in our hip pocket. If you don't cut out all this stalling and let us get down to work, I am going to pull an atomic bomb out of my hip pocket and let you have it." Molotov and the interpreter laughed, although Byrnes's remark suggested the Truman administration's keen awareness of the diplomatic advantages afforded by the bomb. The conference adjourned in deadlock.

The following December 1945, at the Moscow Conference of Foreign Ministers, Soviet attitudes appeared to have softened. Byrnes agreed to recognize the Soviet-controlled Romanian and Bulgarian governments and to recommend an Allied Control

Council for Japan; Stalin accepted a more broadly based representation in Romania and Bulgaria, promised to attend a peace conference in Paris in 1946, and consented to cooperate in the establishment of a program of international atomic supervision. The atmosphere in Moscow was less tense than it had been in London, but the Soviets' aggressive behavior had already made a distinct impression on Truman. Although he had earlier tried to mediate between growing British and Soviet animosities, he now sharply rebuked what he called Byrnes's "appeasement policy" and asserted that the secretary had "lost his nerve in Moscow." In January 1946, Truman disgustedly wrote Byrnes that he was "tired of babying the Soviets."

By early 1946, the nation's attitude toward the Soviet Union had stiffened. Secretary of the Navy James V. Forrestal opposed any attempt to "buy understanding and sympathy" from the Soviets. "We tried that once with Hitler," he caustically remarked. Republican Senator Arthur Vandenberg of Michigan (an isolationist until Pearl Harbor) encouraged the administration to adopt a harder line toward the Soviets and recalled what happened when the West gave in to aggressors during the 1930s. In February 1946, Americans learned that a spy ring in Canada had relayed information on atomic research to the Soviet Union. Armed with the atomic bomb, the Soviets appeared to be capable of anything.

Problems in Iran suggested the ominous direction of international affairs and soon emerged as the first major issue for the newly established UN organization. An Anglo–Soviet agreement in 1942 had approved the wartime occupation of Iran, with the stipulation that each force withdraw six months after the fighting ended. In the meantime, the British retained their virtual monopoly on Iranian oil production and marketing that they had held since the beginning of the century, whereas a U.S. firm had secured a small concession in 1944 and prompted the Soviets to seek the same. When a Communist-inspired revolution broke out late the following year in the northern province of Azerbaijan, the Moscow government sent arms and troops to aid the rebels.

Iran worked with the United States in bringing the matter before the United Nations, which was then meeting in London. The Security Council turned the issue over to the Soviets and Iranians to negotiate. The Soviets demanded the permanent installation of their troops in Iran, control of a proposed oil company, and rights for the Communist Tudeh Party in Azerbaijan. Iran rejected every term. When the deadline for the Soviets' withdrawal came and passed in March 1946, the West became alarmed that both countries had enlarged their armies and had brought in additional heavy military goods.

Yet neither the Soviets nor their cohort made any attempt to overthrow the Iranian government, probably because of U.S. opposition and the worldwide hostility toward the Kremlin's actions. The Soviets pulled out of Iran in May after securing certain rights for the Tudeh in Azerbaijan and gaining the assurance of oil concessions if the Iranian legislature approved (which never materialized). The following December, the United States sent aid to Iran that helped to put down the unrest in Azerbaijan. Although the Soviets did not intervene, the Truman administration recognized that East–West rivalries in the Near East, as well as in Eastern Europe, could escalate tensions to a dangerous level.

In the midst of the Iranian troubles, heated rhetorical exchanges brought greater focus to the growing impasse between East and West. Stalin delivered a spirited speech praising Leninist doctrine and denouncing the West. In it he argued that a clash between communism and capitalism was inevitable and necessitated a massive Soviet military buildup. Emphasis would be on internal development through a series of five-year plans and not on the international economic proposals worked out at Bretton Woods in 1944. Although he probably intended this speech only for domestic consumption, Americans considered it the prelude to a new wave of Soviet aggression. Indeed, Moscow's leaders began to tighten controls in Eastern Europe and at home launched a bitter propaganda campaign against the United States and the West.

Less than two weeks later, on February 22, 1946, the American chargé in Moscow, George F. Kennan, sent his home office the famous "long telegram," an 8,000-word, sixteen-page response to the State Department's request for an analysis of Stalin's fiery speech. Kennan was a career diplomat who had been educated at Princeton and trained in the Foreign Service as one of the first Americans assigned to observe the Soviets from Riga in Latvia. He was also a member of the first U.S. embassy in Moscow when William Bullitt began his nightmarish three-year stint as ambassador in 1933. For more than a decade, Kennan remained in the Soviet Union and Eastern Europe, developing a warm feeling for the Soviet people while enriching his scholarly interest in nineteenth-century Russian literature. But he strongly detested the revolutionary principles of the Bolshevik Revolution and the bloody Stalinist purges of the 1930s—which he had seen firsthand.

Neither friendship nor war with the Soviets was conceivable, Kennan insisted in early 1946. The Soviets had a "neurotic" view of the world and were "committed fanatically to the belief that with [the] U.S. there can be no permanent modus vivendi." Their fear of

George F. Kennan
As chargé in Moscow in 1946, he wrote the "Long Telegram," and as a member of the State Department's Policy Planning Staff wrote an article in *Foreign Affairs* titled "The Sources of Soviet Conduct"—both helping to establish him as the chief architect of America's containment policy. *(Wide World Photos, New York)*

"capitalist encirclement" had now reasserted "the traditional and instinctive Russian sense of insecurity." Americans must work toward securing the industrial and economic nerve centers of Western Europe and Japan while preparing countermeasures short of war to discourage Soviet expansion. The president read the telegram as did many officials in the State Department. Its argument confirmed what they already believed.

In March, former British prime minister Winston Churchill bore witness to a certain East–West confrontation when he came to the United States and delivered a blunt warning of Soviet intentions. Before a Westminster College crowd in Fulton, Missouri, and with Truman on the dais, the august and elderly British statesman dramatically proclaimed in his gravelly voice that "from Stettin in the Baltic to Trieste in the Adriatic, an iron curtain has descended across the continent." The Soviets did not want war; they sought "the fruits of war and the indefinite expansion of their power and doctrines." The only recourse was a "fraternal association of English-speaking peoples." A *Pravda* interview with Stalin soon appeared in the *New York Times*, which carried the Soviet premier's dark assertion that Churchill's appeal for an Anglo-American alliance was a "call to war" as dangerous in its racial implications as Adolf Hitler's hate-filled speeches. Surely, Stalin declared, the European nations did not want to replace the "lordship of Hitler" with the "lordship of Churchill."

Other developments pointed to continually worsening Soviet–American relations during the spring of 1946. The Soviets had wanted a huge loan from the United States for domestic reconstruction purposes, but even though Secretary of Commerce Henry Wallace and Secretary of the Treasury Henry Morgenthau favored the financial measure as a stimulus to trade and better relations, Truman opposed the action without Soviet concessions. The former U.S. ambassador to the Soviet Union, W. Averell Harriman, had won Truman's support for foreign aid as "one of the most effective weapons at our disposal."

The president later asserted that the Soviets would have to come to the United States because "we held all the cards." The United States had offered the enticement of new negotiations regarding Eastern Europe along with the possibility of Soviet involvement in the World Bank, but the Kremlin showed no interest in either idea. The first could lead to concessions to the West, and the second would entail subordination to an organization under U.S. control. But in May, the Soviets suddenly reversed their position and expressed a willingness to discuss Eastern Europe. Their surprising message aroused considerable uncertainty within the Truman administration. The president's advisers did not believe that the Soviet Union was ready to retreat in Eastern Europe, and they realized that funds in the World Bank were too low to permit a major loan. The State Department therefore turned down the Soviet proposal and promptly ended all loan discussions. That same month, the military governor of the U.S. occupation zone in Germany, General Lucius Clay, cut off reparations from that zone to the Soviet Union until it cooperated in promoting German economic unity. The Soviets doubtless interpreted the U.S. rejection of the loan and the termination of German reparations as the first assault of a massive economic offensive by the United States.

Another major source of contention was the Truman administration's proposal for international control of atomic weaponry through the Baruch Plan. The United States, Britain, and Canada had called for an international organization to regulate atomic energy, and Truman responded by asking Undersecretary of State Dean Acheson and David Lilienthal (head of the Tennessee Valley Authority) to draw up a plan. Their proposal called for an international body to supervise both the materiel and the production process involved in developing atomic energy. In June 1946, financier Bernard Baruch, the U.S. representative on the Atomic Energy Commission (recently established by the UN General Assembly), made significant revisions

in the Acheson-Lilienthal Plan that authorized the United States to control the entire
program—including peaceful research on
atomic power *inside* the Soviet Union. Under
what became known as the Baruch Plan, an
International Atomic Development Authority
was to regulate "all atomic energy activities
potentially dangerous to world security"
through licensing and on-site inspections.
Once this agency established controls, the
United States would dispose of its atomic
stockpile and halt further production. The
United States would give up its atomic monopoly—*after* the Soviets stopped their research and permitted on-the-spot verification.
To allow the program to work, Baruch insisted on suspension of the veto in the Security Council. The choice, he declared, was
"World Peace or World Destruction."

Not surprisingly, the Soviet Union rejected
the Baruch Plan. The Kremlin could not approve a program of international atomic control monopolized by the United States, nor
could it allow internal inspection and forgo
use of the veto in such a substantive matter.
The Americans, according to the Moscow
government, should destroy their atomic
stockpile, outlaw atomic weapons, and allow
the veto to apply to atomic energy matters. After months of wrangling, the Soviet delegate
in the Security Council, Andrei Gromyko, declared that suspension of the veto would lead
to "unlimited interference" in "the economic
life of the countries on whose territories this
control would be carried out, and . . . in their
internal affairs." Proponents of the Baruch
Plan, Gromyko charged with considerable justification, "completely ignore national interests of other countries and proceed from . . .
the interests actually of one country; that is,
the United States of America."

There was little hope for international
atomic energy controls. The United States
could not surrender its monopoly on atomic
weapons because of the strength of the Red
Army, and the Soviets refused to cut back on
ground forces because of U.S. possession of
the bomb. One way out of this dilemma was

for the West to build up its land armies; the
other was for the Soviets to develop their
own atomic bomb. As for the Baruch Plan,
it was dead.

By the autumn of 1946, the Truman administration's growing hard-line approach to
Soviet affairs became increasingly evident
during the steadily escalating controversy
over Germany. The only common ground
between East and West was the belief that
Germany should exist as a nation; beyond
that, the two sides vehemently disagreed over
nearly every issue—particularly whether its
government should be democratic or Communist. After the war—and consistent with
the Potsdam reparations agreements—the
Soviets confiscated huge amounts of food-
stuffs, carried away numerous Germans for
forced labor, and dismantled and carted
home entire industrial plants and other materials from their eastern zone. The Soviets
also refused to fulfill the wartime agreements
requiring the occupation forces to send food
and supplies to the other zones, but in doing so they failed to foresee the adverse effect this move would have on their interests:
Germans outside the eastern sector turned
to the United States for assistance.

At Stuttgart in September, Secretary of
State Byrnes signaled a major change in U.S.
policy when he delivered a stirring speech that
called for partitioning Germany between East
and West. The Potsdam agreement aimed at
the economic unity of Germany was not working, he declared, and more U.S. assistance was
needed to secure the continent, restore Germany's economy, and encourage its move toward a federal system of self-government. The
Truman administration had given up on uniting the country economically and now admitted to the seemingly irrevocable partition
between East and West. Thus, a stalemate presented a better option than continued dis-
agreements that might culminate in war. The
punitive spirit so evident at Potsdam had given
way to the overriding necessities of securing
French cooperation by dropping the call for
German reunification and assuring Western

Germany and allies in Europe that the United States intended to safeguard them from Soviet communism. The U.S. and British zones should merge, Byrnes said, and the United States must stay in Europe indefinitely.

In December, Britain and the United States took a big step toward an East–West partition of Germany when they combined their occupied areas into "Bizonia." The Soviet Union charged (correctly) that such a move violated the wartime agreements by promoting the permanent partition of Germany. France feared another resurrection of its longtime enemy and refused to join the merger. Although the reaction from Paris was disturbing to the Truman administration, its chief concern was the Soviet Union. "There's no way to argue with a river," Acheson later declared about negotiating with the Soviets. "You can channel it; you can dam it up. But you can't argue with it."

The Truman administration had meanwhile asked for an in-house study of the motives behind Soviet behavior and the recommended actions by the United States. The result was a lengthy report in September 1946, prepared by presidential counsel Clark Clifford, that the president considered so explosive that he collected all copies and had them locked away. The Clifford memorandum, drawing heavily from Kennan's ideas, advised the United States to prepare for atomic and biological warfare because of Soviet aggressions driven by fear of capitalist encirclement. Moreover, these Soviet aggressions would stop only if checked by U.S. counterpressure, both military and economic. The Clifford report called on the United States to prepare for a war on all fronts. "When you are faced with that kind of crisis," Clifford declared, "you come up with whatever weapons you have—political, military, economic, psychological, whatever they might be."

Secretary of Commerce Wallace was worried that the Truman administration's hardening Soviet policies would lead to war. A former member of Roosevelt's cabinet and his vice president until January 1945, Wallace re-

mained an ardent New Deal liberal and a strong advocate of developing an economic relationship with the Soviets. In a September 1946 speech before a huge crowd of 20,000 in New York's Madison Square Garden, he insisted that "'getting tough' never brought anything real and lasting—whether for schoolyard bullies or businessmen or world powers. The tougher we get, the tougher the Russians will get." Americans must withdraw from Eastern Europe and allow the Soviets to devise their own security apparatus. Wallace had already embarrassed the administration by repeatedly criticizing the new president's domestic and foreign policies, and after some confusion over whether the secretary had had prior approval to deliver the address, Truman secured his resignation. "The Reds, phonies and 'parlor pinks,'" the president recorded in his diary, "seem to be banded together and are becoming a national danger. I am afraid they are a sabotage front for Uncle Joe Stalin."

The Wallace episode suggested deep division within the administration over the direction of foreign policy, but this appearance quickly changed in the spring of 1947 when a sharp deterioration in U.S.–Soviet relations prompted the White House to draw the line against Soviet expansion. After another rancorous Council of Foreign Ministers' meeting in Moscow, the focus of trouble abruptly shifted from Western and Eastern Europe to the fringe area along the top of the Mediterranean—the "northern tier" of Greece, Turkey, and Iran. Rebuffed in Iran a year earlier, the Soviets now seemed determined to stage a Communist takeover in Greece and wrest the straits from Turkey.

Although it is doubtful that the Soviets were either directly involved in the Greek troubles or actually prepared to make a military move against Turkey, the heightened emotional atmosphere resulting from the believed threat encouraged perceptions that distorted reality. Evidence suggests that from mid-1945 through late 1946, the Soviets attempted a political infiltration of Greece, but even that restrained effort failed. Yet the

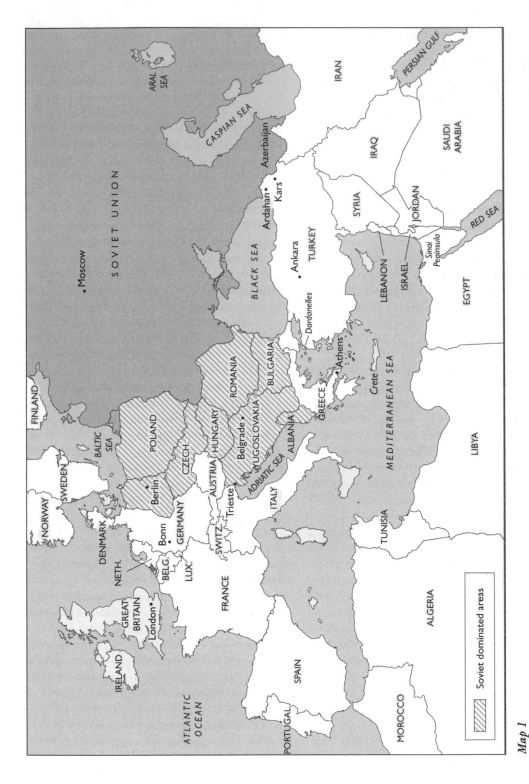

Map 1
Europe and the Near East. These areas, in particular the "northern tier" of Greece, Turkey, and Iran, became the focal points of the Cold War in the early part of the Truman administration. *(Source: author)*

impression remained in Washington that the Soviets exercised considerable control over events. The Truman administration feared that Soviet success in these two ventures would provide access to the Persian Gulf, the Mediterranean, and, ultimately, the entire Middle East. The alarming prospect was that Soviet hegemony in this oil-rich region could promote the collapse of Western Europe without the firing of a single shot. Americans came to perceive Greece and Turkey as the last barrier to a catastrophic break in Britain's Mediterranean lifeline that would permit a dangerous spread of Soviet influence. The controlling power in the eastern Mediterranean would determine the fate of the World Island—that huge area adjoining the Mediterranean, the Near and Middle East, and North Africa.

The Truman Doctrine

The Truman administration's immediate concern was Greece. That small country had been under Nazi occupation until October 1944 and then had experienced sporadic outbreaks of domestic violence that took on the extreme bitterness of a vendetta. The central political issue was whether Greece would remain monarchical or adopt a democratic system of government. King George II had fled the country during World War II and established a government-in-exile, first in London and then in Cairo. The British promised to support his attempt to reoccupy the throne after the German withdrawal, but they encountered staunch opposition from a leftist and Communist-led wartime resistance group called the National Popular Liberation Army, or ELAS, and its political counterpart, the National Liberation Front, or EAM. In the period after the Germans pulled out of the country, the Greek Communist Party— the KKE—boasted of building a Greater Greece. But the new state meant different things to different people. To Greek Nationalists, it heralded territorial expansion northward and the enhancement of Greece as a

nation; to hard-core Communists, it entailed meshing the Greeks into a Balkan federation or Macedonian free state led by Slavs. EAM/ELAS enjoyed considerable popular support as long as it sustained an image of promoting purely Greek interests.

Germany's departure from Greece threatened to set off a civil war in the long-beleaguered country. Major fighting broke out between leftists and rightists in the streets of Athens by December 1944, which led the British to send troops to aid Greek national forces in putting down what was a Communist-led rebellion. Widespread apprehension had developed over whether the Soviets would help the KKE, but they had not done so for several reasons. As pointed out earlier, during the previous October, Stalin and Churchill had negotiated the percentages agreement in Moscow, which recognized a British sphere of interest in Greece in exchange for Soviet hegemony in Romania. Stalin abided by that agreement. According to a contemporary, the Soviet premier refused to interfere with the December uprising because he opposed spontaneous, indigenous or Nationalist revolutions not susceptible to his control. It also seems likely that Stalin realized that Soviet interference in Greece on the eve of the Yalta Conference could have hurt his chances for achieving favorable postwar adjustments in Europe and Asia. For whatever reasons, he did not order the Red Army to intervene in the December revolution in Greece.

The warring parties finally arranged an uneasy truce at Varkiza in February 1946 that called first for a plebiscite to determine the people's will concerning the form of government they wanted and then the election of a constituent assembly. But during succeeding days, the rightist Athens government heated the political atmosphere by brutally repressing all opposition to the monarchy. By March, when the plebiscite was to occur, the British and Americans had reversed the political procedure stipulated at Varkiza. Over KKE protests and its eventual abstention, the general election took place first, which brought in a constituent assembly favorable to the monarchy, and in the following September a plebiscite yielded the same results, seemingly demonstrating great popular support for the king's return. It is impossible to determine the legitimacy of the vote. Americans were part of an international observer team that attested to the fairness of the elections, although the Soviet press joined the KKE and others in criticizing the outcome and blasting the British-supported government in Athens as "monarcho-fascist."

It seems certain now that most of the problems in Greece were of domestic origin, but in this angry atmosphere reason gave way to emotion, causing the March elections to set off a civil war that many Americans automatically assumed was Soviet inspired. In August 1946, the guerrillas launched a number of raids on villages and towns and received valuable assistance from the Communist regimes in Yugoslavia, Albania, and Bulgaria. For territorial ambitions rather than ideological ties, the Communist leader in Yugoslavia, Josip Broz Tito, furnished the bulk of the aid by providing sanctuary, material goods (both military and nonmilitary), and training and hospital facilities. Indeed, according to one of Tito's cohort, the Soviet Union itself contributed a small portion of these goods. Tito hoped to build a Balkan federation by acquiring Trieste at the top of the Adriatic Sea and annexing enough of Greece to permit access to the Mediterranean. The British, however, became convinced that aid to the guerrillas came indirectly from Moscow and warned Americans of Greece's imminent collapse to communism. Although most rebels were Greek Nationalists and not Communists interested in world revolution, the West believed that Communist leadership in the uprising necessarily meant links to the Kremlin. Firsthand observations underlined that point, however unsubstantiated by concrete evidence. The U.S. ambassador to Greece, Lincoln MacVeagh, warned that Yugoslavia, Albania, and Bulgaria were Moscow's puppets and that Greece's fall would open the

Mediterranean to the Soviets. By the spring of 1947, the United States regarded Greece as the supreme test of the Free World's will.

Turkey was also a vital part of the West's concern. Located along the Soviet border, it controlled the straits connecting the Black Sea with the Mediterranean and was vital to the Soviets' push for a warm water link to the Middle East. For 200 years, the Russians had wanted the straits. In the post–World War II period, the Soviet Union sought a revision of the Montreux Convention of 1936, which had recognized Turkish control of the straits. The Soviets wanted the Dardanelles, along with the districts of Kars and Ardahan on the east side of the Black Sea, the last two of which bordered Soviet Georgia and Armenia and had been lost after World War I. During World War II, the Turks had allowed Germany to use the straits to enter the Black Sea and attack the Soviet Union itself. At Yalta, Stalin declared that he could not allow Turkey to have "a hand on Russia's throat," and at Potsdam he sought to salvage the straits by opposing the U.S. call for internationalizing all inland waterways bordered by more than two countries (thereby safeguarding U.S. control over the Panama Canal and British control over the Suez Canal because both waterways touched only a single country). Turkey was anti-Soviet, Stalin told the U.S. ambassador in Moscow, and command of the straits was "a matter of our security."

The Soviets launched an intimidation campaign against Turkey soon after the war. After a series of feverish propaganda attacks, Moscow's leaders amassed Soviet troops along the common border. These events suggested an imminent invasion of Turkey, causing a "war of nerves" that forced the Ankara government to assign most of its already sparse funds to military preparations.

The Turkish crisis of 1946 did not surprise the United States. In the autumn of that year, it had stationed a battleship in nearby waters to demonstrate support for Turkey and had warned the Moscow government that any move toward the straits would cause the United States to take the issue before the UN

Dean Acheson
President Truman's secretary of state who became a Pulitzer Prize–winning author in 1969 for his book *Present at the Creation. (LBJ Library photo by Yoichi R. Okamoto)*

Security Council. Truman had agreed with Undersecretary of State Dean Acheson to stand firm. "We might as well find out whether the Russians were bent on world conquest now," the president declared.

With the United States firmly behind the Turks, the Soviets soon eased their demands. In September, the Truman administration declared that a task force, spearheaded by the aircraft carrier *Franklin D. Roosevelt*, would remain in the Mediterranean on a permanent basis. When Soviet newspapers angrily called this "gangster diplomacy," Admiral William ("Bull") Halsey drew widespread U.S. support with his indignant reply: "It's nobody's damn business where we go. We will go anywhere we please." Although the crisis had passed, the White House believed this only a reprieve and would not relax its vigilance. A State Department study had earlier asserted that Turkish control of the straits "constitutes the stopper in the neck of the bottle through which Soviet political and military influence could most effectively flow into the eastern Mediterranean and Middle East."

The twin crises along the northern rim of the Mediterranean merged into a U.S. problem in February 1947, when the British government informed the United States that it was no longer financially able to maintain long-standing commitments in Greece and Turkey. On Monday, February 24, the State Department received two notes from the British ambassador announcing an end to economic assistance in Greece and Turkey on March 31 and warning that if aid were to continue, the United States would have to assume the responsibility. General Marshall, who had replaced Byrnes as secretary of state in January, had already instructed Acheson to prepare an economic and military assistance plan for Greece. The task of formulating an official reaction to the notes therefore fell to Acheson, who had received word the Friday before that the British were preparing to withdraw from Greece and Turkey. That same day, he had authorized a State Department policy planning group to work around the clock over the weekend to draft a favorable response to London.

Events moved quickly in Washington. The director of the newly organized Near Eastern Affairs Division, Loy Henderson, joined others in the State Department in writing a plan outlining U.S. economic assistance to Greece and Turkey. From Acheson's desk, the draft went before the State-War-Navy Coordinating Committee (SWNCC), which believed that economic rehabilitation in Greece could not succeed until the Athens government wound down the civil war. The SWNCC therefore called for a shift in emphasis to military aid. In the meantime, the Greek government followed the State Department's recommendation to make a formal request for help, and Acheson secured Truman's support by warning that the collapse of Greece and Turkey would throw open the entire Mediterranean to the Soviet Union. "If Greece fell within the Russian orbit," Acheson told his cabinet colleagues, "not only Turkey would be affected but also Italy, France, and the whole of western Europe." Congressional members from both parties received invitations to the White House to join the administration in forming a bipartisan for-

President Truman to Congress, March 12, 1947
Giving Truman Doctrine address asking for aid to Greece and Turkey. (*Harry S. Truman Library, Independence, Missouri*)

eign policy aimed at halting a Communist drive allegedly engineered by the Kremlin.

Although the Middle East's oil (40 percent of the world's reserves) was a crucial factor in U.S. thinking, the administration presumed that everyone understood this fundamental truth and emphasized instead the battle with communism. Senator Arthur Vandenberg, chair of the Foreign Relations Committee, supported the approach and warned that the proposal would succeed only if the administration engaged in a major campaign designed to scare Americans about the dangers of a Communist takeover. What lay ahead, Truman remarked to his advisers, was "the greatest selling job ever facing a President."

This whirlwind of activity in Washington culminated in a revolutionary new policy known as the Truman Doctrine. Before a joint session of Congress on March 12, 1947, the president outlined the dangers in Greece and Turkey and then pointed to the bipolarity of interests in the world. He did not specify the Soviet Union as the cause of unrest in the Mediterranean world, although his allusions were unmistakable. One set of ideas was totalitarian and repressive, Truman asserted, the other democratic and supportive of freedom. Should Greece and Turkey fall to communism, the forces of oppression could stamp out freedom in the Near and Middle East. To save Greece and Turkey, Congress must support a massive military and economic aid program of $400 million, most of which would be military and go to Greece. He also sought authorization for sending military and civilian advisers to each country to administer the aid programs.

Considerable resistance immediately arose against a drastic shift in the nation's foreign policy. Marshall and Kennan, who had been recently recalled from Moscow to serve in the State Department office, thought the anti-Communist tone of the message too severe, but the president had deferred to Clifford's advice in delivering a "blunt" statement of the U.S. position on recent events along the Mediterranean. Kennan did not perceive a military threat in either Greece or Turkey and ar-

The Truman Doctrine promised military and economic assistance to Greece and Turkey in an effort to protect them from communism.

The Truman Doctrine, President Harry S. Truman's special message to the Congress on Greece and Turkey, March 12, 1947, *Public Papers of the Presidents of the United States, Harry S. Truman, 1947* (Washington, D.C.: Government Printing Office, 1963), 176–80.

At the present moment in the world history nearly every nation must choose between alternative ways of life. The choice is too often not a free one.

One way of life is based upon the will of the majority and is distinguished by free institutions, representing government, free elections, guarantees of individual liberty, freedom of speech and religion, and freedom from political oppression.

The second way of life is based upon the will of the minority forcibly imposed upon the majority. It relies on terror and oppression, a controlled press and radio, fixed elections, and the suppression of personal freedoms.

I believe that it must be the policy of the United States to support free peoples who are resisting attempted subjugation by armed minorities or by outside pressures.

I believe that we must assist peoples to work out their own destinies in their own way.

I believe that our help should be primarily through economic and financial aid which is essential to economic stability and orderly political processes. . . .

The seeds of totalitarian regimes are nurtured by misery and want. They spread and grow in the evil soil of poverty and strife. They reach their full growth when the hope of a people for a better life has died.

We must keep that hope alive.

gued that the Soviet challenge was primarily political; economic assistance offered the appropriate remedy. Truman's language was "grandiose" and "sweeping," Kennan warned, and would lead to a worldwide crusade that the United States was neither militarily nor economically prepared to support. When critics inquired why the United States did not act through the United Nations, Acheson explained that the situation was an emergency, that the United Nations had no funds except those provided by the United States, and that once the crisis had passed, the United Nations could assume responsibility. Vandenberg helped to ward off much of this criticism. Failure to act, he warned Congress, would encourage a "Communist chain reaction from the Dardanelles to the China Sea and westward to the rim of the Atlantic." He then sponsored an amendment assuring Americans that the United States would retreat from its commitments to the Truman Doctrine when the United Nations was able to assume them.

Others complained that the United States had made a blanket commitment to worldwide foreign aid that would ultimately bankrupt the country. Acheson countered that the Truman Doctrine applied specifically to Greece and Turkey and that the administration would consider aid to other countries only on their "individual merits." To other skeptics, the administration admitted that neither Greece nor Turkey was democratic but noted that those situations might change if the United States could guarantee both nations' right to choose a government. Isolationist Republican Robert Taft insisted that the United States was taking on Britain's responsibilities; Acheson responded that whatever happened in Greece and Turkey affected the vital interests of the United States.

The arguments continued for weeks, but in May 1947, Congress approved the Greek-Turkish Aid bills in a wide and bipartisan vote. By autumn, U.S. aid was en route to both countries.

Thus, by the summer of 1947, the United States had moved toward a more cohesive foreign policy that gradually became known as "containment," a policy that rested in part on Kennan's theories of attempting to thwart Soviet expansion through any means short of war. In July, he expanded his ideas in an anonymously written article for *Foreign Affairs* magazine that he titled "The Sources of Soviet Conduct." Signing it "X" (a ploy that fooled few people), Kennan warned that the basis of Stalin's behavior was Marxist-Leninist ideology combined with his effort to mobilize popular support for his policies by exploiting the widespread fear of "capitalist encirclement." The Kremlin was in no hurry to achieve world conquest. Its "political action is a fluid stream which moves constantly, wherever it is permitted to move, toward a given goal." The only solution was "a long-term, patient but firm and vigilant containment" in which the United States countered the Soviets "at a series of constantly shifting geographical and political points, corresponding to the shifts and maneuvers of Soviet policy." Such a U.S. response might lead to "either the breakup or the gradual mellowing of Soviet power."

The vagueness of Kennan's argument left him susceptible to the unwarranted charge of favoring a global crusade against communism. He did not clarify whether he meant containment through military or economic means. Nor did he make clear that some areas of the world were vital to U.S. interests and that others lay on the periphery. The result was that policymakers regarded his writings as a warning that all over the world the Soviets intended to instigate crises designed to spread Communist ideology and that the United States had to be militarily ready to halt this new form of aggression wherever it occurred.

The same month that Kennan's article appeared, Congress left little doubt about the aggressive direction of U.S. foreign policy when it passed the National Security Act. This legislation first gave statutory sanction to the Joint Chiefs of Staff and then established several advisory bodies. It created a National Se-

curity Council to advise the president on domestic and foreign policy relating to the nation's security, a secretary of defense to replace the secretary of war and coordinate control over the nation's armed forces, and the Central Intelligence Agency (CIA) to gather and analyze intelligence at home. An amendment to the act in 1949 created the Department of Defense, and the CIA's activities were later expanded to include covert operations outside the country. Indeed, the secret provision condoning "sabotage" and "subversion" also instituted untruths as an official part of policy by declaring that CIA leaders were to craft their activities so carefully that if exposed, there must be room for plausible denial. Containment, whether by military or economic means or both, became the guiding principle of the administration's foreign policy.

Columnist Walter Lippmann was among more than a few Americans who opposed the doctrine of containment. He warned that it would lead to a worldwide ideological crusade because it failed to delineate which areas sought by the Soviets were of vital importance to the United States. In addition, Lippmann believed, Stalin was motivated more by historic Soviet expansionist aims than by Communist ideology. The real issue, Lippmann insisted, was a balance of power. The United States should confront the Soviets with naval bases in the eastern Mediterranean, along with other visible signs of its strength. Danger lay in attempting to stop Soviet expansion with "dispersed American power in the service of a heterogeneous collection of unstable governments and of contending parties and factions which happen to be opposed to the Soviet Union." Such policy would harden the Soviet military presence in Europe while draining U.S. resources and will. It presumed Soviet involvement throughout Europe and Asia, which in turn depended on the questionable premises that the Moscow government had the ability to coordinate its own foreign policy as well as that of its allies. Leaders in Washington and Moscow should arrange a mutual withdrawal of their military forces from Central Europe and thus defuse the explosive situation. Containment, Lippmann concluded, was a "strategic monstrosity."

Despite the much trumpeted fears of globalism and ultimate war, Washington's policymakers had actually fashioned a program that, if carefully used, rested on the principles of flexibility and restraint. Acheson repeatedly assured congressional committees that the Truman Doctrine did not entail an automatic global commitment by the United States and that each applicant for assistance would receive consideration based on the merits of that case alone. The chief guidelines were simple: the area requesting assistance must be both vital to U.S. interests and capable of salvation. Acheson also emphasized that the type of aid depended on the problem under advisement. Greece was in the throes of civil war and needed emergency military assistance. Indeed, the war at first went so badly for the Greek government that some Washington officials seriously considered sending U.S. combat troops. Finally, however, the Greek National Army firmed up its performance in the field as a result of the arrival of U.S. military materiel and uniformed advisers on the operational level. The Soviet threat to Turkey had already eased, permitting that government to handle many of its problems without as much direct U.S. involvement.

The Truman Doctrine eventually stabilized Greece and Turkey, thereby appearing to establish the credibility of the containment policy of the United States. Nearly 300 U.S. military and civilian advisers and a host of support personnel provided advisory assistance to the Greek army in its war against the guerrillas. American advice and firepower proved essential to the ultimate triumph of the government's forces, although Tito's independent posture in the Communist world caused a bitter rift between Yugoslavia and the Soviet Union that was also important in winding down the civil war in Greece. A year after Tito defected from the Communist Information Bureau (Cominform) in July 1948, he closed the border to Greek guerrillas and cut off assistance. The guerrillas no longer had a place of refuge and were forced to raid and pillage the Greek countryside for provisions and seize hostages as military inductees. Popular resistance to their methods grew, increasing support for the king. In October 1949, the fighting came to an end when the royalist forces, aided by U.S. napalm and navy Helldivers, scattered the guerrillas into the northern mountains of Greece and into Albania. The crisis in Turkey likewise passed as U.S. military assistance and advice bolstered the country against Soviet pressure.

Both successes were fortuitous abroad though divisive at home. In May 1948, the United States had extended recognition to the new Jewish state of Israel (discussed in a later chapter), whose creation set off the first of many postwar crises in the Middle East and thereby brought even more stature to the resolution of the Greek–Turkish problems. On the one hand, containment seemed to have yielded a monumental triumph in the Near East and hence in the Cold War. On the other hand, the administration's success in scaring Americans into adopting such an ambitious aid program had a negative and inflammatory effect at home: it encouraged another "red scare" similar to that of 1919 and 1920. Its label during the 1950s became "McCarthyism," however, and its impact proved even more damaging to the blameless Americans caught in the accusatory fallout.

The atmosphere of McCarthyism actually began to develop during the late 1940s, when Whitaker Chambers, senior editor of *Time* news-magazine and a former Communist Party member, accused Alger Hiss, a State Department adviser who had accompanied Roosevelt to Yalta, of being a Communist spy. A widely publicized trial followed that catapulted the young chair of the House Committee on Un-American Activities, Republican Representative Richard M. Nixon of California, into the national limelight as an anti-Communist crusader. To support the charges, Chambers escorted Nixon and a large group of reporters to his farm in Maryland, where he pulled out of a pumpkin several rolls of microfilm containing the State Department documents of the late 1930s allegedly pilfered by Hiss. Although protected from the charge of espionage by the statute of limitations, Hiss was convicted of perjury in January 1950 and sentenced to five years' imprisonment for denying having been a Communist or knowing Chambers. The judicial process, however, failed to resolve the central question of whether Hiss actually was a spy. A pattern of conspiracy seemed to develop when, that same month, British physicist Klaus Fuchs was identified as one of several spies who had participated in developing the atomic bomb and shared information with the Soviets.

Then, in February 1950, Senator Joe McCarthy of Wisconsin, desperately looking for an issue that would assure his shaky bid for reelection, appeared before a Republican Women's Club in Wheeling, West Virginia, and dramatically waved a so-called list of Communists in the State Department. Although he had no such list, his theatrics caused a veritable witch hunt that spread like wildfire throughout the country, lasting for nearly five years and ruining many innocent persons' reputations. In every walk of life, including the government, Hollywood, and the college teaching profession, Americans suspected of being anything less than fiercely anti-Communist were automatically condemned as "pinkos," "fellow travelers," or "hard-core Communists." Fear of subversion at home necessitated a stronger policy abroad, leading Americans to attribute problems in other countries to a monolithic form of communism emanating solely from the Kremlin and not to difficulties arising from within troubled countries. The forecast was deepening U.S. involvement in foreign affairs and a greatly intensified Cold War.

Heightened Cold War: The Marshall Plan and Germany

While the Truman Doctrine was under way, the administration turned toward resolving the massive economic problems in Europe left by World War II. Europe, Churchill lamented, was "a rubble heap, a charnel house, a breeding ground of pestilence and hate." Despite billions of dollars of U.S. assistance through the UN Relief and Rehabilitation Administration (UNRRA) and other organizations by mid-1947, Europe lay open to despair, revolution, and totalitarian exploitation, particularly in France and Italy, where local Communist parties threatened to win national elections. Furthermore, the United States had withdrawn from UNRRA in 1946 because of charges that Communist East European nations were distributing food only to political allies. The last U.S. aid installments arrived the following year, forcing an end to UNRRA and highlighting the desire of Americans, in Acheson's words, to extend relief "in accordance with our judgment and supervised with American personnel." The central dilemma was clear: no recovery could take place in Europe without Germany's playing an integral role in that recovery. And that entailed further alienation of the Soviet Union—as well as France.

In the spring of 1947, after a frustrating Council of Foreign Ministers' conference in Moscow, Secretary of State Marshall visited Western Europe and was visibly shaken by the devastation. Europeans were unable to buy American products, and the drought of 1946 had almost wiped out the grain crop. The ensuing winter brought heavy snowstorms followed by spring floods that threatened the next year's yield and raised the distinct possibility of famine across Europe. The British were also in dire straits. Officials had reserved coal for emergency use only, and they even ordered brief daily shutdowns of electricity to save the sharply diminishing supply. Communist Party victories in the fast-approaching elections in France and Italy would mean that, for a second time within the decade, Britain would stand alone against totalitarian aggression. In exchange for Britain's relaxation of commercial restrictions, the United States had approved a loan of $4.4 billion in July 1946, but even this huge sum was not enough to

George C. Marshall
He eventually became President Truman's
secretary of state and a proponent of the
Marshall Plan in Europe. *(U.S. Army)*

site which feeds only on diseased tissue." Marshall now expressed this same thought, which had already become the prevailing view in the State Department. Following the stand advocated by Undersecretary of State for Economic Affairs William L. Clayton, Marshall called on all European governments—East and West—to draw up a mutual aid program and inform the United States how it could contribute to their recovery. "The initiative," he emphasized, "must come from Europe."

To avoid antagonizing the Soviets, Marshall insisted, the United States must make no distinction between the forms of government receiving assistance. "Our policy is directed not against any country or doctrine but against hunger, poverty, desperation, and chaos." As Acheson noted in an earlier speech in Mississippi, these problems were common to all Europeans. Such a stance, however, raised fears that U.S. aid might go to Communist East Europe and even to the Soviet Union. This was unlikely, according to Kennan and Charles E. Bohlen, who had been with Kennan while witnessing Stalin's brutal purges of the 1930s and was the principal writer of Marshall's Harvard address and later ambassador to Moscow. The Soviets, Kennan believed, could not accept U.S. help, especially when the stipulations for doing so included U.S. participation in planning the recipient's economy and full disclosure of that government's files to verify need. Anxiety remained, however. If the Moscow government accepted the U.S. invitation and Congress refused to approve an aid bill, the United States would suffer a serious propaganda defeat.

Marshall's offer of economic assistance caused a flurry of activity in Europe that culminated in a tripartite conference in Paris. In late June, British Foreign Secretary Ernest Bevin met in that city with French Foreign Minister Georges Bidault and after considerable discussion decided to invite Soviet Foreign Commissar Molotov to join them. Molotov at first hesitated to attend, even though he doubtless realized that failure to do so would increase the chances of a Western

stave off impending disaster. On Marshall's return to Washington, he instructed Kennan, now head of the State Department's new Policy Planning Staff, to prepare a study of the European situation and recommend a policy promoting relief and recovery.

At Harvard University's commencement ceremony on June 5, 1947, the secretary of state delivered an address on European affairs that became the essence of the Marshall Plan. Partly basing his remarks on Kennan's report, Marshall warned that the widespread "economic, social, and political deterioration" of Europe was conducive to political instability, totalitarian exploitation, and the obstruction of peace. Kennan had earlier argued that "world communism is like a malignant para-

alliance. Yet if the Soviet Union became part of that bloc, its allied states would be susceptible to Western penetration. American assistance, Molotov feared, might draw Eastern Europe toward the West, revive Germany, and endanger Soviet military security. Although disgruntled by the situation, he finally accepted the invitation.

Accompanied by eighty-nine economic advisers and clerks, Molotov attended the meeting in Paris, where he blasted the aid proposal as a "new venture in American imperialism" and objected to nearly every aspect of the program. He opposed U.S. control over reconstruction and called for a decentralized approach to preserve the integrity of each participant. He wanted each government to compile its own list of needs and send it directly to the United States. Bevin and Bidault disagreed. "Debtors do not lay down conditions when seeking credits from potential creditors," Bevin remarked to Molotov. "If I went to . . . Moscow with a blank check and ask[ed] you to sign it I wonder how far I would get at your end." The following day, Molotov warned them not to act without Soviet approval. His arguments had no impact. Bevin and Bidault rejected these stipulations, and Molotov stalked out of the conference.

Molotov's decision greatly relieved the Truman administration. Harriman, now secretary of commerce, declared that "Bevin did a superb job of getting Molotov out of Paris— by careful maneuvering. Bidault claims to have had a part in it. But Bevin had the courage to invite Molotov and the bluntness to get rid of him. He could have killed the Marshall Plan by joining it." Kennan confessed to having no faith in Soviet cooperation in attempting to establish trade between East and West. "So, in a sense, we put Russia over the barrel. . . . When the full horror of [their] alternatives dawned on them, they left suddenly in the middle of the night."

After Molotov's departure, France and Britain invited more than twenty European governments to Paris to draft a proposal for U.S. aid. Those governments under Soviet influence—Yugoslavia, Albania, Bulgaria, Poland, Romania, Czechoslovakia, Hungary, and Finland—either did not attend or denounced the aid program as an "imperialist" conspiracy. By September, sixteen Western European governments requested a four-year allotment of $22 billion of assistance aimed at bringing economic stability to the continent by 1951.

Poland and Czechoslovakia had rejected the chance for U.S. aid only with great reluctance and because of Soviet intimidation. Both had initially shown interest in participating in the program but changed their minds because, they declared with more than a little trepidation, acceptance "might be construed as an action against the Soviet Union." A Czech delegation led by Foreign Minister Jan Masaryk had been in Moscow to negotiate a commercial treaty when a question arose about whether their government should accept U.S. assistance. Stalin bitterly attacked the program as an effort "to form a Western bloc and to isolate the Soviet Union." He continued in an icy tone, "We look upon this matter as a question of principle, on which our friendship with Czechoslovakia depends. . . . All the Slavic states have refused. . . . That is why, in our opinion, you ought to reverse your decision." To refuse to do so, Stalin pointedly warned, carried dangerous repercussions: "If you take part in the conference, you will prove by that act that you allow yourselves to be used as a tool against the Soviet Union." Neither the Czech nor the Polish governments sent representatives to Paris.

The Soviet Union tried several tactics to reduce the impact of the proposed Marshall Plan. It negotiated defense pacts with Finland, Bulgaria, Hungary, and Romania, which were additions to those agreements already signed with Poland, Czechoslovakia, and Yugoslavia. It rigged elections in Hungary to ensure Communist victory. In early October 1947, Molotov arranged the establishment of the Cominform in Belgrade, a nine-member organization that succeeded the now defunct Comintern, which the Kremlin had dissolved four years earlier. The new Cominform attempted to disrupt U.S. influence in Europe. Moscow also announced the Molotov Plan, a series of bilateral treaties promising Soviet economic assistance to Communist governments in Europe. Strikes broke out in Italy and France that apparently were Communist efforts to undermine faith in those governments and prevent them from becoming recipients of Marshall Plan aid.

In January 1948, shortly after another abortive Council of Foreign Ministers' meeting in London, Truman sparked a lively debate over the European aid bill when he asked Congress to appropriate $6.8 billion for fifteen months, followed by more than $10 billion during the next three years. The purpose, he stated, was to "contribute to world peace and to its own security by assisting in the recovery of sixteen countries which, like the United States, are devoted to the preservation of the free institutions and enduring peace among nations." Economic and political stability in Europe meant greatly enhanced trade for the United States and a halt to the spread of communism. Wallace, already ousted from the administration after his speech in New York, termed the aid program a "Martial Plan," and Senator Taft denounced it as a "European T.V.A." Too much money had already gone overseas, many charged, and such a program might worsen U.S.–Soviet relations and further divide Europe into hostile camps.

Despite this vocal opposition, it quickly became evident that Congress would approve the aid program. Among its supporters were farmers, laborers, manufacturers, and the press. Also working in its favor was the Cold War itself. In an action strikingly reminiscent of the Munich crisis of a decade before, the Communists overthrew the Czech republic in February 1948 and installed a regime tied to the Kremlin. Masaryk's sudden death, reported as suicide though attributed by Truman to "foul play," especially appalled the West and promoted the bill's passage. Other inducements to congressional support of the Marshall Plan were the forced Russo–Finnish alliance, the expected Communist victory in

the impending elections in Italy, and rising tensions in Germany. General Clay in Berlin noted a "new tenseness in every Soviet individual with whom we have official relations." In an effort to convince Congress to allot more money to the military but that raised fear about the outcome in Germany, he warned that war "may come with dramatic suddenness." The Senate approved the aid bill by a wide margin (sixty-nine to seventeen), and as it went before the House, Truman delivered a speech to Congress calling for a universal military training program and resumption of the selective service.

In March, the House of Representatives overwhelmingly approved the Economic Cooperation Act (ECA), or Marshall Plan (329 to 74), which became a prime example of the administration's containment policy. The act established the European Recovery Program, which eventually provided more than $12 billion of assistance by its termination date of 1952. Congress also restored the selective service, and even though it rejected universal military training, it strengthened the air force. In the meantime, the European governments, as members of the Organization of European Economic Cooperation, prepared to receive U.S. aid.

The Marshall Plan, which the president signed into law on April 3, 1948, resulted from a combination of idealistic and realistic concerns. Although it attempted to help Europe for humanitarian reasons, it also sought to halt the spread of communism. By extending credits to Europeans to purchase American goods, the United States hoped to restore order to the continent, prevent Communist takeover, and enhance U.S. prestige. The United States also aimed to promote economic growth by expanding capitalism through the multilateral trade principles spelled out in the Bretton Woods agreements of 1944. To further ensure free commercial exchange, the United States that same year of 1948 joined twenty-two other nations in establishing the General Agreement on Tariffs and Trade, which rested on the most-favored-nation principle. Thus, liberal trade agreements between two countries extended automatically to the others as well. The key to economic recovery, however, was the integration of Europe and the reintegration of Germany into a system of multilateral world trade.

The Marshall Plan was a success in many ways. Although Western Europe's economic recovery was already under way, it intensified with U.S. assistance. In addition, the aid probably helped to undercut the Communist Party in France while proving instrumental in that party's defeat in Italy's elections. Western Europe did not become commercially interdependent: cartels and other obstacles to trade remained. Yet the Marshall Plan made headway by following many principles underlying the New Deal. In meshing private capital interests with the government, it exemplified the new sense of cooperation between the public and the private sector that led to greater efficiency through planning and control, reduction of commercial barriers, and ready convertibility of currencies. The central objective was to build a multilateral, corporatist system that guaranteed global security by tying together economic, political, social, and strategic interests.

Like the Truman Doctrine, however, the Marshall Plan became heavily military in character and hardened the divisions in the Cold War. When the aid program ended in 1952, 80 percent of its assistance had become military, partly stemming from the outbreak of the Korean War in 1950 and partly because of the 1951 decision to merge the ECA with the Military Defense Aid Program. This broadened program then became the Mutual Security Administration in 1952 and continued to distribute military aid funds to Western Europe. The Marshall Plan brought enormous benefits to its recipients, but it drove the wedge deeper between East and West by helping to reconstruct Germany and thereby encouraged the Kremlin to clamp down even more on Eastern Europe.

The Berlin Crisis

The Marshall Plan heightened the Soviets' fear of a reunified Germany and helped bring on a crisis in Berlin during the summer of 1948 that caused the Truman administration to discuss using the atomic bomb. The city lay almost one hundred miles within the Soviet zone of occupation, landlocked from the West though guaranteed access by air. Only under great pressure from the United States and Britain had France recently joined its occupation forces with theirs in creating "Trizonia," which they believed might save Germany's economy. The Soviets, however, feared that Trizonia would lead to the West's absorption of their economically weaker eastern zone. The entire German economy was in bad shape. The reichsmark was so inflated that American cigarettes had become a medium of exchange. Food supplies and steel production were down, relief costs were rising, and the Communist Party was becoming stronger.

In the spring of 1948, representatives of the United States, Britain, France, Belgium, Luxembourg, and the Netherlands gathered

Postwar Germany
In the rubble of Essen, Germany, was a new citizen who benefited from American aid. *(Harry S. Truman Library, Independence, Missouri)*

in London to establish a government in the western section of Germany. The Ruhr industries would remain under their supervision but in cooperation with the West Germans. Once residents of West Germany elected a parliament, it would draft a constitution for a federal government inviting East German membership. To alleviate fears of a rearmed Germany, the United States and others would maintain restrictions on West Germany's foreign activities, prevent rearmament, and terminate foreign occupation only when calm returned to Europe. The delegates also instituted changes in Germany's currency system designed to ease the inflationary spiral and promote economic recovery and political unification under Western leadership. Such reforms, in combination with the Marshall Plan, would rehabilitate Germany, promote Europe's revival, and, as a matter of course, threaten the Soviet Union.

The United States had meanwhile continued to work toward a military pact in Europe. In March, Britain, France, Belgium, Luxembourg, and the Netherlands signed the Brussels Treaty, which established a fifty-year collective defense system known as Western Union, and shortly afterward Truman urged Congress to support the pact. In June, the Senate overwhelmingly approved the Vandenberg resolution, which called for U.S. cooperation "with such regional and other collective arrangements as are based on continuous and effective self-help and mutual aid, and as affect its national security." The United States, the resolution continued, should make known "its determination to exercise the right of individual or collective self-defense under article 51 [of the UN Charter] should any armed attack occur affecting its national security."

By the summer of 1948, the West's new measures appeared threatening to Moscow. West European nations were banding together under the Marshall Plan and had moved closer to a military alliance with the United States. An independent West Germany meant its eventual incorporation into a military organization opposed to the Soviets. American economic assistance had gone to Yugoslavia, whose Communist regime under Tito had left the Communist bloc and exposed a deep crack in the alleged monolith. With Germany revived, Western Europe strengthened and unified, and Eastern Europe perhaps loosening its loyalties to Moscow, the security of the Soviet Union itself came into question.

In June, the West announced the imminent establishment of the West German Republic, which caused the Soviets to take drastic action. They imposed a blockade of all surface routes into West Berlin (rail, highway, and water) in an effort to intimidate and divide the Western alliance, halt the move toward a West German government, and undermine U.S. influence in Europe. In addition, they froze bank deposits in the city's central bank (located in the Soviet sector) and greatly reduced the flow of electricity into West Berlin from power plants also in the eastern sector of the city. The diminished power carried enormous potential for trouble because it hit everyone by slowing down the pumps handling sewage disposal and maintaining the water supply. The same day the blockade went into effect, the Soviets issued the Warsaw Declaration, which demanded a return to the four-power division of Germany stipulated at Potsdam.

The Soviets appeared to hold the upper hand. The West had no specific guarantee of any surface connections through Soviet-controlled eastern Germany, meaning that, they thought, it had to either pull out of Berlin and leave the Soviets in total control of East Germany or agree to negotiations that restored the four-power wartime agreements on all Germany. The latter measure would assure the Soviets a major governing voice throughout the country because by an earlier agreement, every decision had to come from a unanimous vote. In either case, the Soviets would achieve their chief objective of halting the creation of a West German government. Certainly, Stalin must have reasoned, the West

The Berlin Chess Game
After Stalin imposed a blockade on Germany on
June 24, 1948, Truman countered with the
Berlin airlift. *(Simon and Schuster, New York)*

would not use force in opening the surface
routes and thereby risk the lives of more than
2 million Germans now held hostage in their
own country.

Stalin correctly assumed that the West
would not directly challenge the blockade.
The U.S. military governor in Berlin, General
Clay, called for a strong reaction that his superiors in Washington ultimately rejected.
Clay had warned the Pentagon in early April
that "when Berlin falls, Western Germany will
be next. If we mean . . . to hold Europe
against communism, we must not budge. . . .
If we withdraw, our position in Europe is
threatened. If America does not understand
this now, then it never will and communism
will run rampant. I believe the future of
democracy requires us to stay." The Soviet action was a bluff, Clay believed; the United
States should test the Soviet will by sending
an armed convoy into Berlin. But the army

chief of staff, General Omar Bradley, warned
that the Soviets could impede the passage of
Allied trucks without the use of force. They
could simply close the roads for repairs, or "a
bridge could go out just ahead of you and
then another bridge behind, and you'd be in
a hell of a fix." General Albert C. Wedemeyer,
director of army plans and operations in Washington, noted the Soviets' military superiority
in the region and insisted that "our forces
would have been annihilated." Colonel Frank
Howley, chief of the military government in
the U.S. zone, put it even more bluntly: "We
would have got our *derrieres* shot off."

Truman searched for a response that
would be equivalent to the Soviet blockade
without raising the ante and increasing the
chances for war. He realized the Red Army
outnumbered Allied forces in Germany three
to one, and he knew that reopened negotiations over Germany would endanger the new
West German government. So he adopted a
suggestion posed earlier by the British: a massive airlift, carried out in conjunction with
the British and designed to deliver supplies
into the western part of the city. In addition,
he supported a counterblockade—an embargo on selected industrial items considered
integral to Soviet needs in East Germany (including chemicals and steel). No questions
could arise about the legality of an airlift because the Allied Control Council had earlier
authorized the establishment of three air lanes
connecting West Germany with Berlin. The
West *had* to act, warned a British general on
the scene. Otherwise, it "might wake up
some fine morning to find the Hammer and
Sickle already on the Rhine."

In the event that the airlift failed, however,
the United States seemed prepared to resort
to the atomic bomb—or at least to leave the
impression with the Soviets that it would do
so. Although the United States had fewer
than fifty bombs (and not all of them usable)
and only thirty B-29s capable of delivering
them, the president sent a threatening signal
to the Kremlin by securing Britain's permission to house sixty B-29 bombers, declaring

to the press that they were "atomic-capable," and hinting that they *carried* nuclear warheads. In actuality, the planes were not yet adaptable to a nuclear cargo, but this did not become known until the 1970s. Truman's intimidation tactics might succeed—as long as Stalin did not dismiss them as a mere bluff. The Soviet premier probably remained uncertain whether the United States would use the bomb, but he must have been aware of his adversary's limited nuclear capacity. One of Stalin's top-level spies, Donald Maclean, was in Washington from 1946 to 1948, where, in his capacity as Britain's joint secretary of the Combined Policy Committee on Atomic Energy, he had full access to atomic stockpile information.

By the spring of 1949, the Anglo-American airlift, occasionally harassed but never attacked by Soviet planes, had provided over 13,000 tons of goods per day (more than three times the amount required), enough to meet the needs of Americans plus the city's other 2.5 million residents. From the beginning of the airlift in late June 1948, each citizen in West Berlin received more than half a ton of supplies from planes arriving at three-minute intervals every day.

From Berlin to NATO

Stalin's strategy failed in that the Berlin crisis not only fueled the drive toward a self-governing West German republic tied to the West but also served as an important impetus for the formation of the North Atlantic Treaty Organization (NATO). On April 4, 1949, twelve nations assembled in Washington to sign the North Atlantic Treaty, which established a European defense pact that initially included the United States, Britain, Canada, France, Italy, Belgium, Luxembourg, Norway, Denmark, Iceland, Portugal, and the Netherlands. By the mid-1950s, however, NATO's membership grew to fifteen with the additions of Greece, Turkey, and West Germany. NATO was a military alliance of permanent duration, uniting signatories "by means of

continuous and effective self-help and mutual aid." Article 5 of the treaty declared that "an armed attack against one or more [signatory nations] . . . shall be considered an attack against them all" and promised "such action as it deems necessary, including the use of armed force." The United States alone possessed atomic weapons, and NATO had the Strategic Air Command with its long-range bombers. Direction of the new organization would come through the North Atlantic Council, comprised of the foreign, defense, and finance ministers of member nations. Combined with the Truman Doctrine and Marshall Plan, NATO helped to bring postwar order to the continent.

The ensuing debate over U.S. membership in NATO raised familiar arguments. Critics predicted involvement in European wars and ultimate bankruptcy caused by deepening foreign commitments. Taft warned that NATO would provoke an arms race and, in an argument remindful of the Lodge–Wilson fight over the League of Nations, declared that the pact would tie U.S. soldiers to Europe without constitutional sanction. NATO's advocates countered that the pact contained no provisions for mandatory military action, that the United States had vital interests in Europe's security, and that a Soviet attack was unlikely, largely because only the United States had the bomb. Acheson, now secretary of state after Marshall's resignation in January 1949, assured the Senate that membership in NATO did not require the United States to commit more ground forces to Europe; the new system constituted a warning to the Soviets that NATO and the U.S. presence would have a "trip-wire" effect intended to generate even a nuclear response in an extreme case.

The success of the Berlin airlift, the pressures resulting from the Western counterblockade, and the tightened Western alliance provided by NATO forced the Soviets to call off their blockade in May 1949. Anxious moments had not led to a military confrontation, and the United States had acted calmly, legally, and with resolution. World public opinion had meanwhile judged the Soviet Union to be in the wrong. In exchange for the Soviet retreat, the United States agreed to discuss the German question at another Council of Foreign Ministers's meeting in Paris later that month. Although the conference led to no agreements on Germany, Soviet actions in Berlin had ensured the formation of the West German Republic and encouraged the United States to join the European defense system.

The Senate approved U.S. membership in NATO by a wide margin on July 21, 1949, and two days later the president signed the agreement. That same day, he sent Congress the Mutual Defense Assistance Bill, which provided a one-year appropriation of $1.5 billion to revamp and expand Europe's military strength. Thus, NATO furnished a viable alternative to the bomb in deterring Soviet aggression. At the same time, the pledge to use the bomb secured the much-needed European bases for B-29 bombers. Vandenberg considered NATO "the most important step in American foreign policy since the promulgation of the Monroe Doctrine." The United States had joined its first entangling alliance in Europe since the treaty with France in 1778 and its first formal military alliance in peacetime. It had also become part of a military organization that hardened Cold War divisions and, almost paradoxically, helped to reduce the likelihood of all-out war.

Another objective of the Truman administration's European policy was to win Allied support for rearming West Germany and making it part of NATO's military force. The organization needed German human and industrial resources, although France and the Benelux nations remained concerned about the restoration of their longtime enemy. In September 1949, Trizonia became West Germany, or the Federal Republic of Germany (which included the three Western sectors of Berlin). Its capital was Bonn and its chancellor Konrad Adenauer. The government was civilian in orientation, although Allied military occupation continued under a High Commission of three members, one each from

the Western occupying powers. As noted earlier, the United States approved Marshall Plan assistance for the new republic and agreed to participate in the international administration of the Ruhr Valley. West Germany's 50 million people had not only begun the long process of economic and political recovery, but their new government now seemed on the verge of a major military buildup.

The movement for West German military integration into NATO received a sudden boost in late September 1949, when Truman stunned Americans by announcing that the Soviet Union had exploded an atomic device—ten years earlier than experts had envisaged. While this development unsettled Americans at home, it also severely weakened the central bond of NATO: the atomic monopoly of the United States. The following month, the Soviets announced the formation of the German Democratic Republic of East Germany. Two Germanies and two Berlins—each trying to absorb the other—became symbols of the East–West struggle for Europe. Western Europe's hatred for Germany, the Truman administration was convinced, would have to give way to the immediate need of halting further Soviet advances across the European continent. NATO required the integration of West German soldiers to balance the strength of the Red Army.

Prevailing thought in Washington dictated that with the East and West in atomic deadlock, the United States would have to work harder to block Soviet infiltration of potential new nations and their resources. In the president's inaugural address of the previous January 1949, he had outlined his foreign policy objectives: support the United Nations, Marshall Plan, "freedom-loving nations," and "a bold new program for making the benefits of our scientific advances and industrial progress available for the improvement and growth of underdeveloped areas." The last, a Technical Assistance Program for Latin America, Asia, and Africa, became known as Point Four. It aimed at combating "hunger, misery, and despair" and thus preventing the spread of communism into the southern half of the globe. Congress, however, reacted with little enthusiasm. It implemented Point Four in 1950 by allocating the modest sum of $35 million for technical aid and placing the program under the Technical Cooperation Administration. Despite the dearth of funds, the United States soon negotiated agreements with more than thirty countries and helped fight disease and famine while raising living standards through the building of facilities for hydroelectric power and irrigation. The Soviets responded quickly. Less than a week after the president called for Point Four, they established a Council for Mutual Economic Assistance, designed to help their fellow Communist states.

By 1950, the U.S. emphasis in foreign aid had shifted dramatically from economic to military assistance. The Truman Doctrine had proved the State-War-Navy Coordinating Committee to be correct: crushing the rebellion in Greece was the necessary prerequisite to its economic rehabilitation. Marshall Plan aid gradually became more military oriented, and soon afterward the United States implemented a global military aid program under the Mutual Defense Assistance Act of 1949. Within two years, the West lifted the restraints from Italy, permitting it to rearm. American priorities had also become unmistakably military with the establishment of NATO because that organization's stated purpose was to maintain a ground force large enough to hold off Soviet attack until the United States could engage the Strategic Air Command.

Yet NATO's conventional land forces never became as large as hoped, primarily because France led the movement to integrate Germany's industrial might into a broadly based program of West European control that would, as a necessary by-product, prevent a resurgence of the German military machine. French Foreign Minister Robert Schuman succeeded in instituting the Schuman Plan of 1951, which established the European Coal and Steel Community and was composed of France, West Germany, Italy, and the three Benelux countries. The European allies of the United States seemed satisfied to remain under free nuclear protection while continuing to block the use of West German troops.

The biggest impetus to a militarized U.S. foreign policy was nuclear expansion. The Soviets' challenge to the atomic monopoly of the United States, combined with the Communist victory in China shortly afterward (discussed in the next chapter), seemed too close in time to be coincidental. In January 1950, the president ordered the development of a hydrogen bomb that would be hundreds of times more powerful than either atomic bomb used on Japan. Opposition to the hydrogen bomb (or "Super") came from a long list of scientists that included J. Robert Oppenheimer, who had supervised the building of the atomic bomb and now joined David Lilienthal (chair of the Atomic Energy Commission) in calling the hydrogen bomb "a weapon of genocide." The result, they all warned, would be an arms race that could escalate into nuclear war. Truman, however, pushed for the new bomb, which the United States successfully tested in 1952. A year later, the Soviets did the same.

Toward a Global Strategy: NSC-68

In late January 1950, Truman directed the State and Defense Departments "to make an overall review and reassessment of American foreign and defense policy in the light of the loss of China [to communism], the Soviet mastery of atomic energy and the prospect of the fusion [hydrogen] bomb." Kennan feared a massive arms buildup intended to establish what Acheson called "situations of strength" and resigned as head of the State Department's Policy Planning Staff. His replacement was Paul Nitze, a hard-liner who supervised the preparation of this report, which reached the president's desk in April. There was no foreseeable end to the Communist threat, according to National Security Council Study 68 (NSC-68); conflict was "endemic." As Acheson later noted, the top-secret document "combined the ideology of communist doctrine and the power of the Russian state into an aggressive expansionist drive, which found its chief opponent, and, therefore, target in the antithetical ideas and power of our own country." The Free World faced danger from a "combination of ideological zeal and fighting power."

Kennan had been correct in his prognosis: NSC-68 urged the United States to "strike out on a bold and massive program of rebuilding the West's defensive potential to surpass that of the Soviet world, and of meeting each fresh challenge promptly and unequivocally." Americans were to defend non-Communists from Soviet encroachments through a military-oriented, globalist, and activist policy of containment. Such an objective necessitated expenditures almost four times greater than the budgeted amounts for 1950. Not only did the United States have to develop more "atomic weapons," but it must implement a decision already made by the president to build the infinitely more powerful "thermonuclear" or hydrogen bomb.

NSC-68, not declassified until the mid-1970s (and even then by accident), had defined the world's problems in the broad ideological terms of communism versus democracy. It had called on the United States to take the lead in restoring world stability as the first step toward destroying communism. Once the United States had contained the Communists, it was to "foster the seeds of destruction within the Soviet system." Any distinction between vital and peripheral interests had blurred, meaning that strategic areas included every point along the Soviet perimeter. No longer was there a distinction between the security of the United States and that of the world; they had meshed into a global and offensive policy that condoned any policy necessary to victory. "The integrity of our system will not be jeopardized by any measures, covert or overt, violent or nonviolent, which serve the purposes of frustrating the Kremlin design."

But before the Truman administration could decide how to implement these recom-

---

NSC-68 globalized the Cold War and called for containing the Soviet Union by a massive military buildup by the United States.

NSC-68 [National Security Council Study no. 68], April 14, 1950, U.S. Department of State, *Papers Relating to the Foreign Relations of the United States, 1950, National Security Affairs; Foreign Economic Policy* (Washington, D.C.: Government Printing Office, 1977), vol. 1, 252–92.

As for the policy of "containment," it is one which seeks by all means short of war to (1) block further expansion of Soviet power, (2) expose the falsities of Soviet pretensions, (3) induce a retraction of the Kremlin's control and influence and (4) in general, so foster the seeds of destruction within the Soviet system that the Kremlin is brought at least to the point of modifying its behavior to conform to generally accepted international standards. . . .

In the concept of "containment," the maintenance of a strong military posture is deemed to be essential for two reasons: (1) as an ultimate guarantee of our national security and (2) as an indispensable backdrop to the conduct of the policy of "containment." Without superior aggregate military strength, in being and readily mobilizable, a policy of "containment"—which is in effect a policy of calculated and gradual coercion—is no more than a policy of bluff. . . .

A more rapid build-up of political, economic, and military strength and thereby of confidence in the free world than is now contemplated is the only course which is consistent with progress toward achieving our fundamental purpose. The frustration of the Kremlin design requires the free world to develop a successfully functioning political and economic system and a vigorous political offensive against the Soviet Union. These, in turn, require an adequate military shield under which they can develop . . . a firm policy intended to check and to roll back the Kremlin's drive for world domination.

mendations, its justification for a huge military build-up fortuitously appeared in June 1950, when war suddenly broke out in Korea.

Selected Readings

Acheson, Dean. *Present at the Creation: My Years in the State Department.* 1969.

Alexander, George M. *The Prelude to the Truman Doctrine: British Policy in Greece, 1944–1947.* 1982.

Ambrose, Stephen E., and Douglas G. Brinkley. *Rise to Globalism: American Foreign Policy since 1938.* 8th ed., 1997.

Anderson, Carol. *Eyes Off the Prize: The United Nations and the African American Struggle for Human Rights, 1944–1955.* 2003.

Anderson, Irvine H. *Aramco, the United States, and Saudi Arabia: A Study of the Dynamics of Foreign Oil Policy, 1933–1950.* 1981.

Anderson, Sheldon. "Poland and the Marshall Plan, 1947–1949." *Diplomatic History* 15 (1991): 473–94.

Anderson, Terry H. *The United States, Great Britain, and the Cold War, 1944–1947.* 1981.

Arkes, Hadley. *Bureaucracy, the Marshall Plan, and the National Interest.* 1972.

Backer, John H. *The Decision to Divide Germany: American Foreign Policy in Transition.* 1978.

———. *Winds of History: The German Years of Lucius DuBignon Clay.* 1983.

Ball, S. J. *The Cold War: An International History, 1947–1991.* 1998.

Barker, Elisabeth. *The British Between the Superpowers, 1945–1950.* 1983.

Barnes, Trevor. "The Secret Cold War: The C.I.A. and American Foreign Policy in Europe, 1946–1956. Part I." *The Historical Journal* 24 (1981): 399–415.

———. "The Secret Cold War: The C.I.A. and American Foreign Policy in Europe, 1946–1956. Part II." *The Historical Journal* 25 (1982): 649–71.

Baylis, John. *The Diplomacy of Pragmatism: Britain and the Formation of NATO, 1942–1949.* 1993.

Beisner, Robert L. *Dean Acheson: A Life in the Cold War.* 2006.

Bernstein, Barton J. "American Foreign Policy and the Origins of the Cold War." In Barton J. Bernstein, ed., *Politics and Policies of the Truman Administration,* 15–77. 1970.

Best, Richard A., Jr. *Co-operation with Like-Minded Peoples: British Influences on American Security Policy, 1945–1949.* 1986.

Bill, James A. *The Eagle and the Lion: The Tragedy of American-Iranian Relations.* 1988.

Bird, Kai, and Martin J. Sherwin. *American Prometheus: The Triumph and Tragedy of J. Robert Oppenheimer.* 2005.

Black, Allida M. *Casting Her Own Shadow: Eleanor Roosevelt and the Shaping of Postwar Liberalism.* 1995.

Blum, Robert M. "Surprised by Tito: The Anatomy of an Intelligence Failure." *Diplomatic History* 12 (1988): 39–57.

Bohlen, Charles E. *Witness to History, 1929–1969.* 1973.

Boll, Michael M. *Cold War in the Balkans: American Foreign Policy and the Emergence of Communist Bulgaria, 1943–1947.* 1984.

Borowski, Harry R. *A Hollow Threat: Strategic Air Power and Containment before Korea.* 1982.

Boyer, Paul S. *By the Bomb's Early Light: American Thought and Culture at the Dawn of the Atomic Age.* 1985.

Brands, H. W. *The Devil We Knew: Americans and the Cold War.* 1993.

———. *Inside the Cold War: Loy Henderson and the Rise of the American Empire, 1918–1961.* 1991.

———. *The Specter of Neutralism: The United States and the Emergence of the Third World, 1947–1960.* 1989.

Brands, Henry W., Jr. "Redefining the Cold War: American Policy toward Yugoslavia, 1948–60." *Diplomatic History* 11 (1987): 41–53.

Browder, Robert P., and Thomas G. Smith. *Independent: A Biography of Lewis W. Douglas.* 1986.

Buhite, Russell D., and William C. Hamel. "War for Peace: The Question of an American Preventive War against the Soviet Union, 1945–1955." *Diplomatic History* 14 (1990): 367–84.

Byrnes, James F. *All in One Lifetime.* 1958.

———. *Speaking Frankly.* 1947.

Callahan, David. *Dangerous Capabilities: Paul Nitze and the Cold War.* 1990.

Campbell, Thomas M. *Masquerade Peace: America's UN Policy.* 1973.

Chace, James. *Acheson: The Secretary of State Who Created the American World.* 1998.

Cohen, Michael J. *Truman and Israel.* 1990.

Cohen, Warren I. *America in the Age of Soviet Power, 1945–1991.* 1993.

Conquest, Robert. *Stalin: Breaker of Nations.* 1991.

Costigliola, Frank. *France and the United States: The Cold Alliance since World War II.* 1992.

Couloumbis, Theodore A. *The United States, Greece and Turkey.* 1983.

Craig, R. Bruce. *Treasonable Doubt: The Harry Dexter White Spy Case.* 2004.

Cronin, Audrey K. *Great Power Politics and the Struggle over Austria, 1945–1955.* 1986.

Davison, W. Phillips. *The Berlin Blockade: A Study in Cold War Politics.* 1958.

DePorte, A. W. *Europe Between the Superpowers: The Enduring Alliance.* 1979.

DeSantis, Hugh. *The Diplomacy of Silence: The American Foreign Service, the Soviet Union, and the Cold War, 1933–1947.* 1980.

Deutscher, Isaac. *Stalin: A Political Biography.* 2nd ed., 1967.

Doenecke, Justus D. *Not to the Swift: The Old Isolationists in the Cold War Era.* 1979.

Donovan, John C. *The Cold Warriors.* 1974.

Donovan, Robert J. *Conflict and Crisis: The Presidency of Harry S Truman, 1945–1948.* 1977.

———. *Tumultuous Years: The Presidency of Harry S. Truman, 1949–1953.* 1982.

Edmonds, Robin. *Setting the Mould: The United States and Britain, 1945–1950.* 1986.

Eisenberg, Carolyn. *Drawing the Line: The American Decision to Divide Germany, 1944–1949.* 1996.

Elliott, Mark R. *Pawns of Yalta: Soviet Refugees and America's Role in Their Repatriation.* 1982.

Ellwood, David W. *Rebuilding Europe: Western Europe, America, and Postwar Reconstruction.* 1992.

Evangelista, Matthew A. "Stalin's Postwar Army Reappraised." *International Security* 7 (1982–1983): 110–38.

Evensen, Bruce J. *Truman, Palestine, and the Press: Shaping Conventional Wisdom at the Beginning of the Cold War.* 1992.

Fawcett, Louise L. *Iran and the Cold War: The Azerbaijan Crisis of 1946.* 1992.

Feis, Herbert. *From Trust to Terror: The Onset of the Cold War, 1945–1950.* 1970.

Ferrell, Robert H. *George Marshall.* 1966.

———. *Harry S. Truman: A Life.* 1994.

———. *Harry S. Truman and the Modern American Presidency.* 1983.

Fleming, D. F. *The Cold War and Its Origins, 1917–1960.* 2 vols., 1961.

Folly, Martin H. "Breaking the Vicious Circle: Britain, the United States, and the Genesis of the North Atlantic Treaty." *Diplomatic History* 12 (1988): 59–77.

Freeland, Richard. *The Truman Doctrine and the Origins of McCarthyism: Foreign Policy, Domestic Politics, and National Security, 1946–1948.* 1970.

Fried, Richard M. *Nightmare in Red: The McCarthy Era in Perspective.* 1990.

———. *The Russians Are Coming! The Russians Are Coming! Pageantry and Patriotism in Cold-War America.* 1998.

Gaddis, John L. *The Cold War: A New History.* 2005.

———. "The Corporatist Synthesis: A Skeptical View." *Diplomatic History* 10 (1986): 357–62.

———. "The Emerging Post-Revisionist Synthesis on the Origins of the Cold War." *Diplomatic History* 7 (1983): 171–90.

———. "Intelligence, Espionage, and Cold War Origins." *Diplomatic History* 13 (1989): 191–212.

———. *The Long Peace: Inquiries into the History of the Cold War.* 1987.

———. "NSC-68 and the Problem of Ends and Means." *International Security* 4 (1980): 164–80.

———. *Russia, the Soviet Union, and the United States: An Interpretive History.* 2nd ed., 1990.

———. *Strategies of Containment: A Critical Appraisal of Postwar American National Security Policy.* 1982; rev. ed., 2005.

———. *The United States and the Origins of the Cold War, 1941–1947.* 1972.

———. *We Now Know: Rethinking Cold War History.* 1997.

Gardner, Lloyd C. *Architects of Illusion: Men and Ideas in American Foreign Policy, 1941–1949.* 1970.

Gimbel, John. *The American Occupation of Germany: Politics and the Military, 1945–1949.* 1968.

———. *The Origins of the Marshall Plan.* 1976.

Goedde, Petra. *GIs and Germans: Culture, Gender, and Foreign Relations, 1945–1949.* 2003.

Goldman, Eric F. *The Crucial Decade and After.* 1960.

Goode, James F. *The United States and Iran, 1946–51: The Diplomacy of Neglect.* 1989.

Gori, Francesca, and Silvio Pons. *The Soviet Union and Europe in the Cold War, 1945–53.* 1996.

Gormly, James L. *The Collapse of the Grand Alliance, 1945–1948.* 1987.

——. *From Potsdam to the Cold War: Big Three Diplomacy, 1945–1947.* 1990.

Gray, William G. *Germany's Cold War: The Global Campaign to Isolate East Germany, 1949–1969.* 2003.

Griffith, Robert. *The Politics of Fear: Joseph R. McCarthy and the Senate.* 1970.

Hahn, Peter L. *Caught in the Middle East: U.S. Policy toward the Arab-Israeli Conflict, 1945–1961.* 2004.

——. *The United States, Great Britain, and Egypt, 1945–1956: Strategy and Diplomacy in the Early Cold War.* 1991.

Hamby, Alonzo L. *Man of the People: A Life of Harry S. Truman.* 1995.

Hanhimäki, Jussi M. *Containing Coexistence: America, Russia, and the "Finnish Solution."* 1997.

Harbutt, Fraser J. "American Challenge, Soviet Response: The Beginning of the Cold War, February–May, 1946." *Political Science Quarterly* 96 (1981–1982): 623–39.

——. *The Iron Curtain: Churchill, America, and the Origins of the Cold War.* 1986.

Harper, John L. *America and the Reconstruction of Italy, 1945–1948.* 1986.

Harrington, Daniel F. "The Berlin Blockade Revisited." *International History Review* 6 (1984): 88–112.

——. "Kennan, Bohlen, and the Riga Axioms." *Diplomatic History* 2 (1978): 423–37.

——. "United States, United Nations and the Berlin Blockade." *Historian* 52 (1990): 262–85.

Hathaway, Robert M. *Ambiguous Partnership: Britain and America, 1944–1947.* 1981.

Haynes, John E. *Red Scare or Red Menace? American Communism and Anticommunism in the Cold War Era.* 1996.

Haynes, Richard F. *The Awesome Power: Harry S. Truman as Commander-in-Chief.* 1973.

Herken, Gregg. *Counsels of War.* 1985.

——. *The Winning Weapon: The Atomic Bomb in the Cold War, 1945–1950.* 1980.

Herring, George C. *Aid to Russia, 1941–1946: Strategy, Diplomacy, the Origins of the Cold War.* 1973.

Hershberg, James G. *James B. Conant: Harvard to Hiroshima and the Making of the Nuclear Age.* 1993.

Hess, Gary R. "The Iranian Crisis of 1945–46 and the Cold War." *Political Science Quarterly* 89 (1974): 117–46.

Hitchcock, William I. "France, the Western Alliance, and the Origins of the Schuman Plan, 1948–1950." *Diplomatic History* 21 (1997): 603–30.

Hixson, Walter L. *George F. Kennan: Cold War Iconoclast.* 1989.

Hogan, Michael J. "Corporatism: A Positive Appraisal." *Diplomatic History* 10 (1986): 363–72.

——. *A Cross of Iron: Harry S. Truman and the Origins of the National Security State, 1945–1954.* 1998.

——. *The Marshall Plan: America, Britain, and the Reconstruction of Western Europe, 1947–1952.* 1987.

——. "Revival and Reform: America's Twentieth-Century Search for a New Economic Order Abroad." *Diplomatic History* 8 (1984): 287–310.

——. "The Search for a 'Creative Peace': The United States, European Unity, and the Origins of the Marshall Plan." *Diplomatic History* 6 (1982): 267–85.

Hoopes, Townsend, and Douglas Brinkley. *Driven Patriot: The Life and Times of James Forrestal.* 1992.

Iatrides, John O. *Revolt in Athens: The Greek Communist "Second Round," 1944–1945.* 1972.

Ireland, Timothy P. *Creating the Entangling Alliance: The Origins of the North Atlantic Treaty Organization.* 1981.

Isaacson, Walter, and Evan Thomas. *The Wise Men: Six Friends and the World They Made: Acheson, Bohlen, Harriman, Kennan, Lovett, McCloy.* 1986.

Jackson, Scott. "Prologue to the Marshall Plan: The Origins of the American Commitment for a European Recovery Program." *Journal of American History* 65 (1979): 1043–68.

Jenkins, Roy. *Truman.* 1986.

Jessup, Philip C. "Park Avenue Diplomacy—Ending the Berlin Blockade." *Political Science Quarterly* 87 (1972): 377–400.

Johnson, Robert H. *Improbable Dangers: U.S. Conceptions of Threat in the Cold War and After.* 1994.

Jones, Howard. "The Diplomacy of Restraint: The United States' Efforts to Repatriate Greek Children Evacuated During the Civil War of 1946–49." *Journal of Modern Greek Studies* 3 (1985): 65–85.

———. *"A New Kind of War": America's Global Strategy and the Truman Doctrine in Greece.* 1989.

———, and Randall B. Woods. "Origins of the Cold War in Europe and the Near East: Recent Historiography and the National Security Imperative." *Diplomatic History* 17 (1993): 251–76.

Jones, Joseph. *The Fifteen Weeks (February 21–June 5, 1947).* 1955.

Kaplan, Lawrence S. *A Community of Interests: NATO and the Military Assistance Program, 1948–1951.* 1980.

———. *The Long Entanglement: NATO's First Fifty Years.* 1999.

———. *NATO and the United States: The Enduring Alliance.* 1988.

———. *The United States and NATO: The Formative Years.* 1984.

Kaufman, Burton I. *The Arab Middle East and the United States: Inter-Arab Rivalry and Superpower Diplomacy.* 1996.

Kennan, George F. *American Diplomacy.* Expanded ed., 1984. Originally published as *American Diplomacy, 1900–1950.* 1951.

———. *Memoirs, 1925–1950.* 1967.

———. "The Sources of Soviet Conduct." *Foreign Affairs* 25 (1947): 566–82.

Kent, John. *British Imperial Strategy and the Origins of the Cold War, 1944–49.* 1993.

Kimball, Warren F. *Swords or Ploughshares? The Morgenthau Plan for Defeated Nazi Germany, 1943–1946.* 1976.

Klehr, Harvey, and Ronald Radosh. *The Amerasia Spy Case: Prelude to McCarthyism.* 1996.

Kochavi, Arieh J. *Post-Holocaust Politics: Britain, the United States, and Jewish Refugees, 1945–1948.* 2001.

Kofas, Jon V. *Intervention and Underdevelopment: Greece during the Cold War.* 1989.

Kofsky, Frank. *Harry S. Truman and the War Scare of 1948: A Successful Campaign to Deceive the Nation.* 1993.

Kolko, Joyce, and Gabriel Kolko. *The Limits of Power: The World and United States Foreign Policy, 1945–1954.* 1972.

Krenn, Michael L. *Black Diplomacy: African Americans and the State Department, 1945–1969.* 1999.

Kuklick, Bruce. *American Policy and the Division of Germany: The Clash with Russia over Reparations.* 1972.

Kuniholm, Bruce R. *The Origins of the Cold War in the Near East: Great Power Conflict and Diplomacy in Iran, Turkey, and Greece.* 1980.

Kunz, Diane B. *Butter and Guns: America's Cold War Economic Diplomacy.* 1997.

LaFeber, Walter. *America, Russia, and the Cold War, 1945–1996.* 8th ed., 1997.

Laqueur, Walter. *Stalin: The Glasnost Revelations.* 1990.

Larson, Deborah W. *Anatomy of Mistrust: U.S.-Soviet Relations during the Cold War.* 1997.

———. *Origins of Containment: A Psychological Explanation.* 1985.

Lees, Lorraine M. "The American Decision to Assist Tito, 1948–1949." *Diplomatic History* 2 (1978): 407–22.

———. *Keeping Tito Afloat: The United States, Yugoslavia, and the Cold War.* 1997.

Leffler, Melvyn P. "The American Conception of National Security and the Beginnings of the Cold War, 1945–48." *American Historical Review* 89 (1984): 346–81.

———. *A Preponderance of Power: National Security, the Truman Administration, and the Cold War.* 1992.

———. *The Specter of Communism: The United States and the Origins of the Cold War, 1917–1953.* 1994.

———. "Strategy, Diplomacy, and the Cold War: The United States, Turkey, and NATO, 1945–1952." *Journal of American History* 71 (1985): 807–25.

———. "The United States and the Strategic Dimensions of the Marshall Plan." *Diplomatic History* 12 (1988): 277–306.

Leonard, Thomas M. *The United States and Central America, 1944–1949: Perceptions of Political Dynamics.* 1984.

Leslie, Stuart W. *The Cold War and American Science: The Military-Industrial-Academic Complex at MIT and Stanford.* 1993.

Levering, Ralph B. *The Cold War: A Post-Cold War History.* 1994; rev. ed., 2005.

Lieberman, Joseph I. *Scorpion and Tarantula: The Struggle to Control Atomic Weapons, 1945–1949.* 1970.

Liedtke, Boris N. *Embracing a Dictatorship: U.S. Relations with Spain, 1945–53.* 1998.

Lindee, M. Susan. *Suffering Made Real: American Science and the Survivors at Hiroshima.* 1994.

Loescher, Gil, and John A. Scanlan. *Calculated Kindness: Refugees and America's Half-Open Door, 1945 to the Present.* 1986.

Louis, William R. *The British Empire in the Middle East, 1945–1951: Arab Nationalism, the United States, and Postwar Imperialism.* 1984.

Lukas, Richard C. *Bitter Legacy: Polish-American Relations in the Wake of World War II.* 1982.

Lundestad, Geir. *America, Scandinavia, and the Cold War, 1945–1949.* 1980.

———. *The American Non-Policy towards Eastern Europe, 1943–1947: Universalism in an Area Not of Essential Interest to the United States.* 1975.

Lytle, Mark. *The Origins of the Iranian-American Alliance, 1941–1953.* 1987.

Maddox, Robert J. *The New Left and the Origins of the Cold War.* 1973.

Mark, Eduard. "American Policy toward Eastern Europe and the Origins of the Cold War, 1941–1946: An Alternative Interpretation." *Journal of American History* 68 (1981): 313–36.

Mastny, Vojtech. *The Cold War and Soviet Insecurity: The Stalin Years.* 1996.

———. *Russia's Road to the Cold War: Diplomacy, Warfare, and the Politics of Communism, 1941–1945.* 1979.

———. "Stalin and the Militarization of the Cold War." *International Security* 9 (1984–1985): 109–29.

Max, Stanley M. *The United States, Great Britain, and the Sovietization of Hungary, 1945–1948.* 1985.

Mayers, David A. *Cracking the Monolith: U.S. Policy Against the Sino-Soviet Alliance, 1949–1955.* 1986.

———. *George Kennan and the Dilemmas of US Foreign Policy.* 1988.

Mazuzan, George T. *Warren R. Austin at the U.N., 1946–1953.* 1977.

McAllister, James. *No Exit: America and the German Problem, 1943–1954.* 2002.

McCormick, Thomas J. *America's Half-Century: United States Foreign Policy in the Cold War.* 1989.

McCoy, Donald R. *The Presidency of Harry S. Truman.* 1984.

McCullough, David. *Truman.* 1992.

McFarland, Stephen L. "A Peripheral View of the Origins of the Cold War: The Crises in Iran, 1941–47." *Diplomatic History* 4 (1980): 333–51.

McLellan, David S. *Dean Acheson: The State Department Years.* 1976.

McNeal, Robert H. *Stalin: Man and Ruler.* 1988.

Mee, Charles L., Jr. *The Marshall Plan: The Launching of the Pax Americana.* 1984.

Messer, Robert L. *The End of an Alliance: James F. Byrnes, Roosevelt, Truman, and the Origins of the Cold War.* 1982.

———. "Paths Not Taken: The United States Department of State and Alternatives to Containment, 1945–1946." *Diplomatic History* 1 (1977): 297–319.

Miller, Aaron D. *Search for Security: Saudi Arabian Oil and American Foreign Policy, 1939–1949.* 1980.

Miller, James E. *The United States and Italy, 1940–1950: The Politics and Diplomacy of Stabilization.* 1986.

Milward, Alan S. *The Reconstruction of Western Europe, 1945–1951.* 1984.

———. "Was the Marshall Plan Necessary?" *Diplomatic History* 13 (1989): 231–53.

Miscamble, Wilson D. *George F. Kennan and the Making of American Foreign Policy, 1947–1950.* 1992.

Morgan, Roger. *The United States and West Germany, 1945–1973: A Study in Alliance Politics.* 1974.

Naimark, Norman. *The Russians in Germany: A History of the Soviet Zone of Occupation, 1945–1949.* 1995.

Nelson, Anna K. "President Truman and the Evolution of the National Security Council." *Journal of American History* 72 (1985): 360–78.

Nelson, Daniel J. *Wartime Origins of the Berlin Dilemma.* 1978.

Nesbitt, Francis N. *Race for Sanctions: African Americans Against Apartheid, 1946–1994.* 2004.

Newman, Robert P. *Truman and the Hiroshima Cult.* 1995.

Ninkovich, Frank. *The Diplomacy of Ideas: U.S. Foreign Policy and Cultural Relations, 1938–1950.* 1981.

———. *Modernity and Power: A History of the Domino Theory in the Twentieth Century.* 1994.

Offner, Arnold A. *Another Such Victory: President Truman and the Cold War, 1945–1953.* 2002.

Osgood, Robert E. *NATO: The Entangling Alliance.* 1962.

Ovendale, Ritchie. *The English-Speaking Alliance: Britain and the United States, the Dominions and the Cold War, 1945–1951.* 1985.

Pach, Chester, Jr. *Arming the Free World: The Origins of the United States Military Assistance Program, 1945–1950.* 1991.

Painter, David S. *The Cold War: An International History.* 1999.

——. *Oil and the American Century: The Political Economy of U.S. Foreign Oil Policy, 1941–1954.* 1986.

Paterson, Thomas G. *On Every Front: The Making of the Cold War.* 1979.

——. *Soviet-American Confrontation: Postwar Reconstruction and the Origins of the Cold War.* 1973.

Patterson, James T. *Mr. Republican: A Biography of Robert Taft.* 1972.

Peterson, Edward N. *The American Occupation of Germany: Retreat to Victory.* 1977.

Pfau, Richard. "Containment in Iran, 1946: The Shift to an Active Policy." *Diplomatic History* 1 (1977): 359–72.

Pisani, Sallie. *The CIA and the Marshall Plan.* 1991.

Pogue, Forrest C. *George C. Marshall: Statesman, 1945–1949.* 1987.

Pollard, Robert A. *Economic Security and the Origins of the Cold War, 1945–1950.* 1985.

——. "Economic Security and the Origins of the Cold War: Bretton Woods, the Marshall Plan, and American Rearmament, 1944–50." *Diplomatic History* 9 (1985): 271–89.

Prados, John. *Presidents' Secret Wars: CIA Pentagon Covert Operations from World War II through the Persian Gulf.* 1996.

Rabel, Roberto G. *Between East and West: Trieste, the United States, and the Cold War, 1941–1954.* 1988.

Radzinskii, Edward. *Stalin: The First In-Depth Biography Based on Explosive New Documents from Russia's Secret Archives.* 1996.

Randall, Stephen J. *United States Foreign Oil Policy, 1919–1948: For Profits and Security.* 1985.

Ranelagh, John. *The Agency: The Rise and Fall of the CIA.* 1986.

Rappaport, Armin. "The United States and European Integration: The First Phase." *Diplomatic History* 5 (1981): 121–49.

Raucher, Alan R. *Paul G. Hoffman: Architect of Foreign Aid.* 1986.

Rearden, Steven L. *History of the Office of the Secretary of Defense. Vol. 1: The Formative Years, 1947–1950.* 1984.

Reid, Escott. *Time of Fear and Hope: The Making of the North Atlantic Treaty, 1947–1949.* 1977.

Resis, Albert. *Stalin, the Politburo, and the Onset of the Cold War, 1945–1946.* 1988.

Robertson, David. *Sly and Able: A Political Biography of James F. Byrnes.* 1994.

Rogers, Daniel E. *Politics After Hitler: The Western Allies and the German Party System.* 1995.

Roman, Eric. *Hungary and the Victor Powers, 1945–1950.* 1996.

Rose, Lisle A. *After Yalta.* 1973.

Rosenberg, David A. "American Atomic Strategy and the Hydrogen Bomb Decision." *Journal of American History* 66 (1979): 62–87.

Rubenberg, Cheryl. *Israel and the American National Interest.* 1986.

Rubin, Barry. *The Great Powers in the Middle East, 1941–1947: The Road to the Cold War.* 1980.

Ruddy, T. Michael. *The Cautious Diplomat: Charles E. Bohlen and the Soviet Union, 1929–1969.* 1986.

Ryan, Henry B. *The Vision of Anglo-America: The US-UK Alliance and the Emerging Cold War, 1943–1946.* 1987.

Schlaim, Avi. *The United States and the Berlin Blockade, 1948–1949: A Study in Crisis Decision-Making.* 1983.

Schlesinger, Arthur M., Jr. "Origins of the Cold War." *Foreign Affairs* 46 (1967): 22–52.

Schoenbaum, David. *The United States and the State of Israel.* 1993.

Schwartz, Thomas A. *America's Germany: John J. McCloy and the Federal Republic of Germany.* 1991.

Sibley, Katherine A. S. *Red Spies in America: Stolen Secrets and the Dawn of the Cold War.* 2004.

Siracusa, Joseph M. *Rearming the Cold War: Paul H. Nitze, the H-Bomb and the Origins of a Soviet First Strike.* 1983.

Smith, E. Timothy. *The United States, Italy, and NATO, 1947–52.* 1991.

Smith, Gaddis. *Dean Acheson.* 1972.

Smith, Jean Edward. *The Defense of Berlin.* 1963.

——. "General Clay and the Russians: A Continuation of the Wartime Alliance in Germany, 1945–1948." *Virginia Quarterly Review* 64 (1988): 20–36.

Snetsinger, John. *Truman, the Jewish Vote, and the Creation of Israel.* 1974.

Spanier, John W. *American Foreign Policy since World War II.* 14th ed., 1998.

Stavrakis, Peter J. *Moscow and Greek Communism, 1944–1949.* 1989.

Steel, Ronald. *Walter Lippmann and the American Century.* 1980.

Steinitz, Mark S. "The U.S. Propaganda Effort in Czechoslovakia, 1945–48." *Diplomatic History* 6 (1982): 359–85.

Stephanson, Anders. *Kennan and the Art of Foreign Policy.* 1989.

Stivers, William. "The Incomplete Blockade: Soviet Zone Supply of West Berlin, 1948–49." *Diplomatic History* 21 (1997): 569–602.

Stoff, Michael B. *Oil, War, and American Security: The Search for a National Policy on Foreign Oil, 1941–1947.* 1980.

Stoler, Mark A. *George C. Marshall: Soldier-Statesman of the American Century.* 1989.

Taubman, William. *Stalin's American Policy: From Entente to Détente to Cold War.* 1982.

Theoharis, Athan G. *The Yalta Myths: An Issue in U.S. Politics, 1945–1955.* 1970.

Thomas, Evan. *The Very Best Men: Four Who Dared: The Early Years of the CIA.* 1995.

Thomas, Hugh. *Armed Truce: The Beginnings of the Cold War, 1945–46.* 1987.

Trachtenberg, Marc. *A Constructed Peace: The Making of the European Settlement, 1945–1963.* 1999.

———. "A 'Wasting Asset': American Strategy and the Shifting Nuclear Balance, 1949–1954." *International Security* 13 (1988–89): 5–49.

Troy, Thomas F. *Wild Bill and Intrepid: Donovan, Stephenson, and the Origin of CIA.* 1996.

Truman, Harry S. *Memoirs.* 2 vols., 1956.

Tusa, Ann, and John Tusa. *The Berlin Airlift.* 1988.

Ulam, Adam B. *The Communists: The Story of Power and Lost Illusions, 1948–1991.* 1992.

———. *The Rivals: America and Russia since World War II.* 1971.

Ullmann, Walter. *The United States in Prague, 1945–1948.* 1978.

Wala, Michael. "Selling the Marshall Plan at Home: The Committee for the Marshall Plan to Aid European Recovery." *Diplomatic History* 10 (1986): 247–65.

Walker, J. Samuel. *Henry A. Wallace and American Foreign Policy.* 1976.

Wall, Irwin M. *The United States and the Making of Postwar France, 1945–1954.* 1991.

Walton, Richard J. *Henry Wallace, Harry Truman and the Cold War.* 1976.

Wandycz, Piotr S. *The United States and Poland.* 1980.

Ward, Patricia D. *The Threat of Peace: James F. Byrnes and the Council of Foreign Ministers, 1945–1946.* 1979.

Weiner, Tim. *Legacy of Ashes: The History of the CIA.* 2007.

Wells, Samuel F., Jr. "Sounding the Tocsin: NSC-68 and the Soviet Threat." *International Security* (1979): 116–58.

Westad, Odd Arne. *The Global Cold War: Third World Interventions and the Making of Our Times.* 2006.

Wexler, Immanuel. *The Marshall Plan Revisited: The European Recovery Program in Economic Perspective.* 1983.

White, Graham, and John Maze. *Henry A. Wallace: His Search for a New World Order.* 1995.

Whitnah, Donald R., and Edgar L. Erickson. *The American Occupation of Austria: Planning and Early Years.* 1985.

Wilford, Hugh. *The CIA, the British Left and the Cold War: Calling the Tune?* 2003.

Williams, William A. *The Tragedy of American Diplomacy.* 1959. Rev. ed., 1972.

Williamson, Samuel R., and Steven L. Rearden. *The Origins of U.S. Nuclear Strategy, 1945–1953.* 1993.

Wittner, Lawrence S. *American Intervention in Greece, 1943–1949.* 1982.

———. "The Truman Doctrine and the Defense of Freedom." *Diplomatic History* 4 (1980): 161–87.

Woods, Randall B. *A Changing of the Guard: Anglo-American Relations, 1941–1946.* 1990.

———, and Howard Jones. *Dawning of the Cold War: The United States' Quest for Order.* 1991, 1994.

Yergin, Daniel H. *Shattered Peace: The Origins of the Cold War and the National Security State.* Rev. ed., 1990.

Zubok, V. M., and Constantine Pleshakov. *Inside the Kremlin's Cold War: From Stalin to Khrushchev.* 1996.

CHAPTER 2

Cold War and Containment in East Asia, 1950–1953

Outbreak of War in Korea

Early in the morning of June 25, 1950, more than 100,000 North Korean troops, using Soviet-made tanks and artillery, invaded the Republic of Korea along a 150-mile front and set off the first major military conflict of the Cold War. Succeeding events in East Asia became symbolic of the new military tactics necessitated by the dangers of atomic warfare. Indeed, the sudden and dramatic return to conventional conflict highlighted the irony confronting the United States: it possessed the bomb but could not use it. Americans believed they were fighting the Communists by proxy—that the Moscow government had manipulated the North Koreans into the attack and that the United States had to counter this new threat by any method short of all-out war. Kennan's theories seemed correct: the Soviets were determined to test Americans' will by probing soft spots throughout the world. The United States had shored up the Near East and Western Europe by the Truman Doctrine, Marshall Plan, and NATO; proponents of containment were convinced that the Soviets had now turned to East Asia.

Recent events in East Asia reinforced that belief. The U.S. postwar occupation of Japan

under General Douglas MacArthur had implanted democratic reforms that provided a model of Western ideals in East Asia and thereby threatened Soviet interests in that part of the world. But then, in late 1949, Jiang Jieshi's Chinese Nationalist forces had collapsed before Mao Zedong's Communists and retreated to the island of Formosa. It appeared that a monolithic communism out of the Kremlin had brought the "fall" of China and now tried to counter U.S. successes in Japan as an attempt to restore Soviet influence in East Asia. Washington's leaders perceived the invasion of South Korea as, for practical purposes, a Soviet invasion and sought to resist it by working through a UN force dominated by U.S. soldiers, money, and war materiel. To avoid the label of war, the conflict became officially known as a "police action."

American policy toward East Asia rested on three assumptions, none of them sound. The first was that communism in Korea, China, and everywhere else in East Asia was a single movement directed from Moscow. In fact, there were many Communist movements, some more or less controlled by the Kremlin and others not, and thus the United States failed to exploit these differences to its own strategic advantage. The second assumption was that every revolutionary movement in East Asia was Communist inspired or had communism as its goal. Actually, the most powerful force pushing for revolutionary change in East Asia was nationalism, not ideology, so despite an official (and usually sincere) U.S. policy of anticolonialism, discontented easterners perceived the continued U.S. presence and intervention in East Asia as the same type of Western colonialism practiced earlier by France, Britain, and the Netherlands. The third misguided assumption was the belief that "limited war" furnished a viable method for deterring the spread of communism. In actuality Americans, accustomed to fighting through to victory, were unwilling to endure the frustrations that limited war entails, and thus, in 1952, they voted the Democrats out of power for the first time in twenty years.

Japan

The U.S. occupation of Japan lasted from 1945 through 1952 and left the defeated country with markedly changed features. In December 1945, the United States, Britain, and China met with the Soviet Union in Moscow and established an advisory group in Tokyo known as the Four-Power Allied Council for Japan. The United States rejected the Soviets' call for a share in the occupation of Japan and agreed to their participation only in an advisory role. Authority rested in the Supreme Commander for the Allied Powers in Japan, General Douglas MacArthur. He worked under the supervision of the Far Eastern Advisory Commission in Washington, which was composed of the eleven nations (later expanded to thirteen) that had fought Japan in the war. By a firm and businesslike disposition, MacArthur dominated policy in Japan. His stern, authoritarian, and military manner—along with his sunglasses and the ever-present corncob pipe jutting upward from his mouth—appealed to people accustomed to worshipping an emperor. In truth, however, the war's devastation left the Japanese no choice.

The initial aims of the United States were to reduce Japan to lesser power status and to institute an ambitious democratic reform program. The first intention gradually changed as East Asia became a battleground of the Cold War and the grand hopes for making China into a major power sputtered and failed. The second goal, however, remained constant and soon became integral to restoring Japan to a position strong enough to balance off Soviet influence in East Asia. MacArthur drew up a constitution for Japan in May 1947, patterned after that of the United States. Under it, Japan "forever renounced war as a sovereign right of the nation and the threat or use of force as a means of settling international disputes." Japan also agreed to discard "land, sea, and air forces, as well as other war potential." Americans reformed the education system, barred war makers from official positions in the country, sponsored war crimes trials that led to imprisonment and executions, stripped Japan of overseas possessions, and allowed it to retain only the four islands comprising the homeland. The monarchy remained only in form because final power rested in delegates chosen by the people—including the votes of women (a revolution in itself). The United States also encouraged economic opportunity by breaking up industrial monopolies (the *zaibatsu*) and dividing huge land tracts among the peasants. As the Cold War intensified in East Asia by 1950, the U.S. occupation forces relaxed restrictions on industrial production and encouraged former Japanese leaders to reassume official responsibilities. Japan became a model of democratic reform in East Asia, a growing industrial ally with the United States, and a constant source of embarrassment to the Soviet Union.

China

The resumption of civil war in China after the end of World War II had threatened to cause the government's collapse under Communist

Jiang Jieshi and Wife
Jieshi headed the Chinese Nationalists until defeated in the civil war with Mao Zedong's Communists and driven off the mainland to Formosa in October 1949. *(Roger Viollet)*

attack. Such a possibility stunned Americans. Their longtime paternal policy toward China had expressed itself in continuing missionary and humanitarian interests, in the Open Door with its drive for the fabled "China market," and in Franklin D. Roosevelt's objective of establishing the huge country as a postwar world power. Yet these high trade expectations never materialized, and China did not become the reformed and progressive mammoth capable of bringing a balance of power to East Asia. In August 1945, the Soviets signed a treaty of "friendship" with the Nationalists that sent a signal to the Communists that they were on their own. Jiang's forces meanwhile received increased U.S. assistance in regaining control over the cities and the China coast. Communist forces meanwhile held on to the upper interior and ad-

vanced toward Manchuria, where they confiscated war materiel from the Japanese. Furthermore, Stalin violated his treaty with Jiang by extending secret aid to the Chinese Communists. Mao, however, refused to play a subordinate role to the Moscow government, which led Stalin to remark that the Chinese Communists were "not real communists" but "'margarine' communists." Despite the crack in the alleged Communist monolith, Americans continued to believe that the movement, whether inspired by Stalin or Mao, could cause the collapse of Nationalist China and constitute a major defeat in the Cold War.

The U.S. ambassador to Nationalist China, General Patrick Hurley, thought that the Kremlin's August 1945 decision to help Jiang provided an opportunity to defeat Mao's Communist forces. Hurley first tried to

Mao and Hurley
Arriving at Chongqing airport from Yenan for a conference with the chiefs of the central Chinese
government in August 1945. *(National Archives, Washington, D.C.)*

persuade Jiang and Mao to settle their differences, but after six weeks of negotiations in Chongqing, he failed, largely because Jiang demanded too much. Hurley resigned his post in November and accused the Foreign Service of supporting Mao (whom he disdainfully called "Mouse Dung"). Hurley's rebuke left an erroneous impression of the Foreign Service officers. They had long emphasized that Mao would win the civil war because of the Nationalists' weaknesses and lack of popular support, but their reasoned assessment seemed to question the traditional support of the United States for China, and for that they appeared to be Communist sympathizers.

After Hurley's resignation, President Truman appointed General George C. Marshall, retired army chief of staff and revered World War II figure, to head a special mission to resolve the problems in China. Like Stilwell and Hurley before him, Marshall was to arrange a cease-fire and build a coalition government, but with Jiang's regime standing as "the only legal government" and the "foundation of the new political structure." Marshall tried to bring the opposing groups together, but this objective showed that Washington had failed to recognize Mao's strength. Marshall did secure a truce in January 1946, and the Communists seemed interested in a coalition government—perhaps as a less costly route to victory. Under the truce terms, each side agreed to scale down its armies before combining them into a single force, which was to be trained by a thousand Americans in a Joint U.S. Military Advisory Group situated in

Nanking. Both antagonists would then write a new constitution for China. But the Marshall mission failed because neither the new government nor the army came into being.

Stilwell and the Foreign Service officers in China had been correct: Jiang's army was incapable of winning the war and uniting the country. Peace lasted fitfully through 1946, but in the meantime the Communists had established control over nearly all of Manchuria. Marshall realized that war was imminent and returned to the United States. The following month, he submitted a report attributing the dire situation in China to "extremist elements on both sides." Compromise between Jiang's conservative supporters and Mao's self-proclaimed "Marxists" was out of the question. That same month, January 1947, Marshall became secretary of state.

Fear of a Communist takeover in China and pressure from the opposition Republican Party to save the huge country led Truman to send another mission during the summer of 1947. General Albert C. Wedemeyer, the new appointee, recommended UN supervision of Manchuria; massive "moral, advisory, and material support" to the Nationalists; and a wide range of reforms in the army requiring the help of 10,000 U.S. military advisers. His proposals won no support from the Truman administration. In fact, Marshall prevented their release to the public—which doubtless added to the growing impression that the White House was doing little or nothing to save China from the Communists. Given the magnitude of U.S. commitments in Europe, the secretary of state opposed further involvement in China and warned that UN intervention in Manchuria could cause the Moscow government to call for a reciprocal arrangement in Greece. Past experience, he warned, demonstrated the futility in attempting to reform the Chinese Nationalist Army. The secretary was amenable to limited military and economic aid to the Nationalists, and he authorized a few advisers to upgrade Jiang's army. But this was as far as he would go. The postwar priorities of the United States had become strikingly similar to those before 1941: an emphasis on Europe and a hope that problems in East Asia would take care of themselves.

Marshall's recommendations for China were not sufficient to prevent a Communist victory. In May 1948, Congress appropriated $400 million of military and economic aid under the Foreign Assistance Act. Whereas critics warned that this was not enough, Senator Vandenberg contended that no amount was enough: "China aid is like sticking your finger in the lake and looking for the hole." On August 5, 1949, a State Department White Paper of more than one thousand pages of text and documents attributed China's impending collapse to the ineptitude of Jiang's Nationalists. In covering remarks, Dean Acheson, who had become secretary of state in January 1949, offered an accurate assessment of the situation. "Nothing that this country did or could have done within the reasonable limits of its capabilities could have changed that result," he wrote; "nothing that was left undone by this country has contributed to it. It was the product of internal Chinese forces." Acheson concluded that "a decision was arrived at within China, if only a decision by default." The first loyalty of the Chinese Communists, according to the White Paper, was to the Soviet Union.

Events in China gathered momentum as the Communists tightened their hold on the country. At a September conference in Beijing (Peiping, but now changed back to the title and spelling of ancient days as Peking), they drew up a constitution for the "People's Republic of China," which had the outward markings of democracy but was Communist. Mao declared the regime in effect on October 1, 1949, with himself as head and Zhou Enlai (Chou En-lai) as premier and foreign minister. The Soviet Union extended recognition the next day, leading Jiang's Nationalists to break relations with Moscow on October 3. Although Britain and other non-Communist countries eventually recognized Communist China, the United States again rejected de facto recognition policy and on October 4 affirmed support for the Nationalists as China's legitimate government. After a series of military retreats from Nanking, then from Canton, and finally from Chongqing, the Nationalists withdrew from the mainland for the island of Formosa (also known as Taiwan). In December, they resumed governmental functions in the island's capital city of Taipei.

Several factors contributed to Jiang's failure, none of which the United States could have significantly altered. Americans did not lose China to communism; they never owned or controlled the country. Despite the unfortunate comparison of China to Greece, a proportionate economic and military aid program in China would have required enormous expenditures and countless more military advisers. Ambassador John L. Stuart, born in China and president of Yenching University in Beijing, probably offered the best explanation of China's collapse. In his memoirs, *Fifty Years in China*, he blamed the outcome on "a gigantic struggle between two political ideologies with the overtones of democratic idealism perverted by bureaucratic incompetence on the one side, succumbing to a dynamic socialized reform vitiated by Communist dogma, intolerance and ruthlessness on the other. And the great mass of suffering inarticulate victims cared for neither but were powerless to do anything about it." Neither antagonist, he asserted, had many avid party members. The Chinese people were "merely Chinese" who wanted "to live their own lives with a minimum of government interference or oppression."

The Communist success in China was attributable to a long history of internal troubles, to repeated instances of outside intervention, to the destruction of World War II, and to Jiang's disastrous rule. Group after group had vied for control in Beijing, and in the provinces numerous independent warlords competed for power. Jiang's early military triumphs had come to an abrupt end during the Sino-Japanese War of the 1930s,

which itself meshed into the events of World War II. Billions of dollars of U.S. aid to Jiang disappeared in inflation, bureaucratic inefficiency, nepotism, corruption, and his decision to hoard war materiel for future use against Mao rather than against Japan in the present war. Moreover, he failed to win popular support because of the lack of land reforms, the chronic instability of the country, his own incapacities, and the devastation of the world war. Jiang's strength rested on the landlords, who opposed land reform, whereas the Communists gained widespread peasant support by promising agrarian reforms. Thus, the revolution swept the countryside while Jiang and his forces remained in the cities, insulated from the need for change and failing to grasp the realities of his rule collapsing all around him.

Washington's decision to withhold recognition of Communist China did not necessarily imply protection to Formosa, but the White House soon found that refusal to help the Nationalists left the appearance of tacitly favoring the Communists. In January 1950, Truman informed Jiang's advocates in the United States that he had no plans for furnishing "military aid or advice" to the Nationalists. Indeed, Acheson was quietly searching for steps toward establishing diplomatic relations with the new government in Beijing in view of firsthand reports by Foreign Service officers that Mao sought a policy independent of Stalin and would soon crush Jiang's ill-fated regime. But that realistic stance quickly changed. Members of the Republican Party were already claiming that Communists in Washington had betrayed Nationalist China.

As shown in the previous chapter, the great publicity surrounding the Alger Hiss trial, followed by the sensational charges made by Republican Senator Joe McCarthy, left the impression that communism had infiltrated the very halls of the nation's government. Not long afterward, authorities arrested Julius Rosenberg (who had worked on the Manhattan Project) and his wife Ethel for espionage.

The resulting wave of fear and suspicion aroused by "McCarthyism" thoroughly discredited Acheson, who had remained loyal to Hiss and whose tailored mustache, expensive Ivy League clothing, mincing manner, and arrogant bearing gave him the image of a dangerous intellectual—more European than American. The fallout did not stop with him. As part of the administration's 1947 security program, government employees had to take loyalty oaths. Indeed, anyone suspected of engaging in "radical" activity—including those in academia and Hollywood—was subject to being fired or blacklisted. Books allegedly professing the doctrine of communism were burned or banned from the libraries. In one remarkable instance, *Robin Hood* was pulled from the library shelves because the hero exemplified Communist principles by taking from the rich and giving to the poor. The national hysteria damaged the reputation of the Foreign Service, converted judgmental errors into a believed Communist conspiracy, and made the administration wary of admitting to any mistakes or failures in diplomatic policy that critics could label as treason, or at least as being "soft on communism."

In February 1950, the Soviet Union and the People's Republic of China further alarmed Americans by signing a thirty-year mutual defense pact. The treaty added to the fear in the United States that a single brand of communism, guided by the Kremlin, was spreading throughout the world. Americans became convinced that the Communist Chinese had come under the Soviet heel. Few realized that the agreement of 1950 resulted from mutual need and not from ideological ties. Mao wanted to stem the deepening influence of the United States in East Asia; Stalin sought assurances for the Yalta guarantees and was leery of a strong and independent Communist China. The Soviets demanded that Mao's China replace Jiang's Nationalists in the UN Security Council. When this effort failed, the Soviet delegate walked out, signifying his government's boycott of that organization.

The Korean War

The situations in Japan and China constituted an important and related background to the conflict in Korea, a peninsula that became the hot spot of the Cold War by mid-1950. The ensuing problems quickly raised questions about U.S. resolve in Japan and the effectiveness of its policies in China. Korea, like Germany in Europe, became symbolic of the struggle between East and West.

The Soviet Union and the United States had temporarily divided Korea at the thirty-eighth parallel in 1945, with the understanding that the Soviets would wind down the war against Japanese invasion forces in the north and the United States would do the same in the south. Afterward, full withdrawal would take place, in line with wartime agreements stipulating that Korea was to be "free and independent." The partition at the thirty-eighth parallel was a military decision, even though it cut off the industrialized north from the agricultural south and left the north larger in area though smaller in population. At the time it was a sound decision in Washington's view because the United States was unable to transport soldiers there immediately, and the Soviet agreement to remain above that parallel would perhaps prevent the Red Army from occupying all of Korea.

But problems soon developed over the agreement's implementation. In December 1945 and again in March 1947, the Soviet and U.S. foreign ministers agreed in Moscow that the military commands in Korea should discuss the procedure for installing a government favorable to reuniting the north and south. But each time, the talks failed to resolve the composition of that government. The United States referred the Korean issue to the UN General Assembly, which in November 1947 established a Temporary Commission on Korea to sponsor nationwide elections. The Soviets, however, refused to allow the commissioners above the thirty-eighth parallel. Elections took place in May 1948—but only in the south. Syngman Rhee, seventy-three years old and a longtime resident of the United States who held a doctorate degree in international law from Princeton, emerged as president of the Republic of Korea in Seoul. In September, Kim Il-sung became president of a Soviet-supported regime in Pyongyang, capital of the Democratic People's Republic of Korea. The following December, Rhee signed an economic and military aid pact with the United States. When the question of South Korea's admission to the United Nations came before the Security Council, the Soviet delegate vetoed the measure. As in Germany, the two Koreas became symbolic of the Cold War rivalry.

Meanwhile, the North Korean government had surged ahead of the south in military power. Both Koreas had armies, but whereas the Soviets had provided heavy artillery and tanks to Kim, the Americans had refused to grant Rhee anything more than light defensive weaponry because of his dictatorial rule and undisguised intention to reunite the country. Only after great pressure from Washington did Rhee hold long-promised general elections, and when they did take place, the negative results exposed his shaky control in

Syngman Rhee and Douglas MacArthur
The leader of South Korea greets the top American representative in Asia. *(Library of Congress, Washington, D.C.)*

South Korea. Yet the United States had no feasible alternative to Rhee. The Soviet Union withdrew its troops from Korea in December 1948, and the United States did the same in June 1949, but neither power's commitment had ceased. The Soviets left behind heavy artillery and tanks; the Americans maintained a considerable amount of light military equipment and 400 technical and military advisers.

By early 1950, the United States appeared to have left the South Koreans on their own. The military withdrawal reinforced that impression, as did MacArthur's ill-timed announcement from Japan that he opposed a land war in Asia. The U.S. Army had ten poorly equipped and inadequately manned divisions, and the Joint Chiefs of Staff considered South Korea of only secondary military importance. On January 12, Acheson seemed to affirm his nation's retreat from East Asia. Before the National Press Club in Washington, he defined the "defense perimeter" of the United States in Asia as a line enveloping the Aleutians, Japan, the Ryukyus, and the Philippines, which implied that the United States felt no responsibilities toward either Formosa or the Chinese mainland. Should aggression occur, Acheson emphasized, "the initial reliance must be on the people attacked to resist it and then upon the commitments of the entire civilized world under the Charter of the United Nations which so far has not proved a weak reed to lean on by any people who are determined to protect their independence against outside aggression." The secretary was perhaps attempting to give subtle notification to the Communist Chinese that the United States wished to withdraw support from the Nationalists. Not inconsistent with this supposition, he wished to place emphasis on economic and administrative assistance to South Korea rather than military, exemplifying Washington's belief that sound economies and democratic governments provided the best insurance against communism. Whatever his intentions, the effect was not what he had anticipated. Observers were convinced that Acheson had removed both South Korea and Formosa from the U.S. defense system.

When in the summer of 1950 the North Korean forces launched their invasion of South Korea, they met little resistance. News of the attack reached Washington, which was thirteen hours behind Korean time, late in the evening of June 24. Acheson met with other State Department officers in emergency session and decided the United States would take action through the UN Security Council. Truman was at home in Independence, Missouri, and returned to Washington the following day. Meanwhile, the State Department worked all night drafting a resolution condemning the North Korean aggression that the U.S. delegation would present to the Security Council. The Truman administration ordered Americans in Seoul to evacuate at once.

No debate took place in Washington about the Soviet Union's role in the attack. Everyone held the Moscow government responsible and felt the United States had to act. Washington's officials agreed that the Soviets had begun probing for weak areas susceptible to Communist takeover. Korea therefore loomed as a major test of U.S. will in East Asia. The State Department alerted its foreign offices to this danger: "Possible that Korea is only the first of series of coordinated actions on part of Soviets. Maintain utmost vigilance."

Washington's assumption of Soviet complicity in the attack made it a test of the U.S. commitment to Asia. North Korea's effort to reunify the country by force caused the Truman administration to alter its Korean policy and adopt measures that were stronger than the mere extension of economic aid and military advice. One State Department official, John Foster Dulles, publicly expressed the common belief that the North Koreans "did not do this purely on their own but as part of the world strategy of international communism." The successes of U.S. containment policy in Europe and the Near East had seemingly evoked this aggressive Soviet response.

It is impossible to know the full story behind the North Korean invasion, but some certainties exist. Kim Il-sung and Syngman Rhee were bitter rivals, both fully capable of acting on their own. Border incidents had dramatically increased before June; since 1946, more than 100,000 Koreans had died in what had become by 1950 a bloody civil war. Indeed, the same morning of the attack, South Korean forces had raided a town above the thirty-eighth parallel. Had Moscow known of the impending North Korean attack, its delegate would surely have returned to the Security Council, where he could have vetoed UN military action and bought time for the North Koreans before the General Assembly could act. It also made little sense for Stalin to move so clearly for peace in Europe, only to instigate a war in Asia. Admittedly, he had extended some help to North Korea but probably in an attempt to avert Communist Chinese accusations that he opposed revolutions in Asia. Conceivably, he calculated that even if the United States did nothing to protect the South Koreans, it would certainly continue its protection of Formosa and thereby undermine any chance of a U.S. settlement of that issue with the People's Republic of China. Mao would thus have no choice but to turn to Moscow for assistance.

Questions remain about the Kremlin's assumed role in these events. One theory is that the Soviets were unaware of the imminent North Korean attack and, once aware, even wanted to call it off until its surprising success suddenly offered the opportunity of accomplishing everything they sought in East Asia. Another theory, which is probably nearer the truth, holds that Kim had wanted to strike a posture more independent of Mao's Communists and therefore traveled to the Kremlin twice to talk with Stalin of a planned attack on the south without specifying its timing. The Soviet premier, it seems, approved Kim's intentions and assured him of materiel but made clear he was on his own. Should Kim fail, Stalin could disclaim involvement; if successful, Kim

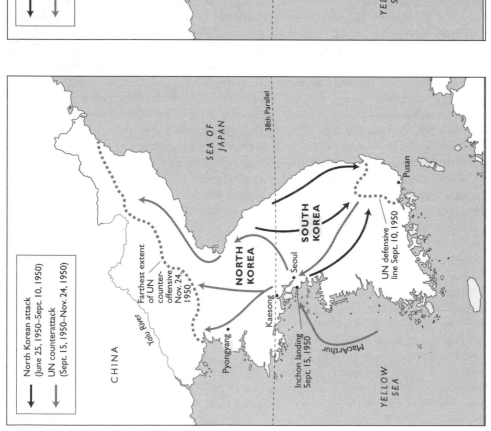

Maps 2 and 3

The Korean War, 1950 and 1951–1953. Over three years of war resulted in a stalemate as the fighting came to a close in almost exactly the same area it began. (*Source: author*)

would stand clear of China's influence and unite Korea under his direction. In either case, the Soviets could cite the success of the attack as further evidence of U.S. military weakness, already exemplified in China. Moreover, the North Koreans' actions threatened to diminish U.S. credibility in Japan. If U.S. prestige fell in Asia, only the Soviet Union would gain—as long as it quietly furnished military assistance to the North Koreans while publicly castigating the United States, the region's unmistakable outsider, as the interventionist aggressor. Soviet, Chinese, and North Korean documentation suggests that Stalin and his generals planned and helped the invasion, and the Soviet premier convinced a reluctant Mao to go along.

Truman never doubted Soviet culpability and called for strong action. Here was an opportunity to regain flagging popular support at home, resulting largely from the Republicans' charges that the administration was "soft on communism." Truman regarded the North Korean attack as another test of the Free World's commitment to liberty. "Communism," he wrote in his *Memoirs*, "was acting in Korea just as Hitler, Benito Mussolini, and the Japanese had acted ten, fifteen, and twenty years earlier." He assured an anxious senator that his administration would not give in to the Soviet Union and told reporters that Korea was "the Greece of the Far East." Acheson explained years afterward that "to back away from this challenge, in view of our capacity for meeting it, would be highly destructive of the power and prestige of the United States."

The perceived Soviet threat in Asia caused both the United States and its NATO allies to move with determination. By the afternoon following the attack, the Security Council had overwhelmingly approved the U.S. resolution (nine to zero, the Soviets absent and Yugoslavia abstaining), labeling the attack a "breach of the peace" and calling on the North Koreans to withdraw from the area below the thirty-eighth parallel. The Council then approved a second resolution urging member nations to "furnish such assistance to the Republic of Korea as may be necessary to repel the armed attack and to restore international peace and security." Truman warned the Communist Chinese not to exploit the Korean situation by attacking the Nationalists on Formosa. To emphasize the point, he approved military assistance to the Philippines and to the French in Indochina. Communism, the president explained, "has passed beyond the use of subversion to conquer independent nations and will now use armed invasion and war." In a single day, he had committed the United States to Nationalist China, the Philippines (granted independence by the United States in July 1946), and Indochina, all three experiencing internal problems believed to be Communist inspired.

On June 27, 1950, Truman ordered the Seventh Fleet to the Chinese coast to "prevent any attack on Formosa" that would cause a resurgence of civil war. Whether to "leash" Jiang or to protect Formosa, Truman's actions angered Communist China because they constituted blatant interference in its domestic affairs. They also upset the UN members who had extended recognition to the Communist regime and believed it justified in wanting to absorb Formosa. But because the Republicans charged the administration with already having "lost" China, the White House had to adopt strong policies to prevent the loss of South Korea. To keep the war limited in nature, Truman emphasized that the United States sought only "to restore peace and . . . the border."

The shocking collapse of the capital city of Seoul to the North Koreans on June 28 exposed the weaknesses in the U.S. containment effort and led to the decision to send U.S. troops to save South Korea. On June 29, Truman approved U.S. air strikes above the thirty-eighth parallel, and the following day in Tokyo, MacArthur recommended that the United States send soldiers, blockade the coast, and bomb areas in North Korea "wherever militarily necessary." In a decision that Truman later called "the most important" of his presidency, he ordered U.S. combat forces into Korea as part of what would become a UN command. The president did not ask Congress for a declaration of war because, he explained, the U.S. soldiers had undertaken a "police action." The situation was desperate. The North Koreans had pushed the South Koreans all the way down to Pusan at the bottom of the peninsula and were on the verge of driving them into the sea. MacArthur, as commander-in-chief in the Far East, received orders on June 30 to secure a port and air base in the Pusan area. Acheson later explained with some satisfaction that the decision to send soldiers to Korea "removed the recommendations of NSC-68 from the realm of theory and made them immediate budget issues." According to that document, the Soviet Union sought "domination of the Eurasian land mass," leaving the United States no alternative to pursuing a global military policy.

Great symbolic importance rested in the U.S. decision to commit troops to Korea. Bases in the peninsula were not vital in a strategic military sense. Soviet control of Korea could not have posed a greater threat to Japan than did Soviet bases in Manchuria or China. Moreover, the limited size of the U.S. military force in 1950 meant that the relocation of ground forces to East Asia would seriously weaken Europe. Yet the symbolism of the commitment was fast approaching the level of the U.S. national interest. The United States had found it necessary to demonstrate assurances to South Korea, Japan, and other nations subject to aggression—especially the Europeans. Failure to do so would constitute a major defeat in the propaganda war with the Communists and perhaps sacrifice all hopes of winning the allegiance of the emerging postwar nations. Furthermore, a weak will would raise doubts among the NATO allies of the United States. The nation's credibility was on the line.

Truman repeatedly emphasized the global context of the war. The decision to use combat troops escalated Korean events into a conflict having international ramifications. On July 8, the Security Council chose MacArthur to head the UN forces in Korea (although all his orders came from Washington), and on August 1, the Soviet representative to the Council, Yakov Malik, returned to his seat. To calm nervous Europeans who were worried that U.S. priorities had shifted to Asia, Truman launched a military buildup on the continent. Acheson horrified the British and French by proposing that Germany contribute ten divisions to the European defense system. To quiet their protests, he assured them that the German forces would be integrated into a European army and that the United States would send four additional divisions to the continent. Finally, the president announced that General Eisenhower had agreed to take leave from the presidency of Columbia University and become NATO's Supreme Commander.

The UN forces now prepared to take the offensive. While South Korean units and a small number of U.S. forces were backed to the water's edge at Pusan, MacArthur made a daring move: on September 15, he launched an amphibious landing at Inchon on the western side of the peninsula, hundreds of miles behind the North Korean front. Most military experts had argued that such a landing could not work because of enormously high tides and rocky cliffs; MacArthur promised that "we shall land at Inchon, and I shall crush them." He succeeded magnificently and soon freed Seoul from the Communists. The counterinvasion broke the advance of the North Koreans and drove them back above the thirty-eighth parallel. Meanwhile, South Korean and U.S. forces gained the initiative in Pusan and severed the enemy's supply line. And despite these successes, Americans noted one telling fact: neither the Soviet Union nor Communist China had intervened.

MacArthur's landing at Inchon had an exhilarating effect in the United States that soon

Inchon
General MacArthur's UN forces launched an
invasion at Inchon on September 15, 1950.
(National Archives, Washington, D.C.)

highlighted a major policy decision in Washington already made in early August: invade the north and reunify Korea. Despite the claim by critics that the general acted on his own, the truth is that the Truman administration had already decided to convert the policy of containment into a liberating force that became known as "rollback," and the new military situation afforded by MacArthur's success provided an excellent opportunity for its implementation. In late September, State Department official H. Freeman Matthews wrote the Joint Chiefs of Staff that if the United States reunified Korea, "the resultant defeat to the Soviet Union and to the Communist world" would be of "momentous significance." Korea would join Japan as a model of national self-determination in East Asia and mark the successful culmination of U.S. policy on Korea established during World War II. Over Kennan's insistence that the Soviets

would never allow MacArthur near the "gates of Vladivostok," the administration approved the military advance across the thirty-eighth parallel that would set an example for the world by liberating all of Korea from Communist control.

The Communist Chinese meanwhile assured the United States, through India's delegate to the United Nations, that they would not "sit back with folded hands and let the Americans come to the border." Washington's leaders ignored the warning. The long civil war in China, they declared with certainty, had depleted that regime's sparse resources and prohibited its involvement. Moreover, Mao's focus was on northern China, where Soviet interests clashed with his and loomed as a far more important danger than that in Korea. Chinese intervention in the Korean War would be "sheer madness," according to Acheson. They had enough problems with the Soviet Union and did not want to alienate "all the free nations of the world who are inherently their friends." MacArthur was also confident that the Chinese would stay out of the conflict. Earlier, at Wake Island, he had assured the president, "We are no longer fearful of their intervention. They have no air force . . . [and] if the Chinese tried to get down to Pyongyang there would be the greatest slaughter. . . . We are the best." To the president's advisers, MacArthur asserted that "the Oriental follows a winner. If we win, the Chinese will not follow the USSR [Union of Soviet Socialist Republics]."

With the Soviet delegate now back in the Security Council, the Truman administration pushed a proposal through the General Assembly that suddenly elevated that body's importance in international affairs. Acheson won support for a "Uniting for Peace" program that authorized General Assembly members to recommend force in maintaining collective security if a Soviet veto blocked Security Council action. On October 9, 1950, the same day two U.S. jets mistakenly strafed a Soviet airstrip near the naval base at Vladivostok (a swift apology eased Soviet protests), the General Assembly resolved that MacArthur push for "a unified, independent and democratic Korea."

The General Assembly's action was pro forma. On September 29, MacArthur had learned that the White House was disgruntled with his apparent decision to stop at the thirty-eighth parallel and await UN approval before moving northward. Marshall, now secretary of defense, cabled MacArthur: "We want you to feel unhampered tactically and strategically to proceed north of [the] thirty-eighth parallel. Announcement above referred to may precipitate embarrassment in the UN where evident desire is not to be confronted with necessity of a vote on passage, rather to find you have found it militarily necessary to do so." MacArthur replied that he had never intended to halt his advance and that the parallel was "not a factor in the mil[itary] employment of our forces." He added that "unless and until the enemy capitulates, I regard all of Korea open for our mil[itary] operations." MacArthur promised reporters that "the war very definitely is coming to an end shortly."

The UN decision to cross the thirty-eighth parallel dramatically elevated the Cold War to a level just short of full conflict. In an effort to avert a wider war, President Truman rejected MacArthur's request to attack strategic spots in China itself and, in an inexplicable move, authorized UN forces to bomb only the southern half of the bridges connecting the Chinese banks of the Yalu River with those of North Korea. "How can we bomb half a bridge?" the general indignantly asked his staff.

The Truman administration seems not to have recognized that the UN invasion of North Korea was tantamount to a thrust toward China that necessitated a strong counteraction. Mao could not have wanted to enter the Korean conflict after his own recent long and costly civil war. His philosophy of survival argued against military confrontation with a superior military force. But Mao recognized that failure to halt the UN drive toward the Yalu River would discredit his regime's claim to the mainland and endanger his own leadership. Furthermore, here was opportunity, perhaps too soon presented, for the Beijing government to come of age. Should it establish hegemony over that area, Mao would gain stature in East Asia approaching that of the Soviets. Pushed into action by the UN decision to move toward the Yalu, Communist China prepared to protect its vital interests in Asia.

The manner of Communist China's intervention in the Korean War suggested Mao's reluctance to act. On October 26, a large number of "Chinese volunteers" attacked the UN forces, thereby maintaining the fiction of no official involvement. The assault halted the UN advance and drove it back. A week later, the Chinese disappeared from the field. The message should have been clear: Mao had warned the UN to confine the fighting to South Korea. His priority was still Formosa, as evidenced by his agreement to send representatives to the United Nations to discuss that situation. MacArthur did not see it that way. He called for an all-out attack and on November 24, the day of the Chinese delegates' arrival at the United Nations, proudly declared that his men had begun an "end-the-war offensive" that would have them "home by Christmas"—after they saw the Yalu. This news infuriated both the Communist Chinese and the Europeans, who accused MacArthur of trying to "wreck the negotiations" over Formosa. Two days later, as UN soldiers again inched northward, the first large contingent of nearly 400,000 Communist Chinese soldiers suddenly swarmed into the seventy-five-mile-wide gap between MacArthur's two advancing and dangerously exposed flanks. Combined with the onset of a blizzard marked by temperatures of thirty degrees below zero, this attack in two weeks drove the remnant of his vastly depleted 20,000 troops back below the thirty-eighth parallel.

Communist China's second entry into the fighting drastically changed the tenor of the

China in the Korean War
Massive human wave assaults by the Chinese resulted in more than 400 casualties at the hands of U.S. Marines wielding machine guns and rifles during one ten hour battle in the spring of 1951. (*U.S. Marine Corps*)

cil as the legitimate Chinese government. The United States rejected all three demands.

The Chinese intervention sparked a major debate within the Truman administration over whether to return to the original objectives of containment. After a massive countereffort, MacArthur's forces stopped the Chinese assault and arduously began another offensive that took them back to the thirty-eighth parallel in March 1951. At that point, Truman called for a negotiated settlement, but MacArthur unilaterally destroyed any chances for a cease-fire by crossing the border again and demanding an unconditional Chinese surrender. To achieve this objective, he asserted, the United States should blockade the Chinese coast, bomb the enemies' "privileged sanctuary" in Manchuria along with China's major industrial centers, permit the Nationalists to attack the mainland, and, as he later noted in his *Reminiscences*, "sever Korea from Manchuria by laying a field of radioactive wastes—the by products of atomic manufacture—across all the major lines of enemy supply." Truman strenuously objected. In accordance with the Joint Chiefs of Staff, he argued that MacArthur's strategy was militarily unsound. First, a blockade and bombings could cause Soviet intervention in accordance with its defensive pact with Communist China. Second, these tactics would not cut inland communication and supply lines. Third, Jiang had already proved his ineptitude on the battlefield. Fourth, the European allies of the United States were not supportive. Finally, and most important, use of atomic materials could bring on World War III.

MacArthur rigidly opposed any restrictions on his military actions. Insisting that Asia would be the next major battleground between communism and the Free World, he argued that the United States should "go it alone if necessary." He publicly implied that Truman was guilty of appeasement, and in a move raising questions about the constitutionality of civilian over military authority, he wrote a letter to the leading Republican in the House of Representatives, Joseph Martin, in

Korean conflict. MacArthur pronounced it "an entirely new war" and sought an air bombardment of China, and the UN General Assembly overwhelmingly condemned China for aggression. When Truman left the impression with reporters that use of the atomic bomb was under consideration, British Prime Minister Clement Attlee frantically rushed to Washington to urge a negotiated settlement. Meanwhile, the president secured additional military appropriations from Congress to bolster Europe and other parts of the world. In a few weeks, the Chinese again pushed the UN forces below the thirty-eighth parallel and once more took Seoul. The United Nations sought a cease-fire, but China refused until the following conditions were met: withdrawal of "foreign troops" from Korea, cessation of U.S. support to Formosa, and admission of Communist China to the UN Security Coun-

which he asserted that "there is no substitute for victory." In Asia, MacArthur wrote, "the communist conspirators have elected to make their play for global conquest. Here we fight Europe's war with arms while the diplomats there still fight it with words." Martin dramatically read the letter before the House on April 5. MacArthur had earlier ignored the president's directive against issuing public statements concerning foreign policy without prior approval from the State Department. He had then undermined his own credibility by assuring the president that the Chinese would not intervene in the war. Although many others had agreed with his assessment of the Chinese, it was MacArthur who as field commander engaged in histrionics and therefore attracted the most attention. Publication of the letter now challenged the president either to remove the seventy-one-year-old general from his East Asian duties on grounds of insubordination or to alter military policy to suit the commander in the field. Truman, with full support from the Joint Chiefs of Staff, chose to relieve MacArthur of his East Asian command. "The son of a bitch isn't going to resign on me," the president hotly told General Omar Bradley, chair of the Joint Chiefs. *"I want him fired."*

The announcement on April 11 of MacArthur's "firing" set off a storm of protest in the United States that led some Americans to demand Truman's impeachment. The furor was attributable to several factors. Frustrations over the no-win nature of containment ("police actions" or "limited wars") headed the list because this seemingly passive approach to war violated the U.S. military tradition of total victory and threatened to undermine the related illusion that the United States had "won" all its wars. The rage over MacArthur's treatment also provided an outlet for some Americans' long-standing isolationist discontent with the nation's interventionist foreign policy and for Republican desperation over losing the White House again in 1948.

Suspicion of Communist infiltration of the government also drove numerous Americans

who regarded the Hiss case and McCarthy's sensational charges as only the surface of a dark and weblike conspiracy. Many events since the Democrats' victory in 1932 had suggested a pattern of un-Americanism: the socialistic nature of the New Deal, diplomatic recognition of the Soviet Union, Roosevelt's "maneuverings" of the United States into World War II, the Yalta "betrayals," the "fall" of China to communism, and now the Truman administration's decision to fire the only person brave enough to insist on victory. McCarthy's accusations took on greater credibility with MacArthur's removal. "How can we account for our present situation," asked the senator, "unless we believe that men high in this government are concerting to deliver us to disaster?" McCarthy's heated charge was a thinly veiled reference to General Marshall, who had long been offended by MacArthur's inordinate vanity and had recommended his dismissal. Marshall, according to McCarthy on the Senate floor, was an integral part "of a great conspiracy on a scale so immense as to dwarf any previous venture in the history of man."

Another reason for the public's wrath was the mistaken impression that all MacArthur wanted was a conventional assault on the Chinese mainland. Not until 1964, a few days after his death, did his earlier private and highly revealing conversations with two reporters become public. In 1951, MacArthur had wanted to drop atomic bombs on North Korea as a prelude to a land offensive led by Americans and Nationalist Chinese. These forces were to invade North Korea from the west and east, he insisted, imposing a stranglehold on the Korean peninsula that would have resulted in total victory in less than two weeks. No reinforcements could have arrived from the north because in the meantime the United Nations would have laid a five-mile-wide strip of cobalt along the Chinese–Korean border. For the lifetime of the cobalt—more than half a century—no one could have entered the zone. MacArthur had no fear of Soviet intervention. "It makes me laugh," he declared, "that Russia would commit its armies to a war in China's behalf at the end of an endless one-track railroad to a peninsular battleground that led only to the sea. Russia could not have engaged us. She would not have fought for China. She is already unhappy and uncertain over the colossus she has encouraged." He concluded that "it was in our power to destroy the Communist Chinese army and Chinese military power. And probably for all time. My plan was a cinch."

MacArthur's popularity in the United States remained high for about six weeks before beginning to recede—in line with the president's prediction. In April 1951, the general received an impassioned public welcome on his return to the United States for the first time since 1937. Congress invited him to speak before a joint session, which became a nationwide media event over radio and television.

In his thirty-four-minute address, he called for a stepped-up war in Asia and included a moving peroration based on the lines of a popular song that "old soldiers never die; they just fade away." At the conclusion, he declared that "like the old soldier of that ballad, I now close my military career and just fade away—an old soldier who tried to do his duty as God gave him the light to see that duty." After a pause, he whispered "good-bye" and left the podium. Not a dry eye remained in the chamber. Former President Herbert Hoover christened MacArthur as the "reincarnation of St. Paul into a great General of the Army who came out of the East." And Missouri Representative Dewey Short, a former preacher educated at Harvard, Oxford, and Heidelberg, told reporters, "We heard God speak here today, God in the flesh, the voice of God."

But soon the emotional reaction wore thin and reason took over. When MacArthur showed up late for a press conference, a reporter snidely remarked that the general's friends had probably experienced some difficulty in removing the nails holding him to the cross. In subsequent Senate inquiries, General Bradley, the highly respected chair of the Joint Chiefs of Staff, gave a persuasive defense of the administration that soon undermined the wisdom of MacArthur's strategy. "Taking on Red China," Bradley declared, would have created "a larger deadlock at greater expense" and without the support of U.S. allies. The Soviet Union was the "main antagonist" and Western Europe the "main prize." In the most telling words, he insisted that an assault on China would have involved the United States "in the wrong war at the wrong place at the wrong

---

In this speech over television, General MacArthur outlined his military strategy for winning the Korean War.

General Douglas MacArthur's address to Congress, April 19, 1951, U.S. Congress, Senate, Joint Committee on Armed Services and Foreign Relations, *Military Situation in the Far East*, 81st Cong., 1st sess. (Washington, D.C.: Government Printing Office, 1951), 3553–58.

I felt that military necessity in the conduct of the war made necessary:

First, the intensification of our economic blockade against China.

Second, the imposition of a naval blockade against the China coast.

Third, removal of restrictions on air reconnaissance of China's coastal areas and of Manchuria.

Fourth, removal of restrictions on the forces of the Republic of China on Formosa with logistical support to contribute to their effective operation against the Chinese mainland. . . .

War's very object is victory—not prolonged indecision. In war, indeed, there can be no substitute for victory.

There are some who for varying reasons would appease Red China. They are blind to history's clear lesson. For history teaches with unmistakable emphasis that appeasement but begets new and bloodier war.

General MacArthur before Congress
In early April 1951, after President Truman had dismissed MacArthur from his Far Eastern command, the general presented his case to Congress and the American people, concluding his remarks with the famous words, "Old soldiers never die; they just fade away." *(National Archives, Washington, D.C.)*

time and with the wrong enemy." Bradley's argument was calm, reasoned, and based on military and political realities, not on emotional charges of Communist subterfuge and U.S. cowardice and stupidity. Truman meanwhile repeatedly reminded Americans that European allies likewise opposed MacArthur's attempt to widen the conflict. But perhaps just as important to the argument, the president emphasized that in the United States the civilian authority outranked that of the military. MacArthur's actions, he declared, were a violation of the Constitution. Faced with such unassailable arguments, the general's credibility began to dip.

Meanwhile, hopes for an end to the Korean conflict arose when the Communists agreed to truce talks in the summer of 1951. On June 23, the Soviet delegate to the Security Council called for a cease-fire. The Chinese Communists approved, but with the stipulation that foreign soldiers pull out of Korea. Armistice discussions began in early July at Kaesong near the thirty-eighth parallel, although the negotiators eventually moved to Panmunjom. In November, the antagonists tentatively accepted an armistice line at the point where the fighting ended, but the United States steadfastly refused to approve a UN withdrawal from South Korea.

General Matthew Ridgway
General Ridgway discusses strategy with Major
General Frank W. Milburn on December 27,
1950, just one day after Ridgway assumed
command of the Eighth Army in Korea.
(*U.S. Army*)

The Communists then heightened their demands and accused the United States of using germ warfare, and violence broke out among the prisoners of war (POWs) in UN camps. The talks stalemated. Over the next year and a half, the antagonists argued about the location of the cease-fire line, the steps necessary to implement an armistice agreement, and the repatriation of prisoners. By the spring of 1952, only the last question remained an issue. Whereas the Communists wanted all prisoners returned, the United Nations refused to repatriate those who did not want to go home. This was no small problem: nearly half of the UN's 170,000 POWs opposed repatriation.

While the fighting continued under the leadership of MacArthur's replacement, General Matthew Ridgway, the United States moved toward a tighter alliance with coun-

tries in East Asia. On August 30, 1951, it signed a security pact with the Philippines, and two days later it became party to the Tripartite Security Treaty with Australia and New Zealand. The Truman administration intended both pacts to allay those countries' anxieties over its real objective of rebuilding Japan as a counterweight to Soviet influence in East Asia.

Thus, the Korean War catalyzed a move already under way in Tokyo to conclude a peace treaty with Japan and make it an ally against communism. More than fifty nations gathered in San Francisco in early September to begin negotiations under the leadership of John Foster Dulles, adviser to the secretary of state. Four days later, the United States secured the Peace of Reconciliation, which recognized Japan's sovereignty over its home islands, awarded the United States a military base on Okinawa, and referred reparations problems to individual negotiations between Japan and concerned countries. There were no longer any prohibitions against Japanese rearmaments, and the United States would continue to occupy the Ryukyu and Bonin islands. That same day, September 8, the United States and Japan signed a Security Treaty permitting U.S. soldiers to remain in Japan as long as necessary "to contribute to the maintenance of international peace and security in the Far East and to the security of Japan." On April 28, 1952, the two treaties with Japan went into effect, marking the close of the U.S. administration of the Tokyo government and officially ending World War II in the Pacific.

The fighting continued in Korea, however, arousing deeper concern about the imminence of a global conflict. American planes bombed hydroelectric plants on the Yalu River in June 1952, and in early October, Truman declared that "we are fighting in Korea so we won't have to fight in Wichita, or in Chicago, or in New Orleans, or in San Francisco Bay." Later that same year, in November, American scientists developed the hydrogen bomb, a thermonuclear device possessing a thousand times more destructive capacity than the atomic bombs dropped over Hiroshima and Nagasaki. Instead of comforting Americans, this news heightened their uneasiness over the military escalation in Korea and intensified demands to end the conflict.

Armistice in Korea

As the presidential election of 1952 approached, Americans became increasingly suspicious that Communist sympathizers in Washington were obstructing the war effort. The campaign tied these issues together when the Republicans used the symbol "K_1C_2" to refer to Korea, communism, and the several instances of corruption recently uncovered among administration officials. At the Re-publican convention, MacArthur delivered the keynote address, in which he denounced the Free World's "headlong retreat from victory." McCarthy followed with a speech blasting Acheson and others for their "abysmal stupidity and treason" and assured listeners that he would never fight communism "with a perfumed silk handkerchief." The party's choice for vice president was Richard M. Nixon, who had led the House committee attack on Alger Hiss and earlier in the campaign had labeled the Democratic candidate, Adlai Stevenson of Illinois, as "a Ph.D. from Dean Acheson's cowardly college of Communist containment." The Republicans' candidate for the top office in the land, Dwight D. Eisenhower, aroused enormous support

President-elect Eisenhower in Korea, December 4, 1952
Eisenhower fulfills his campaign promise that, if elected president, he would "go to Korea." *(Dwight D. Eisenhower Library, Abilene, Kansas)*

by promising that, if victorious, "I shall go to Korea." His unquestioned honesty, disarmingly homespun personality, and numerous military successes in World War II won him the confidence of voters. Eisenhower rolled over the less colorful though highly eloquent Stevenson with 55 percent of the popular vote. In December, the president-elect kept his campaign promise and went to Korea for three days. There he mingled with the soldiers on the front and announced support for the UN decision not to return the POWs who refused to go home.

Shortly after his inauguration in January 1953, President Eisenhower moved toward ending the Korean conflict. His administration took on the image of boldness and resolution, partly because of the outspoken nature of his secretary of state, John Foster Dulles, a Wall Street attorney and chief negotiator of the peace and security treaties with Japan. Seemingly bred as a diplomat (his family had long experience in the State Department), this son of a Presbyterian minister viewed the Cold War as a virtual religious conflict between the forces of good and evil. Dulles guaranteed an aggressive foreign policy and soon became identified with the terms "massive retaliation," "brinkmanship," "liberation," and the "New Look" in suggesting that the United States was willing to use military force and even atomic weaponry to free people from communism.

The Eisenhower–Dulles team left the implication that the United States had rejected containment and returned to the time-honored drive for total victory. The president notified the North Koreans and Communist Chinese through private channels that he wanted an immediate cease-fire; should they fail to comply, he warned, the United States might retaliate "under circumstances of our choosing." In his first State of the Union Address, he announced that the Seventh Fleet would "no longer be employed to shield Communist China," implying that he had "unleashed" Jiang's Nationalist forces to attack the mainland. Eisenhower's resort to the "MacArthur strategy" sounded convincing—so much so that Dulles had to make a sudden trip to London and Paris to calm the worried allies of the United States. Another factor also encouraged peace prospects: Stalin died in March 1953, opening the possibility of a softer line from Moscow. His successor, Georgi Malenkov, seemed moderate in tone and more concerned about his country's internal problems.

In July 1953, armistice talks began in earnest at Panmunjom, and by the end of the month the negotiators reached an agreement. The previous month, Syngman Rhee had almost wrecked the discussions by freeing 27,000 North Korean POWs who opposed communism in an effort to abort a settlement that he knew would not unify the Koreas under his rule. Rhee was a "zealous, irrational, and illogical fanatic," according to a presidential envoy sent from Washington. But the Communists did not break off the talks, which suggested that they wanted to end the war. The antagonists finally agreed to the establishment of a neutral commission to deal with prisoner exchanges. The armistice line was to be the present battle front, which meant that although the North Koreans lost some territory, the war would end at approximately the same place it had begun—the thirty-eighth parallel. A demilitarized zone would serve as a buffer between the Koreas. The United States won Rhee's acquiescence by assuring military and economic aid.

Domestic American politics also played a role in ending the war. As columnist Walter Lippmann observed, President Truman "was not able to make peace, because politically he was too weak at home. He was not able to make war because the risks were too great. This dilemma of Truman's was resolved by the election of Eisenhower. . . . President Eisenhower signed an armistice which accepted the partition of Korea and a peace without victory because, being himself the victorious commander in World War II and a Republican, he could not be attacked as an appeaser."

Impact of the Korean War

The Korean War had an enormous yet mixed effect on international affairs. Unrest remained between the Koreas, which outside nations continued to exploit. If the conflict did little for Soviet prestige in Asia, it greatly enhanced that of the Communist Chinese. Their intervention assumed the appearance of a bold move in defense of the North Koreans and had a powerful impact on nations wanting to be neutral in the world's power struggles. The war also postponed any chance that the United States would extend recognition to Communist China: U.S. support for Nationalist China was stronger than ever. Indeed, it now appears that the Truman administration lost an opportunity to exploit the growing Sino–Soviet rift when it approved the UN advance across the thirty-eighth parallel and forced the Communist Chinese to intervene. Furthermore, the U.S. alienation of the Chinese continued for more than two decades, creating perceptions of an even more harrowing "yellow peril" than that of the Japanese and converting what one contemporary called "700 million potential customers" into "700 million dangerous adversaries."

The war stimulated the U.S. economy, but at great expense for everyone involved. The United States furnished more than half the ground forces (with the South Koreans supplying most of the rest, while only sixteen of sixty UN members made any contributions), 80 percent of the naval assistance, 90 percent of the air power, and more than $15 billion in the war effort. It incurred 36,568 combat deaths, whereas Korea lost more than 2 million lives, civilian and military, and China 600,000.

If the establishment of a truce near the point of the war's origins constituted a victory for containment, it also meant that no one had won the conflict and that the region and the world had become more dangerous. Nuclear weapons did not play a direct role in the war, although their existence surely helped to maintain limitations on the escalation. Years afterward, it became clear that in the course of the Korean War, Soviet and U.S. fighter planes exchanged fire for the only time in the Cold War, but both sides considered it wise at the time to keep these confrontations quiet. The United Nations had gained in stature by containing Communist aggression, yet Korea remained divided and in an uneasy stalemate. The Soviets and the Chinese meanwhile resumed their rivalry, made more sensitive after the latter's involvement in the war. In August 1953, the Soviet Union, too, had exploded a hydrogen bomb, and in October the United States and South Korea signed a mutual defense pact that the Senate overwhelmingly approved the following year. According to physicist Robert Oppenheimer, the two superpowers were like "two scorpions in a bottle, each capable of killing the other, but only at the risk of his own life." Despite the new foreign policy labels associated with the Eisenhower administration, the United States had affirmed its acceptance of the containment doctrine, which meant continued military buildups, repeated refusals to compromise with the Communists, and the virtual guarantee of a long and more militarized Cold War. President Eisenhower offered the most direct appraisal: "We have won an armistice on a single battleground, not peace in the world. We may not now relax our guard nor cease our quest."

Selected Readings

Acheson, Dean. *Present at the Creation: My Years in the State Department.* 1969.

Ambrose, Stephen E., and Douglas G. Brinkley. *Rise to Globalism: American Foreign Policy since 1938.* 8th ed., 1997.

Ball, George W., and Douglas B. Ball. *The Passionate Attachment: America's Involvement with Israel 1947 to the Present.* 1992.

Beisner, Robert L. *Dean Acheson: A Life in the Cold War.* 2006.

Blum, Robert M. *Drawing the Line: The Origins of the American Containment Policy in East Asia.* 1982.

Borden, William S. *The Pacific Alliance: United States Foreign Economic Policy and Japanese Trade Recovery, 1947–1955.* 1984.

Brands, H. W. *The Devil We Knew: Americans and the Cold War.* 1993.

Buhite, Russell D. *Patrick J. Hurley and American Foreign Policy.* 1973.

———. *Soviet-American Relations in Asia, 1945–1954.* 1982.

Callahan, David. *Dangerous Capabilities: Paul Nitze and the Cold War.* 1990.

Caridi, Ronald J. *The Korean War and American Politics: The Republican Party as a Case Study.* 1968.

Carter, Carolle J. *Mission to Yenan: American Liaison with the Chinese Communists, 1944–1947.* 1997.

Chen, Jian. *China's Road to the Korean War: The Making of the Sino-American Confrontation.* 1994.

Christensen, Thomas J. *Useful Adversaries: Grand Strategy, Domestic Mobilization, and Sino-American Conflict, 1947–1958.* 1996.

Cohen, Warren I. *America's Response to China: An Interpretive History of Sino-American Relations.* 2000.

Cumings, Bruce, ed. *Child of Conflict: The Korean-American Relationship, 1943–1953.* 1983.

———. *Korea's Place in the Sun: A Modern History.* 1997.

———. *The Origins of the Korean War. Vol. I: Liberation and the Emergence of Separate Regimes, 1945–1947.* 1981.

———. *The Origins of the Korean War. Vol. II: The Roaring of the Cataract, 1947–1950.* 1990.

Dobbs, Charles M. *The Unwanted Symbol: American Foreign Policy, the Cold War, and Korea, 1945–1950.* 1981.

Donovan, Robert J. *Tumultuous Years: The Presidency of Harry S Truman, 1949–1953.* 1982.

Dower, John W. *Embracing Defeat: Japan in the Wake of World War II.* 1999.

Dulles, Foster R. *American Foreign Policy toward Communist China.* 1972.

Feis, Herbert. *The China Tangle.* 1953.

———. *Contest over Japan.* 1967.

Ferrell, Robert H. *Harry S. Truman and the Modern American Presidency.* 1983.

Finn, Richard B. *Winners in Peace: MacArthur, Yoshida, and Postwar Japan.* 1992.

Fish, M. Steven. "After Stalin's Death: The Anglo-American Debate Over a New Cold War." *Diplomatic History* 10 (1986): 333–55.

Foot, Rosemary. "Anglo-American Relations in the Korean Crisis: The British Effort to Avert an Expanded War, December 1950–January 1951." *Diplomatic History* 10 (1986): 43–57.

———. *The Practice of Power: U.S. Relations with China since 1949.* 1995.

———. *A Substitute for Victory: The Politics of Peacemaking at the Korean Armistice Talks.* 1990.

———. *The Wrong War: American Policy and the Dimensions of the Korean Conflict, 1950–1953.* 1985.

Gaddis, John L. *The Cold War: A New History.* 2005.

———. *The Long Peace: Inquiries into the History of the Cold War.* 1987.

———. *Russia, the Soviet Union, and the United States: An Interpretive History.* 2nd ed., 1990.

———. *Strategies of Containment: A Critical Appraisal of Postwar American National Security Policy.* 1982; rev. ed., 2005.

———. *We Now Know: Rethinking Cold War History.* 1997.

Gallicchio, Marc S. *The Cold War Begins in Asia.* 1988.

George, Alexander L. *The Chinese Communist Army in Action: The Korean War and Its Aftermath.* 1967.

Goncharov, S. N., John W. Lewis, and Xue Litai. *Uncertain Partners: Stalin, Mao, and the Korean War.* 1993.

Goode, James F. *The United States and Iran, 1946–51: The Diplomacy of Neglect.* 1989.

Goulden, Joseph C. *Korea: The Untold Story of the War.* 1982.

Grasso, June M. *Harry Truman's Two-China Policy, 1948–1950.* 1987.

Griffith, Robert. *The Politics of Fear: Joseph R. McCarthy and the Senate.* 1970.

Halberstam, David. *The Coldest Winter: America and the Korean War.* 2007.

Harries, Meirion, and Susie Harries. *Sheathing the Sword: The Demilitarization of Japan.* 1987.

Hart, Robert A. *The Eccentric Tradition: American Diplomacy in the Far East.* 1976.

Hastings, Max. *The Korean War.* 1987.

Herring, George C., Jr. *America's Longest War: The United States and Vietnam, 1950–1975.* 3rd ed., 1996.

———. *The United States' Emergence as a Southeast Asian Power, 1940–1950.* 1987.

Higgins, Trumbull. *Korea and the Fall of MacArthur.* 1960.

Hogan, Michael J. *The Marshall Plan: America, Britain, and the Reconstruction of Western Europe, 1947–1952.* 1987.

Hunt, Michael H. *The Genesis of Chinese Communist Foreign Policy.* 1996.

Iriye, Akira. *The Cold War in Asia: A Historical Introduction.* 1974.

James, D. Clayton. *Refighting the Last War: Command and Crisis in Korea, 1950–1953.* 1992.

——. *The Years of MacArthur. Vol. 3: Triumph and Disaster, 1945–1964.* 1985.

Kaufman, Burton I. *The Korean War: Challenges in Crisis, Credibility, and Command.* 1986.

Keefer, Edward C. "President Dwight D. Eisenhower and the End of the Korean War." *Diplomatic History* 10 (1986): 267–89.

Kusnitz, Leonard A. *Public Opinion and Foreign Policy: America's China Policy, 1949–1979.* 1984.

LaFeber, Walter. *America, Russia, and the Cold War, 1945–1996.* 8th ed., 1997.

——. *The Clash: A History of U.S.-Japanese Relations.* 1997.

Leckie, Robert. *Conflict: The History of the Korean War, 1950–1953.* 1962.

Lee, Chae-jin, ed. *The Korean War: 40-Year Perspectives.* 1991.

Leffler, Melvyn P. *A Preponderance of Power: National Security, the Truman Administration, and the Cold War.* 1992.

——. *The Specter of Communism: The United States and the Origins of the Cold War, 1917–1953.* 1994.

Levering, Ralph B. *The Cold War: A Post-Cold War History.* 1994; rev. ed., 2005.

Levine, Steven I. "A New Look at American Mediation in the Chinese Civil War: The Marshall Mission and Manchuria," *Diplomatic History* 3 (1979): 349–75.

Lowe, Peter. *The Origins of the Korean War.* 1997.

MacDonald, Callum A. *Korea: The War before Vietnam.* 1987.

Martin, Edwin W. *Divided Counsel: The Anglo-American Response to Communist Victory in China.* 1986.

Matray, James I. *The Reluctant Crusade: American Foreign Policy in Korea, 1941–1950.* 1985.

——. "Truman's Plan for Victory: National Self-Determination and the Thirty-Eighth Parallel Decision in Korea." *Journal of American History* 66 (1979): 314–33.

May, Ernest R. *The Truman Administration and China, 1945–1949.* 1975.

May, Gary. *China Scapegoat: The Diplomatic Ordeal of John Carter Vincent.* 1979.

Mayers, David A. *Cracking the Monolith: U.S. Policy Against the Sino-Soviet Alliance, 1949–1955.* 1986.

McGeehan, Robert. *The German Rearmament Question.* 1971.

McLean, David. "American Nationalism, the China Myth, and the Truman Doctrine: The Question of Accommodation with Peking, 1949–50." *Diplomatic History* 10 (1986): 25–42.

McMahon, Robert J. *Colonialism and Cold War: The United States and the Struggle for Indonesian Independence, 1945–1949.* 1982.

Merrill, John. *Korea: The Peninsular Origins of the War.* 1989.

Offner, Arnold A. *Another Such Victory: President Truman and the Cold War, 1945–1953.* 2002.

Oshinsky, David M. *A Conspiracy So Immense: The World of Joe McCarthy.* 1983.

Paige, Glenn D. *The Korean Decision, June 24–30, 1950.* 1968.

Petillo, Carol M. "The Cold War in Asia." In John M. Carroll and George C. Herring, eds., *Modern American Diplomacy,* 127–46. 1986.

Pierpaoli, Paul G. *Truman and Korea: The Political Culture of the Early Cold War.* 1999.

Prados, John. *Presidents' Secret Wars: CIA Pentagon Covert Operations from World War II through the Persian Gulf.* 1996.

Purifoy, Lewis M. *Truman's China Policy: McCarthyism and the Diplomacy of Hysteria.* 1976.

Rees, David. *Korea: The Limited War.* 1964.

Rose, Lisle A. *Roots of Tragedy: The United States and the Struggle for Asia, 1945–1953.* 1976.

Rovere, Richard H., and Arthur M. Schlesinger Jr. *The MacArthur Controversy and American Foreign Policy.* 1965. Revised and expanded version of the authors' *The General and the President.* 1951.

Sandler, Stanley. *The Korean War: No Victors, No Vanquished.* 1999.

Schaller, Michael. *The American Occupation of Japan: The Origins of the Cold War in Asia.* 1985.

——. *Douglas MacArthur: The Far Eastern General.* 1989.

——. "MacArthur's Japan: The View from Washington." *Diplomatic History* 10 (1986): 1–23.

Schwartz, Thomas A. *America's Germany: John J. McCloy and the Federal Republic of Germany.* 1991.

Spanier, John W. *American Foreign Policy since World War II.* 14th ed., 1998.

———. *The Truman-MacArthur Controversy and the Korean War.* 1959.

Spector, Ronald H. *Advice and Support: The Early Years of the U.S. Army in Vietnam: 1941–1960.* 1983.

Stueck, William. *The Korean War: An International History.* 1995.

———. "The Korean War as International History." *Diplomatic History* 10 (1986): 291–309.

———. *Rethinking the Korean War: A New Diplomatic and Strategic History.* 2002.

———. *The Road to Confrontation: American Policy toward China and Korea, 1947–1950.* 1981.

———. *The Wedemeyer Mission: American Politics and Foreign Policy during the Cold War.* 1984.

Theoharis, Athan G. *Seeds of Repression: Harry S. Truman and the Origins of McCarthyism.* 1971.

———. *The Yalta Myths: An Issue in U.S. Politics, 1945–1955.* 1970.

Toland, John. *In Mortal Combat: Korea, 1950–1953.* 1991.

Truman, Harry S. *Memoirs.* 2 vols., 1956.

Tsou, Tang. *America's Failure in China, 1941–1950.* 1963.

Tucker, Nancy B. *Patterns in the Dust: Chinese-American Relations and the Recognition Controversy, 1949–1950.* 1983.

Ulam, Adam B. *The Communists: The Story of Power and Lost Illusions, 1948–1991.* 1992.

———. *The Rivals: America and Russia since World War II.* 1971.

Weiner, Tim. *Legacy of Ashes: The History of the CIA.* 2007.

Weintraub, Stanley. *MacArthur's War: Korea and the Undoing of an American Hero.* 2000.

Westad, Odd Arne. *The Global Cold War: Third World Interventions and the Making of Our Times.* 2006.

Whelan, Richard. *Drawing the Line: The Korean War, 1950–1953.* 1990.

Whiting, Allen S. *China Crosses the Yalu: The Decision to Enter the Korean War.* 1960.

Williams, William J., ed. *A Revolutionary War: Korea and the Transformation of the Postwar World.* 1993.

Zhang, Shu Guang. *Deterrence and Strategic Culture: Chinese-American Confrontations, 1949–1958.* 1992.

———. *Economic Cold War: America's Economic Embargo Against China and the Sino-Soviet Alliance, 1949–1963.* 2001.

———. *Mao's Military Romanticism: China and the Korean War, 1950–1953.* 1996.

CHAPTER 3

Containment Continued:
The Eisenhower Years, 1953–1961

The Rhetoric of Cold War

Despite the Cold War rhetoric of the Eisenhower presidency, U.S. foreign policy remained essentially the same: that of containment. Secretary of State John Foster Dulles, son of a Presbyterian minister and relative of two other secretaries of state before him (John W. Foster and Robert Lansing), was stern and self-righteous in manner, sour in disposition, and less than exciting in demeanor (one contemporary spoke of him as "Dull, Duller, Dulles"). He was also a staunch anti-Communist who saw political value in suggesting that the administration had discarded containment for "liberation" when he called for a cutback in conventional forces and a heavy reliance on nuclear weapons. America's containment policy, Dulles warned in a *Life* magazine article in 1952, endangered civil liberties by necessitating excessive taxes and a refusal to seek victory. The United States needed "a policy of boldness" that enabled Americans "to retaliate instantly against open aggression by Red armies, so that if it occurred anywhere, we could and would strike back where it hurts, by means of our own choosing." Four years later, he elaborated on these ideas in another article in *Life*. "The ability to get to the verge without getting into the war is the necessary art," he asserted. "If you cannot master it, you inevitably get into war. If you try to run away from it, if you are scared to go to the brink, you are lost." Yet the explosive events of the 1950s showed that President Eisenhower recognized the realities of the nuclear standoff and often restrained his secretary of state by implementing a cautious foreign policy that avoided challenges to Soviet spheres of influence. Nikita Khrushchev, who became premier in 1958, later reminisced that Dulles "knew how far he could push us, and he never pushed us too far." Despite the administration's emphasis on the "New Look" in diplomacy, it adhered to the principles of containment.

Eisenhower exercised a greater degree of leadership over his administration than usually acknowledged. He chaired the numerous meetings of the National Security Council and, despite all the public attention Dulles commanded, maintained tight control over foreign policy. Dulles's busy nervousness, along with his numerous trips to Europe and Latin America, left the impression that he alone made the decisions. Indeed, he once drew the comment, "Don't do something, Foster, just stand there!" But it was Eisenhower himself

John Foster Dulles
Holding a press conference on his arrival in Taipei, Taiwan, in October 1958, just before conferring with Generalissimo Jiang Jieshi, president of Nationalist China. *(U.S. Army)*

who made foreign policy though remaining deliberately in the background. It was he who condoned covert action through the CIA (headed by Allen Dulles, brother of the secretary of state) and shepherded the expansion of the country's nuclear warheads eighteen times over their number of 1,000 in 1953. He also approved the development of both the B-52, a jet bomber capable of carrying a nuclear payload, and the Polaris, a ballistic missile fired from a submarine while underwater. Eisenhower considered atomic weaponry to be a vital part of the nation's defense network, not a last resort. His image of do-nothingism (a "national sedative," some declared) fulfilled a much-needed role, however. Given the past crises caused by the Great Depression, World War II, McCarthyism, Korean War, and the ever-heightening Cold War, Eisenhower's unquestioned honesty, disarming personality, and

outwardly calm manner reassured anxious Americans that their nation was once again in safe hands.

The 1950s: An Age of International Turmoil

Several crises during the decade highlighted the growing Cold War and tested the ability of the Eisenhower–Dulles foreign policy team to contain the spread of Soviet communism. Korea (see previous chapter), the Third World, Iran, Guatemala, Indochina, Communist China, Poland, Hungary, Suez, Berlin, the U-2 incident, Latin America—all problems appeared to be Communist in origin. Eisenhower recognized that a balance of nuclear terror had developed that rested precariously on mutual Soviet–American distrust, and he knew that the only way to keep peace lay in a diplomacy dependent on nuclear strength as leverage. While Dulles publicly advocated massive retaliation and maintained an apocalyptic approach to foreign affairs, Eisenhower quietly exercised restraints without abandoning the nuclear alternative. Yet the nation's driving force throughout the decade remained consistent with that of the Truman administration: a Cold War perception of the world that interpreted nearly every troublesome event as part of the epochal struggle with the Soviet Union.

The rising postwar Third World nations played a vital role in the Cold War. By 1960, nearly forty nations had emerged in Asia, Africa, and the Middle East, many rich in natural resources though desperately poor in economic development. Americans and Soviets found these new nations increasingly important to the search for strategic bases in the steadily intensifying rivalry between East and West. The largely uncontrollable factor was the growing number of nationalist revolutions that erupted from the anticolonial sentiment of World War II. Leaders were often leftist, Marxist, and only ostensibly democratic, building a following among peoples who were economically and politically destitute and hence subject to the bidding of Moscow's assumed proxies all over the world. A further complication came from the realization that as these peoples were accorded national status, they often adopted neutralist postures, preferring to play one superpower against the other rather than taking sides and thereby becoming the flashpoints of nuclear war. Indeed, in April 1955, twenty-nine nonaligned Asian and African nations gathered at the Bandung Conference in Indonesia, where Communist China's Zhou Enlai and India's Prime Minister Jawaharlal Nehru expressed the delegates' chief concerns about staying out of Cold War battles, remaining free of Western colonialism, and calling for "peaceful coexistence."

Washington's policymakers found themselves in an unenviable position in relation to the Third World. One could never be sure which direction a social revolution would take, and rather than risk a Communist takeover, the simplest approach was to support those leaders who were anti-Communist and promised stability, even at the cost of personal freedoms. The stakes were too high to allow any revolution to run its course, and for that reason the Eisenhower administration continued and even broadened the Truman policy of interventionism. Arguing that the Soviet Union was meddling in nearly every hot spot in the world, the United States extended military, economic, and political assistance; manipulated governments by virtually establishing surrogates in positions of power; participated in coups through the CIA; and demanded loyalty in the United Nations and other major concerns. Thus, the United States adopted many of the same measures that it criticized the Soviet Union for using. Rather than regarding Third World unrest as local in origin, the Eisenhower administration established a precedent for equating nationalism and neutralism with communism and assuming that the party line emanated solely from the Kremlin. In this respect, the president and his staff failed to come to terms with Third World nationalism and thereby left a dangerous legacy for their successors.

Eisenhower's foreign policy, like that of Truman's, sought to achieve order and stability in the Third World through economic and military measures. Some of the methods changed. The new administration considered reciprocal trade agreements (even with Eastern Europe) to be more important than foreign aid programs in curbing communism, and it depended more on the Export-Import Bank in combating economic problems overseas. American exports doubled from 1952 to 1960, although military aid under the Mutual Security Program averaged more than $3 billion a year in expenditures abroad.

Conservative Republicans fought both reciprocal trade pacts and the use of executive agreements in foreign affairs. Allied with conservative Democrats, they came within a single vote of passing an amendment proposed by Senator John Bricker of Ohio that would have changed the Constitution to allow congressional regulation of executive agreements with foreign countries. The White House maintained control over foreign policy, although it continued to operate within more stringent limitations imposed by a nearly chaotic brand of domestic politics. The irony is that during the remainder of the decade, Eisenhower so cautiously phrased his requests to Congress in matters relating to foreign affairs that it granted him more authority than anyone could have expected.

The frenzied political atmosphere at home resulting from McCarthyism obstructed the formulation of a realistic policy to deal with another major development of the period: the growing diversity in the Communist world. The Kremlin's hold had begun to loosen as local Communist parties preferred national objectives to ideology and threatened to further diffuse the international power structure. The first signal came in mid-1948, when Yugoslavia and the Soviet Union broke relations. A more profound change occurred during the 1950s, when the Communist Chinese intervened in the Korean War, earning them a sudden surge of prestige in Asia at Soviet expense. A U.S. foreign policy built on caution and restraint seemed wise, yet internal politics put pressure on the Washington government to pursue an activist policy braced with rhetoric and warning. Furthermore, the policy's anti-Communist thrust led the United States to support reactionary, repressive regimes, often putting it on the side of those leaders who opposed legitimate domestic reforms.

The nation's racial policies at home also hurt its international standing and promoted Communist propaganda. Race relations were tense. In December 1952, the U.S. attorney general urged the Supreme Court to rule against school segregation on the ground that "it is in the context of the present world struggle between freedom and tyranny that the problem of racial discrimination must be viewed." Two years later, the Supreme Court struck down segregation in the landmark case of *Brown v. Board of Education*, although the

ruling's actual implementation was delayed by ensuing events of the decade. In perhaps the most highly publicized incident threatening to cause racial violence, Eisenhower sent federal troops to Little Rock, Arkansas, in 1957 to protect black schoolchildren from angry white citizens. The state, according to the president, had performed a "tremendous disservice . . . to the nation in the eyes of the world." As the State Department and Voice of America tried to fend off Soviet propaganda, the United States continually fought racial battles at home while competing for Third World support and trying to hold together a Western alliance composed of Britain, France, and other former colonial powers.

If Eisenhower's foreign policy followed many of the same patterns established by his predecessor, it nonetheless was distinctive in attempting to negotiate with the Soviet Union. In April 1953, before the resolution of the Korean War, the president delivered a speech titled "The Chance for Peace" that pushed for improved relations with Stalin's more moderate successor, Georgi Malenkov. Eisenhower's subsequent proposals for disarmament had no immediate effect because in June workers in East Berlin, dissatisfied with increased workloads, set off a crisis in Germany by walking off their jobs. When their bold action grew into protests against the Soviet Union, Red troops and tanks swarmed into the city and brutally crushed the upheaval in less than twenty-four hours. The message seemed clear: disharmony in the Communist world had left the door ajar for easing relations between East and West. By the end of the year, the Korean War had wound down, and the Moscow government had established diplomatic relations with Yugoslavia and Greece, dropped territorial demands on Turkey, relaxed denunciations of the United States, and liberated the captives in Stalin's labor camps. Eisenhower went before the UN General Assembly in early December 1953 to recommend a slowdown in the nuclear arms race and to advocate international cooperation in industrial development.

The CIA in Iran and Guatemala

But before talks could begin, the Eisenhower administration had to turn to growing problems in Iran that many in Washington attributed to Communist infiltration. In 1953, it appeared that Premier Muhammad Musaddiq had edged too closely to the Soviet Union through the Tudeh, the Communist Party in Iran. Two years earlier, Musaddiq had nationalized the Anglo-Iranian Oil Company and in 1953 seized control of the government, forcing the young Muhammad Reza Shah (King) Pahlavi into exile. Although Musaddiq's nationalism was probably his greatest liability to the West, the United States viewed his actions as Communist-inspired and cut off aid in the autumn of that year. The administration worked through the CIA (the venture led by the grandson of Theodore Roosevelt and former member of the Office of Strategic Services during World War II, Kermit Roosevelt, and by General H. Norman Schwarzkopf Sr., who had engineered the establishment of the shah's secret police following the war), the British Secret Intelligence Service, and Iranian royalists in secretly organizing mass demonstrations in Teheran that embarrassed Musaddiq's government and led to his overthrow and imprisonment.

The shah, supported by U.S. military aid, returned to the throne in August 1953 and soon granted oil concessions to the West. Not by coincidence did he agree to the establishment of a consortium that provided for an even division of profits between it and Iran. The arrangement awarded the country's oil production rights primarily to Britain (40 percent) and the United States (five U.S. companies received 40 percent) and split the remainder between a French firm and a Dutch firm. In 1957, the CIA assisted the shah, who was anti-Communist and pro-American, in building a secret police network called SAVAK, which used torture, arbitrary imprisonment, and other repressive measures to guarantee loyalty to the throne. The Eisenhower administration proudly proclaimed that Iran was no longer in danger of a Communist takeover.

Growing unrest in Latin America also seemed to be Communist-induced but was attributable more to economic distress and resentment toward what appeared to be a cold indifference by the United States. Although the United States had extended aid to Europe and Asia by the end of the 1940s, it had done little to help Latin Americans experiencing declining prices on the world market; steadily increasing poverty, illiteracy, and disease; and mounting overpopulation and production problems. Nor did it show interest in meeting their needs for low-term government loans or outright grants, along with help in stabilizing prices. Rather, Washington's leaders favored industrial growth through private funds tied to Latin American guarantees against nationalizing foreign holdings. Many Latin Americans considered private investment akin to imperialist exploitation and reminded the White House that U.S. businesses had traditionally drained the region of natural resources.

The Truman administration had tried to establish better relations with Latin America, but always with the perceived Communist threat as priority. In 1947, U.S. representatives attended a conference in Rio de Janeiro that established a regional defense agreement, encouraged multilateral status for the Monroe Doctrine, and assured help to any American republic undergoing armed assault until the UN Security Council took action. The Inter-American Treaty of Mutual Assistance of September, or Rio Pact, fulfilled the intentions of Article 51 of the UN Charter by providing collective security in the hemisphere. But the first sign of trouble came early the following year, when the United States sought a treaty against communism at the Ninth International Conference of American States at Bogotá, Colombia, and, as a sweetener, offered $500 million of assistance through the Export-Import Bank. Latin Americans had expected considerably more than that. Street riots, driven by hunger and anger with the United States, resulted in the deaths of more than one thousand people and left large parts of the city in ruins. Washington, however, interpreted the violence as Communist inspired and called even more for a military agreement.

After the restoration of order in Bogotá, the delegates of the Latin American republics returned to the conference and signed the charter of the Organization of American States (OAS), which went into effect in 1951. The United States praised this regional defense pact as another triumph over communism; Latin Americans considered it a victory over U.S. interventionism. Over the strenuous objections of the United States, the Latin American delegations exacted a high price for the alliance: they inserted Article 15 of the OAS Charter, which declared that "no State or group of States has the right to intervene, directly or indirectly, for any reason whatever, in the internal or external affairs of any other State."

These agreements did not mollify Latin Americans, who demanded an aid program similar to that of the Marshall Plan in Europe. But despite the economic problems plaguing the Americas south of the United States, the Washington government pursued a policy that lasted into the early 1960s—a Cold War emphasis on Europe. Latin Americans wanted greater access to U.S. markets and bitterly denounced White House priorities.

The Eisenhower administration instituted changes in Latin American policy that, though having the appearance of humanitarian concern, actually reflected an overwhelming emphasis on ridding the hemisphere of communism. In 1953, the president's brother Milton, who was president of Johns Hopkins University, headed a special mission that visited ten South American states and proposed price stabilization, public loans, stimulation of private investment, and increased technical assistance under the Point Four program. But these measures were insufficient to meet the need. By the early 1950s, swelling economic and political unrest in Latin America had com-

bined with growing nationalist fervor to create a highly combustible situation.

Problems in Guatemala became the focal point of concern over Latin America because the White House was convinced that Communists, led by leftist president Jacobo Arbenz Guzmán, had infiltrated the republic. The facts belied the suppositions. Arbenz and his closest advisers were not Communists, only four of fifty-six members of Congress were party members, and neither the Catholic Church nor the army—the chief sources of power in the country—was Communist. Dulles admitted he could not prove a link between the Guatemalan government and the Kremlin, but his sound observation had the perverse effect of proving the Communist influence by suggesting the devious and skillful nature of that clandestine relationship.

The Arbenz regime had aroused massive unrest by calling for land reforms in a country where 2 percent of its people owned 70 percent of the land. The largest landholder in Guatemala was a U.S. firm, United Fruit Company of Boston, which had long enjoyed favored treatment by the government. In 1953, the Arbenz regime expropriated 400,000 acres of the company's holdings not then in use without providing what the company considered to be adequate compensation. To regain its land, United Fruit sought the assistance of the State Department in Washington by warning that if Arbenz succeeded, communism would spread into all of Latin America. Guatemala lay within airstriking distance of the Panama Canal, the company's representatives reminded the Eisenhower administration, and Arbenz was moving close to the Soviet Union in the United Nations. American Ambassador John Peurifoy, who had been in Greece during the civil war of the late 1940s, assured his superiors in Washington that Arbenz "thought like a Communist and talked like a Communist, and if not actually one, would do until one came along."

The White House at first employed diplomatic measures to bring about the fall of

Arbenz. In March 1954, at the Tenth International Conference of American States in Caracas, Venezuela, Dulles secured a nearly unanimous vote (Guatemala the lone dissenter) condemning "the domination or control of the political institutions of any American state by the international Communist movement." The statement was milder than Dulles wanted, and even then, several of those voting for the resolution complained that they had done so only under enormous U.S. pressure. Over the bitter protests of Guatemala's foreign minister that the declaration meant "the internationalization of McCarthyism," the United States cut off aid to his country.

But diplomatic efforts failed to undermine the Arbenz regime, and the White House resorted to surreptitious means. The CIA cooperated with Carlos Castillo Armas—an exiled Guatemalan army colonel and graduate of the U.S. Army's Command and General Staff College in Fort Leavenworth, Kansas—in building a mercenary army based both in Honduras and on an island off Nicaragua. Arbenz appealed to the UN Security Council for help, but the United States blocked any substantive consideration of the issue. Believing that the Eisenhower administration was seeking his overthrow with the help of Nicaraguan dictator Anastasio Somoza, Arbenz requested military assistance from the Communist states and drew a favorable Soviet response. In May, a Swedish vessel arrived in Guatemala carrying machine guns and rifles produced in Czechoslovakia and authorized by the Kremlin. The United States did not interfere with the unloading of the weapons, but the CIA prepared for an imminent coup by airlifting arms and other materials to spots near United Fruit possessions in Guatemala.

The fall of the Arbenz regime came surprisingly easy. In June, Armas opened the military assault while CIA pilots in U.S. planes bombed Guatemala City. Arbenz's army quickly deserted, forcing him to flee the country. Armas took power, United Fruit got back its land, and the new regime honored its debt by moving close to the United States. Although Armas had hundreds executed, the Eisenhower administration hailed Arbenz's demise as a victory over communism. Yet the social, economic, and political situation in Guatemala remained dismal, and the country turned into a virtual police state as perhaps 100,000 died over the next three decades under harsh military rule. The ill feeling generated by the intervention damaged U.S.–Latin American relations for years.

Southeast Asia

Meanwhile, the Eisenhower administration faced another Third World problem: the ongoing insurgent war in Indochina against the French. During the 1860s, France had imposed colonial rule onto the small S-shaped province, and in the early 1880s, it established protectorates over Laos and Cambodia, soon incorporating them—with Vietnam's three colonies of Annam, Tonkin, and Cochin China—into Indochina. The French, meanwhile, extracted vast quantities of rice, rubber, tin, oil, and tungsten from the area but did little to help its people, the great majority of whom were poverty-stricken country peasants. A staunch and learned Vietnamese nationalist, Ho Chi Minh, appeared as a self-appointed representative for Indochina at the Paris Peace Conference ending World War I, where he failed to win support for democratic reforms at home. Disillusioned, he joined the French Communist Party and throughout the 1920s and 1930s lived and campaigned in China, the Soviet Union, Thailand, and Vietnam. During that time, he established the Indochinese Communist Party, which tried unsuccessfully to undermine French rule.

The onset of World War II had a profound effect on Indochina. After Japan seized the area in 1941, Indochinese nationalists formed an underground resistance organization called the Vietminh, which combined the various nationalist groups under Ho's Communist leadership and used China as its base of operations. Toward the end of the war, the Vietminh cooperated with agents of the U.S. Office of Strategic Services against the Japanese, and Ho spoke of impending support from Washington in implanting U.S. ideals in an independent Indochina during the postwar period. In late August 1945, the Vietminh proclaimed the establishment of the Democratic Republic of Vietnam, with its capital in Hanoi. After the war, Ho reiterated his call for Indochinese independence based on the same principles found in the U.S. Declaration of Independence in 1776.

But the Washington government had never looked favorably on Ho Chi Minh's Vietminh forces. Indeed, it was not until the autumn of 1944 that the State Department recognized the growing importance of Southeast Asia to U.S. interests in the Philippines. President Roosevelt opposed the long-standing colonial system and instead tried to establish an international trusteeship over Indochina, but he encountered vehement opposition from Churchill, who feared that such an example would endanger the British Empire's colonial interests. When Roosevelt died, the State Department convinced President Truman that the restoration of French hegemony in Southeast Asia was necessary to win that government's support against the growing Soviet threat in Europe. Consequently, in 1946, after the war wound down in Asia, Indochina returned to French control.

Vietminh resistance immediately formed against the French, leading to what became known as the First Indochinese War. In March 1946, Ho Chi Minh and the French attempted to resolve their differences. Under agreements reached in Hanoi, Vietnam was to become a "free state" within the French Union, in return for joining Laos and Cambodia under a French protectorate called the "Associated States." But the French did not follow through on a promised plebiscite, and conflict broke out in November. The French bombarded Haiphong and seized the cities while Vietminh guerrillas solidified control over the countryside. In 1949, the French installed the emperor of Annam, Bao Dai, as

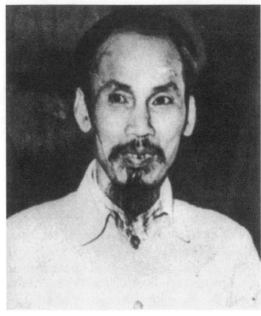

Ho Chi Minh
Leader of the Vietminh during World War II who later fought for Vietnam's independence and reunification until his death in September 1969. *(National Archives, Washington, D.C.)*

ruler of Vietnam and widened his domain to include Cochin China. Although genuinely concerned about his people, Bao Dai did not push for reforms primarily because he was too closely tied to his sponsors in Paris and to wealthy landholders within his regime. The Vietminh meanwhile attracted widespread popular support as the representatives of nationalism. They were also the "rebels," and the war continued.

American interest in Indochina jumped dramatically during the early 1950s because of China's change to communism, the outbreak of the Korean War, and the Truman administration's realization that to win French support for its European policies, it had to back French interests in Indochina. Although Secretary of State Acheson termed this reciprocal arrangement with France "blackmail," the decision to comply with its demands came easier because the State Department believed that the alternative was the spread of communism throughout Southeast Asia. Ho Chi Minh, according to the White House, was Moscow's Communist agent. Acheson, in fact, told the Senate in 1949 that Ho was an "outright Commie." In February 1950, the United States joined Britain in extending recognition to the French-sponsored government of Bao Dai. It also provided $150 million in military assistance that included planes, tanks, and napalm and dispatched a small number of U.S. military advisers to train Vietnamese soldiers loyal to the French. Indochina, declared Assistant Secretary of State Dean Rusk, had become "the most strategically important area of Southeast Asia."

As Southeast Asia became increasingly integral to the Cold War, the United States stepped up military aid to the French. By 1954, the number of U.S. military advisers had grown to more than 300, and its aid proportion now constituted 80 percent of France's war expenditures. Communist China and the Soviet Union countered by extending recognition to the Democratic Republic of Vietnam in the north and granting military assistance. The French commander in Indochina, General Henri Navarre, meanwhile called for a massive military buildup of the Vietnamese National Army and enough additional French soldiers to launch a major offensive against the Vietminh stronghold located in the far northern region of the Red River delta. Although Dulles was confident that the Navarre Plan would "break the organized body of Communist aggression by the end of the 1955 fighting season," the general was not so sure. The best result, he told leaders in Paris, was a stalemate that might lead to a peace treaty with the Vietminh. Even as the United States began its aid program in 1950, the Vietminh controlled two-thirds of the countryside, counted hundreds of thousands within its ranks, and held the offensive in the war.

The showdown in the First Indochinese War came in March 1954 when the Vietminh, armed with Chinese artillery, surrounded a combined French and Vietnamese army of 20,000 in the northwest Vietnamese village of Dienbienphu, a remote valley fortress almost totally encircled by hills a thousand feet high. Navarre had intended to lure the Vietminh into an open engagement where his superior weapons could take their toll. But the guerrillas surprised the French by first closing off air access to the fortress and then, in a superhuman effort, laboriously transporting heavy artillery to the high areas ringing the garrison. The French were isolated and appealed to the United States for an air strike and full-scale military intervention. The alternative, warned the Paris government, would be the fall of Indochina and the rest of Southeast Asia to communism.

The Eisenhower administration was divided in reaction to the French plea but appeared to lean toward intervention. Vice President Richard M. Nixon aroused stiff public opposition in April when he declared in an unauthorized remark that "if to avoid further Communist expansion in Asia and Indochina, we must take the risk now by putting our boys in, I think the Executive has to take the politically unpopular decision and do it." Dulles also wanted to send U.S. soldiers and bomb the area, but Army Chief of Staff Matthew Ridgway staunchly opposed direct military involvement because it would lead to heavy U.S. casualties and seriously undermine the nation's military commitment to Europe through NATO. At a press conference, Eisenhower spoke of the "domino theory," by which he seemed to imply that U.S. military intervention was necessary to prevent the fall of Indochina and an ensuing chain reaction that would cause the collapse of the entire region. Yet he questioned the value of an air strike in guerrilla warfare and in densely forested topography. He also rigidly opposed the emotional argument of Air Force Chief of Staff Nathan Twining, who wanted to drop three atomic bombs on the Vietminh forces at Dienbienphu to "clean those Commies out of there."

In the end, Eisenhower rejected the French request for intervention at Dienbienphu. An

Map 4
French Indochina. When Ho Chi Minh's Vietminh forces defeated the French at Dienbienphu in
1954, they won their independence only in the north. After the Geneva Conference of that same
year, the United States engaged in a policy of "nation building" that was supportive of Ngo Dinh
Diem's government in the south. *(Source: author)*

The Joint Chiefs of Staff
The debate over U.S. intervention at Dienbienphu in 1954. Admiral Arthur W. Radford (on left with back to camera) could convince only U.S. Air Force General Nathan Twining (to Radford's right) to favor intervention on behalf of the French. The other three joint chiefs (moving clockwise from Radford)—General Matthew Ridgway, U.S. Army Chief of Staff, General Lemuel Shepherd of the U.S. Marine Corps, and Admiral Robert Carney—opposed intervention. *(National Archives, Washington, D.C.)*

air strike, he asserted, was "just silly." Years later in a television interview with CBS news commentator Walter Cronkite, Eisenhower explained, "I couldn't think of anything probably less effective . . . unless you were willing to use weapons that could have destroyed the jungles all around the area for miles and that would have probably destroyed Dienbienphu itself." There was no such thing as "partial involvement," Admiral A. C. Davis sharply warned. "One cannot go over Niagara Falls in a barrel only slightly."

Eisenhower refused to act unless he had other countries' assistance, popular support at home, and a French pledge of independence to Indochina. He had none of these. America's al-lies were not interested in Dulles's call for "United Action," and the British in particular refused to believe that the fall of Indochina would bring down all of Southeast Asia. A recent Gallup poll in the United States had shown ten-to-one opposition to the use of U.S. combat troops. Included among the congressional members resisting such a move were future presidents John F. Kennedy and Lyndon B. Johnson, the first declaring that dispatching U.S. soldiers would be "dangerous, futile and self-destructive" and the second warning against "sending American GI's into the mud and muck of Indochina on a bloodletting spree." Finally, the French refused to guarantee independence to Indochina. Eisenhower privately criticized them for using "weasel words in promising independence" and disgustedly referred to France as "a hopeless, helpless mass of protoplasm." American forces would not become "junior partners" to the French. Congress agreed with the president's reasoning.

On May 7, after a fifty-five-day horrendous siege, the French and Vietnamese forces surrendered at Dienbienphu. Although artillery was integral to the victory, the story grew to mythical proportions that a guerrilla army had proved the feasibility of defeating the superior conventional force of a major power.

There is an ominous note about the situation in Indochina: had the Communist Chinese threatened to intervene, Eisenhower was prepared to use nuclear weapons as a deterrent. Communist China, he explained, was "the head instead of the tail of the snake," and its involvement would have necessitated a massive U.S. military response. In June, Dulles warned the Beijing government that its entry in the war "would be a deliberate threat to the United States itself." The early 1970s publication of *The Pentagon Papers*, a huge collection of top-secret Defense Department documents pilfered from the files, shows that the president and his secretary of state were prepared to take these drastic actions. In late May, Eisenhower approved proposals by the Joint Chiefs of Staff for "employing atomic weapons" if China intervened in Indochina. He added, however, that such a move would have taken place only after congressional approval and with the concurrence of the nation's allies. "Unilateral action by the United States in cases of this kind would destroy us," he told an aide. "If we intervened alone in this case we would be expected to intervene alone in other parts of the world."

A conference had meanwhile convened in Geneva to discuss Korea and Indochina, and by July, the nineteen delegations present, including the Soviet Union, North Korea, Communist China, and the United States, had moved toward a series of agreements on Southeast Asia. Despite victory on the battlefield, however, the Vietminh failed in its quest to rid Vietnam of foreign influence. Indeed, the Communist Chinese opposed a total French withdrawal as a prelude to a deeper U.S. involvement. A divided Vietnam fitted Chinese security interests more than did an unfriendly neighbor unified and ready to expand into Laos and Cambodia. The Geneva Accords therefore did little for the Vietminh. They called for an armistice in Indochina, recognition of the independence of Laos and Cambodia, and, most important to the Chinese, the construction of a "provisional military demarcation line" at the seventeenth parallel in Vietnam that would place 13 million Vietnamese above the division and 10 million below. The proposed agreements emphasized that this was a temporary partition, not "a political or territorial boundary." Although the Vietminh retained control over Hanoi and Haiphong in the north, Bao Dai was to remain emperor of the south. Free elections would take place in 1956 to unite the Vietnams, followed by elections in Laos and Cambodia. Neither region of Vietnam was to enter into military pacts or permit foreign occupation.

The United States refused to sign the Geneva agreements, even though it pledged not to interfere with their fulfillment and promised to support elections under UN supervision. The administration did not recognize Communist China and could enter no formal negotiations with its representatives, and it opposed any territorial awards to the Vietminh. The White House also disliked the prohibition against the introduction of new military forces and weaponry and the ruling against a move by either part of Vietnam to join a military pact. Eisenhower realized, however, that the Communists had won the war and agreed with the National Security Council's warning that Communist China would now promote the spread of communism into all of Southeast Asia. A two-year delay in elections was advantageous, the president believed, because he was certain that Ho Chi Minh would easily win if elections took place immediately.

Eisenhower, Dulles, and Diem
President Eisenhower and Secretary of State Dulles greet South Vietnamese Premier Ngo Dinh Diem in Washington, D.C., in May 1957. *(National Archives, Washington, D.C.)*

To prevent a Communist takeover, the Eisenhower administration prepared to aid the non-Communists in the south. This arrangement seemed highly preferable because of the recently installed premier in the south, Ngo Dinh Diem. Even though he was a Catholic in a country overwhelmingly Buddhist, Diem was a fervent nationalist who steadfastly opposed the French and the Communists. Furthermore, he had lived in exile in the United States for years, where he made many valuable contacts with influential political and religious figures. The State of Vietnam (South) joined the United States in refusing to sign the Geneva Accords.

To protect Western interests, the United States took the lead in establishing the Southeast Asia Treaty Organization (SEATO) to safeguard South Vietnam, Laos, and Cambodia from communism. Toward that objective, Dulles called a conference at Manila in September that was attended by the United States, Britain, France, Australia, New Zealand, the Philippines, Thailand, and Pakistan. Other prominent governments in that region—India, Indonesia, Burma, and Ceylon (now Sri Lanka)—did not attend because they preferred remaining neutral to antagonizing the Communist Chinese. Britain's refusal to recognize the Nationalists on Formosa barred that government from the proceedings. On September 6, the delegates approved a recommendation by President Ramon Magsaysay of the Philippines that established a Pacific Charter ensuring support for "equal rights and self-determination of peoples."

Fear of an imminent Communist Chinese invasion of Formosa hurried the proceedings. Two days after approval of the Pacific Charter, the delegates signed the Southeast Asia Collective Defense Treaty, which asserted that in the event of attack, each signatory would "consult immediately" according to each member's "constitutional processes." Unlike NATO, the new organization contained no central armed force and depended almost exclusively on U.S. military support. In addition, it committed the United States to halt subversion coming from outside the Southeast Asian protected states. The ominous implication was the possibility of unilateral U.S. action if other signatories failed to regard communism as an international threat. Headquartered in Bangkok, SEATO went into effect in 1955.

By mid-decade, the United States had adopted a highly precarious policy that rested on a firm commitment to Diem as head of an independent, non-Communist South Vietnam. The organization of SEATO raised questions about the sanctity of the Geneva Accords because it implied that the "temporary" demarcation line had taken on permanent status and had thereby left South Vietnam as a separate country. The United States also violated the Accords by stipulating that in exchange for Diem's assurances of social and economic reforms, it would send military and economic aid. But had Diem *wanted* to do so, he could not have implemented sweeping internal changes because his regime was elitist and nepotistic, overwhelmingly Catholic in a predominantly non-Catholic area, and primarily dependent on the landlords for support. Most important, Diem was a product of the privileged mandarin class and, accordingly, had never professed a belief in democracy. In fact, given Vietnam's devastation from the war, it

is doubtful that the United States could have found a less likely place to engage in what Dulles would herald as a grand experiment in "nation building."

While U.S. military advisers worked to improve Diem's army, the French remained in South Vietnam to carry out the promised elections. They only grudgingly assumed their new secondary status, however, and openly resented the use of Diem by the United States to gain a foothold in Indochina. Indeed, from this time forward, the Eisenhower administration extended aid directly to South Vietnam and not through what Dulles called the French "protected preferential market." Diem faced the monumental task of trying to shore up a fragmented society, increasingly staggered by vast influxes of mostly Catholic northern refugees who were loyal to traditions and cultures vastly different from those already in the south. The south, in fact, soon became a haven for a variety of independent sects, each with its own beliefs and its own warlords and armies. At one point in 1955, Diem had to use brute force to put down a sect crisis led by the Mafia-like Binh Xuyen, which had seized control of the Saigon police force. Dulles had already begun hedging on the likelihood of an election in South Vietnam in 1956. He told reporters that the United States would recognize a government opposed to Diem only if "it seems to be expressive of the real will of the people and if it is truly representative." Dulles further expressed fear that the South Vietnamese did not understand that Ho Chi Minh was an advocate of international communism. In a statement that raised more questions than it answered, he emphasized that until the South Vietnamese recognized Diem's attractions, there could be no valid electoral process. The Communist Chinese, too, made clear their opposition to an election intended to unify Vietnam. By July 1955, most of the French had given up on the chances of an election and had gone home.

The U.S. fear of communism in Southeast Asia led it to overlook many faults in Diem's regime. In October 1955, he held a plebiscite

Proponents of the National Liberation Front argued that its purposes were to unify Vietnam and free it from Diem and outside control.

Manifesto of the South Vietnam National Front for Liberation, December 1960, *Vietnamese Studies* (Hanoi), no. 23, "South Vietnam from the N.F.L. to the Provisional Revolutionary Government," 247–54.

The *South Viet Nam National Front for Liberation* undertakes to unite all sections of the people, all social classes, nationalities, political parties, organizations, religious communities and patriotic personalities, without distinction of their political tendencies, in order to struggle for the overthrow of the rule of the US imperialists and their stooges—the Ngo Dinh Diem clique—and for the realization of independence, democracy, peace and neutrality pending the peaceful reunification of the fatherland.

in South Vietnam, easily winning the presidency over Bao Dai in an obviously fixed proceeding. Massachusetts Senator John F. Kennedy nonetheless called Diem's Republic of Vietnam the "cornerstone of the Free World in Southeast Asia, the keystone in the arch, the finger in the dike." He continued, "It is our offspring, we cannot abandon it, we cannot ignore its needs." Diem worked closely with CIA operative Edward Lansdale in "psywar" (psychological warfare) programs against the Hanoi government, and the Saigon regime instituted reform programs designed to undercut a growing insurgency by herding South Vietnamese peasantry into barbed-wire encampments called "agrovilles." But the situation in the south slowly and then rapidly deteriorated. Diem survived numerous domestic crises (including a coup attempt in November 1960) and consolidated his control only through increasingly repressive measures. The Vietminh in South Vietnam meanwhile followed Hanoi's secret directives in establishing the National Liberation Front (NLF) in December 1960. An anti-Diem organization led by Communists, the NLF attracted a significant following by calling for widespread reforms and the independence of a unified Vietnam. Diem's supporters derisively labeled the NLF as Vietcong, or Vietnamese Communists. Given North Vietnam's unyielding determination to drive out foreign intervention and incorporate the economically richer south, the forecast was a civil war that, to the United States, bore dire international ramifications that necessitated an expanded military and economic commitment.

Communist China and Formosa

In a move that the United States attributed to its deepening involvement in Asia, the Communist Chinese in the autumn of 1954 began bombarding the offshore Nationalist-controlled islands of Quemoy, Matsu, and the Tachens. Such action, Americans thought, marked the first step toward a Communist invasion of Formosa and an ultimate confrontation with the United States. Earlier, in August, Premier Zhou Enlai in Beijing had called for the liberation of Formosa because, he charged, it had become a U.S. military base. Jiang had meanwhile heavily fortified Quemoy, and the Communist Chinese began shelling it on September 3, killing two U.S. military advisers. Eisenhower sternly warned that "any invasion of Formosa would have to run over the Seventh Fleet." Although willing to give up the Tachens (lying 200 miles north of Formosa), he refused to do the same with Quemoy and Matsu, which were much closer to Formosa and hence integral to its safety. The collapse of these two areas, the president later declared, would have endangered "the anti-Communist barrier" in the western Pacific of Japan, South Korea, Nationalist China, the Philippines,

Thailand, and Vietnam and would have led to Communist triumphs in Burma, Cambodia, Indonesia, Laos, and Malaya.

In truth, however, the Eisenhower administration's fears were greatly exaggerated. Much of the tension during the 1950s, particularly in these offshore islands, stemmed from the preceding Chinese civil war, which suggests that the United States wrongfully interpreted these events as another salvo in the Cold War rather than as a continuation of internal troubles. The British government blamed the shelling on longtime animosities between Nationalists and Communists that had heated up during the previous summer. Indeed, the Nationalists had bombed the mainland and had long harassed the Communists by firing on their ships and launching commando expeditions ashore. But the United States regarded the shelling as a challenge to its deterrence policy, especially in light of the West's recent failures in Korea and Indochina. Chinese documentation, however, shows that the Beijing government ordered the shelling of Quemoy not as a prelude to an invasion of the island but as a political move warning against U.S. interference in Chinese domestic affairs. The Communists particularly feared an escalation in U.S. and Nationalist aggressions and the creation of a mutual defense pact between the two governments. The only islands under consideration for a Communist takeover were the Tachens, which were far to the north and under Nationalist control. Mao considered the United States the aggressor and was unaware of U.S.–Nationalist tensions at the time brought on primarily by the White House's wish to restrict Jiang's assaults on the mainland and defuse tensions in the area.

Some members of the Eisenhower administration reacted strongly to these events, insisting that even though the islands were not vital to U.S. interests, they were symbolic of Free World resistance to communism. The Joint Chiefs of Staff recommended that the president instruct the Nationalists to bomb the Chinese mainland; if this measure led to a Communist attack on Quemoy, they continued, the United States should join in its defense. Nixon grimly declared that "we should stand ready to call international Communism's bluff on any pot, large or small. If we let them know that we will defend freedom when the stakes are small, the Soviets are not encouraged to threaten freedom where the stakes are higher." Quemoy and Matsu were important in "the poker game of world politics."

The president, however, agreed with General Ridgway, who warned that such a policy would cause war with China. "We're not talking now about a limited, brush-fire war," Eisenhower asserted to the National Security Council. "We're talking about going to the threshold of World War III. . . . Moreover, if we get into a general war, the logical enemy will be Russia, not China, and we'll have to strike there." Dulles had initially supported the Joint Chiefs' call for action but now had to change course. The president had already ordered him to Formosa to negotiate a treaty promising U.S. protection to Jiang but leaving the welfare of the offshore islands ambiguous. Dulles had wanted to specify them in the pact, but Eisenhower insisted on a vague authorization of a U.S. commitment to "such other territories as may be determined by mutual agreement." In December, the United States and Formosa signed a mutual defense pact to prevent unilateral military action in exchange for a U.S. guarantee to keep forces "in and about" the island. The following month, after the Communist Chinese seized one of the Tachens, Dulles solemnly warned the president of "at least an even chance that the United States will have to go to war."

But Eisenhower had laid the groundwork for a peaceful resolution of the crisis. The defense treaty had allowed him to satisfy Jiang's outspoken supporters within the Republican Party yet at the same time to place restraints on the Nationalists. In January 1955, Congress overwhelmingly approved the "Formosa Resolution," which authorized the president to use military force in defending Formosa and "such related positions and territories" as he considered necessary. Thus, Eisenhower's options remained open, leaving the Chinese uncertain about his intentions to protect Quemoy, Matsu, and the Tachens. In a letter to Churchill, the president expressed concern about his own ability to distinguish "between an attack that has only as its objective the capture of an offshore island and one that is primarily a preliminary movement to an all-out attack on Formosa." American policy depended on "circumstances as they might arise."

The artillery barrage continued, however, suggesting that the Beijing government had interpreted Eisenhower's inaction as an unwillingness to go to war over these islands. In response, the White House issued a public warning that it was considering the use of nuclear weapons. In March, Dulles asserted in a speech that to stop the "aggressive fanaticism" of the Chinese, the United States was prepared to use "new and powerful weapons of precision which can utterly destroy military targets without endangering unrelated civilian centers." Although the CIA argued that a "clean" nuclear assault was an impossibility—that it would kill up to 14 million Chinese civilians—Eisenhower alarmed reporters by declaring that Dulles was correct: nuclear weapons could be used "as you use a bullet or anything else." He later wrote in his memoirs that his intention had been to convince the Chinese Communists that he would defend Formosa. According to his own assessment, his strategy of threatening preventive war worked because the shelling stopped in April. But the Beijing government had relented for reasons having little to do with Eisenhower's implied use of massive retaliation. Its decision makers had already decided to work toward peaceful coexistence with their country's neighbors just before that month's opening of the Bandung Conference in Indonesia. One way to ensure harmony with fellow non-Western nations was to ease the pressure on the offshore islands.

The war scare had mixed results. On the one side, Communist China had succeeded in its political purpose of drawing worldwide attention to U.S. involvement in an internal affair, and it had achieved a longtime objective of opening direct talks with the United States. But the crisis had also hurt China's position by encouraging better U.S.–Nationalist relations through the Mutual Defense Treaty and the Formosa Resolution. On the other side, however, the United States could claim no victory for deterrence because the Communists had never intended to invade either Quemoy or Matsu. And even though the crisis encouraged the Washington government to push for peace through summit negotiations, it established a potentially dangerous precedent through the Formosa Resolution. The president now had authority to decide when to deploy U.S. forces in a troubled area, thereby chipping away at Congress's constitutional power to declare war. On yet another level, the mutual misinterpretation of each other's motives demonstrated the danger of an isolation policy that leaves ideological differences as the only guide for understanding each other. Brinkmanship and deterrence actually encouraged conflict.

The Spirit of Geneva and Europe

By early 1955, the situation had also stabilized in Europe, but at the cost of what appeared to be a permanently divided Germany within a permanently divided continent. The United States had earlier failed to persuade the French to accept the integration of West German soldiers into an organization known as the European Defense Community, but in 1954, the European states had agreed to place West German forces under the control of a Western European Union (WEU). France accepted, but at the high price of a British commitment to send four divisions to Europe and a U.S. promise to retain troops already there since 1951. In turn, West German Chancellor Konrad Adenauer pledged not to produce long-range missiles and atomic, chemical, or bacteriological weapons without the consent of NATO's commander and a two-thirds approval of the WEU Council. The other members guaranteed that West Germany would not use force to reunify the country or modify its present boundaries. This plan went into effect in May 1955 and thereby brought to a close ten years of German occupation. The United States, Britain, and France proclaimed the Federal Republic of West Germany as the country's only legitimate government, effectively denying recognition to East Germany. West Germany also became part of NATO that year. A European standoff developed when the Soviets countered with the Warsaw Pact, a military organization of themselves, East Germany, and loyal East European Communist states.

The time for a Soviet–American agreement seemed auspicious. Premier Malenkov had resigned in February 1955, and his successor was Nikolai Bulganin, although the real power was Nikita Khrushchev, first secretary of the Communist Party. The new Soviet regime seemed amenable to East–West cooperation. It approved a small number of visits by American tourists, and the United States allowed the entry of Soviet agriculturalists and journalists. In May, the Soviet Union joined the United States, Britain, and France in signing the Austrian State Treaty, which ended ten years of joint occupation and established that country's independence and neutral status in international affairs. Although the Soviets simply preferred a neutral Austria to an Austria divided between East and West (like Germany), their withdrawal appeared altruistic and drew a favorable world reaction. On the very day of the treaty-signing ceremony, the Soviets agreed to the first summit since Potsdam when they announced their willingness to meet in July with the United States, Britain, and France in Geneva.

The Geneva Conference of 1955 convened amid an air of optimism tempered by caution and uncertainty. The United States was confident in both its own strength and the Soviet Union's economic weaknesses.

The European allies of the United States were more concerned about stopping the race to war. NATO war games had recently indicated that if fighting broke out on the continent, Western Europe would become a fiery and radioactive holocaust as a result of more than 170 atomic bombs.

Despite the widely heralded "spirit of Geneva," the Big Four reached no important agreements at the weeklong conference. Both sides presented proposals virtually certain to fail. The Soviets called for an end to NATO, the withdrawal of U.S. soldiers from the continent, and a ban on the production and use of atomic weapons. The West pressed for Germany's unification through democratic elections. On arms control, Eisenhower made an "Open Skies" proposal by which the United States and the Soviet Union would furnish maps of each other's military complexes to allow mutual aerial surveillance. The president was not naive. He knew that the Soviets were already aware of most U.S. military sites, and he therefore used this piece of drama to counter their earlier call for disarmament. "We knew the Soviets wouldn't accept it," he later recalled. Yet the president hoped that the proposal might ease international tension by opening the way to less comprehensive arms control measures. In a letter to General Alfred Gruenther, Eisenhower explained that his intention had been to secure "an immense gain in mutual confidence and trust." At Geneva, the United States and the Soviet Union agreed only to encourage cultural exchanges; the other issues they forwarded to a meeting of the Big Four's foreign ministers.

The Geneva Conference left the misguided impression of a thaw in the Cold War. Eisenhower encouraged the optimism by highlighting the "new spirit of conciliation and cooperation," and the Soviets likewise fostered this brief wave of euphoria by extending recognition to West Germany that same year. But recognition of West Germany ensured a divided Germany and led the Soviets to build up the East German army. Moreover, it soon became evident that the conference was a mere publicity show in which photographers' pictures created the illusion of Soviet–American harmony. Khrushchev boasted that "we had established ourselves as able to hold our own in the international arena." Dulles warned against expecting an "era of good feelings," and W. Averell Harriman, former ambassador to Moscow and inveterate critic of its policies, expressed concern that the "free world was psychologically disarmed" by the "spirit of Geneva" and warned that it was a "smoke screen" for Soviet expansion. Khrushchev emphasized that no change had taken place in Soviet attitude. "If anybody thinks that for this reason we shall forget about Marx, Engels, and Lenin, he is mistaken. This will happen when shrimps learn to whistle."

Still, the false image of improved relations continued into the new year, cresting in February 1956 when Khrushchev shocked friends and foes alike by calling for peaceful coexistence and the de-Stalinization of Eastern Europe. Before the Twentieth Congress of the Communist Party in Moscow, the first secretary delivered a speech in which he turned away from Lenin's assertion of the inevitability of war between Communists and capitalists and then denounced Stalin's domestic crimes and urged party members to accept diversity in the Communist world. Khrushchev had several objectives, including an expansion of his power at home, a loosening of restraints on the country's economy to promote production, and a maintenance of domestic control short of outright repression. There was little reason to believe that he had softened. Khrushchev had called for a new approach to the same goal: a Communist triumph by Soviet exploitation of the uncommitted nations of the world, whether or not they were Communist.

In the meantime, the erosion of Communist unity had not gone unnoticed by the Eisenhower administration. Tito's defection, the growing division between the Soviets and the Communist Chinese, and now an admission to "national Communism" all suggested that the United States needed to examine re-

cent instances of unrest throughout the world to determine whether the Soviets were losing their grip on the Communist movement. Khrushchev's recognition of "Titoism" in 1955 was an important sign of change, as were the Soviets' decisions to disband the Cominform, arrange an exchange of visits between Tito and Khrushchev, and negotiate a pact with Yugoslavia that contained the surprising assertion that there were "different roads to socialism."

But before the United States could assess the potential impact of this new Soviet policy, thousands of dissidents in Poland and Hungary seized on Khrushchev's speech as an invitation to self-determination and rose in revolt against Stalinist leaders in their countries. Americans interpreted the upheavals as a fulfillment of Dulles's goal of "liberation" and supported the Voice of America and Radio Free Europe in encouraging further resistance in Eastern Europe. The dangerous implication was that the United States would assist anyone taking the first step toward breaking Soviet ties.

In June 1956, riotous demonstrations among workers in Poland soon developed into a widespread revolt against Soviet dominance in the country. The Soviets threatened to use force to put down the uprising, but in October, Polish Communists led by Wladyslaw Gomulka met with Khrushchev and warned of full-scale armed resistance if the Soviets staged a coup. Khrushchev discreetly agreed to accept Gomulka (earlier rejected by Stalin as "Titoist") as chair of the Polish Communist Party. Poland remained Communist and within the Warsaw Pact, even though its relationship with the Soviet Union was uneasy. Poland appeared to have won autonomy in October when it elected Gomulka chair of the Communist Party. As was the case with Yugoslavia in 1948, the United States extended economic aid to Poland.

The successes in Poland probably had a direct effect on Hungary because in late October 1956, demonstrations in Budapest against Stalinism exploded in violence aimed at the

Communist government and at the Soviet Union. The leader of the insurrection, Imre Nagy, feared Soviet military intervention and tried to restrain the extremism of his followers, but matters quickly got out of hand as the rebels demanded freedom, toppled the huge statue of Stalin in the city, and killed several Stalinist Communists. Nagy soon emerged as head of a new regime that included non-Communist members. It broke with the Warsaw Pact, demanded a Soviet troop withdrawal, and announced a neutralist position in international affairs. The new government then turned to the United States for aid based on the assurances of Eisenhower–Dulles "liberation."

The Eisenhower administration found itself in the uncomfortable position of wanting to see the Hungarians succeed but unable to do anything in an area deemed vital to Soviet interests. Dulles praised the revolution as proof of the "weakness of Soviet imperialism" and noted that these "captive peoples should never have reason to doubt that they have in us a sincere and dedicated friend who shares their aspirations." The secretary, however, was in ill health and would soon undergo emergency surgery for cancer, but even if Dulles had been healthy, the administration would not have intervened in Hungary. It is impossible to determine whether Eisenhower's foreign policy pronouncements influenced the outbreak of the Hungarian revolution, but they doubtless led the rebels to believe that U.S. aid would arrive after they took the initial step toward independence. The United States publicly expressed sympathy, introduced UN resolutions condemning Soviet actions and calling for withdrawal, and threw open its doors to thousands of Hungarian refugees. But that was the extent of U.S. involvement. The White House recognized that intervention could lead to war with the Soviet Union over an area not vital to American security. Besides, troubles had meanwhile erupted in the Middle East, a region regarded as crucial to U.S. interests.

Events in Hungary threatened to establish a dangerous precedent for other Communist states interested in autonomy, and for that reason the Soviet Union had to act. It first installed a Communist regime in Budapest that immediately requested Moscow's help in restoring order. On November 4, at the height of the concurrent crisis in the Middle East, Red tanks and troops stormed into Budapest to put down the revolution. Nagy sought refuge in the Yugoslav embassy but came out after allegedly receiving assurances of a seat in the new government. (The Soviets sent him to Russia and executed him in 1957.) After weeks of street fighting, the Soviets squelched the rebellion at the horrendous cost of 30,000 Hungarian lives. "Poor fellows, poor fellows," Eisenhower lamented to a reporter. "I think about them all the time. I wish there were some way of helping them."

Several revealing aspects about U.S. and Soviet behavior emerged from the Hungarian crisis. Eisenhower "liberation" offered false hopes in areas considered vital to the Soviet Union. The Moscow government permitted nationalist uprisings only if they did not damage Soviet prestige or set precedents dangerous to international communism. The Soviets lost respect among Communists in other countries because their troops had not performed well, their allies' military forces had defected in fairly large numbers, and Hungarian youths had not converted to communism. The revolution resulted in a severe propaganda defeat for the Kremlin, but Hungary remained within the Soviet bloc.

Suez

Toward the last stages of the Hungarian revolution, attention suddenly shifted to the Middle East, where war threatened to develop during the Suez crisis of 1956. Ancient issues in this region, combined with its growing military and strategic importance in the postwar era, created an explosive situation. Volatile ingredients were there: Arab–Israeli conflict,

Anglo–Egyptian rivalry, French concern over the possible loss of Algeria, emerging nationalisms after World War II, big power interests in oil, suspicions between East and West, and divisiveness among the Western powers. As in other trouble spots in the world, the Eisenhower administration feared that continued disorder in the Middle East would invite Soviet involvement.

British policy lay at the root of many problems in the Middle East. During World War I, Britain issued the Balfour Declaration, which offered renewed hope to the Zionist movement by guaranteeing "the establishment in Palestine of a National Home for the Jewish people." The year before, however, the British assured the Arabs an independent state out of the remains of the old Ottoman Empire— including Palestine. The two promises were irreconcilable. At Versailles in 1919, the peacemakers assigned Britain the League of Nations mandate over Palestine, and for years afterward it attempted to resolve these conflicting policies. In more than one instance, the British alienated world opinion by turning away ships bearing Jewish refugees as they approached Palestine. Meanwhile, in September 1922, the U.S. Congress approved a joint resolution endorsing the Balfour Declaration. Two years later, the United States negotiated a treaty recognizing the British mandate over Palestine and thereby set the direction of its own Palestinian policy.

Hitler's persecutions of the Jews during World War II revived Zionism and drove many European Jews toward their "homeland" in the postwar period. In 1947, Britain announced the termination of its Palestinian mandate the following year, leaving the question for the United Nations to resolve. In late November 1947, the General Assembly decided to partition Palestine into Arab and Jewish states and to establish international supervision of the ancient city of Jerusalem. But this plan drew bitter Arab opposition. The Arabs had twice as many people in Palestine as did the Jews, and they claimed the right of

possession by having resided there for centuries. Furthermore, the partition awarded the Jews the largest section of Palestine's farmland, along with most of its urban and railroad areas. The Arab delegation in the General Assembly stalked out in protest. On May 14, 1948, the day before Britain's mandate came to an end, the Jews proclaimed the independent state of Israel. Less than fifteen minutes later, President Truman rejected the advice of his diplomatic and military counselors and extended de facto recognition. Three days afterward, the Soviet Union did the same.

In explaining the rapid recognition of Israel by the United States, Truman emphasized humanitarian concern for the Jews, but he could not have been oblivious to domestic political considerations. He had earlier called on Britain to permit 100,000 Jews to enter Palestine. A few days later, his probable Republican opponent in the presidential election of 1948, New York Governor Thomas Dewey, recommended raising the number to several hundred thousand. The election of 1948, everyone knew, would be close, and the Jewish vote in New York could award the White House to the Republicans for the first time since 1933. The State Department had joined military advisers in opposing the UN partition plan because it would alienate the Arabs. The president supported the partition for humanitarian and political reasons.

In May 1948, the neighboring Arab states invaded Palestine, causing a conflict that threatened to become more than regional in implication. Arab forces soon had to turn back in the face of the smaller yet better-equipped Israelis—most of whose heavy weaponry came from Communist Czechoslovakia. This situation exposed the dilemma facing the United States. Sentiment for Hitler's wartime victims and the need for the Jewish American vote at home had generated a pro-Israel feeling in Washington. Yet two-thirds of the world's oil reserves were in the Middle East, whose borders touched 3,000 miles of the Soviet Union.

West and virtually invited the Soviet Union to exploit Arab hostility toward the Jews. A decline in Western influence became plain by the autumn of 1955. The French were deeply involved in putting down an uprising in Algeria encouraged by Egypt, and British efforts to persuade Jordan to join the Baghdad Pact led to violent demonstrations in its capital of Amman.

In the meantime, the situation worsened in the Suez area. The Israelis had retaliated against repeated border troubles by raiding Egypt's Gaza Strip along their common frontier in February 1955, and in late September, Nasser mortgaged his country's entire year's cotton crop for an arms deal with Czechoslovakia, which was acting as a front for the Soviet Union. The following December, the United States attempted to pull Nasser into the Western camp by agreeing to help finance a massive enlargement of the Aswan Dam (on the Nile River) to promote electricity and irrigation. More than $1 billion was to come from the World Bank plus American and British funds. Jewish Americans put pressure on the Eisenhower administration to cancel the deal, while southern congressional members complained that such a dam would hurt their own cotton manufacturers.

The Eisenhower administration failed to undercut the Soviets and win Egypt's support. The president and his secretary of state were already upset with Nasser for his recent decision to recognize Communist China, and they now feared that the arms deal was proof of his shift from neutralism to a pro-Soviet allegiance. Dulles put it simply: "Do nations which play both sides get better treatment than nations which are stalwart and work with us?" The administration's answer to Nasser's blackmail tactics came in July 1956, when Dulles suddenly and dramatically withdrew the loan offer for the Aswan Dam. He had not consulted the British, who had agreed to share the financial burden, and he had chosen to make the announcement on the very day Nasser's foreign minister arrived in Washington to finalize the arrangement. Dulles was confident that the move would call the Soviet bluff and set a telling example for neutralists.

But the Soviets did not have time to act: Nasser nationalized the canal by taking over the British- and French-controlled Universal Suez Canal Company. The canal tolls, he announced, would finance the dam. To make the move legal, he promised to compensate the stockholders and pledged to keep the passage open. These assurances proved unsatisfactory. Nasser's action humiliated the British and infuriated the French, who already held him responsible for many of the arms used by their Algerian rebels. Dulles immediately flew to London to confer with British Prime Minister Anthony Eden and French Premier Guy Mollet, both of whom had discussed the use of force in regaining control over the canal. At a meeting of the twenty-four nations chiefly dependent on the canal, the vast majority supported the establishment of an international organization to administer the waterway. Nasser, however, rejected the plan because the organization would clearly be under British and French control. Dulles recommended forming a Suez Canal Users Association to collect the tolls and divide the funds between canal maintenance and payments to owners. Nasser likewise turned down this plan. In October, the UN Security Council responded to the Anglo–French request for assistance by establishing guidelines for the canal's administration that included assurances of Egyptian sovereignty, no outside interference with the canal's operation, and "free and open transit through the Canal." Egypt accepted these terms, although Britain and France doubted that Nasser would abide by them. Eden and Mollet decided to act on their own.

By late October, coinciding with the popular upheavals in Poland and Hungary, the rapidly building crisis in the Middle East threatened to cause an East–West confrontation. In a move destined to have long-lasting ramifications, France, England, and Israel secretly collaborated to invade Egypt and bring down Nasser. Israel moved first. Its forces easily overran the Egyptians in the Gaza Strip and Sinai Peninsula, seizing nearly all the Czech arms along with 6,000 Egyptian soldiers and then heading toward the Suez Canal. The day after the invasion, Britain and France feigned surprise at Israel's actions and called for a cease-fire stipulating that Egypt and Israel withdraw ten miles from the canal, thereby giving Israel a hundred miles of Egyptian territory. The British and French had violated the Tripartite Declaration of May 1950, which had guaranteed no border violations of either Israel or the Arab states.

The conflict then threatened to spread beyond the confines of the Middle East. Nasser angrily rejected the Anglo–French proposal and closed the canal by sinking ships in its passageway. Arab militants sabotaged pumphouses that sent oil from the Persian Gulf to the Mediterranean, causing a shortage in Western Europe that necessitated a severe rationing program and underlined the importance of the Middle East. On the same day Nasser turned down the Anglo–French demand, October 30, the United States and the Soviet Union sponsored cease-fire resolutions in the UN Security Council. Both Britain and France vetoed the measures and the next day, according to plan, opened an offensive that culminated in the bombing of Egyptian air strips as the initial step toward seizing Port Said at the northern end of the canal. The timing was not opportune because the Anglo–French military action blunted the concurrent protests by the United States against Soviet attempts to put down the rebellion in Hungary.

Eisenhower, who was in the heat of a reelection campaign, became livid with the British and French when he learned of their actions in the Middle East. With Dulles hospitalized for stomach cancer, Eisenhower took the lead. He called Eden on the phone and gave his wartime friend a verbal lashing that brought the already distraught and physically ailing prime minister to tears. Eisenhower then blasted the British and French over radio and television on October 31 for endangering peace in the Middle East by pulling in

the Soviet Union and blamed the two powers for turning the world's attention from Moscow's brutal suppression of Hungary. In early November, the UN General Assembly overwhelmingly approved a U.S. resolution for cutting back Latin American oil to Britain and France as leverage to force them into a cease-fire and a withdrawal to the previous armistice line. Bulganin and Khrushchev meanwhile sought to exploit the widening rift in the Western alliance by suggesting joint military action with the United States. The Soviets, according to Khrushchev, were prepared to fire rockets onto London and Paris to halt the invasion and to send "volunteers" to evict the "aggressors." Eisenhower dismissed the Soviets' proposal as "unthinkable" but became increasingly disturbed about the possibility of a nuclear confrontation. The president assured the head of the CIA, Allen Dulles, that "if the Soviets should attack Britain and France directly, we would of course be in a major war." During this period of sharply escalating international tensions, the Hungarian and Suez crises rallied Americans around the president and helped sweep him to reelection that week.

The results in the Middle East were not surprising: Britain and France relented to the combined pressure of the United States, the United Nations, and the Soviet Union. On November 5, the General Assembly proposed the establishment of an Emergency Force (UNEF) for Palestine, and the next day, Britain, France, and Israel agreed to a cease-fire. By Christmas, UNEF forces occupied the Gaza Strip and the Gulf of Aqaba, providing the Israelis with both protection from Egypt and a water link to the Red Sea through the port of Elath. But the Israelis had not secured use of the canal. In March 1957, under U.S. pressure, they withdrew behind the original armistice lines.

The Suez crisis furthered Soviet influence in the Middle East and thereby heightened U.S. involvement in the area. The United States had helped to save Nasser, but at the cost of British and French prestige, which put a severe strain on the Western alliance. Although he suffered a humiliating military defeat by the Israelis, Nasser held the canal and enjoyed great respect throughout the Arab world. The U.S. retraction of funds for the Aswan Dam drove Nasser closer to the Soviets, who had acquired stature in the Middle East and now furnished him arms and finances for improving the dam. The United States, however, had protected its oil interests and saw no choice but to assume the responsibilities for maintaining order in the Middle East, formerly undertaken by the British and the French.

The U.S. concern over Soviet penetration into the Middle East led to the announcement of the Eisenhower Doctrine in the spring of 1957. The Moscow government had negotiated economic and military agreements with Egypt and Syria, raising White House fear that with Syria's help Nasser might emerge as leader of the Arab world—and under Soviet influence. In January, the president asked congressional approval to warn that the United States was prepared to defend the Middle East from outside encroachments. After lengthy debates, Congress in March approved a joint resolution that became known as the Eisenhower Doctrine. It empowered the president to use military force if any Middle Eastern government requested protection against "overt armed aggression from any nation controlled by International Communism." Congress also guaranteed economic and military aid for the Middle East. Dulles noted with satisfaction that "gradually, one part of the world after another is being brought into it [America's defense system] and perhaps we may end up with a, what you might call, universal doctrine reflected by multilateral treaties or multilateral worldwide authority from Congress." Although critics complained that Communist subversion was a greater danger than armed attack, the Eisenhower administration had dramatically assumed the longtime Anglo–French peacekeeping role in the Middle East. Its policy marked a commitment to containment, though under a different name.

The Eisenhower Doctrine underwent immediate tests in Jordan and Lebanon, although in both cases Arab nationalism probably posed a greater threat to the Middle East's stability than did Soviet communism. When a leftist coup supported by Egypt and Syria threatened to overthrow Jordan's pro-Western King Ibn Talal Hussein in the spring of 1957, the United States sent economic and military aid and moved the Sixth Fleet to the eastern Mediterranean. The situation eased. Early the following year Egypt, Syria, and Yemen established the United Arab Republic, with Nasser as president, and Jordan and Iraq countered with the Arab Union. In mid-July, a military coup in Iraq led to the installation of a "republican" regime that moved close to the Soviet Union. The West erroneously assumed that Nasser was behind the revolution in Iraq and feared the same in Lebanon, located along the strategically important eastern Mediterranean. Lebanon's pro-Western and Maronite Christian president, Camille Chamoun, held the United Arab Republic responsible for aiding a Muslim armed insurrection and joined Jordan in asking the United States and Britain for protection. American forces could easily move into Lebanon, General Twining assured Dulles. The "Russians aren't going to jump us," and "if they do come in, they couldn't pick a better time, because we've got them by the whing whang and they know it." Eisenhower responded by dispatching 14,000 marines to Lebanon in July 1958 (who waded onto the beach through Lebanon sunbathers). Britain sent 3,000 paratroopers to bolster Jordan's Hussein, again in danger of overthrow.

By the autumn of 1958, both the Jordanian and Lebanese crises had passed without incident. The UN Security Council was stymied, but because the Soviets were accusing the West of imperialism and demanding its withdrawal from the two countries, Arab leaders in the General Assembly took the lead toward peace. They proposed a resolution between the Western nations and the Soviets that pledged nonintervention in one another's domestic affairs, and they asked the UN secretary-general to guarantee its implementation in Jordan and Lebanon. The resolution prepared the way for military withdrawal. Meanwhile, U.S. diplomat Robert Murphy helped mediate an end to Lebanon's internal troubles, allowing the United States to pull out its forces in October. Britain left Jordan the following month. In March 1959, Eisenhower negotiated separate executive agreements with Turkey, Iran, and Pakistan that guaranteed U.S. military assistance should they come under attack. These countries also set up headquarters in Ankara, Turkey, for a joint organization that became known as the Central Treaty Organization and whose members were Turkey, Britain, Iran, and Pakistan. Iraq withdrew from the Baghdad Pact in March 1959 in favor of a neutralist position.

Berlin, Formosa (Again), and the Spirit of Camp David

Despite Eisenhower's easy reelection, Americans remained uneasy about the Democrats' continuing charges that the Soviet Union had surged ahead in the Cold War. The United States faced a paradoxical situation: any move toward peace through disarmament could imply weakness, invite Soviet expansion, and lead to war. Early in 1957, Polish Foreign Minister Adam Rapacki recommended the establishment of a denuclearized zone in Central and Eastern Europe. The Soviets endorsed the plan, but the Eisenhower administration showed no interest. In June, the Senate approved the Atoms-for-Peace Treaty, which Eisenhower had proposed four years earlier. Similar to the abortive Baruch Plan of 1946, it called for the major powers to share atomic materials through an International Atomic Energy Agency. But the safeguards did not work, and the joint contributions of fissionable materials to the agency promoted a highly dangerous move toward nuclear proliferation. In late 1957, the Moscow government shocked Americans twice: first in late August by announcing the development of an intercontinental ballistic missile and then on October 4 by launching the *Sputnik*, the first space satellite of human origin.

The image of Soviet leadership in the space race deeply unsettled Americans. Ironically, the Eisenhower administration knew from secret U-2 reconnaissance planes flying high over the Soviet Union that *Sputnik* posed no threat to the United States, but the president could not say anything for fear of revealing the aerial operations. A second irony is that Khrushchev was aware of the reconnaissance flights but also could say nothing: the U-2s flew above Soviet firing range, and a protest would constitute an admission to his nation's inability to defend itself against espionage. Furthermore, the Soviets would lose ground in their growing rivalry with the Communist Chinese. The British ambassador in Washington noted that "the Russian success in launching the satellite has been something equivalent to Pearl Harbor. The American cocksureness is shaken." The following month the Soviets sent *Sputnik II* into orbit—carrying a canine passenger. Someone wittily remarked that the Soviets would probably send cows on the next flight, thus constituting "the herd shot 'round the world."

The Eisenhower administration quickly moved to regain the lead in the Cold War. The Gaither Report, a top-secret study by the Ford Foundation Commission that the American press uncovered and published, had enormous public impact because of its call for a huge armaments program to counter the Soviets' growing military and economic power. Although researchers were stepping up work on ballistic missiles, the president hesitated to turn the nation into what he termed a "garrison state." Yet he dispatched bombers of the Strategic Air Command to bolster the NATO alliance, agreed to furnish intermediate range ballistic missiles to NATO allies, and approved the continuation of U-2 flights. In January 1958, the United States launched *Explorer I*, the nation's first space satellite, and by July it had established the National Aeronautics and Space Administration (NASA) to promote aerospace research. The following September, Congress passed the National Defense Education Act to provide federal aid for education in science, mathematics, and foreign languages.

As the military and missile buildup threatened to race out of control by late 1957, Soviet specialist George F. Kennan aroused great opposition when he called for a return to a less confrontational form of containment based on the "disengagement" of foreign military forces from Germany and Eastern Europe. In the prestigious BBC Reith Lectures over radio in London in autumn, he urged the major powers to construct a unified, neutral Germany built around the "free city" of Berlin. If the United States could separate the German issue from NATO and the bitter rivalries of the Cold War, Kennan argued, the Soviets might withdraw their armies from Eastern Europe. Should the Eisenhower administration deemphasize NATO and turn to diplomacy, the Soviets might reciprocate by dismantling the Warsaw Pact. Then the much-discussed European Common Market (or European Economic Community), established in June 1958, could promote the economic integration of the continent through the elimination of tariffs and other obstacles to unity.

But the Washington government was not interested in disengagement. Former Secretary of State Dean Acheson expressed the feelings of many when he dismissed the idea as isolationist in thrust. Such a move, he warned, would undercut the Western alliance by encouraging the Red Army to take all of Europe and then negotiate a military agreement with an independent Germany. "Mr. Kennan has never, in my judgment," Acheson remarked, "grasped the realities of power relationships, but takes a rather mystical attitude toward them. To Mr. Kennan there is no Soviet military threat in Europe."

As the Western allies increasingly disagreed over European policy, the Soviets seized the moment in an attempt to win concessions in Berlin. The Western-held sector of the city had become a dangerous example for unhappy East Germans, who suffered severe economic and political hardships. The glaring contrasts in lifestyles between the two Germanies seemed to emphasize the superiority of capitalism over communism. West Berlin was not only prospering but also serving as an espionage and propaganda center for the West. Indeed, nearly 3 million East Germans had defected to West Berlin since 1949. Although the United States refused to recognize East Germany, it openly praised the courage of the East German people; sent armaments to West Germany to bolster the 11,000 U.S., British, and French soldiers occupying West Berlin; and repeatedly called for democratic elections to unite the Germans into a single state. West Berlin was a "bone in the throat," grumbled Khrushchev, now Soviet premier. The arming of West Germany, he charged, was a violation of wartime pledges to prevent the country from again becoming a military power. West Germany's imminent move to join France, Italy, Belgium, Luxembourg, and the Netherlands in the European Common Market finally pushed Khrushchev into action. Germany, he feared, was about to become irrevocably tied to the West.

In November 1958, Khrushchev delivered a blustery speech announcing abrogation of the wartime agreements relating to Germany and demanding an end to Western occupation of West Berlin. Unless negotiations began in six months, he warned, the Soviet Union would sign a separate peace treaty with the East Germans that terminated occupation and, as a matter of course, left West Berlin isolated more than one hundred miles inside a Communist nation. The Allies would then have to work out passage rights into Berlin through the East German government, which, he reminded them, they did not recognize. If they used force, the signatories of the Warsaw Pact stood ready to help East Germany. Berlin should be a "free city" within a confederation of East and West Germany, Khrushchev stated in notes to Washington, London, and Paris.

Khrushchev's ultimatum placed the United States in a bind. Recognition of East Germany would virtually turn it over to the Soviets and permanently divide the country. Kennan's disengagement plan was out of the question.

Furthermore, if the United States pulled out of West Berlin, the Adenauer government's faith in NATO and the European Common Market would diminish, laying the groundwork for another Soviet–German arrangement only slightly less dangerous than the nonaggression pact they had negotiated on the eve of war in 1939. Some Americans, including Acheson and Army Chief of Staff Maxwell Taylor, recommended that the United States determine whether this was a Soviet bluff by sending more soldiers to West Berlin. Dulles told the press that "we are most solemnly committed to hold West Berlin, if need be by military force." General Twining, who had favored the use of atomic weapons during the Dienbienphu crisis and was now chair of the Joint Chiefs of Staff, assured the president that he was ready "to fight a general nuclear war." But Eisenhower was not. "Destruction is not a good police force," he declared. "You don't throw hand grenades around streets to police the streets so that people won't be molested by thugs." The outcome depended largely on the attitude of the Western allies, who had steadily drifted apart over numerous issues.

As in the Berlin crisis of 1948–1949, however, the West surprised the Soviets by uniting against their demands. At first, the NATO allies disagreed over what action to take. President Charles de Gaulle of France did not favor German reunification, but he refused to retreat on Berlin. British Prime Minister Harold Macmillan realized that a Soviet nuclear attack would focus on England and seemed to support West Berlin's conversion into a free city in line with Khrushchev's ultimatum. Eisenhower, however, refused to budge. "Any sign of Western weakness at this forward position could be misinterpreted with grievous consequences." Although first wanting to "give peace forces a chance," Eisenhower made it clear that if the East Germans stopped any U.S. vehicle after the six-month deadline, the United States would order a small armed convoy to Berlin. Should that convoy encounter interference, he would institute an airlift, sever relations with Moscow,

take the matter before the United Nations, and prepare for war. The president privately remarked that "in this gamble, we are not going to be betting white chips, building up the pot gradually and fearfully. Khrushchev should know that when we decide to act, our whole stack will be in the pot."

After many anxious moments the Berlin crisis faded without incident. In December 1958, the foreign ministers of the United States, Britain, France, and West Germany met in Paris and decided not to capitulate, and two days later the NATO Council pledged support. The wartime victory over Germany had been a cooperative Allied effort, the West argued, and the Soviet Union had no right to alter the situation without common consent. Seeing the West unified, Khrushchev backed off from his ultimatum with the lame explanation that he had not meant six months in a literal sense. He agreed that the Big Four's foreign ministers should meet in Geneva to discuss Germany, Europe, and disarmament.

Perhaps because of the U.S. preoccupation with the Lebanon and Berlin crises, the Communist Chinese had in the autumn of 1958 resumed their bombardment of Quemoy, now fortified with 100,000 Nationalists, or a third of Jiang's army. Mao probably intended a resumption of the shelling to demonstrate again the growing U.S. presence in Chinese internal affairs and perhaps attract Soviet support. If so, the strategy appeared successful. Beijing radio threatened to "smash the American paper tiger and liberate Taiwan [Formosa]," and Khrushchev staunchly warned that "an attack on the Chinese People's Republic is an attack on the Soviet Union."

As in late 1954, the United States feared a Communist invasion of the islands and reacted strongly. Dulles was anxious to look strong without provoking a nuclear encounter and recommended mere "air bursts, so that there would be no appreciable fallout or large civilian casualties." The president seemed to agree. His purpose, as he recorded in his memoirs, was to convince the Chinese Communists that the United States would not retreat. Instead of using nuclear weaponry, Eisenhower approved airlifts of Jiang's troops, authorized the Seventh Fleet to convoy the Nationalists' supply ships, and, most ominous, dispatched marines into Quemoy bearing howitzers capable of delivering atomic shells. In September, he asserted over television that the desertion of Quemoy would be a "Western Pacific Munich." Americans would not engage in "appeasement."

Despite war threats, the second crisis over Formosa in less than five years again quickly dissipated. If the Communist Chinese agree to a cease-fire, Dulles proposed, the United States would seek a reduction of the Nationalist forces on Quemoy. He sweetened the offer by publicly declaring that the United States had "no commitment" to support Jiang's return to the mainland. The Communist Chinese responded by calling off the firing for a week, and in return Eisenhower ordered the Seventh Fleet to stop convoying Jiang's supply ships. Dulles traveled to Formosa in October and convinced Jiang to cut back on the number of soldiers on the islands and to renounce forceful attempts to take the mainland. The Beijing government nonetheless announced its intention to shell Quemoy on alternate days, a ploy that permitted Jiang to supply his troops on Quemoy yet allowed the Communist Chinese to maintain a formal protest against the Nationalists' presence on the island. Eisenhower expressed bewilderment over this "Gilbert and Sullivan war." Mao later declared with wonder, "Who would have thought when we fired a few shots at Quemoy and Matsu that it would stir up such an earth-shattering storm?"

After Dulles's death from cancer in the spring of 1959, Eisenhower appointed a much less assertive secretary of state, Christian Herter, and assumed a more visible role in seeking better relations with Moscow. An encouraging sign was Vice President Nixon's visit to the Soviet Union in July, followed by Khrushchev's tour of the United States in September. Not all was harmonious. Nixon, who once characterized Khrushchev as a "bare

knuckle slugger who had gouged, kneed, and kicked" his way to the top, took advantage of television cameras to score a Cold War victory in the famous "kitchen debate." Before a model kitchen at the American National Exhibition in Moscow, he and Khrushchev engaged in an animated discussion of capitalism and socialism in which Nixon shook his finger at Khrushchev, much to the delight of Americans. Eisenhower later welcomed Khrushchev to the United States, hoping to "soften up the Soviet leader." Khrushchev was short-tempered and unpolished in manner and speech, yet Eisenhower considered him a "powerful, skillful, ruthless, and highly ambitious politician" who was "blinded by his dedication to the Marxist theory of world revolution and Communist domination." Khrushchev admitted that Eisenhower was "a good man, but he wasn't very tough."

Khrushchev's visit to the United States left the impression that Soviet–American relations had improved. But there were touchy moments. After touring an IBM plant, the premier visited a Hollywood set and concluded that the scant dress of actresses was proof of capitalism's decay. He also became upset that in the interest of security, he was unable to see the recently opened amusement park at Disneyland. Yet Khrushchev toned down his belligerence by promising "peaceful coexistence" and explaining that his promise to "bury capitalism" did not constitute a military threat. "I say it again—I've almost worn my tongue thin repeating it—you may live under capitalism and we will live under socialism and build communism. The one whose system proves better will win. We will not bury you, nor will you bury us." Khrushchev called for total disarmament in a speech before the UN General Assembly in New York but would permit no inspection of Soviet arms.

After less than two weeks inside the United States, the Soviet premier accepted Eisenhower's invitation to discuss Berlin at his Camp David mountain retreat in Maryland. Although the two heads of state reached no settlement, they clarified their stands on major

Eisenhower and Khrushchev
Soviet Premier Nikita Khrushchev visits Washington, D.C., September 15, 1959. *(Dwight D. Eisenhower Library, Abilene, Kansas)*

issues, expressed interest in negotiating on Berlin, renounced the use of force, and indicated support for disarmament. The "spirit of Camp David" seemed genuine when Eisenhower announced his intention to visit the Soviet Union in the spring of 1960.

The U-2 Incident

After the Camp David meeting, Britain and France joined the United States in calling for a summit conference that never convened when Soviet–American relations suddenly plummeted. On May 1, 1960, an American U-2 reconnaissance plane was soaring more than a thousand miles inside Soviet airspace when engine trouble forced it below its normal flying range and a Soviet surface-to-air missile shot it down. The U-2's pilot, Francis Gary Powers, parachuted safely from the plane. Soviet authorities seized both him and the wreckage.

The Soviets' heated protests over this intrusion of airspace drew a confused and bungled U.S. reaction. On May 3, NASA announced that a weather "research airplane" operating over Turkey had apparently gone down; two days later, Khrushchev coldly declared that Soviet missiles had shot down a U.S. plane over Soviet territory. To this charge, the State Department supported the NASA cover by admitting that a "civilian" piloting a weather plane had mistakenly flown over Soviet airspace. A spokesman for the agency declared emphatically on May 6 that "there was absolutely no— N-O, no—deliberate attempt to violate Soviet air space, and there never has been."

That same day, Khrushchev exhibited photographs of Powers, the downed plane, and its reconnaissance instruments and followed these dramatic revelations with pictures of Soviet military plants taken by U-2 cameras. The State Department then conceded that the U-2 had "probably" been on an intelligence mission, but on May 9, Secretary of State Herter admitted to full knowledge of the flights. When Khrushchev left Eisenhower a face-saving way out by expressing doubt that he was involved,

the president infuriated him and shocked everyone else by accepting full responsibility for the missions and defending them on the basis of national security. Soviet secrecy, Eisenhower declared in his weekly press conference, had necessitated such measures to prevent "another Pearl Harbor."

The summit conference opened in Paris on May 16 in the midst of intense animosity over the U-2 episode. Khrushchev's rage far outweighed the magnitude of the incident. His fury undoubtedly was attributable to his desires to quiet critics at home who were starving for a Cold War victory and to subvert a conference in which his demands on Germany had no chance for success. While in Paris, he bitterly attacked the United States and refused to discuss anything until Eisenhower apologized for the flight, punished those involved, and announced an end to U-2 activities over the Soviet Union. He also canceled the president's invitation to the Soviet Union. Eisenhower guaranteed only that no more U-2 flights would occur during his presidency. When de Gaulle and Macmillan tried to mediate, Khrushchev stormed out, ending the summit conference one day after it began.

The U.S. actions during the U-2 affair helped to intensify the Cold War during the summer and autumn of 1960. Washington's clumsy handling of the incident had invited the verbal attack. Eisenhower's apparent ineptitude had damaged the nation's image abroad. Furthermore, the episode forced accommodations in policy. After Khrushchev warned of a nuclear assault on those neutralist nations permitting U-2 bases, protesters in Japan demonstrated against the presence of three U-2s and opposed a mutual defense pact with the United States. The Washington administration removed the planes before the treaty went into effect in June, but Eisenhower had to cancel a visit to Japan because of security risks. In September, Khrushchev arrived at the United Nations in New York and spent almost a month inside the United States without receiving an invitation to meet with Eisenhower. The Soviet premier bragged

U-2 Crisis
Khrushchev visiting exhibit of U-2 remains in 1960. *(Library of Congress, Washington, D.C.)*

about his country's missile production, shouted down British Prime Minister Macmillan, called the United Nations a "spitoon," and at one point took off his shoe, shook it at the speaker, and pounded it on the table. Khrushchev's angry outbursts deepened the division between East and West and made a Berlin settlement even more remote.

Latin America

Meanwhile, problems in Latin America had heated again. More than two years earlier, Vice President Nixon had made a goodwill visit to eight countries in South America, attempting to assure Latin Americans that they were "not only our neighbors but our best friends." But he encountered angry crowds at every stop, including riotous students at the University of the Republic in Montevideo, Uruguay, and at San Marcos University in Lima, Peru. Confronting what Nixon later called a "bunch of Communist thugs," he barely escaped rocks and eggs thrown by protesters yelling "Nixon get out!" In Caracas, Venezuela, a mob shouting "Death to Nixon!" surrounded his limousine, rocked it, kicked in its sides, and broke the windows before the driver could speed away. Eisenhower dispatched a thousand marines to U.S. bases in the Caribbean to prevent further incidents.

Nixon attributed these ill feelings primarily to Communists, an argument perhaps bolstered by the realization that by the mid-1950s, nearly twenty Latin American republics had signed commercial agreements with either the Soviet Union or its allied states. The former president of Costa Rica, however, explained that Latin Americans hated the United States for backing dictators. In Venezuela, for example, the United States had long supported dictator Marcos Pérez Jiménez; even after his overthrow by a military junta in 1958, it awarded asylum to him and his police chief.

The Eisenhower administration encouraged reforms in Latin America, largely because it believed that the region's economic problems could lead to a Communist takeover. In 1958,

a Brazilian diplomat in Washington complained that since 1946, the State Department had followed "two patterns of action: the Marshall Plan dedicated to Europe and the John Foster Dulles Plan dedicated to Asia and the Middle East." To remedy the situation, the president's brother Milton made a second fact-finding visit to Latin America. The following year, 1959, the United States adopted several measures to cure what the president called "the festering sore of underdevelopment." It established the Inter-American Development Bank to float loans, tried to stabilize coffee prices by restricting U.S. exports, and worked toward ending tariffs and establishing a common market among the Americas. In early 1960, the president visited South America, and the following August, he requested $500 million in economic aid for the region. Congress quickly complied, albeit in a lukewarm manner. In September, twenty-one American states approved the Act of Bogotá, designed to implement the economic and social reform program.

Presidential Election of 1960 and Cold War Rhetoric

Heightened Cold War tensions carried over into the presidential election of 1960. Nixon, vice president for eight years, easily won the Republican nomination, and Senator John F. Kennedy of Massachusetts emerged as the Democrats' candidate. Both men tried to portray the image of youth, vitality, and strength of leadership against communism. Nixon reminded Americans of his longtime experience in the office closest to the presidency, his courage in standing up to Khrushchev in Moscow, and his resistance to the alleged Communists in Latin America. Kennedy, a naval war hero, member of the Senate Foreign Relations Committee, and author of *Why England Slept* and the Pulitzer Prize–winning *Profiles in Courage*, called for a hard-line approach to Soviet affairs and promised to support anyone willing to fight communism. Nixon defended Eisenhower's policies, but

Kennedy accused the Republicans of permitting the United States to fall behind the Soviet Union in economic development and in the missile race. "I think it's time America started moving again," Kennedy declared at the close of his first television debate with Nixon. Pledging victory in the Cold War, Kennedy and the Democratic Party won the election by a narrow margin.

President Kennedy inherited a world pulsating with Cold War tension. Berlin, Southeast Asia, Communist China, the Third World—all areas suggested the need for careful diplomacy rather than angry rhetoric. In all these problem spots, Eisenhower had kept the United States out of war by what many believe were the narrowest of margins. Yet in the Formosa crisis and perhaps others as well, the White House had overreacted by casting all events within a Cold War context. The rhetoric had become more fevered as Dulles emphasized liberation and thereby missed chances to negotiate with the Soviet Union and the People's Republic of China. East–West divisions had hardened, covert actions had threatened to become the norm, and U.S. suspicions had grown that Third World nationalism was a mere front for the spread of communism. Kennedy used his inaugural address to assure Americans that his administration would not shrink from communism anywhere in the world. His challenging words guaranteed the continuation of a volatile international atmosphere.

Selected Readings

Accinelli, Robert. *Crisis and Commitment: United States Policy Toward Taiwan, 1950–1955*. 1996.

Adams, Sherman. *Firsthand Report: The Story of the Eisenhower Administration*. 1961.

Aguilar, Manuela. *Cultural Diplomacy and Foreign Policy: German-American Relations, 1955–1968*. 1996.

Alexander, Charles C. *Holding the Line: The Eisenhower Era, 1952–1961*. 1975.

Allen, Craig. *Eisenhower and the Mass Media: Peace, Prosperity, and Prime-Time TV*. 1993.

Alteras, Isaac. *Eisenhower and Israel: U.S.-Israeli Relations, 1953–1960*. 1993.

Ambrose, Stephen E. *Eisenhower. Vol. 2: The President*. 1984.

———. *Ike's Spies: Eisenhower and the Espionage Establishment*. 1981.

———. *Nixon: The Education of a Politician, 1913–1962*. 1987.

———, and Douglas G. Brinkley. *Rise to Globalism: American Foreign Policy since 1938*. 8th ed., 1997.

Anderson, Carol. *Eyes Off the Prize: The United Nations and the African American Struggle for Human Rights, 1944–1955*. 2003.

Arnold, James R. *The First Domino: Eisenhower, the Military, and America's Intervention in Vietnam*. 1991.

Ashton, Nigel J. *Eisenhower, Macmillan, and the Problem of Nasser: Anglo-American Relations and Arab Nationalism, 1955–59*. 1996.

Ball, George W., and Douglas B. Ball. *The Passionate Attachment: America's Involvement with Israel 1947 to the Present*. 1992.

Ball, Howard. *Justice Downwind: America's Atomic Testing Program in the 1950s*. 1986.

Beisner, Robert L. *Dean Acheson: A Life in the Cold War*. 2006.

Ben-Zvi, Abraham. *Decade of Transition: Eisenhower, Kennedy, and the Origins of the American-Israeli Alliance*. 1998.

Beschloss, Michael R. *Mayday: Eisenhower, Khrushchev and the U-2 Affair*. 1986.

Bill, James A. *The Eagle and the Lion: The Tragedy of American-Iranian Relations*. 1988.

Billings-Yan, Melanie. *Decision against War: Eisenhower and Dien Bien Phu, 1954*. 1988.

Bird, Kai, and Martin J. Sherwin. *American Prometheus: The Triumph and Tragedy of J. Robert Oppenheimer*. 2005.

Borstlemann, Thomas. *The Cold War and the Color Line: American Race Relations in the Global Arena*. 2001.

Botti, Timothy. *Ace in the Hole: Why the United States Did Not Use Nuclear Weapons in the Cold War, 1945–1965*. 1996.

Boyer, Paul S. *By the Bomb's Early Light: American Thought and Culture at the Dawn of the Atomic Age*. 1986.

Bradley, Mark Phillips. *Imagining Vietnam and America: The Making of Postcolonial Vietnam, 1919–1950*. 2000.

Brands, H. W. *The Devil We Knew: Americans and the Cold War*. 1993.

Brands, H. William, Jr. *Cold Warriors: Eisenhower's Generation and American Foreign Policy.* 1988.

Brigham, Robert K. *Guerrilla Diplomacy: The NLF's Foreign Relations and the Viet Nam War.* 1999.

Brinkley, Douglas. *Dean Acheson: The Cold War Years, 1953–71.* 1992.

Broadwater, Jeff. *Adlai Stevenson and American Politics: The Odyssey of a Cold War Liberal.* 1994.

———. *Eisenhower and the Anti-Communist Crusade.* 1992.

Buckley, Roger. *U.S.-Japan Alliance Diplomacy, 1945–1990.* 1992.

Bulkeley, Rip. *The Sputniks Crisis and Early United States Space Policy: A Critique of the Historiography of Space.* 1991.

Burns, William J. *Economic Aid and American Policy toward Egypt, 1955–1981.* 1985.

Burr, William. "Avoiding the Slippery Slope: The Eisenhower Administration and the Berlin Crisis, November 1958–January 1959." *Diplomatic History* 18 (1994): 177–205.

Buzzanco, Robert. "Prologue to Tragedy: U.S. Military Opposition to Intervention in Vietnam, 1950–1954." *Diplomatic History* 17 (1993): 201–22.

Campbell, Craig. *Destroying the Village: Eisenhower and Thermonuclear War.* 1998.

Chang, Gordon H. *Friends and Enemies: The United States, China, and the Soviet Union, 1948–1972.* 1990.

———, and He Di. "The Absence of War in the U.S.-China Confrontation over Quemoy and Matsu in 1954–1955: Contingency, Luck, Deterrence?" *American Historical Review* 98 (December 1993): 1500–24.

Christensen, Thomas J. *Useful Adversaries: Grand Strategy, Domestic Mobilization, and Sino-American Conflict, 1947–1958.* 1996.

Citino, Nathan J. *From Arab Nationalism to OPEC: Eisenhower, King Saud, and the Making of U.S.-Saudi Relations.* 2002.

Clark, Ian. *Nuclear Diplomacy and the Special Relationship: Britain's Deterrent and America, 1957–1962.* 1994.

Clark, Paul C., Jr. *The United States and Somoza, 1933–1956: A Revisionist Look.* 1992.

Clayton, Lawrence A. *Peru and the United States: The Condor and the Eagle.* 1999.

Clowse, Barbara B. *Brainpower for the Cold War: The Sputnik Crisis and the National Defense Education Act of 1958.* 1981.

Clymer, Kenton J. *Quest for Freedom: The United States and India's Independence.* 1995.

Cohen, Warren I. *America's Response to China: An Interpretive History of Sino-American Relations.* 2000.

———, and Akira Iriye, eds. *The Great Powers in East Asia, 1953–1960.* 1990.

Cook, Blanche W. *The Declassified Eisenhower: A Divided Legacy.* 1981.

Cooper, Chester L. *The Lion's Last Roar: Suez, 1956.* 1978.

Costigliola, Frank. *France and the United States: The Cold Alliance since World War II.* 1992.

Cronin, Audrey K. *Great Power Politics and the Struggle over Austria, 1945–1955.* 1986.

Cullather, Nick. *Illusions of Influence: The Political Economy of United States-Philippines Relations, 1942–1960.* 1994.

———. *Secret History: The CIA's Classified Account of Its Operations in Guatemala, 1952–1954.* 1999.

Currey, Cecil B. *Edward Lansdale: The Unquiet American.* 1988.

Davidson, Phillip B. *Vietnam at War: The History, 1946–1975.* 1988.

Diamond, Sigmund. *Compromised Campus: The Collaboration of Universities with the Intelligence Community, 1945–1955.* 1992.

Divine, Robert A. *Blowing on the Wind: The Nuclear Test Ban Debate, 1954–1960.* 1978.

———. *Eisenhower and the Cold War.* 1981.

———. *The Sputnik Challenge: Eisenhower's Response to the Soviet Satellite.* 1993.

Dockrill, Saki. *Eisenhower's New-Look National Security Policy, 1953–61.* 1996.

Donovan, Robert J. *Eisenhower: The Inside Story.* 1956.

Dozer, Donald. *Are We Good Neighbors?* 1961.

Duiker, William J. *The Communist Road to Power in Vietnam.* 1981.

———. *Ho Chi Minh.* 2000.

Eisenhower, Dwight D. *The White House Years: Mandate for Change, 1953–1956.* 1963.

———. *The White House Years: Waging Peace, 1956–1961.* 1965.

Fall, Bernard B. *Hell in a Very Small Place: The Siege of Dien Bien Phu.* 1966.

———. *The Two Viet-Nams: A Political and Military Analysis.* 2nd rev. ed., 1967.

Finer, Herman. *Dulles over Suez: The Theory and Practice of His Diplomacy.* 1964.

Freiberger, Steven Z. *Dawn over Suez: The Rise of American Power in the Middle East, 1953–1957.* 1992.

Fursenko, Aleksandr, and Timothy Naftali. *Khrushchev's Cold War: The Inside Story of an American Adversary.* 2006.

Gaddis, John L. *The Cold War: A New History.* 2005.

——. *The Long Peace: Inquiries into the History of the Cold War.* 1987.

——. *Russia, the Soviet Union, and the United States: An Interpretive History.* 2nd ed., 1990.

——. *Strategies of Containment: A Critical Appraisal of Postwar American National Security Policy.* 1982; rev. ed., 2005.

——. *We Now Know: Rethinking Cold War History.* 1997.

Gambone, Michael D. *Eisenhower, Somoza, and the Cold War in Nicaragua, 1953–1961.* 1997.

Gardner, Lloyd C. *Approaching Vietnam: From World War II through Dienbienphu, 1941–1954.* 1988.

Gasiorowski, Mark J. *U.S. Foreign Policy and the Shah: Building a Client State in Iran.* 1991.

Gendzier, Irene L. *Notes from the Minefield: United States Intervention in Lebanon and the Middle East, 1945–1958.* 1997.

Gerson, Louis. *John Foster Dulles.* 1968.

Giauque, Jeffery G. *Grand Designs and Visions of Unity: The Atlantic Powers and the Reorganization of Western Europe, 1955–1963.* 2002.

Gordon, Leonard H. D. "United States Opposition to Use of Force in the Taiwan Strait, 1954–1962." *Journal of American History* 72 (1985): 637–60.

Graebner, Norman A. *The New Isolationism: A Study in Politics and Foreign Policy since 1950.* 1956.

Gray, William G. *Germany's Cold War: The Global Campaign to Isolate East Germany, 1949–1969.* 2003.

Green, David. *The Containment of Latin America: A History of the Myths and Realities of the Good Neighbor Policy.* 1971.

Greene, Daniel P. O'C. "John Foster Dulles and the End of the Franco-American Entente in Indochina." *Diplomatic History* 16 (1992): 551–71.

Greenstein, Fred I. *The Hidden-Hand Presidency: Eisenhower as a Leader.* 1982.

Grose, Peter. *Gentleman Spy: The Life of Allen Dulles.* 1994.

Gurtov, Melvin. *The First Vietnam Crisis: Chinese Communist Strategy and United States Involvement, 1953–1954.* 1967.

Haddow, Robert H. *Pavilions of Plenty: Exhibiting American Culture Abroad in the 1950s.* 1997.

Hahn, Peter L. *Caught in the Middle East: U.S. Policy toward the Arab-Israeli Conflict, 1945–1961.* 2004.

——. *The United States, Great Britain, and Egypt, 1945–1956: Strategy and Diplomacy in the Early Cold War.* 1991.

Hammer, Ellen J. *The Struggle for Indochina, 1940–1955.* 1966.

Harrison, James P. *The Endless War: Fifty Years of Struggle in Vietnam.* 1982.

Heale, M. J. *McCarthy's Americans: Red Scare Politics in State and Nation, 1935–1965.* 1998.

Heiss, Mary Ann. *Empire and Nationhood: The United States, Great Britain, and Iranian Oil, 1950–1954.* 1997.

Henriksen, Margot A. *Dr. Strangelove's America: Society and Culture in the Atomic Age.* 1997.

Herken, Gregg. *Counsels of War.* 1985.

Herring, George C. *America's Longest War: The United States and Vietnam, 1950–1975.* 4th ed., 2002.

——. "'In the Lands of the Blind': Eisenhower's Commitment to South Vietnam, 1954." In Howard Jones, ed., *The Foreign and Domestic Dimensions of Modern Warfare: Vietnam, Central America, and Nuclear Strategy,* 31–39. 1988.

——, ed. *The Pentagon Papers: Abridged Edition.* 1993.

——. "The Truman Administration and the Restoration of French Sovereignty in Indochina." *Diplomatic History* 1 (1977): 97–117.

——, and Richard H. Immerman. "Eisenhower, Dulles, and Dienbienphu: 'The Day We Didn't Go to War' Revisited." *Journal of American History* 71 (1984): 343–68.

Hess, Gary R. *America Encounters India, 1941–1947.* 1971.

——. "The First American Commitment in Indochina: The Acceptance of the 'Bao Dai Solution,' 1950." *Diplomatic History* 2 (1978): 331–50.

——. *The United States' Emergence as a Southeast Asian Power, 1940–1950.* 1987.

——. *Vietnam and the United States: Origins and Legacy of War.* 1998.

Hixson, Walter L. *Parting the Curtain: Propaganda, Culture, and the Cold War, 1945–1961.* 1997.

Hoopes, Townsend. *The Devil and John Foster Dulles.* 1973.

Hughes, Emmet J. *The Ordeal of Power: A Political Memoir of the Eisenhower Years.* 1963.

Immerman, Richard H. *The CIA in Guatemala: The Foreign Policy of Intervention.* 1982.

———. *John Foster Dulles: Piety, Pragmatism and Power in U.S. Foreign Policy*. 1999.

———. ed. *John Foster Dulles and the Diplomacy of the Cold War*. 1990.

———. "The United States and the Geneva Conference of 1954: A New Look." *Diplomatic History* 14 (1990): 43–66.

Irving, Ronald E. *The First Indochina War: French and American Policy, 1945–1954*. 1975.

Jablon, Howard. *David M. Shoup: A Warrior against War*. 2005.

Johnson, Loch K. *America's Secret Power: The CIA in a Democratic Society*. 1989.

Johnson, Robert H. *Improbable Dangers: U.S. Conceptions of Threat in the Cold War and After*. 1994.

Kahin, Audrey R., and George McT. Kahin. *Subversion as Foreign Policy: The Secret Eisenhower and Dulles Debacle in Indonesia*. 1995.

Kahin, George McT. *Intervention: How America Became Involved in Vietnam*. 1986.

———, and John W. Lewis. *The United States in Vietnam*. Rev. ed., 1969.

Kalb, Madeline. *The Congo Cables: The Cold War in Africa—From Eisenhower to Kennedy*. 1982.

Kaplan, Lawrence S., Denise Artaud, and Mark R. Rubin, eds. *Dien Bien Phu and the Crisis of Franco-American Relations, 1954–1955*. 1990.

Karnow, Stanley. *Vietnam: A History*. Rev. ed., 1991.

Kattenburg, Paul. *The Vietnam Trauma in American Foreign Policy, 1945–1975*. 1980.

Kaufman, Burton I. *Trade and Aid: Eisenhower's Foreign Economic Policy, 1953–1961*. 1982.

Kendrick, Alexander. *The Wound Within: America in the Vietnam Years, 1945–1974*. 1974.

Killian, James R. *Sputnik, Scientists and Eisenhower*. 1978.

Kolko, Gabriel. *Anatomy of a War: Vietnam, the United States, and the Modern Historical Experience*. 1985.

Krenn, Michael L. *Black Diplomacy: African Americans and the State Department, 1945–1969*. 1999.

Kunz, Diane B. *The Economic Diplomacy of the Suez Crisis*. 1991.

LaFeber, Walter. *America, Russia, and the Cold War, 1945–1996*. 8th ed., 1997.

———. *Inevitable Revolutions: The United States in Central America*. 1984.

Langguth, A. J. *Our Vietnam: The War, 1954–1975*. 2000.

Latham, Earl. *The Communist Controversy in Washington*. 1969.

Ledeen, Michael, and William Lewis. *Debacle: The American Failure in Iran*. 1980.

Leonard, Thomas M. *The United States and Central America, 1944–1949: Perceptions of Political Dynamics*. 1984.

Levering, Ralph B. *The Cold War: A Post-Cold War History*. 1994; rev. ed., 2005.

Levey, Zach. *Israel and the Western Powers, 1952–1960*. 1998.

Lind, Michael. *Vietnam the Necessary War: A Reinterpretation of America's Most Disastrous Military Conflict*. 1999.

Little, Douglas. "His Finest Hour? Eisenhower, Lebanon, and the 1958 Middle East Crisis." *Diplomatic History* 20 (1996): 27–54.

Lloyd, Selwyn. *Suez, 1956*. 1978.

Louis, William R., and Roger Owen, eds. *Suez 1956*. 1991.

Lowe, Peter. *Containing the Cold War in East Asia: British Policies towards Japan, China and Korea, 1948–53*. 1997.

Lytle, Mark H. *The Origins of the Iranian-American Alliance, 1941–1953*. 1987.

Maclear, Michael. *The Ten Thousand Day War, Vietnam: 1945–1975*. 1981.

Maldonado, A. W. *Teodoro Moscoso and Puerto Rico's Operation Bootstrap*. 1997.

Manor, Robert. *A Grand Illusion: America's Descent into Vietnam*. 2001.

Marks, Frederick W. "The CIA and Castillo Armas in Guatemala, 1954: New Clues to an Old Puzzle." *Diplomatic History* 14 (1990): 67–86.

———. *Power and Peace: The Diplomacy of John Foster Dulles*. 1993.

Mayers, David A. *Cracking the Monolith: U.S. Policy against the Sino-Soviet Alliance, 1949–1955*. 1986.

Mazuzan, George T. "American Nuclear Policy." In John M. Carroll and George C. Herring, eds., *Modern American Diplomacy*, 147–63. 1986.

McAllister, James. *No Exit: America and the German Problem, 1943–1954*. 2002.

McMahon, Robert J. *The Cold War on the Periphery: The United States, India, and Pakistan*. 1994.

———. *Colonialism and Cold War: The United States and the Struggle for Indonesian Independence, 1945–49*. 1981.

———. "Eisenhower and Third World Nationalism: A Critique of the Revisionists." *Political Science Quarterly* 101 (1986): 453–73.

———. *The Limits of Empire: The United States and Southeast Asia since World War II*. 1999.

Meers, Sharon I. "The British Connection: How the United States Covered Its Tracks in the 1954 Coup in Guatemala." *Diplomatic History* 16 (1992): 409–28.

Melanson, Richard A., and David Mayers, eds. *Reevaluating Eisenhower: American Foreign Policy in the Fifties.* 1987.

Meriwether, James H. *Proudly We Can Be Africans: Black Americans and Africa, 1935–1961.* 2002.

Merrill, Dennis. *Bread and the Ballot: The United States and India's Economic Development, 1947–1963.* 1990.

Mitrovich, Gregory. *Undermining the Kremlin: America's Strategy to Subvert the Soviet Bloc, 1947–1956.* 2000.

Montague, Ludwell L. *General Walter Bedell Smith as Director of Central Intelligence, October 1950–February 1953.* 1992.

Montgomery, Gayle B., and James W. Johnson. *One Step from the White House: The Rise and Fall of Senator William F. Knowland.* 1998.

Morgan, Joseph G. *The Vietnam Lobby: The American Friends of Vietnam, 1955–1975.* 1997.

Neff, Donald. *Warriors at Suez: Eisenhower Takes America into the Middle East.* 1981.

Nelson, Anna K. "The 'Top of Policy Hill': President Eisenhower and the National Security Council." *Diplomatic History* 7 (1983): 307–26.

Nesbitt, Francis N. *Race for Sanctions: African Americans against Apartheid, 1946–1994.* 2004.

Noer, Thomas J. *Cold War and Black Liberation: The United States and White Rule in Africa, 1948–1968.* 1985.

Olson, James S., and Randy Roberts. *Where the Domino Fell: America and Vietnam, 1945–1995.* 3rd ed., 1995.

Oren, Michael. *Origins of the Second Arab-Israeli War: Egypt, Israel, and the Great Powers, 1952–56.* 1992.

Osgood, Kenneth. *Total Cold War: Eisenhower's Secret Propaganda Battle at Home and Abroad.* 2006.

Pach, Chester J., Jr., and Elmo Richardson. *The Presidency of Dwight D. Eisenhower.* Rev. ed., 1991.

Palmer, Dave R. *Summons of the Trumpet: A History of the Vietnam War from a Military Man's Viewpoint.* 1978.

Parmet, Herbert S. *Eisenhower and the American Crusades.* 1972.

Paterson, Thomas G. *Contesting Castro: The United States and the Triumph of the Cuban Revolution.* 1994.

Patterson, James T. *Mr. Republican: A Biography of Robert A. Taft.* 1972.

Patti, Archimedes L. A. *Why Viet Nam? Prelude to America's Albatross.* 1980.

Pickett, William B. *Dwight David Eisenhower and American Power.* 1995.

Plummer, Brenda G. *Rising Wind: Black Americans and U.S. Foreign Affairs, 1935–1960.* 1996.

Poole, Peter. *The United States and Indochina from FDR to Nixon.* 1973.

Porter, Gareth. *Perils of Dominance: Imbalance of Power and the Road to War in Vietnam.* 2005.

Prados, John. *The Blood Road: The Ho Chi Minh Trail and the Vietnam War.* 1999.

———. *Presidents' Secret Wars: CIA Pentagon Covert Operations from World War II through the Persian Gulf.* 1996.

Pruessen, Ronald W. *John Foster Dulles: The Road to Power.* 1982.

Rabe, Stephen G. "The Clues Didn't Check Out: Commentary on 'The CIA and Castillo Armas.'" *Diplomatic History* 14 (1990): 87–95.

———. *Eisenhower and Latin America: The Foreign Policy of Anticommunism.* 1988.

Randle, Robert R. *Geneva 1954: The Settlement of the Indochina War.* 1969.

Ranelagh, John. *The Agency: The Rise and Decline of the CIA.* 1986.

Richardson, Elmo. *The Presidency of Dwight D. Eisenhower.* 1979.

Risse-Kappen, Thomas. *Cooperation among Democracies: The European Influence on U.S. Foreign Policy.* 1995.

Roman, Peter J. *Eisenhower and the Missile Gap.* 1995.

Roosevelt, Kermit. *Countercoup: Struggle for the Control of Iran.* 1979.

Rotter, Andrew J. *Comrades at Odds: The United States and India, 1947–1964.* 2000.

Rubin, Barry. *The Arab States and the Palestine Conflict.* 1981.

———. *Paved with Good Intentions: The American Experience and Iran.* 1980.

Samii, Kuross A. *Involvement by Invitation: American Strategies of Containment in Iran.* 1987.

Saunders, Bonnie F. *The United States and Arab Nationalism: The Syrian Case, 1953–1960.* 1996.

Schick, Jack M. *The Berlin Crisis, 1958–1962.* 1971.

Schlesinger, Stephen, and Stephen Kinzer. *Bitter Fruit: The Untold Story of the American Coup in Guatemala.* 1982.

Schmitz, David F. *Thank God They're on Our Side: The United States and Right-Wing Dictatorships, 1921–1965.* 1999.

Schoenbaum, David. *The United States and the State of Israel*. 1993.

Schoutz, Lars. *Beneath the United States: A History of U.S. Policy toward Latin America*. 1998.

Schraeder, Peter J. *United States Foreign Policy toward Africa: Incrementalism, Crisis, and Change*. 1994.

Schulzinger, Robert D. *A Time for War: The United States and Vietnam, 1941–1975*. 1997.

Shaplen, Robert. *The Lost Revolution: The U.S. in Vietnam, 1946–1966*. 1966.

Sheehan, Michael K. *Iran: The Impact of U.S. Interests and Policies, 1941–1954*. 1968.

Sheehan, Neil, et al., eds. *The Pentagon Papers*. 1971.

Sick, Gary. *All Fall Down: America's Tragic Encounter with Iran*. 1985.

Singh, Anita I. *The Limits of British Influence: South Asia and the Anglo-American Relationship, 1947–56*. 1993.

Smith, Gaddis. *The Last Years of the Monroe Doctrine*. 1994.

Smith, Peter H. *Talons of the Eagle: Dynamics of U.S.-Latin American Relations*. 2nd ed., 2000.

Smith, R. B. *An International History of the Vietnam War. Vol. 1: Revolution versus Containment, 1955–1961*. 1983.

Snead, David L. *The Gaither Committee, Eisenhower, and the Cold War*. 1999.

Snetsinger, John. *Truman, the Jewish Vote, and the Creation of Israel*. 1979.

Spanier, John W. *American Foreign Policy since World War II*. 14th ed., 1998.

Spector, Ronald H. *Advice and Support: The Early Years of the U. S. Army in Vietnam: 1941–1960*. 1983.

Spiegel, Steven L. *The Other Arab-Israeli Conflict: Making America's Middle East Policy, from Truman to Reagan*. 1985.

Stevenson, Richard W. *The Rise and Fall of Détente: Relaxations of Tensions in U.S.-Soviet Relations, 1953–1984*. 1985.

Stookey, Robert W. *America and the Arab States: An Uneasy Encounter*. 1975.

Tananbaum, Duane A. "The Bricker Amendment Controversy: Its Origins and Eisenhower's Role." *Diplomatic History* 9 (1985): 73–93.

Thomas, Evan. *The Very Best Men: Four Who Dared: The Early Years of the CIA*. 1995.

Thomas, Hugh. *The Suez Affair*. 1967.

Tomes, Robert R. *Apocalypse Then: American Intellectuals and the Vietnam War, 1954–1975*. 1998.

Trachtenberg, Marc. *A Constructed Peace: The Making of the European Settlement, 1945–1963*. 1999.

Truong Nhu Tang. *A Vietcong Memoir*. 1985.

Tucker, Nancy B. *Taiwan, Hong Kong, and the United States, 1945–1992: Uncertain Friendships*. 1994.

Tucker, Spencer C. *Vietnam*. 1999.

Turley, William S. *The Second Indochina War: A Short Political and Military History, 1954–1975*. 1986.

Ulam, Adam B. *The Communists: The Story of Power and Lost Illusions, 1948–1991*. 1992.

———. *The Rivals: America and Russia since World War II*. 1971.

Von Eschen, Penny M. *Race Against Empire: Black Americans and Anticolonialism, 1937–1957*. 1998.

Weiner, Tim. *Legacy of Ashes: The History of the CIA*. 2007.

Wells, Samuel F., Jr. "The Origins of Massive Retaliation." *Political Science Quarterly* 96 (1981): 31–52.

Wenger, Andreas. *Living with Peril: Eisenhower, Kennedy, and Nuclear Weapons*. 1997.

Westad, Odd Arne. *The Global Cold War: Third World Interventions and the Making of Our Times*. 2006.

Wilford, Hugh. *The CIA, the British Left and the Cold War: Calling the Tune?* 2003.

Winks, Robin W. *Cloak and Gown: Scholars in the Secret War, 1939–1961*. 1987.

Wise, David, and Thomas B. Ross. *The U-2 Affair*. 1962.

Wittner, Lawrence S. *The Struggle against the Bomb*. 1997.

Wolpert, Stanley A. *Nehru: A Tryst with Destiny*. 1996.

Wood, Bryce. *The Dismantling of the Good Neighbor Policy*. 1985.

Wunderlin, Clarence E. *Robert A. Taft: Ideas, Tradition, and Party in U.S. Foreign Policy*. 2005.

Yaqub, Salim. *Containing Arab Nationalism: The Eisenhower Doctrine in the Middle East*. 2004.

Young, Marilyn B. *The Vietnam Wars, 1945–1990*. 1991.

Zhai, Qiang. *China and the Vietnam Wars, 1950–1975*. 2000.

———. *The Dragon, the Lion, and the Eagle: Chinese-British-American Relations, 1949–1958*. 1994.

Zhang, Shu Guang. *Deterrence and Strategic Culture: Chinese-American Confrontations, 1949–1958*. 1992.

———. *Economic Cold War: America's Economic Embargo against China and the Sino-Soviet Alliance, 1949–1963*. 2001.

CHAPTER 4

Containment at the Brink: Kennedy and Cuba, 1961–1963

A Global Commitment to Freedom

When sworn in on January 20, 1961, President John F. Kennedy called on Americans to resolve the world's problems. "Let every nation know that we shall pay any price, bear any burden, meet any hardship, support any friend or oppose any foe in order to assure the survival and success of liberty." Containment to its fullest extent was the promise of the new administration because Kennedy intended that the doctrine encompass the globe with military force, economic pressure, or both. Staunchly anti-Communist, he was a product of the eras of appeasement and McCarthyism. Kennedy also symbolized a changing of the order, much as Franklin D. Roosevelt did to many Americans almost three decades before. As the youngest elected president—forty-three—Kennedy replaced the oldest person ever to occupy that office up to that time— Eisenhower, at seventy.

Kennedy's campaign program likewise suggested an abrupt change from that of the previous administration: his "New Frontier" assured Americans of a return to government activism in both domestic and foreign affairs. Although a bipartisan "conservative coalition" in Congress blocked much of the new presi-

dent's domestic program, his foreign policy aroused considerable support because it coincided with the basic premise of Americans— that a monolithic communism emanating from the Kremlin threatened to absorb all vulnerable nations. Kennedy's concern was more sophisticated, however, in that he recognized the growing fragmentation among the Communists and regarded Communist China to be as dangerous as the Soviet Union. Yet he believed it the responsibility of the United States to guarantee each people's right to choose their own form of government. In addition to foreign military aid, the administration established a division in the Defense Department that focused on the sale of weapons to non-Communist governments. To expand U.S. trade and investment opportunities while winning allies against communism, Congress in 1962 authorized the president to lower tariffs 50 percent for nations buying American products. Finally, Kennedy came to realize soon after taking office that no "missile gap" existed; indeed, Eisenhower's administration had kept the United States well ahead of the Soviets in nuclear capacity. But to maintain this lead and to win the struggle against communism, the White House guaranteed a deepening involvement in world

White House Meeting
Left to right: Vice President Lyndon B. Johnson, Attorney General Robert F. Kennedy, and President
John F. Kennedy. *(White House)*

affairs, in turn ensuring confrontation with
the Soviet Union.

Kennedy's Foreign Policy

Kennedy's brief tenure in the White House
emphasized image over reality. His presidency
ended abruptly in November 1963 with an
assassin's bullet in Dallas, leaving behind an
image of greatness born of martyrdom. Yet
even before these tragic events set him firmly
in their hearts, Americans spoke of the
"Kennedy style," which was characterized by
numerous attributes. Kennedy had personal
charm, affluence, and a Hollywood aura fostered by his father's investments in the business, and he showed the same grace under

pressure found in the historical figures described in his Pulitzer Prize–winning *Profiles
in Courage*. The nation loved the sound of
children and the flair of a youthful and athletic
family living in the executive mansion, playing
touch football with relatives and reporters on
the White House lawn. He brought the revival
of intellectual leadership, reinforced by the appointment of a historian as special assistant to
the president (Arthur M. Schlesinger Jr., who
wrote a Pulitzer Prize–winning study of
Kennedy's thousand days in office), and his
beautiful wife Jacqueline cultivated interest in
the arts and music. The president also showed
wit and humor, especially during his many
press conferences. Furthermore, Americans
could claim still another military hero in the

White House; during World War II, Kennedy had overcome lifelong back problems to rescue sailors under his command after the Japanese destroyed his torpedo boat, the PT-109. After his assassination, his most avid followers used the utopian musical stage play *Camelot* to idealize Kennedy and his cohorts as veritable knights of King Arthur's mythical Round Table who possessed all wisdom, knowledge, and courage while exuding genuine humanitarian concern.

Only decades after the assassination have observers been able to view the Kennedy administration with some degree of objectivity. As with most images, the Kennedy stories suffer when confronted with reality. Increasing numbers of historians have charged that both of Kennedy's major academic endeavors, *Why England Slept* (his senior thesis at Harvard, which criticized England for failing to use force against the aggressions of the 1930s) and *Profiles in Courage*, could not have been published without the extraordinary assistance of others. The image of "family" has also faded in light of the revelations of Kennedy's numerous sexual ventures (including those with Hollywood starlets), which continued throughout his presidency and were among Washington's best-known secrets. And, as has recently become clear, he supported assassination as an instrument of foreign policy, even to approving the establishment of an "executive action capability" in the CIA. Still, the Kennedy "mystique" has endured. Although the adjectives of youth and vigor suggested advantages in leadership, they carried with them distinct disadvantages in international relations when the fledgling president faced the hardened and gruff Soviet premier, Nikita Khrushchev. In promising to close the alleged missile gap, Kennedy exemplified his belief that only a display of firm resolution and superior strength could discard his image of immaturity and inexperience in office and earn the respect of Moscow's leader. During a staff discussion of a planned summit meeting with Khrushchev, Kennedy declared, "I have to show him that we can be as tough as he is.

. . . I'll have to sit down with him, and let him see who he's dealing with."

Supported by a "brain trust" of advisers, Kennedy appeared capable of turning the irrationality of the Cold War into the paths of reason and peace. Secretary of Defense Robert McNamara, for whom Kennedy had the greatest admiration, was a Republican and a fast-rising business executive from Ford Motor Company who had a well-deserved reputation for quickness of mind and expertise in numbers. Secretary of State Dean Rusk (called "Buddha" by his critics because of his self-effacing personality and near baldness) was the son of a Presbyterian minister and had risen from the poorest confines of Georgia to become a Rhodes scholar, career officer in the State Department, and head of the Rockefeller Foundation. Intensely loyal to the White House, he was a Cold Warrior who viewed the world in 1940s terms and, while secretary of state for eight years, obeyed orders in a quiet, unassuming manner. McGeorge Bundy and Walt Rostow, college professors turned presidential advisers, were hard-line anti-Communists. Kennedy also relied heavily on his younger brother, Attorney General Robert F. Kennedy, and on his chief speechwriter Theodore Sorensen, even though in the opening days of the administration he adhered more closely to diplomatic, military, and intelligence experts. The president's campaign promise to close the missile gap encouraged a huge arms buildup, although U-2 flights soon substantiated U.S. military superiority and confirmed that the Soviets were not engaged in a large missile expansion program.

The Kennedy administration advocated a foreign policy program of "flexible response," which permitted the United States to deal with all types of threats. From 1961 to 1963, the defense budget increased dramatically, allowing American intercontinental ballistic missiles to grow almost sevenfold in number and giving the United States a three-to-one advantage over the Soviet Union. A group of Special Forces in the army, known as the Green Berets, became the object of

Kennedy's special admiration—to the extent that he personally supervised their equipment and dress. Highly romanticized in the gloriously patriotic days of the early 1960s, the Green Berets employed the latest technical advances in developing counterinsurgency measures against guerrilla uprisings believed to be Communist inspired. Kennedy's discovery that there was no missile gap encouraged him to support the maintenance of sufficient conventional strength to deal with limited conflicts, but he nonetheless sought to enlarge the nation's nuclear stockpile as a deterrence to all-out war. In the meantime, civil defense programs provided protection against radioactive fallout in the event of nuclear war. Finally, the administration intended to work closely with the United Nations in keeping peace through collective security. *New York Times* writer David Halberstam characterized the Kennedy people as the "best and the brightest," who believed themselves capable of changing the course of history.

In a special address to Congress in May 1961, the president declared that "the great battleground for the defense and expansion of freedom today is . . . Asia, Latin America, Africa and the Middle East, the lands of the rising peoples." To prevent the spread of communism into the Third World, the administration's foreign aid program encouraged the development of democratic nations through economic progress. Like his predecessor in the White House, Kennedy intended to channel the nationalist fervor of emerging nations into orderly societies capable of resisting leftist revolutions inspired by Communists. Modernization through U.S. aid became the means for converting potential revolutionary situations into evolutionary developments that would bring the domestic stability vital to elections and economic advance. Mao Zedong's explanation of his success in China struck Kennedy as correct: "Guerrillas are like fish, and the people are the water in which fish swim. If the temperature of the water is right, the fish will thrive and multiply."

The 1960s were a turbulent era at home and abroad, best exemplified at the outset of the new presidency by the growing problems with Cuba. Kennedy's activist foreign policy and his concern for halting communism carried his administration into a Caribbean venture that colored his remaining days in office. In fact, the president tended to base his assessment of nearly every hot spot in the Cold War—Berlin, the Third World, and Southeast Asia, and particularly Vietnam—on his experiences with Fidel Castro's Cuba beginning in early 1961.

Cuba and the Bay of Pigs

Kennedy's troubles with Cuba were under way even before he became president. During the 1950s, the United States, interested in maintaining economic and political stability in the Caribbean as conducive to trade and security, sold arms to Cuba's longtime dictatorial ruler Fulgencio Batista and furnished military advisers through the Mutual Security Program. But whereas the image of Cuba highlighted gambling casinos, tourism, and a general nightclub atmosphere, the reality was rampant corruption, Mafia domination, drug running, and unbridled prostitution. The overwhelming majority of islanders were poverty stricken. The best lands belonged to American businesses, and the Havana government callously ignored the need for reform. Cuba was ready for revolution.

Fidel Castro, a young middle-class law school graduate, called for far-reaching reforms and with eighty followers initiated guerrilla operations against the government in 1956. Within two years, his cohort had grown in number and strength, armed with weapons provided by Cubans in the United States. A coup seemed imminent, causing the United States to begin pulling away from Batista by cutting off his arms supply. In the ensuing popular revolution that became known as the "26th of July Movement," Castro forced Batista into exile the following January 1959 and seized control. Within a week, the Washington government extended recognition to the new regime, which had ensured democratic elections and freedom of speech and press. To many Americans, Castro became a highly romanticized revolutionary figure who had risen from the people to institute reform.

But by the spring of 1959, the enchantment had worn off, as many suspected that Castro had been a Communist from the start. Their suppositions were not entirely wrong. Castro likely used the weak Communist Party on the island to further his own interests but leaned toward Marxist principles developed in his college days at the University of Havana. The cardinal objective of the new regime was to push out the United States before making an effort to revive the Cuban economy. To bring changes to the island, Castro instituted an agrarian reform program and expropriated more than $1 billion worth of American holdings. Should there be doubt about his intentions, Castro boasted that "we will take and take, until not even the nails of their shoes are left." In the meantime, thousands of Cubans fled to the United States: democratic freedoms had not materialized in Cuba, and mock trials led to mass executions of Batista's followers. By the summer, Castro's need for a broader political base had driven him closer to the Communists on the island. Director of the CIA Allen Dulles warned President Eisenhower that "communists and other extreme radicals appear to have penetrated the Castro movement." Indeed, two Communists were part of his regime: Ernesto (Che) Guevara and Raúl Castro, Fidel's brother. Washington could not shake the impression that Cuba threatened to become a propaganda center and training ground for promoting Communist revolutions throughout Latin America.

The United States became Castro's particular object of scorn because it had exploited the island for so long and now protested the executions and granted asylum to refugees. Washington responded by placing an embargo on nearly all Cuban goods and appealing for collective defensive action under the Rio Pact of 1947. But in August 1959, when the American foreign ministers met in Santiago, Chile, the United States failed to arouse full Latin American support against the alleged threat of communism in Cuba. Many leftists favored Castro, and numerous other Latin Americans simply enjoyed seeing the United States in an uncomfortable position. The meeting resulted in only a vague pronouncement against totalitarian rule that made no reference to Cuba.

Castro soon consorted openly with the Soviets while intensifying his radio and television attacks on the United States. He demanded U.S. withdrawal from Guantanamo and gave the U.S. embassy in Havana forty-eight hours to reduce its staff of 300 to a mere eleven. He called Eisenhower a "gangster" and a "senile White House golfer," extended recognition to Communist China, and in February 1960 concluded a treaty with the Soviets by which Cuba agreed to exchange 5 million tons of sugar over the next five years for arms, oil, machinery, and technical advisers. In less than two years, Cuba's trade with Soviet-controlled countries grew from 2 to 80 percent of its total commerce. Khrushchev bragged of his new Communist brother and warned that he would rain rockets on the United States if it interfered in Cuban affairs. Although he later claimed the warning was only "symbolic," he pronounced the Monroe Doctrine dead and urged the United States to "bury it, just as you bury anything dead, so it will not poison the air."

Toward the end of the Eisenhower presidency, the United States devised plans for Castro's overthrow. In March 1960, Eisenhower approved a secret $13 million fund for the preparation of a small group of Cuban refugees to invade their homeland and stage a coup. The CIA, in accordance with the plan, began training 1,400 Cuban exiles in Guatemala and Nicaragua.

As an essential part of the overthrow, the White House approved Castro's assassination as the spark to set off a popular insurrection considered critical to the invasion's success. With that objective in mind, the CIA's deputy director of plans, Richard Bissell, concocted a unique scheme in late 1960 of collaborating with the Mafia in finding Cuban exiles capable of killing Castro. The underworld, or so Bissell reasoned, had strong motives for seeing Castro dead: under Batista, Mafia figures had controlled the highly lucrative casino, drug, and prostitution businesses, only to see Castro force them off the island after his takeover. Not only did the Mafia chieftains seek vengeance, but they knew the island well enough to locate an assassin willing to poison Castro's food. The CIA's involvement would remain hidden, for no operative was to participate in either the invasion or the assassination.

Shortly before Kennedy assumed office, the United States and Cuba broke diplomatic relations on January 3, 1961, and to Washington, Castro's regime became synonymous with communism. The U.S. ambassador to Cuba, Philip Bonsal, attempted to downplay this fear. Although he opposed Castro, Bonsal attributed the dictator's Soviet leanings to the unbending policies of the United States, not to communism. Castro's purpose, Bonsal later declared, "was radically and exclusively nationalistic; it became oriented toward de-

Castro and Khrushchev
A warm embrace at the United Nations in New York in late 1960. *(Wide World Photos, New York)*

pendence on the Soviet Union only when the United States, by its actions in the spring of 1960, gave the Russians no choice other than to come to Castro's rescue." Bonsal's reasoned assessment did not convince Washington. Kennedy had chastised the Republicans during the presidential campaign for allowing a "communist satellite" at "our very doorstep." Americans, he defiantly declared, would not be "pushed around any longer."

Kennedy had virtually announced his intention to rid the hemisphere of Castro's communism. Not by coincidence had the president's national security adviser, McGeorge Bundy, instructed the CIA to establish an executive action program in the CIA that targeted "dangerous" foreign leaders such as Castro. Arkansas Senator J. William Fulbright, influential chair of the Foreign Relations Committee, assured Kennedy the Castro regime was "a thorn in the flesh" and "not a dagger in the heart." Yet the new administration continued to treat the regime as a dire threat to U.S. prestige and security. Shortly after Kennedy's arrival in the White House, the CIA informed him of its invasion plans and insisted that the landing of Cuban exiles would set off a full-scale insurrection against Castro, just as an earlier coup had succeeded in Guatemala and erased another Communist menace. The CIA had already helped to establish a Cuban Revolutionary Council to take over the government after Castro's overthrow. After considerable discussion, the White House selected the invasion point at Cochinos Bay (Bay of Pigs), located on the southwest side of the island. D-day was April 17, 1961.

At first, Kennedy appeared hesitant about the invasion plan and approved it only as a "contingency" operation, subject to cancellation at any time. Such blatant interventionism bothered him: not only would it raise widespread criticism both inside and outside the United States, but it might fail. And even given the attributes of plausible deniability, there would be no way, Kennedy realized, to deny complicity, whether direct or indirect in nature. Yet if the plan were successful, his administration would score an early victory in the Cold War and force the Soviets to sense the determination of the new leaders in Washington. Besides, the young president had become an advocate of the CIA as a result of his admiration for the fictional James Bond of Ian Fleming's bestselling spy thrillers. Had not the CIA in 1954 performed masterfully in Guatemala? asked Allen Dulles—without also noting that it had failed miserably four years later in Indonesia, when it attempted to bring down the suspected leftist-leaning regime of President Achmed Sukarno. Kennedy instructed Schlesinger to draft a White Paper justifying the U.S. decision to intervene in Cuba. The State Department meanwhile published a pamphlet titled "Cuba," which outlined Castro's broken promises and labeled his alleged Communist regime "a fateful challenge to the inter-American system." Without attempting to open negotiations with Castro and without consulting Congress, the Kennedy administration embarked on a dangerously uncharted course that had little assurance of success.

The secret plan was anything but secret. Rumors had spread that U.S. Marines were preparing Cuban exiles in Guatemala for an invasion of Cuba. Details were so widely known that two American reporters, working independently of each other, had written stories for national publication that were amazingly accurate. Only after direct appeals from the White House did the journals refrain from releasing them. Less than a week before the invasion, Kennedy assured journalists of "no intervention in Cuba by United States armed forces."

Kennedy had told the truth, if only in a literal sense aimed at erecting a basis for plausible denial: *U.S.* armed forces did not intervene in Cuba. About 1,400 Cuban exiles, sixteen to sixty-one in age, poorly equipped, and largely inexperienced and untrained in military matters, set out by trucks from Guatemala to Nicaragua, where they boarded boats headed for the Bay of Pigs. Everything went wrong. American-sponsored air strikes on Cuba's air force two days before had not had the softening effect claimed by the CIA, and Kennedy's doubts about the expedition had become so deep that he called off a second wave of strikes on D-1 as well as the air cover scheduled for the day of the invasion. When the landing party hit the beaches, Castro's planes, tanks, and ground forces swarmed all over them. No general uprising had welcomed their arrival, largely because the CIA had failed to set up a network of communications on the island and the Mafia's chosen assassin had backed out at the last moment. Finally, contrary to the CIA's earlier assurances, there were no mountains nearby for refuge: the ragtag army had landed on the edge of a crocodile-infested swamp. Castro's army, air force, and militia units killed 114 and captured 1,179; U.S. destroyers rescued around 30 stragglers sometime afterward, but the others disappeared. In an effort to save those taken captive, the president authorized an airborne expedition that likewise failed because, incredibly, no one took into account the change in time zones when arranging the rendezvous of the rescue planes. Most of the captives won their freedom nearly two years later, but, in a further humiliation, the United States had to pay $53 million in food and medicine as ransom. Castro's agents among the rebels had forewarned him of the attack, and his forces had fought far better than the CIA had expected, awarding his regime a phenomenal military and propaganda triumph at Kennedy's expense.

With his nation's prestige reeling badly, Kennedy accepted full blame for the Cuban disaster, recognizing that his greatest task now was to convince the Soviet Union that the Bay of Pigs episode was not a barometer of U.S. weakness. "How could I have been so stupid, to let them go ahead?" he moaned afterward. "All my life I've known better than to depend on the experts." Kennedy held the CIA and the Joint Chiefs of Staff responsible because of their careless planning and clumsy implementation of the operation. One can attribute part of the blame to his

newness in office, yet the fact remains that the idea of such an invasion was not alien to Kennedy's worldview. The rub was the plan's inept execution by so-called intellectuals, exposing the youthful president to charges not only of failure but also of stupidity and weakness. In the biting words of Cyrus Sulzberger in the *New York Times*, "We looked like fools to our friends, rascals to our enemies, and incompetents to the rest." Latin Americans denounced Yankee imperialism and raised uncomfortable questions about whether this infamous action was consistent with the UN Charter and the principles of the Organization of American States (OAS). "Fair Play for Cuba" rallies in the United States drew numerous Americans who blasted the administration for participating in such a zany scheme and sarcastically denounced the CIA as the "Cuban Invasion Authority." Most embarrassed was UN Ambassador Adlai Stevenson, who had not known of the impending attack and just two days before had gone before member nations to deny rumors of an invasion.

The Kennedy administration was especially concerned about image. Even though the Soviets had in reality gained nothing on the United States, they publicly warned the White House to stay out of Cuban affairs, leaving the appearance that a dramatic shift was under way in the world balance of power. Attorney General Robert F. Kennedy recognized the danger. "We just could not sit and take it," he warned; the Soviets would consider Americans to be "paper tigers." White House adviser Walt Rostow tried to console the distraught president that "we would have ample opportunity to prove we were not paper tigers in Berlin, Southeast Asia, and elsewhere." In the minds of administration members, the Communist danger loomed larger than ever.

To restore faith in the United States, the president asserted that the nation's "restraint" was "not inexhaustible" and that it would continue to fight communism "in every corner of the globe." Responding to

Khrushchev's warnings of war if the United States invaded Cuba, Kennedy insisted that *Americans* would determine the business of the hemisphere. "In the event of any military intervention by outside force we will immediately honor our obligations under the inter-American system to protect this hemisphere against external aggression." A few days later, he told the American Society of Newspaper Editors that the patience of the United States had limitations. "Should it ever appear that the inter-American doctrine of noninterference merely conceals or excuses a policy of non-action—if the nations of this hemisphere should fail to meet their commitments against outside Communist penetration—then I want it clearly understood that this Government will not hesitate in meeting its primary obligations, which are to the security of our Nation."

Cuba remained a major irritant to the Washington administration because Castro used the Bay of Pigs fiasco as propaganda against the United States and swore to spread communism throughout the hemisphere. The White House tightened its economic restrictions on the island, continued to withhold recognition, criticized Castro through the U.S. Information Agency and other means, assisted his opponents in Miami, and, in a striking move, renewed interest in his assassination. Castro meanwhile proclaimed Cuba a "socialist" state under single-party control of the Popular Socialist (Communist) Party. "I am a Marxist-Leninist and will be one until the day I die," he insisted over radio and television. Castro's professed socialism caused Colombia and Peru to assemble the American foreign ministers at Punta del Este, Uruguay, in late January 1962, where all delegations except Cuba's pronounced communism alien to the hemisphere and barred Cuba from the Inter-American Defense Board. Also by a large margin, the ministers halted the arms trade with Cuba and secured its ouster from the OAS by the minimum two-thirds majority. Finally, the United States imposed a trade embargo on Cuba in February 1962 that remains in effect to the present. Even then, these measures had little effect because they drew no support from the larger, more populated Latin American states of Argentina, Bolivia, Brazil, Chile, Ecuador, and Mexico. Chastised but not leashed, Castro continued to accept Soviet aid and repeated his promise to spread communism into all Latin America.

The Third World

Kennedy's ordeal with Cuba deeply affected his administration's policies toward the Third World. To prevent other Castro-like revolutions, the president deemed it necessary to control the nationalist energies of these emerging peoples by emphasizing calm, orderly development through U.S. aid and advice. Washington's policymakers continued to believe that the Third World's peculiar susceptibility to revolution furnished an invitation to communism. The remedy was a nation-building process aimed at spreading democracy.

To bring stability to the new postwar nations, Kennedy had issued an executive order in March 1961 establishing the Peace Corps, which sent Americans to Latin America and Africa to aid in social and economic development. In the autumn, after the Bay of Pigs episode, Congress approved a bill giving the organization permanent standing. Within two years, nearly 5,000 Americans had joined the Peace Corps, working as teachers, doctors, and agricultural and technical advisers to bring about flood control, irrigation, and general community development. The goal was to alleviate poverty through economic and social uplift and thereby reduce the attraction of communism, although few recipients converted to U.S. ideals in return.

In an even more ambitious attempt to combat growing unrest in Latin America, the Kennedy administration pushed through a social and economic program known as the Alliance for Progress. Based on the Act of Bogotá of 1960, the idea of a new aid program first appeared in the president's inaugural address. To Latin American diplomats meeting in the White House, Kennedy praised the hemisphere's revolutions for independence and then asserted that the work was not over: "For one unfulfilled task is to demonstrate to the entire world that man's unsatisfied aspiration for economic progress and social justice can best be achieved by free men working within a framework of democratic institutions." In August 1961, Secretary of the Treasury Douglas Dillon told an Inter-American Economic and Social Conference at Punta del Este that nearly $20 billion of assistance was necessary over the next decade. The money would come from the United States, Europe, and Japan, although his government agreed to provide a major share of the funds. The resulting Charter of Punta del Este established the Alliance for Progress, whose purpose, according to the accompanying Declaration to the Peoples of America, was "to bring a better life to all the peoples of the Continent."

Despite high hopes and considerable publicity, the Alliance for Progress never fulfilled expectations. Within two years, the United States had furnished nearly $2 billion for improvements, yet the program did not achieve the desired economic changes in Latin America. Several considerations account for this failure. Private investors in the United States were afraid of the certain disorder emanating from a program that encouraged such sweeping social and economic changes. Latin American landowners held authority and resisted land reforms, and the rest of the people resented U.S. intervention under any name. The region lacked the skilled workers needed to carry out the program, and the Alliance funds never reached those in need because of bureaucratic inertia in Washington and the tendency of Latin Americans in power to keep the money for themselves. In addition, few Roman Catholics in Latin America were willing to adopt birth-control practices; indeed, they were encouraged to promote large families by exorbitant infant mortality rates and by leaders who insisted that the United States sought a reduction in family size as part of its effort

to maintain control over the region. Within the decade of its mandated existence, the Alliance for Progress virtually died out as military coups continued and political democracy remained elusive.

Congo (now Zaire) in central Africa also raised apprehension in the Kennedy administration that the region was a potential breeding ground for communism. As the largest African state, Congo's political direction would undoubtedly influence others on the continent. Under the threat of racial violence, Belgium had granted independence to the colony in June 1960, but civil war broke out, and Moise Tshombe, an anti-Communist backed by Belgian mining interests, led the mineral-rich southern province of Katanga (gold, diamonds, and uranium) in a separatist movement. The United States supported a UN Security Council decision to send peacekeeping forces to Congo, but it did not favor Katanga's return to the central government. Congo's premier, the staunch nationalist Patrice Lumumba, bitterly opposed the UN action as a conspiracy against him and appealed to the Soviet Union for help. Director of the CIA Allen Dulles disgustedly referred to Lumumba as "a Castro, or worse" and won White House approval to engineer Lumumba's demise through the CIA. But in September 1960, Congolese President Joseph Kasavubu, regarded as conservative and pro-American, overthrew Lumumba and ordered the Soviets out of the country.

When Kennedy became president, he infuriated the Belgians by calling for a "middle-of-the-road government" in Congo. To avert a Soviet–American confrontation, he added, the United Nations must maintain order through a trusteeship until the Congolese could administer the government. In January 1961, a Belgian captain of a mercenary force acted without CIA involvement in shooting and killing Lumumba when Congolese troops refused to do so. Less than six months later, a moderate was elected premier and received U.S. support in his attempt to reunify the country. When continued efforts failed, the

United Nations reversed its stance and authorized forces to put down the government's opposition. They succeeded and in 1963 restored Katanga (now Shaba) to Congo. Although problems persisted, Americans interpreted Congo's reunification as a victory over communism, ignoring the probability that supporters of nationalism were the chief victims of their actions. The results of such alienation threatened to have serious ramifications in the United Nations, where by the spring of 1963 the Afro-Asian nations made up the majority.

Berlin

The reverberations from the Bay of Pigs failure became evident during the first summit meeting between Kennedy and Khrushchev, held at Vienna in June 1961. The announced purposes of the two-day gathering were to discuss a nuclear test ban treaty and growing problems in Berlin and Laos, but the conference degenerated into caustic exchanges designed to assess the will of the other. Except for Khrushchev's agreement to seek a negotiated settlement in Laos, neither man retreated on any issue. After the Soviet premier suggested that the United States had exposed a basic weakness by refusing to launch a military invasion of Cuba, he suddenly announced an ultimatum on Berlin that resurrected the crisis of 1958. Berlin should be a "free city," Khrushchev declared. If Western occupation did not terminate within six months, his government would sign a separate peace with the East Germans, forcing the West to negotiate with them for continued access to West Berlin. Kennedy was determined to show strength, although newsreels and cameras revealed a nervousness that stood in sharp contrast to Khrushchev's calm and paternalistic bearing. The president realized he had lost the battle at Vienna, but he was not about to lose the war. "If Khrushchev wants to rub my nose in the dirt," Kennedy angrily declared, "it's all over."

By mid-July, the Berlin issue had stirred up a war scare in the United States as the Kennedy administration took a hard-line position that outdid the measured response of his predecessor in 1958. The president insisted that his country, along with Britain and France, had "a fundamental political and moral obligation" to West Berlin. Any action endangering the city "would have the gravest effects upon international peace and security and endanger the lives and well-being of millions of people." Over television, he proclaimed that "we cannot and will not permit the Communists to drive us out of Berlin, either gradually or by force." Americans "do not want to fight, but we have fought before."

Whereas Eisenhower had rejected any thought of expanding U.S. military strength in preparation for a ground war in Europe, Kennedy seemed willing to take that hard step. He activated 250,000 reserves, asked Congress to expand the country's military forces by 25 percent, and aroused fears of a nuclear holocaust by calling for a nationwide civil defense program based on fallout shelters in case of attack. Congress approved the president's requests and added 45,000 troops for assignment to Europe. Meanwhile, France and West Germany bolstered their numbers in NATO. "If we don't meet our commitments in Berlin," Kennedy warned, "it will mean the destruction of NATO and a dangerous situation for the whole world. All Europe is at stake in West Berlin."

As escalation fed escalation during that tense summer of 1961, the Soviets in the nighttime hours of August 13 erected a twenty-eight-mile-long barricade of barbed wire (later reinforced with concrete slabs) between East and West Berlin to stop the vast and ongoing exodus of East Berliners into the free section of the city. The effort succeeded. The influx of refugees into West Berlin came to a sudden halt, but for the first time the Cold War had a visible symbol of totalitarianism that the United States could advertise to the world. Whereas the "iron curtain" was abstract and arguable in terms of actual existence, the Berlin Wall was physical and irrefutable. The United States could claim a

Berlin Wall
Construction of the Berlin Wall around the Brandenburg Gate, November 20, 1961. *(U.S. Army)*

victory in the Cold War in that the very construction of the wall signified the Soviets' admission to Western control over West Berlin. The city, it appeared, would follow the path of Germany itself by becoming permanently divided. During the first trying moments of this new crisis in Germany, the United States ordered more soldiers through the East German passageway that led into West Berlin.

At the end of August, Khrushchev raised the ante by announcing an end to the three-year moratorium on nuclear tests in the atmosphere, a decision that ultimately led to the Soviets' explosion of a weapon 3,000 times more powerful than the bomb dropped over Hiroshima. Although the United States still had a far superior delivery capability, the impression was that the Soviets had surged ahead in nuclear capacity. Kennedy, under enormous pressure to resume testing, finally agreed to underground tests in September

1961 and in the following April extended them to the atmosphere.

As in 1958, however, neither nation wanted war, and the problems over Berlin did not graduate beyond mere rhetoric and shows of force. According to some reports, the president took a strong stand on Berlin without fear of a holocaust because he had learned from a spy, Soviet Colonel Oleg Penkovsky, that the Soviets lacked the nuclear strength claimed by Khrushchev. If so, the crisis nonetheless conjured up a war scare. But Khrushchev had apparently bluffed again, and the United States was reluctant to fight over East Berlin, particularly when the wall provided visible proof of Soviet repression and a superb source of propaganda. Kennedy defused the taut situation by asking for a negotiated settlement, which in turn suggested his willingness to forgo serious efforts to reunify Germany. Although the tension eased,

Kennedy's offer to negotiate over Berlin further weakened NATO's unity by upsetting both Charles de Gaulle in France and Konrad Adenauer in West Germany. As for the Soviets, the December deadline set by Khrushchev (as during the Eisenhower administration) came and passed without incident.

The Cuban Missile Crisis

The long-feared Soviet–American showdown came not in Berlin but in Cuba. In April 1962, Khrushchev made a stunning move: he arranged the construction of missile sites to test the Kennedy administration's resolve while protecting the island against an expected U.S. invasion. Doubtless encouraged by the president's apparent lack of fortitude at the Bay of Pigs and in Vienna and Berlin, the Soviet premier calculated that any leverage gained in Cuba could set examples for allies of both the United States and the Soviet Union, force concessions in Berlin and elsewhere, facilitate the spread of socialist doctrine throughout Latin America, and salvage his own tenuous position in Moscow. Khrushchev was under fire at home because of his failing economic programs and his calls for "peaceful coexistence," which seemed to abdicate Communist leadership to the Chinese. Indeed, he could achieve the impression of nuclear parity with the United States (although the United States had a seventeen-to-one advantage in atomic weaponry) by placing missiles within the Western Hemisphere. The United States had missiles in Britain, Turkey, and Italy, he groused, and the presence of Soviet missiles in Cuba would now show Americans "what it feels like to have enemy missiles pointing at you." Even though Khrushchev later insisted that his paramount purpose had been to defend his Cuban ally against an imminent U.S. assault, this objective was probably only part of a broader program designed to regain prestige at home while establishing a strategic balance of power in world affairs.

Khrushchev's concern about his Caribbean comrade was not groundless: the president seemed obsessed with toppling the Cuban dictator. Kennedy had condoned the trade embargo early in 1962 and had secured Cuba's ban from the OAS. The U.S. Marines were on secret maneuvers in the Caribbean that April, training to free an island from a mythical ruler called "Ortsac"—"Castro" spelled backward. But even more inventive was the president's earlier approval of "Operation Mongoose," a CIA-sponsored covert operation supported by a $50 million annual budget. Guided by his brother, the attorney general, and run by air force general and legendary psywar figure Edward Lansdale, the program sought to bring down Castro by spreading propaganda, running paramilitary operations, contaminating Cuban sugar headed for the Soviet Union, and sabotaging the island's economy by burning cane fields and blowing up department stores, oil tanks, and factories. In one of Mongoose's most imaginative schemes, it suggested convincing the Cuban peasants of the imminent Second Coming of Christ by lighting up the night sky with incendiaries launched by submarines while the CIA spread the word that the Lord was not pleased with their leader in Havana and wanted his immediate overthrow. Finally, the administration tacitly revived its support for assassination with the Mafia's help or by using exploding cigars and either pens, pills, or needles laced with poison.

The Cuban missile crisis had its origins in July 1962, when American U-2 flights detected a growing number of Soviet ships in the island's waters. Refugees from Cuba and secret agents from the United States had also noted what might have been missile sites under construction. Furthermore, an extraordinary Soviet troop buildup seemed to be under way on the island, substantiated years later at 42,000 troops and a number of armed, short-range nuclear missiles. In August, U-2 reconnaissance discovered the construction of a missile site, but the CIA director, John McCone, was on a honeymoon in France and could not authenticate the findings. Finally, someone in the CIA leaked the information to

U-2 Photo of Cuban Missile Site
One of the aerial surveillance pictures that helped to set off the "thirteen days" of the Cuban missile crisis that threatened nuclear war between the United States and the Soviet Union. *(CIA)*

a reporter for the *Buffalo Evening News* who failed to convert disbelievers with his published account of late August. The following month, the president, who was then more concerned about problems in Europe and Southeast Asia, repeatedly assured the press that there was no evidence that the Soviets were establishing offensive military installations in Cuba. But in early October, U-2 commanders were under orders to photograph western Cuba, and by the middle of the month, they had located missile sites close to San Cristóbal. The pictures revealed over forty IL-28 (Ilyshin-28) light bombers (capable of carrying nuclear payloads), the same number of strategic missiles, and nine missile sites in

preparation. There was no sign of nuclear warheads, although evidence later showed that twenty of the planned forty warheads were already on the island and that the balance was en route by sea. The early warning systems of the United States against air attacks lay in the distant Arctic north, leaving the southern part of North America dangerously exposed. The crucial point was that missiles fired from Cuba could reach Washington within eight minutes, considerably faster than the near half hour required when launched from the Soviet Union.

President Kennedy, then on the campaign trail, learned of these startling developments on October 16. Within the next few days, he raised the matter of the Soviet military buildup in Cuba (but not the missiles) in meetings with Soviet Foreign Minister Andrei Gromyko and Soviet Ambassador Anatoly Dobrynin. Neither man, however, knew of the Kremlin's missile plans on the island and assured the president that the military additions were for defensive purposes only. Kennedy had not yet settled on a course of action regarding the missiles and decided against confronting either Soviet official with the photographs.

Thus, the most serious legacy of the Bay of Pigs fiasco became the supreme test of will during the ensuing Cuban missile crisis of October 1962. To deal with the problem, Kennedy established an Executive Committee of the National Security Council ("Ex Comm"), which met in an adjunct office of the State Department to avoid press detection and included current administration figures along with some from the Truman presidency. Rusk chaired the proceedings, although he encouraged free discussion. President Kennedy avoided the meetings as much as possible to promote an open interchange of ideas among a varied group of individuals that included his brother, Rusk, McNamara, Bundy, General Maxwell Taylor as chair of the Joint Chiefs of Staff, Air Force General Curtis LeMay, speechwriter Theodore Sorensen, former Secretary of State Dean Acheson, and, intermittently, UN Ambassador Adlai Stevenson.

During an emotion-packed week in October, Ex Comm met almost continuously to discuss Soviet motives for placing the missiles in Cuba and to decide how to resolve the crisis. Khrushchev, the committee members surmised, could not have expected to keep the weapons installation a secret. He was surely aware of the U-2 flights over Cuba yet made no effort to conceal the arrival of Soviet ships and soldiers, along with the construction of missile sites. The placement of missiles in Cuba might not have actually changed the world power balance, Sorensen noted, but they would have forced an alteration "*in appearance*; and in matters of national will and world leadership, as the President [himself] said later, such appearances contribute to re-

ality." The Soviets would leave the impression that they were supporting an ally against invasion, blunting the Communist Chinese claim that Khrushchev was reluctant to support "liberation" movements. At the same time, the missiles' presence in Cuba would damage U.S. prestige by raising questions about the nation's military power. One truth was certain: the United States could not allow the missiles to remain in Cuba. "The 1930s," President Kennedy observed, "taught us a clear lesson: aggressive conduct, if allowed to go unchecked and unchallenged, ultimately leads to war."

Ex Comm's discussions of the missile crisis were free and open, as Robert F. Kennedy's memoir *The Thirteen Days* dramatically attests. Its members were uncertain about Soviet motives but considered them dangerously provocative. Some believed that Khrushchev sought leverage to force the West out of Berlin; others thought he wanted the United States to remove its Jupiter missiles from Turkey. The latter suggestion brought a sharp reaction from the president. Kennedy recognized that those missiles were outmoded and had earlier called for their removal, but he now realized his directive had not yet been implemented and that taking them out now would appear to be a capitulation. Furthermore, under the 1959 agreement that authorized the missiles' installation, the Turks owned the missiles and the Americans the nuclear warheads. Any attempt to remove the missiles would inflict domestic political damage on the Turkish government while drawing negative reactions from other NATO members. Khrushchev, several Ex Comm members believed, did not seek a nuclear showdown, but as the president and his brother realized late one night, war could come through whim or miscalculation.

After considerable debate, Ex Comm focused on two options for the president aimed at preventing the arrival of nuclear warheads: either order an immediate air strike against the missile sites (promoted by Acheson and the Joint Chiefs of Staff), or impose a blockade of

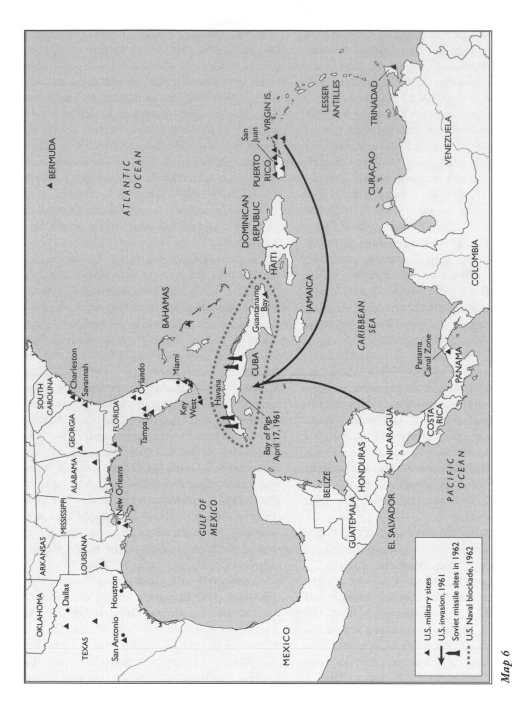

Map 6
The United States and Cuba, 1961–1962. Cuba became the center of the Cold War early in the Kennedy administration. After the United States failed to achieve the overthrow of Castro, it went to the brink of nuclear war with the Soviet Union when it implanted missile sites on the island. (*Source: author*)

the island (advocated by Undersecretary of State George Ball). At one point, the Joint Chiefs called for an all-out invasion to rid the hemisphere of both the missiles and Castro. Opponents countered that this measure would lead to a lengthy and costly war with Cuba while leaving the Soviets free to take Berlin. Suggestions for arranging private talks with Castro or turning over the matter to the United Nations led to staunch opposition, as did Stevenson's recommendation that in exchange for withdrawing the missiles, the United States should pull its missiles from Turkey and Italy and give up its naval base in Guantanamo. General LeMay argued that the Soviets would do nothing if the United States bombed their missile sites in Cuba. The president strongly disagreed. To a friend, he tersely remarked, "Can you imagine LeMay saying a thing like that? These brass hats have one great advantage in their favor. If we listen to them, and do what they want us to do, none of us will be alive to tell them later they were wrong." The U.S. Air Force admitted that it could not ensure total destruction through air strikes and warned that the missiles left undamaged would be capable of hitting the United States. It also allowed that bombings might kill Soviet nationals and lead to war. Ball was leery of the air force's ability to carry out a "surgical air strike." Its questionable performance in World War II, he observed, suggested that the outcome in Cuba might be similar to that of a surgeon who intended to remove an appendix but took out the kidneys and lungs instead. "My brother is not going to be the Tojo of the 1960s," the attorney general asserted in clinching the argument for a blockade.

Ex Comm actually decided on a "quarantine" of Cuba, which would deny the island arms and supplies while, as McNamara argued, leaving the administration some flexibility to either escalate or mitigate the situation. Robert F. Kennedy and others had recommended using the term "quarantine" rather than "blockade" to avoid the international language of war, although some warned that in either case the Soviets could retaliate by shutting off Berlin without removing the missiles from Cuba. Proponents of the quarantine pointed out that Article 51 of the UN Charter permitted the use of force in "self-defense if an armed attack occurs" and argued that the installation of missiles was tantamount to an attack. The United States had to move quickly and alone. Attempts to work through either the United Nations or the OAS would lead to interminable delays, although the United States kept its allies informed and won their support along with that of the OAS and the Third World. De Gaulle was disgruntled about being informed rather than consulted, but he joined others in realizing that missiles aimed at the United States could also be turned toward Western Europe.

While U.S. air, land, and naval forces prepared for action, President Kennedy appeared over nationwide television on the evening of October 22, 1962, to deliver a chilling address on the crisis in Cuba. Kennedy's knowledge of the Soviets' nuclear capabilities rested heavily on pilfered information provided by the spy Penkovsky, who was in Soviet military intelligence and was soon thereafter arrested and executed. Indeed, Richard Helms of the CIA declared that Penkovsky's microfilmed materials from the Soviet Defense Ministry allowed the president to resist the pressure for an air strike because the CIA was able to tell him that "this is what we've got here and it will take them X days to be ready to fire." Thus assured of a few days of maneuverability, Kennedy first outlined to Americans the revelations of the past few days and declared that the Soviet Union's purpose in planting missiles in Cuba was "none other than to provide a nuclear strike capability against the Western Hemisphere." The missiles already there could hit Washington, Cape Canaveral, and the Panama Canal, and others under construction could reach as far north as Hudson Bay and as far south as Lima, Peru. Such aggressive Soviet action came under the "cloak of secrecy and deception" and constituted "an explicit threat to the peace and security of the

Americas." The United States therefore would "regard any nuclear missile launched from Cuba against any nation in the Western Hemisphere as an attack by the Soviet Union on the United States requiring a full retaliatory response upon the Soviet Union." He called on Khrushchev to "halt and eliminate this clandestine, reckless and provocative threat to world peace and to stable relations between our two nations." To encourage the premier to reverse his dangerous policy, the United States would establish "a strict quarantine on all offensive military equipment under shipment to Cuba," effective on the morning of October 24.

The United States adopted other measures as well. It reinforced Guantanamo, evacuated dependents of military personnel, and requested public declarations of support from the OAS and the United Nations. President Kennedy meanwhile approved the State Department's plans to draw up a blueprint for civil rule over the island in the event of occupation. In the United Nations, Stevenson dramatically confronted Soviet Ambassador Valerian Zorin (who, like Dobrynin, knew nothing of the missiles) with giant photographs of the missile sites and challenged him to work toward a settlement before nuclear war developed. While nearly 200 U.S. ships gathered in the Caribbean to enforce the quarantine, 7,000 additional U.S. Marines headed for Guantanamo, and the Strategic Air Command for the first time went into full-

To end the missile crisis, President Kennedy announced a quarantine of all offensive military materials entering Cuba and promised instant retaliation against the Soviet Union if it launched a nuclear attack anywhere in the Western Hemisphere.

President John F. Kennedy, radio and television address on Cuban missile crisis, October 22, 1962, *Public Papers of the Presidents of the United States: John F. Kennedy, 1962* (Washington, D.C.: Government Printing Office, 1963), 806–9.

I have directed that the following *initial* steps be taken immediately:

First: To halt this offensive buildup, a strict quarantine on all offensive military equipment under shipment to Cuba is being initiated. All ships of any kind bound for Cuba from whatever nation or port will, if found to contain cargoes of offensive weapons, be turned back. . . .

Second: I have directed the continued and increased close surveillance of Cuba and its military buildup. . . .

Third: It shall be the policy of this Nation to regard any nuclear missile launched from Cuba against any nation in the Western Hemisphere as an attack by the Soviet Union on the United States, requiring a full retaliatory response upon the Soviet Union.

Fourth: As a necessary military precaution, I have reinforced our base at Guantanamo, evacuated today the dependents of our personnel there, and ordered additional military units to be on a standby alert basis.

Fifth: We are calling tonight for an immediate meeting of the Organ of Consultation under the Organization of American States, to consider this threat to hemispheric security and to invoke articles 6 and 8 of the Rio Treaty in support of all necessary action. . . .

Sixth: Under the Charter of the United Nations, we are asking tonight that an emergency meeting of the Security Council be convoked without delay to take action against this latest Soviet threat to world peace. . . .

Seventh and finally: I call upon Chairman [Nikita] Khrushchev to halt and eliminate this clandestine, reckless, and provocative threat to world peace and to stable relations between our two nations. I call upon him further to abandon this course of world domination, and to join in an historic effort to end the perilous arms race and to transform the history of man. He has an opportunity now to move the world back from the abyss of destruction. . . .

war readiness. Hundreds of huge B-52s were airborne, each carrying nuclear bombs.

The greatest concern, of course, was whether the Soviets already had nuclear warheads in Cuba and, if so, that some officer on the island could order their use. To the press shortly after the president's speech, McNamara somberly noted that nuclear warheads were "of such a size that it is extremely unlikely we would ever be able to observe them by the intelligence means open to us." But he thought it "almost inconceivable" that the Soviets would send missiles without warheads. The following day, the CIA told Kennedy that even though it could not confirm the presence of warheads, U-2 photos had detected the construction of buildings near the missile sites that probably were meant for nuclear storage. One day later, the CIA noted that the Soviets were building such storage sites at the rate of one per missile regiment. There was another, more immediate danger that the White House recognized. The missiles, it now seems clear, had no "permissive-action-link" device, a safety measure instituted by the United States to guarantee that only the president could authorize the firing of nuclear warheads. Years afterward, McNamara remembered his concern in 1962 that "some second lieutenant could start a nuclear war."

The minutes ticked by loudly during the following days. The day after the president's television appearance, the OAS Council met with Rusk and voted nearly unanimous support for a resolution urging "the immediate dismantling and withdrawal from Cuba of all missiles and other weapons with any offensive capability." It also called on member states to use any means necessary to stop a further missile buildup; the Rio Treaty of 1947, the Council pointed out, permitted assistance to any American state threatened by aggression. That same day, the White House received a letter from Khrushchev asserting that the blockade was illegal. "The actions of [the] U.S.A. with regard to Cuba," he alleged, "are outright banditry or, if you like, the folly of degenerate imperialism." Kennedy, he charged, was pushing the nations into nuclear war.

October 24 loomed as the day of reckoning: two Soviet ships, with a submarine between them, were approaching U.S. naval patrols in the Caribbean, only an hour away from Cuba. The U.S. aircraft carrier *Essex* prepared to contact the submarine by sonar and ask it to surface; on refusal, the U.S. captain was to employ small-scale depth charges to force it up. Robert F. Kennedy described his brother's tense waiting:

> His hand went up to his face and covered his mouth. He opened and closed his fist. His face seemed drawn, his eyes pained, almost gray. We stared at each other across the table. For a few fleeting seconds, it was almost as though no one else was there and he was no longer the President. Inexplicably, I thought of when he was ill and almost died; when he lost his child; when we learned that our oldest brother had been killed; of personal times of strain and hurt. The voices droned on.

The Soviet vessels suddenly stopped just shy of the quarantine line and turned back, a last-minute preemption of Khrushchev's order to run the blockade that resulted from the intervention of Anastas Mikoyan, the Soviet first deputy premier and second in command to the premier himself. Whether Mikoyan reversed the original decision on his own or somehow convinced Khrushchev to do so remains unclear. But either way, the October 24 confrontation at sea brought the two superpowers close to war.

Still the tension persisted, even while signs of an impending Soviet retreat became evident. United Nations Secretary-General U Thant called for negotiations, and Khrushchev sought a summit conference to resolve the question, but President Kennedy insisted that removal of the missiles had to come first. On October 26, Washington received encouraging news. A high official in the Soviet embassy informed the administration through ABC news correspondent John Scali that the Soviet Union would remove the missiles under UN auspices if the United States lifted the quarantine and guaranteed not to invade Cuba. That same Friday night, Khrushchev sent a long, rambling letter offering similar conditions. "If you have not lost your self-control," he wrote the president, "we and you ought not to pull on the ends of the rope in which you have tied the knot of war." Insisting he did not want war, Khrushchev appealed to Kennedy to "let us not only relax the forces pulling on the ends of the rope, let us take measures to untie that knot. We are ready for this."

Yet the conciliatory tone of these developments was puzzling because it did not coincide with other events. The FBI discovered the day afterward (October 27) that Soviet officials in New York City were destroying sensitive papers (a move signifying the possibility of war), a Soviet surface-to-air missile shot down a U-2 over Cuba (later found to have resulted from a Soviet general in Cuba who violated orders), and no slowdown had occurred in the construction of the missile sites. Most ominous, a second note had arrived from Khrushchev, more belligerent than the first. The Soviets, asserted the premier, would pull their missiles from Cuba only if the United States withdrew its missiles from Turkey.

Khrushchev's second note threatened to heighten the crisis because the White House responded with a virtual ultimatum to the Soviets. President Kennedy of course could not agree to Khrushchev's new proposal, but his brother and Sorensen followed the advice of others in suggesting a way out: disregard the second letter and reply to the first with an ultimatum. On October 27, the president notified Khrushchev that in return for withdrawing the missiles from Cuba, the United States would promise not to invade the island. The implication was clear: if the Soviets refused this offer, the United States would itself take out the missiles (and thousands of Soviet soldiers) with an air strike that would, in turn, have forced a military retaliation by the Kremlin. That same night, Robert F. Kennedy met privately with Dobrynin and assured him (a pledge approved beforehand by the president and several close advisers but

unknown to many members of Ex Comm until publication of the attorney general's memoirs in 1969) that even though the president could not immediately remove the missiles from Turkey and Italy, he would do so shortly after the Cuban crisis had passed. If Khrushchev publicly divulged this offer, it would become null and void.

Another pivotal moment had presented itself. Would a Soviet refusal to accept this arrangement result in a nuclear confrontation? First, it seems clear now (although not clear then) that even though Khrushchev often engaged in adventurism, he would not go to war when the opposition held an overwhelming logistic and atomic superiority. Second, evidence now suggests that had Dobrynin rejected the administration's terms, the president was prepared to make a concession designed to avert war: he would ask the United Nations to propose a withdrawal of the U.S. missiles from Turkey in exchange for the Soviet withdrawal of missiles from Cuba. Thus could the White House argue that the United Nations, not the United States, had made the explicit link between the missiles in Turkey and those in Cuba. But this step never became necessary. Dobrynin expressed satisfaction with the original terms and the next day made clear that the Soviet missiles would be withdrawn.

Thus, on Sunday, October 28, thirteen days after the first confirmation of missiles in Cuba, the crisis was over. Just two days before the United States would have launched an air strike, Khrushchev accepted Kennedy's assurance against an invasion of Cuba in exchange for on-site UN inspection of the withdrawal of Soviet missiles. As events would show, this verification never took place because of Castro's angry opposition, a stand that, in turn, released the United States from its pledge against invasion. Indeed, U.S. military forces remained on alert until November 20, when Castro at last approved the departure of the Soviet IL-28 bombers. Furthermore, Kennedy had conditioned his promise against invasion on the removal of "all offensive weapons" from Cuba and its pledge against committing "aggressive acts" in the hemisphere. Finally, recent documentation shows that the Soviets had nine short-range nuclear missiles specifically intended to stop a U.S. invasion of the island. Had the United States attempted such an operation, according to McNamara years afterward, there would have been "a ninety-nine percent probability" of nuclear war.

But these considerations now seem academic: the United States and the Soviet Union had narrowly averted the most serious threat to global peace since the period prior to World War II. Rusk later reminded Scali to "remember when you report this—that eyeball to eyeball, they blinked first." Rostow pointedly remarked that Khrushchev had relented only when "he felt the knife on his skin."

President Kennedy has received praise for courage under fire, yet many critics have raised searching questions about whether he might have averted the Cuban missile crisis through careful diplomacy. Castro incisively remarked that "if the United States had not been bent on liquidating the Cuban revolution, there would not have been an October crisis." The Kennedy administration made no effort to open discussions with the Castro regime before approving the disastrous course leading to the Bay of Pigs. Even had the invasion succeeded, it is doubtful that the certain unfavorable publicity surrounding U.S. involvement would have been worth the victory. Succeeding events do not substantiate the fear that Castro was spreading communism throughout Latin America. In fact, critics insist, the aggressive actions of the Kennedy administration were largely responsible for the new wave of anti-Americanism in the southern half of the hemisphere. Kennedy's critics also note other diplomatic breakdowns in the autumn of 1962. Washington's leaders made no attempt to talk privately with Cuba before the October confrontation despite this repeated suggestion during the Ex Comm meetings by two former ambassadors to the Soviet Union, Charles E. Bohlen and Llewellyn Thompson.

As early as October 25, columnist Walter Lippmann wondered why the president, in his private meetings the week before with Gromyko and Dobrynin, did not reveal the U-2 photos and warn of public disclosure should the Soviets refuse to withdraw the missiles. Finally, the president's televised ultimatum virtually ruled out the chances for compromise.

The irony is that a presidential administration composed of what writer Theodore H. White termed "action intellectuals" was determined to change the course of events, yet its members became themselves captives of those events. The central force clouding the administration's foreign policy was the Bay of Pigs disaster: President Kennedy refused to sustain another loss of prestige. If he relied on Penkovsky's stolen information about the Soviets' weaknesses in nuclear capability, his decision to do so nevertheless rested on a risk-filled gamble that the information was accurate and up to date. Kennedy thus engaged in a policy of brinkmanship much more dangerous than that pursued by the Eisenhower administration during the 1950s. Khrushchev, too, had pursued the same hard-line tactics and had failed either to redress the nuclear balance of power or to break the stalemate over Berlin. Fortunately, he chose to retreat. Economist John Kenneth Galbraith wrote afterward, "We were in luck, but success in a lottery is no argument for lotteries."

The Cuban missile crisis constituted the most dangerous series of events in the Cold War and for that reason led both powers to take steps designed to avoid another direct confrontation. To reduce the chances of miscalculation, President Kennedy installed a "hotline" that directly connected the White House and the Kremlin by a private teletype. He also worked toward an arms limitations agreement with the Soviet Union. To weaken Castro's rule, the United States banned travel to Cuba and prohibited international monetary exchange; the Soviets countered by increasing aid to Cuba. Despite Kennedy's directive against boasting of a U.S. victory in the missile crisis, the fact remained that the

Soviet Union had suffered a heavy blow to its prestige. Khrushchev had foolishly challenged the United States in an area vital to its security and where it held conventional military superiority. One Soviet official eerily commented, "Never will we be caught like this again."

The missile crisis had severe repercussions. It exposed the Soviet Union's nuclear inferiority and led to a program of Soviet military expansion, contributed to a change in its leadership that saw Khrushchev ousted from power in 1964, and encouraged the governments in both Moscow and Washington to turn toward indirect and less dangerous policies in the Third World. The Communist Chinese ridiculed Khrushchev's capitulation on Cuba, leading the Soviet premier to retort that if the United States was a "paper tiger," it had "nuclear teeth." The new premier, Alexei Kosygin, was less belligerent than his predecessor, making this an opportune moment for the United States to pursue détente, or a reduction of tensions, and at the same time exploit the growing Sino–Soviet rift. Cuba meanwhile remained a Soviet protectorate as nearly 17,000 Soviet soldiers and technicians stayed on the island. If the Monroe Doctrine was not dead as Khrushchev had charged, it suffered a near lethal blow.

Southeast Asia

While Cuba monopolized the attention of the Kennedy administration, concurrent problems in Laos and Vietnam continued to grow. Laos, a landlocked agricultural country, had become independent under the Geneva Accords of 1954 and soon assumed a neutral position in international affairs. Three years later, under Prince Souvanna Phouma, the nationalists established a coalition regime composed of neutralists and a former wartime resistance group, now Communist, known as the Pathet Lao ("Lao nation"). The Eisenhower administration countered with military assistance to the rightist Laotian army, which was concentrated in the towns, but the money did little to improve its performance in the field and in fact

contributed to the country's inflated economy and widespread graft. Yet there seemed no choice. Eisenhower wrote in his memoirs that "the fall of Laos to Communism would mean the subsequent fall—like a tumbling row of dominoes—of its still-free neighbors, Cambodia and South Vietnam and, in all probability, Thailand and Burma. Such a chain of events would open the way to Communist seizure of all Southeast Asia." Eisenhower considered the Laotian problem so serious that he did not even mention Vietnam to President-elect Kennedy during the transition briefing of January 19, 1961.

Americans attributed the struggle in Laos to communism. In 1958, the CIA worked with rightists in bringing down Phouma and installing a pro-American government clear of Pathet Lao representation. American military advisers arrived to stabilize the new government, but trouble continued. The Laotian government asked the United Nations for help, and matters calmed when the Security Council sent a team of inquiry. In August 1960, Phouma and the Pathet Lao regained control and soon received Soviet and North Vietnamese aid. But Phouma's regime collapsed again, forcing him to flee to Cambodia. Phouma later lamented, "The Americans say I am a Communist. All this is heartbreaking. How can they think I am a Communist? I am looking for a way to keep Laos non-Communist."

The Kennedy administration was also concerned that problems in Laos would spill into surrounding countries and spread communism throughout Southeast Asia. Guerrilla activities had intensified in both Laos and Vietnam by the spring of 1961, causing White House adviser Walt Rostow to urge the president to use counterinsurgency measures in restoring stability. In line with previous policy, Kennedy blamed the Communists for Laos's problems and supported the rightist regime as the basis of "a neutral and independent Laos." He stationed the Seventh Fleet in the South China Sea, had 500 marines helicoptered into Thailand, and ordered American soldiers to Okinawa to be ready for action.

The Cuban fiasco had influenced the president's thinking on Southeast Asia, making him more cautious than he might otherwise have been about intervening in Laos. "I just don't think we ought to get involved," Kennedy told Nixon, "particularly where we might find ourselves fighting millions of Chinese troops in the jungles." Furthermore, he could not justify taking action in Laos, which was thousands of miles away, when he had not done so in Cuba, only ninety miles from American shores. The president, however, could not appear weak in Laos after the Bay of Pigs episode and made a show of force by ordering several hundred U.S. military advisers in Laos to don military uniforms. That same month of April, the Soviet Union supported the president's call for a cease-fire, but the Pathet Lao refused to follow the Soviet lead. Kennedy asked the Joint Chiefs of Staff if U.S. combat troops could deliver a victory in Laos. Although most of the commanders were skeptical, the chair, General Lyman Lemnitzer, argued that "if we are given the right to use nuclear weapons, we can guarantee victory." When someone asked what "victory" entailed, Kennedy called the meeting to a close.

In May, fourteen governments gathered in Geneva for more than a year before they could devise a solution to the Laotian problem. Arguments focused on the guidelines for a coalition government composed of the three dissident groups—neutralists, rightists, and leftists. The conference took place against a background of trouble because the Pathet Lao was close to forcing the rightists out of Laos and into neighboring Thailand. In June, the delegations reached an agreement: Laos would be neutral and could neither enter military pacts nor house foreign military bases, and its government would be a coalition of neutralists, rightists, and leftists, with Phouma as premier. The situation was not auspicious: the Pathet Lao held two-thirds of the country and was armed with Soviet weapons. The Kennedy administration continued to send military materiel to the rightists, justifying the aid on the basis of a believed North Vietnamese infiltration of upper Laos.

Then a strange mixture of events took place: Washington's decision to negotiate over Laos seemed to combine with the embarrassment of the Bay of Pigs fiasco to transform Vietnam into a symbol of the U.S. stand against communism. "At this point we are like the Harlem Globetrotters," Bundy remarked, "passing forward, behind, sidewise, and underneath. But nobody has made a basket yet." Elections had not taken place in Vietnam in 1956, as stipulated in the Geneva Accords of 1954, partly because the Eisenhower administration believed that Ho Chi Minh would win but also because, as the North Vietnamese Communists later asserted, Communist China preferred a divided, weaker Vietnam and cut off military aid to the Hanoi government to ensure compliance. In either case, a succession

Ngo Dinh Diem
South Vietnamese President Diem reviews air force officers shortly after two pilots assaulted the presidential palace in February 1962. *(National Archives, Washington, D.C.)*

of terrorist activities had transpired in the south during the late 1950s that Americans thought Communist instigated. The United States, it appeared, was about to undergo another test of will.

Controversy still exists over the ensuing troubles in Vietnam. Were they due more to Diem's repressive regime than to alleged North Vietnamese aggression? Or was the fighting of a civil war between northern and southern Vietnamese made worse by U.S. intervention? The truth seems to be that the Vietcong waged a revolutionary war—or people's war—which was a domestic conflict aimed at building a new social order based on changing the state or government. Thus, the guerrilla warfare of the early 1960s constituted the first stage in a process beginning with terror and violence, graduating into a transitional mixture of guerrilla tactics and conventional warfare, and then climaxing with a popular uprising supported by all-out military operations. But this more accurate description of the war remained unclear to Washington, at least in part attributable to the confusion stemming from the Kennedy administration's inconsistent policies. The State Department implied that South Vietnam was a separate nation (contrary to the Geneva Accords of 1954) when it recommended U.S. aid to counter the believed threat from outside forces (in line with the same Geneva agreements). Several French and U.S. writers, however, called it a local rebellion against Diem that the Hanoi government indeed aided by 1960, but only after Ho Chi Minh's former Vietminh forces in the south sought his assistance against U.S. intervention in Vietnamese domestic affairs.

The U.S. interpretation of the conflict in Vietnam was vital in justifying assistance to the south because under the SEATO Treaty, the White House had guaranteed the Senate that it would not become involved in the domestic troubles of Southeast Asian nations. If the North Vietnamese had intervened in the south as either Beijing's or Moscow's agent, of course, such action would have constituted

a threat from the outside. Rusk was convinced that this was the case. Reflecting the Munich mentality regarding the dangers of appeasement, he argued that Communist China had incited the war in Vietnam as part of its effort to control all Asia. Thus, Diem's Army of the Republic of Vietnam (ARVN) had become locked in a guerrilla war with the Chinese-assisted Vietcong (Vietnamese Communists), who in December 1960 became the military arm of the National Liberation Front (NLF) in South Vietnam and had gained control over nearly all rural areas. The primary threat was therefore *external*, requiring the United States to honor its SEATO obligations. A recently published history of the war by the People's Army of Vietnam tends to support the U.S. case. It asserts that Hanoi's leaders played an earlier part in promoting the Vietcong's military development in the south. Even then, the Hanoi government claimed it was helping fellow Vietnamese in a civil war that did not concern the United States. This was the heightened military activity in the south that Kennedy faced when he became president in 1961.

The Kennedy administration soon made Vietnam a test of America's will to combat communism. In January, former OSS agent Edward Lansdale returned from an inspection of Vietnam with recommendations that the new president develop a counterinsurgency force to combat the Vietcong and that he maintain U.S. support for Diem. The following May, the president sent Vice President Lyndon B. Johnson on a fact-finding tour of Southeast Asia that focused on assuring Diem that negotiations over Laos did not imply the same approach to South Vietnam. If communism penetrated that region of the world, Johnson reported to Kennedy, the United States would have to "surrender the Pacific and take up our defenses on our own shores." The United States had to protect "the forces of freedom in the area." Such involvement could lead to "the further decision of whether we commit major United States forces to the area or cut our losses and withdraw should our efforts fail." Johnson urged "a clear-cut and strong program of action" in behalf of Diem—whom the vice president praised in his effusive Texas manner as the "George Washington of Vietnam" and the "Winston Churchill of Southeast Asia." Although never explaining how Diem's collapse would automatically strip the United States of its Pacific bases and threaten national security, Johnson exuded an Alamo mentality in warning of encirclement and insisting that the choice was either to "help these countries . . . or throw in the towel in the area and pull back our defenses to San Francisco and a 'Fortress America.'"

In response to Johnson's inquiry, Diem sought neither U.S. combat troops nor a bilateral treaty with the United States. Diem wanted more technical advisers and more U.S. aid but not U.S. soldiers. He already felt too closely identified with Americans. North Vietnamese propaganda continually berated him for consorting with the United States and fostering what Hanoi derided as "American-Diem imperialism." That same month, Kennedy sent another hundred military advisers and, in accordance with Lansdale's recommendation, 400 Green Berets to train the Vietnamese in counterinsurgency warfare. "If we can save Vietnam," Bundy declared, "we shall have demonstrated that the communist technique of guerrilla warfare can be dealt with."

Over the next few months, conflicting reports from Vietnam led the president to inquire deeper into the situation. Although Rusk and others argued that the south was in danger from the outside, U.S. intelligence agents claimed that nearly 90 percent of the 17,000 Vietcong in the south had come from South Vietnam itself. As the Joint Chiefs of Staff and the National Security Council considered sending combat troops, Kennedy dispatched two of his advisers to South Vietnam: Walt Rostow and General Maxwell Taylor. They returned in October with a dismal report. The South Vietnamese army seemed incapable of taking the offensive, but Diem still intended to maintain control over the grim

military situation. Rostow called for U.S. bombings of North Vietnam and joined Taylor in recommending an 8,000-person "logistic task force" of engineers, medical personnel, and infantry to assist the ARVN in closing North Vietnam's supply lines to the Vietcong in the south. The introduction of this thinly disguised combat unit, Taylor believed, would raise South Vietnamese morale by standing as a "visible symbol of the seriousness of American intentions." Indeed, these U.S. forces would provide an important source of military assistance if needed. To conceal their purpose, the Americans could arrive under the euphemistic title of a "flood control unit."

Kennedy, however, decided against sending combat forces to Vietnam no matter what garb or title they wore. Such a provocative move, he feared, would jeopardize the Laotian negotiations and escalate the war in Vietnam. Besides, as Kennedy trenchantly remarked, "The troops will march in; the bands will play; the crowds will cheer; and in four days everyone will have forgotten. Then we will be told we have to send in more troops. It's like taking a drink," he declared. "The effect wears off, and you have to take another." Instead, Kennedy compromised between negotiations and combat troops by approving Diem's call for more advisers. Yet he realized a further escalation might be necessary to save South Vietnam. By the end of 1961, over 3,000 U.S. military advisers were in South Vietnam, more than triple the number of a year before.

In December 1961, the U.S. military presence in Vietnam became increasingly visible. A U.S. carrier brought in four single-engine training planes, more than thirty helicopters, and 400 operations and maintenance personnel. Eventually, minesweepers and reconnaissance planes would arrive. Meanwhile, the Green Berets trained the South Vietnamese in guerrilla warfare and worked with Diem in establishing a "strategic hamlet" program intended to undermine the Vietcong's war effort. According to proponents, the program (similar to the agrovilles tried during the 1950s) would isolate the peasants by relocating them in bamboo stake encampments encircled by moats and soldiers and therefore deny the Vietcong any assistance, recruits, and places of refuge. Its greatest effects, however, were negative: the program failed to provide security along with promised medical, educational, and land reform benefits, and it tore peasants from their ancestral grounds and thereby allowed the Vietcong to assume the role of "liberators." The strategic hamlets nonetheless remained the heart of the counterinsurgency effort. Kennedy emphasized to Diem that "the campaign of force and terror now being waged against your people and your Government is supported and directed from the outside by the authorities at Hanoi." North Vietnam's actions had violated the Geneva Accords of 1954, the president explained, and the United States felt compelled to help South Vietnam.

Despite optimistic reports, the Vietnamese situation continued to deteriorate. McNamara visited Vietnam in the summer of 1962 and declared that "every quantitative measurement we have shows we're winning this war." A few months later, Rusk proclaimed that the war was coming to an end. Yet a Senate subcommittee had visited Southeast Asia and warned that a cut in U.S. aid would lead to domestic upheaval and the establishment of Chinese influence. The South Vietnamese, it appeared, could not win the war by themselves, although the subcommittee cautioned the administration against converting the conflict into "an American war, to be fought primarily with American lives." The United States, under "*present circumstances*," had no interests in Vietnam that justified sending combat troops.

In the spring of 1963, Diem's long-standing problems with the Buddhists erupted in a crisis that drew the United States deeper into South Vietnamese affairs. His Catholicism had long been a focal point of opposition from the Buddhists, who made up more than 80 percent of the country's population. But then Diem stirred up a wave of angry protests by prohibiting the Buddhists from flying their religious flags in commemorating Buddha's birth, and in May the government's forces, armed with clubs and guns, turned on 10,000 protesters in the city of Hué, killing nine in the melee. The following month, an elderly Buddhist monk protested the government's actions by having himself doused in gasoline and, as an American photographer and television crew recorded the grisly event (alerted beforehand by Buddhists), setting himself afire before horrified crowds in downtown Saigon. Madame Nhu, Diem's vitriolic sister-in-law and a former Buddhist, coldly dismissed such actions as "Buddhist barbecues," and her husband and Diem's closest confidant, Ngo Dinh Nhu, callously remarked that if more Buddhists wanted to immolate themselves, he would gladly furnish the gasoline and matches. "Let them burn," Madame Nhu added, "and we shall clap our hands." Nationwide raids on Buddhist pagodas followed, engineered by Nhu, whose own private and U.S.-trained Special Forces (Can Lao, or Vietnamese Bureau of Investigation) disguised themselves in army apparel and destroyed religious shrines, ransacked the pagodas, killed anyone who resisted, and arrested more than 1,400 Buddhists, including numerous children of Diem's own civilian and military officials. Diem, as advised by Nhu, blamed the Vietcong for the Buddhist unrest. The United States, however, was already disenchanted with Diem's domestic failures and began to cut back assistance in an effort to force him into reform programs.

The Kennedy administration still opposed a direct military involvement in South Vietnam, but it had come to realize that Diem was not the solution to the problem but the problem itself. The president told CBS newsman Walter Cronkite, "In the final analysis, it is their war. They are the ones who have to win or lose it. We can help them, give them equipment, send our men out there as advisers, but they have to win it." On another occasion, Kennedy explained that "strongly in

The Buddhist Crisis
The self-immolation of a Buddhist monk in Saigon in June 1963 brought worldwide focus to Diem's problems and moved the United States closer to government opposition elements in South Vietnam. *(Wide World Photos, New York)*

our mind is what happened in the case of China at the end of World War II, where China was lost. . . . We don't want that." Diem had not instituted democratic reforms in South Vietnam, as Americans had hoped. Indeed, nothing in his background suggested that he supported democracy. The "revolution" Diem envisioned called for the restoration of an imperial Vietnam that rested on his Chinese mandarin philosophy of personalist rule by a privileged and educated elite. Introverted, stubborn, cold, self-righteous, unwilling to compromise, and devoid of charisma, Diem had aroused deep resentment by ending longtime elections in the villages, brutally repressing his opposition, exploiting

the strategic hamlet program to establish greater control over the peasants, engaging in rampant nepotism, and rejecting U.S. advice as interference in domestic affairs. "No wonder the Vietcong looked like Robin Hoods when they began to hit the hamlets," a U.S. civilian official commented.

The American commitment became nearly irreversible in the autumn of 1963, when the Kennedy administration became identified with a conspiracy against Diem led by South Vietnamese army generals. Dissatisfied officers, headed by General Duong Van Minh, were angry over Nhu's attempt to affix blame for the pagoda raids on the army and notified the CIA in late August that he intended to have them executed and then negotiate away South Vietnam's independence by working out some sort of arrangement with Hanoi. They intended to overthrow Diem and wanted to know what the U.S. reaction would be. In a cable cleared by Kennedy, his newly arrived ambassador to Saigon, Henry Cabot Lodge, received instructions to persuade Diem to dismiss his brother Nhu from the regime. Should Diem refuse, the United States had to "face the possibility that Diem himself cannot be preserved." In that event, Lodge was to inform the generals that Diem no longer could count on U.S. aid and that they would receive "direct support in any interim period of breakdown of central government mechanism." Lodge was not to engage in the "active promotion of [a] coup" but "to identify and build contacts with possible alternative leadership as and when it appears." The cable found a receptive reader. Lodge had been appalled by the pagoda raids, and when Diem did not remove Nhu, the U.S. embassy dispatched a CIA operative to assure the generals of White House support if their scheme succeeded—but *no* assistance if it failed. The generals became uncertain about their prospects and called off the coup.

The next month was a confusing period for the Kennedy administration. McNamara wanted to investigate Diem's chances for winning the war and sent a mission of inquiry to South Vietnam led by General Victor Krulak of the Defense Department and State Department official Joseph Mendenhall. But this effort only underlined the administration's dilemma. Krulak was optimistic about the war, Mendenhall was disenchanted with Diem, and Kennedy was frustrated with both emissaries. "You two did visit the same country, didn't you?" he asked with exasperation.

By late October, the generals had revived their plot to overthrow Diem and this time went through with it. On November 1, again with the tacit approval of the Kennedy administration, they staged their coup, afterward killing both Diem and his brother Nhu. Suddenly, the reality of the Vietnamese situation hit the White House. On learning of the murders of Diem and Nhu, Kennedy, according to Taylor, "leaped to his feet and rushed from the room with a look of shock and dismay on his face which I had never seen before."

The U.S. promise of support to the generals made it an accomplice in the assassinations. The president and Lodge denied culpability by reasoning that the making of a coup centered on its planning and implementation and *not* its encouragement. But the administration had promoted the coup at its most critical point—

In this document, approved by President Kennedy, the United States supported Diem's overthrow as a last resort.

Telegram from Department of State to Ambassador Henry Cabot Lodge in South Vietnam, August 24, 1963, U.S. Department of State, *Foreign Relations of the United States, 1961–1963, Vol. 3: Vietnam January–August 1963* (Washington, D.C.: Government Printing Office, 1991), 628.

It is now clear that whether military proposed martial law or whether [Ngo Dinh] Nhu [South Vietnamese Premier Ngo Dinh Diem's brother] tricked them into it, Nhu took advantage of its imposition to smash pagodas with police and [Colonel Le Quang] Tung's Special Forces loyal to him, thus placing onus on military in eyes of world and Vietnamese people. Also clear that Nhu has maneuvered himself into commanding position.

US Government cannot tolerate situation in which power lies in Nhu's hands. Diem must be given chance to rid himself of Nhu and his coterie and replace them with best military and political personalities available.

If, in spite of all of your efforts, Diem remains obdurate and refuses, then we must face the possibility that Diem himself cannot be preserved.

when its leaders needed the final assurance of support. The White House had signaled its approval by reducing aid to Diem in October, and Lodge had assured the generals of American support if they overthrew the regime. In either directly or indirectly participating in the coup, all generals shared guilt, as did the United States.

The White House was also directly responsible for the welfare of the South Vietnamese government. The new regime in Saigon was civilian in form only. Power remained in the military, but the leaders promised elections and a free press, released political prisoners, and made much-needed changes in the war effort. When the United States extended recognition to the new government and restored full trade relations, the impression grew that it had been involved in the assassinations. The presence of nearly 17,000 U.S. military advisers and 8,000 other Americans in South Vietnam seemed proof of a deepening commitment. Shortly after Diem's death, the NLF in North Vietnam proposed negotiations with Saigon aimed at a cease-fire, to be followed by "free general elections" designed to establish a "national coalition government composed of representatives of all forces, parties, tendencies, and strata of the South Vietnamese people." Although some ARVN officials seemed interested, the United States opposed the offer. By November 1963, U.S. prestige was on the line: both the successes and the failures of the South Vietnamese government now belonged to the United States.

But Kennedy was assassinated that same November of 1963, leaving questions about the potential direction of U.S. policy on Vietnam. Several signs suggest that he had matured in office because of the Cuban and Berlin war scares and would have worked for a more cooperative relationship with the Soviet Union that might have allowed a greatly reduced U.S. involvement in Vietnam. Indeed, the president had authorized the drafting of a plan that called for a phased withdrawal beginning in December 1963 and resulting by the end of 1965 in a return to the

U.S. military levels of January 1961. He never advocated a total withdrawal, however. In one of his last press conferences, Kennedy asserted that "for us to withdraw from that effort would mean a collapse not only of South Vietnam but Southeast Asia. So we are going to stay there." Rusk, one of the president's most trusted confidants, insisted that during their many conversations Kennedy never discussed withdrawing from Vietnam. But Rusk had told the truth only in a technical sense. The president repeatedly resisted pressure from within his administration to send combat troops and was prepared to reduce the U.S. commitment to numbers that complied with the Geneva Accords of 1954 while Americans trained the ARVN to deal with the situation.

Whatever the outcome might have been, the U.S. commitment had greatly expanded by the end of November 1963. Eisenhower's less than a thousand so-called advisers in Vietnam had grown to nearly 17,000 under Kennedy and included a large number of Special Forces who were steadily enlarging their role in the war while maintaining the fiction that they were only advising. Indeed, seventy-five Americans had died in combat by the end of 1963. Furthermore, the ARVN now had napalm and defoliants to go with all other types of war materiel coming regularly from the United States. And, most of all, the major share of the blame for the Diem coup had fallen on the White House, despite its insistence that the regime had self-destructed. The U.S. involvement in Vietnam was now much more extensive and volatile than when Kennedy came into office.

A Mixed Verdict

It remains unclear whether by late 1963 Kennedy had moved away from his initial foreign policy—built on challenge and response—and toward one emphasizing diplomacy and restraint. In June, he delivered an address at American University, asserting that all peoples could live together peacefully and calling for disarmament and an end to the Cold War. Yet the nation's military arsenal had increased dramatically at every level during his brief presidency. Shortly after his June speech, in fact, the president tried to revive support for NATO, which had entered a state of decline largely because of Europe's fears brought on by the two superpowers' near clash over Cuba. Kennedy was especially worried that France would assert leadership on the continent, a concern justified by its recently developed nuclear device and an alliance with West Germany. De Gaulle had already blocked Britain's membership in the European Common Market because, he declared, "it would appear as a colossal Atlantic community under American domination and direction." West Germany's decision to remain closely aligned with the United States was due partly to Kennedy's efforts. In June 1963, he appeared before the Berlin Wall and defiantly challenged defenders of communism to "come to Berlin." To a wildly enthusiastic audience, he concluded with these famous words: "All free men, wherever they may live, are citizens of Berlin, and, therefore, as a free man, I take pride in the words 'Ich bin ein Berliner'" ("I am a Berliner").

Even while Kennedy made provocative statements in Berlin that sent a clear warning to the Kremlin, he softened their impact by supporting negotiations over other important matters. The following August, the United States, Britain, and the Soviet Union signed the Nuclear Test Ban Treaty, bringing a close to testing underwater and in the atmosphere and outer space. Although its prohibitions did not apply to underground testing because of continued opposition to on-site inspection, this ban was the first arms limitations agreement between the nations after nearly two decades of attempts. Despite Kennedy's declaration that the pact was a great step forward on "the path of peace," the Joint Chiefs of Staff agreed to it only after McNamara assured them of a big program of underground tests and presented a written promise to begin nuclear tests anew in the atmosphere "should they be deemed essential to our national security." In October, the United States sold $250 million of surplus wheat and flour to the

Soviet Union and Eastern Europe. Tensions seemed to have eased by the end of 1963.

Despite the Bay of Pigs fiasco followed by the Cuban missile crisis, the Kennedy administration did not give up its obsession with removing Castro. Recent research suggests that the White House had secretly moved toward an accommodation with Castro, yet the documents show more conclusively that it remained so angry with him for allowing the implantation of Soviet missiles that invasion and assassination remained on the Kennedy agenda and outweighed any chances for normalizing relations. Indeed, the very day Kennedy died in Dallas, a CIA operative was meeting in Paris with a Cuban dissident about assassinating Castro.

On Vietnam, the rhetoric had receded, yet it still seems doubtful that had Kennedy lived, he would have taken the monumental step of fully withdrawing. It would have been a sharp reversal indeed for him to have shed the past in such a bold manner. Had not President Truman prevailed over Communist forces in both Greece and South Korea? Kennedy's administration had already paid the price of hesitation at the Bay of Pigs. It had then compromised in Laos. He could not abandon Vietnam, although he leaned toward a phased withdrawal that would have greatly alleviated tensions in Southeast Asia. The hard truth is that much of Kennedy's Vietnam policy resulted from his failures in Cuba and Laos. His sense of U.S. righteousness remained, and he remained supportive of world order and stability in preventing the spread of totalitarian rule by either the Soviets or the Communist Chinese. Kennedy, like others before and after him, remained a hostage of the Cold War. If his administration never developed a plan for winning the war in Vietnam, it certainly refused to be the one to lose that war.

Selected Readings

Abel, Elie. *The Missile Crisis.* 1968.
Allison, Graham T. *Essence of Decision: Explaining the Cuban Missile Crisis.* 1971; 2nd ed., with Philip Zelikow, 1999.

Ambrose, Stephen E. *Nixon: The Education of a Politician, 1913–1962.* 1987.

——, and Douglas G. Brinkley. *Rise to Globalism: American Foreign Policy since 1938.* 8th ed., 1997.

Ball, George W., and Douglas B. Ball. *The Passionate Attachment: America's Involvement with Israel 1947 to the Present.* 1992.

Baritz, Loren. *Backfire: A History of How American Culture Led Us into Vietnam and Made Us Fight the Way We Did.* 1985.

Bass, Warren. *Support Any Friend: Kennedy's Middle East and the Making of the U.S.-Israel Alliance.* 2003.

Beisner, Robert L. *Dean Acheson: A Life in the Cold War.* 2006.

Ben-Zvi, Abraham. *Decade of Transition: Eisenhower, Kennedy, and the Origins of the American-Israeli Alliance.* 1998.

Beschloss, Michael R. *The Crisis Years: Kennedy and Khrushchev, 1960–1963.* 1991.

Bill, James A. *George Ball: Behind the Scenes in U.S. Foreign Policy.* 1997.

Bird, Kai. *The Color of Truth: McGeorge Bundy and William Bundy, Brothers in Arms: A Biography.* 1998.

Blair, Anne E. *Lodge in Vietnam: A Patriot Abroad.* 1995.

Blight, James G., Bruce J. Allyn, and David A. Welch. *Cuba on the Brink: Castro, the Missile Crisis, and the Soviet Collapse.* 2002. Revised ed. Originally published in 1993.

——, and David A. Welch. *On the Brink: Americans and Soviets Reexamine the Cuban Missile Crisis.* 1989.

Brands, H. W. *The Devil We Knew: Americans and the Cold War.* 1993.

Brigham, Robert K. *Guerrilla Diplomacy: The NLF's Foreign Relations and the Viet Nam War.* 1999.

Brinkley, Douglas. *Dean Acheson: The Cold War Years, 1953–71.* 1992.

Brugioni, Dino A. *Eyeball to Eyeball.* 1992.

Burchett, Wilfred. *Catapult to Freedom: The Survival of the Vietnamese People.* 1978.

Busch, Peter. *All the Way With JFK? Britain, the U.S., and the Vietnam War.* 2003.

Buttinger, Joseph. *Vietnam: A Dragon Embattled.* 2 vols., 1967.

Buzzanco, Robert. *Vietnam and the Transformation of American Life.* 1999.

Cate, Curtis. *The Ides of August: The Berlin Wall Crisis, 1961.* 1978.

Catton, Philip E. *Diem's Final Failure: Prelude to America's War in Vietnam.* 2002.

Catudal, Honor, M. *Kennedy and the Berlin Wall Crisis: A Case Study in U.S. Decision Making.* 1980.

Chayes, Abram. *The Cuban Missile Crisis: International Crises and the Role of Law.* 1974.

Cobbs, Elizabeth H. *All You Need Is Love: The Peace Corps and the Spirit of the 1960s.* 1998.

Cohen, Warren I. *America's Response to China: An Interpretive History of Sino-American Relations.* 2000.

——. *Dean Rusk.* 1980.

Conboy, Kenneth, and Dale Andradé. *Spies and Commandos: How America Lost the Secret War in North Vietnam.* 2000.

Costigliola, Frank. "The Failed Design: Kennedy, de Gaulle, and the Struggle for Europe." *Diplomatic History* 8 (1984): 227–51.

——. *France and the United States: The Cold Alliance since World War II.* 1992.

Currey, Cecil B. *Edward Lansdale: The Unquiet American.* 1988.

Davidson, Phillip B. *Vietnam at War: The History, 1946–1975.* 1988.

Detzer, David. *The Brink: Cuban Missile Crisis, 1962.* 1979.

DiLeo, David L. *George Ball, Vietnam, and the Rethinking of Containment.* 1991.

Dinerstein, Herbert S. *The Making of a Missile Crisis: October 1962.* 1976.

Duiker, William J. *The Communist Road to Power in Vietnam.* 1981.

——. *Ho Chi Minh.* 2000.

——. *U.S. Containment Policy and the Conflict in Indochina.* 1994.

Ernst, John. *Forging a Fateful Alliance: Michigan State University and the Vietnam War.* 1998.

Evans, John W. *The Kennedy Round in American Trade Policy.* 1973.

Fairlie, Henry B. *The Kennedy Promise.* 1973.

Fall, Bernard B. *Anatomy of a Crisis: The Laotian Crisis of 1960–1961.* 1969.

Ferrell, Robert H. *Ill-Advised: Presidential Health and Public Trust.* 1992.

Firestone, Bernard J. *The Quest for Nuclear Stability: John F. Kennedy and the Soviet Union.* 1982.

Fischer, Fritz. *Making Them Like Us: Peace Corps Volunteers in the 1960s.* 1998.

FitzGerald, Frances. *Fire in the Lake: The Vietnamese and the Americans in Vietnam.* 1972.

FitzSimons, Louise. *The Kennedy Doctrine.* 1972.

Frankel, Max. *High Noon in the Cold War: Kennedy, Khrushchev, and the Cuban Missile Crisis.* 2004.

Freedman, Lawrence. *Kennedy's Wars: Berlin, Cuba, Laos, and Vietnam.* 2000.

Fursenko, Aleksandr, and Timothy Naftali. *Khrushchev's Cold War: The Inside Story of an American Adversary.* 2006.

———. *"One Hell of a Gamble": Khrushchev, Castro, and Kennedy, 1958–1964.* 1997.

Gaddis, John L. *The Cold War: A New History.* 2005.

———. *The Long Peace: Inquiries into the History of the Cold War.* 1987.

———. *Russia, the Soviet Union, and the United States: An Interpretive History.* 2nd ed., 1990.

———. *Strategies of Containment: A Critical Appraisal of Postwar American National Security Policy.* 1982; rev. ed., 2005.

———. *We Now Know: Rethinking Cold War History.* 1997.

Gaiduk, Ilya V. *The Soviet Union and the Vietnam War.* 1996.

Garthoff, Raymond L. *Reflections on the Cuban Missile Crisis.* 1987.

———, Barton J. Bernstein, Marc Trachtenberg, and Thomas G. Paterson. "Commentaries on 'An Interview with Sergo Mikoyan,'" in "The Cuban Missile Crisis Reconsidered." *Diplomatic History* 14 (1990): 223–56.

Gelb, Leslie H., and Richard K. Betts. *The Irony of Vietnam: The System Worked.* 1979.

George, Alice L. *Awaiting Armageddon: How Americans Faced the Cuban Missile Crisis.* 2003.

Giglio, James N. *The Presidency of John F. Kennedy.* 1991.

Goh, Evelyn. *Constructing the U.S. Rapprochement with China, 1961–1974: From "Red Menace" to "Tacit Ally."* 2005.

Goodman, Allan E. *The Lost Peace: America's Search for a Negotiated Settlement of the Vietnam War.* 1978.

Gray, William G. *Germany's Cold War: The Global Campaign to Isolate East Germany, 1949–1969.* 2003.

Greenstein, Fred I., and Richard H. Immerman. "What Did Eisenhower Tell Kennedy about Indochina? The Politics of Misperception." *Journal of American History* 79 (1992): 568–87.

Greiner, Bernd. "The Soviet View: An Interview with Sergo Mikoyan," in "The Cuban Missile Crisis Reconsidered." *Diplomatic History* 14 (1990): 205–21.

Gurtov, Melvin. *The United States against the Third World.* 1974.

Halberstam, David. *The Best and the Brightest.* 1972.

———. *Ho.* 1971.

———. *The Making of a Quagmire: America and Vietnam during the Kennedy Era.* Rev. ed., 1984.

Hallin, Daniel C. *The "Uncensored War": The Media and Vietnam.* 1986.

Hammer, Ellen J. *A Death in November: America in Vietnam, 1963.* 1987.

Hammond, William H. *Reporting Vietnam: Media and Military at War.* 1998.

Harrison, James P. *The Endless War: Fifty Years of Struggle in Vietnam.* 1982.

Heath, Jim F. *Decade of Disillusionment: The Kennedy-Johnson Years.* 1975.

Hendrickson, Paul. *The Living and the Dead: Robert McNamara and Five Lives of a Lost War.* 1996.

Herring, George C., Jr. *America's Longest War: The United States and Vietnam, 1950–1975.* 4th ed., 2002.

———, ed. *The Pentagon Papers: Abridged Edition.* 1993.

———. "The Vietnam War." In John M. Carroll and George C. Herring, eds., *Modern American Diplomacy,* 165–81. 1986.

Hersh, Seymour M. *The Dark Side of Camelot.* 1997.

Hershberg, James G. "Before 'The Missiles of October': Did Kennedy Plan a Military Strike against Cuba?" *Diplomatic History* 14 (1990): 163–98.

Hess, Gary R. *Vietnam and the United States: Origins and Legacy of War.* 1998.

Higgins, Trumbull. *The Perfect Failure: Kennedy, Eisenhower, and the CIA at the Bay of Pigs.* 1987.

Hilsman, Roger. *To Move a Nation: The Politics of Foreign Policy in the Administration of John F. Kennedy.* 1967.

Jablon, Howard. *David M. Shoup: A Warrior against War.* 2005.

Jacobs, Seth. *America's Miracle Man in Vietnam: Ngo Dinh Diem, Religion, Race, and U.S. Intervention in Southeast Asia.* 2004.

———. *Cold War Mandarin: Ngo Dinh Diem and the Origins of America's War in Vietnam, 1950–1963.* 2006.

Jones, Howard. *The Bay of Pigs.* 2008.

———. *Death of a Generation: How the Assassinations of Diem and JFK Prolonged the Vietnam War.* 2003.

Kahin, George McT. *Intervention: How America Became Involved in Vietnam.* 1986.

——, and John W. Lewis. *The United States in Vietnam.* Rev. ed., 1969.

Kaiser, David E. *American Tragedy: Kennedy, Johnson, and the Origins of the Vietnam War.* 2000.

Kalb, Madeleine G. *The Congo Cables: The Cold War in Africa—From Eisenhower to Kennedy.* 1982.

Kaplowitz, Donna R. *Anatomy of a Failed Embargo: U.S. Sanctions against Cuba.* 1998.

Karnow, Stanley. *Vietnam: A History.* Rev. ed., 1991.

Kattenburg, Paul M. *The Vietnam Trauma in American Foreign Policy, 1945–1975.* 1980.

Kendrick, Alexander. *The Wound Within: America in the Vietnam Years, 1945–1974.* 1974.

Kennedy, Robert F. *The Thirteen Days: A Memoir of the Cuban Missile Crisis.* 1969.

Kern, Montague, Patricia W. Levering, and Ralph B. Levering. *The Kennedy Crisis: The Press, the Presidency, and Foreign Policy.* 1983.

Kochavi, Noam. *A Conflict Perpetuated: China Policy during the Kennedy Years.* 2002.

Kolko, Gabriel. *Anatomy of a War: Vietnam, the United States, and the Modern Historical Experience.* 1985.

Krenn, Michael L. *Black Diplomacy: African Americans and the State Department, 1945–1969.* 1999.

Krepinevich, Andrew F., Jr. *The Army and Vietnam.* 1986.

LaFeber, Walter. *America, Russia, and the Cold War, 1945–1996.* 8th ed., 1997.

Langguth, A. J. *Our Vietnam: The War, 1954–1975.* 2000.

Langley, Lester D. "Latin America from Cuba to El Salvador." In John M. Carroll and George C. Herring, eds., *Modern American Diplomacy,* 183–200. 1986.

Latham, Michael E. "Ideology, Social Science, and Destiny: Modernization and the Kennedy-Era Alliance for Progress." *Diplomatic History* 22 (1998): 199–229.

——. *Modernization as Ideology: American Social Science and "Nation Building" in the Kennedy Era.* 2000.

Levering, Ralph B. *The Cold War: A Post-Cold War History.* 1994; rev. ed., 2005.

Levinson, Jerome, and Juan de Onís. *The Alliance That Lost Its Way.* 1970.

Lewy, Guenter. *America in Vietnam.* 1978.

Lind, Michael. *Vietnam the Necessary War: A Reinterpretation of America's Most Disastrous Military Conflict.* 1999.

Logevall, Fredrik. *Choosing War: The Lost Chance for Peace and the Escalation of War in Vietnam.* 1999.

Maclear, Michael. *The Ten Thousand Day War, Vietnam: 1945–1975.* 1981.

Maga, Timothy P. *John F. Kennedy and New Frontier Diplomacy, 1961–1963.* 1994.

——. *John F. Kennedy and the New Pacific Community, 1961–63.* 1990.

Mahoney, Richard D. *JFK: Ordeal in Africa.* 1983.

Mangold, Tom, and John Penygate. *The Tunnels of Cu Chi: The Untold Story of Vietnam.* 1985.

Mann, Robert. *A Grand Illusion: America's Descent into Vietnam.* 2001.

May, Ernest R., and Philip D. Zelikow, eds. *The Kennedy Tapes: Inside the White House during the Cuban Missile Crisis.* 1997.

McMahon, Robert J. *The Cold War on the Periphery: The United States, India, and Pakistan.* 1994.

——. *The Limits of Empire: The United States and Southeast Asia since World War II.* 1999.

McNamara, Robert S. *In Retrospect: The Tragedy and Lessons of Vietnam.* 1995.

Merrill, Dennis. *Bread and the Ballot: The United States and India's Economic Development, 1947–1963.* 1990.

Miroff, Bruce. *Pragmatic Illusions: The Presidential Politics of John F. Kennedy.* 1976.

Morgan, Joseph G. *The Vietnam Lobby: The American Friends of Vietnam, 1955–1975.* 1997.

Morley, Morris. *Imperial State and Revolution: The United States and Cuba, 1952–1985.* 1987.

Munton, Don, and David A. Welch. *The Cuban Missile Crisis: A Concise History.* 2007.

Nash, Philip. *The Other Missiles of October: Eisenhower, Kennedy, and the Jupiters, 1957–1963.* 1997.

Neese, Harvey, and John O'Donnell, eds. *Prelude to Tragedy: Vietnam, 1960–1965.* 2001.

Nesbitt, Francis N. *Race for Sanctions: African Americans Against Apartheid, 1946–1994.* 2004.

Newman, John M. *JFK and Vietnam: Deception, Intrigue, and the Struggle for Power.* 1992.

Noer, Thomas J. *Cold War and Black Liberation: The United States and White Rule in Africa, 1948–1968.* 1985.

Oliver, Kendrick. *Kennedy, Macmillan, and the Nuclear Test-Ban Debate, 1961–1963.* 1998.

Olson, James S., and Randy Roberts. *Where the Domino Fell: America and Vietnam, 1945–1995.* 3rd ed., 1995.

Palmer, Dave R. *Summons of the Trumpet: A History of the Vietnam War from a Military Man's Viewpoint.* 1978.

Parmet, Herbert S. *JFK: The Presidency of John F. Kennedy.* 1983.

Paterson, Thomas G., ed. *Kennedy's Quest for Victory: American Foreign Policy, 1961–1963.* 1989.

Pérez, Louis A., Jr. *Cuba and the United States: Ties of Singular Intimacy.* 1997.

Poole, Peter. *The United States and Indochina from FDR to Nixon.* 1973.

Porter, Gareth. *Perils of Dominance: Imbalance of Power and the Road to War in Vietnam.* 2005.

Prados, John. *The Blood Road: The Ho Chi Minh Trail and the Vietnam War.* 1999.

———. *Presidents' Secret Wars: CIA Pentagon Covert Operations from World War II through the Persian Gulf.* 1996.

Prochnau, William. *Once upon a Distant War: David Halberstam, Neil Sheehan, Peter Arnett—Young War Correspondents and Their Early Vietnam Battles.* 1995.

Rabe, Stephen G. *The Most Dangerous Area in the World: John F. Kennedy Confronts Communist Revolution in Latin America.* 1999.

Reeves, Richard. *President Kennedy: Profile of Power.* 1993.

Reeves, Thomas C. *A Question of Character: A Life of John F. Kennedy.* 1991.

Rice, Gerald T. *The Bold Experiment: JFK's Peace Corps.* 1985.

Risse-Kappen, Thomas. *Cooperation among Democracies: The European Influence on U.S. Foreign Policy.* 1995.

Rotter, Andrew J. *Comrades at Odds: The United States and India, 1947–1964.* 2000.

Rusk, Dean. *As I Saw It.* 1990.

Rust, William J. *Kennedy in Vietnam.* 1985.

Schaffer, Howard B. *Chester Bowles—New Dealer in the Cold War.* 1993.

———. *Ellsworth Bunker: Global Troubleshooter, Vietnam Hawk.* 2003.

Schecter, Jerrold L., and Peter S. Deriabin. *The Spy Who Saved the World: How a Soviet Colonel Changed the Course of the Cold War.* 1992.

Schick, Jack M. *The Berlin Crisis, 1958–1962.* 1971.

Schlesinger, Arthur M., Jr. *A Thousand Days: John F. Kennedy in the White House.* 1965.

Schoenbaum, David. *The United States and the State of Israel.* 1993.

Schoenbaum, Thomas J. *Waging Peace and War: Dean Rusk in the Truman, Kennedy, and Johnson Years.* 1988.

Schoutz, Lars. *Beneath the United States: A History of U.S. Policy toward Latin America.* 1998.

Schulzinger, Robert D. *A Time for War: The United States and Vietnam, 1941–1975.* 1997.

Schwab, Orrin. *Defending the Free World: John F. Kennedy, Lyndon Johnson, and the Vietnam War, 1961–1965.* 1998.

Seaborg, Glenn T., and Benjamin S. Loeb. *Kennedy, Khrushchev, and the Test Ban.* 1981.

Shaplen, Robert. *The Lost Revolution: The U.S. in Vietnam, 1946–1966.* 1966.

Shapley, Deborah. *Promise and Power: The Life and Times of Robert McNamara.* 1993.

Sheehan, Neil. *A Bright Shining Lie: John Paul Vann and America in Vietnam.* 1988.

———, et al., eds. *The Pentagon Papers.* 1971.

Shultz, Richard H., Jr. *The Secret War against Hanoi: Kennedy's and Johnson's Use of Spies, Saboteurs, and Covert Warriors in North Vietnam.* 1999.

Slusser, Robert M. *The Berlin Crisis of 1961: Soviet-American Relations and the Struggle in the Kremlin, June–November 1961.* 1973.

Smith, R. B. *An International History of the Vietnam War. Vol. 2: The Kennedy Strategy.* 1985.

Sorensen, Theodore C. *Kennedy.* 1965.

Spanier, John W. *American Foreign Policy since World War II.* 14th ed., 1998.

Stern, Sheldon. *Averting 'the Final Failure': John F. Kennedy and the Secret Cuban Missile Crisis Meetings.* 2003.

Stevenson, Richard W. *The Rise and Fall of Détente: Relaxations of Tensions in U.S.-Soviet Relations, 1953–1984.* 1985.

Summers, Harry G., Jr. *On Strategy: A Critical Analysis of the Vietnam War.* 1982.

Szulc, Tad, and Karl E. Meyer. *The Cuban Invasion: The Chronicle of a Disaster.* 1962.

Taylor, Sandra C. *Vietnamese Women at War: Fighting for Ho Chi Minh and the Revolution.* 1999.

Tomes, Robert R. *Apocalypse Then: American Intellectuals and the Vietnam War, 1954–1975.* 1998.

Trachtenberg, Marc. *A Constructed Peace: The Making of the European Settlement, 1945–1963.* 1999.

Truong Nhu Tang. *A Vietcong Memoir.* 1985.

Tucker, Spencer C. *Vietnam.* 1999.

Turley, William S. *The Second Indochina War: A Short Political and Military History, 1954–1975.* 1986.

Turner, Karen G. *Even the Women Must Fight: Memories of War from North Vietnam.* 1998.

Ulam, Adam B. *The Communists: The Story of Power and Lost Illusions, 1948–1991.* 1992.

———. *The Rivals: America and Russia since World War II.* 1971.

U.S. Information Agency. "Back from the Brink: The Correspondence between President John F. Kennedy and Chairman Nikita S. Khrushchev on the Cuban Missile Crisis of Autumn 1962." *Problems of Communism* 41 (1992).

Vandenbroucke, Lucien S. *Perilous Options: Special Operations as an Instrument of U.S. Foreign Policy.* 1993.

Walton, Richard J. *Cold War and Counterrevolution: The Foreign Policy of John F. Kennedy.* 1972.

Weiner, Tim. *Legacy of Ashes: The History of the CIA.* 2007.

Weissman, Stephen. *American Foreign Policy in the Congo, 1960–1964.* 1974.

Welch, Richard E., Jr. *Response to Revolution: The United States and the Cuban Revolution, 1959–1961.* 1985.

Weldes, Jutta. *Constructing National Interests: The United States and the Cuban Missile Crisis.* 1999.

Wenger, Andreas. *Living with Peril: Eisenhower, Kennedy, and Nuclear Weapons.* 1997.

Westad, Odd Arne. *The Global Cold War: Third World Interventions and the Making of Our Times.* 2006.

White, Mark J. *The Cuban Missile Crisis.* 1996.

———, ed. *Kennedy: The New Frontier Revisited.* 1998.

———. *Missiles in Cuba: Kennedy, Khrushchev, Castro, and the 1962 Crisis.* 1997.

Winters, Francis X. *The Year of the Hare: America in Vietnam, January 25, 1963–February 15, 1964.* 1997.

Wyatt, Clarence R. *Paper Soldiers: The American Press and the Vietnam War.* 1993.

Wyden, Peter. *Bay of Pigs: The Untold Story.* 1979.

———. *Wall: The Inside Story of Divided Berlin.* 1989.

Young, Marilyn B. *The Vietnam Wars, 1945–1990.* 1991.

Zeiler, Thomas W. *Dean Rusk: Defending the American Mission Abroad.* 2000.

Zhai, Qiang. *China and the Vietnam Wars, 1950–1975.* 2000.

Zhang, Shu Guang. *Economic Cold War: America's Economic Embargo against China and the Sino-Soviet Alliance, 1949–1963.* 2001.

CHAPTER 5

Containment in Collapse: Johnson and Vietnam, 1963–1969

The Tragedy of LBJ

"Let us continue," the tall and robust Texan declared as he assumed his new duties as president in November 1963. In an attempt to retain the Kennedy effect, Lyndon B. Johnson promised to work toward implementing his predecessor's domestic and foreign programs and persuaded several members of his staff to remain. McNamara, Rusk, Bundy, Rostow, and others stayed until many of them could no longer support the new administration's policies. Try as he did, the new president could not capture the "magic" of the Kennedy years. Part of the reason was personal. Johnson came from a barren and poor south-central sector of Texas and was boisterous, crude, and often ill-mannered. Whereas Kennedy had gone to Harvard and engaged in numerous extracurricular activities that did not include politics, Johnson attended a local teachers' college and, while there, developed an inordinate skill in campus politics that he carried throughout his life. Kennedy was glamorous; Johnson was political.

As president, Johnson lived in the shadow of the wealthy and cultured Massachusetts-bred Kennedy, never managing to throw off the image of wheeler-dealer politician and riverboat gambler that resulted from decades in Congress. The new president was grounded in the humanitarian principles of Franklin D. Roosevelt's New Deal program and implemented a similarly ambitious range of domestic reforms under the label of the "Great Society." Johnson was hard-working, demanding, stubborn, egotistic, self-righteous, and exceedingly sensitive to criticism. He expected total loyalty and used his famous "Johnson treatment" to achieve that objective. According to a fellow Texan, "Lyndon got me by the lapels and put his face on top of mine and he talked and talked and talked. I figured it was either getting drowned or joining." Benjamin Bradlee of the *Washington Post* once declared that when administered the "Johnson treatment, you really felt as if a St. Bernard had licked your face for an hour, had pawed you all over."

Johnson's central tragedy was his acceptance of unrestrained assumptions about containment that led him relentlessly deeper into Vietnam. Meanwhile, he tried to maintain the costly Great Society—and not by taking the politically unpopular route of raising taxes but by borrowing huge sums of money that ultimately led to rampant inflation. Like Truman, Eisenhower, and Kennedy, Johnson became

President Johnson and Advisers on Vietnam
Left to right: Ambassador Henry Cabot Lodge, Secretary of State Dean Rusk, President Johnson, Secretary of Defense Robert McNamara, and Undersecretary of State George Ball. *(Lyndon B. Johnson Library, Austin, Texas)*

the captive of appeasement and McCarthyism, and like them he was convinced that communism posed a threat in nearly every trouble spot in the world. Most social revolutions in the Third World, Johnson believed, were Communist tinged if not inspired, necessitating a rigid U.S. stand for order and stability.

As Cuba had been the supreme test of Kennedy's will, Vietnam became that of Johnson's. "I want to leave the footprints of America there," he declared. "We're going to turn the Mekong [River delta] into a Tennessee Valley" and democratize the surrounding area. In fact, however, he gave U.S. Vietnam policy a greater military orientation than Kennedy had conceived. By mid-1965,

the United States found itself locked in a major land war in Southeast Asia that escalated into a bloody stalemate and made democracy one of its many casualties. Johnson, meanwhile, encountered other issues that often became intertwined with the Vietnam involvement and starkly showed the dangers in overcommitment: problems in the Dominican Republic; secret attempts to reestablish diplomatic relations with Cuba; de Gaulle's challenges to U.S. influence in Southeast Asia and Europe; riots in Panama over the U.S. presence; the timeless Arab–Israeli struggle in the Middle East; the effort to promote détente with the Soviet Union, built on nuclear proliferation treaties and other measures; and

Soviet repression of an uprising in Czechoslovakia similar to that in Hungary. The Vietnam War brought down Johnson's presidency in 1968 and ushered in Republican Richard M. Nixon and the promise of a new direction in foreign policy.

"Americanizing" the War in Vietnam, 1963–1965

The deepening involvement of the United States in Vietnam ultimately consumed the Johnson presidency. Although the president considered Vietnam a "raggedy-ass fourth-rate country," he feared that if the United States failed to "stop the Reds in South Vietnam, tomorrow they will be in Hawaii, and next they will be in San Francisco." Along with former Kennedy advisers, he was convinced that Communist China sought to control Southeast Asia and that North Vietnam's aggressions were part of that objective. "I am not going to lose Vietnam," Johnson promised soon after becoming chief executive. "I am not going to be the president who saw Southeast Asia go the way China went." But Johnson, also like Kennedy, had no strategy for victory, except to escalate involvement while avoiding defeat.

Johnson firmly believed that U.S. military strength would resolve the problems in Vietnam, but he failed to recognize that since its peak year of power in 1945, the United States had been steadily losing its capacity to influence global events. The world's power structure was becoming increasingly diffused as the Soviet Union grew in military strength, as NATO members acted more independently, and as the Third World stepped up demands for a greater voice in international affairs. But the most baffling dilemma was how the small country of North Vietnam could handcuff the mighty United States, denying it a military victory ensured by every resource statistic available. After Diem's assassination in November 1963, the pressure had grown for the establishment of a coalition government and a neutral stance for Vietnam in international affairs. But Johnson insisted on victory. The "neutralization of South Vietnam," he declared, "would only be another name for a Communist takeover." To the new South Vietnamese leader, General Duong Van Minh, he wrote, "The United States will continue to furnish you and your people with the fullest measure of support in this bitter fight."

Despite U.S. aid, the situation in Vietnam continued to unravel in early 1964. General Minh had fallen in a military coup in January that resulted in a long period of political uncertainty complicated by repeated changes in leadership and rapid intensification of the war. The South Vietnamese raided North Vietnam and hit its sources of supplies in Laos, but by April the Vietcong had gained control of most Vietnamese villages in the south and had taken the offensive. Indeed, the Vietcong had established a checkpoint a bare fifty miles outside Saigon, forcing the city to become a veritable armed fortress, complete with barbed wire and concrete sentry barricades bolstered by sandbags and heavily armed soldiers. In retrospect, it seems clear that the most crucial ingredient in achieving victory was not the field of battle but popular political support gained by satisfying the legitimate needs of the peasantry. The Washington government, however, emphasized the use of superior firepower to stop a Communist threat believed to originate from Hanoi—an approach that had the adverse impact of alienating the surrounding peoples, whose support the South Vietnamese government could least afford to lose.

In the autumn of 1964, the Johnson administration encountered a series of incidents in the Gulf of Tonkin off North Vietnam that led to a more direct involvement in the war. The U.S. destroyer *Maddox* was engaged in a top-secret program of electronic espionage (a "DeSoto Mission" that was part of "Operation 34-A," actually developed under Kennedy in 1962 though not approved until January 1964) in the Gulf of Tonkin when, on the morning of August 1, it underwent fire by several North Vietnamese torpedo

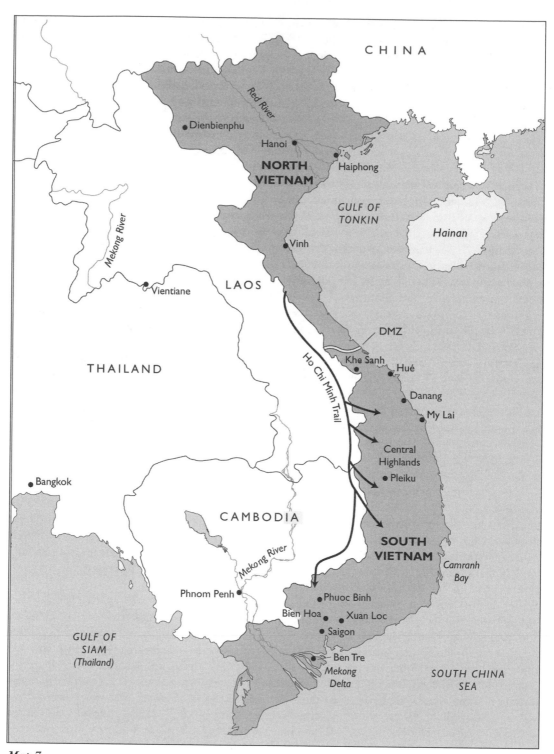

Map 7

North and South Vietnam. America's involvement in Indochina began in 1950 during the Korean War, escalated with combat troops in 1965, and officially ended with a cease-fire agreement in 1973 that the Nixon administration termed "peace with honor." (*Source: author*)

boats in an area close to the offshore islands but nonetheless in international waters. American air fire drove away the assailants, but Johnson was outraged and ordered the *Maddox* to return to those waters, accompanied by another destroyer, the *C. Turner Joy*. On the evening of August 4, according to U.S. accounts, North Vietnamese torpedo boats fired on both vessels, then cruising sixty miles at sea, but failed to hit either one.

Considerable doubt exists about the authenticity of a second attack. The Hanoi government had admitted to the first assault on the *Maddox* as retaliation for U.S. collaboration with recent South Vietnamese commando raids, but it vehemently denied the second incident. Indeed, U.S. commanders were probably mistaken about whether an attack had actually occurred. The fog was thick and the night so black that one sailor termed it "darker than the hubs of Hell." Star shells had failed to light up the sky because they exploded above the low and extremely dense cloud cover. One pilot flying directly overhead, James B. Stockdale, held what he called "the best seat in the house from which to detect boats" and saw "no boat wakes, no ricochets, no torpedo wakes—nothing but the black sea and American firepower." The Americans had fired into the blackness for several hours, during which time the "enemy" had appeared only on sonar and radar, and the captain of the *Maddox* later admitted that both detection systems were unreliable in such

General Nguyen Khanh
In the summer of 1964, South Vietnamese General Khanh alarmed the White House by calling for attacks on North Vietnam. *(National Archives, Washington, D.C.)*

Senator J. William Fulbright and President Johnson
Fulbright listens to the president in the White House in late July 1965. *(Lyndon B. Johnson Library, Austin, Texas)*

bad weather. Because there had been no "visual sightings," he strongly urged a "complete evaluation" before taking action. Each U.S. vessel could have been firing at the wakes of the other. Johnson later put it more directly to an aide: "Hell, those dumb stupid sailors were just shooting at flying fish."

But the truth became academic because the Johnson administration had already decided to upgrade its involvement in the war and take it north, as later shown in *The Pentagon Papers*, a pillaged collection of secret Defense Department documents on Vietnam that the *New York Times* published in 1971. This material suggests that the president and his advisers had been frustrated with South Vietnam's war effort and were looking for an opportunity to justify direct U.S. action. In a matter of hours, the Washington administration, without launching an investigation, au-

thorized a "firm, swift retaliatory [air] attack" on North Vietnamese torpedo boat bases. American planes thus took the war into the north for the first time by bombing North Vietnamese torpedo boat bases and oil supply depots at Vinh, which lay well above South Vietnam's upper border at the seventeenth parallel. Johnson appeared on television that same evening—August 4, 1964—to inform Americans of recent events in the Gulf of Tonkin and accuse North Vietnam of "open aggression on the high seas." Although the SEATO Treaty pledged only *consultation* about military aid, the president asserted that it was the duty of the United States to help any member "requesting assistance in defense of its freedom." Johnson relied on his old friend Senator J. William Fulbright, chair of the Foreign Relations Committee, to steer a resolution through Congress asking for authorization to use military force. But the president did not reveal to either Fulbright or Congress that the *Maddox* had been involved in espionage and raiding expeditions, pointing instead to official reports that the vessel had been on patrol in international waters and had not provoked an attack.

After virtually no debate in either chamber, Congress took the first major step toward "Americanizing" the conflict when it approved the Gulf of Tonkin Resolution on August 7—three days following the U.S. assault on Vinh. By a unanimous vote in the House and the wide margin of eighty-eight to two in the Senate (the only negative votes coming from Ernest Gruening of Alaska and Wayne Morse of Oregon), Congress empowered the president to "take all necessary measures to repel any armed attacks against the forces of the United States and to prevent further aggression." A high-ranking official in the State Department called the resolution "a functional equivalent of a declaration of war." Johnson, however, had no intention of broadening the war effort. He still thought it possible to achieve success in Vietnam through what his advisers called "graduated overt pressures."

The administration believed the Tonkin Resolution would accomplish both foreign and domestic objectives. It would show the North Vietnamese that Americans were determined to uphold their commitments in Southeast Asia. The White House would also appear resolute and in control, which would help Johnson fend off his challenger in the presidential contest of 1964, conservative Republican Barry Goldwater of Arizona. In the heat of the campaign, Johnson attacked Goldwater for wanting to escalate the war by authorizing air strikes on North Vietnam and reviving MacArthur's claim that there was no substitute for victory. In response to the Republican campaign slogan, "In your heart, you know he's right," the Democrats countered with, "In your heart, you know he might." Such an unreasoned approach, the president warned, could lead to the use of U.S. fighting forces. He pledged against sending Americans "nine or ten thousand miles away from home to do what Asian boys ought to be doing for themselves."

This resolution supported by President Lyndon B. Johnson was the closest the United States came to declaring war on North Vietnam.

The Gulf of Tonkin Resolution, August 7, 1964, U.S. Department of State, *Bulletin*, August 29, 1964, 268.

Whereas naval units of the Communist regime in Vietnam, in violation of the principles of the Charter of the United Nations and of international law, have deliberately and repeatedly attacked United States naval vessels lawfully present in international waters, and have thereby created a serious threat to international peace; and

Whereas these attacks are part of a deliberate and systematic campaign of aggression that the Communist regime in North Vietnam has been waging against its neighbors and the nations joined with them in the collective defense of their freedom; and

Whereas the United States is assisting the peoples of southeast Asia to protect their freedom and has no territorial, military or political ambitions in that area, but desires only that these peoples should be left in peace to work out their own destinies in their own way: Now, therefore, be it

Resolved by the Senate and House of Representatives of the United States of America in Congress assembled,

That the Congress approves and supports the determination of the President, as Commander in Chief, to take all necessary measures to repel any armed attack against the forces of the United States and to prevent further aggression.

Walt Rostow and President Johnson
Rostow and the president confer in the Oval Office in March 1967. *(Lyndon B. Johnson Library, Austin, Texas)*

Perhaps out of fear of a Goldwater victory or because of the Tonkin Resolution, the Hanoi government had secretly offered to negotiate, but the president refused. As a former White House aide later explained, "The very word *negotiations* was anathema in the Administration." National security affairs adviser Walt Rostow belligerently insisted that "it is on this spot that we have to break the liberation war—Chinese type. If we don't break it here, we shall have to face it again in Thailand, Venezuela, elsewhere." In a statement that expressed the administration's central feeling, Rostow pronounced Vietnam "a clear testing ground for our policy in the world." There were other considerations. The country's strategic location, some believed, was vital to the U.S. position in Southeast Asia. Neither the Johnson administration nor the leaders of the Army of the Republic of Vietnam (ARVN) in Saigon were interested in establishing a coalition government. Nor would Johnson subject himself to charges of appeasement and the possible loss of Vietnam—especially on election eve.

Johnson won a massive victory in November, and soon afterward his administration made a highly secretive decision to use air power in Vietnam. The objectives were mixed. Some officials thought that bombings would raise morale in South Vietnam; others hoped that aerial attacks would reduce suspected North Vietnamese army infiltration from the north and perhaps even cause the Hanoi regime to suspend its aid to the Vietcong.

The decision to bomb did not come without opposition. Undersecretary of State George Ball strongly objected to such tactics as pointless in dealing with a primitive industrial country and useless in trying to close the infinite number of infiltration routes into the south that wound through the dense jungles of Laos and Cambodia as the "Ho Chi Minh Trail." It was certain, Ball said, to unite *all* Vietnamese on the ground against the intruder from the sky. Intelligence reports likewise warned that air assaults would have minimal effect on the fighting in South Vietnam. The Vietcong were an insurgency group with no air force, he reminded his colleagues, and bombings aimed at their believed whereabouts on the ground would alienate the area's inhabitants and result in political calamity. Some observers pointed out that if the Vietcong's tools were primarily nonmilitary—propaganda, terror, and political subversion—then the key to victory lay in winning the people's support. Bombings lacked that potential. One U.S. artilleryman noted that in World War II "there were real targets to aim at—enemy artillery or fortresses or fortified positions or massed enemy-troop formations or even bridges." But in Vietnam, such targets did not exist. Artillery fire "did nothing but kill a lot of innocents and alienate us from those we were supposedly trying to help." By implication, bombing would have the same effect—except on a wider scale. Ball warned that the United States would find it impossible to control events in the midst of military escalation. "Once on the tiger's back," he prophetically declared, "we cannot be sure of picking the place to dismount."

But these counterarguments did not change the direction of the Johnson administration, and by the end of the month it had secretly adopted a bombing program that lay midway between all-out assaults and nothing at all—what one adviser proudly called a "carefully orchestrated bombing attack" on North Vietnam. Proponents of the new strategy dismissed the fears of a widened war with the assertion that restrained bombing raids would not endanger North Vietnam's existence and thus would furnish no grounds for a Chinese intervention. Air assaults would also allow the South Vietnamese government a "breathing spell and opportunity to improve." Communist China's recent development of a nuclear device made it imperative to protect South Vietnam, and, according to a telling argument presented by some in the White House, the use of air power would greatly diminish the chances of having to send U.S. combat troops. Although the bombing decision turned out to be one of the most monumental moves in the war, it came with surprisingly little confidence in its impact. Presidential adviser William Bundy noted that

bombing offered "at least a faint hope of really improving the Vietnamese situation."

On the night of February 6, 1965, Vietcong forces provided the Johnson administration with a reason for implementing its bombing program when they attacked the huge U.S. army barracks and air base at Pleiku in central South Vietnam, inflicting more than a hundred U.S. casualties that included nine dead. National security adviser McGeorge Bundy, then on an investigative mission in Saigon, rushed to the scene. He joined two others there—the U.S. ambassador to South Vietnam, General Maxwell Taylor, and the commander of U.S. forces, General William Westmoreland of the Military Assistance Command, Vietnam (MACV)—in calling for instant retaliation. As fate would have it, Johnson authorized air strikes on North Vietnam at precisely the time that the new Soviet premier after Khrushchev's ouster, Alexei Kosygin, was in Hanoi—perhaps discussing whether to increase military aid. The president's need for a show of force, however, overrode the risk of creating a confrontation with the Soviets. "We have kept our guns over the mantel and our shells in the cupboard for a long time now," Johnson declared. "I can't ask our American soldiers out there to continue to fight with one hand behind their backs."

The attack on Pleiku had thus provided the pretext rather than the cause for U.S. bombing operations that grew into a massive campaign known as "Rolling Thunder." McGeorge Bundy later remarked that "Pleikus are like streetcars," suggesting that if that incident had not occurred, another one would have come along soon. Within twelve hours of the Vietcong attack, the first of nearly fifty U.S. jets penetrated North Vietnamese airspace and raided military installations above the seventeenth parallel. Initially referred to as "Flaming Dart," the air raids graduated from individual retaliatory missions to a sustained bombing campaign by the summer of 1965 that lasted until the end of the U.S. involvement in the war in 1973. In the course of eight years, Rolling Thunder dropped 8 million tons of bombs on the whole of Vietnam—four times the amount used in World War II. Besides hitting key military targets, the bombs eventually struck Hanoi, Haiphong (with Soviet vessels in the harbor), and the railroad from Hanoi to China, inflicting damage just ten miles outside China's borders.

Despite the pilots' claims that they hit military targets with "surgical" accuracy, their bombing expeditions ultimately became indiscriminate and inadvertently included civilian centers. Still, this was not enough for the hard-line Air Force Chief of Staff, General Curtis LeMay. "We are swatting flies when we should be going after the manure pile." To counter the effects of the bombings, the North Vietnamese moved urban civilians to the countryside; spread out industrial and storage centers, often placing them in caves or underground; and dug thousands of miles of tunnels (many there since the Vietminh's war against the French) for transportation and living purposes. United Nations Secretary-General U Thant urged an end to the bombing, and French President Charles de Gaulle ignored his own country's past plundering of Vietnam in calling it "detestable" for "a great nation to ravage a small one." The United States became subject to the charge of atrocity as up to a thousand Vietnamese civilians a week were added to casualty lists. Within the United States, Americans were shocked by the apparent suddenness of the decision to bomb North Vietnam. Some wondered whether the United States might not be the aggressor.

The bombings escalated the war in another way: recently declassified documents suggest that the U.S. decision to bomb above the seventeenth parallel made the administration's charge of North Vietnamese interference in the south a self-fulfilling prophecy. Rolling Thunder proved integral to the first military involvement of North Vietnamese army regulars (People's Army of Vietnam [PAVN]) in May 1965. The PAVN quickly numbered 6,500 and fought with the Vietcong guerrillas in the war.

The growing emphasis on bombing had another unforeseen and bitterly ironic effect: whereas the Johnson administration had counted on the new strategy to rule out the need for ground forces, U.S. soldiers now became necessary to protect air bases from Vietcong assaults. Thus did the administration find itself in the anomalous position of needing to send troops to protect an air offensive intended to avoid the use of troops. General Taylor understood the necessity of defending such air bases, but he warned about the dire implications of such a move. "Once we brought any troops in, that was the nose of the camel. Never would we know how many were enough." Furthermore, the troop introduction raised another danger: Americans could not be sure which Vietnamese were Vietcong, whereas the Vietcong would have no trouble identifying their enemy.

In February 1965, the president gave in to Westmorcland's requests for protection of the air base at Danang and ordered two battalions of marines, accompanied by tanks and eight-inch howitzers, to South Vietnam. The highly publicized arrival of 3,500 marines near Danang on March 8 (Westmoreland had wanted a dramatic "re-enactment of Iwo Jima") further Americanized the conflict. "When we marched into the rice paddies on that damp March afternoon," according to Marine Lieutenant Philip Caputo in his highly acclaimed autobiographical account *A Rumor of War*, "we carried, along with our packs and rifles, the implicit convictions that the Viet Cong would be quickly beaten and that we were doing something altogether noble and good." Less than a week after their landing, an equally ebullient Johnson spoke to an assistant about the U.S. offer of economic aid to the Mekong. Patting his knee, the president declared that "Old Ho can't turn that down."

Although U.S. forces were at first restricted to patrol duty, Westmoreland soon enlarged their role and ultimately completed the job of Americanizing the war. "The first troops were invited in to protect our air bases," he de-

America at War
U.S. Marine engaged in counterinsurgency action near Danang in March 1965. *(National Archives, Washington, D.C.)*

clared. "Now once those troops were at those bases, it made no sense at all to have them dig in and go strictly on the defensive." They soon engaged in "search-and-destroy" missions that more deeply alienated the populace and paradoxically diminished chances for winning the war, almost in direct relation to their military success. Taylor supported the use of U.S. combat troops, but he warned of the inherent danger of taking the war away from the ARVN. "There was every tendency," he asserted, "to push the little brown men to one side" and proclaim, "Let us go do it."

Surprisingly, the Johnson administration thought it could conceal the steady escalation of the war from Americans and others outside the country. Its goal of imperceptibly widening the war rested on a policy of gradualness intended to avoid a confrontation with either Communist China or the Soviet Union. Johnson also wanted to prevent a vicious congressional debate over Vietnam that would, in the president's words, destroy "the woman I really loved—the Great Society." The White House efforts were largely unsuccessful. A growing chorus of protests against the war came from the *New York Times*, numerous university students, and leading Democratic senators such as Frank Church of Idaho, Mike Mansfield of Massachusetts, and George McGovern of South Dakota. Outside the United States, UN Secretary-General U Thant of

Burma (now Myanmar) called for a negotiated end to the war, as did Britain, Canada, and seventeen neutralist nations.

The expanded involvement of the United States in Vietnam developed out of a strange mixture of the olive branch and the sword. In early April 1965, Johnson delivered a speech at Johns Hopkins University in which he warned that "the appetite of aggression is never satisfied" and declared that the United States had a "promise to keep." The nation's primary stipulation for peace was "an independent South Vietnam—securely guaranteed and able to shape its own relationships to all others—free from outside interference—tied to no alliance—a military base for no other country." Once peace was restored, he added, the United States would provide $1 billion for

the economic development of the Mekong Delta. "We want nothing for ourselves—only that the people of South Vietnam be allowed to guide their own country in their own way." Johnson warned of "the deepening shadow of Communist China" and reaffirmed the U.S. commitment. Failure to take action would lead to a "Red Asia" and a dangerous shift in the global balance of power. "Let no one think for a moment that retreat from Vietnam would bring an end to the conflict. The battle would be renewed in one country and then another. . . . We must say in southeast Asia—as we did in Europe—in the words of the Bible: 'Hitherto shalt thou come, but no further.'"

The next day a reply came from Hanoi that both mystified and angered the White House. The North Vietnamese government de-

U.S. Soldiers on Search-and-Destroy Mission
U.S. Marines in rice paddies looking for Vietcong. *(National Archives, Washington, D.C.)*

manded that the United States sever military ties with Saigon, withdraw from South Vietnam and allow it to become neutralized, guarantee no "foreign interference" in the reunification of the Vietnams, and accept the establishment of a coalition government based on the National Liberation Front's social, political, and economic reform program. Furthermore, the United States had to stop the bombing before peace talks could begin. With the United States committed to an independent, non-Communist South Vietnam and with the North Vietnamese determined to unify the country under their lead, the differences between the antagonists in the war were nonnegotiable.

Revolution in the Dominican Republic

While the bombing went on, a problem in the Dominican Republic suddenly interjected itself into the concerns of the Johnson administration, the successful resolution of which doubtless contributed to its decision to adopt even stronger military measures in Vietnam. The crisis grew out of a leftist revolution in the spring of 1965 that the White House considered Communist-inspired. The goals and methods of the United States were the same there as in Vietnam: halt the spread of communism by intervening with military force to uphold domestic stability. After a brutal and murderous dictatorship of more than thirty years, Dominican President Rafael Trujillo (trained by U.S. Marines) was assassinated with CIA weapons by dissidents in 1961, and the following year the islanders elected liberal reformer Dr. Juan Bosch as president. Although a military coup forced Bosch into exile less than a year later, his leftist supporters mounted an insurrection against the military regime in April 1965 that brought on civil war. "Men and women like this," warned the U.S. ambassador to the Dominican Republic, John Bartlow Martin, "have nowhere to go except to the Communists." Military action by Washington seemed necessary to prevent the establishment of another Castro-like regime in the Caribbean.

Johnson quickly dispatched over 20,000 troops to support a conservative government and thereby safeguard U.S. interests on the island. Having decided against first consulting either the United Nations or the Organization of American States (OAS), he defended his action in a nationwide address over television on April 28. The soldiers were to not only restore order and bring citizens home, the president explained, but also deal with a new menace. The Dominican revolution had taken a Communist turn, an argument he buttressed with a dubious list of over fifty "identified and prominent Communist and Castroite leaders" among the rebels. Another Cuba seemed likely. "We don't intend to sit here in our rocking chair with our hands folded and let the Communists set up any governments in the Western Hemisphere." Lest there be doubt about his determination, he reiterated his stand in May in a statement later referred to as the "Johnson Doctrine": "American nations cannot, must not, and will not permit the establishment of another Communist government in the Western Hemisphere."

Despite bitter opposition in the United States and Latin America, the American soldiers remained and predictably became enmeshed in the Dominican conflict. Many critics claimed that the U.S. action violated the OAS Charter, which stipulated that "no State or group of States had the right to intervene, directly or indirectly, for any reason whatever, in the internal or external affairs of any other State." Johnson countered with an argument that had a highly questionable foundation in fact: "People trained outside the Dominican Republic are seeking to gain control." Senator Fulbright doubted that the Communist danger was real and denounced the intervention as the work of hard-line *anti*-Communists who had seized control of U.S. foreign policy. In an observation that perhaps applied to numerous instances outside the hemisphere, the influential chair of the Foreign Relations Committee declared that Americans had become "the prisoners of the Latin American oligarchs who are engaged in a vain attempt to preserve the status quo—reactionaries who habitually use the term *communist* very loosely, in part . . . in a calculated effort to scare the United States into supporting their selfish and discredited aims."

The United States finally turned to the OAS as a way out of the imbroglio. In early May, the American foreign ministers' deputies met in Washington, where after a week of debate the United States narrowly won the two-thirds support needed (despite the opposition of the larger states) to establish a five-nation OAS Inter-American Peace Force. Most U.S. soldiers could now leave, although some stayed with the force as it tried to build a new regime composed of military and civilian leaders.

Although the Dominican intervention had been costly in credibility and prestige, the Johnson administration claimed a victory in blocking the installation of a leftist president. The unilateral action of the United States, however, had violated a number of assurances given to Latin America as early as Franklin D. Roosevelt's Good Neighbor policy and as late as John F. Kennedy's Alliance for Progress. In June 1966, moderate rightists, led by Joaquín Balaguer, defeated Bosch for the presidency. Bosch bitterly asserted that his had been "a democratic revolution smashed by the leading democracy of the world." Johnson, however, remained convinced that his forceful actions had prevented a Communist takeover in the Dominican Republic and that the same resolute action in Vietnam could bring similar results.

Continued Escalation in Vietnam

Meanwhile, the war in Southeast Asia threatened to escalate again as the governments in

Nguyen Cao Ky and President Johnson
The president conferring with the vice president of South Vietnam in early February 1966. *(Lyndon B. Johnson Library, Austin, Texas)*

both Saigon and Washington adopted harder positions. For nearly a week in May 1965, the United States called off the bombing to encourage negotiations, but with no results. In June, Saigon's government came under the control of the flamboyant and dashingly attired Air Marshal Nguyen Cao Ky, who had fought with the French against the Vietminh during the First Indochinese War. Ky became premier, and his cohort, the ruggedly capable and less pretentious General Nguyen Van Thieu, became commander-in-chief of the armed forces. Although Americans attested to Thieu's abilities, they could not do the same with Ky. The CIA dismissed Ky as grossly irresponsible and concerned only about "drinking, gambling and chasing women." It was "the bottom of the barrel, absolutely the bottom of the barrel," one of Johnson's advisers recalled. Less than a week before Ky took over, the war took another dramatic turn upward: U.S. soldiers received authority to engage in full combat duty.

In the pivotal month of July, Johnson, without congressional approval, made an open-ended commitment to a ground war in Asia by assuring Westmoreland of as many troops as he needed. By the end of the year, U.S. combat troops in Vietnam numbered more than 184,000, a figure that more than doubled a year later and continued growing. The U.S. economy could support a guns-and-butter policy, he declared. In justifying the momentous decision to inject so many more Americans, McNamara first admitted that such a heavy troop presence would make it more difficult to withdraw later on; yet, in a statement that revealed the administration's failure to develop a cohesive strategy for conducting the war, he added that the move might "stave off defeat in the short run and offer a good chance of producing a favorable settlement in the longer run."

Thus had the administration Americanized the war by bombings that offered a slim chance of improving the situation and by combat troops who might promote an acceptable resolution of the war. The effort had become an all-out war of attrition that sought to pass the "enemy's threshold of pain" by the graduated use of superior manpower and resources. Not the least among the considerations underlying this objective was the widespread belief that the Vietnamese were racially and materially inferior rather than cunning, wily, and amazingly resilient. In retrospect, however, such a monumental decision conjures up the dark words of British writer Rudyard Kipling, which were openly displayed in U.S. clubs and bars in South Vietnam during the war. In his famous piece titled "The Ballad of East and West," Kipling included these piercing lines:

> Now it is not good for the Christian's health
>   to hustle the Aryan [Asian in Vietnam]
>   brown
> For the Christian riles, and the [Asian] smiles
>   and weareth the Christian down;
> And the end of the fight is a tombstone white
>   with the name of the late deceased
> And the epitaph drear: "A fool lies here who
>   tried to hustle the East."

That same month of July, several key Great Society programs had reached critical junctures in the legislative process, leading some writers to believe that Johnson feared he would lose South Vietnam at precisely the time he needed leverage to force through his reform program at home. Therefore, the argument goes, the president raised the level of involvement in Vietnam out of both domestic and foreign considerations. Whatever the truth, it appears that without a coherent military strategy, the administration simply followed the day-to-day developments in an effort to wear down the enemy while avoiding defeat. His decision to escalate the involvement in Vietnam transformed the conflict into an American war, narrowing succeeding options and making his nation's commitment virtually unlimited.

As the fighting in Vietnam intensified in 1965, the United States defended its involvement on several grounds. First and foremost, it sought to halt outside "aggression" through military action while shoring up a rapidly deteriorating South Vietnam. The State Department argued that the Tonkin Resolution

McNamara and Westmoreland
Secretary of Defense McNamara in South Vietnam to discuss General Westmoreland's call for more than 100,000 U.S. troops. *(National Archives, Washington, D.C.)*

was a natural extension of the SEATO Treaty, by which signatory nations agreed to aid members whose "peace and safety" were in jeopardy. The Johnson administration, like Kennedy's, believed that North Vietnam had infiltrated South Vietnam, thereby constituting an armed attack requiring protection by SEATO's members. In addition, Article 51 of the UN Charter allowed "collective self-defense" and justified U.S. action. Furthermore, a failure to protect South Vietnam would breach a moral duty, setting an example injurious to U.S. prestige and security throughout the world. There was "light at the end of the tunnel" and victory "just around the corner," according to McNamara after vis-its to Vietnam in 1965 and 1966. Conflicting reports came from Hanoi's Premier Pham Van Dong, who solemnly warned, "There's no light at the end of the tunnel." Washington's most dangerous assumption was that a mere show of U.S. military strength would shatter the Vietcong and end the war.

Growing numbers of Americans questioned the wisdom of the nation's commitment to South Vietnam. In view of the widening rift between Moscow and Beijing (as best shown by the rising number of border clashes between Soviet and Chinese troops in early 1966), the traditional argument of halting a Kremlin-directed Communist monolith suddenly rang hollow. Questions arose about containment's open-ended premise that vital U.S. interests encompassed every area of the world threatened by communism—which meant that the United States was in danger of over-extending itself. The United States had assumed the uncomfortable position of opposing all social revolutions simply because they opened the door for Communist subversion; the only safe situation seemed to be the status quo, which meant upholding stability even at the price of reform. By the mid-1960s, the justification for U.S. involvement in Vietnam, begun by the Truman administration in 1950, had to come from other sources. The United States could not pull out of Vietnam without losing prestige and honor. The first intervention necessitated a deeper commitment, which in turn grew because of the first involvement: the longer the United States remained in Vietnam, the longer it had to stay.

Seeds of "Vietnamization," 1966–1969

Continuation of the bombings had serious repercussions inside the United States because it tended to divide Americans into two broadly defined camps: the "doves," a mixed group of liberals and others who wanted a negotiated withdrawal, and the "hawks," primarily right-wing Republicans and conservative Democrats who advocated victory through increased military force. Protest demonstrations grew into a firestorm as the escalated involvement forced major cutbacks in foreign aid, threw the nation's budget into disarray by draining the dollar and feeding inflation, and threatened the Great Society's reform programs. "Teach-ins" began in 1965 at the University of Michigan and spread to other places of learning as faculty members opposed to the war held informal classes that analyzed the reasons for U.S. involvement. Many youths either burned their draft cards and chanted "Hell no, we won't go" or avoided the draft by going to Canada or to jail. "Hey, hey, LBJ, how many kids have you killed today?" chanted demonstrators around the White House as they called

the United States immoral, racist, and imperialist. The U.S. government, they bitterly complained, was killing reform at home and innocents abroad. The presidency was becoming imperial in callously ignoring the wishes of Congress and the people. Involvement in Vietnam, the doves argued, was wrecking the Western alliance and undercutting U.S. authority and prestige. Furthermore, it was unconstitutional because Congress had not declared war. Withdrawal from Vietnam was the only solution.

Although the hawks accused the doves of being led by Communists, criticism of the administration's Vietnam policies came from all parts of the nation and were attributable to factors beyond mere propaganda. The most vocal opponents of the war included Senators Fulbright, Mansfield, and Morse; containment architect George F. Kennan; journalist Walter Lippmann; civil rights leader Dr. Martin Luther King Jr.; numerous notables from both major political parties; and leading newspapers, such as the *New York Times* and the *Washington Post*. Others who emphasized the immoral nature of the war included "New Left" writers already critical of the country's alleged capitalist and exploitative "ruling class," longtime pacifist A. J. Muste and radical Tom Hayden, writer Norman Mailer, pediatrician Benjamin Spock, heavyweight boxer Muhammad Ali, popular rock singers Joan Baez and Bob Dylan, Hollywood actress Jane Fonda, and great masses of college students. The United States, they claimed, was guilty of aggression in a civil war that had no relation to the SEATO charter.

The war's opponents presented many arguments that were difficult to refute. They charged that the United States was the only SEATO member that felt a responsibility to South Vietnam and that it was doing so by helping a repressive government crush a movement of the people. Furthermore, the United States had not supported the elections called for by the Geneva Accords of 1954, and Diem and his successors had released the United States from its commitments by failing to implement reforms. Johnson, they argued, had broken his word in sending soldiers to an Asian war. Moreover, they concluded, "victory" could come only at the cost of annihilating Vietnam: the United States could not win the war through conventional means, and the bombings would devastate the land in the name of peace. The most fundamental failure, some argued, was that the village pacification program had alienated the vast majority of peasants, encouraging the Vietnamese people to hate Americans. The bombings had now underlined the problem by thoroughly antagonizing the victims below. American "globalism" was the root of the problem, many asserted, a feeling of superiority characterized by Fulbright as "arrogance of power."

Defeat, the doves admitted, might allow Vietnam to become Communist, but that did not mean the country would automatically become Communist China's puppet. The Chinese confronted many problems at home and abroad that hampered their involvement in Southeast Asia. Serious foreign policy reverses had helped set off widespread domestic upheaval, causing Mao to initiate a "cultural revolution" that necessitated a less active foreign policy while he worked to squelch his opposition at home. Furthermore, ancient hatreds between Vietnam and China blocked their cooperation—an argument the Johnson administration could not counter because of its refusal to recognize the Beijing government and its resultant inability to gain firsthand information about that Communist regime's real feelings about the war.

In any case, the very multiplicity of arguments against the war guaranteed division among the doves, preventing unified resistance and helping the hawks stay in command. The hawks' defense of the war was formidable because they based their arguments on the fear of global communism and on Americans' fictional belief that they had won all their wars. Americans insisted that withdrawal from Vietnam would constitute their first military defeat, and Johnson refused to be the first chief executive to lose a war. Furthermore, the

hawks declared, the president as commander in chief could send U.S. soldiers anywhere, a power confirmed by the Tonkin Resolution. On the charge of immorality, the hawks declared that the Vietcong were the aggressors and that South Vietnam had asked for U.S. help. It was not a civil war any longer—if indeed it ever had been—because the North Vietnamese depended on Chinese and Soviet assistance. The hawks insisted that Johnson's pledge against using U.S. combat forces was no longer applicable because conditions had deteriorated so rapidly that South Vietnam needed direct assistance. Containment of communism was vital to U.S. security because failure in Southeast Asia would have a "domino" effect that ultimately reached Pacific shores. Appeasement in Vietnam, the hawks concluded, would show a lack of U.S. will, inviting direct intervention by the Soviet Union and Communist China.

Unrest over the war continued to grow throughout 1966 and 1967. In early 1966,

The Anguish of America's Longest War
A U.S. infantryman buries his head in his hands after reading a letter from home. *(Associated Press)*

Fulbright chaired a series of televised hearings by the Senate Foreign Relations Committee regarding U.S. involvement in Vietnam. Asking probing questions of administration supporters, he could get no satisfactory answer regarding which country's communism the United States was trying to contain in Southeast Asia. The major spokesman for the administration, Secretary of State Rusk, argued that the United States was fighting the spread of Chinese communism, ignoring growing reports that by the mid-1960s China's domestic and foreign troubles had permitted the Soviet Union to assume a major burden of aid for North Vietnam. In a move that struck many listeners as utterly anachronistic, he quoted from the Truman Doctrine of 1947 in justifying the U.S. presence in Southeast Asia: "I believe it must be the policy of the United States to support free peoples who are resisting attempted subjugation by armed minorities or by outside pressures."

Criticisms of the administration's Vietnam policies were steadily intensifying. Kennan asserted that he never intended the containment doctrine to entail the use of military force at virtually any point in the world. There was "no reason why we should wish to become so involved" in Vietnam. The United States should begin a phased withdrawal, he declared; containment was not the solution to Asian problems as it had been to Europe's crises of the 1940s. Communism was too diverse and the world's problems too monumental for the United States alone to resolve. Even McNamara, one of Johnson's closest supporters, changed his stance. In 1967, he declared his intention to resign in protest over the administration's policies in Vietnam, joining McGeorge Bundy, George Ball, and the president's political adviser and friend Bill Moyers, all having already left Washington.

While the arguments drummed on, the United States slowly sank into what writers later called the "quagmire" of Vietnam. By 1967, after three years of direct military involvement, the situation in South Vietnam had not improved, and the United States had sustained great losses, including growing casualty lists that reached 13,500 by the end of the year and $6 billion worth of aircraft downed in North Vietnam. But General Westmoreland was calling for more soldiers. Johnson was reluctant. "When we add divisions," he asked in April, "can't the enemy add divisions? If so, where does it all end?" The search-and-destroy missions had led to heavy loss of life and property but had failed to root out villagers suspected of helping the Vietcong. On television news programs, Americans heard grisly accounts of skyrocketing "body counts" of enemy dead that allegedly proved the imminence of victory. And they watched with shock and dismay as their soldiers cleared the Vietcong from villages and countryside (many areas declared "Free Fire Zones" and hence subject to all-out assault) by using napalm, tear gas, flame throwers, saturation bombing, chemical defoliants that included "Agent Orange," and firepower of all kinds.

The prospects of the United States in Vietnam were dismal at best. "Pacification" centers (the once-heralded strategic hamlets erected to guarantee peasant security) were filled and failing, and increasing numbers of U.S. soldiers had fallen victim to mines and booby traps (packed with shrapnel called "American spaghetti," which consisted of short strips of barbed wire chopped off posts) set by peasants and by the ghostlike enemy referred to as "Charlie" (the "Orwellian unperson," as dubbed by French news correspondent and author Bernard Fall). Corruption and governmental incompetence in Saigon continued its upward spiral, the Vietcong found sustenance and sanctuary in Laos and Cambodia, and the Ho Chi Minh Trail, according to one special forces soldier, reminded him of the "Long Island expressway—during rush hour." The number of refugees by the beginning of 1968 had soared to 4 million, or a quarter of the country's population. Even the environment worked to the advantage of the Vietcong. To Americans, Vietnam was an unfamiliar and foreboding land called "Apache country"—a dense tropical jungle characterized by insufferable heat and humidity, countless legions of leeches and fire ants, towering elephant grass that made passage extremely difficult, deadly diseases such as malaria and jungle fever, and monsoons and heavy fog cover that severely hampered both ground and air operations. All the while, the fiercely determined enemy countered the superior artillery and air power of the United States by what one U.S. officer called "violent, close-quarters combat." Thus did the Americans as outsiders wage a war of attrition that almost inevitably alienated the great masses of native people, whose support was critical to success.

As General Taylor had warned, the Americanization of the war carried the seeds of its own destruction. The move had indeed reduced the role of the ARVN and made it less effective, and Ky's Saigon government had further embarrassed the United States by imprisoning thousands of political enemies because of another Buddhist upheaval. In the meantime, the political battle over the people's support was being lost as mounting numbers of peasants, including refugees, flocked into the ranks of the Vietcong, thereby disproving the theory of Westmoreland's advisers that the number of enemy killings would eventually reach that highly coveted "crossover point" at which more died than the Hanoi government could replenish. Ironically, as U.S. firepower became more effective, the chances for gaining popular support and winning the war seemed to decline correspondingly. Johnson claimed he felt like a hitchhiker on a road in a Texas hailstorm: "I can't run. I can't hide. And I can't make it stop."

American relations with most other Asian countries also steadily deteriorated in almost direct proportion to its military escalation in Vietnam. The United States accused Cambodia of providing sanctuary for the Vietcong, leading that government to break relations with Washington in 1965. Americans meanwhile bombed supply lines in neutral Laos

(a top-secret operation code-named "Steel Tiger") to close the Ho Chi Minh Trail. Japan increasingly questioned U.S. involvement in Southeast Asia, especially after Okinawa became the headquarters for launching aerial attacks on North Vietnam. Thailand was an exception to the region's growing anti-American feeling: fearing Communist guerrillas in the east, it permitted the establishment of U.S. military plants and bombing bases. As in the Korean War, Americans made up the great bulk of fighting forces in Vietnam, although 50,000 soldiers from South Korea joined the few contributed by Thailand, Australia, New Zealand, and the Philippines. SEATO, as many feared, had become a transparent cover for what was fast becoming a unilateral U.S. involvement.

The Agony of War
President Johnson's reaction to news of more Americans killed in Vietnam. (*National Archives, Washington, D.C.*)

Johnson continued his call for peace (more than 2,000 attempts between 1965 and 1967) while refusing to condone any appearance of capitulation to aggression. But the administration insisted on an independent, non-Communist South Vietnam, whereas the North Vietnamese demanded an end to the bombing, a total U.S. withdrawal, and the ultimate unification of the entire country "in accordance with the program of the National Liberation Front." The opposing stands were irreconcilable. The United Nations, the Vatican, and Poland offered to mediate an end to the war, and several times the United States authorized bombing pauses to encourage negotiations. During a month-long bombing halt that began on Christmas Eve of 1965, Johnson sent a much-publicized peace mission to forty foreign capitals to explain the U.S. stand and to seek these governments' help in ending the war. The delegation's membership was impressive—Vice President Hubert Humphrey, UN Ambassador Arthur Goldberg, and Ambassador-at-Large W. Averell Harriman—and its program sounded irresistibly Wilsonian in carrying the name of the "Fourteen Points." Rusk boasted, "We put everything into the basket but the surrender of South Vietnam." But to Hanoi, this was everything. The effort failed, and the bombings resumed. Under no conditions would the United States permit the Vietcong into the government. That would be like "putting the fox in a chicken coop," Humphrey publicly scoffed. The president then instructed Goldberg to take the issue before the UN Security Council, but that body took no action.

The United States stood virtually alone in Vietnam, yet the Johnson administration still refused to relent. In an interview, the president explained his position in Rooseveltian language: "I deeply believe we are quarantining aggression over there, just like the smallpox. Just like FDR and Hitler, just like Wilson and the Kaiser. . . . What I learned as a boy in my teens and in college about World War I was that it was our lack of strength and failure to show stamina that got us into that war."

The Six Day War in the Middle East

In the spring of 1967, the danger of a U.S. overcommitment in Vietnam became evident when in the Middle East, Israeli forces again grappled with those of Egypt in a fierce but abbreviated conflict known as the Six Day War. The region had remained unstable after the Suez crisis of 1956. The United States had continued its dual policy toward the Israelis and Arabs, including the sale of arms to both sides to maintain a power balance, but Nasser had also received Soviet planes and tanks, worked with other Arab leaders in 1964 in establishing the Palestine Liberation Organization (PLO) to tear Palestine from Israel, and demanded that the UN peacekeeping force withdraw from the Egyptian–Israeli border. When the United Nations complied with his wishes in May 1967, the two age-old antagonists directly confronted each other again for the first time since Britain's departure in 1956. Shortly afterward, Nasser moved his forces into the Sinai Peninsula and seized Sharm el-Sheikh, a camp strategically overlooking the entrance into the Gulf of Aqaba. His actions effectively closed the gulf and denied Israel its only port.

Nasser seemed to be preparing for an invasion of Israel. His seizure of Sharm el-Sheikh had brought the United States into the matter because in 1956 the Eisenhower administration had secured Israel's withdrawal from the area with a promise to support its access to the Gulf of Aqaba. Meanwhile, PLO terrorist groups from Syria and Jordan began guerrilla raids on Israel that drew immediate reprisals and threatened to engulf the entire region in war.

As Egyptian, Syrian, and Jordanian troops massed along Israel's borders, the Israelis decided to repeat their strategy of 1956 by striking first. On the morning of June 5, 1967, Israeli planes, evading Egyptian radar by approaching over the Mediterranean rather than the Sinai, launched a series of devastating raids on Nasser's air force, which was still on the ground. They then did the same with those of

Jordan, Syria, and Iraq. Israeli tanks and soldiers meanwhile crossed the Sinai desert and within six days had blocked the Suez Canal and controlled Sharm el-Sheikh, the old city of Jerusalem, the West Bank of the Jordan River, the Golan Heights along Syria's border, and parts of Jordan and Syria. Neither the Soviet Union nor the United States intervened, although their use of the "hotline" between Moscow and Washington perhaps reduced the chances of a misunderstanding that could have widened the war. With the Arabs defeated, the Soviets recommended a cease-fire, and on June 11, the UN Security Council accepted it. The fighting was over.

The United Nations managed a shaky agreement in late November 1967. The vaguely worded document, Security Council Resolution 242, stipulated that in exchange for the Israelis' withdrawal from recently occupied Arab territories, they would receive guarantees of border security and free use of regional waterways. To ensure peace, the resolution called for the establishment of "demilitarized zones," the nondiscriminatory use of international waters in the area (the Suez Canal was closed again because, as in 1956, Nasser sank ships at its entrance), and "a just settlement of the refugee problem," which the Palestinians interpreted as the establishment of a homeland. Resumption of the age-old conflict seemed predictable—particularly when the antagonists did not implement the terms of the resolution.

In the aftermath of the Six Day War, the Middle East remained unstable, further revealing the incapacity of the United States to keep peace all over the world. American relations with the Arabs plummeted. Nasser broke relations after making erroneous charges that U.S. and British planes had aided the Israeli offensive, and several Arab nations responded by instituting a short-lived oil embargo against the West. Meanwhile, the Israelis argued that Security Council Resolution 242 meant that satisfactory security treaties must *precede* their withdrawal from the newly occupied lands, and they continued to hold the Sinai Penin-

sula (part of Egypt for more than 5,000 years), the Gaza Strip, and the east bank of the Suez Canal. Furthermore, they barred access to the waterway until it was open to everyone. The Soviet Union finally broke relations with Israel after warning it to return all Arab lands before negotiations could begin. Although the United States refused to recognize the Israelis' occupation of the old sector of Jerusalem, it understood their need for security and tried to persuade them to return the lands taken in exchange for guaranteed access to the canal and the Gulf of Aqaba. But neither the Soviets nor the Americans were able to arouse enough support for their program, and Israel steadfastly refused to return territories taken during the Six Day War.

While several mediation attempts failed, sporadic border incidents and increasing terrorist acts by the rapidly growing PLO underlined the need for a permanent settlement. Peace continued to elude the region throughout Johnson's tenure in office, further draining the energy his administration needed to deal with the ongoing war in Vietnam.

Attempted Negotiations with Hanoi and the *Pueblo* Incident

By the end of 1967, the imminence of hostilities in the Middle East had highlighted the dangers of the growing global commitments of the United States and provided renewed impetus to the search for an honorable way out of Vietnam. Indeed, peace prospects had improved. Earlier that year in June, the president had met with Soviet Premier Kosygin at Glassboro State College in New Jersey, and even though the two leaders failed to reach agreements on either Vietnam or the ongoing Middle East crisis, they left the image of a friendly atmosphere conducive to détente. In autumn, opinion polls showed that a majority of Americans considered intervention in Vietnam to have been a mistake.

That September in San Antonio, Texas, Johnson set out a plan for peace that became known as the "San Antonio formula." The

United States, he declared, was "willing to stop all aerial and naval bombing of North Vietnam when this will lead promptly to productive discussions. We, of course, assume that while discussions proceed, North Vietnam would not take advantage of the bombing cessation or limitation." The White House now demanded only an end to new infiltration as a prerequisite to negotiations and, in a remarkable turnaround, dropped its rigid opposition to Vietcong participation in the political process. Two months later, the United States withdrew its opposition to negotiating with the National Liberation Front as a separate organization. North Vietnam, in turn, also retreated from some of its stringent conditions for talks. No longer did it demand a total U.S. military withdrawal, although it still insisted on a bombing halt before any discussions could begin. The Hanoi government also seemed willing to accept a long-range reunification plan.

Yet neither side was willing to concede anything on the premier issue of South Vietnam's future, and that bitter standoff dictated a prolongation of war. The United States reiterated its call for an independent non-Communist South Vietnam, and North Vietnam repeated its demand for a reunited country free from foreign influence. The U.S. ambassador to South Vietnam, Ellsworth Bunker, nonetheless assured superiors in Washington that the pacification program was working. That same year of 1967, the CIA station chief in Saigon, William Colby, had helped to create the "Phoenix Program," which allegedly promoted pacification by undermining the "Vietcong Infrastructure" in South Vietnam through mass arrests and trials of civilians accused of helping the enemy. But all too quickly "Phoenix" became synonymous with assassinations: due process was discarded, and thousands of suspected Vietcong and their sympathizers were "neutralized" every month as part of the "Accelerated Pacification Campaign." On the surface, however, the prognosis looked good. "We are winning a war of attrition," Westmoreland declared. Figures compiled by MACV suggested that the U.S. military effort was about to reach the magical "crossover point," when American and ARVN armies were killing more North Vietnamese regulars than the Hanoi government could replace. Although the CIA argued that MACV's calculations were misleading and that North Vietnam's military force included many fighters not in uniform, Westmoreland chose to accept MACV's findings and thereby offered the president an optimistic assessment of the war's progress. Within two years, the general asserted, the United States could begin a gradual withdrawal that would allow South Vietnam to take over the war. But even though the chief U.S. diplomatic and military representatives in South Vietnam had finally discerned a timetable for withdrawal, two more years of fighting seemed interminable to those who wanted out immediately.

Several events in early 1968 suddenly complicated the U.S. involvement in Vietnam. An American B-52 disappeared in Greenland carrying four H-bombs, Democratic Senator Eugene McCarthy from Minnesota entered the presidential race on an antiwar platform and gained a surprising amount of support, and new troubles developed in Berlin that perhaps necessitated more U.S. troops. But most exasperating was the incident involving the U.S. intelligence vessel *Pueblo*. On January 23, North Korean forces seized the *Pueblo* in the Sea of Japan, charging it with invading their territorial waters and imprisoning the ship's eighty-two officers and sailors. Although Americans demanded prompt military action, the Johnson administration could not risk a war in Korea while immersed in one in Vietnam. After nearly a year of negotiations, the U.S. sailors, clearly under duress, admitted to violating North Korean waters and signed an apology. In a bizarre twist, the U.S. commander had permission from his captors to renounce the confession before and after signing it. The men were freed, although the Communists kept the ship and won a major propaganda victory that further underlined the finite nature of the superpower status of the United States.

U.S. Embassy in Saigon
With their dead comrades lying nearby, these American soldiers held out against the Vietcong's attack on the embassy during the Tet Offensive of January 1968. *(Wide World Photos, New York)*

Tet—and After

A week after the *Pueblo* incident, on January 30, 1968, Vietcong and North Vietnamese forces broke the long-honored truce during Tet (lunar new year holiday) by launching a massive surprise offensive against the cities and provinces of South Vietnam that the Hanoi regime hoped would generate a popular uprising against the Americans and the ARVN. At 2:45 A.M., nineteen Vietcong exploded a hole in the thick-walled, eight-foot-tall barricade around the U.S. embassy in Saigon, invading American territory inside South Vietnam and killing two military policemen on duty at the time. Using antitank guns and rockets that had been brought surreptitiously into the city weeks earlier, the Vietcong en-

tered the courtyard but never managed to seize the embassy building, which at the time housed only a few CIA and Foreign Service officers. American soldiers retaliated at daybreak. Marines and paratroopers landed by helicopter on the embassy roof and regained control of the grounds a little after 9:00 A.M. Five Americans died in the heated exchange; all nineteen Vietcong were either killed or seriously wounded.

The greatest casualty of the Tet Offensive was the Johnson administration's credibility at home. Americans were shocked to see televised coverage of their embassy grounds overrun by Vietcong and of U.S. soldiers and civilians frantically running through the carnage and gunfire, searching out other assailants. The timing of the assault was particularly traumatic. Westmoreland had just returned to the United States in late 1967 to report imminent victory, and the president himself had declared just two weeks before Tet in his State of the Union Address that South Vietnam was nearly all "secure." In surveying the damage on the embassy grounds (which one journalist called "a butcher shop in Eden"), Westmoreland presented a coldly formal statement over television during which he asserted that the Communists had "very deceitfully" exploited the holiday truce "to create maximum consternation." He then drew groans of disbelief among reporters by dismissing the assault as the Vietcong's "last gasp" and claiming that the enemy's "well-laid plans" had met a crushing defeat.

The urban offensive had completely surprised the United States and South Vietnam, primarily because both had thought that the central North Vietnamese assault was the ongoing siege on the huge marine garrison at Khe Sanh. Located in the far northwest section of South Vietnam and close to the Laotian border, the military fortress was an imposing part of the continuing effort to end infiltration through the Ho Chi Minh Trail. Some observers considered Khe Sanh to be the chief object of North Vietnam's offensive, another Dienbienphu—a ruse that North Vietnamese military chieftain and strategist Vo Nguyen Giap later claimed he had intended. The North Vietnamese army's offensive against Khe Sanh was a diversionary move, he

General William Westmoreland
The leader of American forces in Vietnam (second from left) talks to military personnel in the U.S. embassy in Saigon after the Vietcong siege during Tet, January 31, 1968. *(U.S. Army)*

argued, designed to draw Americans' attention from the plan's central thrust: a massive Vietcong assault on South Vietnam's major urban areas that would set off the revolution basic to a people's war and liberate the south by bringing down the Saigon government and sending the Americans home. As is the goal of any sound military strategist, Giap attempted to strike at his antagonist's most vulnerable point. Tactically, he knew he could not prevail over the vastly superior firepower of the United States, but psychologically and politically, he could win a crucial battle by convincing Americans at home that the war was not winnable. The Johnson administration's continued optimism in the face of such adversity would then open a credibility gap that the president could not close. With the decline of domestic support for the war, Giap

reasoned, the United States would have no choice but to withdraw.

Westmoreland was correct in terming the outcome of Tet a military victory for the United States, but he missed the point: Americans refused to believe him. Renowned CBS newsman and staunch administration supporter Walter Cronkite stormed, "What the hell is going on? I thought we were winning the war!" He soon called the war a stalemate and urged the White House to negotiate "as an honorable people who lived up to their pledge to defend democracy, and did the best they could." Although Johnson agreed with his field commander that the assault was a "complete failure," he quietly admitted that the Vietcong had won a "psychological victory." Nor was Westmoreland naive. Privately, he conceded that Tet was a "severe blow" to

Battle of Khe Sanh
U.S. Marines under siege by the North Vietnamese at Khe Sanh in 1968. *(National Archives, Washington, D.C.)*

South Vietnam, yet the U.S.–South Vietnamese counterassault also dealt the Vietcong a near lethal blow. No revolution occurred, and local television accounts of the stacks of Vietcong bodies in Saigon sent a horrifying message to many villagers in South Vietnam that it would be wiser to send their young males into the local defense units than to have them forced into the Vietcong.

But despite the unquestioned success in the field, most talk of victory in the war came to an abrupt end as U.S. leaders took the first important turn toward a negotiated peace based on the reality of a stalemate. Perhaps the critics were correct: the United States could not win the war because the Hanoi government adamantly refused to negotiate until the Americans left the Vietnamese to resolve their own problems. Yet the presence of U.S. troops upheld the Saigon government and thereby denied the North Vietnamese a victory. Most important, the Tet Offensive raised the question that many Americans had been silently asking for some time: if the war was going so well, why was it lasting so long?

Although the furious U.S.–ARVN counteroffensive was enormously successful, it further highlighted the ghastly nature of the fighting and, almost paradoxically, increased opposition to U.S. involvement in the war. Using rockets and gas, the combined armies regained control of the city of Hué, but only at the heavy cost of three weeks of vicious street-to-street fighting that led to 4,000 civilian deaths and added more than 100,000 refugees to the already bloated list. "Nothing I had seen during the Second World War in the Pacific, during the Korean War, and in Vietnam," journalist Robert Shaplen wrote, could compare to the "destruction and despair" in Hué. By the middle of March, according to perhaps inflated estimates, more than 40,000 Vietcong, or half

The Totality of War
South Vietnamese civilians evacuating the village of My Tho in Dinh Tuong province during the Tet Offensive of 1968. *(National Archives, Washington, D.C.)*

their forces, lay dead throughout the country. The American dead numbered a thousand, and the ARVN's total was twice that amount. The war seemed to have reached a new level of atrocity. Mass graves uncovered in Hué yielded close to 3,000 bodies of civilian men, women, and children, all executed by the North Vietnamese and Vietcong and many buried alive. Another 2,000 of Hué's citizens were missing and probably murdered. But even more shocking was an NBC news program in February that showed footage of Saigon's police chief executing a handcuffed Vietcong prisoner in the street by a pistol shot to the head. In the provincial capital of Ben Tre, U.S. and ARVN troops killed a thousand civilians while rooting out the Vietcong, causing one U.S. officer to capsulize the new nightmarish direction of the war in these words: "We had to destroy the town to save it."

By March, North Vietnamese army units had resumed their earlier attack on Khe Sanh, but even though the Americans held on to the garrison, people in the United States were convinced that their soldiers were on the defensive. In fact, it now appears that the U.S. and ARVN counterattack was so successful that North Vietnamese regulars had to fill the Vietcong's sharply diminished ranks, finally converting the fighting into a conventional war between North and South Vietnam.

By early 1968, skepticism about the U.S. involvement in Vietnam had permeated the top echelons of the Johnson administration. In late February, the president asked his new secretary of defense, Clark Clifford, to assess

The TV War in Vietnam
Vietcong guerrilla executed by South Vietnamese national police chief, Brigadier General Nguyen Ngoc Loan, in Saigon on February 1, 1968. Associated Press photographer Eddie Adams took the picture that brought the war home to Americans and others around the world. *(Wide World Photos, New York)*

the nation's Vietnam policy. Westmoreland had just called for 206,000 more soldiers to join the 535,000 already there, in preparation for a major offensive. To send such a large military contingent, Johnson realized, required the politically unpopular moves of mobilizing the reserves and enlarging the draft. Indeed, he had already dismissed the idea of a massive troop buildup, only to see that someone in the administration had leaked the request to the press and thereby set off another barrage of criticism. In March, Rusk suggested a cease-fire based on a bombing halt, and presidential hopeful Eugene McCarthy, calling for an immediate U.S. withdrawal, made a strong showing in the New Hampshire Democratic primary. His success may have been due to the votes of unhappy hawks rather than doves, but it nonetheless showed Americans' mounting displeasure with the administration.

Meanwhile, even the strongly supportive foreign policy "establishment" had changed its views on the war. Former Secretary of State Dean Acheson assured the president that "the Joint Chiefs of Staff don't know what they're talking about" in asking for more men, and Clifford bolstered this charge by reporting that the generals could give him no specific answers regarding when and how victory would come or at what cost. In early March, Clifford recommended the addition of only 22,000 more U.S. soldiers, the call-up of an undetermined number of reserves, and a "highly forceful approach" to Ky and Thieu to take over more of the fighting. Support for the "gradual disengagement" of Americans from the war (later called "Vietnamization") came from the Senior Informal Advisory Group on Vietnam (the "Wise Men"), a collection of fourteen diplomatic and military figures of the Truman years who stunned the president by expressing doubt about the nation's ability to win the war.

Thus, by 1968, serious misgivings about the U.S. role in Vietnam had reached the White House, where the lack of progress in the war and its tremendous expense soon forced a change both in tactics in Vietnam and in leadership in Washington. The ARVN's

Dean Rusk
Secretary of state at cabinet meeting in September 1968. *(Lyndon B. Johnson Library, Austin, Texas)*

surprising recovery from the Tet Offensive upheld the argument that scaling down U.S. involvement to its pre-1965 level might be the
most feasible way out of the war. Johnson, believing that his generals had misled him in
Vietnam, decided against sending even the
22,000 men Clifford had recommended and
then ordered Westmoreland home and promoted him to Army Chief of Staff to spare
him the blame for failure to win the war. Finally, in view of marked domestic unrest over
the war, the president announced in a televised broadcast on March 31 that he would

call off much of the bombing of North Vietnam to encourage peace talks. Lest his plea appear to be a cheap political effort to ensure
reelection, he surprised the nation and most
of his advisers by adding that he would neither seek nor accept his party's nomination
for the presidency.

Within a week of the president's withdrawal
from the 1968 campaign, the North Vietnamese surprised the White House by agreeing to
peace talks, which began in Paris on May 13.
But high hopes just as suddenly dissipated as
snags immediately developed. The U.S. dele-

McNamara and Clifford
McNamara was secretary of defense from 1961 to 1968, when he resigned and Clifford took his place
and worked toward America's withdrawal from the war in Vietnam. *(U.S. Army)*

gation, headed by veteran diplomat W. Averell Harriman, encountered resistance from the North Vietnamese, who refused to discuss terms until the United States stopped *all* bombing. The Johnson administration declined on the same ground as earlier: the North Vietnamese might exploit the truce to strengthen their forces and therefore endanger U.S. soldiers. With neither side willing to retreat, the United States and South Vietnam intensified their pacification and de-Americanization programs, leaving the peace talks for a new presidential administration in Washington.

The Presidential Election of 1968

With Vietnam as the major issue of the 1968 presidential election, the Republicans met in Miami Beach in early August and nominated the staunch anti-Communist Richard M. Nixon for the office. Trying to walk down the political middle, the former vice president offered experience in office and a hard-nosed tenacity in seeking his objectives. Had he not risen from the political grave after his presidential defeat in 1960, followed just two years later by a gubernatorial defeat in California? Most important, he promised reductions in government spending and no retreat in Vietnam. In a reminder of the Eisenhower strategy of 1952, Nixon assured Americans that he had a "secret plan" designed to "end the war and win the peace." When pressed to reveal the plan, Nixon explained that secrecy was essential because of the ongoing Paris negotiations.

The Democrats prepared for battle. With Johnson out of the race, Vice President Humphrey declared his intention to run, as did Senator Robert F. Kennedy of New York, who announced his candidacy on an antiwar platform and took most of McCarthy's supporters. Kennedy won the June primary in California but, like his brother five-and-a-half years earlier, was assassinated that very evening. His death shocked the nation and left the antiwar campaign in disarray. Had

the United States become a nation of violence? asked many Americans, who had just witnessed the riots and burning cities (including Washington) in the aftermath of the murder of civil rights leader Martin Luther King Jr. in Memphis the previous April. Kennedy's followers had no choice but to shun the campaign in frustration or fall back with McCarthy: Humphrey was locked into administration policies that called for continued bombing until concessions from North Vietnam allowed peace with honor.

Later that August, the Democratic Party gathered in Chicago, where a siegelike atmosphere prevailed both inside and outside the convention hall. Inside, an extremely bitter political battle developed over the Democratic platform on Vietnam. McCarthy's followers demanded an end to the bombing, immediate negotiations, and withdrawal of U.S. forces; Humphrey's supporters countered with the administration's hard-line argument and after a bitter three-hour debate defeated the peace plank. In celebration of their victory, Democratic hard-liners on Vietnam tactlessly showed film on the wide auditorium screen of air force action as the band struck up the tune, "Up We Go, into the Wild, Blue Yonder." Outside the hall, antiwar protesters carrying Vietcong flags called the police "pigs," sang the popular song "I Ain't Marchin' Anymore," and chanted "Ho, Ho, Ho Chi Minh," "Sieg Heil, Sieg Heil, Sieg," and "The Whole World Is Watching." In what an investigative commission afterward termed a "police riot," violence broke out in Chicago's streets as thousands of troops and hundreds of club-wielding policemen swarmed into the crowd, injuring hundreds of demonstrators, bystanders, and reporters, and taking many to jail. Out of concern for personal safety, President Johnson did not attend the nomination proceedings. Symbolism took center stage when NBC-TV interjected clips of the violence on the streets just as Humphrey's nomination was to receive a second, thus adding an appropriate bloody context for the chaos erupting all around him.

The political sides had not yet been fully drawn because a third party entered the contest. The American Independence Party (AIP) nominated Alabama Governor George Wallace for the presidency on a "law and order" campaign, which many called a euphemism for a "white backlash" against the civil rights movement. The AIP demanded continued racial segregation and a crackdown on all protesters. Wallace insisted on victory in Vietnam, and his vice-presidential running mate, General Curtis LeMay, lamented the "phobia" of the United States over nuclear weapons and told observers that he favored bombing North Vietnam "[back] into the stone age." One wag labeled the AIP candidates as "the bombsy twins."

Nixon's "hawkish" candidacy suddenly received a big boost when, on the night of August 20–21, Soviet tanks and troops stormed into Czechoslovakia to put down an uprising similar to that of the late 1940s. To justify this action, Soviet General Secretary Leonid Brezhnev asserted in what became known as the "Brezhnev Doctrine" that the Soviets had the right to intervene in any allied country to defend "proletarian internationalism." Although Johnson protested, he could not fend off the strongly indignant counterattacks pointing to the recent U.S. military intervention in the Dominican Republic and its ongoing war in Vietnam. The Soviet intervention in Czechoslovakia seemed to have undermined hopes for détente. It heightened the Cold War by dredging up the black memories of Stalinism, stimulated a missile and arms buildup that threatened to interfere with the Senate's approval of the nuclear nonproliferation agreement, drew the NATO alliance closer together again, and underscored the inability of the United States to determine world events. The hawks in the United States cited the Czech crisis as evidence of the need to stand up to the Communists in Vietnam, and many Americans became convinced that Nixon's long record of fighting communism made him the best choice in 1968.

With Nixon running ahead in the polls, Johnson announced late in the campaign, on October 31, that all bombing would end the following day. His move suddenly lifted Humphrey's chances for winning and offered new hope for the staggering peace talks in Paris. But the change of course came too late. On November 5, Nixon won a narrow victory despite Humphrey's rapid surge following the bombing halt. With 302 electoral votes but only 43.4 percent of the popular vote and with Democratic majorities in both Houses of Congress, Nixon prepared to assume the presidency and "win the peace" in Vietnam. Prospects looked good: on January 16, 1969, four days before the inauguration, the Paris conferees agreed to sit at a round table, resolving a long and bitter dispute by awarding all participants equal status, and the three delegations from South Vietnam, North Vietnam, and the National Liberation Front agreed with the Americans to turn to substantive matters.

Containment in Free Fall

The containment policy followed since the Truman era had virtually collapsed during the Johnson presidency. All its assumptions had come into question: that a huge Communist monolith existed under Moscow's direction; that the United States had to defend "vital interests" in whatever area in the world the Communists sought (never seeming to doubt, for example, South Vietnam's strategic importance, its viability as a nation-state, or the popularity of its government); that the instability resulting from social revolutions was an automatic breeding ground for communism and had to be resisted with either military or economic means; that the American sense of mission necessitated the exportation of democracy into every nation in the world; and, above all, that the United States could leave no indications of a weakened will. The Vietnam crisis had gone on for so long that the future of the world appeared to rest in that small country, which dictated a total commitment that forced the collapse of containment. Fighting without the ideological belief in containment proved devastating to Americans' morale, moral fiber, and sense of right-

Nguyen Van Thieu and President Johnson
The president of South Vietnam listens to President Johnson in July 1968. *(Lyndon B. Johnson Library, Austin, Texas)*

eousness. The consolation was that the new presidential administration seemed to offer a different direction in foreign policy.

Selected Readings

Ambrose, Stephen E., and Douglas G. Brinkley. *Rise to Globalism: American Foreign Policy since 1938.* 8th ed., 1997.

Anderson David L., ed. *Facing My Lai: Moving beyond the Massacre.* 1998.

Ashby, LeRoy, and Rod Gramer. *Fighting the Odds: The Life of Senator Frank Church.* 1994.

Ball, George W., and Douglas B. Ball. *The Passionate Attachment: America's Involvement with Israel 1947 to the Present.* 1992.

Baritz, Loren. *Backfire: A History of How American Culture Led Us into Vietnam and Made Us Fight the Way We Did.* 1985.

Barrett, David M. *Uncertain Warriors: Lyndon Johnson and His Vietnam Advisers.* 1993.

Ben-Zvi, Abraham. *Decade of Transition: Eisenhower, Kennedy, and the Origins of the American-Israeli Alliance.* 1998.

Berman, Larry. *Lyndon Johnson's War: The Road to Stalemate in Vietnam.* 1989.

———. *Planning a Tragedy: The Americanization of the War in Vietnam.* 1982.

———. *William Fulbright and the Vietnam War.* 1988.

Bernstein, Irving. *Guns or Butter: The Presidency of Lyndon Johnson.* 1996.

Bill, James A. *George Ball: Behind the Scenes in U.S. Foreign Policy.* 1997.

Bird, Kai. *The Color of Truth: McGeorge Bundy and William Bundy, Brothers in Arms: A Biography.* 1998.

Blair, Anne E. *Lodge in Vietnam: A Patriot Abroad.* 1995.

Bornet, Vaughn Davis. *The Presidency of Lyndon B. Johnson.* 1983.

Brands, H. W. *The Devil We Knew: Americans and the Cold War.* 1993.

———. *The Wages of Globalism: Lyndon Johnson and the Limits of American Power.* 1995.

Brigham, Robert K. *Guerrilla Diplomacy: The NLF's Foreign Relations and the Viet Nam War.* 1999.

Brinkley, Douglas. *Dean Acheson: The Cold War Years, 1953–71.* 1992.

Burchett, Wilfred. *Catapult to Freedom: The Survival of the Vietnamese People.* 1978.

Buttinger, Joseph. *Vietnam: A Dragon Embattled.* 2 vols., 1967.

———. *Vietnam: A Political History.* 1968.

Buzzanco, Robert. *Masters of War: Military Dissent and Politics in the Vietnam Era.* 1996.

———. *Vietnam and the Transformation of American Life.* 1999.

Cable, Larry. *Unholy Grail: The US and the Wars in Vietnam, 1965–8.* 1991.

Caputo, Philip. *A Rumor of War.* 1977.

Cincinnatus [pseudonym for Currey, Cecil B.]. *Self-Destruction: The Disintegration and Decay of the United States Army during the Vietnam Era.* 1981.

Clifford, Clark. *Counsel to the President: A Memoir.* 1991.

Clodfelter, Mark. *The Limits of Air Power: The American Bombing of North Vietnam.* 1989.

Cohen, Warren I. *America's Response to China: An Interpretive History of Sino-American Relations.* 2000.

———. *Dean Rusk.* 1980.

Conboy, Kenneth, and Dale Andradé. *Spies and Commandos: How America Lost the Secret War in North Vietnam.* 2000.

Cooper, Chester L. *The Lost Crusade: America in Vietnam.* 1970.

Costigliola, Frank. *France and the United States: The Cold Alliance since World War II.* 1992.

Currey, Cecil B. *Edward Lansdale: The Unquiet American.* 1988.

Dallek, Robert. *Flawed Giant: Lyndon Johnson and His Times, 1961–1973.* 1998.

Davidson, Phillip B. *Vietnam at War: The History, 1946–1975.* 1988.

DeBenedetti, Charles. "The Antiwar Movement in America, 1955–1965." In Howard Jones, ed., *The Foreign and Domestic Dimensions of Modern Warfare: Vietnam, Central America, and Nuclear Strategy,* 76–93. 1988.

———. *The Peace Reform in American History.* 1980.

DiLeo, David L. *George Ball, Vietnam, and the Rethinking of Containment.* 1991.

Draper, Theodore. *The Dominican Revolt.* 1968.

Duiker, William J. *The Communist Road to Power in Vietnam.* 1981.

———. *Ho Chi Minh.* 2000.

———. *U.S. Containment Policy and the Conflict in Indochina.* 1994.

Fall, Bernard B. *Last Reflections on a War.* 1967.

———. *The Two Vietnams: A Political and Military Analysis.* 2nd ed., 1967.

FitzGerald, Frances. *Fire in the Lake: The Vietnamese and the Americans in Vietnam.* 1972.

Gaddis, John L. *The Cold War: A New History.* 2005.

———. *The Long Peace: Inquiries into the History of the Cold War.* 1987.

———. *Russia, the Soviet Union, and the United States: An Interpretive History.* 2nd ed., 1990.

———. *Strategies of Containment: A Critical Appraisal of Postwar American National Security Policy.* 1982; rev. ed., 2005.

———. *We Now Know: Rethinking Cold War History.* 1997.

Gaiduk, Ilya V. *The Soviet Union and the Vietnam War.* 1996.

Gardner, Lloyd C. *Pay Any Price: Lyndon Johnson and the Wars for Vietnam.* 1995.

Gelb, Leslie H., and Richard K. Betts. *The Irony of Vietnam: The System Worked.* 1979.

Geyelin, Philip. *Lyndon B. Johnson and the World.* 1966.

Gleijeses, Piero. *The Dominican Crisis.* 1978.

Goh, Evelyn. *Constructing the U.S. Rapprochement with China, 1961–1974: From "Red Menace" to "Tacit Ally."* 2005.

Goldman, Eric F. *The Tragedy of Lyndon Johnson.* 1968.

Goodman, Allan E. *The Lost Peace: America's Search for a Negotiated Settlement of the Vietnam War.* 1978.

Gray, William G. *Germany's Cold War: The Global Campaign to Isolate East Germany, 1949–1969.* 2003.

Gurtov, Melvin. *The United States against the Third World.* 1974.

Halberstam, David. *The Best and the Brightest.* 1972.

Hallin, Daniel C. *The "Uncensored War": The Media and Vietnam.* 1986.

Hammond, Paul Y. *LBJ and the Presidential Management of Foreign Relations.* 1992.

Hammond, William H. *Reporting Vietnam: Media and Military at War.* 1998.

Harrison, James P. *The Endless War: Fifty Years of Struggle in Vietnam.* 1982.

Havens, Thomas R. H. *Fire Across the Sea: The Vietnam War and Japan, 1965–1975.* 1987.

Heath, Jim F. *Decade of Disillusionment: The Kennedy-Johnson Years*. 1975.

Hendrickson, Paul. *The Living and the Dead: Robert McNamara and Five Lives of a Lost War*. 1996.

Herring, George C., Jr. *America's Longest War: The United States and Vietnam, 1950–1975*. 4th ed., 2002.

———. *LBJ and Vietnam: A Different Kind of War*. 1994.

———, ed. *The Pentagon Papers: Abridged Edition*. 1993.

———, ed. *The Secret Diplomacy of the Vietnam War: The Negotiating Volumes of the Pentagon Papers*. 1983.

———. "The Vietnam War." In John M. Carroll and George C. Herring, eds., *Modern American Diplomacy*, 165–81. 1986.

Hess, Gary R. *Vietnam and the United States: Origins and Legacy of War*. 1998.

Hoopes, Townsend. *The Limits of Intervention: An Inside Account of How the Johnson Policy of Escalation in Vietnam Was Reversed*. Rev. ed., 1987.

Hunt, Michael H. *Lyndon Johnson's War: America's Cold War Crusade in Vietnam, 1945–1968*. 1996.

Johnson, Robert D. *Ernest Gruening and the American Dissenting Tradition*. 1998.

Kahin, George McT. *Intervention: How America Became Involved in Vietnam*. 1986.

———, and John W. Lewis. *The United States in Vietnam*. Rev. ed., 1969.

Kaiser, David E. *American Tragedy: Kennedy, Johnson, and the Origins of the Vietnam War*. 2000.

Kalb, Marvin, and Elie Abel. *Roots of Involvement*. 1971.

Karnow, Stanley. *Vietnam: A History*. Rev. ed., 1991.

Kattenburg, Paul M. *The Vietnam Trauma in American Foreign Policy, 1945–1975*. 1980.

Kearns, Doris. *Lyndon Johnson and the American Dream*. 1976.

Kendrick, Alexander. *The Wound Within: America in the Vietnam Years, 1945–1974*. 1974.

Kolko, Gabriel. *Anatomy of a War: Vietnam, the United States, and the Modern Historical Experience*. 1985.

Krenn, Michael L. *Black Diplomacy: African Americans and the State Department, 1945–1969*. 1999.

Krepinevich, Andrew F., Jr. *The Army and Vietnam*. 1986.

LaFeber, Walter. *America, Russia, and the Cold War, 1945–1996*. 8th ed., 1997.

———. *The Deadly Bet: LBJ, Vietnam, and the 1968 Election*. 2005.

Langguth, A. J. *Our Vietnam: The War, 1954–1975*. 2000.

Lanning, Michael L., and Dan Cragg. *Inside the VC and the NVA: The Real Story of North Vietnam's Armed Forces*. 1992.

Lerner, Mitchell B. *The Pueblo Incident: A Spy Ship and the Failure of American Foreign Policy*. 2002.

Levering, Ralph B. *The Cold War: A Post-Cold War History*. 1994; rev. ed., 2005.

Lewy, Guenter. *America in Vietnam*. 1978.

Lind, Michael. *Vietnam the Necessary War: A Reinterpretation of America's Most Disastrous Military Conflict*. 1999.

Logevall, Fredrik. *Choosing War: The Lost Chance for Peace and the Escalation of War in Vietnam*. 1999.

Lowenthal, Abraham F. *The Dominican Intervention*. 1972.

Maclear, Michael. *The Ten Thousand Day War, Vietnam: 1945–1975*. 1981.

Mangold, Tom, and John Penygate. *The Tunnels of Cu Chi: The Untold Story of Vietnam*. 1985.

Mann, Robert. *A Grand Illusion: America's Descent into Vietnam*. 2001.

McMahon, Robert J. *The Cold War on the Periphery: The United States, India, and Pakistan*. 1994.

———. *The Limits of Empire: The United States and Southeast Asia since World War II*. 1999.

McMaster, H. R. *Dereliction of Duty: Lyndon Johnson, Robert McNamara, the Joint Chiefs of Staff, and the Lies That Led to Vietnam*. 1997.

McNamara, Robert S. *In Retrospect: The Tragedy and Lessons of Vietnam*. 1995.

Moise, Edwin E. *Tonkin Gulf and the Escalation of the Vietnam War*. 1996.

Moore, Harold G., and Joseph L. Galloway. *We Were Soldiers Once . . . And Young: Ia Drang: The Battle That Changed the War in Vietnam*. 1992.

Morgan, Joseph G. *The Vietnam Lobby: The American Friends of Vietnam, 1955–1975*. 1997.

Neese, Harvey, and John O'Donnell, eds. *Prelude to Tragedy: Vietnam, 1960–1965*. 2001.

Nesbitt, Francis N. *Race for Sanctions: African Americans Against Apartheid, 1946–1994*. 2004.

Oberdorfer, Don. *Tet!* 1971.

Olson, James S., and Randy Roberts. *Where the Domino Fell: America and Vietnam, 1945–1995.* 1995.

Oren, Michael B. *Six Days of War: June 1967 and the Making of the Modern Middle East.* 2002.

Page, Caroline. *U.S. Official Propaganda During the Vietnam War, 1965–1973: The Limits of Persuasion.* 1996.

Palmer, Bruce, Jr. *Intervention in the Caribbean: The Dominican Crisis of 1965.* 1989.

Palmer, Dave R. *Summons of the Trumpet: A History of the Vietnam War from a Military Man's Viewpoint.* 1978.

Pérez, Louis A., Jr. *Cuba and the United States: Ties of Singular Intimacy.* 1997.

Pike, Douglas. *PAVN: People's Army of Vietnam.* 1986.

———. *Viet Cong: the Organization and Techniques of the National Liberation Front of South Vietnam.* 1966.

Pisor, Robert L. *The End of the Line: The Siege of Khe Sanh.* 1982.

Poole, Peter. *The United States and Indochina from FDR to Nixon.* 1973.

Porter, Gareth. *Perils of Dominance: Imbalance of Power and the Road to War in Vietnam.* 2005.

Prados, John. *The Blood Road: The Ho Chi Minh Trail and the Vietnam War.* 1999.

———. *Presidents' Secret Wars: CIA Pentagon Covert Operations from World War II through the Persian Gulf.* 1996.

Prochnau, William. *Once upon a Distant War: David Halberstam, Neil Sheehan, Peter Arnett—Young War Correspondents and Their Early Vietnam Battles.* 1995.

Race, Jeffrey. *War Comes to Long An: Revolutionary Conflict in a Vietnamese Province.* 1972.

Redford, Emmette S., and Richard T. McCulley. *White House Operations: The Johnson Presidency.* 1986.

Risse-Kappen, Thomas. *Cooperation among Democracies: The European Influence on U.S. Foreign Policy.* 1995.

Rusk, Dean. *As I Saw It.* 1990.

Rystad, Göran. *Prisoners of the Past? The Munich Syndrome and Makers of American Foreign Policy in the Cold War Era.* 1982.

Schaffer, Howard B. *Chester Bowles—New Dealer in the Cold War.* 1993.

———. *Ellsworth Bunker: Global Troubleshooter, Vietnam Hawk.* 2003.

Schandler, Herbert Y. *The Unmaking of a President: Lyndon Johnson and Vietnam.* 1977.

Schlesinger, Arthur M., Jr. *The Imperial Presidency.* 1973.

Schmitz, David F. *The Tet Offensive: Politics, War, and Public Opinion.* 2005.

Schoenbaum, David. *The United States and the State of Israel.* 1993.

Schoenbaum, Thomas J. *Waging Peace and War: Dean Rusk in the Truman, Kennedy, and Johnson Years.* 1988.

Schoutz, Lars. *Beneath the United States: A History of U.S. Policy toward Latin America.* 1998.

Schulzinger, Robert D. *A Time for War: The United States and Vietnam, 1941–1975.* 1997.

Schwab, Orrin. *Defending the Free World: John F. Kennedy, Lyndon Johnson, and the Vietnam War, 1961–1965.* 1998.

Seaborg, Glenn T., and Benjamin S. Loeb. *Stemming the Tide: Arms Control in the Johnson Years.* 1987.

Shaplen, Robert. *The Lost Revolution: The U.S. in Vietnam, 1946–1966.* 1966.

———. *The Road from War: Vietnam, 1965–1970.* 1970.

———. *Time Out of Hand: Revolution and Reaction in Southeast Asia.* Rev. ed., 1970.

Shapley, Deborah. *Promise and Power: The Life and Times of Robert McNamara.* 1993.

Sheehan, Neil. *A Bright Shining Lie: John Paul Vann and America in Vietnam.* 1988.

———, et al., eds. *The Pentagon Papers.* 1971.

Shultz, Richard H., Jr. *The Secret War against Hanoi: Kennedy's and Johnson's Use of Spies, Saboteurs, and Covert Warriors in North Vietnam.* 1999.

Slater, Jerome. *Intervention and Negotiation: The United States and the Dominican Revolution.* 1970.

Small, Melvin. *Covering Dissent: The Media and the Anti-Vietnam War Movement.* 1994.

———. *Johnson, Nixon, and the Doves.* 1988.

Spanier, John W. *American Foreign Policy since World War II.* 14th ed., 1998.

Spector, Ronald H. *After Tet: The Bloodiest Year in Vietnam.* 1993.

Spiegel, Steven L. *The Other Arab-Israeli Conflict: Making America's Middle East Policy, from Truman to Reagan.* 1985.

Stevenson, Richard W. *The Rise and Fall of Détente: Relaxations of Tensions in US-Soviet Relations, 1953–1984.* 1985.

Summers, Harry G., Jr. *On Strategy: A Critical Analysis of the Vietnam War.* 1982.

Taylor, Sandra C. *Vietnamese Women at War: Fighting for Ho Chi Minh and the Revolution.* 1999.

Thies, Wallace J. *When Governments Collide: Coercion and Diplomacy in the Vietnam Conflict, 1964–1968.* 1980.

Thompson, James C. *Rolling Thunder: Understanding Policy and Program Failure.* 1980.

Tomes, Robert R. *Apocalypse Then: American Intellectuals and the Vietnam War, 1954–1975.* 1998.

Truong Nhu Tang. *A Vietcong Memoir.* 1985.

Tucker, Spencer C. *Vietnam.* 1999.

Turner, Karen G. *Even the Women Must Fight: Memories of War from North Vietnam.* 1998.

Turner, Kathleen J. *Lyndon Johnson's Dual War: Vietnam and the Press.* 1985.

Ulam, Adam B. *The Communists: The Story of Power and Lost Illusions, 1948–1991.* 1992.

——. *The Rivals: America and Russia since World War II.* 1971.

Valentine, Douglas. *The Phoenix Program.* 1990.

VanDeMark, Brian. *Into the Quagmire: Lyndon Johnson and the Escalation of the Vietnam War.* 1991.

Vandenbroucke, Lucien S. *Perilous Options: Special Operations as an Instrument of U.S. Foreign Policy.* 1993.

Vandiver, Frank E. *Shadows of Vietnam: Lyndon Johnson's Wars.* 1997.

Weiner, Tim. *Legacy of Ashes: The History of the CIA.* 2007.

Weis, W. Michael. *Cold Warriors and Coups D'Etat: Brazilian-American Relations, 1945–1964.* 1993.

Wells, Tom. *The War Within: America's Battle over Vietnam.* 1994.

Westad, Odd Arne. *The Global Cold War: Third World Interventions and the Making of Our Times.* 2006.

Westmoreland, William C. *A Soldier Reports.* 1976.

Winters, Francis X. *The Year of the Hare: America in Vietnam, January 25, 1963–February 15, 1964.* 1997.

Wirtz, James J. *The Tet Offensive: Intelligence Failures in War.* 1991.

Woods, Randall B. *Fulbright: A Biography.* 1995.

——. *J. William Fulbright, Vietnam, and the Search for a Cold War Foreign Policy.* 1998.

——. *LBJ: Architect of American Ambition.* 2006.

Wyatt, Clarence R. *Paper Soldiers: The American Press and the Vietnam War.* 1993.

Young, Marilyn B. *The Vietnam Wars, 1945–1990.* 1991.

Zaroulis, Nancy, and Gerald Sullivan. *Who Spoke Up? American Protest against the War in Vietnam, 1963–1975.* 1984.

Zeiler, Thomas W. *Dean Rusk: Defending the American Mission Abroad.* 2000.

Zhai, Qiang. *China and the Vietnam Wars, 1950–1975.* 2000.

CHAPTER 6

Vietnamization through Détente: A New Containment, 1969–1977

Détente: A Structure of Peace

The Nixon administration's primary objective was to build what the president called a "structure of peace" through détente, which would allow the United States to end its involvement in Vietnam and turn to other problems both at home and abroad. The task would not be easy. The new Republican White House faced a Democratic Congress, a shattered consensus of popular support for the Washington government, and an American people thoroughly disenchanted with containment. Détente's supporters heralded its ideas as the basis of a new foreign policy, but this was not the case. Actually begun during the 1960s, détente aimed to reduce tensions with both the Soviet Union and Communist China by avoiding confrontations, supporting nuclear nonproliferation, and calling for an end to the struggle against monolithic communism. But there was more. To the United States, détente offered an honorable way out of Vietnam. The growth of a multipolar world order helped to promote détente because the forces of nationalism had encouraged neutralism among numerous Third World countries and also created a polycentric system within the Soviet bloc that reduced depend-

ence on the Kremlin. If the United States could establish good relations with the Soviet Union and Communist China, even by playing one against the other, it might be able to wind down involvement in Asia. "I'm not going to end up like LBJ," Nixon proclaimed, "holed up in the White House afraid to show my face in the street. I'm going to stop that war. Fast."

The president's closest adviser in foreign affairs was Henry Kissinger, who rigidly adhered to *realpolitik* in foreign relations and became the chief architect of détente. Basing his philosophy of foreign policy in part on his doctoral studies in political science at Harvard, Kissinger sought to erect a balance of power patterned after the Congress of Vienna of 1815. All states had legitimate rights, he admitted, but no state could have "absolute security" because such a situation meant "absolute insecurity for all the others." He understood, as did the continental powers after the Napoleonic Wars, that peace could come only through a world order based on shared interests and the major powers' determination to defuse international troubles. Rather than reconstruct a traditional balance of power system, however, Kissinger wanted to replace ideology with an emphasis on geopolitical considerations designed to achieve what he termed an "equilibrium of strength" conducive to world peace. His plan rested not on specific, unyielding commitments and treaty terms but on a general frame of mind or attitude that repeatedly adjusted to constantly shifting power realities. Détente constituted an ongoing attempt to find new grounds for agreements that promoted a general peace. As he told a congressional committee in 1974, it was "a process of managing relations with a potentially hostile country in order to preserve peace while maintaining our vital interests." The underlying stipulation was clear: the big powers had to renounce the use of nuclear weapons in achieving their objectives.

As national security affairs adviser until September 1973, when he took on the additional duties of secretary of state, Kissinger initially enjoyed an independence in foreign affairs that someone tied to the State Department could not have. This arrangement suited the White House because, as the president remarked, "no Secretary of State is really important. The President makes foreign policy." New York attorney William Rogers headed the State Department but was continually upstaged by Kissinger and therefore had little impact on foreign affairs. Nixon privately assessed the situation in these words: "Henry thinks Bill [Rogers] isn't very deep and Bill thinks that Henry is power crazy. In a sense they are both right."

For a time, Kissinger seemed to dominate foreign affairs. Critics considered the German-born and heavily accented adviser to be arrogant and intensely loyal to "the Establishment," yet they admitted that his individualism, wit, charm, and personal style of diplomacy allowed him to avert the entrapments of State Department bureaucracy and get things done. Those same critics warned, however, that Kissinger did not formalize many of his agreements and that his word was good only as long as he was in a position of power. Because he held no formal office during the first four years of the Nixon adminis-

tration, Kissinger took advantage of "executive privilege" to engage in secret diplomacy, approve wiretappings of underlings and journalists, avoid congressional hearings (leaving an uninformed Rogers to testify), and answer only to the president. In fact, he seldom consulted his own staff. An observer remarked that "Henry's chief lieutenants are like mushrooms. They're kept in the dark, get a lot of manure piled on them, and then get canned."

Nixon and Kissinger favored détente for several reasons, the most fundamental being to halt a dangerously escalating arms race. They were aware of certain realities: the declining prestige of the United States, brought on primarily by the war in Vietnam; the Cold War's constant drain on human and material resources; the Soviet Union's rapid military expansion after the Cuban missile crisis; the rising importance of the Third World; the fruitlessness of refusing to recognize Communist China; the steady descent of the dollar; and the growing economic and political strength of Western Europe and Japan. A number of agreements with the Soviet Union had pointed to better relations, yet the all-important element of trust was still missing. In the mid-1960s, the United States found that the Soviet Union supported the development of antiballistic missiles (ABMs), which, if successful, would undermine the deterrence capacity of the United States by permitting the destruction of approaching intercontinental ballistic missiles (ICBMs). The Soviet Union's ABMs would raise the chances of a nuclear confrontation by reducing the level of its own "assured destruction" to an "acceptable" casualty figure of a few million. In 1969, the Nixon administration pushed for an improved ABM system, called "Safeguard," to protect U.S. missile sites. More alarming, both superpowers sought to develop a greater offensive capability through the multiple independently targeted reentry vehicle (MIRV), a first-strike ICBM carrying up to ten independently fired nuclear warheads and thus able to counteract ABMs by its sheer number and diversified direction of projectiles. Although each side had a satellite reconnaissance system, neither could determine the number of warheads in a MIRV and therefore could not know the other's nuclear capability. With the two nations approaching strategic parity, détente was not a choice but a necessity.

Détente carried both advantages and disadvantages. First and foremost, it offered diminished international tensions as a major step toward leaving Vietnam. If instituted as policy, the United States could lower arms expenditures and encourage negotiations over cutbacks, reduce the need for combat forces and end the draft, curtail the assumed necessity for intervening in other countries, and build a greater international trade system leading to global order. Kissinger explained that the world consisted of five major areas of power—the United States, the Soviet Union, China, Japan, and Western Europe—and that each should have hegemony in its own locale. None would interfere in another's region, and all would cooperate in preventing neutralist nations from manipulating the superpowers. Détente called for a continuously shifting global balance of power in which the leading nations discouraged aggressions within their own spheres. As Nixon put it in 1971, the "five great economic superpowers will determine the economic future" as well as "the future of the world in other ways in the last of this century."

Détente worked better in theory than in application. The Third World preferred diplomatic nonalignment and increasingly resisted efforts by either the Soviets or the Americans to dictate its policies. Thus emerging nationalist movements in Asia, the Middle East, and Africa caused major problems for the big powers. Indeed, the developing nations of the "South" put pressure on the more advanced nations of the "North" to forgo huge profits in the interests of helping the less fortunate peoples close the gap between them and the wealthy. Economic troubles stemmed from many sources—including competition from Europe and Japan, the balance-of-payments deficit, devaluation of the dollar in 1971 and

1973, and recurring inflation. But the most immediate problem emanated from the Organization of Petroleum Exporting Countries (OPEC), whose oil-producing members aggravated an energy crisis during the early 1970s by raising prices for consumer nations. At the same time, terrorists and hijackers repeatedly posed dilemmas seemingly incapable of resolution. Especially alarming were the massive hunger problems that took millions of lives in the economically destitute and poverty-stricken "Fourth World." Critics in the United States complained that détente was a new form of globalism that would again overextend the nation's foreign involvement in economic, political, and military affairs. Others wondered what would happen if the Communist Chinese tried to play off the Soviets against the Americans or if the Soviets attempted the same with the Americans and the Chinese. Yet despite the pitfalls of détente, there seemed to be no viable alternative.

Kissinger used the idea of "linkage" in trying to reduce his country's tensions with the Soviet Union and Communist China. By exerting economic pressure on the Moscow and Beijing governments, the United States might convince them to halt their arms supply to North Vietnam and force Ho Chi Minh into a compromise settlement of the war. Despite the apparent new direction in foreign policy, this approach actually looked backward because it assumed that the North Vietnamese lacked a will of their own and that the United States could manipulate and control history. Another premise of linkage was the indivisibility of peace—that an act of aggression in any part of the world constituted a threat to the overall network of peace. Kissinger hoped that the three major powers might tie all facets together in one magnificent design for peace. According to theory, the United States would furnish economic assistance to the Soviets in exchange for helping to wind down the war in Vietnam and accepting arms limitations. The Washington government would then open negotiations with Beijing's leaders to guarantee peace. By linking economic aid to military events in Southeast Asia, the United States would lay the basis for détente by improving relations with the Soviet Union and inaugurating a new era with the People's Republic of China. Military withdrawal from Vietnam would also unite Americans at home and allow the United States to negotiate from a position of strength. Détente and linkage sought to alleviate tensions; distrust and rivalry would remain.

Linkage came laden with questionable premises that offered little assurance of success. Policymakers during the Franklin D. Roosevelt presidency had had minimal effect on achieving world order when they tried to tie together seemingly unrelated issues. Furthermore, the amount of war materiel that the Soviets and Communist Chinese furnished to the North Vietnamese was small compared to the help provided by the Americans to the Army of the Republic of Vietnam (ARVN). In truth, linkage was little different from containment in that both rested on the highly dubious assumption that world events depended primarily on the decisions of the major powers. The Nixon administration nonetheless sought a Soviet–American arms control agreement and expanded commercial relations, which it claimed would end the war in Vietnam and ease world unrest. Washington's policymakers still ignored the central truth repeatedly hammered home by the nation's ongoing experience in Vietnam: the United States was unable to determine the world's events. Although its destructive capacity was greater than it had been in 1945, its leverage over global affairs had steadily declined since the war because of the world's constantly shifting balance of power. Détente and linkage were attempts to deal with these developments, but the central objective of U.S. foreign policy remained the same—to contain communism.

Vietnam and Détente

Meanwhile, the war in Vietnam continued. Nixon's alleged "secret" plan turned out to be more of the same—"Vietnamization" of the war, a term created by Secretary of Defense Melvin Laird but reflecting a process of de-Americanization of the conflict first sought by Kennedy but dropped and then begun anew in the latter stages of the Johnson administration. Vietnamization ensured a scaled withdrawal in proportion to expanded aid to Saigon or, as one U.S. official cynically put it, "changing the color of the corpses." The scheme rested on the improved fighting skills of the ARVN, which so far had displayed little evidence of such prowess. No longer was there any debate about *whether* the United States would pull out of Vietnam; the question was how to do so without marring U.S. respect throughout the world. If the United States appeared weak in Vietnam, détente had little chance for success. President Nixon therefore adopted an unyielding stance in the Paris peace talks and at the same time sought leverage by resuming the bombing. Both measures, he assured Americans, would promote Vietnamization. Privately, however, he had already observed to Laird that "there's no way to win the war. But we can't say that, of course." Like Kennedy and Johnson, Nixon refused to allow the appearance of defeat to cloud his administration, and like those before him, his central goal remained an independent, non-Communist South Vietnam. Above all, he could not condone a coalition government because it would eventually come under Communist control. Impatient critics, however, soon charged that the administration sought only a "decent interval" between the time the United States withdrew its combat forces and when South Vietnam collapsed to the Communists—presumably two to three years.

Nixon tried to promote the peace process by exerting more military pressure on the battlefield. Little hope came out of Paris, where the talks had bogged down over several issues that included procedural matters, whether the Vietcong and the Saigon government should have representatives at the proceedings, the timing of U.S. and North Vietnamese withdrawals, and Vietnam's postwar political framework. The president feared that a premature U.S. withdrawal meant immediate Communist victory and decided to exploit his hard-line anti-Communist image as a critical bargaining point with the North Vietnamese. As he told an adviser, "They'll believe any threat of force Nixon makes because it's Nixon. We'll just slip the word to them that 'for God's sake, you know Nixon's obsessed about Communism . . . and he has his hand on the nuclear button.'" Yet he realized that the use of nuclear weapons would arouse worldwide condemnation, foment opposition among Americans, and create a situation conducive to total war. The only alternative was Vietnamization because it would leave the impression that the United States had fulfilled its objectives in Vietnam while reserving the option of escalating the war.

The North Vietnamese did not make the problem easy for the United States: in February 1969, a month after Nixon's inauguration, they launched a massive offensive across the demilitarized zone (DMZ) that took a heavy toll on Americans. The war's end seemed nowhere in sight. Television reporters pointed out that U.S. forces in Vietnam numbered nearly 542,000, the most there during the entire war, and that its death totals were now more than 40,000, a figure higher than that of the Korean War. Nixon emphasized that U.S. withdrawal depended on success in Paris and on the behavior of North Vietnamese forces in the field. Yet just as the Hanoi regime had earlier baffled Washington's leaders by standing up to American firepower, it now refused to reduce military actions in proportion to any U.S. steps toward withdrawal. The reason was simple though totally unacceptable to the White House: any termination of the war short of a reunified Vietnam under Hanoi's leadership constituted a defeat.

The North Vietnamese assault in February evoked a strong response from the Nixon administration, both on the battlefield and at the peace table. The United States bombed North Vietnam's supply routes out of Cambodia (Operation MENU), an action kept secret from Congress and the American people

for four years. When the *New York Times* exposed the campaign, the White House plugged the leaks by ordering FBI wiretaps on reporters and government officials. As in the earlier phases of the war, the B-52s were unable to stop the transportation of goods by humans and bicycles over countless winding and largely hidden jungle trails. In mid-May 1969, Nixon presented what he termed a "comprehensive peace plan" that called for the reestablishment of the DMZ between the antagonists and the mutual withdrawal of U.S. and North Vietnamese forces from South Vietnam within a year of a cease-fire agreement. Internationally supervised elections would follow, although South Vietnam's military president, Nguyen Van Thieu, would remain in office during the interim.

But Nixon's proposals had no effect. North Vietnam angrily rejected them as a "farce" and warned that it was prepared to stay in Paris "until the chairs rot." The Hanoi government remained firm in its demands for a total U.S. withdrawal, the establishment of a provisional coalition regime that did *not* include Thieu, and the final disposition of Vietnam to be settled by the "Vietnamese parties among themselves." There was still no basis for a settlement, which meant that Vietnamization would take longer than expected.

In the summer of 1969, the White House announced the first of several troop reductions in Vietnam and called for a program of greater assumption of international responsibility by the allies that eventually became known as the "Nixon Doctrine." The president met with Thieu in June at Midway Island, where Nixon declared that as of August 1, 25,000 combat forces would pull out of Vietnam, followed by more in relation to the ARVN's improved battle performance. Shortly after the announcement, on July 20, the nation's prestige received a huge lift when worldwide television covered two U.S. astronauts from the Apollo 11 mission who became the first human beings to land on the moon. Two days later, Nixon was en route to Asia and Europe, stopping at Guam and delivering an address on July 25 that called for a new direction in foreign policy. Speaking within the context of Vietnam, the president asserted that in the future the United States would avoid heavy military involvement in Asian affairs, but he added that the principles he expounded would apply "to all our international relationships." Lest some worry about a return to isolationism, Nixon promised to honor treaty obligations, provide military and economic aid in combating aggression, and furnish a nuclear shield to any ally or nation deemed vital to U.S. security. The key point in the Nixon Doctrine was the president's pledge to "look to the nation directly threatened to assume the primary responsibility of providing the manpower for its defense." His administration called for partnerships based on "shared burdens and shared responsibilities."

The Nixon Doctrine did not signal an end to U.S. global commitments, but it marked another step toward détente and a withdrawal from Vietnam because it constituted an admission of power limitations and an invitation to antagonists to wind down the Cold War. Laird explained that "America will no longer try to play policeman to the world. Instead, we will expect other nations to provide more cops on the beat in their own neighborhood." The United States would rely more on Japan in Asia, Iran in the Middle East, and Zaire (formerly Belgian Congo), Angola, and South Africa in Africa.

The Nixon administration's program also encompassed massive arms sales—with nearly predictable repercussions. The arms influx encouraged the use of military force in the Middle East, Latin America, and Africa; tied the Nixon administration to white regimes in Africa and to the shah in Iran; hurt other nations financially; and endangered relations with Japan, which refused to accept the upgraded role the United States wanted it to assume in Asia. The inflated prices charged by arms producers, in fact, encouraged Iran, a U.S. ally, to raise oil prices to facilitate the purchase of war materiel. At these heavy costs,

the United States struggled toward an honorable withdrawal from Vietnam.

While the Nixon administration maintained a strong public position in the war, Kissinger secretly opened new peace talks in Paris with North Vietnam's representative, Xuan Thuy. Virtually ignoring South Vietnam, Kissinger in August 1969 called for a cease-fire, the return of American prisoners of war (POWs), and Thieu's retention as president in Saigon. In exchange, the United States would withdraw, implicitly recognizing Communist control over much of South Vietnam. The offer aroused no interest. North Vietnam wanted both the United States and Thieu out of the country, and it was in the strong military position to demand the entire south. Still another problem appeared: Thieu felt betrayed by Washington's attempt to get out of Vietnam "with honor."

As the secret talks went on, so did the war. Ho Chi Minh died in September 1969, causing great mourning throughout North Vietnam and turning over leadership to longtime nationalists Pham Van Dong (premier), Vo Nguyen Giap (general), and Le Duan (leader of the Lao Dong, or Communist Workers' Party, in North Vietnam). Nixon continued to defend his policies to Americans becoming increasingly impatient with the pace of Vietnamization. Antiwar demonstrations spread during October and November, attracting thousands of participants to "The Vietnam Moratorium" in Boston and Washington. In a television appearance on November 3, Nixon repeated that the United States would pull out "on an orderly scheduled timetable" that depended on progress in Paris, "the level of enemy activity," and the speed with which the South Vietnamese assumed responsibilities. Should North Vietnam step up resistance, he promised, the United States would adopt "strong and effective measures." At the end of his speech, Nixon asserted that "North Vietnam cannot humiliate the United States. Only Americans can do that." The establishment of a draft lottery system that month helped to take the fire out of the protest movements by making the system fairer in application.

Nixon cited several reasons for insisting that the United States remain in Vietnam as long as necessary. Moving out too quickly would endanger the lives of U.S. troops and supporters in Saigon. Defeat in South Vietnam would threaten other U.S. interests in Asia. The United States had treaty obligations and moral commitments to honor. It had to ensure the return of the POWs. To Congress in January 1970, Nixon proclaimed that "when we assumed the burden of helping South Vietnam, millions of South Vietnamese men and women placed their trust in us. To abandon them would risk a massacre that would shock and dismay everyone in the world who values human life."

Suddenly, the war seemed to take a turn in South Vietnam's favor. Faced with U.S. troop withdrawals, Thieu had announced a general mobilization that called in all men eighteen to thirty-eight years of age, placing more than half of South Vietnam's male population in military service and raising the army's rolls from 700,000 to more than a million. Refugees flocked into the cities, where they worked in the ARVN or for Americans and added to the outward appearance that the metropolitan centers were thriving. The truth was otherwise. Saigon was only a facade of industrial growth because the peasants had fled there for safety from the "Free-Fire Zones" in which U.S. armed forces tried to root out pockets of help for the Vietcong. American dollars were the country's sole financial base, and the only bustling industry was the war machine underwritten almost entirely by the United States. If the soldiers pulled out now, the South Vietnamese economy would collapse.

The irony was that whereas the United States had not intended to make South Vietnam a colony, its very existence depended almost totally on the United States. Americans had not drained the country's wealth as had the French, but they had established a widespread network of services for themselves that the Vietnamese filled through the armed forces as well as through household duties, office work, and other menial tasks. The United States had also failed to encourage the production of rice and other commodities, handing Thieu a government without an economic base. As long as the Americans required services, the Vietnamese people remained in a state of dependency that had nothing to do with patriotism or ideals. In 1969 and 1970, the United States cited statistics allegedly proving Vietnamization a success—climbing Vietcong body counts, an expanded ARVN, and increasing supplies of weapons. But the new South Vietnamese soldiers were poor fighters because they were there without choice and lacked morale and a cause. The essential ingredient of U.S. victory—"winning the hearts and minds of the people"—had little chance in this uncertain atmosphere.

Hopes for détente seemed to brighten with the Strategic Arms Limitations Talks (SALT) with the Soviet Union, which began in Helsinki, Finland, in November 1969 and shifted back and forth between there and Vienna for the next two-and-a-half years. Although the U.S. triad strategic force had ICBMs, submarine-launched ballistic missiles (SLBMs), and long-range bombers, the Soviet Union had made rapid advances, passing the United States in ICBMs though remaining behind in the other two categories. Rather than seek superiority in strategic weapons, Nixon appeared satisfied with parity. Kissinger emphasized that "an attempt to gain a unilateral advantage in the strategic field" was "self-defeating." Yet the policy seemed inconsistent. Nixon had campaigned in 1968 on dealing only "from a position of superiority" and had secured the Senate's narrow passage of the Safeguard ABM system in August, just before he notified the Moscow regime of the readiness of the United States to discuss issues. To ensure leverage in the SALT talks, he approved development of the MIRV. The president nonetheless reassured Congress in February 1970 that his administration sought a partnership in maintaining world peace. "America cannot—and will not—conceive *all* the plans, design *all* the programs, execute *all* the decisions and undertake *all* the defense of the free nations of the world." Détente was the only way out of Vietnam, and that process began with arms limitations agreements.

But before the SALT talks could make headway, attention dramatically returned to the war in Southeast Asia. On April 30, 1970, Nixon shocked the nation by declaring that the United States and South Vietnam had extended the military effort into Cambodia to destroy the enemy's bases of operation. The United States had known of the Cambodian sanctuary for some time, he explained over television, but had done little for fear of pushing the neutralist Cambodian regime of Prince Norodom Sihanouk into the Communist camp. Sihanouk, however, had fallen in a coup assisted by the United States and led by a pro-Western general named Lon Nol, who now sought U.S. help against a possible military takeover by the thousands of North Vietnamese forces inside his country.

Nixon's speech was filled with misleading statements and, according to some critics, deceptions and falsehoods. Should the North Vietnamese overthrow the Lon Nol regime, Nixon warned, "Cambodia would become a vast enemy staging area and springboard for attacks on South Vietnam along 600 miles of frontier." Lon Nol had asked for assistance, and the United States intended to "go to the heart of the trouble" by destroying the enemy's military "nerve center"—the Central Office for South Vietnam (COSVN)—which was "the headquarters for the entire Communist military operation in South Vietnam." There was no choice. "We will not be humiliated. We will not be defeated." In true Cold War language, complete with allusions to Armaggedon, he warned Americans that, "if when the chips are down, the world's most powerful nation . . . acts like a pitiful helpless giant, the forces of totalitarianism and anarchy will threaten free nations and free institutions throughout the world." This was not an in-

President Richard M. Nixon at Press Conference
Explaining American incursion into Cambodia on April 30, 1970. *(National Archives, Washington, D.C.)*

In this nationwide television address, President Nixon declared that the U.S. and South Vietnamese military entrance into Cambodia was not an invasion but, rather, an attempt to clear out the North Vietnamese and Vietcong and thus facilitate an end to the war in Vietnam.

President Richard Nixon's television speech on Cambodia, April 30, 1970, *Public Papers of the Presidents of the United States: Richard Nixon* (Washington, D.C.: Government Printing Office, 1971), 405–9.

For the past five years as indicated on this map that you see here North Vietnam has occupied military sanctuaries all along the Cambodian frontier with South Vietnam. Some of these extend up to twenty miles into Cambodia. . . . In cooperation with the armed forces of South Vietnam, attacks are being launched this week to clean out major enemy sanctuaries on the Cambodian Vietnam border.

A major responsibility for the ground operations is being assumed by South Vietnamese forces. . . .

There is one area, however, immediately above Parrot's Beak, where I have concluded that a combined American and South Vietnamese operation is necessary.

Tonight, American and South Vietnamese units will attack the headquarters for the entire Communist military operation in South Vietnam. This key control center has been occupied by the North Vietnamese and Vietcong for five years in blatant violation of Cambodia's neutrality.

This is not an invasion of Cambodia. The areas in which these attacks will be launched are completely occupied and controlled by North Vietnamese forces. Our purpose is not to occupy the areas. Once enemy forces are driven out of these sanctuaries and once their military supplies are destroyed, we will withdraw. . . .

We take this action not for the purpose of expanding the war into Cambodia but for the purpose of ending the war in Vietnam and winning the just peace we all desire. . . .

The action that I have announced tonight puts the leaders of North Vietnam on notice that we will be patient in working for peace; we will be conciliatory at the conference table, but we will not be humiliated. We will not be defeated. We will not allow American men by the thousands to be killed by an enemy from privileged sanctuaries. . . .

I would rather be a one-term President and do what I believe is right than to be a two-term President at the cost of seeing America become a second rate power and to see this Nation accept the first defeat in its proud 190-year history.

vasion of Cambodia, he insisted; the assault force would concentrate only on locations "completely occupied and controlled by North Vietnamese forces. . . . Once enemy forces are driven out of these sanctuaries and their military supplies destroyed, we will withdraw." The military operation in Cambodia, Nixon assured, would further promote a U.S. withdrawal from Vietnam.

Nixon's speech drew such an angry reaction inside the United States that he felt compelled to impose limits on the new military campaign. Americans were enraged that the administration's way out of Vietnam seemed to be through Cambodia. Demon-

strations broke out in hundreds of colleges and universities across the United States, and in the Senate a move began toward prohibiting funds for the military effort in Cambodia after June 30. On May 4, an explosive atmosphere at Kent State University in Ohio caused National Guardsmen to fire into a group of students, killing four and injuring nine. As legions of protesters stormed the streets of Washington, U.S. soldiers moved into the White House basement, ready to defend it from attack by fellow Americans. The day following the events at Kent State, Nixon attempted to defuse the national anger by promising that U.S. combat forces would go no farther than twenty-two miles into Cambodia without congressional approval and that troops and their advisers would pull out of the country by June 30. In addition, he assured Americans that there would be no secret deals with the Lon Nol regime and asserted that U.S. assistance to Cambodia would consist only of war materiel and air cover. Privately, however, Nixon was furious at the growing protests at home and directed the FBI and CIA to intensify their search for connections between radical organizations in the United States and those abroad. "Don't worry about divisiveness," he told aides. "Having drawn the sword, don't take it out—stick it in hard."

After June 30, and with the U.S. troops withdrawn as promised, Nixon proclaimed the Cambodian mission a huge success. South Vietnamese forces had killed or taken prisoner thousands of North Vietnamese and Vietcong, confiscated or destroyed great amounts of war materiel, and cleared the enemy from miles of jungle. Yet he did not mention that U.S. and allied units had failed either to close the supply route or to locate the alleged COSVN. In fact, the Defense Department in Washington was unsure whether such a nerve center actually existed. The North Vietnamese and Vietcong, it now seems clear, never operated out of a central command headquarters comparable to anything in the West. Nor did the president point out that the campaign had set off widespread unrest in Cambodia, providing cause for a brutal Communist insurgency movement led by the Khmer Rouge and thus breathing life into the domino theory. The invasion widened the war in Southeast Asia by committing the United States to another weak regime, this one in Cambodia.

In the meantime, the Senate infuriated Nixon by acting to curb the war-making activities of the White House. On June 24, it had overwhelmingly voted to repeal both the Eisenhower Doctrine of 1957 and the Tonkin Resolution of 1964 and had forwarded the bill to the House. Nixon had not fought these moves because, he argued, his policies in Vietnam and Cambodia were justified by his constitutional duty to safeguard members of the armed forces. But evidence was growing that the Executive Office was becoming isolated from the rest of the country and increasingly suspicious of any calls for change. One of Nixon's aides later recalled that during the summer of 1970, a "siege mentality" was developing "quite unknowingly" inside the White House. "It was now 'us' against 'them.' Gradually, as we drew the circle closer around us, the ranks of 'them' began to swell."

In the autumn of 1970, Nixon asserted that the Cambodian venture had opened new peace avenues in Vietnam. Both North Vietnam and the National Liberation Front (NLF) had boycotted the Paris proceedings because of the invasion, but in mid-September the North Vietnamese returned to the talks with repeated demands for an unconditional U.S. military withdrawal from Vietnam and the assurance of Vietcong participation in a political settlement. Nixon countered with a "major new initiative for peace" that drew bitter reactions in Hanoi and Moscow and among the Vietcong. On television on October 7, he called for a "standstill" cease-fire and the immediate exchange of POWs; inclusion of Cambodia and Laos in the peace talks, thereby establishing the war in Vietnam as an Indochinese conflict and not a civil war; total U.S. military withdrawal according to a determined schedule; and assurances that Thieu would remain in control until elections took place. Thus, neither side would make concessions. Nixon's effort attracted no interest. The Hanoi government joined the Vietcong in refusing to consider the proposals and spokespersons in Moscow called them "a great fraud."

A month later the war in Vietnam intensified again as the United States bombed the DMZ and the Hanoi–Haiphong region in an extensive campaign that Nixon termed "protective reaction strikes." According to the White House, the bombings would continue until the North Vietnamese stopped firing at U.S. reconnaissance planes over North Vietnam. This announcement drew a sharp reaction from Hanoi's defense minister and long-time military strategist Vo Nguyen Giap, who indignantly declared North Vietnam "a sovereign independent country, and no sovereign independent country will allow its enemy to spy freely upon it." Congress also opposed the bombings. The House had meanwhile approved the Senate's bill repealing the Tonkin Resolution (a move Nixon dismissed as unnecessary to his continuing the war) but would not repeal the Eisenhower Doctrine. The modified measure became law in January 1971. Although Congress refused to deny funds to U.S. soldiers, it prohibited the use of money to broaden the war in Vietnam and barred the deployment of U.S. troops in either Cambodia or Laos. Congress did not prohibit the use of planes, however, and when in February 1971 the ARVN invaded Laos to close the Ho Chi Minh Trail, Nixon authorized air cover. But South Vietnam's field performance was disastrous. In less than two months, the North Vietnamese inflicted 50 percent casualties and drove the ARVN out of Laos—with some of the retreating soldiers hanging onto the skids of the escaping helicopters.

By the spring of 1971, Americans at home had again mobilized against the war. Nearly 200,000 antiwar activists, including Vietnam War veterans, demonstrated in Washington, only to draw Nixon's cutting remark that they were "mobs" who did not speak for "the great silent majority." But a Gallup poll in May suggested that the president was wrong. According to the survey, six of ten Americans thought the United States should not be in Vietnam, which was an exact reversal of the opinion expressed in the autumn of 1965. Furthermore, the opposition was bipartisan. Later studies revealed that contrary to popular belief, the war's greatest critics by the early 1970s were not the country's youths but older Americans, women, lower-class Americans, and blacks. The black population argued with justification that a disproportionate share of black soldiers were fighting and dying in Vietnam.

Other revelations had meanwhile deepened Americans' resentment of the war and, in some cases, of the actions of their soldiers. In early 1971, a court-martial had found Army Lieutenant William Calley guilty of "at least twenty-two murders" of men, women, and children in the South Vietnamese village of My Lai in 1968. The village, Calley alleged, had been Vietcong infested and was therefore a legitimate military target. Nixon soon added to the widespread indignation over the massacre and army cover-up by ordering Calley's release while the decision came under review and by ultimately extending him a full pardon. The image of the U.S. fighting man took another severe blow when CBS News reported large numbers of American soldiers in Vietnam using drugs and nearly 15,000 as heroin addicts. Furthermore, the advent of Vietnamization meant a winding down of the war, which had the unexpected result of making U.S. soldiers reluctant to engage in combat. No one wanted to be the last American killed in Vietnam.

Still other issues soured the U.S. experience in Vietnam. The American economy reeled from recession, inflation, a steady outflow of dollars from the country, and an unfavorable balance of trade that found the United States for the first time since the 1890s importing more than it exported. Finally, in June 1971, the *New York Times* published *The Pentagon Papers*, selections from classified documents that government employee Daniel Ellsberg had illegally removed from the Defense Department in an effort to halt the war in Vietnam. The Pentagon materials supported the longtime allegations that Kennedy and Johnson had been less than truthful about their nation's involvement in Southeast Asia. When the Supreme Court refused to prevent publication of the documents, the White House used its special task force called the "plumbers" to halt further leaks and to discredit Ellsberg. Ultimately, a federal judge dismissed charges against him when it became clear that the Justice Department, with CIA help, had illegally wire-tapped his phone and burglarized the files of his psychiatrist to "find some dirt" about Ellsberg.

High Tide of Détente: Communist China, the Soviet Union, SALT I, and Vietnamization

To encourage détente, President Nixon made a stunning announcement in July 1971: he had accepted an invitation from Beijing to visit China to "seek the normalization of relations," which were in total disarray following the Communist triumph of 1949. Considerable quiet preparation had taken place for this pathbreaking decision. In early 1969, Nixon had directed Kissinger to reassess the situation with China for the purpose of restoring relations. That same year, the United States eased commercial and travel restrictions with China, pointedly referred to its regime as the People's Republic of China, and terminated the Seventh Fleet's regular patrol of the Taiwan Strait. The following year, the United States resumed talks with China in Warsaw, adjourned since early 1968 as a result of friction over Vietnam. When war broke out in 1971 between India (supported by the Soviet Union) and Pakistan (which received help from China), the Nixon administration leaned toward Pakistan. That same year, in April, American table tennis players then in Japan accepted an invitation to China, where they played a match and lost to the world champions. Their trip to China, however, popularized the term "Ping-Pong diplomacy" as a breakthrough to détente. Shortly afterward, the United States ended its trade embargo on China. Kissinger had secretly traveled to Beijing less than a week before Nixon's announcement, where he made arrangements with Zhou Enlai, second only to Mao Zedong in the Chinese Communist Party. "What we are doing now with China," Kissinger later declared, "is so great, so historic, the word *Vietnam* will be only a footnote when it is written in history." In August, the State Department announced support for Communist China's admission into the United Nations with the simultaneous membership of the Republic of China. This "Two-Chinas policy" lasted until October, when the UN General Assembly approved the admission of Communist China and, with only a mild U.S. protest, expelled Taiwan.

Numerous factors account for this revolution in U.S. foreign policy, but as in all reciprocal arrangements, the basic consideration was mutual need. Since 1969, both nations had given subtle indications of interest in establishing relations, based on the common grounds of halting Soviet expansion and promoting trade. China was alarmed over recent clashes with Soviet troops stationed along the nations' common border. It was also concerned about Japan, fearing that the establishment of relations with the United States might either reduce the Tokyo government's belligerence or promote a foundation for Sino–Japanese relations—still broken since the two sides went to war in 1937. The prime objective of the United States, however, was to widen the rift in Sino–Soviet relations and develop a power balance conducive to détente and world peace. The resulting stimulus to trade might also revive the ailing U.S. economy by securing it a greater share of the China market before Japan established a monopoly. As the *New York Times* declared, "The President is in the position of the lovely maiden courted by two ardent swains, each of whom is aware of the other but each of whom is uncertain of what happens when the young lady is alone with his rival."

Nixon also had personal reasons for wanting to normalize relations with China. Such a dramatic move would award him a place in history that only he could occupy because of his staunch anti-Communist reputation. The presidential election of 1972 was another factor. Nixon had still not extricated the United States from Vietnam, and peace-minded Democrats led by Senator George McGovern were making gains, as evidenced by their strong showing in the New Hampshire primary of the previous March. Nixon, however, remained in a sound political position. Right-

Henry Kissinger at the Great Wall of China, October 1971
In preparation for President Nixon's visit, the national security adviser went to China with orders to avoid any publicity that would upstage his superior's place in history. The president was enraged when this picture appeared worldwide—as was UN Ambassador George Bush, who, at the time, was trying to save Taiwan's seat in the organization. *(National Archives, Washington, D.C.)*

wing Republicans could not accuse him of being "soft on communism," and liberal Democrats could not be critical because many of them had advocated recognition of China for some time. Although the powerful China lobby and much of the U.S. labor lobby favored the Chinese in Taiwan, Nixon realized that Americans' emotions over that issue had calmed considerably. During the mid-1960s, about a quarter of Americans had not even known that the mainland Chinese government was Communist.

But the most immediate goal in Nixon's China decision was to promote détente and allow a U.S. withdrawal from Vietnam. Rela-

tions with Beijing might force the Moscow government to ease its anti-American stance and cause both the Soviets and China to cut aid to North Vietnam and the Vietcong, thereby permitting the United States to complete the Vietnamization of the war and turn to other matters. If handled correctly, détente would heighten concern within the Soviet Union about the consequences of a U.S. alliance with China. The basic goal was to leave the Thieu regime intact and permit U.S. withdrawal from Vietnam.

Nixon's trip to China in February 1972 received worldwide attention. According to the president as he left the United States, his visit would "signal the end of a sterile and barren interlude in the relationship between two great peoples." Accompanying him on the 20,000-mile journey were nearly ninety journalists plus almost forty members of the mission, including Secretary of State Rogers, who remained conspicuously subordinate to Kissinger in discussing foreign policy.

Nixon's landing in China on February 21 aroused little outward enthusiasm, although the Chinese had probably staged this quiet reception to suggest that the United States was more eager to establish relations than were the Chinese. Premier Zhou Enlai greeted Nixon with a formal handshake and then warmly welcomed Kissinger as his "old friend." No ceremony took place, although the band played America's National Anthem, followed by China's "The March of the Volunteers." That same day, Nixon and Kissinger met with Mao and Zhou for nearly an hour, and later that evening they attended a huge banquet in the Great Hall of the People, where numerous toasts to good relations set the tone of succeeding discussions. "What we do here," Nixon proclaimed, "can change the world."

The image fostered by the White House and the news media was that Nixon's visit to China was monumental in importance. As the presidential party stood before the Great Wall, Nixon made the inane remark before television cameras that "I think that you would have to conclude that this is a great wall. . . . As we look at this wall, we do not want walls of any kind between peoples." On February 27 in Shanghai, the two nations signed a vaguely worded joint communiqué that offered assurances of normal relations. The United States declared that its goal was peace in Asia with "social progress for all peoples . . . [and] free of outside pressure or intervention." After reiterating the desire to withdraw from Vietnam, the United States affirmed that its "ultimate" goal was "the withdrawal of all U.S. forces and military installations from Taiwan" to promote "a peace-

ful settlement of the Taiwan question by the Chinese themselves." China approved, emphasizing that Taiwan was the "crucial question obstructing the normalization of relations." The two nations probably aimed this statement at the Soviet Union: "Neither should seek hegemony in the Asia-Pacific region and each is opposed to efforts by any other country or group of countries to establish such hegemony." The United States and China concluded the Shanghai communiqué with a call for expanded commerce and cultural interchange. Formal recognition seemed imminent. As Nixon departed for home the next day, he triumphantly pronounced this "the week that changed the world."

Nixon's China visit had mixed consequences for détente. Japan was stunned about the imminent establishment of Sino–American diplomatic relations, particularly because it remained technically at war with China (since 1937). But the time had come to break with the past. In the autumn of 1972, the Japanese premier traveled to Beijing to repair relations and soon afterward severed ties with Taiwan. Both Vietnams felt threatened by the new accord between China and the United States—the north because it depended on Beijing for arms and the south because the Chinese were its avowed enemy. The Chinese action, in fact, aroused considerable suspicion among numerous Third World peoples who were undecided about whom to trust. But if the central purpose of Nixon's China trip was to promote détente by placing pressure on Moscow, it was successful. Shortly after he had announced his intention to travel to China, the Soviets invited him to Moscow. The president decided to go in May 1972, just three months after the trip to Beijing.

If the Nixon administration felt confident that détente's success had established a firm grasp on the direction of events, it soon found out that lesser powers can exert considerable influence as well. In late March 1972, North Vietnam challenged both the claimed accom-

Nixon and Zhou Enlai
The president called his visit to the People's Republic of China "the week that changed the world."
(Wide World Photos, New York)

plishments of Vietnamization and the new U.S.–China arrangement by launching the mammoth "Easter Offensive" against the south. In an assault that approximated the Tet Offensive in ferocity and posed a severe test to détente, nearly 200,000 North Vietnamese forces, with Soviet tanks and heavy artillery, hit South Vietnam across the DMZ, into the Central Highlands, and out of Cambodia just northwest of Saigon. The invaders came within sixty miles of the capital, convincing many observers that the Saigon government was on the verge of collapse. To counter the widespread offensive, Nixon approved the largest bombing campaigns of the war—later called "Linebacker I," a reflection of his avid love of football—which lasted from May through October and included the use of computer-guided "smart bombs" to hit railway lines to China. As American B-52s struck Hanoi and Haiphong for the first time since 1968, Nixon ignored fears of involving Communist China and the Soviet Union and authorized the mining of the port of Haiphong and the imposition of a naval blockade of the north. "The bastards have never been bombed like they're going to be bombed this time," he asserted. If the United States lost in Vietnam because of failure to use the power it possessed, "there would have been no respect for the American President. . . . We must be credible."

Like Johnson, Nixon coupled the stick with the carrot, and, like Johnson, Nixon succeeded in safeguarding the Saigon regime but at the heavy cost of escalating the destructive level of the war. Nixon prohibited the bombing of civilian targets and held out the possibility of peace by assuring the Hanoi government that if it agreed to return all American POWs and accept an internationally supervised cease-fire, the United States would pull out of Vietnam within four months. For the first time, the White House had set a timetable for withdrawal, and for the first time, it had made no demand that the North Vietnamese leave the south. Furthermore, the long-standing stipulation of Thieu's survival was noticeably missing. But North Vietnam, perhaps testing détente's resilience, turned down the offer. In the meantime, even though the Soviets lost four merchant vessels during the bombardment of Haiphong, they raised no objections—doubtless because of ongoing border problems with China and their desire for détente with the United States. China publicly criticized the Nixon administration but likewise took no action on behalf of North Vietnam. The reluctance of either Communist power to intervene must have put Hanoi's leaders into a quandary. Although the new fighting again resulted in a stalemate, the North Vietnamese undoubtedly had become more amenable to a cease-fire. Pummeled and exhausted by the bombs and the fighting, they now found themselves alone: neither the Chinese nor the Soviets had come to their side during the U.S. offensive.

The Soviets' restraint over the escalated U.S. military actions demonstrated that they attached great importance to Nixon's impending arrival in May. Soviet General Secretary Leonid Brezhnev had signaled his readiness for détente a year before, when at the Twenty-Fourth Party Congress he spoke of peace measures for the 1970s. The Soviet economy was in dire shape, as shown by the recent failure of a Five-Year Plan that had underlined his people's need for grain and technological assistance. Revolutionaries in several Communist states were still bitter over the Red Army's heavy-handed tactics in putting down the 1968 uprising in Czechoslovakia. Poland and Romania, for example, increasingly leaned toward the West for trade. In August 1970, the Moscow government had signed a nonaggression pact with West German Chancellor Willy Brandt that smoothed the path toward détente with the United States and also allowed the dispatch of additional Soviet troops to the tense Chinese frontier. The treaty terms relieved Soviet fears of a revived, powerful Germany by conceding the reality of two Berlins and two Germanies. Three months later, West Germany signed a nonaggression agreement with Poland that recognized the Oder-Neisse River as the common border, a move restoring Polish control over territories lost in 1945. Finally, in September 1971, Brezhnev signed a pact pledging Western access to Berlin in exchange for West Germany's recognition of the East European borders established by the Red Army in 1945. Fear of encirclement was a major Soviet concern, especially after China began negotiations with the United States and Japan.

Nixon's visit to the Soviet Union in May led to agreements more substantial than any reached with China. The atmosphere in Moscow was more cordial than in Beijing, and Nixon was even allowed to speak to the Soviet people over radio and television. He and Brezhnev agreed to cooperate in space exploration, environmental protection, medical and scientific research, and other matters of common concern. They also discussed Vietnam but would only state that small nations should not stand in the way of détente. The major accords related to arms limitations. On May 26, Nixon and Brezhnev signed a document proclaiming their goal of "peaceful coexistence" and then reached an agreement based on more than two years of SALT talks. Known as SALT I, it included two pacts: the Treaty of Anti-Ballistic Missiles Systems and the Interim Agreement on Limitation of Strategic Offensive Arms. The first agreement, aimed at those systems designed to intercept and neutralize approaching nuclear warheads, initially restricted each party to no more than two ABM systems but later cut them to one. According to the theory appropriately known as MAD (mutual assured destruction), both sides' major cities would be vulnerable to attack, ensuring that neither would choose to begin war. The second—the Interim Agreement—attempted to establish a five-year ceiling on the construction of offensive missiles. Bombers were not part of these agreements, however, leaving the United States at a distinct advantage. By September 1972, both agreements had received formal U.S. approval by wide margins. The following month, the two nations negotiated a commercial pact that included the sale of U.S. grain and the Soviet Union's agreement to pay back its Lend-Lease debt of World War II by 2001.

The appearance of compromise in Moscow was deceptive, however, because the SALT I agreements had actually encouraged an arms race in new weapons—American cruise missiles and Soviet "Backfire" supersonic bombers. The ABMs were costly yet ineffective, thus constituting no concession by either side. The United States maintained the upper hand in technology because the agreements had no bearing on the multiple-headed MIRVs. A single U.S. submarine (of which the United States had thirty) could carry MIRVs capable of delivering the impact of Hiroshima 160 times over. Within a year, the United States had 6,000 nuclear warheads to the Soviets' 2,500, and by the time the SALT I agreements expired as scheduled in 1977, the Americans' weapons doubled those of the Soviets.

Thus, the SALT discussions in Moscow paradoxically stimulated an arms race by placing limitations on older models and diverting attention from the ongoing development of newer, more sophisticated weapons. To pre-

vent interference with the MIRVs, Nixon prohibited his negotiating team from discussing them during the SALT talks in Helsinki. In addition, each side was capable of "overkill" numerous times, and both possessed satellite surveillance systems that made secret testing a phenomenon of the past. The terms of agreement were forwarded to Helsinki, where the intent of SALT II was to convert the interim agreement into a permanent pact.

Yet the SALT I agreements in Moscow encouraged the image of détente, which in turn had favorable repercussions in Europe. The improvement of Soviet–American relations offered the opportunity to resolve problems in Germany remaining from World War II. In June 1972, the Quadripartite Treaty, or Berlin Agreement, went into effect when the four occupying powers—the United States, the Soviet Union, Britain, and France—extended recognition to East Germany. Two years later, the United States established formal diplomatic relations, making divided Germany a fact and ending the wartime goal of reunification. Détente also furthered the Helsinki Accords of 1972, which called for recognition of boundaries in East European Communist states in exchange for the signatory nations' pledge of respect for human rights. These agreements likewise endorsed the results of World War II in Eastern Europe by admitting to Soviet domination of the area, a fact resisted since the Truman years.

Détente also affected events in the Pacific because by the 1970s Japan had stepped up demands that the United States relinquish Okinawa, held by the Americans as a military base since 1945. In addition to the Tokyo government's wish to reestablish control over a million of its people on the island, the return of Okinawa would remove the last reminders of defeat in World War II while reducing the chances of being drawn into an Asian conflict. In November 1969, the Nixon administration had agreed to return Okinawa and the other Ryukyu Islands sometime in 1972, thereby completing the process begun

May 1972: High Point of Détente
Just three months after his visit to China, President Nixon was in Moscow drinking a toast to the SALT I agreement with Premier Alexei Kosygin and Chairman Leonid Brezhnev. *(Wide World Photos, New York)*

by President Johnson when he had given up the Bonin Islands. The official transfer of the Ryukyus took place in May 1972.

Despite these concessions by the United States, détente had not yet freed it from Vietnam, and as the presidential election of 1972 approached, Nixon stepped up the pressure by approving an air offensive against North Vietnam, Cambodia, and Laos. The use of ground forces was out of the question because by the autumn of 1972, the Vietnamization program had left only 70,000 U.S. troops in the country, and the overwhelming majority of them were in noncombat roles. The outlook still seemed promising. Nixon was a certain winner in the election, the Soviets and Chinese were following détente, and the North Vietnamese were reeling badly from the new assault. The Hanoi government decided to negotiate. It

apparently thought that the Washington administration might permit better terms before the election than afterward.

Cease-Fire in Vietnam

Kissinger had meanwhile continued peace talks in Paris with North Vietnam's chief negotiator, Le Duc Tho, and finally, in October, a break seemed imminent. The Hanoi government expressed willingness to turn over the POWs simultaneously with a U.S. withdrawal sixty days after a cease-fire. An international commission was to supervise elections and implement treaty terms. The North Vietnamese had dropped their demands for Thieu's immediate removal from office, and the Americans had not insisted on North Vietnam's withdrawal from the south. Nixon accepted a cease-fire at the points of present military occupation and approved an electoral commission, both major concessions from his previous stance.

On October 26, less than two weeks before the election, Kissinger returned from Paris and triumphantly proclaimed that "peace is at hand." At almost the same time, North Vietnam published the terms worked out in the talks, probably to prevent leaders in Washington and Saigon from making private arrangements. North Vietnam set a deadline of October 31 for signing an agreement, a move that was designed to place pressure on Nixon before the election but that also had the unintended effect of further undercutting his Democratic opponent, Senator George McGovern, who had promised to end the war as soon as he took office. The president assured Americans that he would accept only "peace with honor."

But South Vietnam sensed a sellout to the Communists and blocked the settlement. Thieu vehemently opposed any arrangement that approved U.S. withdrawal while permitting North Vietnamese forces to remain in the south during the cease-fire period. He also complained that an electoral commission was tantamount to a coalition government that the Communists would ruthlessly seek to dominate. Restoration of the DMZ between the Vietnams, he declared, was vital. Although Kissinger was furious with Thieu, Nixon worried that the South Vietnamese premier might complain of a betrayal and wreck the Republicans' promise of "peace with honor." The president, however, sought more than extrication from Vietnam. He considered Thieu's objections defensible and, based on that stand, would permit a delay in the negotiations until after the election had provided a mandate to press for additional concessions from the Hanoi regime. In the meantime, the United States could send more aid to Saigon, eliminate the undesirable parts of the treaty, and further impair North Vietnam's capacity to break the peace. To save face, Nixon announced his refusal to bend to North Vietnam's pressure tactics. The dead-

line came and passed, and on November 2, he declared that he would sign "only when the agreement is right."

Nixon overwhelmingly won reelection and then, to revive the Paris peace talks, sharply escalated the war by what Kissinger termed "jugular diplomacy"—a series of air assaults that became known as "Linebacker II," or the "Christmas bombings." After the election in the United States, each side in Vietnam moved quickly to expand its holdings before a cease-fire in place went into effect. On December 15, Le Duc Tho walked out of the Paris discussions in disgust. Three days later, Nixon explained that to promote the release of the POWs, he had ordered immediate large-scale bombings on North Vietnamese cities (attempting to avoid populated areas by the use of smart bombs) and military points—including Hanoi and Haiphong. To the chair of the Joint Chiefs of Staff, Admiral Thomas Moorer, Nixon sternly declared, "I don't want any more of this crap about the fact that we couldn't hit this target or that one. This is your chance to use military power to win this war, and if you don't, I'll consider you responsible." For nearly two weeks (except for Christmas Day), American B-52s, carrying huge bomb loads and possessing all-weather flying ability, thundered around the clock more than 30,000 feet over North Vietnam. They unloaded more than 36,000 tons of bombs (more than the amount dropped from 1969 to 1971), killed close to 2,000 civilians, and damaged or destroyed numerous military and nonmilitary sites. All the while, Air Force F-4s used smart bombs in attacking the Hanoi Rail Yard and destroying its surface-to-air missile assembly plant. During the bombing, nearly thirty B-52s and fighter-bombers were shot down, adding almost one hundred to the POW list and supporting the arguments of the generals in Washington who had warned the administration that the Soviets had effectively safeguarded the North Vietnamese capital against an air attack.

The Christmas bombings drew bitter protests from all over the world. According to critics, Nixon was a "madman" who waged "war by tantrum." Tom Wicker of the *New York Times* expressed the feelings of the international press in calling the air offensive "Shame on Earth," and Senate Democratic Majority Leader Mike Mansfield denounced this "Stone Age tactic." Admiral Moorer later denied that the U.S. planes had engaged in blanket bombing and insisted that the pilots had specific strategic targets in mind that were located primarily on Hanoi's periphery. But he could say nothing during the bombing campaign for fear of alerting the North Vietnamese as to which areas to protect with their limited number of surface-to-air missiles. A journalist noted Nixon's private declaration that he "did not care if the whole world thought he was crazy for resuming the bombing." The Soviets and Chinese "might think they were dealing with a madman and so better force North Vietnam into a settlement before the world was consumed into a larger war."

Nixon's brutal tactics had seemingly worked: the day after Christmas, Kissinger was in Washington when he received a call from Hanoi asking for a resumption of his talks with Le Duc Tho. Kissinger observed that "we had not heard such a polite tone from the North Vietnamese since the middle of October." The bombings above the twentieth parallel ceased on December 30.

For several reasons, the Nixon administration was also ready to talk. American generals warned that North Vietnam's air defenses were inflicting long-range damages on the strategic strength of the United States, worldwide revulsion had developed for the bombings, the Hanoi government's peace conditions seemed the best possible, and the Democrats now controlled Congress and in January would doubtless cut off funds for future bombings. Nixon boasted that the Christmas assault had brought peace, although one of his administration officials disagreed. "We were in an embarrassing situation. Could we suddenly say we'll sign in January what we wouldn't in October? We

had to do something," he declared. "So the bombings began, to try to create the image of a defeated enemy crawling back to the peace table to accept terms demanded by the United States." Whatever the truth, the terms were strikingly similar to those of the previous October.

The question of whether Linebacker was instrumental in bringing the peace remains unclear. Nixon's credibility soared in view of the massive air assault, and not purely by coincidence did the Hanoi government consent to resuming the Paris talks. Kissinger noted that Le Duc Tho repeatedly insisted that what brought him back to the peace table was "the President's firmness and the North Vietnamese belief that he will not be affected by either congressional or public pressures." The North Vietnamese no longer had enough food to survive a prolonged attack, and by the end of December they had used all their surface-to-air missiles and were totally vulnerable to destruction. Also important was the diplomatic and military isolation that North Vietnam experienced while under siege. Linebacker I had destroyed rail access from China, and even though the North Vietnamese had restored the lines and managed to stockpile large amounts of Soviet materiel before December, Linebacker II had quickly destroyed those supplies and, combined with the mining of ports, cut off Hanoi and Haiphong from the rest of the world. Just as important, however, was North Vietnam's feeling that a settlement with the United States might lead to its withdrawal and permit the Vietnamese to settle their problem by themselves. Finally, Nixon was convinced that soon after Linebacker II, North Vietnam had learned of his ultimatum to Thieu as a result of their infiltration of the Saigon government. The bombing campaign bought more time for Vietnamization to work and more likely complemented other realities in achieving a settlement.

On January 27, 1973, the Paris negotiators signed a cease-fire agreement in the old Hotel Majestic in Paris, twenty-three years after the initial U.S. commitment in Vietnam and eight years following its first assignment of combat troops. In the pact signed by Kissinger, the foreign ministers of North and South Vietnam and the "South Vietnamese Provisional Revolutionary Government," or PRG (formerly the NLF), accepted the following terms: an immediate cease-fire in place; U.S. withdrawal of its final 27,000 troops from South Vietnam and the return of all American POWs (nearly 600), both within sixty days; enforcement of treaty provisions through an international commission; general elections carried out through the establishment of a National Council of Reconciliation and Concord; an international conference on Vietnam to convene within thirty days; and authorization for the United States to replace South Vietnam's damaged or worn-out military equipment but not to add to existing stores. In an unofficial, semisecret arrangement that was not part of the pact, the United States agreed to furnish Hanoi $4.75 billion of reconstruction assistance. To secure Thieu's compliance with the treaty, the United States threatened to withdraw all aid.

The agreement came with mixed blessings. The atmosphere in Paris was so bitter that the South Vietnamese and the PRG refused to sign the same copy of the treaty. Although the Nixon administration had assured Americans of open agreements in Paris, the president had earlier made a private pledge of military aid to Thieu if North Vietnam violated the cease-fire. To the South Vietnamese premier, Nixon wrote that if you will "go with us, you have my assurance of continued assistance in the post-settlement period and that we will respond with full force should the settlement be violated by North Vietnam." The alternative was equally clear: a little over a week later, Nixon assured Thieu that the United States would sign the pact by itself if necessary. "In that case," Nixon declared, "I shall have to explain publicly that your Government obstructs peace. The result will be an inevitable and immediate termination of U.S. economic and military assistance which cannot be fore-

stalled by a change of personnel in your government." Just one week before the treaty-signing session, Thieu sent his foreign minister to take part in the Paris negotiations, thereby indicating acquiescence to the president's pressure tactics. With Thieu in line, Nixon sent him additional arms that same year.

Even the peacemakers recognized that the cease-fire they had crafted bore no relation to honor, and thus did they turn their backs on the praise that some accorded to them. Kissinger and Le Duc Tho received the Nobel Peace Prize in 1973 for their roles in the Vietnam agreement. Le Duc Tho rejected the award, and Kissinger declined to attend the awards proceedings at the University of Oslo and then gave the $65,000 cash prize to a scholarship designed to aid the Amerasian children of U.S. soldiers killed in Vietnam. Longtime critic of the war and former Undersecretary of State George Ball cynically remarked that "the Norwegians must have a sense of humor."

The Nixon administration hailed the January 1973 agreements as a victory for détente, although it quickly became clear that the United States had won neither "peace" nor "honor." Conflict went on in Vietnam, even while people all over the world praised the cease-fire. The treaty left North Vietnamese forces in the south, without specifying which areas belonged to whom, and Hanoi's leaders were more determined than ever to seize control of the entire country. In March 1973, twelve nations met in Paris—including the United States, China, and the Soviet Union—and formally approved the cease-fire agreement. The U.S. presence in Vietnam was still visible though altered: numerous U.S. military advisers remained in South Vietnam, albeit hurriedly discharged from the service and no longer in uniform as part of a poorly disguised effort to circumvent the Paris terms, and rather than dismantle its military installations as required, the White House transferred the titles to the South Vietnamese. The United States also continued sending military goods but designated them

Kissinger and Le Duc Tho
Both Kissinger and Le Duc Tho received the Nobel Peace Prize in 1973 for their efforts in arranging the cease-fire of January that year. *(Wide World Photos, New York)*

as nonmilitary, and the U.S. Air Force maintained its bombing of Cambodia to protect the Lon Nol regime from the Communist Khmer Rouge. Resentment for Linebacker II continued to grow in the United States despite the revelations that in comparison with the damage caused, the civilian casualties were remarkably low. These findings affirmed not only successful evacuation proceedings by the North Vietnamese but also the Nixon administration's directives to avoid nonmilitary targets. A journalist toured Hanoi in March 1973 and declared that "pictures and some press reports had given a visitor the impression Hanoi had suffered badly in the war—but in fact the city is hardly touched." When Congress cut off funds for the bombing, Nixon angrily vetoed the measure in late June, but he soon had no choice other than

to sign a bill requiring an end to all U.S. combat in Indochina by August 15.

Congress's attempt to reassert itself in foreign affairs contributed to the nation's subdued global presence in the period following its direct involvement in Vietnam. Impeachment proceedings then under way for the president's role in Watergate may have pushed him into a retreat. But another development was also important. That November of 1973, Congress narrowly overrode Nixon's veto in passing the War Powers Act, which marked an effort to make any armed venture by the United States a joint responsibility of Congress and the Executive Office. It asserted that "in every possible instance" the president was to consult Congress before sending soldiers into situations "where imminent involvement in hostilities is clearly indicated by

Nixon and Thieu
President Nixon and President Nguyen Van Thieu at San Clemente, California, "White House" in early April 1973. *(National Archives, Washington, D.C.)*

circumstances." Should he intervene outside the country without a formal declaration of war, he must "report" his actions to Congress within forty-eight hours. Unless that body endorsed the intervention, the military forces had to pull out within sixty days—extended to ninety days if the president certified "unavoidable necessity." In effect, however, the president could still react immediately to a crisis and wage war for sixty to ninety days without congressional approval—a period so long, critics warned, that the United States might find extrication difficult if not impossible. But this was not the real problem, Kissinger warned. Congress was too closely tied to public opinion to formulate meaningful, long-range foreign policies. Although severely criticized by Nixon and Kissinger, the War Powers Act illustrated the inseparability of domestic and foreign policy and therefore pro-

vided an appropriate epitaph for the U.S. military experience in Southeast Asia.

Disintegration of Détente, 1973–1977

The new peace seemingly ushered in by détente paradoxically eroded from within because of problems with the Western alliance, among Third World nations, and within both the Western Hemisphere and the United States. France and other West European governments were hurting economically and had become unhappy with the U.S. emphasis on non-European affairs and its insistence on dictating their policies in line with Cold War strategy. West Europeans joined the Japanese in complaining about the decline of the dollar, Washington's high balance-of-payments deficits, and U.S. accusations that they were guilty of commercial discrimination. Nixon and Kissinger hoped that détente's umbrella effect would bring peace to countries outside the major power blocs. Freed of Vietnam, they sought to patch relations with their continental allies by heralding 1973 as "The Year of Europe." Yet Italy was becoming Communist in orientation, Portugal was angry over criticisms of its African policies, and Greece and Turkey were bitter rivals over the Mediterranean island of Cyprus. In the Middle East, Latin America, and Africa, pressures for social reforms likewise created explosive situations that the White House attributed to Communist influence. Furthermore, the United States faced deepening recession and spiraling inflation, and the seemingly endless unraveling of the Watergate scandals (explained later) undermined the Nixon administration's credibility at home, dividing Americans and further undercutting the nation's foreign policy.

The most immediate threat to détente came in the Middle East. As discussed earlier, the center of controversy was the Arab–Israeli feud, kept under control only by a series of fragile agreements. Three times—in 1948, 1956, and 1967—the Arabs attempted to destroy Israel, and in every instance they failed. After the Six Day War of 1967, Jews inside the United States exerted pressure on Washington to approve the sale of fifty F-4 Phantom jets to Israel. A number of Arab states responded by severing relations with the United States and opening their ports to Soviet ships. The growing crisis in the Middle East endangered détente because of competing Soviet–American economic and strategic interests in the area, along with the persistent U.S. fear of Communist infiltration.

Conflict again loomed in the Middle East as the Nixon administration moved into the White House in early 1969. Israel refused to withdraw from areas occupied during the war of June 1967, and in the spring of 1969, Suez once more became the trouble spot. Nasser brought in heavy weapons, and the newly created Palestine Liberation Organization (PLO) promised death to any Arab leader who called for a peaceful settlement of the Israeli dispute.

Under the leadership of Yasir Arafat, the PLO intensified demands for a homeland in Palestine and, using Syria and Jordan as bases, launched a series of raids on Israel. The Israelis retaliated by bombing those neighboring states helping the PLO, with some of the strikes touching the outskirts of Cairo. The Moscow government sent troops and antiaircraft materiel to Egypt, including SAM-3 (surface-to-air) missiles operated by Soviets to counter Phantom jet attacks and Soviet pilots to fly MIGs earlier furnished to Nasser. As the problems escalated, the Israelis appealed to the United States for help, and in July 1970, President Nixon responded with 125 Phantom and Skyhawk jets. "We will do what is necessary to maintain Israel's strength," he declared over television. "Not because we want Israel to be in a position to wage war—that isn't it—but because that is what will deter its neighbors from attacking it."

By the autumn of 1970, the Arabs and Israelis had managed another cease-fire that, like the others, was short lived. Nasser had visited Moscow in July and afterward agreed to the U.S. proposal for a UN-supervised, ninety-day armistice. The Israelis accepted, but only after the United States guaranteed their security. Discussions then broke down over charges that Nasser, with Soviet help, had moved missiles into the cease-fire area west of the Suez Canal, exposing Israel to attack along the east bank. The Israelis withdrew from the talks until Nasser removed the missiles.

The same day the Israelis left the negotiations, September 6, Palestinian guerrillas initiated a new wave of terrorism that was followed by the outbreak of civil war in Jordan. The PLO hijacked four commercial airliners, including a Pan American 747 jumbo jet, and after evacuating all passengers destroyed the planes. Nearly sixty people, including Americans, Israelis, British, Swiss, and West Germans, were held hostage to secure the freedom of imprisoned Arab terrorists. Negotiations quickly began with the help of the International Red Cross, but these talks were hampered by the conflict in Jordan between government forces and Palestinians living inside the country. As Syrian tanks roared into Jordan to help the guerrillas, the Nixon administration reinforced the Sixth Fleet in the Mediterranean and readied its airborne forces at home and in West Germany. But the Syrians, perhaps as a result of Soviet pressure, suddenly pulled out of Jordan, leaving the Palestinians to defeat and exile to Lebanon, where they became a continuing source of instability in the region. After a cease-fire in Cairo on September 25, the Red Cross soon won the hostages' freedom in exchange for the release of the Arab terrorists.

The end of both the Jordanian civil war and the hostage crisis once again temporarily eased the situation in the Middle East. But during that same month of September, Nasser died, leaving the office of premier to Anwar el-Sadat, who promised to continue Egypt's hard-line policies toward Israel. With Soviet backing, he refused to remove the missiles from the cease-fire zone; Israel subsequently built up defenses along the east bank and secured a promise of U.S. military assistance. Israel then returned to the peace negotiations after the United States guaranteed support against excessive Arab demands. Sadat intended to open a new offensive against Israel, but he was unable to persuade the Soviets to furnish more arms because of their desire for détente with the United States. Exasperated with the Moscow government, he expelled thousands of Soviet military advisers and technicians from Egypt in the summer of 1972. Although the PLO continued its terrorist acts—including killing Israeli athletes at the Munich Olympics that same year—Sadat's move again relieved the situation in the Middle East.

The peace did not last, however, for on October 6, 1973, the Arabs invaded Israel for the fourth time in what became known as the Yom Kippur War. To regain lands lost in the 1967 war, Egypt, aided by Jordan, Iraq, Morocco, and Saudi Arabia, relied heavily on Soviet materiel and advice to surprise both Israel and the United States on Yom Kippur (Jewish holy day, the Day of Atonement) by attacking Israeli armies in the Sinai and at the Golan Heights. With Israel nearly split in two by the assault, Prime Minister Golda Meir appealed for U.S. military assistance and considered using her country's atomic bomb against the Arabs. The Nixon administration called for an immediate meeting of the UN Security Council, but a series of unfriendly sessions on October 8 and 9 brought no results. Forgetting their past differences, the Soviets sent military aid to Egypt and prepared to airlift a ground force into the combat zone. Although the Nixon administration was reeling from Watergate and other domestic scandals, it approved an airlift of planes, tanks, and war materiel, enabling Israel to hold its ground.

The Arabs only briefly enjoyed their military successes because the Israelis once again quickly reversed the fortunes of the war. Soviet Premier Alexei Kosygin rushed to Cairo, hoping to convince Sadat to accept a cease-fire, but instead aroused U.S. fears by providing visible evidence of Soviet sympathies in the war. Meanwhile, Arab forces overran the east bank and swept toward Israel across the Sinai desert, where for five days they engaged in the fiercest tank battles since World War II. At the same time, Syrian ground troops aided by tanks advanced across the Golan Heights and toward Israel. The Israelis, however, soon turned back the assault both at the canal and along the Syrian front. Israeli forces won a stretch of land along the western side of the canal, positioning them within seventy miles of Cairo. In doing so, they surrounded 20,000 Egyptian soldiers on the east bank, cutting them off from the main force and putting them in danger of destruction.

The Israelis' reversal of the war's direction forced new peace talks. Sadat appealed to Brezhnev for help, and on October 20 the Soviet general secretary met with Kissinger in Moscow to draft a peace proposal for presentation to the Security Council. En route home, Kissinger stopped in Israel to assure its leaders that the plan was fair. But the only way he could secure an Israeli cease-fire was to threaten a cutoff in military aid. The following evening, the Security Council met in emergency session and early the next morning approved the peace resolution. It called for an immediate cease-fire in place; the implementation of UN Resolution 242, which in 1967 called for Israeli withdrawal from lands occupied in the Six Day War in exchange for defensible borders; a large peacekeeping force comprising soldiers from non–Security Council member nations; and the promise of negotiations aimed at a permanent peace.

Although Egypt and Israel accepted the truce, the Israelis provided a rationale for direct Soviet intervention when they violated the cease-fire lines by seizing more territory and threatening to crush the Egyptian army. Israel's minister of defense, General Moshe Dayan, later explained to the *New York Times* that if he had captured several thousand Egyptian soldiers, "Sadat would have had to admit it to his people. We might only have held them for a day and let them walk out without their arms, but it would have changed the whole Egyptian attitude about whether they had won or lost the war." Kissinger was irate because such a humiliation would upset the delicate balance between Arabs and Israelis and abort a negotiated peace. Furthermore, Brezhnev and Sadat proposed a joint Soviet–American military contingent to supervise the cease-fire, which the Nixon administration flatly rejected as a thinly disguised excuse for Soviet intervention. That evening, a Soviet note jolted the White House by declaring that if the United States did not join, "we may be obliged to consider acting alone." Israel, the note insisted in a menacing tone, "cannot be permitted to get away with the violations." The White House feared a Soviet push into Suez and, without informing NATO allies, placed U.S. armed forces and nuclear strike commands on "precautionary alert." The United States, Nixon asserted, "would not accept any unilateral move" by the Soviets. Two days later, on October 24, the Security Council approved a

second peace resolution. Under threat of a U.S. arms embargo, the Israelis complied with the resolution.

As in the earlier Arab–Israeli wars, no one was satisfied with the outcome. The Arabs did not regain territories lost in 1967, and the Israelis did not feel secure. Most Arab nations in OPEC were angry with the United States for aiding Israel and with the West European nations for allowing the Americans to use NATO bases on the continent. Acting without Iran, the OPEC nations stunned the United States with an oil embargo that lasted until March 1974 and raised prices dramatically for U.S. allies in Japan and Europe. OPEC's oil embargo of 1973–1974 led to gasoline shortages in the United States (which had recently begun to import most of its oil and thus felt the crunch), but it placed a severe strain on the Western alliance. Whereas the United States was committed to Israel and received only 12 percent of its oil from the Middle East, Western Europe and Japan were almost totally dependent on the Arabs. When allies chose not to support the United States in the Middle East, Kissinger called them "contemptible."

Kissinger, meanwhile, tried to arrange a permanent peace in the Middle East by flying back and forth between Egypt and Israel in a series of visits that became known as "shuttle diplomacy." For two years, he attempted to secure a pact that would exclude Soviet and Palestinian participation and end the Arab oil embargo. In November 1973, Kissinger left for Egypt, where he arranged the restoration of diplomatic relations with the United States (broken in 1967). A few days later, he helped bring about an Egyptian–Israeli cease-fire, and in May 1974, he managed the same between Israel and Syria. In September 1975, the two antagonists initialed an agreement whereby Israel was to evacuate part of the Sinai to enable it to become a UN-guaranteed buffer area, and a detachment of 200 U.S. "civilian technicians" would be assigned to "early warning" stations to watch for trouble. To maintain a balance of power in the region, the United

States made general assurances of military assistance to Israel and Egypt. Finally, the oil flow would resume—at quadrupled prices.

Kissinger's diplomacy had mixed results. Boundaries remained uncertain because the Israelis remained in the Sinai, the Golan Heights, and the West Bank of the Jordan. The PLO's demands for a homeland were still unfulfilled, and both the Soviets and the Palestinians were unhappy over being shut out of negotiations affecting their interests in the Middle East. Kissinger's efforts also widened the gulf between Arab moderates and extremists. Yet there was a saving factor: Sadat was disenchanted with the Soviets and had turned to the United States for help. The Washington government now assumed the role of chief mediator in the Middle East, a move that improved the prospects for peace.

Lack of unity within the Western Hemisphere also threatened détente. Canada began to follow policies that opposed those of the United States. It opened trade with China and the Soviet Union, established rigid controls on foreign investments, and raised its export prices for oil and natural gas sold to the United States while retaining enough at home to ensure cheaper energy for Canadians. The situation in Latin America was more serious. Anti-American feeling remained strong, as exemplified by the unfriendly reception accorded New York Governor Nelson Rockefeller during his fact-finding tour of 1969. Although he recommended more economic help by the United States, the Alliance for Progress was virtually dead, and the Nixon administration had shown little interest in reviving it. Mexico was upset over the U.S. economic embargo of Cuba and the intervention of the United States in the Dominican Republic in 1965, and Venezuela sought to use its OPEC membership and rich oil deposits to win economic independence from the United States. The Panamanians still demanded a renegotiation of the canal treaty of 1903, and discussions were under way toward formalizing an agreement arranged by Kissinger in 1974. Terrorists and guerrillas meanwhile exploited

Latin America's dire economic and political situation, and new regimes increasingly expropriated U.S. holdings without providing suitable compensation. Washington's leaders responded to the alleged Communist threat by selling arms to friendly governments.

Cuba remained a special obstruction to détente. Pressure had grown in the United States for lifting the trade embargo and reestablishing diplomatic relations, despite Castro's continued refusal to compensate Americans whose properties had fallen victim to expropriation. "Skyjacking" incidents grew in number because Castro permitted hijacked planes to return to the United States but granted refuge to perpetrators on the basis of the U.S. failure to return Cubans who had hijacked boats and escaped to the United States. In the early 1970s, however, the United States agreed to block attempts by Cuban exiles in the United States to invade the island if Cuba extradited or punished hijackers and returned victimized properties and people. Two years later, with representatives of the Castro regime, Kissinger began secret talks in the United States aimed at settling differences between the countries. But in 1975, a Senate committee inquiring about CIA activities in Cuba found evidence of "at least eight" plots in the past to kill Castro, leading some to wonder if Castro had countered by arranging the assassination of President Kennedy. In December, Castro sent nearly 20,000 soldiers and military advisers to aid a leftist insurrection in Angola, and the United States later found that he had sent thousands more to Ethiopia. Cuba, it appeared, had become a base for spreading communism overseas as well as throughout the hemisphere.

The Nixon administration's greatest concern in Latin America was Chile, where in the autumn of 1970, Salvador Allende, a Marxist and a founder of the Socialist Party, overcame CIA interference to win election as president on the Popular Unity Party ticket. Allende's coalition government, which included Communists and soon leaned toward Moscow, promised constitutional amendments barring totalitarian rule and instituted a reform program designed to free the country from the control of large landowners and U.S. multinational corporations. In so doing, Allende nationalized $1 billion of U.S. holdings, although with assurances of compensation. International Telephone and Telegraph and other business corporations nonetheless put pressure on the Nixon administration to take action against Allende.

Both Nixon and Kissinger regarded Allende as another Castro and hence a potential ally of the Soviet Union. While the White House maintained what it called a "cool but correct" stance toward Allende, it worked surreptitiously to destabilize his regime. The U.S. government persuaded the World Bank and Inter-American Bank to deny funds to Chile, and the CIA collaborated with American businesses to take action against Chile. Together they halted the flow of credit and other materials, secretly paid the Chilean press and opposing political parties to criticize Allende's rule, sent arms to the military, and then cooperated with its leaders in staging a coup. In September 1973, the Chilean army overthrew the government, resulting in Allende's death—by suicide, according to the U.S. ambassador. A brutally repressive but staunchly anti-Communist and rightist military regime under General Augusto Pinochet came to power. When the American ambassador complained about the new government's use of torture, Kissinger abruptly told him "to cut out the political science lectures." There was no "right for people to vote in Communists," he coldly asserted; the United States must not "let a country go Marxist just because its people are irresponsible." The following year, Americans learned that the CIA had participated in the coup that led to Allende's death. Two major investigations into the organization's conduct led to revelations in 1975 that mobilized Congress to restrict CIA activities overseas.

Another serious threat to détente had come from within the United States because by late 1973, the Watergate scandal had greatly weakened the Nixon administration's effectiveness in foreign affairs and soon led to a change in national leadership. During the presidential campaign of 1972, veteran CIA operative E. Howard Hunt (who had helped engineer both the Guatemalan invasion of 1954 and the Bay of Pigs disaster seven years later) led the White House "plumbers" in breaking into the Democratic National Committee's headquarters at the Watergate Hotel in Washington, apparently intending to pilfer political plans. Public knowledge of the break-in fostered the perception of a presidential pattern of abuse of power that led to demands for Nixon's impeachment or resignation. To turn the nation's attention from Watergate as well as to revive détente, the president appointed Kissinger secretary of state (while maintaining him as national security affairs adviser) in the autumn of 1973 and soon attended another well-publicized summit meeting in Moscow. But the political scandals had undermined presidential authority, leading to a virtual abdication of domestic and foreign policy formation to Congress. Faced with certain impeachment, Nixon resigned the presidency in August 1974, leaving as chief executive Vice President Gerald Ford (who had just assumed this position after Spiro Agnew resigned because of revelations that he had accepted bribes while governor of Maryland).

Ford and Kissinger continued the struggle for détente, but in the wake of Watergate and Vietnam, their actions were severely curtailed. As mentioned, Congress had restricted the president's authority with the War Powers Act. Furthermore, the Senate had tied his hands even tighter by stipulating that in exchange for U.S. trade, the Soviets had to respect the human rights of all dissidents—including Jews. The Senate also tried to establish a maximum amount on loans the United States could authorize for the Soviet Union. But these attempts at linkage did not work. The Soviets resented U.S. intervention in their domestic affairs and, instead of relaxing their treatment of Jews, sharply reduced the number allowed to leave the country. The Senate's conditions ultimately blocked Soviet approval of the commercial treaty. To avoid further offense to the Soviet Union, President Ford even refused a White House visit to Alexander Solzhenitzyn, a famous Soviet writer who had been exiled for exposing widespread brutality inside his homeland.

In late 1974, Ford and Kissinger tried to revive détente by accepting guidelines for SALT II, begun in Geneva two years earlier. The president met with Brezhnev in Vladivostok in November and tentatively agreed to a ten-year limit of 2,400 each on the total number of ICBMs, SLBMs, and big bombers. Of the 2,400 on each side, a maximum of 1,320 could have multiple warheads. In effect, SALT II blanketed the arms race with legal issues, ensuring drawn-out discussions over what kinds of weapons fell within the boundaries.

Meanwhile in Vietnam, the most damaging blow to détente came as the Thieu regime approached its final days in early 1975. The Third Indochina War had begun in late 1973 with the ARVN's surprisingly successful attacks on North Vietnam's holdings in the south, but the optimism was unfounded: the Hanoi government had restricted its military response until sure the Americans were gone. In January 1975, the North Vietnamese felt free of a U.S. threat and launched a crushing offensive that succeeded primarily because of the rapid disintegration of the ARVN owing to poor leadership and widespread corruption but also because of the huge cutbacks in U.S. assistance, South Vietnam's excessive dependence on the United States, and, according to Communist accounts, the popular support given the advancing forces. Thieu appealed to Ford to deliver the "full force" promised by Nixon two years before. But the

Secretary of State Henry Kissinger, Vice President Nelson A. Rockefeller, and President Gerald R. Ford Oval Office discussion of the American evacuation of Saigon, April 28, 1975. *(Gerald R. Ford Library, Ann Arbor, Michigan)*

Saigon Airport and Evacuation, April 29, 1975
Vietnamese militants and civilians await air evacuation from South Vietnam as the North Vietnamese
forces close in on the city. *(National Archives, Washington, D.C.)*

letter Thieu alluded to had not been made public, and Kissinger had earlier told the press that such a pledge did not exist. In the meantime, Phuoc Binh, the capital of Phuoc Long Province, collapsed in January, confirming North Vietnam's suspicions that the United States would not reenter the war. Thieu's retrenchment attempt turned into a full-fledged rout as terrified ARVN soldiers and panicky civilians fled what they feared as certain death. The U.S. decision not to intervene in the new fighting meant that the Vietnamese would settle the matter among themselves.

The ensuing collapse of South Vietnam was so sudden that it surprised the Hanoi regime and aroused suspicions of a trap. On March 26, Hué fell, followed by Danang within a week, and on April 21, Thieu resigned, bitterly charging over radio and television that the United States was responsible for the de-

bacle. After he escaped with friends and relatives to Taiwan, the Saigon government fell into the hands of Duong Van Minh, who had been instrumental in the Diem coup of 1963. The ARVN pulled out of Xuan Loc, forty miles east of Saigon, and on April 28, Ford approved emergency helicopter evacuations of Americans in Saigon. Meanwhile, Bien Hoa air base fell to the Vietcong, who were now only fifteen miles outside the city. Nearly 150,000 Vietnamese managed to escape the country, many of them by boats or American planes in the days just before the fall of Saigon. But not enough transportation was available to save everyone from a predicted slaughter. American marines used rifle butts to fight off frantic Vietnamese outside the gates of the U.S. embassy in Saigon as Americans and Vietnamese pushed and shoved their way into the helicopters taking off from a rooftop near

Fall of Saigon, April 1975
An apartment building on Gia Long Street near the U.S. embassy served as a launching pad for Vietnamese fleeing to U.S. aircraft carriers waiting off the coast. *(United Press International)*

the embassy. The final spectacle was that of angry ARVN soldiers shooting at Americans as they left the country.

On April 30, Saigon fell, and the Third Indochina War was over. The expected bloodbath had not occurred, largely because Duong Van Minh had agreed to the unconditional surrender of South Vietnam. In their elation, the Vietcong renamed the South Vietnamese capital Ho Chi Minh City. Twenty-one years after the Geneva Accords of 1954, Vietnam was reunited in an epochal victory for Hanoi. Almost simultaneously, the domino theory appeared to become a

fact. The Lon Nol regime in Cambodia fell to the Communist Khmer Rouge, and soon afterward Laos also came under Communist control. The fall of these three Southeast Asian countries to communism sounded the death knell of SEATO and ended the long ordeal of the United States in Asia.

America's Asian policy lay in shambles. At tremendous costs, successive administrations in Washington had fought to preserve the Saigon regime as a symbol of the Free World's resistance to Communist takeover. Yet South Vietnam had collapsed. North Vietnam seized $5 billion in U.S. military goods to become the leading military regime in Southeast Asia, although its government, like that of the Khmer Rouge in Cambodia, became repressive and caused thousands to flee the country. Although Cambodia and Laos had also changed leadership, there was little unity among the new Communist regimes. Less than a year after the fall of Saigon, Communist Vietnam was at war with Communist Cambodia, and in 1978, it was at war with Communist China. Vietnam's invasion of Cambodia led to the collapse of the Khmer Rouge as well as the onset of a famine that threatened to decimate the population. Japan, South Korea, and Taiwan were stunned by the U.S. withdrawal from Vietnam and feared that it might pull out of South Korea and expose Japan to Communist assault. Thailand told Americans stationed in the country to leave because it now had to deal regularly with other Asian nations.

The Vietnam War left numerous legacies, most of which were bitter and long-lasting. First and foremost, the United States did not win, exploding the myth that it had never lost a war and never would. Second, the cost of the war was heavy in U.S. armed forces and materiel, immeasurable in national spirit, and nearly devastating to the nation's image abroad. More than 58,000 Americans died (more than 20,000 during the Nixon years of Vietnamization), 300,000 had been wounded, at least 1,400 (including civilians) were missing, and the United States expended more than $150 billion, much of it in support of corrupt regimes. Third, U.S. involvement dealt a serious blow to the presidency, which, combined with the Watergate scandals, provided an impetus to congressional power that itself was restricted by widespread distrust for public officials. Fourth, the war encouraged the continued shift in U.S. foreign policy from its dominating role in containing communism to calls for partnerships and détente.

Intervention in Vietnam, like that in other countries, had proved far more complex than ever imagined. Perhaps long-time presidential adviser Clark Clifford said it best: "What we thought was the spread of Communist aggression in my opinion now seems very clearly to have been a civil war in Vietnam. The domino theory proved to be erroneous." Tragically, he observed, the United States had made an "honest mistake."

In the face of growing lack of respect for the United States, the Ford administration took advantage of an incident involving an American merchant vessel, the *Mayaguez*, to make a show of force. In May 1975, Cambodian patrol boats seized the *Mayaguez*, then in the Gulf of Siam, for allegedly violating their country's territorial waters. Occurring barely a month after the fall of Vietnam, the episode afforded the president a chance to restore his country's military credibility. Without allowing time for either a full investigation or a Cambodian response to his demand for the return of ship and crew, he denounced the act as piracy and approved military action. Not realizing that the captors had already freed the thirty-nine Americans aboard, Ford ordered marines to the islands off Cambodia's coast. American warships sank three Cambodian gunboats, and planes bombed an air base and oil depot. At the cost of forty-one American lives (soldiers killed in an accidental explosion during a raid), the Ford administration proudly announced that it had saved both the *Mayaguez* and its men. The American public, as frustrated as the White House over the Vietnam War and other foreign policy failures, praised the president's use of force.

There were other attempts to bolster the staggering policy of détente. In July 1975, Ford joined the representatives of more than thirty nations in Helsinki at the Conference on Security and Cooperation in Europe to tie together the loose ends of World War II. In exchange for Soviet pledges to respect human rights and allow cultural interchange between East and West, the signatories approved the wartime borders of the Baltic States, Poland, and Eastern Europe. The following September, the SEATO Council met in New York and voted to phase out the organization; its central reason for existence, South Vietnam, was gone. Before the United Nations in September 1976, Kissinger called for "coexistence with the Soviet Union" and for "reciprocal [restraint], not just in bilateral relations but around the globe." Finally, the death of Mao Zedong that same year preceded the installation of a moderate government in Beijing that was more receptive to establishing formal Sino–American relations.

Another threat to détente came in Africa, where the United States became convinced that the Soviet Union intended to spread communism among the new postwar nations. Angola's recently won independence from Portugal had led to a civil war in which the United States worked with China and South Africa in covertly aiding the rightists. The Soviet Union meanwhile helped the leftist MPLA—the Popular Movement for the Liberation of Angola—by sending thousands of Cuban soldiers to Angola in late 1975. Kissinger angrily condemned this new Soviet action as expansion by proxy and asked Congress to appropriate aid. Africa's rich mineral resources, he explained to a Senate committee, made the continent important to the United States. But Congress feared another Vietnam, and the public was indignant over revelations that its government had already become secretly involved in Angola. Even though some representatives and senators had earlier known of the intervention and privately concurred, Congress responded to the growing public outcry by cutting off funds for military assistance. Ford reverted to Cold War language in chiding that body for failing to perceive that "resistance to Soviet expansion by military means must be a fundamental element of United States foreign policy."

The MPLA emerged victorious in early 1976 and then surprised Washington by seeking American technological assistance in developing Angola's oil resources. Instead of recognizing a fundamental reality—that the Angolans were concerned more about their own welfare than about communism and the Cold War—the Ford administration rebuked the Soviet Union for the outcome of the civil war and ceased talking about détente.

The U.S. experience in Angola promoted a reassessment of its policies toward Africa. Americans had invested nearly $4 billion in the huge continent, but about 40 percent of the money had gone to the white government of South Africa, which was strategically located at the Cape of Good Hope and was rich in gold and uranium. South Africa, however, posed an embarrassing liability: its government in Pretoria had created a police-state atmosphere by pursuing the racial segregationist policies of apartheid (apartness) against blacks, who outnumbered whites by almost four to one. The United States had alienated most black regimes in Africa, especially by its decision to trade with Rhodesia for its chrome ore (to avoid dependence on the other chief source of the product, the Soviet Union) despite the UN economic boycott of that country's white minority regime. In early 1976, Kissinger visited South Africa, although violence had broken out in Rhodesia, and won concessions for South African blacks. The United States, he explained, had reversed its African policies to "avoid a race war" and "to prevent foreign intervention." But the Washington administration's central objective remained that of preventing Soviet exploitation of what Kissinger called "the radicalization of Africa."

Toward a New Foreign Policy

Détente seemed even more remote by late 1976 as Ford lost his bid for election to a newcomer on the national political scene, a successful peanut farmer, former governor of Georgia, and born-again Baptist—James Earl Carter Jr. During the campaign, right-wing Republicans denounced détente so vehemently that Kissinger referred to it as "a word I would like to forget." Ford had dropped it from his speeches in preference for the phrase "peace through strength." His administration's strong showing in the *Mayaguez* affair had only temporarily soothed the national frustration over Vietnam. Furthermore, Ford had alienated many Americans by pardoning Nixon for his role in Watergate and by making the surprising assertion during his television debates with Carter that "there is no Soviet domination of Eastern Europe, and there never will be under a Ford administration." When Carter challenged this misguided observation, Ford refused to retreat, citing his recent visit to Eastern Europe as proof of his claim. Carter also took advantage of Watergate and U.S. foreign policy failures to promise to run an honest administration, freed from Washington's bureaucracy and prepared to restore the nation's domestic and foreign credibility.

Some of Carter's charges were not consistent, but they were effective. He attacked Kissinger's secret diplomacy, his support for repressive regimes, and the Republicans' exorbitant defense spending. Yet at the same time, he criticized the Ford administration for conceding too much during arms discussions and for the failure of the Helsinki Agreements to guarantee civil liberties within the Soviet Union. The Soviets, he asserted, had exploited détente to the disadvantage of the United States. Carter's strategy was nonetheless successful. He won a little more than half the popular vote, defeating Ford by about a 2 percent margin. The effects of Watergate and Vietnam doubtless influenced Americans to choose Jimmy Carter—a president determined to revive faith in the country by Wilsonian appeals to respect human rights.

Selected Readings

Alexander, Robert J. *The Tragedy of Chile.* 1978.

Ambrose, Stephen E., and Douglas G. Brinkley. *Rise to Globalism: American Foreign Policy since 1938.* 8th ed., 1997.

Asselin, Pierre. *A Bitter Peace: Washington, Hanoi, and the Making of the Paris Agreement.* 2002.

Ball, George W., and Douglas B. Ball. *The Passionate Attachment: America's Involvement with Israel, 1947 to the Present.* 1992.

Baritz, Loren. *Backfire: A History of How American Culture Led Us into Vietnam and Made Us Fight the Way We Did.* 1985.

Baskir, Lawrence M., and William A. Strauss. *Chance and Circumstance: The Draft, the War and the Vietnam Generation.* 1978.

Bell, Coral. *The Diplomacy of Détente: The Kissinger Era.* 1977.

Bill, James A. *The Eagle and the Lion: The Tragedy of American-Iranian Relations.* 1988.

Bilton, Michael, and Kevin Sim. *Four Hours in My Lai.* 1992.

Brandon, Henry. *The Retreat of American Power.* 1972.

Brands, H. W. *The Devil We Knew: Americans and the Cold War.* 1993.

Brigham, Robert K. *Guerrilla Diplomacy: The NLF's Foreign Relations and the Viet Nam War.* 1999.

Brown, Seyom. *The Crises of Power: Foreign Policy in the Kissinger Years.* 1979.

Burchett, Wilfred. *Catapult to Freedom: The Survival of the Vietnamese People.* 1978.

———. *Grasshoppers and Elephants: Why Vietnam Fell.* 1977.

Butler, David. *The Fall of Saigon: Scenes from the Sudden End of a Long War.* 1985.

Cahn, Anne H. *Killing Détente: The Right Attacks the CIA.* 1998.

Campagna, Anthony S. *The Economic Consequences of the Vietnam War.* 1991.

Cannon, James M. *Time and Chance: Gerald Ford's Appointment with History.* 1994.

Clodfelter, Mark. *The Limits of Air Power: The American Bombing of North Vietnam.* 1989.

Cohen, Warren I. *America's Response to China: An Interpretive History of Sino-American Relations.* 2000.

Coker, Christopher. *The United States and South Africa, 1968–1985.* 1986.

Conboy, Kenneth, and Dale Andradé. *Spies and Commandos: How America Lost the Secret War in North Vietnam.* 2000.

Costigliola, Frank. *France and the United States: The Cold Alliance since World War II.* 1992.

Dallek, Robert. *Nixon and Kissinger: Partners in Power.* 2007.

Davidson, Phillip B. *Vietnam at War: The History, 1946–1975.* 1988.

DeBenedetti, Charles, and Charles Chatfield. *An American Ordeal: The Antiwar Movement of the Vietnam Era.* 1990.

DeForest, Orrin, and David Chanoff. *Slow Burn: The Rise and Bitter Fall of American Intelligence in Vietnam.* 1990.

Duiker, William J. *The Communist Road to Power in Vietnam.* 1981.

———. *U.S. Containment Policy and the Conflict in Indochina.* 1994.

DuPuy, Trevor N. *Elusive Victory: The Arab-Israeli Wars, 1947–1974.* 1978.

Ellsberg, Daniel. *Secrets: A Memoir of Vietnam and the Pentagon Papers.* 2003.

Ely, John H. *War and Responsibility: Constitutional Lessons of Vietnam and Its Aftermath.* 1993.

Engelmann, Larry. *Tears before the Rain: An Oral History of the Fall of South Vietnam.* 1990.

FitzGerald, Frances. *Fire in the Lake: The Vietnamese and the Americans in Vietnam.* 1972.

Foot, Rosemary. *The Practice of Power: U.S. Relations with China since 1949.* 1995.

Ford, Gerald R. *A Time to Heal: The Autobiography of Gerald R. Ford.* 1979.

Franck, Thomas M., and Edward Weisband. *Foreign Policy by Congress.* 1979.

Freedman, Robert O. *Soviet Policy toward the Middle East since 1970.* 1978.

Froman, Michael B. *The Development of the Idea of Détente: Coming to Terms.* 1991.

Gaddis, John L. *The Cold War: A New History.* 2005.

———. *The Long Peace: Inquiries into the History of the Cold War.* 1987.

———. *Russia, the Soviet Union, and the United States: An Interpretive History.* 2nd ed., 1990.

———. *Strategies of Containment: A Critical Appraisal of Postwar American National Security Policy.* 1982; rev. ed., 2005.

———. *We Now Know: Rethinking Cold War History.* 1997.

Gaiduk, Ilya V. *The Soviet Union and the Vietnam War.* 1996.

Garthoff, Raymond L. *Détente and Confrontation: American-Soviet Relations from Nixon to Reagan.* 1994.

Gelb, Leslie H., and Richard K. Betts. *The Irony of Vietnam: The System Worked.* 1979.

Glassman, Jon D. *Arms for the Arabs: The Soviet Union and War in the Middle East.* 1975.

Goh, Evelyn. *Constructing the U.S. Rapprochement with China, 1961–1974: From "Red Menace" to "Tacit Ally."* 2005.

Goldman, Marshall I. *Détente and Dollars: Doing Business with the Soviets.* 1975.

Goode, James F. *The United States and Iran: In the Shadow of Musaddiq.* 1997.

Goodman, Allan E. *The Lost Peace: America's Search for a Negotiated Settlement of the Vietnam War.* 1978.

Gottlieb, Sherry G. *Hell No, We Won't Go! Resisting the Draft during the Vietnam War.* 1991.

Greene, John R. *The Limits of Power: The Nixon and Ford Administrations.* 1995.

———. *The Presidency of Gerald R. Ford.* 1995.

Guimarês, Fernando A. *The Origins of the Angolan Civil War: Foreign Intervention and Domestic Political Conflict.* 1998.

Hallin, Daniel C. *The "Uncensored War": The Media and Vietnam.* 1986.

Hammond, William H. *Reporting Vietnam: Media and Military at War.* 1998.

Hanhimäki, Jussi. *The Flawed Architect: Henry Kissinger and American Foreign Policy.* 2004.

Harding, Harry. *A Fragile Relationship: The United States and China since 1972.* 1992.

Harrison, James P. *The Endless War: Fifty Years of Struggle in Vietnam.* 1982.

Harrison, Michael M. *The Reluctant Ally: France and Atlantic Security.* 1981.

Haslam, Jonathan. *The Soviet Union and the Politics of Nuclear Weapons in Europe, 1969–87.* 1990.

Havens, Thomas R. H. *Fire Across the Sea: The Vietnam War and Japan, 1965–1975.* 1987.

Hellmann, John. *American Myth and the Legacy of Vietnam.* 1986.

Herring, George C., Jr. *America's Longest War: The United States and Vietnam, 1950–1975.* 4th ed., 2002.

———, ed. *The Pentagon Papers: Abridged Edition.* 1993.

Hersh, Seymour M. *The Price of Power: Kissinger in the Nixon White House.* 1983.

Hess, Gary R. *Vietnam and the United States: Origins and Legacy of War.* 1998.

Hoff-Wilson, Joan. *Nixon Reconsidered.* 1994.

Holloway, David. *The Soviet Union and the Arms Race.* 1983.

Hyland, William. *Mortal Rivals: Superpower Relations from Nixon to Reagan.* 1987.

Isaacs, Arnold R. *Without Honor: Defeat in Vietnam and Cambodia.* 1983.

Isaacson, Walter. *Kissinger: A Biography.* 1992.

Jeffreys-Jones, Rhodri. *Peace Now! American Society and the Ending of the Vietnam War.* 1999.

Jiang, Arnold X./Hsiang-tse Chiang. *The United States and China.* 1988.

Joiner, Harry M. *American Foreign Policy: The Kissinger Era*. 1977.

Kalb, Bernard, and Marvin Kalb. *Kissinger*. 1974.

Kaplan, Robert D. *The Arabists: The Romance of an American Elite*. 1993.

Karnow, Stanley. *Vietnam: A History*. Rev. ed., 1991.

Kattenburg, Paul M. *The Vietnam Trauma in American Foreign Policy, 1945–1975*. 1980.

Keith, Ronald C. *The Diplomacy of Zhou Enlai*. 1989.

Kendrick, Alexander. *The Wound Within: America in the Vietnam Years, 1945–1974*. 1974.

Kimball, Jeffrey. *Nixon's Vietnam War*. 1998.

———. *The Vietnam War Files: Uncovering the Secret History of Nixon-Era Strategy*. 2004.

Kissinger, Henry. *White House Years*. 1979.

———. *Years of Upheaval*. 1982.

Kolko, Gabriel. *Anatomy of a War: Vietnam, the United States, and the Modern Historical Experience*. 1985.

Kunz, Diane B. *Butter and Guns: America's Cold War Economic Diplomacy*. 1997.

Krepinevich, Andrew F., Jr. *The Army and Vietnam*. 1986.

LaFeber, Walter. *America, Russia, and the Cold War, 1945–1996*. 8th ed., 1997.

———. *The Clash: A History of U.S.-Japan Relations*. 1997.

———. *The Panama Canal: The Crisis in Historical Perspective*. Updated ed. (with Scott LaFeber), 1989.

Lake, Anthony. *The "Tar Baby" Option: American Policy toward Southern Rhodesia*. 1976.

Landau, David. *Kissinger: The Uses of Power*. 1972.

Langguth, A. J. *Our Vietnam: The War, 1954–1975*. 2000.

Lanning, Michael L., and Dan Cragg. *Inside the VC and the NVA: The Real Story of North Vietnam's Armed Forces*. 1992.

Larson, Thomas B. *Soviet-American Rivalry*. 1978.

Levering, Ralph B. *The Cold War: A Post-Cold War History*. 1994; rev. ed., 2005.

Lewy, Guenter. *America in Vietnam*. 1978.

Lind, Michael. *Vietnam the Necessary War: A Reinterpretation of America's Most Disastrous Military Conflict*. 1999.

Litwak, Robert S. *Détente and the Nixon Doctrine*. 1984.

Lomperis, Timothy J. *From People's War to People's War: Insurgency, Intervention, and the Lessons of Vietnam*. 1996.

———. *The War Everyone Lost—And Won: America's Intervention in Vietnam's Twin Struggles*. 1984.

Lukas, J. Anthony. *Nightmare: The Underside of the Nixon Administration*. 1976.

Maclear, Michael. *The Ten Thousand Day War, Vietnam: 1945–1975*. 1981.

Mandelbaum, Michael. *The Nuclear Question: The United States and Nuclear Weapons, 1946–1976*. 1979.

Mangold, Tom, and John Penygate. *The Tunnels of Cu Chi: The Untold Story of Vietnam*. 1985.

Mann, Jim. *About Face: A History of America's Curious Relationship with China from Nixon to Clinton*. 1999.

Mann, Robert. *A Grand Illusion: America's Descent into Vietnam*. 2001.

Matusow, Allen J. *Nixon's Economy: Booms, Busts, Dollars, and Votes*. 1998.

McMahon, Robert J. *The Cold War on the Periphery: The United States, India, and Pakistan*. 1994.

———. *The Limits of Empire: The United States and Southeast Asia since World War II*. 1999.

Melanson, Richard A. *American Foreign Policy since the Vietnam War: The Search for Consensus from Nixon to Clinton*. 2000.

Moran, Theodore H. *Multinational Corporations and the Politics of Dependence: Copper in Chile*. 1974.

Morgan, Joseph G. *The Vietnam Lobby: The American Friends of Vietnam, 1955–1975*. 1997.

Morley, Morris H. *Washington, Somoza, and the Sandinistas: State and Regime in U.S. Policy Toward Nicaragua, 1969–1981*. 1994.

Morris, Roger. *Uncertain Greatness: Henry Kissinger and American Foreign Policy*. 1977.

Nelson, Keith L. *The Making of Détente: Soviet-American Relations in the Shadow of Vietnam*. 1995.

Nesbitt, Francis N. *Race for Sanctions: African Americans against Apartheid, 1946–1994*. 2004.

Newhouse, John. *Cold Dawn: The Story of SALT*. 1973.

Nixon, Richard. *No More Vietnams*. 1985.

———. *RN: The Memoirs of Richard Nixon*. 1978.

Olmsted, Kathryn. *Challenging the Secret Government: The Post-Watergate Investigations of the CIA and FBI*. 1996.

Olson, James S., and Randy Roberts. *My Lai: A Brief History with Documents*. 1998.

———. *Where the Domino Fell: America and Vietnam, 1945–1990*. 1991.

Page, Caroline. *U.S. Official Propaganda during the Vietnam War, 1965–1973: The Limits of Persuasion*. 1996.

Palmer, Dave R. *Summons of the Trumpet: A History of the Vietnam War from a Military Man's Viewpoint.* 1978.

Pérez, Louis A., Jr. *Cuba and the United States: Ties of Singular Intimacy.* 1997.

Petras, James, and Morris Morley. *The United States and Chile: Imperialism and the Overthrow of the Allende Government.* 1975.

Pike, Douglas. *PAVN: People's Army of Vietnam.* 1986.

Pipes, Richard. *U.S.-Soviet Relations in the Era of Détente: A Tragedy of Errors.* 1981.

Podhoretz, Norman. *Why We Were in Vietnam.* 1982.

Polk, William R. *The Arab World Today.* 5th ed., 1991.

Poole, Peter. *The United States and Indochina from FDR to Nixon.* 1973.

Porter, Gareth. *A Peace Denied: The United States, Vietnam, and the Paris Agreement.* 1975.

Powers, Thomas. *The Man Who Kept the Secrets: Richard Helms and the CIA.* 1979.

Prados, John. *The Blood Road: The Ho Chi Minh Trail and the Vietnam War.* 1999.

———. *Lost Crusader: The Secret Wars of CIA Director William Colby.* 2003.

———. *Presidents' Secret Wars: CIA Pentagon Covert Operations from World War II through the Persian Gulf.* 1996.

Quandt, William B. *Decade of Decisions: American Policy toward the Arab-Israeli Conflict, 1967–1976.* 1977.

Rabe, Stephen G. *The Road to OPEC: United States Relations with Venezuela.* 1982.

Reich, Bernard. *Quest for Peace: United States–Israeli Relations and the Arab-Israeli Conflict.* 1977.

Risse-Kappen, Thomas. *Cooperation among Democracies: The European Influence on U.S. Foreign Policy.* 1995.

Ross, Robert S. *Negotiating Cooperation: The United States and China, 1969–1989.* 1995.

Rubin, Barry. *Paved with Good Intentions: The American Experience and Iran.* 1980.

Safran, Nadav. *Israel.* 1978.

Sarotte, Mary E. *Dealing with the Devil: East Germany, Détente, and Ostpolitik, 1969–1973.* 2001.

Sayigh, Yezid. *Armed Struggle and the Search for State: The Palestinian National Movement, 1949–1993.* 1997.

Schaller, Michael. *Altered States: The United States and Japan since the Occupation.* 1997.

———. *The United States and China in the Twentieth Century.* 2nd ed., 1990.

Schell, Jonathan. *The Time of Illusion.* 1976.

Schlesinger, Arthur M., Jr. *The Imperial Presidency.* 1973.

Schoenbaum, David. *The United States and the State of Israel.* 1993.

Schoutz, Lars. *Beneath the United States: A History of U.S. Policy toward Latin America.* 1998.

Schulzinger, Robert D. *Henry Kissinger: Doctor of Diplomacy.* 1989.

———. *A Time for War: The United States and Vietnam, 1941–1975.* 1997.

Schurmann, Franz. *The Foreign Politics of Richard Nixon: The Grand Design.* 1987.

Searles, P. David. *The Peace Corps Experience: Challenge and Change, 1969–1976.* 1997.

Shaplen, Robert. *Bitter Victory.* 1986.

Shawcross, William. *Sideshow: Kissinger, Nixon and the Destruction of Cambodia.* 1979.

Sheehan, Edward R. F. *The Arabs, Israelis, and Kissinger.* 1976.

Sheehan, Neil, et al., eds. *The Pentagon Papers.* 1971.

Sigmund, Paul E. *The Overthrow of Allende and the Politics of Chile, 1964–1976.* 1977.

———. *The United States and Democracy in Chile.* 1993.

Small, Melvin. *Covering Dissent: The Media and the Anti-Vietnam War Movement.* 1994.

———. *Johnson, Nixon, and the Doves.* 1988.

Smith, Gerard. *Doubletalk: The Story of the First Strategic Arms Limitation Talks.* 1980.

Smith, Peter H. *Talons of the Eagle: Dynamics of U.S.-Latin American Relations.* 2nd ed., 2000.

Snepp, Frank. *Decent Interval: An Insider's Account of Saigon's Indecent End Told by the CIA's Chief Strategy Analyst in Vietnam.* 1978.

Sorley, Lewis. *A Better War: The Unexamined Victories and Final Tragedy of America's Last Years in Vietnam.* 1999.

———. *Arms Transfers under Nixon: A Policy Analysis.* 1983.

Spanier, John W. *American Foreign Policy since World War II.* 14th ed., 1998.

Spiegel, Steven L. *The Other Arab-Israeli Conflict: Making America's Middle East Policy, from Truman to Reagan.* 1985.

Stares, Paul B. *The Militarization of Space: U.S. Policy, 1945–1984.* 1985.

Stevenson, Richard W. *The Rise and Fall of Détente: Relaxations of Tensions in US-Soviet Relations, 1953–84.* 1985.

Stockwell, John. *In Search of Enemies: A CIA Story.* 1979.

Stookey, Robert W. *America and the Arab States.* 1975.

Sulzberger, C. L. *The World and Richard Nixon.* 1987.

Szulc, Tad. *The Illusion of Peace: Foreign Policy in the Nixon Years.* 1978.

Taylor, Sandra C. *Vietnamese Women at War: Fighting for Ho Chi Minh and the Revolution.* 1999.

Terriff, Terry. *The Nixon Administration and the Making of U.S. Nuclear Strategy.* 1995.

Todd, Olivier. *Cruel April: The Fall of Saigon.* 1987.

Tomes, Robert R. *Apocalypse Then: American Intellectuals and the Vietnam War, 1954–1975.* 1998.

Truong Nhu Tang. *A Vietcong Memoir.* 1985.

Tucker, Nancy B. *Taiwan, Hong Kong, and the United States, 1945–1992: Uncertain Friendships.* 1994.

Tucker, Spenser C. *Vietnam.* 1999.

Turley, William S. *The Second Indochina War: A Short Political and Military History, 1954–1975.* 1986.

Turner, Karen G. *Even the Women Must Fight: Memories of War from North Vietnam.* 1998.

Ulam, Adam B. *The Communists: The Story of Power and Lost Illusions, 1948–1991.* 1992.

Valentine, Douglas. *The Phoenix Program.* 1990.

Weiner, Tim. *Legacy of Ashes: The History of the CIA.* 2007.

Wells, Tom. *The War Within: America's Battle over Vietnam.* 1994.

Westad, Odd Arne. *The Global Cold War: Third World Interventions and the Making of Our Times.* 2006.

Whitaker, Arthur P. *The United States and the Southern Core: Argentina, Chile, and Uruguay.* 1976.

Wills, Garry. *Nixon Agonistes: The Crisis of the Self-Made Man.* 1970.

Wittner, Lawrence S. *Toward Nuclear Abolition: A History of the World Nuclear Disarmament Movement, 1971 to the Present.* 2003.

Wyatt, Clarence R. *Paper Soldiers: The American Press and the Vietnam War.* 1993.

Young, Marilyn B. *The Vietnam Wars, 1945–1990.* 1991.

Zaroulis, Nancy, and Gerald Sullivan. *Who Spoke Up? American Protest against the War in Vietnam, 1963–1975.* 1984.

Zhai, Qiang. *China and the Vietnam Wars, 1950–1975.* 2000.

CHAPTER 7

The New World Order: Jimmy Carter and the Diplomacy of Human Rights, 1977–1981

Carter and the New World Order

The Carter administration's foreign policy was more vocal about a world order based on human rights than any presidency since that of Woodrow Wilson, even though the underlying objective remained the containment of Soviet expansion. Human rights, the new executive declared, was "the soul of our foreign policy." Indeed, he called on the United States to repent of its past sins by exercising leadership through example rather than through domination. The change in public emphasis partly resulted from the limitations on U.S. power imposed by the recent military growth of other nations, particularly that of the Soviet Union. But the human rights emphasis was also consistent with ideas growing during the past four decades, most notably those highlighted in Franklin D. Roosevelt's Four Freedoms of 1941, the UN Charter of 1945, the Universal Declaration of Human Rights of 1948, and the Helsinki Agreements of 1975. To guarantee "no more Vietnams," Carter asserted, the United States must no longer be directed by "an inordinate fear of communism." His administration would concentrate on tying the world together by economic and social means, including the establishment of a

law of the seas. It would seek to "replace balance of power politics with world order politics." The ultimate objective was to reduce the chances for nuclear war by achieving success in the SALT talks and halting arms sales to other countries.

Problems plagued the administration from the outset because of conflicts between the goals of Soviet containment and the support of human rights. First, containment of the Soviet Union dictated the development of new weapons, the recognition of China, and aid to non-Communist regimes, whereas the drive for human rights led to the encouragement of nationalism, the establishment of a North–South economic relationship between advanced countries and the Third World, public denunciations of the Soviets' policies toward dissidents at home, and support for the SALT talks. Second, morality rarely fit with the government's strategic and economic interests, often exposing the administration to charges of hypocrisy. Carter attacked the repressive tactics of Fidel Castro in Cuba and Idi Amin in Uganda, and he angered Leonid Brezhnev by criticizing his civil liberties policies. But the president ignored similarly harsh practices in countries important to U.S. interests, such as Iran,

Nicaragua, the Philippines, South Korea, and Zaire (formerly Congo). Although the U.S. ambassador to the United Nations, Andrew Young, asserted that the human rights program was never "thought out and planned," the administration spent an enormous amount of time formulating these policies. Finally, the administration never succeeded in establishing a law of the seas that regulated their use and created a sense of interdependence among users.

The Vietnam experience encouraged the new executive to adopt a diplomacy of restraint. The war in Southeast Asia and the Watergate scandals had destroyed the nation's political consensus, allowing the emergence of numerous special interest groups that often operated independently of Washington. The declining global influence of the United States since World War II added to its inability to steer events. Disillusionment and a sense of national guilt over the war in Vietnam meanwhile fostered a greater disengagement in foreign affairs and bred skepticism over the reality of a Communist danger. The new attitude manifested itself in an aversion to foreign intervention and in a call for cooperation in furthering human rights and helping poverty-stricken peoples, especially those in the so-called Fourth World countries having few resources. Indeed, Americans seemed to develop a sense of collective amnesia about the war in Vietnam, preferring to focus on almost any issue other than their nation's longest war. The Washington government was confident that the Kremlin would have to relax its offensive because of the growing aspirations of China, NATO, and the Third World. The United States, it appeared, had finally accepted the limits of power.

The Carter administration encountered numerous problems in foreign policy. The new president was a novice in national politics and was unable to work effectively with Congress. Many Democrats in Congress had won their seats by greater margins than Carter had and did not feel bound to him. The domestic political structure was in constant flux because of shifting alliances that obstructed the formation of a new national consensus. The economy continued to suffer from recession and skyrocketing inflation, a predicament exacerbated by OPEC's periodic raising of oil prices. The nation's allies meanwhile distanced themselves from Washington because its leaders seemed unable to manage their own political and economic situation. Carter's emphasis on human rights hurt détente because a return to idealism in foreign affairs not only disrupted Soviet relations but also caused trouble in Latin America and Europe. Moreover, a call for human rights could lead to policies similar to those of President Wilson: self-righteous interference in other countries' internal affairs. As Carter's policies eventually floundered in indirection and indecisiveness, his performance ratings plunged.

Carter at first leaned toward the views of Secretary of State Cyrus Vance, who preferred an orderly, behind-the-scenes formulation of policy through the State Department. American foreign policy underwent a marked change from Kissinger's independent, flashy style of diplomacy to that of patient and quiet negotiations led by experienced career diplomats. Vance had been deputy secretary of defense from 1964 to 1967 and had participated in the Paris peace talks of 1968–1969 relating to Vietnam. A wealthy New York attorney from West Virginia, he opposed military interventionist policies, refused to hold the Soviets responsible for all the world's problems, advocated disarmament measures, emphasized the need for dealing with change in developing nations outside the competitive context of the Cold War, and believed that the Vietnamese War had demonstrated the principle that Americans could not "prop up a series of regimes that lacked popular support." With the diminished role of the United States in world politics, he declared publicly, "there can be no going back to a time when we thought there could be American solutions to every problem." Peace could come only through negotiations and the establishment of economic ties. SALT II became his premier objective.

Vance relied heavily on his chief adviser for Soviet affairs, Marshall Shulman, on leave from his position as professor of Russian studies at Columbia University. Shulman argued that the United States should emphasize "soft linkage"—discreet suggestions to Moscow that U.S. economic aid would be forthcoming only if the Soviets respected human rights at home and allowed international matters to calm. He hoped that "within-the-system-modernizers" inside the Soviet Union—youthful and middle-aged professionals and technicians—would bring internal changes conducive to cooperation with the West. But time and patience were required. He and Vance agreed that troubles in emerging nations were attributable more to nationalist tendencies than to Soviet instigation. Change in Eastern Europe, they continued, had to come slowly. Otherwise, the Soviets would use military force to settle questions as they had done in Hungary in 1956 and Czechoslovakia in 1968.

But the president's national security adviser, Zbigniew Brzezinski, sharply disagreed with Vance, prompting a division in the administration's foreign policy. A political science professor from Columbia University who specialized in Soviet affairs, Brzezinski was born in Poland and held hard-line anti-Communist views. He saw the world as bipolar and regarded the Soviet Union as the central threat to peace. An early critic of détente, Brzezinski was skeptical about SALT, especially if the Soviets continued their aggressive policies in Africa and the Middle East. Furthermore, he did not believe "that the use of nuclear weapons would be the end of the human race. . . . That's egocentric."

Carter seldom found a common ground between these opposing viewpoints and therefore failed to develop a firm and consistent foreign policy. He promised peaceful resolutions of world problems, cooperation with Congress, restraints on the CIA, a more open foreign policy, restrictions on arms sales, gradual military withdrawal from South Korea, and curtailment of foreign aid to nations refusing to respect human rights. Past experiences suggested that these objectives were impractical. But for Carter, they seemed attainable on an individual basis. One official noted that the president looked at problems "like an engineering student thinking you can cram for the exam and get an A." To Carter, a graduate of the Annapolis Naval Academy and a nuclear engineer, long hours of studying and mastering details left him with a comfortable feeling of understanding the issues. But his approach was virtually meaningless without a corresponding understanding of how the issues were interrelated and that dealing with them required knowledge of both general strategy and history. In 1979, Carter tried to correct the latter deficiency when he admitted to having read more history since becoming president than at any time in his life. Yet the president's fundamentalist religious views influenced him to adopt a simplified world outlook in which morality became the primary determinant in foreign policy. Thus, those nations not professing idealism rejected Carter's calls for human rights as unwarranted attempts to meddle in their domestic affairs. The president sincerely believed in his pleas for human decency, but he was hampered by practical global politics, by his country's diminished world prestige, and by the conflicts between his advisers. The gap between idealistic objectives and realistic policies proved too wide to close.

Perhaps Carter's central difficulty was a lack of vision and direction. A former speechwriter noted that the president "holds explicit, thorough positions on every issue under the sun . . . but he has no large view of the relations between them." Carter "fails to project a vision larger than the problem he is tackling at the moment." The president correctly argued that a "national malaise" had caused a "crisis of the American spirit," but he never laid out a general course of action designed to combat the problem.

The Carter administration sought to counter Soviet military expansion in Eastern Europe by tightening the Western alliance and

In echoing Wilsonian ideas, President Carter called for a new emphasis on human rights diplomacy.
"Human Rights and Foreign Policy," President Jimmy Carter's commencement speech at Notre Dame University, June 1977, *Public Papers of the Presidents of the United States: Jimmy Carter* (Washington, D.C.: Government Printing Office, 1977), vol. 1, 954.

I believe we can have a foreign policy that is democratic, that is based on fundamental values, and that uses power and influence, which we have, for humane purposes. We can also have a foreign policy that the American people both support and, for a change, know about and understand. . . .

In less than a generation, we've seen the world change dramatically. The daily lives and aspirations of most human beings have been transformed. Colonialism is nearly gone. A new sense of national identity now exists in almost 100 new countries that have been formed in the last generation. Knowledge has become more widespread. Aspirations are higher. As more people have been freed from traditional constraints, more have been determined to achieve, for the first time in their lives, social justice.

The world is still divided by ideological disputes, dominated by regional conflicts, and threatened by danger that we will not resolve the differences of race and wealth without violence or without drawing into combat the major military powers. We can no longer separate the traditional issues of war and peace from the new global questions of justice, equity, and human rights. . . .

First, we have reaffirmed America's commitment to human rights as a fundamental tenet of our foreign policy. In ancestry, religion, color, place of origin, and cultural background, we Americans are as diverse a nation as the world has ever seen. No common mystique of blood or soil unites us. What draws us together, perhaps more than anything else, is a belief in human freedom. . . .

This does not mean that we can conduct our foreign policy by rigid moral maxims. We live in a world that is imperfect and which will always be imperfect. . . .

I understand fully the limits of moral suasion. We have no illusion that changes will come easily or soon. . . .

Our policy is based on an historical vision of America's role. Our policy is derived from a larger view of global change. Our policy is rooted in our moral values, which never change. Our policy is reinforced by our material wealth and by our military power. Our policy is designed to serve mankind. And it is a policy that I hope will make you proud to be Americans.

furthering the SALT talks. The Moscow government had apparently matched that of Washington in nuclear power, necessitating a greater U.S. reliance on allies and arms limitations programs. In January 1977, Carter attempted to draw the nation's allies closer together by calling for a program of "trilateralism"—social and economic cooperation among North America, Western Europe, and Japan that also helped the Third World. Less than a week after the inauguration, Vice President Walter Mondale promoted the idea during his goodwill visit to Western Europe and Japan. This program was no surprise; during the early 1970s, Carter and

Vance had been members of the Trilateral Commission, a private group of Americans, West Europeans, and Japanese brought together by Brzezinski and U.S. banker David Rockefeller to rebuild economic and political ties hurt by the Nixon administration's willingness to deal with enemy nations. But the commission rarely agreed on anything. In the spring of 1977, President Carter attended an economic conference in London of seven industrial nations—the United States, Britain, Canada, France, Italy, West Germany, and Japan—that agreed to work toward halting inflation, promoting trade, creating employment, and helping underdeveloped nations. Afterward, he reaffirmed ties with NATO as a core of U.S. foreign policy.

The White House spent most of 1977 trying to advance the SALT negotiations in Moscow. Vance led the delegation in late March as it promoted the principles of November 1974, worked out by Ford and Brezhnev in Vladivostok. Vance offered a well-publicized plan containing several proposals: formal approval of the Vladivostok principles, a specific program calling for a joint cutback in missile launchers and multiple warheads, cessation of the development of new weapons, and a freeze on intercontinental ballistic missiles (ICBMs) at their present level of about 550. Vance also recommended an end to mobile missiles, limits on the scope of cruise missiles, and restrictions against the Soviets' new supersonic "Backfire" bomber. His proposals unleashed a furious reaction in Moscow because they reversed the Ford–Brezhnev understandings by calling for massive reductions in the exact areas of Soviet strengths. Vance's plan was preposterous, Soviet Foreign Minister Andrei Gromyko announced in a televised news conference, because it required the Soviets to phase out their largest missiles. Although the two nations agreed to continue studying the problems relating to nuclear materials, they abruptly terminated the SALT talks. SALT I was due to expire in October 1977, but the governments in Washington and Moscow agreed to extend its life until SALT II became effective. Soviet–American relations had taken a sharp downward turn.

In an effort to defuse the East–West division, Carter relied on UN Ambassador Andrew Young to build a meaningful North–South relationship. Young, a black minister, civil rights leader, and former congressman from Georgia, promoted closer relations with the Third World by advancing the Vance–Shulman position that new nations could seek help from the United States as long as Cold War issues did not intervene. But Young had to leave office in 1979 in the wake of revelations that he had secretly initiated unauthorized communications with the Palestine Liberation Organization (PLO) (not recognized by the United States) to arrange its participation in settling the Middle East crisis.

The administration's human rights stance toward the Third World necessitated understandings with the Soviet Union. There seemed little choice by the late 1970s: Americans were weary of foreign policy commitments and the so-called imperial presidency. According to this argument, the nation's presidents had for too long operated independently of the people's wishes and needed to come under congressional restraints. The Cold War was over, many wanted to believe. Détente was crucial to the new world order.

The United States thus prepared to deal with the realities of a multipolar political and economic system. Should it oppose international cooperation in resolving global problems, growing instability would lead to more political unrest injurious to trade and investment. The world's economy was in a downspin, and Fourth World peoples needed massive assistance to combat droughts, famines, and other natural disasters. Thousands of "boat people" from Vietnam, Laos, and Cambodia sought refuge in the United States from repressive Communist governments; at the same time, however, Third World nations controlled valuable natural resources such as oil and demonstrated a strong desire to use their economic leverage against the great powers. The new postwar nations had become a majority in the United Nations by the 1970s, and the continued proliferation of nuclear weapons was alarming. The Western alliance was shaky, and Latin Americans were increasingly resentful of Washington's exploitative policies. Finally, Watergate, Vietnam, and the manipulative activities of the CIA and multinational corporations caused an erosion of respect for the United States. Carter appeared to recognize these realities, but his rhetorical and often inconsistent appeals to human rights so badly interfered with his positions on events that even the nation's allies viewed his administration as devious, self-righteous, and undependable.

The Third World:
Africa and Latin America

The Carter administration made noteworthy strides toward establishing good relations with Third World countries. Vance, Young, and others in the administration tried to deal with the troubles of the underdeveloped nations on their own merits; not every problem, they argued, was Soviet inspired. Nationalist upheavals did not always relate to great power rivalries. During the first half of his presidency, Carter was receptive to these arguments, even restraining those advisers who called for interventionist policies designed to curb believed Soviet expansionism. The White House tied economic assistance to assurances of human rights reforms, making this principle the central thrust of Third World policies.

Africa was a major concern of the United States. Politically, the representation in the United Nations was already one-third African, and inside the United States blacks pressed for a policy recognizing African nationalism. Economically, the continent was rich in minerals and an excellent source of trade and investment. Nigeria, in fact, had become the second-largest supplier of oil for the United States. Strategically, Africa offered airstrips and ports at key points interconnecting the world. Should the Washington administration continue to support white regimes, however, the Soviets would be in the position to exploit black nationalism and become a major force in Africa.

Young ultimately convinced the president that Africans should resolve their own problems. Both the Kennedy and the Johnson administration had told the UN that they disliked white minority rule in Rhodesia (Zimbabwe after 1980) and South Africa. But despite Johnson's opposition, Congress permitted Americans to purchase Rhodesia's chrome, violating a UN embargo that the United States itself had helped to institute. The Nixon administration then refrained from criticizing white rule in Africa because it believed that whites would remain dominant for

years. But a shift in policy had begun under Kissinger in 1976 that Carter continued. After Young visited black regimes in Africa, Carter denounced the racist policy of apartheid and argued that an independent Africa bolstered by U.S. aid posed a strong obstacle to Soviet infiltration. Congress, under immense White House pressure, restored the embargo on Rhodesian chrome. In the meantime, the Carter administration worked with the British government to persuade Rhodesia's prime minister, Ian Smith, to approve a gradual change to majority rule. As a result, British and American negotiations led to an election in April 1980 that installed a government in Rhodesia headed by a black insurgent and Marxist, Robert Mugabe. In South Africa, however, the Washington government failed to persuade the white regime to change its policies toward blacks, who made up 85 percent of the population.

A conflict between the Marxist regimes of Somalia and Ethiopia dramatically exposed Soviet–American differences over Africa. In 1977, Somalia, the Kremlin's closest ally in Africa since 1969, sent soldiers to fight with the insurgent Western Somali Liberation Front in the Ogaden area of Ethiopia, then populated by a number of Somalis. The Soviets had to choose between the antagonists. Although Somalia had a naval base and air facilities along the Indian Ocean, the Soviets leaned toward Ethiopia because it was much larger than Somalia and its location would facilitate Soviet access to the strategically important Horn of Africa on the central eastern coast of the continent. In November, Somalia's president abrogated his country's friendship with the Soviet Union. The Moscow government promptly sent Ethiopia $1 billion in military assistance, a thousand advisers, and 20,000 Cuban soldiers to put down the Ogaden insurrection. By March 1978, the effort had succeeded in driving Somali regulars out of Ogaden. The Carter administration now feared that if the Soviet Union won greater influence in Ethiopia and went on to seize the southern end of the Red Sea, it would endanger the Suez Canal and Israel and cut off the oil flow from the Persian Gulf to the West.

Growing division within the Carter administration led to a confused reaction to events in Africa. Brzezinski and the Defense Department wanted to send military assistance to Somalia, whereas Vance and the State Department argued that Africa's problems were internal and that U.S. intervention would alienate the entire continent. Although Ethiopia had invited Moscow's help, Vance and Young argued that Somalia was the aggressor. Carter therefore wavered before lashing out at the Soviet Union and Cuba, hurting détente by warning that if the Soviets did not withdraw the Cuban forces from Africa, SALT II was in danger. The United States did not intervene but urged a moderate policy in Ogaden and a peaceful settlement of Somali–Ethiopian difficulties. Somalia, meanwhile, eased the situation by agreeing to keep its soldiers out of Ogaden. But the Soviets entered a twenty-year pact with Ethiopia that condoned their involvement and that of the Cubans.

Despite Young's unceremonious departure from the administration in 1979, U.S. relations with Africa had improved. Commercial ties were growing, and the United States soon secured port and airfield rights in Somalia. In another part of the continent, the Carter administration airlifted supplies to Belgian and French forces in Zaire (the chief source of cobalt for the United States) during May 1978 after Soviet- and Cuban-aided Katangans had invaded the province through Angola, but that was the extent of U.S. military action. The restraint paid off. Numerous African regimes voted with the United States in matters before the UN General Assembly, and although the Soviets and Cubans remained influential in Angola and Ethiopia, the Angolans showed signs of wanting to deal with the West. Africans, the Carter administration seemed to realize, had one overriding objective: never again to become colonials.

Latin America likewise continued to be a major source of U.S. concern. Persistent problems of poverty and overpopulation had stimulated nationalist drives that were, in turn, repeatedly squelched by harsh military regimes often maintained by U.S. arms and materiel. Brazil, Cuba, and Mexico became more independent, although the majority of Latin Americans still sought U.S. help in securing technological assistance, reduced tariffs, higher prices for their goods, and more controls over multinational corporations. Like Africa, Latin America commanded votes in the United Nations and was an important source of trade and investment. The United States could no longer ignore the problem.

The Carter administration sought to relieve Latin America's problems by using economic pressures to force right-wing regimes to respect human rights. In a speech before the Permanent Council of the Organization of American States (OAS) in April 1977, the president called for greater consultation among the American states that rested on three principles: "a high regard for the individuality and sovereignty of each Latin American and Caribbean nation," "respect for human rights," and the intention to resolve "the great issues which affect the relations between the developed and developing nations." Carter urged commercial cooperation in stabilizing prices and building a sound economy and promised U.S. help in securing loans through the American Development Bank. These efforts, however, were contingent on a firm Latin American commitment to human rights.

Carter's first diplomatic offensive in Latin America—to reestablish formal relations with Cuba—was a failure. As prerequisites for U.S. recognition, Castro first had to guarantee respect for human rights, and, second, he had to cease sending troops to Africa. In Havana from April through June 1977, U.S. and Cuban delegates discussed their countries' difficulties. A short time earlier, the Carter administration lifted the ban on travel to Cuba, and Castro promised to continue efforts to discourage airplane hijacking. But by the close of the Havana negotiations, the two delegations had succeeded only in creating "diplomatic interest sections" in the nations' capitals. The U.S. trade embargo was still in effect, Cuban troops remained in Angola and Ethiopia, and Soviet military and economic influence was conspicuous in Cuba. In fact, more than $20 million of economic aid arrived in Havana every week. Although secret U.S.–Cuban discussions continued through 1980, they neither lifted the commercial embargo nor restored diplomatic relations.

The Carter administration's most ambitious effort to build a better relationship with Latin America was a success: the termination of U.S. control over the Panama Canal established by the Hay-Bunau-Varilla Treaty of 1903. A longtime source of resentment, the pact had been the subject of negotiations during the Johnson and the Nixon presidencies. By mid-century, controversy had focused on a local disagreement over the flying of Panamanian and U.S. flags on high school

grounds. In January 1964, U.S. high school students in Panama tore down and allegedly desecrated the Panamanian flag. Angry Panamanians stormed the Canal Zone, where U.S. soldiers drove them back at the cost of twenty-six lives, including those of three Americans. The Panamanian government broke relations with the United States and turned for help to the United Nations and the OAS. An OAS committee tried to mediate the dispute, but Johnson refused the Panamanian government's demand to renegotiate the old Panama Treaty. After his election victory in November, he announced his country's intention to build a sea-level canal through either Panama, Nicaragua, or Colombia. The Panama Canal, he explained, was susceptible to sabotage, unable to service the huge volume of ships passing through daily, and not equipped to accommodate America's large aircraft carriers. But Panamanians objected to America's insistence

President Jimmy Carter and Omar Torrijos
Signing the Panama Canal Treaty, June 16, 1978. (*Jimmy Carter Library, Atlanta, Georgia*)

on controlling the canal and retaining its bases in the area, and the issue remained unsettled. The Nixon administration pledged support for a new treaty, and now Carter as president promised an agreement combining "Panama's legitimate needs as a sovereign nation" with America's "interests in the efficient operations of a neutral canal, open on a nondiscriminatory basis to all users." His administration had a chance to improve relations with Latin America with one bold stroke: turning over the canal to Panama.

The resulting treaties between the United States and Panama were the work of many people, most notably Sol Linowitz as head of the U.S. delegation, Secretary of State Vance, and two senators, Democrat Robert Byrd of West Virginia and Republican Howard Baker of Tennessee. The two pacts, drawn in 1977 and approved in Panama by a two-to-one margin in October of that same year, would abrogate the 1903 treaty, raise Panama's share of the canal tolls, and grant the United States the perpetual right to protect the canal's "neutrality." By the first treaty, the "Panama Canal Treaty," the United States would retain central responsibility for the canal until 2000, at which time Panama was to assume all duties associated with the Canal Zone but with the guarantee that Americans already employed would keep their jobs. The second pact, the "Treaty concerning the Permanent Neutrality and Operation of the Panama Canal," authorized the United States to ensure the permanent "neutrality of the waterway" and promised "no discrimination" against any country wishing to use the canal. An attached statement provided that after 2000, the United States could use the canal to move warships as well as "defend the canal against any threat to the regime of neutrality."

American resistance to the canal treaties was nationwide and emotional. Opponents denounced the agreements as another retreat similar to that in Vietnam; the treaties would become monuments to appeasement. The United States owned the canal, others proclaimed. One senator bluntly stated that "we

stole it fair and square." Republican Ronald Reagan of California, presidential hopeful in the 1980 election, showed no awareness of the historical record in asserting that the Canal Zone was "sovereign United States territory just the same as Alaska . . . and the states that were carved out of the Louisiana Purchase." Loss of the canal, critics charged, would hurt the U.S. economy, undercut the nation's defense, and invite Soviet involvement in the regime of Panamanian President Omar Torrijos, which already seemed to be leaning toward communism.

With public opinion polls showing nearly 80 percent of Americans against giving up the canal, the Carter administration faced an imposing uphill battle. Proponents of the treaties concurred with Carter that their handiwork would establish goodwill throughout Latin America. They also argued that the canal's economic advantages were no longer substantial and that the United States had a moral obligation to relinquish an area belonging to Panama. Less than 10 percent of U.S. trade, in fact, depended on the canal. It offered even less in strategic advantages, asserted the Joint Chiefs of Staff. The canal was subject to sabotage, aircraft carriers and tankers were too large for the waterway, and nuclear submarines wishing to use it would have to surface and reveal their location. To one critic who questioned what the United States would do if Panama declared the canal "closed for repairs," Brzezinski pointedly replied that, "according to the provisions of the Neutrality Treaty, we will move in and close down the Panamanian government for repairs."

Arguments over canal ownership lay at the heart of the controversy. The head of the North American negotiating team in 1976, Ellsworth Bunker, correctly argued that "we bought Louisiana; we bought Alaska. In Panama, we bought not territory, but rights. . . . It is clear that under law we do not have sovereignty in Panama." Carter underlined this point in a "fireside chat" when he asserted that "we do not own the Panama Canal Zone. We have never had sovereignty over it. We have only had the right to use it." Defenders of the treaties rallied behind the Committee of Americans for the Canal Treaties, which numbered among its membership the noted diplomat W. Averell Harriman and a former director of the CIA, William Colby. Indeed, actor John Wayne helped to ease the fears expressed by fellow conservative Ronald Reagan by supporting the treaty and offering assurances about the trustworthy nature of his new acquaintance General Torrijos. Even more impressive, leading Republicans, including former President Ford and Secretary of State Kissinger, joined the nation's big businesses in favoring the treaties.

During the spring of 1978, the two Panama Canal treaties won narrow approval in the Senate. On March 16, that body approved the neutrality treaty by a margin of sixty-eight to thirty-two, a scant one vote more than the two-thirds majority needed. To secure its passage, however, supporters attached a statement reserving the right of the United States to keep the canal open, "including the use of military force in the Republic of Panama." Despite this blatant violation of Panamanian sovereignty, Torrijos accepted this reservation after a special appeal from Carter. In a "Statement of Understanding" in October that became part of the neutrality treaty, Torrijos agreed to the U.S. right after 2000 to halt "any aggression or threat directed against the Canal or against the peaceful transit of vessels through the Canal." In addition, he assured the United States that in times of trouble, its vessels could "go to the head of the line." Carter in turn guaranteed against any claimed U.S. right to intervene in Panama's internal affairs. By the same thin margin, on April 18, the Senate approved the other treaty, turning over the canal to Panama in 2000. Had the United States rejected the treaties, Torrijos later declared, he would have had the canal destroyed.

Thus, after three-quarters of a century of disagreement with Panama, the United States had accepted the abrogation of the treaty of 1903. In a single move, the Carter administration had taken a major step toward estab-lishing U.S. credibility in the southern half of the hemisphere. But succeeding events would show that more than one agreement was necessary to remove the ill will engrained among Latin Americans by the long history of interventionism by the United States.

In the same part of the hemisphere, the Central American state of Nicaragua, the Carter administration's diplomatic efforts were likewise a mixture of idealism and realism that for only a brief time seemed to approximate an effective foreign policy. Since 1936, the United States had supported the anti-Communist dictatorship established by General Anastasio Somoza García. Over the years, Americans ignored the Somoza dynasty's repressive practices and sold it arms, in return receiving Nicaragua's cooperation in interventionist actions in Guatemala in 1954, Cuba in 1961, and the Dominican Republic in 1965. But while the Somozas thrived, the oppressed Nicaraguan people suffered from this tyrannical regime, which had alienated the Catholic Church, middle class, and peasants by its systematic plunder and its ruthless National Guard. Finally, in 1978, a leftist organization known as the Sandinista National Liberation Front rose in rebellion. Named after Augusto César Sandino, who had led insurgents against U.S. forces from the 1920s until his death at the hands of General Somoza in 1934, the Sandinistas picked up widespread support from the people, the Catholic Church, and business interests. The Carter administration at first tried to mediate the dispute, but it was unsuccessful. The Sandinistas launched a major offensive in 1979 and soon took over the government. In mid-July, Anastasio Somoza Debayle, a West Point graduate and son of the original patriarch, Anastasio Somoza Garcia, fled the country, only to be assassinated in Paraguay.

To persuade the Sandinistas to promote reform, Carter asked Congress to appropriate $75 million for economic aid to Nicaragua. In July 1980, that body approved his request over numerous heated protests that Sandinista leader Daniel Ortega was Communist.

The Sandinistas, however, promised open political and economic affairs and continued to receive U.S. assistance until early 1981. Despite inconclusive CIA findings, the Washington government cut off aid after accusing them of arming anti-American insurgents in El Salvador.

The problems in El Salvador, as in other desperately poor Latin American states, had developed over a long period. Five million people were jammed into the tiny country, mostly in poverty-stricken areas characterized by a high birthrate and rampant disease. Calls for reform had gone unheeded by rightist regimes, which were comprised of a small minority of landowners allied with the army and relying on repressive measures to stay in power. But in October 1979, young, reformist, middle-grade officers in the army won control. They installed an anti-Communist regime headed by a civilian president who had been educated at the University of Notre Dame, José Napoleón Duarte of the Christian Democratic Party. The Carter administration sent economic and military assistance to Duarte, who had himself undergone torture years earlier at the hands of the military and now promised land reform and other social and political changes. A brutal reaction by the former ruling minority led to a wave of assassinations by right-wing terrorists known as "death squads," which prevented Duarte from establishing control over the internal security groups within the government and forced him to rely on the military to stay in power. Finally, the death squads assassinated the archbishop of El Salvador during Mass in March 1980 and in December raped and killed four American Catholic missionaries (all women, including three nuns). Carter angrily stopped further assistance to Duarte when his regime failed to punish those responsible.

But Carter soon had to reverse this decision: civil war had broken out after the leftists joined other dissatisfied groups in forming the Democratic Revolutionary Front in April 1980 to oppose the regime. According to some estimates, in trying to put down the uprising, government security forces killed 13,000 Salvadorans by the end of that year, and there was no end in sight. The military in El Salvador, complained U.S. Ambassador Robert E. White in the *New York Times*, was "one of the most out-of-control, violent, bloodthirsty groups of men in the world."

Mexican–U.S. relations also remained uneasy. Millions of illegal aliens had entered the United States by 1980, many of them young men in search of temporary jobs. Americans complained that Mexicans either took the few jobs available and drove down wages or failed to find employment and went on welfare. In August 1977, Carter recommended that Congress grant amnesty to illegal aliens already in the United States and then upgrade border patrols and fine American businesses that hired illegal aliens. Congress established a study commission.

Economic problems also interfered with U.S. relations with Mexico. Nationalists in Mexico sought to break U.S. domination over trade and investment in their country by persuading the United States either to lower tariffs or to place more restrictions on foreign investment. Mexico had won bargaining power during the late 1970s as a result of its vast holdings of oil and natural gas. Although it was not a member of OPEC and Americans expected to buy these resources at low prices, the Mexican government charged higher prices than did Saudi Arabia. After several disputes, the United States agreed to Mexico's prices in late 1979. Within a year, oil and natural gas made up half of Mexico's exports to the United States.

Despite the Panama Canal treaties, Latin Americans continued to regard the United States with suspicion. One act could not erase nearly 160 years of resentment stemming from the assumed role of the United States as guardian of the hemisphere. Whether or not the charges of imperialism were just, its southern neighbors believed they were. The United States appeared callous, arrogant, and exploitative, ignoring the plight of Latin Americans while extending massive aid programs to other parts of the world. Critics warned that if communism was indeed a threat in the Western Hemisphere, that situation was in large part the result of the longtime neglect by the United States of its neighbors. Rather than interpret every insurrection as Communist inspired, they argued, America's leaders must recognize that the region's economic problems had spawned desperate political and military measures that their government might have prevented by astute diplomacy. The treaties with Panama suggested that the United States had taken a new direction in Latin America; only time and additional bold actions could provide proof.

The Middle East

The Carter administration, meanwhile, worked toward a second breakthrough in foreign policy, this time in the Middle East. There the president personally intervened and apparently achieved the first major move toward peace. The region was beset with numerous troubles and increasing troubles by the late 1970s. Besides the ancient Arab–Israeli feud, civil conflict in Lebanon, growing PLO terrorism, and widespread unrest in Iran, the West's needs for oil from the Persian Gulf had escalated. Even Israel's military successes in 1967 came at unexpected expense. The "annexation" of the West Bank imposed severe strains on Israel. Not only did the military occupation program involve heavy financial obligations, but it entailed restrictions on fundamental freedoms that violated Israel's democratic principles. In addition, a refugee problem continued to grow that was both Palestinian and Israeli in scope. The war of 1948–1949 had displaced about 900,000 Palestinians, leading the United Nations to establish refugee camps in Egypt, Jordan, Syria, and Lebanon. The Six Day War of 1967 complicated the refugee problem because more than 800,000 Palestinian Arabs inhabited the areas occupied by Israeli forces—the West Bank and the Old City of Jerusalem. By the late 1970s, displaced Palestinians numbered perhaps 4 million, pro-

viding a large mass of dissatisfied people susceptible to PLO recruitment. The Israelis noted another side to the refugee issue: nearly a million Jewish refugees had left the Arab states, many forced into Israel after the war of 1948–1949 and still holding legitimate claims against Arab governments. There were too many issues to resolve in the Middle East, according to one European observer. It is "something like playing billiards on a small boat in a rough sea—and each ball with a shifting center of gravity."

President Carter was convinced that the key to a comprehensive peace in the Middle East was an Arab–Israeli settlement and in March 1977 told reporters that the United States sought a general agreement based on establishing fair boundaries and a "homeland" for the Palestinians. Although he insisted that such a homeland did not entail a separate Palestinian state, he could not assuage the Israelis' fear that the White House would enter negotiations with the PLO, which they regarded as a fanatical revolutionary group dedicated to their violent overthrow. Two months later, the chances for peace seemed to diminish when the Israelis elected a new government—a coalition regime led by Menachem Begin as prime minister. Begin was himself a former terrorist who had long resisted concessions to the Arabs. In October, the Carter administration joined the Soviet Union in a statement admitting to the "legitimate rights of the Palestinian people." Carter believed that Kissinger had made a mistake in leaving out the Soviets in a Middle East settlement because of their influence with the PLO and the Syrians. But Carter's new line of action with the Moscow regime did not interest either Israel or Egypt.

In November 1977, peace prospects suddenly brightened when Egyptian President Anwar el-Sadat took an unprecedented step toward peace: he risked assassination (which did occur at the hands of his own soldiers in October 1981) by visiting Jerusalem and appearing before the Israeli Knesset, or Parliament. There he delivered a worldwide televised speech in which he made the surprising concession that "Israel has become an established fact." Optimism seemed justified because the Israelis had earlier proclaimed that if the Arabs dealt with them directly, which constituted recognition, Israel would return the territories occupied during the Six Day War of 1967. Sadat proposed Israeli withdrawal from these lands, followed by the establishment of a Palestinian state derived from the West Bank and Gaza. In exchange, Egypt would sign a peace treaty ensuring Israel's security and legitimacy as a nation. But there was an ominous sign: only one other Arab nation showed interest in Sadat's proposal—Saudi Arabia, an ally of the United States.

The initial optimism faded as Begin announced that he did not favor the terms. Although willing to withdraw from the Sinai desert, he refused to concede self-determination to the Palestinians on the West Bank and in the Gaza Strip. The Israeli army must remain in the West Bank, Gaza, and the Golan Heights. Begin did not consider the West Bank (which he called by its Hebrew names Judea and Samaria) to be occupied. The West Bank was a liberated area, he proclaimed, now part of Israel along with Gaza. Begin agreed only to postpone the issue for five years and then negotiate the final status of the disputed areas, but many believed that in the meantime he intended to enlarge Israel's control over them by establishing new settlements.

Not surprisingly, the talks stalemated. Sadat complained that Begin's proposal would prolong Israeli occupation of the West Bank and Gaza. There could be no separate peace with Israel unless the Palestinians received self-rule and the Israelis withdrew from all Arab areas. In March 1978, the situation worsened when Israeli forces attacked the PLO in Lebanon, killing more than a thousand noncombatants in response to a recent PLO terrorist act that led to the deaths of thirty-five Israeli civilians. In this heated atmosphere, Sadat realized that to approve Israel's demands made him a traitor, adding to the widespread condemnation of him in the Arab world caused by his visit to Jerusalem. The leader of Libya, Colonel Muammar al-Qaddafi, demanded Sadat's assassination.

When the negotiations broke down, Carter intervened. He had hesitated because of diverging U.S. interests in Israeli security and Arab oil. But fear of Soviet infiltration became decisive. American involvement in the matter, however, carried a built-in danger: it exposed the Washington government's differences with Israel on how to achieve peace. Carter argued that Sadat had offered security to Israel and warned Begin that failure to accept would worsen matters. West Europeans, the president noted, had long called for Arab recognition of Israel in exchange for the evacuation of lands taken in 1967. After reminding the Israelis that only the United States supported them, he called for the implementation of UN Resolution 242 of 1967, which had stipulated their withdrawal from areas occupied in the Six Day War. To Carter, this meant the return of most Arab territories taken in 1967 (with some adjustments for security reasons), the creation of a Palestinian homeland, and the establishment of diplomatic relations between Israel and the Arab states. Begin, however, interpreted the UN resolution to mean that for security reasons Israel had to retain the West Bank and Gaza and could not permit the establishment of a Palestinian homeland. As for the Old City of Jerusalem, that too must remain in Israeli hands. With the eastern sector occupied in 1967 and now inhabited by 43,000 Israelis, it was, according to Israeli decree, "one city indivisible, the capital of the State of Israel."

The settlements issue underlined the differences between Israel and the United States. Since 1967, the Washington government had considered it illegal for Israel to establish settlements in wartime-occupied lands. Carter now criticized the Israelis' efforts to add to them while negotiations were under way. Although Vance denounced the new settlements as an "obstacle to peace," the Israelis refused to halt the practice, leading the Carter administration to suspect Begin of using the security argument as a guise for annexation. To show dissatisfaction with the Israelis, the White House approved the sale of fighter planes to Israel but also, for the first time, did the same for Egypt and the Saudis. There was still no break in the situation.

Carter, his prestige already low, took a high political risk and arranged a meeting between Begin and Sadat at the presidential retreat in Camp David, Maryland. After nearly two weeks of discussions in which Carter worked as a full partner, the negotiators emerged with a compromise on September 17, 1978. Their general program aimed at completing a formal treaty before Christmas and Israeli withdrawal from Arab territory within three years.

The president had mediated two path-breaking settlements: "A Framework for Peace in the Middle East" and a "Framework for the Conclusion of a Peace Treaty between Egypt and Israel." According to the agreements, there would be "transitional arrangements for the West Bank and Gaza for a period not exceeding five years." To implement "full autonomy to the inhabitants," Israel was to withdraw "as soon as a self-governing authority has been freely elected by the inhabitants of these areas." Thus, the full autonomy question was to become the subject of negotiations after Egypt and Israel had signed a peace treaty. But the accords contained no resolution to the two most explosive issues between the antagonists: Palestinian self-rule and the status of Jerusalem. Furthermore, the wording of the agreements stood open to competing interpretations that would block a meaningful settlement. What were the "legitimate security concerns" of the parties involved? The "legitimate rights" of the Palestinians? Was Israeli security compatible with Palestinian autonomy?

The PLO issue was the basis of most Arab–Israeli troubles. If that organization dominated a Palestinian state in the West Bank and Gaza, it could launch terrorist attacks on Israeli families. Begin refused to approve PLO participation in either the negotiations or the establishment of a homeland; Sadat hoped the Israelis would withdraw from the West Bank and Gaza and that the Palestinians there would win a governing voice. The first step, Sadat believed, was Israeli withdrawal from the Sinai settlements, the second was a peace treaty between Israel and Egypt, and the third was Israeli withdrawal from the Sinai Peninsula. Sadat counted on Jordan to enter the negotiations concerning the West Bank, and he hoped the Saudis would remain supportive. Most of all, he relied on the United States to persuade Israel to accept the terms.

But the Arab states bitterly opposed the settlement because Israel, they believed, would gain too much. A separate peace with the strongest Arab state, Egypt, would ensure Israeli security by reducing the likelihood of attack by other Arabs. Israel would retain the West Bank, Gaza, and the Golan Heights, and the Palestinians would never gain self-rule. The Saudis, unwilling to stand alone among their Arab neighbors, banded together with Algeria, Iraq, Jordan, Libya, and Syria in denouncing Sadat, virtually isolating him and paradoxically making Israel's position even stronger.

At this crucial point, Carter again intervened, this time to visit Egypt and Israel and make a personal appeal for the treaty. His bold strategy worked. Less than a month later, on March 26, 1979, Sadat and Begin signed an agreement at the White House. Anxious moments had developed during the intervening days. Sadat repeated his demands for Palestinian autonomy in the West Bank, and Begin declared before his country's parliament that Israel would not retreat to the 1967 borders, that Jerusalem was Israel's "eternal capital," and that the Palestinians would never establish a state in the West Bank or Gaza. Although Begin's provocative speech nearly scuttled the treaty proceedings, Carter convinced the two leaders to sign.

The Egyptian-Israeli Peace Treaty was an important first step toward a general settlement. According to terms, Israel would begin a scaled withdrawal from the Sinai Peninsula,

Presidents Sadat and Carter and Prime Minister Begin
Celebrating the signing of "Treaty of Peace between the Arab Republic of Egypt and the State of Israel," March 26, 1979. *(Jimmy Carter Library, Atlanta, Georgia)*

to be completed in 1982. United Nations forces were to supervise the boundary, assisted by U.S. air surveillance. The countries established diplomatic and economic relations and agreed to free passage through international waterways. Israel could buy oil from the Sinai after the region went back to Egypt, and negotiations were to begin on Palestinian rights in the West Bank and Gaza. To smooth potential difficulties, the United States repeated its pledges to defend Israel and furnished $5 billion in economic and military aid to the two countries. Critics complained that the United States had bribed the antagonists; proponents countered that any peace was better than continued fighting. Although Carter hailed the pact as "the first step of peace," it only indirectly touched on Jerusalem, the Golan Heights, and the PLO. He had earlier hoped for a sweeping settlement, yet his recent approach had adopted Kissinger's call for

piecemeal procedures. If the antagonists could first settle the less inflammatory issues, Carter hoped, they might build a momentum leading to resolution of the other matters and end three decades of bitter unrest.

The Arab states, however, immediately condemned the Egyptian-Israeli Peace Treaty. Jordan's King Hussein denounced the pact as a "dead horse" because it did not guarantee a Palestinian homeland. Israel's policies, the Arabs contended, were baldly annexationist. The Arab League expelled Egypt and imposed an economic boycott, and most of the Arab states severed diplomatic relations. Israel's actions did not ease the precarious situation. Although it withdrew from the Sinai in early 1982, it announced the establishment of new settlements in the West Bank, incorporated the Golan Heights into Israel in 1982, prepared to take additional land from the large number of Arabs in the region, staunchly refused self-determination to the Palestinians, and intensified military measures against the PLO.

The United States praised the treaty, even though two of its friends in the Middle East, Saudi Arabia and Jordan, moved deeper into the Arab camp. The Saudis held a quarter of the world's known oil reserves and were pro-West and anti-Communist, but they could not support the treaty because it contained no Israeli concessions on the Old City of Jerusalem and failed to provide political autonomy for Palestinians. The Saudis were small in population and depended on an outside labor force to modernize their country, and the result was that numerous foreigners lived in Saudi Arabia, many of them Palestinians or other Arabs. The Saudis did not want to break with Egypt, nor did they seek to loosen ties with the United States. But they had to avoid charges of treason by fellow Arab states. King Hussein joined King Khalid of Saudi Arabia in emphasizing to the White House that Israel was their chief antagonist, not the Soviet Union. The Egyptian-Israeli Peace Treaty shook the Saudis' faith in U.S. policies, but it nonetheless edged the principal antagonists toward some solution short of war.

Declining Soviet–American Relations

For several reasons, Soviet–American relations markedly deteriorated throughout 1979. Economically, the Soviets were in deep trouble. Although leading the United States in the production of cement, coal, oil, and steel, they had added to their own problems by investing too much in Cuba and Vietnam and in vast military improvements, none of which brought profitable returns. Much of the Soviets' land was suited for agriculture, but the ongoing process of collectivization had not yielded sufficient food. In fact, nearly half of the Soviet Union's farm products came from privately owned concerns that made up only 3 percent of the country's agricultural area. Soviet industry, meanwhile, demonstrated lit-

tle innovation, and in technology it lagged behind the United States, West Germany, and Japan. The Soviets also suffered from an inefficient and poorly managed labor force as well as from ethnic divisions obstructing the integration of workers outside Greater Russia. Furthermore, a drop in the birthrate during the 1950s and 1960s had caused a dip in the size of the labor force by the 1980s. Finally, economists projected that the Soviets might have to import oil before the decade was over. Outside the country, problems with China threatened to worsen because of the changed leadership in Beijing, the closer ties between China and Japan, and the imminent establishment of formal diplomatic relations between the United States and China. The Carter administration tried to exploit the Kremlin's troubles. After the early setbacks in the SALT talks in Moscow, the White House criticized Soviet activities in Africa, implied that it would consider arms sales to China, and warned that Soviet military actions in Eastern Europe would encourage a buildup of NATO.

The Soviets' central concern was the establishment of Sino–American relations. Shortly after Carter's inauguration, the United States moved toward completing the recognition process begun by Nixon's visit to China in 1972. Liaison officers had been established soon after the initial contact, and Carter now sought to remove final obstacles. In April 1977, a congressional delegation traveled to China accompanied by one of the president's sons, and in late August, Vance visited Beijing to talk with Vice Premier Deng Xiaoping. More than a year later, President Carter announced in a televised speech that the two nations would establish diplomatic relations on January 1, 1979. According to the joint communiqué of December 15, 1978, the United States severed relations with Taiwan, agreed to withdraw "its remaining military personnel [about 700 soldiers] from Taiwan within four months," and served the required one-year notice of terminating the

Mutual Defense Treaty of 1954 with Taiwan. Although the communiqué asserted that Taiwan was "part of China," the United States maintained "cultural, commercial, and other official relations with the people of Taiwan." The Taiwanese accused the United States of breaking commitments, and right-wing Americans joined a few congressional members in expressing anger over the move, but on January 1, 1979, the United States and the People's Republic of China exchanged ambassadors and announced formal relations.

Carter emphasized that the agreement offered commercial possibilities and the potential of easing the tense situation in East Asia. There already seemed to be proof of the latter claim. In December 1978, Vietnamese Communist forces invaded Kampuchea (formerly Cambodia) to depose Pol Pot, leader of a repressive Communist regime that favored China. The following February, Chinese forces invaded upper Vietnam, and even though the Pentagon and other Americans wanted the United States to act, Carter refused. After the Chinese administered what they called "punishment" to the Vietnamese, they withdrew. In the meantime, the Soviets signed an amity treaty with the Vietnamese, demanded an earlier Chinese pullout, and threatened to take military action. The crisis passed without a confrontation, but the Soviet threats aroused more U.S. skepticism about the SALT talks and increased the call for an arms buildup.

The establishment of relations with China, along with the Soviet desire to avoid a costly arms race and curb the U.S. development of new weapons, promoted the signing of SALT II in Vienna in June 1979. The treaty aimed to equalize the total number of strategic nuclear delivery missiles by permitting each nation to have 2,400 long-range missiles and bombers, to be lowered to 2,250 by 1981. It also set MIRVed ballistic missiles (ICBMs and submarine-launched ballistic missiles [SLBMs]) at a ceiling of 1,200, established maximum warhead figures for other launch-

ers, drew up verification procedures, and made clear that SALT III would focus on reducing nuclear stockpiles.

Like most agreements, both parties could claim advantages. On the U.S. side, the Soviets would have to cut back on 250 delivery vehicles already in existence, whereas the United States could add to its supply of 2,060. Furthermore, the Soviets failed to halt the U.S. development of the intercontinental MX (missile experimental), a mobile missile capable of carrying ten MIRVs and designed to move ICBMs through a maze of underground tunnels in an effort to confuse Moscow on their location. Despite Carter's campaign assurances of arms cutbacks, he approved the MX—at nearly $30 billion in cost. SALT II also placed no restrictions on several missile types: the cruise missile, which carried a single warhead and was capable of striking the Soviet Union; the Pershing II ballistic missile, guided by radar to evade obstacles in hitting targets more than a thousand miles away; and the Trident-II SLBM, which could carry fourteen warheads. The Americans, however, were unable to halt Soviet development of either the Backfire supersonic bomber or the SS-20 intermediate-range nuclear missile, the latter carrying three warheads and able to reach Western Europe.

Widespread disagreement was evident inside the United States over the wisdom of SALT II. Some Americans warned that the maximum limits were too high and sought to link the pact with Soviet behavior elsewhere. Many did not trust the Moscow government and argued that verification was impossible. Others supported the arguments of the "Committee on the Present Danger," which was led by veteran hard-line policymaker Paul Nitze (who helped write NSC-68) and accused Carter of appeasement and endangering U.S. security. Still others wondered whether the MX might cause an arms race. At tremendous costs in dollars and in environmental damage, they declared, the MX would not even be ready until 1990. It seemed wise to continue negotiations aimed at establishing more controls. The president countered that SALT II would stem the Soviets' buildup and benefit the United States because restrictions on its own program were less prohibitive. He added that the U.S. ICBMs were not highly susceptible to destruction because the Soviets were unlikely to achieve the extreme accuracy and timing vital to attack. Besides, the United States would have a twenty-minute warning that enabled it to move the ICBMs from their silos to places of safety. Other than land-based ICBMs, Carter noted, the remaining 70 percent of the triad strategic system—the SLBMs and big bombers—would be intact and ready for a counterstrike.

While the national debate went on over SALT II, its approval seemed ever more unlikely when the Carter administration announced in the summer of 1979 that U.S. intelligence sources had discovered a Soviet brigade of 2,500 combat troops in Cuba. White House spokesmen hotly asserted that until the Soviet soldiers withdrew from the island, ratification of SALT II was out of the question. The "status quo was not acceptable," the president insisted. The Moscow government argued that the soldiers had been on the island for years solely to train Cubans. Furthermore, it accused Carter of choosing to publicize the matter at a particularly opportune time—when his reelection possibilities were down and he needed an issue to rally Americans around him.

Whether or not the president had acted too hastily in an effort to rebuild his image, the outcome proved damaging both to his prestige and to SALT II. The Democratic chair of the Senate Foreign Relations Committee, Frank Church, postponed hearings on SALT II and noted that approval was doubtful until the Soviet troops left Cuba. It soon became evident, however, that the Soviet forces had indeed been there for years and were not about to leave, and Carter had no choice but to accept the status quo that he had earlier found objectionable. In a vain attempt to save SALT II, he told the American people that "I have concluded that the brigade issue is certainly no reason for a return to the Cold War." In January 1980, the president admitted defeat by withdrawing the treaty from the Senate.

The arms rivalry continued to escalate as Europe increasingly became the focal point of concern. In the previous December, NATO made a "two-track" decision calling for the deployment of 572 Pershing IIs in Western Europe (track one) that would proceed until their readiness in 1983—unless the United States and the Soviet Union meanwhile reached an arms control agreement (track two) that secured the continent by requiring the removal of the hundreds of Soviet SS-20s recently installed in Eastern Europe. As this issue intensified, so did antinuclear demonstrations spread across the continent and into the United States.

In the meantime, the Cuban episode and the arms controversy suddenly fell from Americans' attention as the focus of trouble dramatically shifted again to the Middle East.

Hostage Crisis in Iran

On November 4, 1979, 400 student militants in Iran stormed into the U.S. embassy in Teheran, seizing sixty-six U.S. diplomats and military personnel as hostages and causing a crisis that staggered and finally brought down the Carter presidency. Americans' frustrations over recent foreign policy failures seemed to culminate in this national humiliation, which the *New York Times* called "a metaphor for American decline." Although most Americans were shocked that their long-time Iranian ally had permitted such an act, the truth was that relations between the countries had been in serious trouble for years.

By the time Carter became president, Iran had become vital to U.S. strategic and economic interests in the Middle East. Besides offering the advantage of lying just south of the Soviet Union, Iran was second only to the Saudis in oil production among non-Communist countries. Over the years, the CIA installed listening devices along the

Iranian–Soviet border, designed to detect Soviet nuclear and military activity. To solidify U.S. ties with Iran, Carter visited Teheran in late 1977 and on New Year's Eve toasted the country as "an island of stability." He then praised Mohammed Riza Shah Pahlavi as deserving "the respect and the admiration and love which your people give to you." The Iranian people, however, had developed an intense hatred for the shah that was magnified by the U.S. aid he continued to receive after the CIA facilitated his return to power in the early 1950s. Fundamentalist Shiite Muslims (90 percent of the population) were appalled by the shah's efforts to improve the place of women in society and import Western lifestyles into Iran. Youths detested the absence of civil liberties and wanted a constitutional government to replace the shah's corrupt regime. Merchants, land owners, and young laborers opposed his "white revolution," which had allegedly modernized the economy by instituting land reform, profit sharing in industry, women's right to vote, and other measures, and all groups resented the 50,000 Americans in Iran who trained the military, constructed industries, and ran the rich oil reserves. Ethnic rivalries, severe economic problems, increasingly crowded and slum-ridden urban areas, and heightening terrorist actions by the secret police (SAVAK) added to the growing resentment, which was exacerbated by foreigners' monopoly on the few good jobs in Iran and the government's spending on weaponry from the United States that militarized the country at the expense of helping the Iranian people. Some observers argued that the shah's arms purchases alienated more of his subjects than any other single act.

The Shah and President Nixon
American assistance to Iran greatly increased during the Nixon administration. (*Nixon Presidential Library*)

Despite Carter's glowing praise for the shah, U.S. relations with his regime were dangerously uneasy. The shah complained that he did not receive enough military aid, leading him to buy a nuclear reactor from France after the United States turned him down. By the mid-1970s, Americans were unhappy that Iran joined other OPEC nations in raising the price of oil, and in 1976, Congress protested when the Ford administration sold fighter planes to the shah. Carter's public adulation for the shah resulted from poor intelligence sources that were grossly out of touch with reality. By late 1978, SAVAK was hated, the shah was despised, and Iran stood on the verge of a revolution instigated by both the leftist "fedayeen," which had close ties to the PLO, and the rightist Islamic clergy, or mullahs, who sought a return to traditional customs and lifestyles. Animating this strange alliance was a mutual hatred of the shah and the United States.

In 1978, violence finally erupted in Iran, causing the shah to impose martial law and further feed the revolutionary fervor. Striking groups halted oil production, which hurt the United States, and Carter whipped up more anger among Iranians by following Brzezinski's advice to send military assistance to the regime. By the end of the year, Americans in Iran feared for their lives as the shah, now stricken with cancer and increasingly unable to take strong action, steadily lost ground to his rapidly growing political and religious opposition. The anti-shah forces became too powerful to contain, and U.S. diplomats in Iran urged him to abdicate the throne.

In January 1979, the revolutionaries forced the shah to flee the country, leaving Iran to the victorious Muslims. The Muslims' chief religious leader, the Ayatollah Ruhollah Khomeini, was eighty-one years old, with black eyes glowing above his long white beard. Even at that moment in January, he was still in France as part of sixteen years of exile. For years, Khomeini had directed his followers to use any destructive means to bring down the throne, and he now announced the formation of the Islamic Republic. These events shook

Americans' confidence in the Carter administration because the unexpectedness of the revolution raised serious questions about both the abilities of intelligence sources in Iran and the failure of the White House to heed warnings. The U.S. ambassador in Iran, William Sullivan, recommended a meeting with Khomeini, but the White House suspected its emissary of disloyalty to its policies and ignored the suggestion. Instead, the administration infuriated Sullivan by considering Brzezinski's call for a military coup intended to restore the shah.

On February 1, Khomeini returned triumphantly to Iran as the informal head of state and promptly declared that the new regime would cleanse the country of the westernizing and secular influences stemming from the shah's "white revolution." Despite public outcries against the United States, it was evident that the Muslims hated the Communists' atheism as much as the West's capitalism and that Sullivan's proposed meeting with the ayatollah had perhaps been worth pursuing. But if an opportune time for negotiations had existed, its moment had passed. The new Iranian regime, a theocracy, lacked governing experience, and the country quickly moved to the edge of administrative disintegration. The United States faced the unhappy prospect of intervening to safeguard Iranian oil, which Khomeini prepared to cut off from Americans while selling it to Japan and Western Europe. Worse, Marxists were among the anti-shah groups, causing anxiety in Washington that the Soviets had gained an opening into the Persian Gulf and oil-rich Middle East.

The shah, meanwhile, moved from one country to another, looking for refuge but finding none: any government welcoming him would surely alienate Iran or other Arab states and lose access to the region's oil. Carter at first invited the shah to the United States, but Vance convinced him to withdraw the offer as it became plain that the United States was the chief source of resentment in Iran. In October 1979, however, the shah was in Mexico, dying of cancer and in need of medical attention. Even though the embassy in Teheran warned that moving the shah to the United States would endanger the lives of Americans in Iran, Carter yielded to the pressure of Brzezinski, David Rockefeller of Chase Manhattan Bank in New York (which had monetary connections with Iran), and Kissinger, who had personal and financial ties with the Rockefeller family and whose support the White House valued in securing passage of SALT II. Carter's decision to admit the shah into the country, where he entered a New York hospital, "threw a burning branch into a bucket full of kerosene," according to an embassy worker in Teheran. Khomeini angrily told his people that the shah would now conspire first-hand with the hated Americans. Two weeks later, on the Sunday morning of November 4, Iranian students seized the U.S. embassy in Teheran.

The reasons cited for the break-in were many and varied. Khomeini called the embassy a "nest of spies" and denounced the "Great Satan Carter." The militants, who refused to believe that the shah was ill, demanded his wealth and announced that they would free the Americans in exchange for his return to Iran to stand trial for past crimes. Iranian custody of the shah would also prevent his collaboration with the United States in a counterrevolutionary move to regain the throne. Furthermore, taking hostages promoted a diplomatic break with Washington that freed Iran from U.S. domination. Khomeini could exploit anti-American feeling and establish control over the moderates and clerics who had opposed him in the revolution.

Whatever the reasons for taking the embassy, it was the first time that diplomats did not receive immunity in times of trouble. Americans were shocked to see televised coverage of huge crowds of angry Iranians denouncing the United States as the "Great Satan" and yelling "Death to America." They were more appalled to see American hostages blindfolded and apparently undergoing unspeakable treatment by their captors. In television interviews Khomeini and others condemned the long-time support of the United States for the shah and criticized the U.S. naval presence in the Indian Ocean. The ayatollah even accused the United States of planning an assault on the ancient Muslim religious city of Mecca, an unfounded charge that set off anti-American demonstrations in Muslim areas stretching from the Middle East to the Philippines and resulted in the deaths of two Americans in Pakistan.

The Carter administration reacted to the hostage crisis with a confused mixture of shock and dismay that critics considered symbolic of the declining position of the United States in the world. No nation expecting to command the respect of others could permit such a dastardly act to occur, Americans indignantly complained. Yet as Carter later lamented, the seizure revealed "the same kind of impotence that a powerful person feels

The Ayatollah Khomeini
The Muslims' religious leader who, after the shah's departure, came home from exile in 1979 to proclaim the Islamic Republic of Iran. *(Wide World Photos, New York)*

when his child is kidnapped." American honor, commitment, and the certainty of the shah's execution dictated that the president could not send the shah home. Besides, the shah had entered the United States legally, providing Carter with no legal right either to deport him or confiscate his wealth. Nor would the United States apologize for past policies toward the Iranians and allow a UN investigation of its conduct in those matters. Although many Americans demanded military action to free the hostages, the White House realized that such a course could lead to their deaths, stir up more Muslim violence against Americans throughout the Middle East, and cause a war that benefited only the Soviets.

The United States initially responded with a series of steadily escalating pressures on Iran that nonetheless failed to force its government (under various prime ministers of only nominal power) to intervene and secure the release of the hostages. First, the visas of 50,000 Iranian students in the United States underwent examination; those not enrolled in school would be sent home. This approach, however, necessitated deliberation through the courts, which not only proved slow and cumbersome but ultimately resulted in decisions supporting the students' rights. Second, the United States froze nearly $8 billion of Iranian assets inside the country. Third, the Carter administration suspended the sale of arms to Iran, which had no impact because its government no longer sought them. Fourth, the White House covertly enlisted the aid of PLO leader Yasir Arafat, who convinced the Iranian regime to free thirteen of the hostages, mostly female and black Americans. Fifth, the United States sought the assistance of other nations and private individuals in securing the freedom of the remaining fifty-three hostages. Sixth, it worked through the United Nations and the International Court of Justice in calling for the hostages' release. None of these measures succeeded.

On April 7, 1980, the United States broke diplomatic relations with Iran and imposed an economic embargo. These steps likewise had no effect. Western Europe and Japan needed Iranian oil and refused to join the embargo, and by the spring of that year, the Iranian cutoff of oil to the United States (at least in part the result of the government's inability to produce enough oil for its own use) had already led to a 130 percent price rise that heightened U.S. inflation and unemployment. In the meantime, the shah left the United States for Panama in late 1979, and negotiations with the Iranians never got under way. A stable government did not emerge from the revolution, as the Carter administration had hoped, and Khomeini, whether he outright refused to free the hostages or had no choice in view of his supporters' fervor, did not intervene on their behalf.

On April 24, the Carter administration authorized a daring rescue attempt that ended in a humiliating failure and further underlined the helplessness of the United States. Vance had objected to the idea. Not only had he assured European allies against the use of force, but he warned of certain casualties. Even if successful, he noted, the Iranians could seize other Americans. The president nonetheless directed the Joint Chiefs of Staff to organize a rescue mission code-named "Eagle Claw." Eight helicopters embarked from the U.S.S. *Nimitz*, a carrier then based in the Arabian Sea, while six C-130 Hercules transports left their Middle East base, both military teams eluding radar detection and heading for a rendezvous in the Iranian desert south of Teheran. The plan called for marine commandos to burst into the embassy, kill all the Iranian guards, and free the hostages. But everything went wrong. Three helicopters threatened to break down in a swirling dust storm before reaching the desert and had to turn back, one of them colliding with a C-130 and killing eight Americans. By now frustrated with the initial stages of the operation, Carter called it off. In a final embarrassment, the C-130s left so hurriedly in the night that they abandoned helicopters, weapons, maps, and a batch of secret documents. A few days afterward, Americans watched television coverage of Iranians exhibiting the charred remains of the Americans who had died in the midair collision.

Over television the following morning, Carter informed the American people of the

Iranian Hostage Crisis
The U.S. embassy compound in Teheran as Iranians release some American hostages.
(Wide World Photos, New York)

abortive rescue expedition, his somber tone suggesting the administration's concession that the hostage crisis would last until the Iranians themselves brought it to an end. The captors separated and relocated the hostages in different hiding places, making it nearly impossible to consider another rescue attempt, and Khomeini darkly warned that the cost of another such operation would be their deaths. In the meantime Vance quietly resigned from the administration, partly because of the rescue fiasco but also because of growing dissatisfaction over steadily worsening relations with the Soviet Union. SALT II seemed dead, and the United States and its allies were drifting

farther apart. The Carter administration, mired in a crisis over which it had no control, underwent criticism from Americans who believed it had gone too far in a rescue effort that could have led to the deaths of the hostages as well as from Americans who were exasperated that the president seemed too squeamish to take the hard military actions called for in such a situation.

While the Carter administration stood helpless in the hostage crisis, another issue took over the front pages of U.S. newspapers: Soviet military forces invaded neighboring Afghanistan in late December 1979 in an effort to support a tottering leftist regime and by the following spring were locked in battle with Afghan resistance groups.

Last Days: Crisis in Afghanistan and Resurgence of the Cold War

The Soviets' military invasion of Afghanistan had its roots in a coup of 1978, when they established a Marxist regime that soon caved in because of assaults from Muslim rebels unhappy with its antireligious emphasis. Islamic teachings in Iran and Pakistan might sweep across Afghanistan and into the Soviet Union, the Moscow government seemed to fear. The growing crisis attracted U.S. attention because Afghanistan bordered China, Iran, and Pakistan, the last of which fluctuated in and out of Washington's graces. Although Afghan revolutionary forces became stronger in 1979, the Soviets at first hesitated to make a military move. One factor was the imminent possibility of a successor problem in Moscow: Brezhnev was seventy-three years of age and in ill health. Another was Soviet concern about the effect military intervention would have on SALT II. But the Muslim insurgency in Iran and now in Afghanistan raised fears in Moscow that a similar uprising would develop among the millions of Muslims inside the Soviet Union.

Thus, during the Christmas holidays of 1979, nearly 85,000 Red Army troops rolled into Afghanistan to put down the mounting unrest. Soviet authorities immediately executed the failing Marxist leader and within six months established an occupation force of more than 100,000 troops. The result was a lengthy guerrilla war with Muslim rebels and a brutal clampdown on resistance at home to the Kremlin's new policies. Numerous Soviet dissidents were imprisoned, including Andrei Sakharov, the Nobel Prize–winning physicist who led the human rights movement inside the Soviet Union. Soon the Moscow regime resurrected the Brezhnev Doctrine, announced after the Soviet military invasion of Czechoslovakia in 1968, which defended the use of force in

halting any "deviation from socialism" in Marxist states. The Soviets had used similar tactics in Hungary, but this was the first time they had done so outside Eastern Europe.

The Soviet invasion of Afghanistan shattered the Carter administration's illusions about détente. In response, the White House adopted stringent measures that erroneously raised the specter of imminent Soviet troop expansion into the entire Middle East and succeeded only in again calling attention to the diminished influence of the United States on world events. The act, Carter admitted, had "made a more dramatic change in my opinion of what the Soviets' ultimate goals are than anything they've done in previous time I've been in office." The Afghanistan invasion appeared to be a "steppingstone to their possible control over much of the world's oil supplies"—including those of Iran. Brzezinski's hard-line, anti-Soviet stance won instant credibility in the White House as Vance lost influence and departed the administration. Carter, meanwhile, took several courses of action that were more shadow than substance but that the American people at first favored because of the impression of a resolute response. His approach had seven parts: 1) he withdrew the almost defunct SALT II treaty from the Senate and broadened commercial, financial, and military ties with China; 2) he cut off sales of grain (which hurt U.S. farmers) and high-technology items to the Soviet Union; 3) he restricted Soviet fishing rights in U.S. waters and temporarily suspended the opening of new consulates in the United States; 4) he sent more arms to Pakistan and approved covert CIA help to the Afghan rebels; 5) he supported the establishment of a Rapid Deployment Force to stand ready for immediate action in time of crisis; 6) he asked Congress to require registration of both men and women for a possible draft; and 7) in one of the most controversial moves of the time, he called for a boycott of the Olympic Games scheduled in Moscow that summer of 1980.

The president's most provocative action was his proclamation of the Carter Doctrine, which revived memories of the early Cold War by warning the Soviets to halt their expansionist activities in the Middle East. In his State of the Union Address of January 24, 1980, the president warned that "an attempt by any outside force to gain control of the Persian Gulf region will be regarded as an assault on the vital interests of the United States of America, and such an assault will be repelled by use of any means necessary, including military force." Carter declared that the Soviet invasion of Afghanistan threatened the Persian Gulf–Indian Ocean oil supply line and asserted that the United States would act alone if necessary to protect Middle East oil from Soviet takeover. Thus, the administration broke with the Nixon Doctrine, which had called for partnership (albeit with the United States as senior partner), in preference for a return to the unilateral approach inherent in the Truman and Eisenhower doctrines. The United States appeared ready to contain the Soviets by establishing military strongholds in the Indian Ocean, East Africa, and the Middle East.

The Soviet Union must have expected that its invasion of Afghanistan would end hopes for SALT II. Carter warned Brezhnev over the hotline that the Soviet action constituted the most serious threat to world peace since 1945. About a third of U.S. oil came from the Persian Gulf, but, even more important, Western Europe and Japan received the overwhelming bulk of their supplies from that region. The Soviet move, according to Washington officials in a statement dramatically reminiscent of the Cold War 1940s, was part of a concerted effort to take over the whole region. Regional and national issues again threatened to become pawns of big power confrontation.

The Carter administration's reaction to the Afghan crisis was undercut by resistance from U.S. allies, who refused to support either an economic embargo on the Soviet Union or the Olympic boycott. West Germany and Japan had heavy trade with Moscow and Eastern Europe and argued that Soviet military action had been predictable because no country could permit trouble along its borders. The Afghan invasion was a localized matter, they insisted. West German Chancellor Helmut Schmidt told the *New York Times* that he opposed "nervousness, war cries, or excited or provocative speeches." The reaction by allies in Western Europe was understandable: they stood vulnerable to military retaliation by having agreed to allow the United States to deploy nearly 600 intermediate-range ballistic missiles aimed at the Soviet Union. Despite U.S. pressures, European defense allotments had remained distressingly low. Inflation and economic problems were also important considerations, but the fact was that, above all, the Europeans sought to avert a confrontation with the Soviets.

The Carter administration encountered other obstacles. The president had not consulted Congress before announcing his "doctrine." Many Americans chastised him for resurrecting the domino theory and insisted that the Soviets were merely trying to bolster a friendly regime. Others warned that Carter had needlessly revived the Cold War by attempting to force the Persian Gulf states to choose between East and West. Some wanted the White House to pull back and allow the Kremlin to expend itself in a guerrilla war in Afghanistan that they termed "Russia's Vietnam." Argentina and Brazil took advantage of the U.S. grain embargo to increase their sales to the Soviet Union. Pakistan complained that the U.S. offer of military aid was too low, and Saudi Arabia turned down a U.S. request for bases. Furthermore, numerous countries ignored Carter's call for an Olympic boycott and prepared to participate in the games, and the director of the international committee, Lord Killanin, publicly denounced the United States for using athletes "as pawns in political problems that politicians cannot solve themselves." One White House official admitted that the Carter Doctrine had resulted from demands for a presidential statement on the matter, not from a careful assessment of the Middle East situation.

While Carter's policies toward the Afghan crisis settled into grim failure, numerous signs in the United States pointed to a Republican victory in the presidential race of 1980. Many Americans attributed the country's decline in prestige to the Carter administration. Four years of international embarrassment now capitalized by the hostage crisis, they lamented, had underlined the world's lack of respect for the United States. In fairness to Carter, most Americans were unaware of the changes forcing the United States out of its 1945 position of unquestioned unilateral world leadership into that of increased cooperation with allies. But whereas the Nixon and Ford administrations had acted in accordance with the new forced guidelines in foreign policy, Carter only briefly adhered to them before wandering into threatening policies that were virtually incapable of enforcement. After initially accepting the new limitations on U.S. policies, he wavered back and forth between the polarized stances advocated by Vance and Brzezinski until chronic internal division led to frustration and finally the declaration of a hard-line position that had little chance for success.

During the spring of 1980, the president's human rights efforts angered Americans, particularly those in Florida, when he welcomed Cuban refugees into the country. Castro had permitted dissident Cubans to leave the island if they secured visas from Peru, and as thousands pushed into the Peruvian embassy and Carter threw open the doors to the United States, Castro announced that Cubans could leave the island by boat. Soon a "freedom flotilla" of 100,000 Cubans flocked into the United States, creating havoc and riots at processing and detention centers and posing economic problems to a country already burdened with inflation, unemployment, and lengthening welfare rolls. As Castro emptied Cuba's jails, Miami's mayor moaned that "Fidel has flushed his toilet on us."

The Republican presidential candidate, Ronald Reagan of California, exploited Carter's plummeting popularity by drumming away at contradictions and inconsistencies in policy. Despite Carter's campaign assurances in 1976, he did not scale down military expenditures, reduce foreign arms sales, or abide by nuclear nonproliferation. Neither did he cut back on U.S. forces overseas or order military withdrawal from South Korea—the latter decision in part attributable to dramatic revelations of South Koreans' attempted bribes of congressional members. On the human rights issue, the administration did not uniformly criticize allies along with the Soviet Union, and it sold arms to repressive regimes. While welcoming Cubans into the United States, the White House ran afoul of the State Department in attempting to deport thousands of Haitians who had fled the oppressive rule of Jean-Claude ("Baby Doc") Duvalier. The Haitian regime, State Department advisers warned the president, was a friend of the United States.

Carter, Reagan insisted, had contributed to the waning respect for the United States. Inflation and the faltering economy were the results of Democratic fiscal and bureaucratic mismanagement. The United States, Reagan declared, had to adopt a hard-nosed, consistent policy toward the Soviet Union. It was time to expand U.S. military forces to counter the Soviet Union's global "game of dominoes." Although Carter's popularity had briefly surged upward after his initial Iranian and Afghan policies, it lasted only long enough to contribute to victories in the primaries.

These lingering difficulties led Americans to elect Reagan to the presidency by a wide margin and award the Senate to the Republicans for the first time since 1952. Carter's defeat, in a bitter twist of fate, took place on November 4, the first anniversary of the hostage crisis.

Epitaph to a Presidency: Release of the Hostages

Several events combined to force a resolution of the Iranian hostage question. First, in July 1980, the shah died in Egypt after having moved there from Panama, thus eliminating the most inflammatory issue between the United States and Iran. Second, Khomeini's Islamic followers won control over the Iranian Parliament, making the hostages irrelevant to his political fortunes. Third, war broke out between Iraq and Iran in September 1980, leaving Iran with sparse outside help, little money, and virtually no income from oil sales after saboteurs wrecked the pipeline. In addition, Iran fought with U.S.-made planes and tanks and no longer had a source for replacement parts. For the first time, U.S. economic pressures had a positive effect, particularly the freeze on Iranian funds in U.S. banks. Fourth, Reagan was a hard-liner who had blasted the Iranians as "barbarians" and "kidnappers." Military force to free the hostages, it seemed, was likely after his inauguration on January 20, 1981.

As a final epitaph, the Carter administration was not even able to claim fair credit for gaining the hostages' release. On January 19, just one day before Reagan's inauguration, Algerian mediators secured an agreement freeing the Americans in exchange for the release of the $8 billion of frozen Iranian assets in the United States (but with $5 billion of the amount earmarked to pay Iran's debts to U.S. and European banks). The United States met none of the other Iranian demands: an apology for past interference in their affairs during the 1950s and a promise not to engage in such activity again, an international investigation of alleged U.S. violations in Iran, and a return of the shah's vast holdings. As a calculated final insult to Carter, the following day, just moments after Reagan took the presidential oath, the Iranians freed the final fifty-two hostages (one earlier released for health reasons) after 444 days in captivity.

In retrospect, Carter perhaps should have down-played the hostage issue at its beginning and dealt with it through quiet diplomatic channels. This was not feasible, however. Continuous television and newspaper publicity, along with Carter's own sense of compassion and Kissinger's repeated condemnations of U.S. failures in foreign policy, stirred up a na-

tional sense of outrage and indignation requiring an immediate resolution that the administration found impossible to achieve. Suspicions of permanent physical injury to the hostages or sexual violations by the Iranian captors proved unfounded, but the hostages had suffered lengthy denials of personal freedom underlined by mock executions, some instances of solitary confinement, and more than a few cases of physical abuse. The Iranian mobs' daily insults to the United States, combined with the continued affronts to the Carter administration, added to the mood of national insult and frustration that helped sweep out the Democrats in 1980.

Selected Readings

Allin, Dana H. *Cold War Illusions: America, Europe, and Soviet Power, 1969–1989.* 1995.

Ambrose, Stephen E., and Douglas G. Brinkley. *Rise to Globalism: American Foreign Policy since 1938.* 8th ed., 1997.

Armony, Ariel C. *Argentina, the United States, and the Anti-Communist Crusade in Central America, 1977–1984.* 1997.

Arnson, Cynthia. *Crossroads: Congress, the President, and Central America, 1976–1993.* 1994.

Berman, William C. *America's Right Turn: From Nixon to Clinton.* 2nd ed., 1998.

Bermann, Karl. *Under the Big Stick: Nicaragua and the United States since 1848.* 1986.

Bill, James A. *The Eagle and the Lion: The Tragedy of American-Iranian Relations.* 1988.

Bradsher, Henry S. *Afghanistan: Soviet Invasion and U.S. Response.* 1981.

Brands, H. W. *The Devil We Knew: Americans and the Cold War.* 1993.

Brinkley, Douglas. *The Unfinished Presidency: Jimmy Carter's Journey beyond the White House.* 1998.

Brzezinski, Zbigniew. *Power and Principle: Memoirs of the National Security Adviser, 1977–1981.* 1983.

Buckley, Roger. *U.S.-Japan Alliance Diplomacy, 1945–1990.* 1992.

Carter, Jimmy. *Keeping Faith: Memoirs of a President.* 1982.

Christopher, Warren, Harold H. Saunders, Gary Sick, et al. *American Hostages in Iran: The Conduct of a Crisis.* 1985.

Clark, Paul C., Jr. *The United States and Somoza, 1933–1956: A Revisionist Look.* 1992.

Cohen, Warren I. *America's Response to China: An Interpretive History of Sino-American Relations.* 2000.

Coker, Christopher. *The United States and South Africa, 1968–1985.* 1986.

Coleman, Kenneth M., and George C. Herring, eds. *The Central American Crisis: Sources of Conflict and the Failure of U.S. Policy.* 1985.

Cornelius, Wayne. *Building the Cactus Curtain.* 1980.

Cottam, Richard W. *Iran and the United States: A Cold War Case Study.* 1988.

DeRoche, Andrew J. *Andrew Young: Civil Rights Ambassador.* 2003.

Diederich, Bernard. *Somoza and the Legacy of U.S. Involvement in Central America.* 1981.

Dumbrell, John. *The Carter Presidency: A Re-Evaluation.* 1995.

Dupree, Louis. *Afghanistan.* 1978.

Engstrom, David W. *Presidential Decision Making Adrift: The Carter Administration and the Mariel Boatlift.* 1997.

Erb, Richard D., and Stanley R. Ross. *United States Relations with Mexico.* 1981.

Furlong, William L., and Margaret E. Scranton. *The Dynamics of Foreign Policymaking: The President, the Congress, and the Panama Canal Treaties.* 1984.

Gaddis, John L. *The Cold War: A New History.* 2005.

———. *The Long Peace: Inquiries into the History of the Cold War.* 1987.

———. *Russia, the Soviet Union, and the United States: An Interpretive History.* 2nd ed., 1990.

———. *Strategies of Containment: A Critical Appraisal of Postwar American National Security Policy.* 1982; rev. ed., 2005.

Garthoff, Raymond L. *Détente and Confrontation: American-Soviet Relations from Nixon to Reagan.* 1994.

Gasiorowski, Mark J. *U.S. Foreign Policy and the Shah: Building a Client State in Iran.* 1991.

Gaushon, Arthur. *Crisis in Africa.* 1981.

Glad, Betty. *Jimmy Carter: In Search of the Great White House.* 1980.

Goode, James E. *The United States and Iran: In the Shadow of Musaddiq.* 1997.

Grayson, George W. *The Politics of Mexican Oil.* 1981.

Halliday, Fred. *Iran: Dictatorship and Development.* 1979.

Hansen, Roger D. *Beyond the North-South Stalemate.* 1979.

Harding, Harry. *A Fragile Relationship: The United States and China since 1972.* 1992.

Hargrove, Edwin C. *Jimmy Carter as President.* 1989.

Harrison, Michael M. *The Reluctant Ally: France and Atlantic Security.* 1981.

Hellmann, John. *American Myth and the Legacy of Vietnam.* 1986.

Hogan, Michael J. *The Panama Canal in American Politics: Domestic Advocacy and the Evolution of Policy.* 1986.

Hull, Richard W. *American Enterprise in South Africa: Historical Dimensions of Engagement and Disengagement.* 1990.

Hyland, William. *Mortal Rivals: Superpower Relations from Nixon to Reagan.* 1987.

Ismael, Tareq Y. *Iraq and Iran: Roots of Conflict.* 1982.

Jabber, Paul. *Not by War Alone: Security and Arms Control in the Middle East.* 1981.

Jordan, Hamilton. *Crisis: The Last Year of the Carter Presidency.* 1982.

Jorden, William J. *Panama Odyssey.* 1984.

Kaufman, Burton I. *The Presidency of James Earl Carter, Jr.* 1993.

Kennedy, Paul. *The Rise and Fall of the Great Powers: Economic Change and Military Conflict from 1500 to 2000.* 1987.

Khalid, Walid. *Conflict and Violence in Lebanon.* 1980.

Korn, David A. *Ethiopia, the United States, and the Soviet Union.* 1986.

LaFeber, Walter. *America, Russia, and the Cold War, 1945–1996.* 8th ed., 1997.

———. *The Clash: A History of U.S.-Japan Relations.* 1997.

———. *Inevitable Revolutions: The United States in Central America.* 1984.

———. *The Panama Canal: The Crisis in Historical Perspective.* Updated ed. (with Scott LaFeber), 1989.

Lake, Anthony. *Somoza Falling, The Nicaraguan Dilemma: A Portrait of Washington at Work.* 1989.

Ledeen, Michael, and William Lewis. *Debacle: The American Failure in Iran.* 1981.

Lenczowski, George. *The Middle East in World Affairs.* 1980.

LeoGrande, William M. *Our Own Backyard: The United States in Central America, 1977–1992.* 1998.

Levering, Ralph B. *The Cold War: A Post-Cold War History.* 1994; rev. ed., 2005.

Litwak, Robert S. *Détente and the Nixon Doctrine.* 1984.

Love, Janice. *The U.S. Anti-Apartheid Movement: Local Activism in Global Politics.* 1985.

Major, John. *Prize Possession: The United States and the Panama Canal, 1903–1979.* 1993.

Mann, Jim. *About Face: A History of America's Curious Relationship with China from Nixon to Clinton.* 1999.

Massie, Robert. *Loosing the Bonds: The United States and South Africa in the Apartheid Years.* 1997.

McLellan, David S. *Cyrus Vance.* 1985.

Melanson, Richard A. *American Foreign Policy since the Vietnam War: The Search for Consensus from Nixon to Clinton.* 2000.

Meredith, Martin. *In the Name of Apartheid: South Africa in the Postwar Period.* 1988.

Moffett, George D., III. *The Limits of Victory: The Ratification of the Panama Treaties.* 1985.

Morley, Morris H. *Washington, Somoza, and the Sandinistas: State and Regime in U.S. Policy toward Nicaragua, 1969–1981.* 1994.

Morris, Kenneth E. *Jimmy Carter, American Moralist.* 1996.

Moses, Russell L. *Freeing the Hostages: Reexamining U.S.-Iranian Negotiations and Soviet Policy, 1979–1981.* 1996.

Mower, A. Glenn. *Human Rights and American Foreign Policy: The Carter and Reagan Experiences.* 1987.

Nesbitt, Francis N. *Race for Sanctions: African Americans Against Apartheid, 1946–1994.* 2004.

Newell, Nancy P., and Richard S. Newell. *The Struggle for Afghanistan.* 1981.

Pastor, Robert. *Condemned to Repetition: The United States and Nicaragua.* 1987.

Payne, Samuel, Jr. *The Soviet Union and SALT.* 1980.

Pérez, Louis A., Jr. *Cuba and the United States: Ties of Singular Intimacy.* 1997.

Pierre, Andrew J. *The Global Politics of Arms Sales.* 1982.

Pipes, Richard. *U.S.-Soviet Relations in the Era of Détente: A Tragedy of Errors.* 1981.

Prados, John. *Presidents' Secret Wars: CIA Pentagon Covert Operations from World War II through the Persian Gulf.* 1996.

Quandt, William B. *Camp David: Peacemaking and Politics.* 1986.

Raat, W. Dirk. *Mexico and the United States: Ambivalent Vistas.* 1996.

Ramazani, Rouhollah K. *Revolutionary Iran: Challenge and Response in the Middle East.* 1986.

Reimers, David. *Still the Golden Door: The Third World Comes to America.* 1985.

Rosati, Jerel A. *The Carter Administration's Quest for Global Community.* 1987.

Rotberg, Robert I. *Suffer the Future: Policy Choices in Southern Africa.* 1980.

Rubin, Barry. *Paved with Good Intentions: The American Experience and Iran.* 1980.

Ryan, Paul B. *The Iranian Rescue Mission: Why It Failed.* 1985.

———. *The Panama Canal Controversy.* 1977.

Saikal, Amin. *The Rise and Fall of the Shah.* 1980.

Sayigh, Yezid. *Armed Struggle and the Search for State: The Palestinian National Movement, 1949–1993.* 1997.

Schoutz, Lars. *Beneath the United States: A History of U.S. Policy toward Latin America.* 1998.

———. *Human Rights and United States Policy toward Latin America.* 1981.

———. *National Security and U.S. Policy toward Latin America.* 1987.

Shawcross, William. *The Shah's Last Ride: The Fate of an Ally.* 1988.

Sick, Gary. *All Fall Down: America's Tragic Encounter with Iran.* 1985.

———. *October Surprise: America's Hostages in Iran and the Election of Ronald Reagan.* 1991.

Sikkink, Kathryn. *Mixed Signals: U.S. Human Rights Policy and Latin America.* 2004.

Skidmore, David. *Reversing Course: Carter's Foreign Policy, Domestic Politics, and the Failure of Reform.* 1996.

Smith, Gaddis. *The Last Years of the Monroe Doctrine, 1945–1993.* 1994.

———. *Morality, Reason, and Power: American Diplomacy in the Carter Years.* 1986.

Smith, Peter H. *Mexico: The Quest for a U.S. Policy.* 1980.

Spanier, John W. *American Foreign Policy since World War II.* 14th ed., 1998.

Spiegel, Steven L. *The Other Arab-Israeli Conflict: Making America's Middle East Policy, from Truman to Reagan.* 1985.

Stares, Paul B. *The Militarization of Space: U.S. Policy, 1945–1984.* 1985.

Stempel, John D. *Inside the Iranian Revolution.* 1981.

Stevenson, Richard W. *The Rise and Fall of Détente: Relaxations of Tensions in US-Soviet Relations, 1953–84.* 1985.

Sullivan, William H. *Mission to Iran: The Last U.S. Ambassador.* 1981.

Talbott, Strobe. *Endgame: The Inside Story of SALT II.* 1979.

Ulam, Adam B. *The Communists: The Story of Power and Lost Illusions, 1948–1991.* 1992.

———. *Dangerous Relations: The Soviet Union in World Politics, 1970–1982.* 1983.

Vance, Cyrus. *Hard Choices: Critical Years in America's Foreign Policy.* 1983.

Vogelgesang, Sandy. *American Dream, Global Nightmare: The Dilemma of U.S. Human Rights Policy.* 1980.

Walker, Thomas W. *Nicaragua: The Land of Sandino.* 1982.

———. *Revolution and Counterrevolution in Nicaragua, 1977–1989.* 1990.

Weiner, Tim. *Legacy of Ashes: The History of the CIA.* 2007.

Wesson, Robert. *Communism in Central America and the Caribbean.* 1982.

Westad, Odd Arne. *The Global Cold War: Third World Interventions and the Making of Our Times.* 2006.

Wittner, Lawrence S. *Toward Nuclear Abolition: A History of the World Nuclear Disarmament Movement, 1971 to the Present.* 2003.

Wolfe, Thomas W. *The SALT Experience.* 1979.

Wolpert, Stanley. *Roots of Confrontation in South Asia: Afghanistan, Pakistan, India, and the Superpowers.* 1982.

Zonis, Marvin. *Majestic Failure: The Fall of the Shah.* 1991.

CHAPTER 8

Cold War II: Reagan and the Revival of Containment, 1981–1989

The Return of the United States

As Ronald Reagan assumed the presidency on January 20, 1981, the nearly seventy-year-old former Hollywood movie actor and California governor dramatically pronounced an end to the "era of self-doubt" and called on Americans to counter the growing Soviet menace by reasserting their nation's "ideals and interests" throughout the world. In a provocative speech strikingly reminiscent of Kennedy's 1961 inaugural call for a New Frontier, President Reagan warned of a missile gap, emphasized the hardening lines of bipolarity, and revived the combative rhetoric of containment. The Soviets, he had earlier declared, were the basis of "all the unrest going on." At his first press conference in the Oval Office, he charged that they were "prepared to commit any crime, to lie, to cheat." The Soviet Union, he proclaimed before various public groups, was "an evil empire."

Thus did Reagan draw the battle lines immediately on becoming president. Early in his administration, his focus on countering the Kremlin even led him to put great strains on the Western alliance by blocking an effort to build a Soviet pipeline intended to provide Western Europe with Soviet natural gas. The

pipeline, he feared, would make the continental allies of the United States so economically dependent on the Soviet Union that NATO would lose its force. In addition, opposition to the pipeline was part of the administration's strategy to isolate the Soviets economically and surpass them technologically. Although the pipeline opened anyway in January 1984, it ran only from Siberia to France and was much smaller than hoped. White House relations with the Kremlin became so bitter that Reagan reversed his initial opposition to dealing with the Chinese and visited Beijing in 1984 in an effort to restore the ties cultivated by Nixon and Carter. American disillusionment with Soviet détente, Reagan made clear, was complete.

Some writers have argued that the president's real intention in this heightened assault on the Soviet Union was to drive its government into a ruinous arms race that would destroy its struggling economy and end the Cold War. If so, this brinkmanship strategy was extremely risky. The Reagan administration's anti-Communist, anti-Soviet thrusts ensured an upsurge of Cold War tensions, making negotiations secondary to a major buildup of U.S. strategic and conventional military forces. To restore faith in the United States,

President Reagan caused a furor in suggesting that the Soviet Union was evil.

President Ronald Reagan's "Evil Empire" speech, Remarks at the Annual Convention of the National Association of Evangelicals in Orlando, Florida, March 8, 1983, Ronald Reagan Presidential Library, Simi Valley, California.

It was C. S. Lewis who, in his unforgettable "Screwtape Letters," wrote: "The greatest evil is not done now in those sordid 'dens of crime' that [Charles] Dickens loved to paint. It is not even done in concentration camps and labor camps. In those we see its final result. But it is conceived and ordered (moved, seconded, carried and minuted) in clear, carpeted, warmed, and well-lighted offices, by quiet men with white collars and cut fingernails and smooth-shaven cheeks who do not need to raise their voice."

Well, because these "quiet men" do not "raise their voices," because they sometimes speak in soothing tones of brotherhood and peace, because, like other dictators before them, they're always making "their final territorial demand," some would have us accept them at their word and accommodate ourselves to their aggressive impulses. But if history teaches anything, it teaches that simple-minded appeasement or wishful thinking about our adversaries is folly. It means the betrayal of our past, the squandering of our freedom.

So, I urge you to speak out against those who would place the United States in a position of military and moral inferiority. You know, I've always believed that old Screwtape reserved his best efforts for those of you in the church. So, in your discussions of the nuclear freeze proposals, I urge you to beware the temptation of pride—the temptation of blithely declaring yourselves above it all and label both sides equally at fault, to ignore the facts of history and the aggressive impulses of an evil empire, to simply call the arms race a giant misunderstanding and thereby remove yourself from the struggle between right and wrong and good and evil.

the president insisted that its democratic aims were just and that "Marxism-Leninism" would ultimately take its place on "the ash heap of history." Americans had to discard their "no more Vietnams" syndrome and recognize that the war in Southeast Asia had been "a noble cause." If Reagan intended his aggressive foreign policy to force the Soviet Union to spend itself into submission, his approach came at the heavy price of creating an intense adversary relationship that contemporaries soon termed Cold War II.

The new president's call for a military buildup to halt Soviet expansion did not come without opposition. Numerous critics agreed with Soviet specialist George F. Kennan that the president's assessment of the Kremlin's behavior was a sign of "intellectual primitivism." But Reagan pointed out that the Soviets had surpassed the United States in intercontinental ballistic missiles (ICBMs), submarine-launched ballistic missiles (SLBMs), and megatonnage (total explosive force carried as

warheads) and argued that they could soon forge ahead in numbers and size of warheads. Skeptics insisted his statistics were misleading and that a general nuclear balance existed between the superpowers. Soviet production costs were higher than those of the United States, leaving the erroneous impression that the Kremlin's greater military expenditures meant military superiority. Moreover, they added, Reagan's prognosis did not take into account either the contributions of NATO's defense expenditures or the proportion of Soviet strength directed at China.

Reagan nonetheless called for the largest peacetime defense budget in the country's history. The nation's priority, he asserted, was to safeguard its Minuteman land-based ICBMs and B-52 bombers. He also directed the production of the B-1 bomber, thus revoking Carter's cancellation of the project, and went ahead with NATO's plans in December 1979 to install Pershing IIs (single-warhead missiles capable of striking the Soviet

to show Western support. Increasing signs of discontent behind the Iron Curtain dictated encouragement from the outside.

Poland provides the most striking example of heightening problems within the Soviet bloc. In 1980, longtime unrest had peaked in a workers' upheaval that soon included demands for civil liberties and thereby threatened the ruling Communist Party. Polish workers had wanted an independent trade union, and after a series of strikes threatened to upend the government, that body recognized the legitimacy of the Solidarity workers' union led by Lech Walesa. But as the Communist regime in Poland conceded some of its economic and political power, Solidarity increased its demands and attracted support from Catholics and nationalists who hated the Soviets. The organization soon counted 10 million members, or about a third of the Polish population, which raised questions about whether the Communist Party had to use force to remain in control.

In a series of events similar to those in Hungary a quarter of a century earlier, Solidarity risked a Soviet military crackdown by pushing for a national referendum on the present government in Warsaw and its military ties with the Soviet Union. The Kremlin must have considered the use of force. Poland bordered the Soviet Union and had served as a well-trodden roadway in numerous past invasions. It was more vital to Soviet interests than either Hungary or Czechoslovakia and certainly more so than Afghanistan. In December 1981, Polish military and police forces, perhaps reacting to Moscow's pressure, imposed martial law and imprisoned Walesa and other labor leaders. The Polish government then outlawed Solidarity and adopted other stringent measures to break the movement. Solidarity, Soviet leaders realized, was not a mere trade union; it was a broadly based and well-run organization attempting to take Poland toward a socialist form of democracy. Solidarity's success could set a dangerous example for workers in other East European countries or in the Soviet Union itself.

President Ronald Reagan in Oval Office
Calling the war in Vietnam a "noble cause," he attempted to heal divisiveness by restoring faith in America at home and respect for the nation abroad. *(Ronald Reagan Library, Simi Valley, California)*

Union) and ground-launched cruise missiles in Western Europe, reaffirming Europeans' fears that the superpowers had made Europe the battleground in a nuclear Armageddon. Finally, he approved massive arms sales around the world that virtually ensured a rash of regional conflicts.

But the Reagan White House, despite a whopping 40 percent boost in military spending during its first three years in office, fully realized that in areas vital to the Soviet Union all the sophisticated weaponry in the world could have little impact on undermining Communist control. Consequently, the administration resorted to covert operations to stir up reform movements in Czechoslovakia, Hungary, and Poland. It made financial aid available to Warsaw Pact countries willing to protect human rights and move toward political and economic changes based on democracy and a free-market system. It also relied on Radio Free Europe

Vietnam Memorial
On May 28, 1984, veterans form an unofficial color guard at the Vietnam Memorial in Washington, D.C., on the day of the State Funeral for Unknown Serviceman of the Vietnam Era. *(U.S. Army)*

Despite widespread U.S. support for Solidarity, the Reagan administration could do nothing except place mild economic sanctions on Poland and the Soviet Union. Neither the United States nor the other Western nations took steps that amounted to more than a token protest: they did not call in more than $25 billion of late debts, and the White House did not impose a grain embargo—because such a measure would hurt U.S. farmers. White House criticisms of the Kremlin's policies in Poland had attracted little support from NATO countries, which refused to take any action that might encourage full-scale Soviet intervention in Poland or damage their own trade with the Soviets and their allies. After the Polish military relaxed some of its restrictions, the Reagan administration revoked most of its economic sanctions in August 1984. The new administration realized what both President Truman and President Eisenhower had understood in Cold War I: the United States could not implement any effective military strategy toward Eastern Europe because it lay within the Soviet sphere of influence.

Internal division in the Reagan administration, like that of his predecessors, also impeded the president's intention to restore a firm foreign policy. Reagan's secretary of state, General Alexander Haig, was the most outspoken member of the cabinet and soon found himself at odds with many of his colleagues, including Secretary of Defense Caspar Weinberger, who like Haig had served in the Nixon presidency and was likewise vocal. Haig competed for control of foreign policy with the national security affairs adviser, Richard Allen, who also was a staunch anti-Soviet but soon left the White House under charges of having used his office for personal gain.

Haig was almost obsessed with the Soviets' recent military buildup and growing first-strike capability, and he sought to enhance the deterrent strength of the United States by greatly expanding its strategic and conventional forces. The Kremlin, he claimed, sought influence in the Third World by using proxies such as the Vietnamese in Kampuchea (Cambodia) and the Cubans in Africa and by supporting a growing band of international terrorists who were state sponsored by Iran and other nations having connections with the Palestine Liberation Organization (PLO). In an argument consistent with Kennan's analysis of Soviet behavior during the Cold War 1940s, Haig attributed the Soviets' aggressive foreign policy to rising internal problems. But in a stance opposing Kennan's, Haig insisted that the United States had to contain the Soviets through a major military buildup. He concluded that "there are more important things than peace. . . . There are things which we Americans must be willing to fight for."

By the summer of 1982, Haig had resigned as secretary of state, and the office went to George Shultz, whose "team player" reputation and calm demeanor exemplified a White House effort to close the breach in its foreign policymaking apparatus. Haig, mercurial in temperament and accused of being a power seeker (critics tagged him CINCWORLD, or "Commander in Chief of the World"), had failed in a widely publicized effort to mediate a dispute between the United Kingdom and Argentina over the sovereignty of the Falkland Islands in the South Atlantic. After several clashes with other administration members, he departed in June following a disagreement with the president over policies in Europe and the Middle East.

The change in secretaries of state did not bring harmony to the administration. Shultz had a background in business and economics and a Ph.D. from the Massachusetts Institute of Technology, and although he was also concerned about Soviet expansion, he was not as brusque and impatient as Haig. Yet, like Haig, Shultz soon found himself in bitter disagreement with Weinberger over the nation's defense system. Whereas Shultz sought arms reduction talks that would quietly wind down the Cold War, Weinberger insisted that the United States *win* the contest by a massive nuclear expansion program that far surpassed that of the Soviets and drove them into bankruptcy. For most of Reagan's two terms in office, U.S. foreign policy was torn between these two conflicting themes of arms reduction and nuclear expansion.

But even bigger issues confronted the new administration. On Reagan's ascension to the presidency in 1981, the United States faced a new and far more challenging international situation. His harsh Cold War rhetoric belied the fact that bipolarity had receded, only to be replaced by the unpredictable and uncontrollable tensions caused by a multipolar world. Both the United States and the Soviet Union encountered serious difficulties at home as well as in areas previously considered part of their spheres of influence. Furthermore, many formerly subjugated nations exemplified strong feelings of nationalism that encouraged a long pent-up drive for independence. Americans' confidence in their government and culture had been shaken by Watergate and Vietnam, by expanding economic problems at home, and by declining worldwide respect for their nation. The Reagan administration intended to overcome these realities by implementing a strongly militant foreign policy.

The central problem was that U.S. global dominance, so evident in 1945, was less evident in the post-Vietnam years. Part of the explanation rested in the Soviet Union's great advances since World War II; another element was the increasing leverage in world affairs held by Western Europe, Japan, and the Third World countries, particularly OPEC members. Soviet military growth, stimulated especially by the outcome of the Cuban missile crisis of 1962, had brought a precarious balance of power in the world that necessitated arms limitations talks and overtures to Third World nations. The horrors of nuclear war left no alternative to drawn-out negotiations and big power competition for Third World support. The courted nations, however, found non-alignment more advantageous to their interests and in that way managed to dictate much of the superpowers' policy.

The Reagan administration proved reluctant to accept either the need for arms limitations talks or the growing prominence of the Third World. The White House chose instead to expand its nuclear arsenal and deemphasize Carter's attempts to establish North–South relationships based on U.S. economic assistance. It aimed to swell trade and investment through private enterprise and hard work, and it looked with little interest on the SALT talks or the recent call for a New International Economic Order, which amounted to the Third World's claim for compensation for its long history of exploitation by the West. Within the Western Hemisphere, the Reagan administration in early 1982 called for the Caribbean Basin Initiative, which promoted private trade in an effort to help non-Communist governments in the Caribbean and Central America. Globalism again dominated White House policy, intensifying the rivalry between the superpowers for Third World allegiance and paradoxically allowing the smaller nations to wield inordinate influence on world events.

President Reagan's attempt to restore pride in the United States raised high expectations about reclaiming a global leadership role that proved impossible to fulfill. Escalating the arms race, whether or not to undermine the Soviet economy, constituted a high-risk approach that, even if successful, could likewise exhaust the United States while leaving its people under the illusion of having regained its 1945 position. In truth, this policy offered false hopes of total victory in the Cold War and a wishful look back to the days when the United States had solitary superpower status. The multipolar nature of the world meant that the United States could no longer intervene anywhere it chose and virtually dictate the outcome. Failure to win the war in Vietnam

had demonstrated the need to limit commitments to areas indisputably vital to U.S. security. But this fundamental truth got lost in the evangelical revival of patriotism that the new president engendered with his eloquent speech and confident manner.

The Search for a Soviet–American Arms Agreement

To enhance its position in the Cold War struggle, the Reagan administration postponed the SALT talks and made several proposals designed to expand the nation's strategic force. Opposing an arms freeze, the president called for the development of the MX, as Carter had done. Some of the new missiles, Reagan declared, would be located in old Minuteman ICBM silos in Wyoming and Nebraska; the others would await further decision. Congress, however, rejected this plan as making the MX as vulnerable as the Minuteman. Reagan proposed the "dense pack plan," which called for deploying a hundred MIRVed MX missiles in a fifteen-square-mile area in Wyoming on the theory that onrushing Soviet attack missiles would enter the small air space above the MXs and destroy each other. Not surprisingly, Congress likewise turned down this plan. As an option to the controversial MX, Reagan supported the development of a new single-warhead mobile missile dubbed "Midgetman," which would be distributed over a wide area to ensure its safety against attack. He also ordered a hundred B-1 bombers to be ready by 1986, even though experts thought the B-1 expensive and the projected "Stealth" bomber more effective because it was not as susceptible to radar detection. Finally, Reagan insisted on the production of cruise missiles, despite warnings that their capacity to avoid verification would escalate the arms race by encouraging the Soviets to develop them as well.

Arms control attempts during the 1970s, the president thought, had endangered national security. He argued that their purpose had been to slow the Soviets' growth in numbers while the United States developed more sophisticated strategic weapons—better MIRVs, longer-range SLBMs, and highly mobile air-launched cruise missiles. But this approach had not worked, and the Soviet Union had surged dangerously ahead. It was now time to revamp the U.S. military program. Thus, the Reagan administration adopted a time-consuming course of action that would likely encourage a sharp rise in the arms race before it had any effect on curbing the Cold War by undermining the Soviet economy.

To mollify growing popular concern about the arms buildup, the Reagan administration in the spring of 1982 replaced SALT with the Strategic Arms Reduction Talks (START). In actuality, this new program aimed at quieting public criticisms while introducing an idea that the Soviets would have to reject: reducing the stockpile of U.S. and Soviet ICBMs and missile warheads. Such an approach would serve as excellent propaganda while buying time for the United States to expand its nuclear arsenal. But the White House did not seem to take into account that while the START discussions were under way, the Soviet Union could join the United States in a military buildup. Although both superpowers had for years sought to avert nuclear war by maintaining a strategic balance based on the concept of MAD, or mutual assured destruction, the danger now was that each power would strive for superiority and thereby escalate the arms race. The Reagan administration's insistence on greater military security and additional limitations on Soviet strategic growth raised Moscow's fears about U.S. motives and added to the tension. But the president countered that the only way to achieve arms reductions was through a U.S. military buildup intended first to regain Soviet respect.

In an effort to resolve one of Reagan's greatest problems—keeping the NATO alliance intact—his administration presented a plan known as the "zero option." Called for in late 1981 at the Geneva Conference on Intermediate-Range Nuclear Forces (INFs), the plan proposed that the United States deploy none of its planned 572 Pershing II and cruise missiles in Western Europe if the Soviets agreed to dismantle all their 613 INFs aimed at Europe. The Kremlin rejected the plan on the grounds that its missiles lacked the range to strike the United States, whereas the new NATO missiles (Euromissiles) could reach the Soviet Union. The NATO allies of the United States meanwhile hotly complained that the president's proposal would leave them unprotected.

To ward off a dangerous division between the United States and its allies, the president urged an interim solution requiring the Soviet Union to withdraw a large number of its 351 triple-warhead missiles, in exchange for which the United States would scale down the number of missiles scheduled to go into Western Europe in December 1983. The United States would put in enough to match the Soviets, warhead for warhead. In mid-April, West German Chancellor Helmut Kohl offered some hope for European support when he commented that the president's interim solution provided "a basis for flexible and dynamic negotiations."

Not surprisingly, Reagan's interim solution met bitter opposition from the Soviet Union, which sought to promote a NATO split and prolong arms discussions while the growing antinuclear movement in Europe gained more momentum. Foreign Minister Andrei Gromyko called a rare news conference in Moscow to denounce the president's proposal. Reagan's interim solution was "absurd," Gromyko declared. If the United States insisted on such a plan, there was "no chance of an agreement" at the INF proceedings in Geneva. Furthermore, it was ridiculous for Reagan to repeat his earlier argument that French and British missiles should not be counted in any attempt to limit warheads in Europe. If an attack took place on the Soviet Union, "will a French missile have a stamp on it, 'I am French. I was not to be taken into account?'" Should the United States deploy its missiles in Europe, Gromyko darkly warned, the Soviet Union would "take the necessary measures in order to defend its legitimate interests."

In late March 1983, Reagan unveiled a new and much more ambitious defense plan that critics soon derided as "Star Wars." To erase the Soviet Union's "margin of superiority," he declared, the United States would give up deterrence through MAD in favor of a defensive strategy known as SDI, or the strategic defense initiative, which, he explained, offered a highly effective "layered defense" that depended on satellites to "intercept and destroy" enemy missile attacks by lasers or particle beams in the initial stage—*before* the warheads separated from the missiles and headed for an array of targets. As for the warheads that made it through the nuclear shield, the antiballistic missile (ABM) defense system on the ground would provide the final safeguard. Most U.S. scientists claimed that the plan necessitated such sophisticated technology that it would not work. Even if SDI destroyed nearly all the missiles, the few that got through could render enormous destruction—particularly as the Soviets countered the new U.S. defense program by simply increasing their number of missiles and warheads. Over these objections, Reagan asserted that confrontations in space offered the attractive prospect of sparing the earth from a nuclear holocaust.

The Soviet reaction to SDI was sharply negative. Yuri Andropov, a former head of the Soviet state security committee or secret police (KGB), had recently become leader of the Communist Party after Brezhnev's death and now warned that Reagan's highly touted plan "would actually open the floodgates of a runaway race of all types of strategic arms, both offensive and defensive." A push for a major missile defense system could undermine the basis of peace—the mutual fear of instant retaliation in the event of attack. Even if SDI were impractical, Andropov declared, research into its development could yield other technological advances that placed his nation farther behind in the arms race. Indeed, if SDI was not foolproof, the Americans might be tempted to launch a first strike and then rely on SDI as a defense against any shrunken

counterstrike ability that the Soviet Union had left after sustaining the initial assault.

The European allies of the United States likewise opposed the plan, despite Reagan's insistence that the new emphasis on defense would result in a reduction in offensive weapons. Critics warned that the opposite would occur. Should either the United States or the Soviet Union appear ready to deploy an ABM system, the very danger of that occurring would encourage a frantic search for new offensive weaponry by the other superpower and increase the likelihood of war. West Europeans denounced what the *Times* of London called "one of the most fundamental switches in American policy since the Second World War." A British colonel complained that the president's plan would lead to "Fortress America," leaving Europeans "out in the cold" because they no longer posed a nuclear threat to the Soviet Union. The president's message was alarming because it called for replacing MAD with an "ABM umbrella." Devised to prevent nuclear attack, the new plan actually threatened to cause such an attack by setting off a greatly intensified arms race in space that would dangerously upset the present balance of nuclear power.

The arms control situation remained uncertain and explosive. SALT II was still not ratified, and the ABM Treaty of 1972, the only binding arms-control agreement in existence, now stood in jeopardy because of the president's new defense recommendations. The ABM Treaty, based on the fear that defensive systems could disturb the nuclear balance, ensured that "each party undertakes not to develop, test, or deploy ABM systems or components which are sea-based, air-based, space-based, or mobile-land-based." When critics charged that Reagan's plan for a defensive buildup would violate the above provision against space-based ABMs, the White House countered that mere research into such a project did not constitute a treaty violation. In mid-1983, the president and Congress tried to ease growing concerns about a nuclear war by showing interest in a "build-down" strategy, which guaranteed the destruction of a certain number of nuclear weapons for every new one developed. Reagan also leaned toward the recommendation of a bipartisan commission that warned against the production of MIRVs because their destructive capacity would alarm the Soviets and make the United States increasingly subject to a first strike. Some observers argued that a proposed reduction in the number of warheads, rather than in the number of missiles, would move the United States closer to the Soviet Union in the START talks.

Relations between the United States and the Soviet Union continued their uneven and dangerous course. In September 1983, Soviet planes shot down a South Korean jumbo jet (KAL 007), killing all 269 aboard—including a member of Congress among sixty Americans. When the United States and other nations bitterly denounced the act, the Moscow government refused to apologize because, it charged (without justification), the civilian plane was fitted with spy equipment and had purposely violated Soviet airspace over military installations on Sakhalin Island. In November, when the United States began installing the promised Pershing II and cruise missiles in Britain and West Germany, the Soviets broke off the START discussions in Geneva after angrily declaring that the missile placement left them only ten minutes' warning time in the event of attack. By the end of the year, relations between the superpowers were, according to a Soviet high government official, "white hot, thoroughly white hot."

As the U.S. defense budget grew, many observers questioned whether the Reagan administration had developed a comprehensive strategy to deal with the Soviets other than to build more arms and insist that in a "protracted" nuclear war the United States would somehow emerge the victor. A high-ranking Pentagon official promised safety if Americans would "dig a hole, cover it with a couple of doors, and then throw three feet of dirt on top." Another administration official assured Congress that in the aftermath of nuclear war, mail would go through "even if the survivors ran out of stamps." He was not taken aback by a congressional member who cynically noted the difficulty in delivering mail where there were "no addresses, no streets, no blocks, no houses." A large group of doctors warned that nuclear war would bring the "last epidemic," and scientific studies supported that terrifying view by showing that a nuclear holocaust would cause countless deaths and lead to a "nuclear winter." During that bleak period, scientists somberly predicted, a contagion of fires and smoke resulting from the nuclear blasts could destroy the chain of life on earth by blackening the skies for a year, causing a global freeze and disrupting the sun's capacity to provide the basis for food. Despite these dire forecasts, an escalated arms race seemed likely as the United States continued to push for SDI as an alternative to deterrence theory and as the Soviets made greater efforts at building offensive missiles to outdistance the massive U.S. defense buildup.

More than a few observers hoped that a recent change in Soviet leadership would enhance the possibility of arms reductions. Andropov died after a long illness in early 1984 and was succeeded by Konstantin Chernenko. But Chernenko was also elderly and ill and continued the party's rigid control at home and hard-line policies abroad. On Chernenko's death in March 1985, Mikhail Gorbachev became the Soviet general secretary of the Communist Party. Considerably younger than his predecessors (in his early fifties), Gorbachev was warm and charismatic; well-educated in Western philosophy, law, and agriculture; and a Christian whose wife, Raisa, held a doctorate in philosophy. Furthermore, he was experienced in dealing with the West in foreign affairs and sought reform in both Soviet domestic and foreign policy. Most important, he realized his country faced serious internal and external problems that required immediate rectification. Such objectives necessitated an end to the debilitating arms race and a winding down of the Cold War.

At home, Gorbachev sought to maintain socialism by interlocking a restructured Soviet economy (*perestroika*) based on decentralization and market orientation, with a liberalized domestic political system stemming from a policy of openness (*glasnost*). Although the Communist Party would remain dominant, it would move toward democratization and an emphasis on persuasion rather than force. Such an ambitious program required a relaxation of tensions with the United States that permitted a greater focus on economic and political reforms inside the Soviet Union.

Toward these ends, Gorbachev adopted several measures designed to prove his sincerity. He stopped nuclear testing and called for on-site verification, unilaterally halted the installation of Soviet intermediate-range missiles trained on Western Europe, and sought technological assistance from Japan and West Germany. He also removed the Cold War hard-liner, Andrei Gromyko, from his twenty-eight-year-long post as foreign minister, replacing him with the much more accommodating Eduard Shevardnadze of Georgia. Gorbachev then went on a goodwill trip to Europe, Latin America, and the United States, everywhere impressing his counterparts with his compassion and earning high praise from the staunch anti-Soviet British prime minister, Margaret Thatcher, who hailed him as a "friend."

But Gorbachev's announced objectives encountered great skepticism in the United States. In November 1985, he and Reagan (reelected a year earlier by a wide margin) attended a summit meeting in Geneva, the first since 1979. Although the two leaders reached no agreements, they developed a warm, personal relationship that only their wives sullied by finding each other insufferable. During the negotiations, Gorbachev displayed a superior deftness and familiarity with detail that proved embarrassing to the less agile and not equally knowledgeable president. They failed to find common ground on either SDI or SALT II,

even though their lack of hostilities toward each other encouraged hope for a better international relationship.

With the nuclear deadlock remaining a danger, Reagan and Gorbachev agreed to try again—this time at Reykjavik in Iceland—where they developed a general framework of understanding that might yield specific agreements at later meetings. Gorbachev had publicly declared his intention to eradicate all nuclear weapons by the turn of the century, thereby providing a challenging backdrop to his meeting with Reagan in October 1986. At one point, they seemed close to an agreement removing all intermediate-range missiles from Europe and phasing out ballistic missiles over the next ten years. Although such a pact would not eliminate nuclear weapons, it would constitute a first step toward a meaningful arms reduction. But then Gorbachev offered what became known in White House circles as the "grand compromise"—a halt in research toward SDI in exchange for major reductions in strategic arms. Reagan refused to consider any proposal endangering the development of SDI and thereby curtailed all progress toward a meaningful settlement. Still, the two heads of state had further cultivated their cordial personal relationship and in so doing went home convinced of a mutually sincere interest in ending the nuclear standoff.

To most observers, however, the outlook for nuclear arms reductions seemed as dismal as ever. Critics on the left denounced the president for holding on to a defense system that was astronomically expensive and eminently unworkable; those on the right found it difficult to believe that he was willing to give up the nation's nuclear arsenal when its conventional weapons lagged so far behind those of its chief rival. Many wondered about the administration's growing ineffectiveness—especially as Secretary of State Schultz, visibly worn and disappointed, informed the press of the failed negotiations and the White House followed with several muddled and contradictory statements about the results. The chilling prophecy made by Winston Churchill some years earlier remained valid: "Safety will be the sturdy child of terror, and survival the twin brother of annihilation."

Despite the shattered hopes at Reykjavik, the necessity of détente drove the superpowers back to the peace table. Both leaders endorsed a statement that provided a guide for their talks: "A nuclear war cannot be won and must never be fought." At still another summit meeting, in Washington in December 1987, the two leaders agreed on less ambitious terms contained in what became known as the Intermediate-Range Nuclear Forces (INF) Treaty. Rather than eliminate all missiles, it stipulated the disbandment of only those U.S. and Soviet INF missiles in Europe and then, in an epochal move, authorized onsite inspections to verify their destruction.

Gorbachev took the first real step toward this historic agreement by accepting the president's "zero option" and then convincing him of the Soviets' sincere desire for arms reduction. The two superpowers had taken the initial step toward that grand objective and thereby eased tensions in Europe. With Shultz's strong support and Weinberger's earlier resignation from the defense post, the INF Treaty went into effect on June 1, 1988, after sailing through the Senate by the overwhelming margin of ninety-three to five.

Gorbachev undertook other changes, all aimed at ending the Cold War. In April 1988, he agreed to a UN mediation proposal calling for a Soviet troop withdrawal from Afghanistan by the beginning of the new year. Although the Soviets left behind military advisers and a

Toward the End of the Cold War
Soviet leader Mikhail Gorbachev and wife Raisa visit President Reagan and wife Nancy in Washington during the ceremonial signing of the INF Treaty in December 1987. *(Ronald Reagan Library, Simi Valley, California)*

friendly government, they had experienced their own Vietnam, complete with soldiers' addictions to drugs and alcohol, a casualty list of more than 40,000, and a defeat that was partly attributable to another country's intervention—the introduction of U.S. "Stinger" antiaircraft missiles sent by the Reagan administration to the Afghan rebels (*mujahedeen*, or "holy warriors"). In May, the president met again with Gorbachev, this time in Moscow, where in a scene eerily suggestive of an impending Armaggedon, the two men walked through Red Square and talked with people on the street while each leader's military aide lagged not far behind, carrying the codes required to order a nuclear attack.

But in an astounding about-face, Reagan returned to Washington with the glowing report that his cohort was a "friend" and that the Soviets had "changed." Gorbachev meanwhile reinforced Reagan's revelation by cutting aid to the Sandinistas in Nicaragua and working with Castro to pull his troops from Angola. In December 1988, Gorbachev visited the United States, where he became the first Soviet premier since 1960 (when Khrushchev pounded his shoe at the United Nations) to speak before the UN General Assembly in New York. Gorbachev used that august occasion to announce a huge reduction in the Soviet military establishment of half a million ground troops and 10,000 tanks. That same day, a devastating earthquake took the lives of 25,000 Soviet Armenians, drawing a phenomenal outpouring of sympathy and assistance from the United States and other countries in the West.

The whirlwind of events was mind boggling, suggesting that Thatcher was correct in asserting that "the cold war is over." In the brief span of eight years, the Soviet Union and the United States, primarily because of Gorbachev's courageous initiatives, had moved from a dangerously revived Cold War to perhaps its demise. More than forty years earlier, Kennan had argued that America's containment policy would eventually force a mellowed atmosphere in the Soviet Union.

Gorbachev's sweeping reforms had already gone too far to be reversed; his regime was moving toward democracy and a free-market system. Kennan's prediction appeared correct because the Cold War seemed to be drawing to an end.

Central America and the Caribbean

Even as the two chief rivals in the world worked toward settling their differences, the Reagan administration regarded the ongoing civil war in the small Central American country of El Salvador as Communist inspired and hence an integral part of the Cold War. The Salvadoran conflict raised many of the most hotly debated issues during the Cold War years, particularly during the latter period of the U.S. involvement in Vietnam. El Salvador was desperately poor and the most densely populated country in Central America. Its government, Reagan warned, was threatened by a Communist insurgent movement aided by Soviet and Cuban weapons filtered into the country through neighboring Nicaragua. In retrospect, it is clear that internal economic and political problems threatened El Salvador more than did alleged Communist infiltration. But in the heightened atmosphere of Cold War II, realities gave way once again to perceptions.

To counter this claimed Communist menace in the hemisphere, the Reagan administration engaged in several policies. It ignored Castro's interest in restoring relations and continued an economic embargo on Cuba in an effort to stop him from harboring Soviet troops and exporting revolutionary principles throughout the hemisphere. In 1981, the United States agreed to support a land reform program in El Salvador started by President José Napoleón Duarte and sent fifty-five military advisers to help his army put down Marxist and Social Democratic insurgents. Finally, the White House reversed the Carter administration's policy by cutting off economic assistance to the leftist Sandinista government in Nicaragua—although Mexico and France lightened the impact of that measure by offering aid.

El Salvador had emerged as a vital ingredient in the global considerations of the United States. Should El Salvador fall to communism, the president explained to reporters and others gazing at a huge map of Central America, the neighboring American states would collapse, one by one, until the entire region became Communist and endangered the United States. The Soviets must not achieve a victory · in the Western Hemisphere, he emphasized to Congress. Although offering assurances that no U.S. combat soldiers would go to El Salvador, Reagan unsettled listeners by warning that everything was at stake: "We are the last domino."

Skeptics countered that the administration was taking the same treacherous path that had earlier led to Vietnam: a steady escalation of U.S. economic and military aid, the assignment of advisers (referred to as "trainers" by the Reagan administration in an effort to dispel the Vietnam analogy) and administrators,

and the ultimate dispatch of combat troops. The Salvadorans' problems were internal in origin, critics insisted, and the United States was again helping an unpopular elitist regime that opposed reforms. Americans could not accomplish a "victory" for democracy by repeatedly seeking military solutions to social, political, and economic problems. In fact, administration opponents pointed out, Western Europe and many Latin American countries, particularly Mexico, believed that the guerrillas themselves offered more hope for an improved society. Whether a Soviet threat existed in El Salvador or, as some White House officials privately admitted, the United States wanted to use the issue to exemplify a strong course against Communist aggression, the Reagan administration found that its chief obstacle to assuming a greater role in El Salvador was the cry of "No more Vietnams."

The White House further altered Carter's policy regarding El Salvador by sending more military aid and shifting the emphasis from land reform to victory in the war. The State

War in Central America—El Salvador
U.S. Army officer demonstrating map reading to Salvadoran soldiers during field training exercise.
(*U.S. Army*)

Department justified this harder stance by proclaiming the situation a "textbook case of indirect armed aggression by Communist powers." The present regime in El Salvador, the Reagan administration insisted, would lead the way to reform, whereas the left-wing guerrillas were simply Soviet proxies. This was an example of "international terrorism" emanating from the Soviet Union: encouragement to radical groups promoting political changes through violence. Reagan insisted that the United States wanted to help the Salvadoran government because it sought peaceful reforms and was under siege by leftists.

The Reagan administration attempted to make a distinction between "authoritarian" and "totalitarian" regimes in justifying its assistance to El Salvador. The president drew from the earlier writings of now UN Ambassador Jeane Kirkpatrick, who argued that even though authoritarian governments prohibited political freedoms, they offered stability and the chance of becoming democratic while welcoming foreign investments and most often favoring the United States. Totalitarian governments, she noted, were usually Communist and therefore opposed to democracy, capitalism, and the United States. Acting on these premises, Reagan conceded that authoritarian regimes, such as that in El Salvador, had to stamp out criticisms in civil wars, but, he continued, they were not totalitarian in the sense of seeking to squelch all dissent and close their doors on outside involvement. Religious beliefs, family matters, cultural pursuits, and economic concerns—much latitude remained for individual development in authoritarian countries as long as these activities did not grow into a dangerous form of political instability that hampered the development of democracy and markets for investment and trade. Thus could the Reagan administration support governments on the right and oppose those on the left.

The United States, according to the White House, had no choice but to support the military government of El Salvador. Whereas authoritarian regimes exercised varying degrees of repression and therefore had the leeway to become more democratic, those of a totalitarian nature could not change. The best proof was Nicaragua, Reagan asserted. The Carter administration had mistakenly supported the Sandinistas over the Somozan government. Once the Sandinistas gained power, they suppressed civil liberties and moved close to the Soviet Union and Cuba. Congress gave in to the president and agreed to send economic and military assistance along with advisers, but it added one stipulation: improvements in human rights.

Although Kirkpatrick's ideas seemingly provided a clear guideline to foreign assistance programs, they did not work. Any U.S. emphasis on human rights fell victim to the higher priority of encouraging authoritarian regimes to permit evolutionary democratic changes. According to theory, the tenure of such regimes constituted an unavoidable step in a long transition period leading to democracy. It followed that Americans must overlook human rights abuses and sham elections as only temporary detours on the road to democracy. And, as in all imperfect theories, the administration at times had to engage in contradictory actions that raised questions about its direction. In 1982, the United States supported Britain's efforts to hold on to its Falkland Island possessions when they came under attack from the "authoritarian" government of Argentina. Furthermore, sharply deteriorating relations with the Soviet Union led the White House to reestablish ties with the "totalitarian" regime in China. Most important, however, a strict adherence to Kirkpatrick's dictum ensured continued embarrassment for the administration because it required an endorsement of authoritarian and hence repressive regimes all over the world.

For a time, however, the theory seemed sound. Secure in its logic, the Reagan administration asked Congress during the spring of 1983 to approve more military aid to El Salvador as part of a global effort to combat communism. The year before, Americans had met

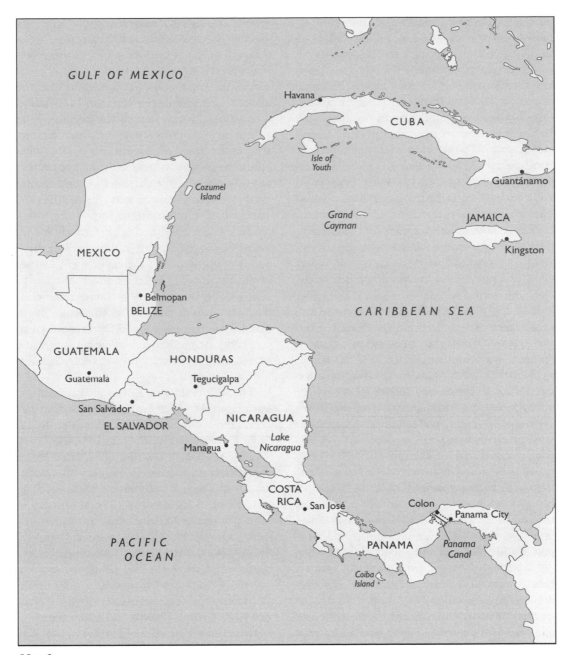

Map 8
Central America. Whether caused by internal problems or by outside interference—or both—the fighting in Central America deeply divided the United States over what remedies to offer. *(Source: author)*

with Mexican emissaries, and a short time afterward, in March 1982, elections took place in El Salvador. Although the insurgents refused to take part, Duarte's moderate Christian Democrats lost control of the National Assembly to a coalition of right-wing leaders who brought the land reform program to a halt. The problems, according to the Reagan administration's distorted assessment, were attributable to the Communists. The Soviets had infiltrated Nicaragua and now El Salvador and soon would concentrate on Honduras and Guatemala. This threatening activity had global implications, Reagan warned: "Soviet military theorists want to destroy our capacity to resupply Western Europe in case of an emergency." They intend "to tie down our attention and forces on our own southern border and so limit our capacity to act in more distant places such as Europe, the Persian Gulf, the Indian Ocean, the Sea of Japan." Central America was "simply too close and the strategic stakes . . . too high, for us to ignore the danger of governments seizing power there with ideological and military ties to the Soviet Union." American assistance was necessary.

Central America had become an integral part of White House foreign policy. To placate those Americans who feared "another Vietnam," Reagan explained in March 1983 that he was willing to have Salvadoran troops trained inside the United States so they could conduct the war themselves. Although repeating his pledge against sending U.S. combat troops to the troubled country, he warned that he would increase the number of advisers if Congress failed to comply with his requests for more military aid. "Two-thirds of all our foreign trade and petroleum pass through the Panama Canal and the Caribbean," the president explained in May. Should a crisis develop in Europe, "at least half of our supplies for NATO would go through these areas by sea." The Caribbean basin was a "magnet for adventurism."

Despite the heavy influx of U.S. aid, the situation in Central America continued to deteriorate, leading the White House into sterner measures. Charges grew that the United States secretly aided the contras (an anti-Sandinista force of perhaps 2,000 soldiers based in Honduras) in an attempt to overthrow the regime in Nicaragua and ease the alleged Communist pressures on El Salvador. The White House denied the accusation as a "myth," claiming that the new fighting was indigenous. American aid to the anti-Sandinistas, the administration continued, aimed only at "interdicting" or prohibiting further military assistance to the Sandinistas' cohort in El Salvador, the Communist insurgents. "The United States isn't invading anybody," UN Ambassador Kirkpatrick declared. But in November 1981, the president had secretly authorized the expenditure of close to $20 million by the CIA to prepare the contras for action against a government in Nicaragua that the United States, strange to say, officially recognized as legitimate. Some of the contras' military leaders received training in Florida.

The White House noted an increasingly dangerous situation in El Salvador that necessitated more active U.S. intervention. A State Department representative warned congressional committees that the United States might have to escalate its military and political involvement in Nicaragua because of the possible introduction into Central America of either Soviet or Cuban "modern fighter aircraft" or "even Cuban combat troops." Should Soviet and Cuban intervention take place, he asserted, the Reagan administration was prepared to launch air strikes, increase aid to friendly nations, and invoke the Rio Treaty of 1947, which authorized U.S. participation in the collective defense of Latin America. The president declared, however, that "we do not view security assistance as an end in itself, but as a shield for democratization, economic development and diplomacy." Shortly afterward, the White House announced that a hundred military advisers had left for Honduras to train Salvadoran troops.

Tensions rose in the summer of 1983 when a U.S. military adviser was assassinated in El

Salvador, but the United States continued to act with outward restraint. The Reagan administration pursued a strategy called "symmetry," which sought to buy time for democratic development in the Central American country. According to theory, the United States would treat the Sandinista regime in Nicaragua in the same way it treated the U.S.-supported government of President Alvaro Magaña in El Salvador: because the Sandinistas sought Magaña's overthrow, the United States would help the guerrilla group in Nicaragua (that is, the contras) seeking to oust the Sandinistas. In late July, Reagan appointed former Secretary of State Henry Kissinger as head of a twelve-member bipartisan commission instructed to develop a long-range policy on Central America. The president also made a show of force by sending an aircraft carrier battle group to engage in military maneuvers along Nicaragua's Pacific coast. Perhaps these demonstrations of U.S. interest in Central American affairs would convince the governments and rebels in both Nicaragua and El Salvador to consider a cease-fire, negotiations, and democratic elections.

At least in part to send a message to the Sandinistas, the Reagan administration in October 1983 took military action in nearby Grenada to thwart what it termed a threatened Communist takeover on that tiny island in the British Commonwealth. Four years earlier, in March 1979, leftists led by Maurice Bishop had overthrown the repressive and corrupt but anti-Communist government in a bloodless coup. In less than a week, a Cuban ship arrived with Soviet arms and ammunition. The following November, Bishop announced that Castro would help Grenada build an "international airport." After construction of the airstrip began, Bishop signed a treaty with Moscow allowing the Soviets to land long-range reconnaissance planes. Although the Reagan administration complained that these moves endangered peace in the hemisphere, Bishop visited Moscow in July 1982 and declared that he had received assurances of long-term financial assistance.

War in Central America—Nicaragua
Contras standing guard in Matagalpa in eastern Nicaragua in September 1985. *(Wide World Photos, New York)*

Over national television in March 1983, Reagan displayed a photograph of the Cuban barracks and airstrip on the island. Grenada had no air force, he asserted. "The Soviet-Cuban militarization of Grenada can only be seen as power projection into the region."

An outbreak of violence on the island provided the opportunity for the United States to act. White House pressure on Bishop had forced him to ease his criticisms of the United States, but Cuba's insistence on a hard-line policy encouraged dissidents on Grenada to seize control in mid-October and place Bishop under house arrest. Bishop's followers soon stormed the building and freed him, whereupon he spoke before a huge rally in the capital city of St. George's. But so-called revolutionary armed forces fired into the crowd, killing several before capturing and executing Bishop. As the militants imposed martial law, the White House declared that close to a thousand Americans on the island, more than half of them students at St. George's University School of Medicine, were in mortal danger.

With the approval of an obscure group of six member nations, the Organization of Eastern Caribbean States, Reagan resorted to military force—without consulting the British government. Probably spurred by news from Lebanon just two days earlier of a terrorist bombing in Beirut that took the lives of 241 U.S. soldiers (discussed later), the president defiantly declared, "We cannot let an act of terrorism determine whether we aid or assist our allies in the region. If we do that," he asked, "who will ever trust us again?" On October 25, 1983, a naval task force of 1,900 marines en route for Lebanon turned instead toward Grenada. There they encountered brief and surprisingly strong resistance at the airstrip from Grenadan troops and nearly 800 Cuban construction workers. The Americans soon secured the island, but only after the dispatch of 4,000 additional troops and 6 hard days of fighting that resulted in 134 U.S. casualties, including 18 dead, along with 396 Cuban and Grenadan casualties that included 69 dead.

Reagan capitalized on the success to issue a warning to those who interfered in the Western Hemisphere. Documents and weapons captured in the assault, he claimed, proved that the Marxist government had become increasingly reliant on Cuba, the Soviet Union, and North Korea—particularly for arms. The White House believed that Castro had intended to use Grenada as a staging ground for spreading communism into the entire region. Most important, however, the president hoped the use of force had demonstrated to the Sandinistas that Nicaragua itself was not immune to harsh treatment. The "rescue mission," as Reagan called it, was necessary to save the Americans and liberate the island from the threat of communism.

Searching questions remained about the Grenada expedition, even though the administration's supporters hailed the outcome as a victory for Reagan's foreign policy. Democra-

tic Speaker of the House Thomas P. O'Neill accused the president of violating the War Powers Act of 1973 by not consulting with Congress. New York Senator Daniel P. Moynihan, also a Democrat, denounced the assumed right of the United States to invade another sovereign nation. While seven members of the House prepared a resolution of impeachment against the president (which failed to win sufficient support), other observers wondered if the White House had too readily resorted to the military option. They remained dubious about the danger to the hemisphere and asked embarrassing questions about the battlefield performance of U.S. military forces. Many disputed Reagan's argument that the new airfield would primarily serve Cuban and Soviet military forces, claiming instead (and probably correctly) that its chief purpose was to support tourism. Still others remained skeptical about the president's defense of the invasion as vital to the safety of Americans on the island. British Prime Minister Thatcher had opposed the military action as a violation of Grenada's sovereignty and urged economic sanctions, and numerous Latin American governments denounced the move as a revival of nineteenth-century "gunboat diplomacy." The UN Security Council had opposed the action, only to have the United States veto the measure. The Grenada expedition nonetheless won widespread public approval in the United States—especially when television cameras showed American medical students arriving home and falling on their knees at the airport to kiss the ground.

With a pro-American group in charge, the troops sent the Cubans home and shut down the Soviet embassy. In late December, the Americans began their departure from the island, following seven weeks of occupation and a total cost of nearly $80 million.

Shortly afterward, in early 1984, the Kissinger Commission presented conclusions that indirectly lent credence to the Reagan administration's assessment of the danger in Grenada. The United States, according to the findings, had vital interests in Central America that required an expansion of its economic and military commitment in an effort to curtail the Soviets' "gradualist" policy. The commission recommended that Congress authorize $8 billion in economic aid to Central America over a five-year period. Most members of the commission took exception to the president's emphasis on the role of private business and urged the United States to condition all aid on changes in human rights. Kissinger warned, however, that the United States must not emphasize the "conditionality" of aid "in a manner that leads to a Marxist-Leninist victory." It would be "absurd," he told reporters, to cut off military assistance to El Salvador in defense of human rights if the move ensured a Communist victory that led to more killing. Reagan approved the report but spoke favorably of Kissinger's warning. Congress responded by approving an aid package of less than half the amount recommended but urged continued assistance to the Salvadoran military and contras in Nicaragua.

The situation in El Salvador, meanwhile, showed signs of easing in intensity. In May 1984, with the United States supervising election proceedings and the CIA providing funds in strategic places, Duarte emerged victorious as president. The following year, his Christian Democratic Party won control over the National Assembly, and the military appeared receptive to his moderate policies and assurances of reforms. The death squads decreased their activity, and Duarte seemingly surprised the White House by meeting with the rebels to explore the possibilities of a negotiated settlement that included their participation in government. The discussions failed, however, and the United States expanded its assistance to Duarte's military forces—which had the unforeseen effect of weakening his appeal to the country's moderates and encouraging the civil war to continue throughout the remainder of the Reagan administration.

The White House, meanwhile, continued to help the contras in Nicaragua as part of the overall effort to bring down the Sandinistas and ease the pressure on El Salvador. It sent aid, supported training the army, and urged land reform. In mid-August 1983, the first of nearly 6,000 army and marine troops landed in Honduras to begin "training exercises." Despite a congressional act of 1982 banning the use of classified funds in trying to undermine the Nicaraguan government (the Boland Amendment, presented by Democrat Edward Boland of the House Intelligence Committee), the White House relied on the other part of the Boland Amendment that permitted overt help to any government in the region endangered by insurgents receiving military assistance from Cuba or Nicaragua. Consequently, the CIA clandestinely participated in the fighting by directing assaults into Nicaragua, flying air missions, sabotaging oil depots, plotting assassinations of Sandinista leaders, and cooperating with the contras in mining the country's harbors.

But in late 1983, the secret war waged by the Reagan administration became public and threatened to come to an end. The mines damaged several neutral vessels and injured ten sailors, exposing the CIA's covert operations and leading an outraged Congress to take preventive measures. The Sandinista government took the matter to the World Court, where it accused the United States of violating Nicaragua's sovereignty. The Reagan administration, however, rejected the Court's right to deal with such matters. Without U.S. involvement in the ensuing judicial process, the World Court in June 1986 found the United States in violation of international law by aiding the contras and mining the harbors and ordered it to make compensation to Nicaragua. The president refused to comply. An irate Congress responded with a second Boland Amendment, which prohibited the use of government funds to undermine the Nicaraguan government and by late 1984 effectively stopped all aid to the contras.

The White House, however, insisted that the Boland Amendment did not apply to the work of the National Security Council (which Congress hotly disputed) and continued to maintain pressure on the Sandinistas in Nicaragua. The president carefully circumvented the wording of the Boland Amendment by calling for an end to arms shipments to insurgents in El Salvador while no longer mentioning the overthrow of the Nicaraguan government. Congress adamantly opposed Reagan's transparent maneuverings. Although agreeing to assist Duarte and El Salvador, it repeatedly turned down the president's requests to aid the contras. Not to be denied, members of the Reagan administration appealed to private groups of Americans, who donated $5 million of supplies to the contras in 1984 and 1985. The president meanwhile solicited contributions from Texas oil magnates, wealthy widows (both groups able to claim tax write-offs), and Arab leaders, including the king of Saudi Arabia.

The situation in Central America continued to deteriorate. The Sandinistas held an election in late 1984 that solidified their control over Nicaragua by putting their leader, Daniel Ortega, into the presidency. The following year, he took measures that substantiated the Reagan administration's worst fears. Ortega imposed martial law, imprisoned many members of his opposition, and shut down media criticism. When the Sandinistas edged closer to Cuba and the Communist bloc, Reagan warned that Nicaragua had become "a Communist totalitarian state" and declared that the United States must help the contras, who were, he insisted, the "moral equal of our Founding Fathers."

The president authorized several actions intended to undermine the Sandinistas. He ordered the contras based in Honduras into maneuvers and stationed U.S. warships off the Nicaraguan coasts. He instituted an economic embargo on Nicaragua in May 1985 and soon afterward blocked Nicaragua's effort to secure funds from the World Bank and Inter-American Development Bank. Under the International Emergency Economic Powers Act of 1977, the president explained, he could impose sanctions without congressional approval once he declared a "national emergency." Reagan announced that Nicaragua's "aggres-

sive activities" were clear from its "continuing efforts to subvert its neighbors, its rapid and destabilizing military buildup, its close military and security ties to Cuba and the Soviet Union and its imposition of Communist totalitarian internal rule." In the summer of 1985, Congress still refused to open its military coffers to the contras, although it agreed to extend $27 million in "humanitarian" aid.

In his December 1985 State of the Union Address, the president kept the heat on Congress by announcing what became known as the "Reagan Doctrine." His administration, he proclaimed, would support anti-Communist "freedom fighters" as part of the nation's "self-defense." Reagan's pronouncements resurrected memories of the Eisenhower fifties, when Secretary of State John Foster Dulles called for the "rollback" of communism and its replacement with Wilsonian ideals of freedom aimed at liberating oppressed peoples everywhere. "Our mission," Reagan declared, "is to nourish and defend freedom and democracy." Covert assistance to counterinsurgents (in what some called "low-intensity conflict") would ultimately unseat dangerous regimes and allow the growth of democracy. To facilitate this moral and ideological process, Reagan seemed to imply, the CIA could use congressional funds to assist the contras in Nicaragua and insurgents anywhere else who resisted totalitarian rule.

Meanwhile, Soviet ties with Nicaragua seemed to tighten. Two days before the United States announced the economic sanctions, Ortega visited Gorbachev in the Kremlin and, before television cameras, openly displayed their friendship. In this visit, Ortega's fourth since the Sandinista takeover in July 1979, he sought new economic assistance. The Soviet Union had delayed news of the planned visit until after Reagan's recent contra aid defeat in Congress. The Soviet news agency TASS confirmed the president's suspicions by announcing the establishment of a Soviet–Nicaraguan commission on economic, commercial, and scientific-technical cooperation.

In March 1986, Reagan again appealed for congressional money for arms to the contras. Three months later, Congress (doubtless in reaction to Ortega's visit to Moscow) approved $100 million but restricted the package to "nonlethal" aid. For a brief time, the problems in Central America dropped from the headlines.

The Middle East

Despite the enormous difficulties in U.S.–Soviet relations and the immediacy of the alleged Soviet connection with Central America, the most perplexing problem facing the United States continued to be the Middle East. The Egyptian-Israeli Treaty of 1979 had not resolved the region's difficulties; indeed, it added still more complications to a list that was already long. The pact negotiated by the Carter administration had actually strengthened Israel's stature in the Middle East by alienating Egypt from the other Arab nations, and at the same time it kept the United States in the awkward position of having to honor commitments to the Israelis while trying to maintain ties with the oil-rich Saudis and other Arabs. If the treaty constituted a first step toward peace, it also brought more focus to the numerous problems that stood in the way.

As in the 1970s, the Reagan administration followed what seemed to be the only feasible approach: extend military and economic aid to both major antagonists (the Israelis and the Arabs), hoping to maintain a balance of power designed to avert conflict. To counter longtime military aid to Israel, the White House permitted the Saudis to buy U.S. tanks and air-to-air missiles for their F-15 fighter planes, which took away Israel's control of the skies. The new sale angered Congress because the administration had earlier pledged against such an act to win congressional support for the original sale of the F-15s. Furthermore, in response to the Saudis' fear of an assault by Iran during its ongoing war with their political ally Iraq, the Reagan administration prepared to sell them Sidewinder missiles and five Airborne Warning and Control System planes (AWACS), which were Boeing 707s equipped with disk-shaped radar antennas capable of tracking up to 400 aircraft within a 350-mile radius. The White House pushed through the hotly debated AWACS sale by a slim four-vote margin in the Senate.

The Reagan administration's arms sales to Saudi Arabia greatly exacerbated the precarious Middle East situation. Israel was angry with the United States over the AWACS deal, which further undercut the hopes of the treaty with Egypt. Although Israel reaffirmed its intention to withdraw from the Sinai in April 1982, uncertainty remained. Then, in October 1981, matters became even more complicated: Muslim extremists in the Egyptian army assassinated Sadat, forcing his successor, Hosni Mubarek, to seek credibility at home by affirming that his loyalties to Egypt were more important than the treaty with Israel. His new regime must restore relations with moderate Arab states.

When Begin visited Washington shortly after the AWACS deal, Reagan recommended a policy called "strategic collaboration," which sought to revive the Camp David accords by offering more security assurances to Israel. The president hoped that such a move would make Begin more open to compromise on the Palestinian issue and relax his resistance to the AWACS agreement. But this effort failed. Begin remained determined to annex the West Bank, and in December he ordered the virtual annexation of the Syrian portion of the Golan Heights by integrating the area into the Israeli administrative and judicial system. When the Reagan administration reacted by suspending the discussions over strategic collaboration, Begin angrily denounced the United States as anti-Semitic and accused it of treating Israel as a "banana republic." Instead of returning to pre-1967 borders in exchange for promises of security, he intended to win the war by strengthening his country's hold on East Jerusalem, the Golan Heights, the West Bank, and Gaza.

Although the central issue in the Middle East remained the Arab–Israeli conflict, the Reagan administration tried to draw the two peoples together by emphasizing the Soviet threat to the entire region and calling for a "strategic consensus" against Moscow. If the United States could convince the ancient antagonists that the Soviet menace superseded their own difficulties, it might be able to maintain relations with both the Arabs and the Israelis and keep peace in the region. The Reagan administration therefore undertook the formidable tasks of deemphasizing Arab–Israeli differences and postponing the Palestinian issue in hope of shifting the focus to containing the Soviet Union. Success would bring greater security to the region's pro-Western nations, in turn ensuring peace in the Middle East and a continued oil supply for the West.

The policy of strategic consensus proved a dismal failure. Not even the Soviet–American rivalry could overshadow Arab–Israeli hostilities. Israel's major concerns, Reagan's critics argued, were the Palestinians and U.S. arms sales to the Arabs. The Arab states declared that only the establishment of a Palestinian state would ease anti-American sentiment in the Middle East and improve economic and military ties with the United States. Despite the Reagan administration's efforts to ignore history and inject the Cold War as a sedative for easing the Middle East's problems, it could not diminish the centrality of Arab–Israeli strife.

Lebanon soon became the focal point of another Middle East crisis. Located north of Israel on the eastern side of the Mediterranean, Lebanon had recently been rocked by a bitter civil war between Christians and Muslims. The Christians, more powerful and wealthy than their hated enemy, had demanded restrictions on the Palestinians in south Lebanon, who had grown in number after their forced departure from Jordan during the early 1970s. The Palestinians now posed a threat to Lebanon because they were armed and therefore attractive to left-wing Muslim militants who sought PLO help against the Christians. Should war develop between Israel and a Muslim-controlled Lebanon, neighboring Syria would become involved. Syria considered it imperative to keep Lebanon intact, first by mediation and then, failing that, by military force.

The United States made a major effort to mediate the growing dispute—especially after Israeli forces raided southern Lebanon to destroy the PLO centers and then armed the Christians as a step toward creating a friendly buffer state between Israel and the PLO. Israel had just complied with the Camp David accords in withdrawing from the Sinai in April 1982, and Begin now felt free to turn toward the festering problem in Lebanon. Internal conflict erupted on an even wider scale: the Syrians emplaced ground-to-air missiles in Lebanon, and the Israelis countered by destroying the missiles in a preemptive strike. War between Israel and Syria, the Reagan administration knew, would drive the Arab states into Syria's arms and leave the United States alone with Israel, thus alienating the Saudis. The Soviet Union, which had recently entered an amity pact with Syria, would then align with the other Arab states and gain a major inroad into the Middle East.

Heightening tensions finally exploded into conflict in mid-1982, when PLO agents assassinated the Israeli ambassador in London and the Israelis retaliated in June by launching a massive invasion of Lebanon. Israeli forces entered Lebanon for the ostensible reason of crippling the PLO's ability to endanger Jewish settlements in the north; in reality, the Israelis sought to destroy the PLO in West Beirut, undermine the hopes of Palestinian nationalists on the West Bank, force the Syrians out of Lebanon, and put the beleaguered country under the control of the Christians, whose close ties with Israel could guarantee some measure of security along their common frontier. At the same time, the Israelis further shocked the White House by bombing the nuclear reactor that Iraq had recently acquired from France to prevent Iraqi production of nuclear bombs capable of destroying Israel.

The timing of the Israeli attack on Lebanon thoroughly embarrassed the United States. President Reagan was on a goodwill visit in Europe, and his administration was involved in the Middle East peace talks. The widespread impression was that the United States either had been unable to restrain Israel or, even worse, had tacitly approved the invasion. The Israeli offensive violated the recent fragile and unwritten cease-fire with the PLO secured after long and delicate negotiations by U.S. Special Envoy Philip Habib. Now more problems lay ahead. A State Department spokesman insisted that "Israel will have to withdraw its forces from Lebanon, and the Palestinians will have to stop using Lebanon as a launching pad for attacks on Israel." A British diplomat was blunt: Israel was "acting as recruiter in chief for the PLO."

The Israeli military offensive in Lebanon threatened to wreck U.S. hopes for peace in the Middle East. World condemnation of the siege developed as nightly news programs televised the Israeli air and ground assaults, which, to most observers, appeared to be unprovoked aggression. Israel once more stood alone against the Arab world, restricting Reagan's attempts to build a sweeping consensus against the Soviet Union. The Israeli actions added weight to the charge that Egypt's earlier treaty had been a betrayal of fellow Arab states. It made U.S. mediation of the Lebanese dispute more remote and, by raising the possibility of war with Syria, virtually invited Soviet intervention in the region.

Israel's behavior also threw American domestic politics into turmoil. White House support of Israel would alienate the Arabs and stop the oil flow, but lack of support would anger the powerful Jewish lobby at home and cost votes. A compromise of sorts was the result. Inside the United Nations, the United States joined Iraq in condemning Israel, but the White House did not support sanctions, except for a delayed delivery of seventy-five promised F-16 fighter planes. Even then, this mild rebuke had no effect because the planes were not due to arrive until 1985.

The Reagan administration meanwhile hoped for a victory by the moderate Labor Party in the 1982 elections in Israel, but the Labor Party lost to the hard-line Likud Party, and Begin continued as prime minister. To his cabinet he appointed a foreign minister who had resisted the treaty of 1979 with Egypt and a defense minister who, as minister of agriculture, had pushed for rapid Israeli settlement of the West Bank. Begin also placed the minister of the interior in charge of the Palestinian autonomy discussions, which implied that the issue was internal in nature and annexation of the West Bank imminent. Begin's renewal in office elevated the Arab–Israeli problem to prominence again and further damaged the Reagan administration's declining hopes for the anti-Soviet strategic consensus in the Middle East. The Arab radicals' position was confirmed, the Palestinians in the West Bank became more embittered, and the Soviet standing in the Middle East seemed to become stronger in proportion to the diminishing position of the United States.

The Middle East remained a steaming cauldron of trouble. The Israelis' attack on the PLO in West Beirut led to the deaths of numerous civilians, and when Israel began a steady shelling of the city's PLO camps in August, many Americans demanded that their government renounce the action. The public's mood helped lead to the resignation of Secretary of State Haig, who was openly pro-Israel. Habib meanwhile arranged a compromise in September by which the Israelis ended the barrage in exchange for a PLO evacuation from Beirut to Jordan and Tunisia under American, British, French, and Italian troop protection. Yasir Arafat, the PLO leader, warned that the Israeli army would seize control of Beirut as soon as the PLO and the international force were gone—and he was correct. On September 14, 1982, Muslim terrorists assassinated the recently elected pro-Israel president of Lebanon, Bachir Gemayel of the Christian, or Phalangist, militia. The following day, under the guise of protecting the Muslims from Christian retaliation, Israeli

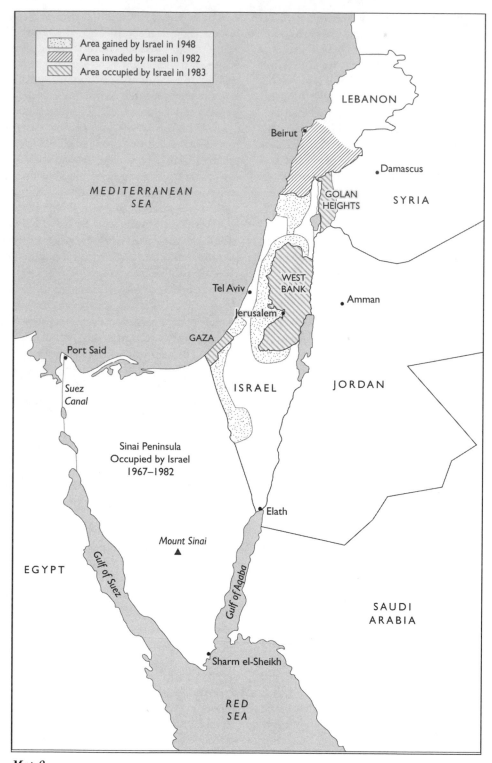

Legend:
- Area gained by Israel in 1948
- Area invaded by Israel in 1982
- Area occupied by Israel in 1983

LEBANON

Beirut

Damascus

MEDITERRANEAN
SEA

GOLAN
HEIGHTS

SYRIA

WEST
BANK

Tel Aviv

Amman

Jerusalem

GAZA

Port Said

ISRAEL

JORDAN

Suez
Canal

Sinai Peninsula
Occupied by Israel
1967–1982

Elath

EGYPT

Mount Sinai

Gulf of Suez

Gulf of Aqaba

SAUDI
ARABIA

Sharm el-Sheikh

RED
SEA

Map 9

The Middle East in 1983. From ancient times to the present, the Middle East has remained impervious to a peaceful resolution of its many problems. *(Source: author)*

forces violated the truce and occupied the Muslim sector of West Beirut. On September 17, Gemayel's Christian militia adhered to Israel's urgings to clear out PLO terrorists from the refugee camps and, in a brutal act of vengeance, machine-gunned nearly 800 Palestinian civilians in what became known as the "Sabra-Shatila Massacres." The episode led to the return of U.S. Marines as part of another multinational peacekeeping force.

Suspicion grew that the Begin ministry had been involved in the slaughter. The main responsibility for the massacres, many argued, lay with the extremist Lebanese Christian Phalangists, but these same observers noted that the killings could not have occurred without Israeli connivance. They had taken place in an area under Israel's military control and with Israeli observation posts nearby. Furthermore, the critics declared, Israeli army officers and government ministers knew about the impending act some thirty-six hours beforehand and had done nothing to stop it. A stormy session followed in the Israeli government, after which a commission of inquiry eventually called for the resignation of the country's fiery defense minister, Ariel Sharon, longtime veteran of Israeli–Arab clashes. Sharon admitted to having permitted Lebanese militia into the camps to clear out Palestinian guerrillas—but, he insisted, only after securing their promise not to harm civilians. Even if Sharon had not actually condoned the killings, he had certainly recognized the danger in sending the Phalangists into the PLO camps in the direct aftermath of Gemayel's death. After a bitter fight inside Israel's highest governing circles, Begin reluctantly accepted an inquiry into the massacres. The judicial commission found Israel "indirectly responsible."

Supported by an angry Jewish community in the United States, the White House stepped up its efforts toward peace by first securing the withdrawal of Israeli military forces from Lebanon. Reagan proposed that the 720,000 Palestinians in the West Bank and Gaza receive self-rule under Jordanian supervision. Begin argued instead for a neutralized Lebanon free of PLO and Syrian involvement, a government dominated by the Christian Phalangists, a Lebanese special force to patrol the country's southern border, a buffer zone policed by an international peacekeeping unit, and the right of Israeli forces to enter Lebanon at any time for searches and arrests. The United States joined Lebanon, which was now under shaky Christian control and fearful of alienating its large Arab population, in rejecting Begin's proposals. The White House then attempted to persuade Jordan's King Hussein to represent the Palestinians in the talks. This plan likewise failed. The PLO opposed the arrangement, and Hussein refused to act without the support of other Arab leaders. In any case, his prior stipulations had not been fulfilled: the United States had not convinced Begin either to withdraw his military forces from Lebanon or to halt the spread of Jewish settlements on the West Bank. "If the U.S. cannot push the Israelis out of Lebanon," a baffled Jordanian politician asked, "why should anyone believe it can get them out of the West Bank?"

Time was not on the side of the peacemakers. The West Bank Palestinians warned that further delay would promote Begin's long-range goal of settling 100,000 Jews in the area, effectively annexing Jordan and all of the West Bank. As a Jordanian official warned, "If we do not force the Israelis to negotiate about the West Bank now, they will force us to negotiate over the East Bank later." The Reagan administration called for a freeze on new Israeli settlements in the West Bank, which had already raised the number of Jewish inhabitants in the area from 5,000 in 1977 to nearly 30,000 by the summer of 1983. Begin dismissed Reagan's proposal with the remark that "it is as impossible to freeze the settlements as it is to freeze life." The Arabs held President Carter responsible for their troubles because he had failed to insist on a settlements freeze in the Camp David accords. As an Israeli admitted, "Begin started the rapid expansion after Camp David because nowhere does the treaty rule settlements out."

With the Middle East talks stalemated, Begin felt no pressure to halt the settlements.

Meanwhile, the situation in Lebanon continued to deteriorate. In mid-April 1983, terrorists blew up a large sector of the U.S. embassy in Beirut, killing more than sixty people (including seventeen Americans) and injuring more than a hundred others also in the building. Although the White House assured the participants that this terrorist act would not interrupt the peace talks over Lebanon, there was little progress, if any. The Israelis and the Lebanese concurred on the need for a security zone in south Lebanon that was free of Palestinian guerrillas and could safeguard northern Israel from attack. The Israelis, however, wanted their soldiers to accompany Lebanese patrols and to have military or police powers, whereas the Lebanese approved Israeli participation only in "joint supervisory teams" having no such powers. The Syrians opposed any form of Israeli–Lebanese agreement as an obstruction to their aim of regaining the Golan Heights, taken by Israel in the Six Day War of 1967 and formally annexed in 1981. The Reagan administration feared that the Christian and pro-Israeli Lebanese government would collapse and give way to one having close ties to Iran, Libya, and the Soviet Union. By mid-1983, there remained in Lebanon a dangerous combination of 38,000 Israeli troops and 50,000 Syrian troops, along with perhaps 15,000 PLO commandos—a situation hardly amenable to the control of a small peacekeeping contingent of U.S., British, French, and Italian soldiers.

The multinational force in Lebanon soon became involved in another terrorist crisis. Arab dissidents regarded the Americans as the chief enemy and began pummeling the U.S. quarters at Beirut International Airport. On the Sunday morning of October 23, 1983, a Muslim suicide mission drove a truck laden with dynamite through the barricade and into the U.S. Marines' command center, blowing up the main military barracks and killing 241 sleeping marines. Two miles from the U.S. compound, another explosion a few minutes later killed more than fifty French paratroopers. The president refused to evacuate the remaining military personnel: their presence, he declared, was "central to our credibility on a global scale." To pull out now would make "others feel confident they can intimidate us and our allies in Lebanon" and encourage the terrorists to "become more bold elsewhere."

But Reagan's hard talk brought no results: the government in Lebanon fell, wiping out its treaty with Israel and leaving Beirut in utter disarray. As the violence intensified among warring factions, the 1,600 marines still there found themselves isolated, trapped, and virtually defenseless in the garrison, and in February 1984, the president ordered their withdrawal to nearby U.S. naval vessels. The U.S. retreat sent an alarming message to friends in the region. With the Americans' departure, Lebanese groups joined Syria in expressing interest in peace talks. The following September a more moderate government took over in Israel and directed the withdrawal of its own soldiers from southern Lebanon.

On December 6, 1987, the Palestinians revolted against the Israelis occupying the West Bank and Gaza Strip in an uprising by Arab young men called the *intifada*, which had far-reaching effects. The following July, as the Israelis escalated their response to the *intifada* with a brutal military force that repelled many of the world's observers, Jordan's King Hussein made a surprising move: he withdrew all claims to the West Bank, effectively turning over the disputed area to the Palestinians for a homeland.

Jordan's action placed the initiative in PLO hands. Arafat came under enormous pressure to accept the offer: a refusal would alienate leaders of the *intifada* in the West Bank and, with Syrian assistance, allow the more extreme wing of the Palestinians to gain control of the PLO. Consequently, in November 1988, he went before the Palestine National Council (PNC) in Algiers and proclaimed the establishment of an independent Palestinian state, a move resting on the UN General Assembly's partition plan of 1947. On the surface,

Arafat's two-state plan proved attractive in that it grounded the legitimacy of Palestine in the same UN resolution that had legitimized Israel. But it also meant that he was speaking of the Israel of 1947, which was only a third of its present size. The resulting "Political Communiqué" (approved overwhelmingly by the PNC) reiterated this point by calling for an international peace conference as provided by UN Security Council Resolution 242, which in 1967 had stipulated Israeli withdrawal from lands occupied in the Six Day War in exchange for secure borders.

Only at first did the Reagan administration reject the seemingly imminent creation of a Palestinian state. Israel, of course, adamantly refused to negotiate with the PLO or to accept boundaries defined before 1967. As the violence spread, Secretary of State Shultz offered a plan in 1988 that rested on the principle of "land for peace" but, not surprisingly,

Beirut Rescue, October 23, 1983
A rescue mission at work after a dynamite-filled truck driven by Muslims blew up the main military barracks in Beirut, killing 241 sleeping U.S. Marines. *(National Archives, Washington, D.C.)*

aroused no interest from either Israel or the PLO. When Arafat requested a chance to present his own peace plan before the UN General Assembly in New York, Shultz in late November refused to grant him a visa. Other members of the United Nations, however, were infuriated with Shultz's action and agreed to meet with Arafat in Geneva. There, on December 7, 1988, Arafat renounced terrorism and any intention to interfere with Israel. But critics noted that his apparent change in policy had come with two distinct qualifications: his renunciation of terrorism did not include Palestinian actions inside Israel, and he meant the Israel *before* the Six Day War. Shultz nonetheless regarded these concessions as potentially pathbreaking, and in a move that shocked the world and enraged the Israelis, he agreed to negotiate with the PLO. Talks began in Tunis in mid-December 1988, shortly before Reagan completed his second term in office, and therefore carried over into the administration of his successor.

The ongoing war between Iran and Iraq meanwhile complicated the already tangled situation in the Middle East by threatening to drag in other nations. Long-standing differences between these two Arab states had exploded in an incredibly bloody conflict in 1980 that imperiled passage through the Persian Gulf and thus affected oil interests all over the world. The Soviets had tried to play both sides by providing Iraq with planes and ammunition while approving Syria's delivery of Soviet arms to Iran. As a result, neither antagonist trusted the Soviet Union. The United States claimed to be neutral, although its relations with Iraq had improved when the State Department took that government off the list of countries supporting terrorism and thus permitted the extension of export credits.

American arms sales to the antagonists caused the greatest furor. Although the White House publicly refused to approve the sale of weapons to Iraq, evidence now shows that huge supplies of American arms went to Iraq's military ruler, Saddam Hussein. Indeed, for a time in 1985 and 1986, the

Reagan administration also secretly sent arms to Iran until exposure of this policy (the Iran-Contra Affair, discussed later) unleashed a furious reaction. Americans still resented the hostage crisis of the Carter years, and Iranian-supported terrorists had stirred up more hard feelings by recently kidnapping other Americans in the Middle East, including news correspondents and State Department and CIA employees. As the Iranian–Iraqi fighting settled into a bitter war of attrition, the chances for a negotiated settlement became increasingly elusive. The president of Iran during the early part of the Khomeini regime, Abolhassan Banisadr, put it bluntly when he declared from outside Paris that "for us, the war will only end with a general embargo on arms deliveries to both belligerents."

Tensions in the Gulf mounted, however, as the Reagan administration became more deeply involved in the fighting and showed an unmistakable tilt toward Iraq. In May 1987, the United States tried to maintain the flow of commerce by flying its flag on Kuwaiti tankers carrying oil to Japan. American planes then strafed two Iranian oil decks in retaliation for the Iranians' firing missiles at one of these tankers. That same month, however, an Iraqi plane hit the U.S. destroyer *Stark* with two French missiles, killing thirty-seven and drawing vehement White House protests. The Baghdad government responded with an apology and reparations. American assistance to Iraq continued even while the president directed minesweepers and helicopters to protect U.S. vessels in the troubled waters. The following July 1988, the commander of the U.S.S. *Vincennes* erroneously thought he was under attack and fired on what turned out to be a civilian Iranian airliner. All 290 aboard died in the fiery blast. The Reagan administration accepted blame for the mistake and, in a move that did not appeal to an American public still bitter over the long hostage crisis, awarded compensation to the victims.

The heightening threat of a widened war in the Persian Gulf hurried the ongoing efforts of the United Nations to secure a cease-fire.

In August, barely a month after the *Vincennes* tragedy, the two totally exhausted warring nations laid down their arms, effectually admitting to the existence of a long and ghastly stalemate that had consumed 2 million lives and inestimable treasure. Iraq had gained a small piece of territory from the fighting, but even that did not change the reality: the war had not yielded a victor and thereby intensified the bitterness in the region.

Other problems had surfaced over Libya, which, though not part of the Middle East, bordered Egypt and compounded the region's difficulties by supporting terrorism. In the spring of 1981, the Reagan administration accused Libyan ruler Muammar Qaddafi of engineering international terrorism with the help of Soviet money. In May, it ordered his diplomats out of Washington in retaliation for the burning of the U.S. embassy in 1980 and for the dismissal of the U.S. diplomats. The following August 1981, Qaddafi accused U.S. forces on maneuvers in the Mediterranean off Libya's shores of violating his country's territorial waters, and in an ensuing aerial exchange, U.S. jets downed two Libyan planes. Relations worsened by the end of the year when the White House announced that Qaddafi had ordered Libyan terrorists in the United States to assassinate Reagan (a charge never confirmed). In early 1982, the administration (without European allied support) stopped Libyan oil imports into the country and placed an embargo on all goods to Libya. "We have to put Qaddafi in a box and close the lid," Shultz told reporters.

Problems intensified between the United States and Libya. In December 1985, terrorist attacks at the Rome and Vienna airports killed 19 (including 5 Americans and 1 Israeli) and injured 112 others. Responsibility seemed to belong to a Palestinian group based in Libya and openly supported by Qaddafi. Sensing an imminent U.S. attack, he warned that government and Israel that a strike against his country would cause Libyans to take action against Americans "in their own streets" and lead to the spread of terrorism throughout the Mediterranean area. In early 1986, U.S. naval vessels in the Mediterranean made another show of force off Libya's coast. When Libyan patrol boats approached the Americans, U.S. planes fired on the boats as well as on Libyan military positions ashore.

In April 1986, relations between the countries reached the breaking point. An explosion rocked a West Berlin discotheque, killing one U.S. soldier and a Turkish woman and injuring 230, including dozens of off-duty U.S. soldiers. Suspicions of Libya's involvement in the bombing grew, encouraged by electronic eavesdropping by the United States that revealed Qaddafi's intentions to launch more terrorist attacks. At a news conference, President Reagan denounced the Libyan ruler as the "mad dog of the Middle East."

That same April, the White House (with the support of Britain, Canada, and Israel) retaliated against Libya's alleged complicity in the West Berlin killings by approving a surprise air raid on its capital of Tripoli. Using bases in Britain, thirteen F-111s began a 5,600-mile round-trip (lengthened by 2,400 miles because France and Spain refused to allow the planes to use their airspace) and bombed Qaddafi's living quarters and his command and communications center. In less than twelve minutes, the planes destroyed several military targets, but they also hit some non-military areas and killed a number of civilians, including one of Qaddafi's children. Although the Arabs and many Europeans denounced the assault, U.S. allies on the continent soon exerted diplomatic pressure on the Libyans, and the terrorist threat eased for a few months. The sense of satisfaction was misplaced, however, because evidence later showed that the Syrians, not Qaddafi, were responsible for the violence in West Berlin.

Time had appeared to stand still in the Middle East. All its problems seemed to be as unsolvable during the 1980s as in the immediate period after World War II. Ancient issues remained, complicated by Cold War rivalries, international terrorism, and the endemic lack of trust.

The Iran-Contra Affair

In an ironic twist, the issues in the Middle East and Central America merged in the 1980s in a zany scheme freighted with illegalities and soon called the Iran-Contra Affair. Public exposure of the escapade began in October 1986, when the Sandinistas shot down a plane flown by three Americans and carrying materiel to the contras. Curiously, the sole survivor admitted to being a CIA agent. A month afterward, a Lebanese newspaper revealed a White House attempt to secure the freedom of six American hostages in Lebanon taken by Iranian-supported terrorists after 1983 by arranging the sale of arms to Iran through the Israelis. As the story unwound, suspicions grew that the president had become as obsessed with the hostages' fate as had Carter—particularly when news arrived of the torture of the captured CIA station chief in Beirut, William Buckley. Later, when the president asked for Buckley's release in accordance with the delivery of arms to Iran, it became clear that he had died from the torture. Indeed, only a single American won his freedom as a result of all the intricate work put into the Iran-contra plan—clergyman Benjamin Weir.

The president decided to admit to the basics of the plan. To win the freedom of Iran's U.S. hostages in Lebanon, he told shocked Americans, his administration had sent a small number of "defensive weapons" to Iran in an effort to establish contact with "moderates" in Teheran (never named) who might serve as intermediaries in negotiations. He had also wanted to help Iraq win its war with Iran, whose Islamic fundamentalists threatened to spread their anti-American and revolutionary doctrines throughout the Middle East. The White House, he insisted, had broken no laws, agreed to no "ransom" payments, and remained determined not to deal with terrorists. Yet as the secret process unfolded, it became clear that the terrorists had intended to free the hostages one at a time rather than all at once and then had kidnapped three others to replenish their leverage for additional arms.

Less than a month later, the White House added a bizarre twist to the story by announcing that money from the arms sales had been deposited in a Swiss bank account earmarked for the contras in Nicaragua. Accusations flew as numerous groups wondered about presidential involvement and drew comparisons with the Watergate scandal. A conspiracy seemed evident—one involving the CIA, nameless arms dealers, and perhaps the White House itself.

By the end of the year, Reagan's foreign policy team was in deep trouble. The previous May 1986, it became clear that National Security Adviser Robert McFarlane had secretly traveled to Iran to offer military hardware in exchange for assistance in freeing the U.S. hostages in Lebanon. Soon, like the Watergate scandal, the entire story began to unravel, threatening to leave the administration's foreign policy in shambles. The White House had blatantly violated the Boland Amendments in attempting to undermine the Nicaraguan government. McFarlane's successor in December 1985, Admiral John Poindexter, had to resign under presidential pressure: without congressional knowledge, he had authorized a National Security Council staff member, Vietnam veteran Marine Lieutenant Colonel Oliver North, to oversee the illegal covert operation.

North soon became the focal point of nationwide interest. Not only had he worked with Israel and private arms dealers in sending missiles and other kinds of military materiel to Iran in 1985 and 1986, but he had also collaborated with Panama General Manuel Noriega (later convicted of international drug trafficking) in illegally funneling up to $30 million of war materiel directly to the contras. In addition, North raised millions of dollars from conservatives at home and supervised an elaborate system of air and water communications with Central America while arranging the construction of a huge airfield in Costa Rica. Indeed, he had worked under the close supervision of the president's longtime friend, CIA Director William Casey, who

had taken the Reagan Doctrine to heart and, with a greatly escalated budget, carried out these clandestine Iran-contra actions in willing contravention of the law. Giving in to growing public pressure, Reagan also called for North's resignation, even while heralding him as a "national hero" who deserved to be the subject of a Hollywood movie.

Was the president directly involved in this singular episode? Reagan admitted to knowledge of the arms-for-hostages negotiations but appeared befuddled in declaring that he could not recall when he had made a decision on the matter. Furthermore, he professed surprise at the alleged Iran-contra connection. If not skirting the truth, he at least promoted the growing image of ineptness in office. Secret aid to the contras, of course, was a violation of the congressional prohibition of trafficking in military goods, and assistance in this unorthodox piece of foreign policy would have broken his own assurances against dealing with Iranian terrorists. Critics declared that the arms-for-hostages deal was tantamount to blackmail. Numerous observers complained that the hard-nosed Reagan administration had reversed its position on terrorism and negotiated with, of all nations, the detested Iran. Had he not called that government an "outlaw state" dominated by "misfits, Looney Tunes, and squalid criminals"? Still others wondered why White House Chief of Staff Donald Regan, Secretary of Defense Weinberger, and Secretary of State Shultz, who all knew about the arrangement before its public exposure and roundly condemned it, did not stop the operation. How much did Vice President (and former CIA head) George Bush know? North's diaries and an independent investigation, it later became clear, suggested Bush's awareness of the Iran arms sale. But the big question related to the president himself. Could he have been oblivious to such a far-fetched scheme?

Various investigations turned up many fascinating details about the operation, but nothing that could lead to an indictment of the president for criminal behavior. A Senate

Intelligence Committee in December 1986 summoned Poindexter and North, who appealed to the Fifth Amendment in declining to answer questions. The following February, a special commission appointed by the president and chaired by former Republican Senator John Tower of Texas reported that the plan had emanated from the machinations of McFarlane, Casey, North, some Israelis, and a single Iranian. The Tower Commission found "no direct evidence" that the president knew of the illegal diversion of funds to the Nicaraguan rebels. In remarkably obtuse language, the commission concluded that Reagan had "a concept of the initiative that was not accurately reflected in the reality of the operation." But its members questioned his defense argument that the weapons transactions were mere diplomatic ventures intended to encourage ties with moderates in the Iranian government. The Tower Commission left nearly all key questions unanswered, thereby turning national attention to a congressional inquiry over television from May through July 1987 that proved reminiscent of the Watergate hearings. The tangled web of intrigue pointed to the White House and was akin to the worst sort of dime novel.

For a brief moment, however, the lengthy congressional testimony seemed to confirm the president's pronouncement of a real hero—Lieutenant Colonel Oliver North—who testified for four days that in the name of justice he had participated in the Iran-contra deal. But North's flirtation with stardom quickly burned out when he admitted to having lied to Congress and to shredding evidence just before Justice Department agents arrived to seize the incriminating materials. It was later discovered that much of the alleged grassroots support expressed for North through an avalanche of telegrams had been manufactured by deep-pocketed Republicans who used Western Union to advantage.

The Iran-contra scandal thus moved to some still-unknown end without lifting the cloud of suspicion over the president. To avoid criminal prosecution, North suddenly turned on his superiors and unveiled his close ties with Casey and Poindexter. Shortly afterward, Poindexter effectively stifled any further inquiry into the president's role when he informed the committee that he had destroyed the findings of a presidential investigation into the matter. Poindexter then told the congressional committee that he had not shared the plan with the president and took full blame for the operation. The committee agreed with the Tower Commission that McFarlane (who tried to commit suicide under the strain) had received verbal approval from the president to make the arms arrangements with the Israelis and Iran. But no one could establish a contra connection. As for Casey, he died of a brain tumor before the testimonies began. Without hard evidence, the congressional investigation into the executive's role came to a close.

The U.S. judicial system ultimately took over the case. In March 1988, McFarlane pleaded guilty to withholding information from Congress, a misdemeanor, and was sentenced to two years' probation. North was convicted in mid-1989 of giving false information to Congress, a felony, and received a three-year suspended sentence. The following year, Poindexter was found guilty of five felonious charges of conspiracy, obstructing congressional inquiries, and lying to Congress. The judge ordered him to prison for six months, making Poindexter the only Iran-contra participant to receive a jail sentence.

While the Iran-contra controversy dominated the news in the United States, the crisis in Central America began to ease as the Latin American states themselves developed a plan of settlement between El Salvador and Nicaragua. In January 1983, Colombia, Mexico, Panama, and Venezuela (the "Contadora group") had met on the island of Contadora off Panama and agreed to work toward convincing the five Central American republics to oppose the further involvement of outside powers and to develop a peace resting on democratic principles. Negotiations between Nicaragua and El Salvador, according to the mediators, were the key to a far-reaching regional settlement.

After four years of deliberation, the president of Costa Rica, Oscar Arias Sánchez, offered a settlement in 1987 based on a cease-fire and a general amnesty. Even though Sánchez won the Nobel Peace Prize for his attempt, the White House did not actively support the plan because it provided for continued Sandinista control in Nicaragua while requiring the contras to disband.

Although the crisis had eased, peace in Central America still seemed unattainable. In March 1988, El Salvador and Nicaragua agreed to a truce followed by negotiations aimed at implementing a democratic political process in both countries. The following year, the cancer-stricken Duarte lost the presidential election to the extreme right, making a permanent peace as elusive as ever. The fighting was under way again as Reagan left the presidency.

Other Global Trouble Spots

In other regions of the world, the Reagan administration attempted to exercise U.S. influence, only to encounter obstacles that were often insurmountable. The problems in the Philippines, Africa, Japan, Haiti, and South Korea all lay beyond U.S. control.

Growing popular unrest in the Philippines provides a striking illustration of the Reagan administration's entanglements in foreign affairs. Hesitating to accept the reality of widespread discontent with longtime ally Ferdinand Marcos, the White House continued to support him out of Cold War considerations. In August 1983, Marcos's chief opponent, Benigno Aquino, was assassinated in the Manila airport as he returned from exile in the United States. That event, carried out by Marcos's supporters, became known to the Filipinos primarily through U.S. and Japanese newscasts recorded on VCRs smuggled into the islands, and it quickly set off a wave of bitter protests against his dictatorial, corrupt, and inept rule. The White House recognized that U.S. economic and strategic interests were in danger. Not only were commercial and financial investments heavy in the islands,

but strategic considerations required the United States to hold on to Clark Air Base and the Subic Bay Naval Station—leased from Marcos under terms scheduled to expire in the autumn of 1991. The White House advised Marcos to institute badly needed reforms in the Philippines; Marcos instead continued his despotic policies and thereby stimulated more protests—including the revival of a Communist insurgency under the label of the Nationalist People's Army.

Facing a now thoroughly alienated public, Marcos sought to regain U.S. faith in his rule by permitting elections in February 1986 that he intended to orchestrate. But the opposition put up the widow of the martyred Aquino, Corazon Aquino, who drew widespread popular support in calling for democratic reforms. Marcos's henchmen engaged in massive and unquestioned fraud to salvage his victory, but the Reagan administration blandly affirmed the fairness and honesty of the outcome as proof of "a strong two-party system now in the islands." It soon had to reverse this stance when numerous U.S. observers, including the media, exposed the wrongdoing in the midst of heightening demonstrations and defections by Marcos's top military leaders. Marcos's refusal to accept the verdict of the elections, it became clear, would lead to a long and bloody civil war injurious to U.S. interests on the islands. His long dictatorial reign had to end.

Reagan found this reality difficult to accept. He had liked Marcos since their first meeting in 1969 and believed his fabricated story that he and Filipino guerrillas had heroically helped Americans against the Japanese in World War II. Now, in a remarkable turn of events, Reagan relented to the urgings of Shultz and other advisers in asking Marcos by phone to resign and leave the country. By the end of the month, Marcos gave in to U.S. pressure and, transported on a U.S. Air Force plane with his wife Imelda and a cargo of wealth amassed by racketeering and other such activities, arrived in Hawaii to live in exile. The new president of the Philippines was Corazon Aquino.

The Philippines remained a serious concern for the White House that it could not resolve. Aquino received an enthusiastic welcome in the United States when she addressed Congress in September 1986, but she proved unable to stem either the rampant corruption or the Communist insurgency that had spread into almost every one of the country's provinces. In 1990, the Communists even forced the Peace Corps to withdraw after threatening to kidnap its workers. As one Aquino supporter quipped, "Ali Baba Marcos fled, leaving behind the forty thieves." American aid funds all but dried up, primarily because of its own economic troubles at home. Natural calamities then struck the islands, further obstructing the chances for change.

There was reason for hope, however. Aquino managed to introduce some political and economic reforms, and in the next election she cast her support for its winner, General Fidel Ramos, who had been one of the early defectors from Marcos. Under Marcos's rule, the Philippines had been a democracy in name only, forcing the White House to break with an ally having no popular base of support. In 1992, the United States went even farther in placing the Philippines more on its own: it implemented a huge reduction in military commitment to Asia that included giving up its two bases in the Philippines after almost a century of control.

Africa posed another major problem that the Reagan administration found impossible to manage. Not only did famine and civil wars threaten to devastate large parts of the huge continent, but Soviet and Cuban soldiers continued to influence events in Angola and Ethiopia while apartheid lay at the heart of increasing racial violence in South Africa. With regard to South Africa, many Americans criticized President Reagan for failing to react strongly enough against the white government's segregationist policies. Instead of calling on American business leaders to "divest" their holdings in South Africa, Reagan argued that the United States lacked sufficient leverage to force a rapid change and supported a calm and business-oriented approach called "constructive engagement." Under this program, he intended to build better diplomatic and economic ties in an effort to influence leaders to alter their racial policies over an extended period of time. In all instances, however, the Reagan administration found itself unable to exert real leadership, largely because these matters lay beyond its control.

Reagan's policies toward Africa were a failure. As most of the 350 American businesses in South Africa rejected divestiture, Congress reacted to public pressure and imposed economic sanctions on that nation in mid-1986—but only after overriding the president's veto. The measure proved effective. Soon more than half of the American firms had pulled out of South Africa. Two-and-a-half years later, in December 1988, pressure eased in Africa when Angola, Cuba, and South Africa agreed to a UN plan supported by both the United States and the Soviet Union. Within the next two years, according to terms, Cuban troops would withdraw from Angola, and the last colony in Africa, uranium-rich Namibia, would become independent of South African rule. Apartheid remained in South Africa, but the white government in Pretoria under President F. W. de Klerk showed signs in early 1990 of relenting to the pressure. It ended a thirty-year ban on the highly influential black organization the African National Congress and, over worldwide television, released its leader, Nelson Mandela, who had been in prison for twenty-seven years and immediately resumed his political battle against apartheid.

Still another problem raised questions about the effectiveness of Reagan's foreign policy: the ever-growing trade deficit with Japan. The United States maintained military bases in the possessions of its former foe in World War II and considered Japan a valuable ally against Soviet influence in Asia. But Japan had expanded its commercial arm so rapidly that the United States soon confronted a powerful Cold War supporter who had become an even more powerful commercial rival. The

Japanese offered better products at lower prices, which created a highly unfavorable balance of trade for the United States and resulted in a slowed U.S. economy and the loss of jobs.

As the ranks of the unemployed increased in the United States, Americans blamed Japan for much of their troubles. In truth, numerous other factors contributed to this dire economic situation: the higher cost of U.S. goods in foreign markets along with the lower cost of foreign goods in the U.S. market, foreign ownership or control of U.S. industrial and financial assets as well as foreign claims on the national debt, and the greatly restricted capacity of Third World peoples to buy U.S. goods because of their own governments' heavy debts, which endangered the Western banking system by putting billions of dollars into possible default. But it was *Japan* that drew the brunt of Americans' anger.

Again, the Reagan administration found itself groping for a policy. As increasing numbers of Americans (many of them speaking for special interest groups) placed pressure on Congress to pass high protective tariffs to keep out Japanese goods, the Tokyo government tried to stem this move in 1985 by announcing limits on certain key exports to the United States (including automobiles) and ensuring reductions in its own tariff barriers. President Reagan did not regard these actions as enough, however, and in 1987 he barred the further entry of selected Japanese goods. The following year, Congress passed the Omnibus Trade and Competitiveness Act, which allowed retaliatory tariffs against countries pursuing a program of commercial restrictions. American–Japanese commercial animosity remained a major sore spot as Reagan left the presidency.

The Reagan administration could claim some credit in early 1986 for the demise of other long-time dictators considered "friendly" to the United States. To Congress in March, the president suggested a new direction in foreign policy when he broke from the Kirkpatrick dictum favoring authoritarian over totalitarian regimes and proclaimed that "the American people believe in human rights and oppose tyranny in whatever form, whether of the left or the right." In Haiti, the White House warned Jean-Claude ("Baby Doc") Duvalier not to use force on Haitians demonstrating against his rule, and when it became evident that he had lost control, it facilitated his departure to France. The following year, the White House applied the new principles to South Korea, where the military regime encountered violent protests and, under U.S. pressure, agreed to democratic elections for the presidency. Reagan denied having taken the approach advocated by Carter in Iran and Nicaragua—that of undermining rightist regimes favorably inclined to the United States. The changes in government, Reagan insisted, had emanated from domestic pressures that his administration regarded as too strong to resist.

The White House had found it exceedingly difficult to influence other countries' policies. In the Philippines, the president at first insisted on maintaining ties with Marcos but finally relented after popular resistance to his rule became impossible to contain. And in 1986 and 1987, Reagan had no choice but to support popular demands for changes in Haiti and South Korea that led to the ousting of regimes long supported by the White House. Problems in Africa were also beyond the capacity of the United States to control or guide. Indeed, the Reagan administration's reluctance to support divestiture in South Africa placed it on the opposite side of a black majority that continued to move toward a dominant leadership role. Finally, the administration failed to accept Japan's growing economic prominence and made no concerted effort to establish a reciprocal trade relationship. The increasingly diffused power structure in the world dictated that no single nation had the resources to determine all events.

Reagan in Perspective

Although the Reagan White House made military and economic efforts to restore the

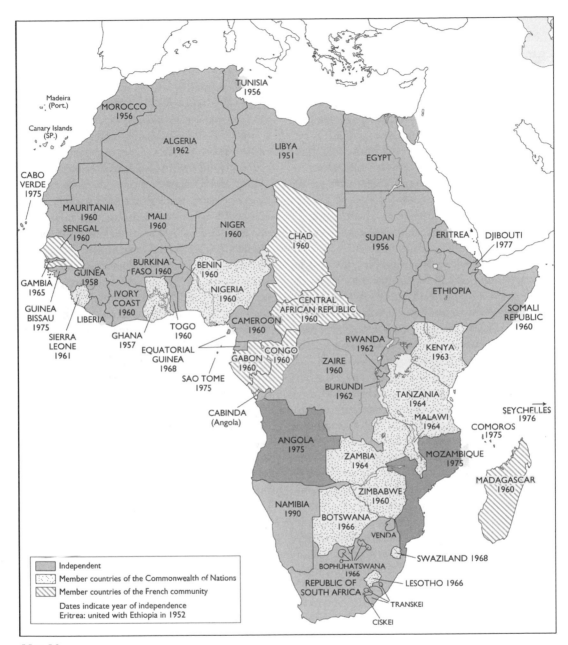

Independent

Member countries of the Commonwealth of Nations

Member countries of the French community

Dates indicate year of independence
Eritrea: united with Ethiopia in 1952

Map 10
Post–World War II Africa. The emerging nations in postcolonial Africa made that huge continent a vital part of the new world order. *(Source: author)*

global status of the United States and keep the Western alliance intact, it too quickly relegated diplomacy to a military-oriented foreign policy. Indeed, the military-industrial complex was vital to the president's political coalition and guided most of his decision making. Early in his first administration, Reagan publicly and unnecessarily whipped up bitter animosity toward the Soviet Union. He then tied Central America's longtime troubles to the Cold War, globalizing a local or regional issue and further intensifying his problems with the Soviet Union and with Congress. Moreover, his aid to the contras prolonged the bloody conflict in Central America. The Middle East remained a tinderbox, also made worse by Reagan's ill-advised attempt to inject the Cold War into ancient indigenous issues by his tragic misjudgment in sending U.S. troops to Lebanon and by his involvement (whether total or partial) in the shadowy Iran-contra affair. Indeed, his administration managed to link two failing policies into one: that in Central America with that in the Middle East.

As Reagan's second term came to a close, the Cold War appeared to be winding down, but even that monumental result was attributable primarily to the efforts of Soviet Leader Mikhail Gorbachev. If Reagan's supporters were correct in declaring that the U.S. arms buildup had put such severe strains on the Soviet Union that it had to call off the Cold War and give priority to domestic affairs, they could not deny that such an approach had proved enormously costly: the United States stirred up nightmarish fears of nuclear destruction and likewise diminished its own power by lowering taxes while raising military defense expenditures and thereby tripling the national debt to $3 trillion in 1989 (a third of which was run up in the Reagan years alone). In just four years, the United States had undergone a revolutionary change in position from the world's number one creditor nation in 1981 to the world's largest debtor nation in 1985. Not since World War I had the United States been in debt.

Two years later, in October 1987, fears of another Great Depression developed when the stock market collapsed in response to global financial problems encouraged by Reagan's economic policies. Even as the Soviet Union's drive for *perestroika* and *glasnost* had unleashed powerful nationalist forces both at home and abroad that required diplomatic rather than military solutions, the United States found itself shackled by enormous domestic and foreign problems that necessitated the same sort of reasoned diplomatic response. Gorbachev confronted these issues by looking ahead to a new world order; Reagan looked backward in trying to restore the old.

Still unlearned was the central truth resulting from the nation's Vietnam experience and now underlined by the dramatic thawing of the Cold War: the United States was no longer the chief determinant in international affairs. Among the entities vying for the top role was the revitalized United Nations, which was composed of many peoples and had slowly but steadily grown in prominence by mediating settlements in numerous trouble spots in the world. Perhaps the grand hope of 1945—that the United Nations would become the supreme arbiter of world difficulties—was about to transpire. All these problems and more awaited Reagan's successor, former Vice President George Bush.

Selected Readings

Allin, Dana H. *Cold War Illusions: America, Europe, and Soviet Power, 1969–1989.* 1995.

Ambrose, Stephen E., and Douglas G. Brinkley. *Rise to Globalism: American Foreign Policy since 1938.* 8th ed., 1997.

Armony, Ariel C. *Argentina, the United States, and the Anti-Communist Crusade in Central America, 1977–1984.* 1997.

Armstrong, R., and J. Shenk. *El Salvador: The Face of Revolution.* 1982.

Arnson, Cynthia. *Crossroads: Congress, the President, and Central America, 1976–1993.* 1994.

———. *El Salvador: A Revolution Confronts the United States.* 1982.

Baker, Pauline H. *The United States and South Africa: The Reagan Years.* 1989.

Ball, George W. *Error and Betrayal in Lebanon.* 1984.

Barrett, Lawrence I. *Gambling with History: Ronald Reagan in the White House.* 1983.

Bell, Coral. *The Reagan Paradox: American Foreign Policy in the 1980s.* 1989.

Berman, Larry, ed. *Looking Back on the Reagan Presidency.* 1990.

Berman, William C. *America's Right Turn: From Nixon to Clinton.* 2nd ed., 1998.

Bermann, Karl. *Under the Big Stick: Nicaragua and the United States since 1848.* 1986.

Bialer, Seweryn, and Michael Mandelbaum, eds. *Gorbachev's Russia and American Foreign Policy.* 1988.

Bill, James A. *The Eagle and the Lion: The Tragedy of American-Iranian Relations.* 1988.

Blacker, Coit D. *Reluctant Warriors: The United States, the Soviet Union and Arms Control.* 1987.

Bonner, Raymond. *Waltzing with a Dictator: The Marcoses and the Making of American Policy.* 1987.

Bradlee, Ben, Jr. *Guts and Glory: The Rise and Fall of Oliver North.* 1988.

Brands, H. W. *Bound to Empire: The United States and the Philippines.* 1992.

———. *The Devil We Knew: Americans and the Cold War.* 1993.

Buckley, Roger. *U.S.-Japan Alliance Diplomacy, 1945–1990.* 1992.

Burns, E. Bradford. *At War in Nicaragua.* 1987.

Burton, Sandra. *Impossible Dream: The Marcoses, the Aquinos, and the Unfinished Revolution.* 1989.

Cannon, Lou. *President Reagan: The Role of a Lifetime.* 1991.

Chace, James. *Endless War: How We Got Involved in Central America.* 1984.

Cimbala, Stephen J. *The Reagan Defense Program.* 1986.

Cockburn, Leslie. *Out of Control: The Story of the Reagan Administration's Secret War in Nicaragua, the Illegal Arms Pipeline, and the Contra Drug Connection.* 1988.

Cohen, Warren I. *America's Response to China: An Interpretive History of Sino-American Relations.* 2000.

Coker, Christopher. *The United States and South Africa, 1968–1985.* 1986.

Coleman, Kenneth M., and George C. Herring, eds. *The Central American Crisis: Sources of Conflict and the Failure of U.S. Policy.* 1985.

Dallek, Robert. *The American Style of Foreign Policy.* 1983.

———. *Ronald Reagan: The Politics of Symbolism.* 1984.

Dallin, Alexander. *Black Box: KAL 007 and the Superpowers.* 1985.

Didion, Joan. *Salvador.* 1983.

Diederich, Bernard. *Somoza and the Legacy of U.S. Involvement in Central America.* 1981.

Drell, Sidney, et al. *The Reagan Strategic Defense Initiative.* 1985.

Drew, Elizabeth. *Portrait of an Election: The 1980 Presidential Campaign.* 1981.

Duignan, Peter, and Lewis H. Gann. *The United States and Africa: A History.* 1984.

Ehrman, John. *The Rise of Neoconservatism: Intellectuals and Foreign Affairs, 1945–1994.* 1995.

Emerson, Steve. *Secret Warriors: Inside the Covert Military Operations of the Reagan Era.* 1988.

Ewell, Judith. "Barely in the Inner Circle: Jeane Kirkpatrick." In Edward P. Crapol, ed. *Women and American Foreign Policy: Lobbyists, Critics, and Insiders,* 153–71. 1987; 2nd ed., 1992.

Falcoff, Mark, and Robert Royal. *Crisis and Opportunity: U.S. Policy in Central America and the Caribbean.* 1984.

Fisk, Robert. *Pity the Nation: The Abduction of Lebanon.* 1990.

Friedman, Thomas L. *From Beirut to Jerusalem.* 1989.

Gaddis, John L. *The Cold War: A New History.* 2005.

———. *The Long Peace: Inquiries into the History of the Cold War.* 1987.

———. *Russia, the Soviet Union, and the United States: An Interpretive History.* 2nd ed., 1990.

———. *Strategies of Containment: A Critical Appraisal of Postwar American National Security Policy.* 1982; rev. ed., 2005.

Gardner, Lloyd C. *A Covenant with Power: America and World Order from Wilson to Reagan.* 1984.

Garthoff, Raymond L. *Détente and Confrontation: American-Soviet Relations from Nixon to Reagan.* 1994.

———. *The Great Transition: American-Soviet Relations and the End of the Cold War.* 1994.

Gettleman, Marvin E., et al., eds. *El Salvador: Central America in the New Cold War.* 1981.

Goode, James E. *The United States and Iran: In the Shadow of Musaddiq.* 1997.

Gorbachev, Mikhail. *Perestroika: New Thinking for Our Country and the World.* 1987.

Greenstein, Fred I., ed. *The Reagan Presidency: An Early Assessment.* 1983.

Gutman, Roy. *Banana Diplomacy: The Making of American Policy in Nicaragua, 1981–1987.* 1988.

Haig, Alexander M., Jr. *Caveat: Realism, Reagan, and Foreign Policy.* 1984.

Harding, Harry. *A Fragile Relationship: The United States and China since 1972.* 1992.

Haslam, Jonathan. *The Soviet Union and the Politics of Nuclear Weapons in Europe, 1969–87.* 1990.

Hersh, Seymour M. *"The Target Is Destroyed": What Really Happened to Flight 007 and What America Knew about It.* 1986.

Hull, Richard W. *American Enterprise in South Africa: Historical Dimensions of Engagement and Disengagement.* 1990.

Hunt, Michael H. *Ideology and U.S. Foreign Policy.* 1987.

Hyland, William. *Mortal Rivals: Superpower Relations from Nixon to Reagan.* 1987.

Jabber, Paul. *Not by War Alone: Security and Arms Control in the Middle East.* 1981.

Jentleson, Bruce. *Pipeline Politics.* 1986.

Johnson, Haynes. *Sleepwalking through History: America in the Reagan Years.* 1991.

Karnow, Staley. *In Our Image: America's Empire in the Philippines.* 1989.

Kenworthy, Eldon. *America/Américas: Myth in the Making of U.S. Policy toward Latin America.* 1995.

Kikkink, Kathryn. *Mixed Signals: U.S. Human Rights Policy and Latin America.* 2004.

Kirkpatrick, Jeane J. *Dictatorship and Double Standards.* 1982.

Klare, Michael T., and Cynthia Arnson. *Supplying Suppression: U.S. Support for Authoritarian Regimes Abroad.* 1981.

Kolko, Gabriel. *Confronting the Third World.* 1988.

LaFeber, Walter. *America, Russia, and the Cold War, 1945–1996.* 8th ed., 1997.

———. *The Clash: A History of U.S.-Japan Relations.* 1997.

———. *Inevitable Revolutions: The United States in Central America.* 1989.

Lake, Anthony. *Somoza Falling, The Nicaraguan Dilemma: A Portrait of Washington at Work.* 1989.

Laqueur, Walter. *The Age of Terrorism.* 1987.

Ledeen, Michael A. *Perilous Statecraft: An Insider's Account of the Iran-Contra Affair.* 1988.

LeoGrande, William M. *Our Own Backyard: The United States in Central America, 1977–1992.* 1998.

Levering, Ralph B. *The Cold War: A Post-Cold War History.* 1994; rev. ed., 2005.

Love, Janice. *The U.S. Anti-Apartheid Movement: Local Activism in Global Politics.* 1985.

Lowenthal, Abraham F. *Partners in Conflict: The U.S. and Latin America.* 1987.

Mann, Jim. *About Face: A History of America's Curious Relationship with China from Nixon to Clinton.* 1999.

Martin, David C., and John Walcott. *Best Laid Plans: The Inside Story of America's War against Terrorism.* 1988.

Massie, Robert. *Loosing the Bonds: The United States and South Africa in the Apartheid Years.* 1997.

Mayer, Jane, and Doyle McManus. *Landslide: The Unmaking of the President, 1984–1988.* 1988.

Melanson, Richard A. *American Foreign Policy since the Vietnam War: The Search for Consensus from Nixon to Clinton.* 2000.

———, ed. *Neither Cold War nor Détente? Soviet-American Relations in the 1980s.* 1982.

Menges, Constantine C. *Inside the National Security Council: The True Story of the Making and Unmaking of Reagan's Foreign Policy.* 1988.

Meredith, Martin. *In the Name of Apartheid: South Africa in the Postwar Period.* 1988.

Montgomery, Tommie S. *Revolution in El Salvador.* 1982.

Morley, Morris. *Imperial State and Revolution.* 1987.

Morris, Roger. *Haig: The General's Progress.* 1982.

Mower, A. Glenn. *Human Rights and American Foreign Policy: The Carter and Reagan Experiences.* 1987.

Nesbitt, Francis N. *Race for Sanctions: African Americans against Apartheid, 1946–1994.* 2004.

Oberdorfer, Don. *From the Cold War to a New Era: The United States and the Soviet Union, 1983–1991.* 1998.

———. *The Turn: From the Cold War to a New Era. The United States and the Soviet Union, 1983–1990.* 1991.

Olson, Robert. *U.S. Foreign Policy and the New International Economic Order.* 1981.

Oye, Kenneth A., Robert J. Lieber, and Donald Rothchild, eds. *Eagle Resurgent? The Reagan Era in American Foreign Policy.* 1987.

Pastor, Robert A. *Condemned to Repetition.* 1987.

Peretz, Don. *Intifada: The Palestinian Uprising.* 1990.

Pérez, Louis A., Jr. *Cuba and the United States: Ties of Singular Intimacy.* 1997.

Pierre, Andrew J. *The Global Politics of Arms Sales.* 1982.

Prados, John. *Presidents' Secret Wars: CIA Pentagon Covert Operations from World War II through the Persian Gulf.* 1996.

Prestowitz, Clyde V., Jr. *Trading Places: How We Are Giving Our Future to Japan and How to Reclaim It.* 1989.

Pryce-Jones, David. *The Closed Circle: An Interpretation of the Arabs.* 1989.

Raat, W. Dirk. *Mexico and the United States: Ambivalent Vistas.* 1996.

Reagan, Ronald. *Speaking My Mind.* 1989.

Rubin, Barry. *Secrets of State: The State Department and the Struggle over U.S. Foreign Policy.* 1985.

Sayigh, Yezid. *Armed Struggle and the Search for State: The Palestinian National Movement, 1949–1993.* 1997.

Schell, Jonathan. *The Fate of the Earth.* 1982.

Schoutz, Lars. *Beneath the United States: A History of U.S. Policy toward Latin America.* 1998.

———. *National Security and U.S. Policy toward Latin America.* 1987.

Schulzinger, Robert D. *The Wise Men of Foreign Affairs: The History of the Council on Foreign Relations.* 1984.

Scranton, Margaret E. *The Noriega Years: U.S.-Panamanian Relations, 1981–1990.* 1991.

Shafer, Michael D. *Deadly Paradigms: The Failure of U.S. Counterinsurgency Policy.* 1988.

Shipler, David K. *Arab and Jew: Wounded Spirits in a Promised Land.* 1986.

Shultz, George P. *Turmoil and Triumph: My Years as Secretary of State.* 1993.

Sick, Gary. *October Surprise: America's Hostages in Iran and the Election of Ronald Reagan.* 1991.

Sklar, Holly. *Washington's War on Nicaragua.* 1988.

Smith, Gaddis. *The Last Years of the Monroe Doctrine, 1945–1993.* 1994.

Spanier, John W. *American Foreign Policy since World War II.* 14th ed., 1998.

Spiegel, Steven L. *The Other Arab-Israeli Conflict: Making America's Middle East Policy, from Truman to Reagan.* 1985.

Stares, Paul B. *The Militarization of Space: U.S. Policy, 1945–1984.* 1985.

———. *Space and National Security.* 1987.

Stevenson, Richard W. *The Rise and Fall of Détente: Relaxations of Tensions in US-Soviet Relations, 1953–84.* 1985.

Talbott, Strobe. *Deadly Gambits: The Reagan Administration and the Stalemate in Nuclear Arms Control.* 1984.

———. *The Master of the Game: Paul Nitze and the Nuclear Peace.* 1988.

———. *The Russians and Reagan.* 1984.

Ulam, Adam B. *The Communists: The Story of Power and Lost Illusions, 1948–1991.* 1992.

Van Crefeld, Martin. *Nuclear Proliferation and the Future of Conflict.* 1993.

Vanderlaan, Mary B. *Revolution and Foreign Policy in Nicaragua.* 1986.

Walker, Thomas W. *Nicaragua: The Land of Sandino.* 1982.

———. *Revolution and Counterrevolution in Nicaragua, 1977–1989.* 1990.

———, ed. *Reagan versus the Sandinistas.* 1987.

Weinberger, Caspar. *Fighting for Peace: Seven Critical Years in the Pentagon.* 1990.

Weiner, Tim. *Legacy of Ashes: The History of the CIA.* 2007.

Westad, Odd Arne. *The Global Cold War: Third World Interventions and the Making of Our Times.* 2006.

Wills, Garry. *Reagan's America: Innocents at Home.* 1987.

Wittner, Lawrence S. *Toward Nuclear Abolition: A History of the World Nuclear Disarmament Movement, 1971 to the Present.* 2003.

Woodward, Bob. *Veil: The Secret Wars of the CIA, 1981–1987.* 1987.

CHAPTER 9

The End of the Cold War and the Outbreak of Regional Conflicts, 1989–2001

Overview

When Vice President George Bush became president in January 1989, he showed little understanding of the ongoing revolutionary events that brought the Cold War to a close. A staunch Cold Warrior, he had served as a naval pilot in World War II before becoming involved in Texas oil and politics and then arriving in Washington as a congressional representative in 1968. After losing a bid for the Senate, his fortunes changed during the 1970s as he served as ambassador to the United Nations, U.S. representative to China, and director of the CIA before becoming vice president in 1981. Enormous changes in the Cold War atmosphere had begun during the latter half of the Reagan presidency when Mikhail Gorbachev launched his reform programs of *perestroika* and *glasnost* while pursuing massive arms reductions, drastic cutbacks in his own conventional forces, and surprising withdrawals from foreign commitments. But skeptics wondered if this were not another Soviet trick designed to relax the guard of the United States or, if true, whether Gorbachev's successors would (or could) continue such a liberal program. The Bush strategy emerged from an internal policy review following the

Malta Summit of December 1989. In the words of U.S. Ambassador to the Soviet Union Jack Matlock, "Our marching orders are clear: Don't do something, stand there!" The Soviets dubbed it the *pauza*—the pause.

Given the long and bitter history of the Cold War, the new president initially adopted a standoffish policy toward these dramatic events. Whether he simply failed to fathom their importance or shrewdly pursued a careful if not dubious reaction, he continued the Reagan administration's emphasis on national defense and chose not to encourage or exploit these world-shaking events by taking any diplomatic or economic initiative. Still, an unmistakable pattern in executive leadership soon emerged. Even as the United States sank deeper into a major economic recession, Bush preferred to let problems take care of themselves while often denying that they existed. In one of the most momentous events of the twentieth century—the approaching end of the Cold War—Bush sat quietly by as Gorbachev almost single-handedly wound down international tensions in a desperate effort to save the remnants of a once-proud Soviet empire.

The rapidly changing global situation dictated a flexible U.S. approach to foreign affairs, but Bush continued his predecessor's rigid Cold War policy, leaving little room for adjustments to changing realities. Long-time friend James Baker became secretary of state. A master politician, Baker knew little about foreign policy, which meant that Bush would take the lead. Most important, Bush intended to seek a Soviet détente while supporting the U.S. military buildup and the Strategic Defense Initiative. He planned to tighten the NATO alliance, continue the fight against communism in Central America, press for peace in the Middle East, maintain the gradualist approach in dealing with apartheid in South Africa, seek commercial accommodations with Japan, strive for better relations with China, and wage war on the escalating international drug trade. Despite a vastly changing world, the Bush administration intended to perpetuate a military-oriented foreign policy that aimed at stemming a shrinking Soviet influence.

The president thus stood as a passive observer of nearly all the epochal developments that ended the Cold War era. Despite landmark changes in the Soviet Union and Eastern Europe, he formulated no comprehensive strategy for dealing with a nascent post–Cold War period. Instead, he exercised a cautious wait-and-see policy that reflected the weakened U.S. economic situation as much as an effort to restrict his country's involvement in these historic events. The United States was the world's leading debtor nation, and the new president had pledged throughout the campaign that he and his Republican Party would never raise taxes. He also prided himself as unemotional and extremely cautious, hesitant to take any action until events had assumed a meaningful form. As the world stumbled toward a new order, the United States failed to exert effective leadership.

Disintegration of the Soviet Union and the End of the Cold War

Developments inside the Soviet Union continued to assume world-shattering propor-

tions. Shortly after Bush became president, democratic elections took place in the Soviet Union for the first time since the Russian Revolution of 1917. Most surprising to Gorbachev and outside observers, the Communist Party lost a large number of seats in the national assembly. Gorbachev's call for *perestroika* did not revive the economy and thoroughly discredited his cohort. Despite his confidence that the Soviet people would work with his party in instituting economic reform, they broke with the long-hated and increasingly impotent Communist regime and moved toward a decentralized government and a free-market economy.

The fallout from *perestroika* thus went farther than Gorbachev could have anticipated. It unleashed powerful forces of nationalism inside the sprawling Soviet empire that threatened to tear it apart and leave behind a multitude of ethnic, racial, and religious disputes. In the far northwest, the three Baltic States of Estonia, Latvia, and Lithuania sought to regain their independence, lost a half-century before; and in the oil-rich area lying south between the Black and Caspian seas, ancient animosities between Muslims in Azerbaijan and Christians in Armenia exploded in a bitter conflict. Gorbachev reacted only mildly to events along the Baltic, but when Azerbaijan threatened to secede from the Soviet Union and come under the control of the popular front, he sent 30,000 soldiers to restore order.

In truth, President Bush could have done little to shape these epoch-making events. The dire economic situation in the United States precluded substantial assistance to the great masses of people seeking change. Besides, these unstable areas lay within the Soviet sphere of influence. Bush and his advisers studied the developments inside the Soviet Union and adopted what they called a "status-quo plus" approach. Whatever the administration's policymakers meant by that innocuous term, they intended primarily to watch. In the meantime, the president claimed victory in the Cold War and attributed that success to the containment strategy. Gor-

bachev, Bush asserted, must now cut back Soviet influence in Eastern Europe and the Third
World as well.

To the president's surprise, Gorbachev
abandoned his country's interventionist policy. Moscow extended no military assistance to
the tottering Communist regime in Poland,
which had no choice but to legalize Solidarity under Lech Walesa's leadership. Soon afterward, Solidarity demanded and received a
primary leadership role in Warsaw, adding
more weight to the Nobel Peace Prize won by
Walesa in 1981 for bringing peaceful reform
to his country. Then, in an astonishing move,
Gorbachev in July 1989 renounced the right
of any nation to interfere with the sovereignty
of another, thus laying to rest the roundly despised Brezhnev Doctrine that had led to the
military subjugation of Czechoslovakia and
other East European countries.

Gorbachev's restraint astounded observers
in both East and West. The Hungarian government, long regarded as the most liberal of
those behind the Iron Curtain, tore down the
150 miles of barbed wire that made up its border with Austria. Almost immediately, thousands of East Germans looking for family and
loved ones flocked into Hungary and then
into Austria before relocating in West Germany. Soon afterward, a massive popular uprising in Czechoslovakia (with participants
chanting "We are not like them" in the streets
of Prague) likewise brought an end to Communist control and culminated in the election
of playwright Václav Havel as president. For
a time, the Communist parties in Bulgaria and
Romania held on to power only by changing
their names in the first democratic elections
after the Soviet collapse and assuring their
reform-minded people that they too had

President Bush and Lech Walesa
The president meets with Poland's Solidarity leader in the residence of the White House, November 14,
1989. *(George Bush Library, College Station, Texas)*

President Bush and Václav Havel
The president greets the Czech president outside
the White House on February 20, 1990. *(George
Bush Library, College Station, Texas)*

reformed. Only in Romania did violence
erupt. The aged tyrant Nicolae Ceaucescu was
the only Communist ruler in Eastern Europe
to resist the reformers with military force; the
effort failed, albeit just barely, and he and his
wife were executed following a quick trial.

On November 9, 1989, the East German
government set off the most dramatic series
of events of all when it admitted to the reality of the mass exodus already under way by
announcing the right of its people to leave
the country. Within a week, on November
15, East German workers began tearing
down the Berlin Wall, the drab twelve-foot-
tall concrete and barbed-wire barrier that had
been the ultimate symbol of Soviet oppression for twenty-eight years. More than any
single act, the human demolition of this tan-

gible reminder of the dark past marked the
end of the Cold War.

In the face of such great changes, Bush
maintained a course of what he termed "prudence," which his detractors derisively called
"timidity." Critics argued that he should seize
the moment to work closely with Gorbachev
in establishing good post–Cold War relations
by extending economic aid to the crumbling
Soviet empire. At the least, many declared, he
could grant most-favored-nation status to the
Soviet Union and thereby give its commerce
an advantage in the U.S. market. Did not the
administration permit this same privilege to
China, even after its Communist regime had
brutally unleashed tanks and soldiers against
students in Beijing (discussed later) who had
peacefully demonstrated for freedom that previous June? The president was correct in declaring that the nation's containment policy
had encouraged the Soviet demise, but, un-
fortunately for the White House in 1989, the
architect of that policy, George F. Kennan,
had not provided guidelines for a U.S. response should those sweeping changes actually occur.

Bush realized that any sort of aid package
to the Soviet Union would be problematic.
The United States had its own economic troubles, and Americans would be reluctant to
help a longtime distrusted empire that still adhered to Communist principles. Moreover,
Bush could not have known whether the Soviet Union would survive the rapidly spreading political assault at home. Even if a
decentralized and much weakened Soviet
Union remained in the aftermath, its deep
structural changes would have international
repercussions not necessarily beneficial to the
United States. The imminent collapse of the
Soviet threat to European security meant that
NATO would lose its chief reason for existence; indeed, the European nations had already begun to work out their own problems.
They established the European Community
to advance economic development through a
single market, and they turned more to an organization founded in Helsinki in 1975 to

deal with political and human rights issues, the Conference on Security and Cooperation in Europe (CSCE). The United States was only one of thirty-five CSCE participants and did not wield a deciding influence.

If the times had changed, the Bush administration refused to change with them. In a crucial period that required new approaches to a world no longer burdened by the Cold War, the president continued Reagan's example of working with Gorbachev toward a greater nuclear arms reduction. On December 2 and 4, 1989, the two heads of state met on an informal basis off Malta in the Mediterranean, where they agreed to work toward limitations on both their nuclear stores and conventional weaponry and to integrate the Soviet Union into the global economy. But Bush, on his return to Washington, rejected proposals to reduce the long-standing twenty-four-hour airborne defense system and to cut the defense budget for 1990. Furthermore, he intended to maintain the heavy military presence of the United States in Germany. The White House should have established good relations with the Soviet Union, according to Kennan's testimony before the Senate Foreign Relations Committee in 1989; instead, it maintained the U.S. military arsenal for a possible confrontation with a Red Army then beating a fast retreat in Eastern Europe.

The chief European issue throughout the Cold War—the status of Germany—now emerged as the chief point of divisiveness between Bush and Gorbachev. Bush was at first hesitant to support reunification until it became clear he could do nothing to stop it. He then did an about-face to argue that failing to support Germany's unification could force it to become neutral in the East–West struggle and thereby endanger continental stability. A unified Germany must be part of both NATO and the European Community. Gorbachev, however, joined France and Britain in staunchly opposing German reunification. If his efforts failed, Gorbachev preferred a neutral Germany rather than one allied with NATO. He also sought limitations on the size

of Germany's army, a ban on its acquisition of nuclear arms, its acceptance of the boundary fronting Poland that the victorious powers had drawn in 1945 (farther west of the Soviet Union), and a continued U.S. military presence in Europe that prevented the rise of another militarized German nation. In all these aspects, however, neither superpower had the capacity to determine the outcome. Gorbachev finally accepted a reunited Germany in NATO—a decision facilitated by Germany's extending $8 billion of credit to the Soviet Union.

In February 1990, the revolutionary changes inside the Soviet Union brought the most stunning news of all: the Communist Party lost control of the government it had held since 1917. Opposition parties won a series of elections in the spring that included the installation of Gorbachev's onetime protégé turned bitter political rival, Boris Yeltsin, as the leader of the Russian Federation. As the largest Soviet republic, Russia made up two-thirds of the former Soviet Union in size and nearly half its people and was rich in oil and other natural resources. Gorbachev regarded Yeltsin, who had risen from abject poverty, as too strongly reformist and had effectively undermined his influence in the Communist Party by a Stalinist-type purge just three years earlier. But Yeltsin bounced back as a virtual martyr of *perestroika*, demanding a complete restructuring of the country and openly brandishing a popular mandate that Gorbachev himself could not claim: Gorbachev's presidential position had resulted primarily from the closed-door maneuverings of Communist Party leaders in the Supreme Soviet. Gorbachev now stood in the unenviable position of having to balance the demands of reformers and the complaints of embittered Communist Party members. As the hard-liners used military force to prevent Lithuania's departure from the Soviet Union, he realized that further moves toward reform could spark stronger actions against dissidents.

Bush continued to support Gorbachev, even while Yeltsin's steadily growing influence

President Bush and Boris Yeltsin
The president and the Russian Republic president speak to the press from the colonnade in the Rose Garden of the White House on June 20, 1991. *(George Bush Library, College Station, Texas)*

became evident. The president felt a personal tie with the Soviet leader that was matched only by his equally strong personal distaste for Yeltsin. More important, Yeltsin's reformist ideas encouraged the further breakup of the Soviet Union, which ensured uncertainty and confusion. Gorbachev was a known quantity, popular with Americans and a recipient of the Nobel Peace Prize in 1990 for his work in ending the Cold War. White House stories at first sharply criticized Yeltsin, and then, in another remarkable reversal of tactics, the president hosted the Russian challenger in an effort to convince him of the wisdom of developing close ties with Gorbachev. To enhance Gorbachev's image, Bush cut back on U.S. nuclear expenditures and placements of the arsenal and then cooperated with him in reducing nuclear and conventional weaponry on the European continent in 1991.

Bush's decision to stay with Gorbachev turned out to be a mistake. While the United States was in peace negotiations ending its Gulf War with Iraq in 1991 (discussed later), Soviet hard-liners rose in rebellion against Gorbachev, placing him under house arrest and clamping down on the country's people and news media. Military officers had long been angry at Gorbachev for doing nothing to deter the surrender of Eastern Europe and reunification of Germany and thereby giving up all they had won in World War II. Then, in the Gulf War, Gorbachev infuriated Soviet military officers by working closely with Bush against an Iraqi force that they had advised and supplied. Their disgust with the recent turn of events grew into a suspicion that their leader intended to tie the Soviet Union to the United States. When Gorbachev agreed with nine of the fifteen Soviet republics to establish a confederation that decentralized authority by guaranteeing sovereignty to each member, eight disgruntled civilian and military leaders took over the government on the day before the treaty-signing proceedings of August 20, 1991.

The August 19 coup only at first appeared to be successful. After seizing Gorbachev, the military turned on Yeltsin and his Russian colleagues, who were in a building close to the Kremlin. But Yeltsin's group proclaimed support for Gorbachev's legitimacy and refused to capitulate to the old guard. By that time, thousands of Yeltsin's supporters had gathered outside the building, forcing the military into making the hard decision of whether to launch an assault. The army decided not to do so. At that point, the coup attempt fell apart, the victim not only of diminishing numbers and aging ideas but also of liquor: several leaders were intoxicated. Gorbachev, however, paid a heavy price for clinging to office. Shortly after arriving on the scene, he declared victory over the coup when he found that seven of its leaders were under arrest and the eighth had committed suicide. But the crisis only seemed to have passed. Observers now questioned Gorbachev's judgment. It was he, after all, who had placed these same traitorous men in top-level positions. More important, Gorbachev faced a country that had taken on a radically different political complexion—one no longer supportive of the Communist Party and ideology.

Yeltsin suddenly emerged as the stronger of the two men and drew widespread support as he purged the country of Communist influence. Down came statues of Lenin and other Communist patriarchs, and up went a new name for Leningrad—once again St. Petersburg, in honor of Czar Peter the Great of pre-revolutionary days. In a dramatic move that came too late to stop Yeltsin's acquisition of power, Gorbachev resigned from the Communist Party and worked toward abolishing its once-dominant Central Committee. In December, however, Yeltsin led the creation of the Commonwealth of Independent States

(CIS), which allied his Russian Federation with the Ukraine and Belarus (formerly Byelorussia). Before the month was over, the CIS counted eleven former Soviet republics among its membership, leaving outside the new organization only the three Baltic States (who remained insistent on their own independence) and Georgia (dominated by hard-liners and beset by civil war).

On Christmas Day 1991, the red flag with hammer and sickle came down from the Kremlin, signaling the death of the Soviet Union. Gorbachev was president of a once-powerful nation that no longer existed. That same day, he presided over its interment when he resigned his position over nationwide television. As a final stamp of legitimacy, Russia replaced the Soviet Union as one of the five permanent members of the UN Security Council. The revolution set off by Gorbachev's reform programs had taken the path of so many other upheavals in the past: it consumed its founder en route to greater changes than the founder had originally envisioned.

By now, in early 1992, the direction of European events had become clearer, but the Bush administration still failed to exert leadership. Yeltsin visited the White House in February, where he joined the president in pronouncing an end to the Cold War and promising to work toward more arms reductions. But when the Russian leader asked for economic assistance, Bush offered no encouragement to what many analysts hailed as burgeoning liberal and democratic tendencies. He did not suggest either high-profile help in the form of technical assistance and advice or an exchange program for training Russians in the many skills needed to establish a democratic political system and free-market economy. Yeltsin went away empty-handed but nonetheless determined to push for liberal market reforms at home. The Russian economy, however, continued to stumble in the face of resistance from conservatives, national and ethnic divisions within the CIS, an endemic poverty that pervaded a third of the Russian people, and threats of massive starvation during the exceptionally brutal winter of

1991–1992 that only a U.S.–West European airlift prevented. As Bush completed his term in office, he remained determined to establish his country's primacy in what a classified document secured from the Pentagon called a "one-superpower world."

East Asia

As these events were under way in Europe, Bush dealt with a host of issues regarding East Asia. While attending the funeral of the aged Emperor Hirohito in January 1989, the new president urged Japan's leaders to work toward improving commercial relations with the United States. Almost half of the U.S. trade deficit came from a trade imbalance with Japan, which had enabled its businesses to accumulate huge stocks of American dollars and buy all types of holdings in the United States. The Bush administration had to handle the growing economic problems with Japan with great care: the United States considered it vital to maintain more than 50,000 military personnel in Japan, the Japanese had assumed a larger share of defense expenditures and needed encouragement to continue doing so, and they were extending welcome aid to needy countries. In South Korea, where nationalist feeling focused on reducing the U.S. military presence, Bush intended to maintain the 40,000 American personnel while working with the Seoul government to establish a better commercial relationship that tipped heavily in South Korea's favor. And in North Korea, the White House became especially concerned that the Communist regime there would develop nuclear weaponry and threaten Japan and the entire region.

Rapidly escalating unrest inside China likewise caused serious concern. The president had once served as the U.S. diplomat to that country and still had warm relations with its leaders. During a visit to Beijing in early 1989, he emphasized the need for expanded commercial relations and came back to assure Americans that an approaching Sino–Soviet summit would not endanger U.S. interests.

But the ruling Communist regime in Beijing had recently countered a Tibetan move for independence by imposing martial law to halt the growing violence. When the Senate in Washington passed a resolution condemning this crackdown, the Chinese snapped back that their internal affairs were not subject to U.S. scrutiny.

Then, in the spring of 1989, students' demands for an open and democratic society in China led to huge demonstrations in Beijing's Tiananmen Square that even drew the support of numerous Communist Party leaders. At first, the government outlawed the public protests, but when the students ignored the edict and boycotted classes, police swarmed into the square to break up the crowd. The move succeeded only in swelling the number of participants to more than 200,000. By the time Gorbachev arrived on May 15 to begin a scheduled summit meeting with Communist leader Deng Xiaoping, the students counted among their supporters a large contingent of workers, intellectuals, and government employees that skyrocketed the total to well over a million. As the demonstrators chanted and marched within sight of the huge picture of Mao Zedong, they carried signs hailing Gorbachev as a pioneer of reform whose example might convert Communist China to democracy.

But conservative Chinese leaders staunchly opposed democracy—particularly when an outsider, Gorbachev, loomed as inspirational leader. Had he not termed the uprising a necessary part of a "painful but healthy" process pointing to democracy? Furthermore, the timing of the protests proved embarrassing: television crews from all over the world were on hand to cover the summit and were conveniently in place to broadcast the demonstrations. Deng had witnessed the national chaos caused by the Cultural Revolution just two decades earlier and regarded the students' demands as injurious to governmental order. On May 19, his regime imposed martial law and attempted to halt live telecasts of the protests. That move stirred up more resistance. The next day, soldiers and tanks moved into Tiananmen Square to seize control, but the demonstrators clogged the streets and refused to move. Deng did not hesitate. On June 3 his military forces fired machine guns into the crowd, inflicting thousands of casualties. The Communist regime then attempted to cover up the number hurt and killed while engaging in a round of arrests and executions, authorizing government purges of those seeking reform, and holding indoctrination sessions for students who supported what Deng harshly denounced as "bourgeois liberalization."

Television coverage, however, had exposed the Beijing government's oppressive policies and inflamed world opinion. The United States joined other nations, both Communist and non-Communist, in condemning China's brutal actions. President Bush publicly criticized the use of force against what television cameras showed as nonviolent demonstrations for democracy. Two days later, on June 5, he stopped the sale of military goods to China and within a week declared that the United States would not consider reestablishing good relations until Beijing's leaders acknowledged "the validity of the pro-democracy movement." On June 20, the White House effectually broke relations with China by ordering a halt to governmental contacts.

In a short time, however, the priorities of power politics overruled human rights considerations, and Bush retracted his punitive actions. That July, he secretly directed his national security adviser, Brent Scowcroft, to meet with China's leaders in Beijing and, in effect, restore relations. When this surreptitious move was exposed months afterward, Americans in both political parties became infuriated. Bush then vetoed a congressional bill that would have extended the visas for about 40,000 Chinese students who had supported the pro-democracy movement and now feared punishment on their return to China. Soon afterward, Bush lifted the ban on weapons sales and approved loans to businesses dealing with China, thereby canceling a congressional pro-

hibition against such practices. In that December of 1989, Scowcroft returned to Beijing, this time in a highly publicized mission to demonstrate U.S. ties. The administration even maintained China's most-favored-nation relationship—a commercial right not granted to the Soviets.

The Bush administration was convinced that its new policies were correct. Three decades of isolating China had not brought democratic reform after the Communist takeover in 1949; there was no reason to think that such an approach would work now. A punitive policy, according to the White House, would alienate those in control and undermine U.S. interests in nuclear nonproliferation and the future of Asia. Early in 1990, China ended martial law in Beijing, drawing skepticism from most Americans but praise from Bush's supporters as the calculated result of his careful policy. A fair analysis, however, reveals that the White House once again pursued an uncertain course in foreign affairs, adopting one position before reversing itself and setting out on another. Whether prudence or indecision, such a waffling approach did little to assure allies of resolute U.S. leadership.

Latin America

The Bush administration also had to improve relations with Latin America, where poverty remained the dominant reality and caused many problems that spilled over into neighboring countries. Many Latin Americans migrated northward, hoping to circumvent U.S. immigration laws and find employment above the Rio Grande. Others participated in the enormously profitable narcotics trade, prompting the Bush administration to send troops to help the governments in Colombia, Bolivia, and Peru combat powerful drug cartels that were producing and selling cocaine and crack. In addition, the United States tried to cut off the growing importation of marijuana and heroin from Mexico. When Americans complained that Mexico had become a virtual conduit for narcotics into their country, that government bitterly charged that it was U.S. demand and not Mexican supply that prolonged the problem. Indeed, huge supplies of heroin came into the United States from the Middle East. Although various governments' efforts to halt the international drug traffic had led to scattered successes, they had been unable to destroy either its sources or its demand.

In Central America, the Bush administration boldly broke with its predecessor's policies by lifting the heavy hand of the United States in that region and thereby encouraging an end to the long struggle between Nicaragua and El Salvador. Secretary Baker drew on the ideas expressed in the Arias peace plan of 1987 by halting U.S. assistance to the contras and urging the Sandinistas to permit free elections in February 1990. Then, with Soviet cooperation, he intended to put pressure on the Salvadoran government to work out its differences with the leftist rebels. The key to success was Nicaragua. Baker felt confident that its people would turn out the Sandinistas—a belief encouraged by Gorbachev's secret assurances that he would stop military assistance to Nicaragua and put pressure on Daniel Ortega to accept the popular verdict.

The Bush administration's diplomacy led to some measure of success. In the elections of early 1990 that former President Jimmy Carter and other international observers certified as honest, Ortega and the Sandinistas suffered a crushing defeat. Eleven years of incompetent rule by the Sandinistas had combined with sustained economic hardship throughout Nicaragua to account for this result. The U.S. economic embargo on Nicaragua had further devastated its economy and forced Ortega into a retrenchment program that cut the country's budget more than 40 percent and left thousands of government workers unemployed. Ironically, the winner was Violeta Chamorro, the widow of Pedro Joaquín Chamorro, the slain editor of *La Prensa*. Her husband's writings had helped drive the Sandinistas into overthrowing Somoza's oppressive regime.

In February 1992, the rightist government of President Alfredo Cristiani in El Salvador met with the insurgents and arranged a ceasefire that established only a fitful peace. After twelve years of fighting and the loss of 75,000 lives, the beleaguered country entered what contemporaries aptly called "the crisis of peace." Both Nicaragua and El Salvador were a long way from a reconciliation of the warring parties.

Despite the diplomatic approach to the Salvadoran–Nicaraguan imbroglio, the Bush administration returned to the use of military force in Latin America when it dealt with Panama. On December 20, 1989, the president approved an invasion by 27,000 U.S. troops whose objectives, according to Bush, were to safeguard the canal and American citizens in the area and to stop the passage of drugs through the country by unseating their chief sponsor, dictator Manuel Noriega. Skeptics argued that the real reason for such a massive military strike was personal: Noriega had alienated both Reagan and Bush. Throughout much of the decade, Noriega had helped the contras while also working undercover for Cuba's Fidel Castro. Noriega had actually been in the secret employ of the CIA since the 1960s, which raised questions about how many of his activities Bush knew about when becoming CIA director in 1976. During the Reagan years, the Panamanian strongman played both sides of the drug scene, on the one hand cooperating with dealers from Colombia and other countries and on the other hand working with the U.S. Drug Enforcement Agency in seizing drug shipments.

By the time Bush became president, Noriega's history of personal and government corruption had embarrassed the United States. In early 1988, two grand juries in Florida indicted him for drug-running activities that included smuggling the Colombian product into the United States, accepting bribes for laundering drug money in his country's banks, and permitting Colombians to produce cocaine inside Panama. Revelations of Noriega's venal conduct soon became known in Panama, inciting demonstrations against his rule that led to a brutal government crackdown. As was the case with Ferdinand Marcos in the Philippines, the Reagan administration put pressure on Noriega to resign. But economic sanctions did not work, nor did a suspension of both economic and military aid. During the presidential campaign of 1988, Bush came under constant questioning about how the White House could allow Noriega to deal with drug lords.

As Bush settled into the presidency, the pressure heightened to remove Noriega. Elections in Panama (fraudulent, according to former President Carter and other international observers) went against the general in May 1989, awarding victory to the vice-presidential candidate, Guillermo Endara. Noriega, however, nullified the results and proclaimed his candidate the victor. Bush protested that "the Panamanian people have spoken. And I call on General Noriega to respect the will of the people." Noriega ignored the plea and ordered his personal police force, the Dignity Battalions, to use an iron bar in administering a public beating to Endara. American television and newsmagazines highlighted the bloody affair that turned Endara's white shirt to crimson. President Bush angrily called on Panamanians to throw out Noriega and "his Doberman thugs," and Americans in Panama urged officers in his Panamanian Defense Force (PDF) to rise in rebellion. But a coup attempt in October failed, partly because its leaders received no U.S. assistance against the soldiers who remained loyal to Noriega. As the news carried stories of the officers' executions, critics denounced Bush as a "wimp" for refusing to act.

Then, in mid-December 1989, the Bush administration decided to oust Noriega after he proclaimed himself Panama's "maximum leader" and declared the two American nations (Panama and the United States) in a "state of war." The president approved "Operation Just Cause," which sought to depose Noriega by U.S. military action. But the intervention proved more difficult than expected, leading to massive destruction in an already economically ravaged country. Only after several days of fighting did the Noriega regime fall, leaving behind a death list that included 24 U.S. soldiers, 139 PDF troops, and more than 300 Panamanian civilians. In the wake of the PDF's collapse came widespread lawlessness and rampant looting. Hospitals overflowed with the injured, most of them receiving inadequate care because of a severe shortage of food and medical supplies. Especially frustrating was Noriega's elusiveness. At long last, the Americans located him in the Vatican embassy in Panama City, where he had sought refuge. After protracted negotiations, he agreed to surrender and was taken to Miami to stand trial on the two indictments for drug trafficking.

The U.S. invasion of Panama was a revealing episode. For the first time in four decades, the United States carried out a forceful intervention that did not rest on Cold War considerations. The administration accomplished its main objective in removing Noriega: he ultimately stood trial in the United States and was convicted in April 1992 and sentenced to jail. Not surprisingly, the military action earned Bush extraordinarily high praise from most of his nation's people. But despite the assurances by Washington's leaders to assist the new Endara government in Panama City, they could do little because of the economic shortfall in the United States. As in the past, the new regime held on to power only with the assistance of the 13,500 U.S. soldiers who were on the scene before the invasion and remained behind after the others pulled out in February 1990.

And, as in the past, the image was that of a U.S. surrogate put in place by White House military action. Numerous Latin American observers denounced the use of force by the United States, even as they welcomed the results. The Soviet Union questioned Bush's heavy-handed methods, particularly after Americans had criticized Moscow's use of military force in neighboring Afghanistan. West Europeans wondered about the wisdom of resurrecting the Roosevelt Corollary, particularly when the Soviet Union seemed to have buried its own interventionist apparatus—the Brezhnev Doctrine—in refusing to put down the anti-Communist movement erupting throughout Eastern Europe. Both the Organization of American States and the UN Security Council moved to condemn the U.S. action; the latter failed to do so only because of the veto exercised by the U.S. delegate.

In still another look backward, the president had sanctioned the invasion of Panama without consulting Congress. The War Powers Act of 1973 authorized that body to put restraints on unilateral military action by the president, yet neither house in Congress challenged the measure or inquired into the reasons behind it. The explanation seemed clear: the move stirred up the martial spirit among Americans and drew widespread support because of the removal of an unpopular dictator. To question the president's action was politically unwise.

By the time Bush left the presidency, U.S. relations with Latin America had improved, however slightly. The White House had withdrawn from the conflict between Nicaragua and El Salvador, allowing it to come to a close and thereby encourage a democratic process that Latin Americans themselves devised. The cease-fire in El Salvador brought some semblance of peace to the economically destitute country. But in Panama, the U.S. military presence remained unmistakable, even as the two nations moved closer to the change in canal control scheduled in 2000. Economic problems persisted, helping the drug business continue despite government efforts to close it down. In Cuba, Castro was still chief of state, though older and grayer and less active in pushing his revolutionary ideas in areas outside his own domain. He now stood as the only Communist dictator in office outside Asia, but, without Soviet assistance, his island was in dire economic straits and internationally isolated. Signs of growing disillusionment among Cuba's ruling elite led more than a few observers to believe this "Castro's final hour." In the meantime, the number of illegal aliens migrating from Mexico into the United States remained high, even while the two nations continued to work toward the proposed North American Free Trade Agreement (or NAFTA, signed by Canada, Mexico, and the United States in October 1992), aimed at bringing the same benefits afforded by the U.S. free-trade agreement with Canada in 1988. The growing numbers of Haitian refugees entering the United States remained a hot issue, although signs pointed to the restoration of democracy and perhaps a greater chance of a settlement. And the drug problem persisted, even as the White House provided funds to help the Colombian government defeat the drug lords.

Beneath all these matters and more, however, the poverty that ran throughout Latin America required more attention from Washington. Indeed, by the close of the Bush administration, the United States was sending more economic assistance to Latin America than to all of Europe. As Western Europe and Japan moved toward a dominant economic position in each of their respective regions, so did Washington's policymakers finally realize that their nation's vital interests were also rooted in the region of its location—that is, North America and the Caribbean basin—and that only economic improvement offered hope for success.

The Gulf War in the Middle East

White House attention suddenly turned to the Middle East in the autumn of 1990 when, on August 2, nearly 100,000 Iraqi forces, escorted by tanks and armed with Soviet weapons, Chinese missiles, and poison gas, invaded their oil-rich southeastern neighbor of Kuwait and set off a crisis in the Persian Gulf that had global repercussions. Iraqi dictator Saddam Hussein attempted to justify this military move in several ways. His country had owned Kuwait until Western imperialists wrested it away many years earlier, leaving Iraq without adequate access to the sea. Kuwait's massive production of oil had driven prices down, preventing him from marketing his own oil at prices high enough to meet $80 billion of debts resulting from the arms and materiel acquired from the United States and other nations during his long war with Iran. No less critical was his need for money to rebuild his nation's economy and finance the huge army and police state that underpinned his stay in power. Most important, he could become leader of the Arab states. His armies rolled on to the northeast border of equally oil-rich Saudi Arabia, seemingly poised to launch an invasion of the long-time ally of the United States.

Until the very moment of his assault on Kuwait, Saddam remained confident that the Bush administration would do nothing. The United States had not responded with force to either the Iranian hostage crisis or the killing of marines in Lebanon. Furthermore, he had both public and private assurances that the White House intended to stay out of the ongoing boundary crisis between Iraq and Kuwait. But after some initial hesitation, President Bush felt compelled to take action. Saddam's invasion of Kuwait endangered international peace by threatening the world's oil flow. If he seized Saudi Arabia as well, Saddam would control more than half the world's crude oil deposits. Aggression unchallenged, Bush declared in harkening back to the pre–World War II decade, fed on itself and ensured wider conflict. "What is at stake," he insisted, "is more than one country, it is a big idea—a new world order" based on "peace and security, freedom and the rule of law." The United States, he declared, did not wish to be "the world's policeman." It sought to cooperate with other nations in combating the instability and disorder that imperiled the world community. As Bush saw it, Saddam was another Hitler whom the United Nations must stop.

Bush received surprising support from a large number of nations that feared a takeover of the Middle East's oil reserves by Saddam. The Iraqi ruler was a ruthless and mercurial tyrant who was willing to crush his neighbors and who chose Stalin (not Hitler) as his model in creating a personality cult based on fear and terror. Most members of the United Nations and all those on the Security Council approved strong action against Iraq. Among those in the U.S. camp were the Soviets (who needed Western economic assistance and broke with their longtime ally Iraq), the British (who had oil interests in Kuwait), and the Chinese (who sought economic ties with the United States). Bush wanted to create and command a UN coalition of powers that would deliver a military response if necessary. What became clear was that the demise of the Cold War meant increased stature for the United Nations. No longer would the bitter U.S.–Soviet exchanges within the Security Council block its efforts to guarantee collective security. The United Nations gave Saddam until midnight of January 15, 1991, to withdraw his forces from Kuwait.

In the meantime, Bush mobilized a massive UN military force that had two objectives: liberate Kuwait and protect Saudi Arabia. The allied powers first worked through the United Nations to impose an international economic boycott on Iraq that most Arab governments supported—including the Syrians, who had aligned with Iran in its war with Iraq and whose assistance the United States cultivated despite their longtime involvement in terrorism. Only Iran and the Palestinians in Jordan supported Iraq, the former because of territorial concessions offered by Saddam (withdrawal from all lands won in their recent war) and the latter out of a chance to destroy Israel. Bush persuaded Kuwait and Saudi Arabia to underwrite U.S. military costs in the Middle East—although the Saudis simply raised their production of oil as prices escalated and then used half the income to meet financial obligations to the United States while keeping the rest.

Eventually, President Bush masterminded the establishment of a highly unusual coalition of

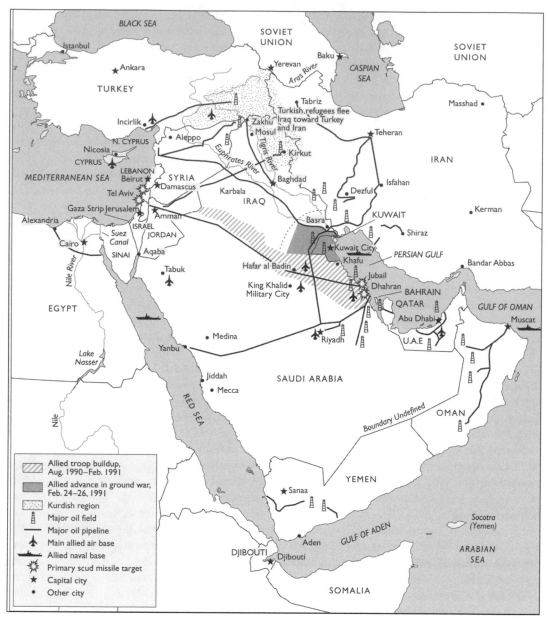

Map 11
The Gulf War. A prime example of regional conflicts that developed in the post–Cold War period.
(Source: author)

forty-eight countries from the Middle East, Europe, and Asia. To help finance the anticipated UN military operation, he put great pressure on several nations to make contributions—including Germany and Japan, both of which drew heavily from the Middle East's oil supply and yet required considerable persuasion before promising billions in monetary assistance. American war mobilization meanwhile raised opposition at home, with thousands of marchers in New York City's Times Square chanting, "Hell, no, we won't go—we won't fight for

Iraqi Invasion of Kuwait
Exiled Sheik Jaber al-Ahmed of Kuwait discusses the Gulf crisis with President Bush in the White
House on September 28, 1990. *(White House)*

Texaco." Others warned, "Speak out now—remember Vietnam." Bush at first hesitated to ask the Democrat-controlled Congress to authorize him to use force. What if it rejected his request? He finally decided to seek congressional approval for participation in any military action, although he would surely have followed the same course regardless of the outcome. The result of a long and bitter debate was a narrow victory for the president that proved vital to maintaining the shaky union of Americans, Europeans, Arabs, and Soviets. In many ways, Bush performed admirably as commander in chief of a unique mixture of allies.

Soon, close to 250,000 U.S. combat troops (including a large number of activated reserves), along with planes and aircraft carriers, were en route to Saudi Arabia, the Persian Gulf, and the Red Sea. Their first tasks were to set up the defense of Saudi Arabia ("Operation Desert Shield") and establish a naval blockade of Iraq. In a pointed reference to a major command flaw during the Vietnam War, Bush assured the chair of the Joint Chiefs of Staff, General Colin Powell, that his military operations would encounter no political interference.

The deadline for the UN ultimatum came and passed without an Iraqi evacuation of Kuwait, thus activating a mammoth air and land campaign known as "Operation Desert Storm." To roll back the Iraqi offensive,

In this paper, President George H. W. Bush implemented measures toward forcing Iraq out of Kuwait and outlined the objectives of the Gulf War of 1991.

National Security Directive 54, January 15, 1991: Response to Iraqi Aggression in the Gulf, George Bush Presidential Library, College Station, Texas.

I hereby authorize military actions designed to bring about Iraq's withdrawal from Kuwait. These actions are to be conducted against Iraq and Iraqi forces in Kuwait by U.S. air, sea and land conventional military forces, in coordination with the forces of our coalition partners, at a date and time I shall determine and communicate through National Command Authority channels. This authorization is for the following purposes:

 a. to effect the immediate, complete and unconditional withdrawal of all Iraqi forces from Kuwait;
 b. to restore Kuwait's legitimate government;
 c. to protect the lives of American citizens abroad; and
 d. to promote the security and the stability of the Persian Gulf.

To achieve the above purposes, U.S. and coalition forces should seek to:

 a. defend Saudi Arabia and the other GCC [Gulf Cooperation Council] states against attack;
 b. preclude Iraqi launch of ballistic missiles against neighboring states and friendly forces;
 c. destroy Iraq's chemical, biological, and nuclear capabilities;
 d. destroy Iraq's command, control, and communications capabilities;
 e. eliminate the Republican Guards as an effective fighting force; and
 f. conduct operations designed to drive Iraq's forces from Kuwait, break the will of Iraqi forces, discourage Iraqi use of chemical, biological or nuclear weapons, encourage defection of Iraqi forces, and weaken Iraqi popular support for the current government.

General Powell orchestrated a month-long bombing of key Iraqi positions, including air defense and ground force command and control centers, providing the prelude to a massive ground assault by 550,000 coalition forces under the command of General H. Norman Schwarzkopf Jr. The land attack on Kuwait and eastern Iraq began on February 23, 1991.

As the UN forces headed into Kuwait, Saddam defiantly promised the "Mother of All Battles"; instead, his troops put up little resistance and sustained a crushing and humiliating defeat. In a vain attempt to draw Israel into the war, Saddam hit that country with ground-launched Scud missiles, confident that the Arab members of the UN coalition would switch sides if he converted the struggle into a contest between Arab and Jew. But Bush convinced Israeli leaders not to retaliate, probably by ensuring a quick victory and increased

U.S. aid following the war. For more than a month, three Cable News Network (CNN) reporters stayed bunkered in a Baghdad hotel, televising live shots of U.S. Tomahawk cruise missiles hammering Iraq (some within yards of the hotel) and U.S. Patriot missiles intercepting and downing the incoming Scud missiles. American tank commanders found it surprisingly easy to maneuver through Iraqi minefields; Saddam's leaders had marked their own path through the area with wire that the invasion forces quickly discovered. "Once we found that," a U.S. officer declared, "the only thing missing was a neon sign saying 'start here.'" Coalition troops, meanwhile, advanced easily into the occupied kingdom of Kuwait, liberating it from quickly retreating Iraqi soldiers who had looted the country of nearly everything of value—even devouring most of the animals in the national zoo. In a spectacle of destruction, Saddam ordered his departing

Secretary of Defense Richard Cheney and General Colin Powell, Chair of the Joint Chiefs of Staff
Meeting with troops in Saudi Arabia on December 21, 1990. *(U.S. Department of Defense)*

troops to set fire to nearly 650 Kuwaiti oil wells, unleashing a fiery holocaust that blackened the sky and took nearly nine months to extinguish. Not all enemy soldiers ran. They had undergone a terrific pounding from the bombing program and were so badly shell-shocked and demoralized that thousands surrendered with little or no opposition.

In less than a hundred hours of ground fighting, Iraq agreed to a UN cease-fire. The coalition had freed Kuwait and went on to take southern Iraq—at the cost of 148 American lives along with 92 allied soldiers. Even then, the Iraqis were not responsible for all coalition casualties. About a quarter of its deaths resulted from "fratricide," or friendly fire. Despite the U.S. claims to pinpoint ac-

curacy, nearly half of the 167 laser-guided bombs dropped from F-117s during the first five nights of conflict missed their targets completely. Other errant air attacks hit oil tankers, milk trucks, and, according to the Iraqis, a factory that made baby formula. More than 100,000 Iraqis died, including numerous civilians. An epidemic of cholera and typhoid soon blanketed the Iraqi nation, adding to the horrid situation.

A wave of euphoria over the surprisingly easy victory momentarily threatened to widen the war's objectives. The coalition command underwent considerable pressure to order its troops into Baghdad to topple Saddam. During his long, tyrannical reign, he was responsible for numerous atrocities against his own

Kuwaiti Oil Fields Afire
U.S. Marines pushing into Kuwait found its oil fields ablaze as a result of demolition charges set off by retreating Iraqi soldiers. *(U.S. Army)*

people, particularly chemical warfare against Kurdish rebels (including women and children) in northern Iraq and the thousands of young men ordered into suicidal attacks on Iranians in the recent war. In the Gulf War, supporters of the UN coalition were appalled by the brutalities committed by Iraqi soldiers on Kuwaiti civilians, by the Scuds lobbed indiscriminately on urban centers in Israel and Saudi Arabia, and by Saddam's decision to use Western captives (including women and children) as "human shields" in preventing enemy bombing of Iraqi military targets. Although British Prime Minister Margaret Thatcher ridiculed Saddam for "hiding behind women's skirts," he had to be taken seriously. Saddam possessed chemical and biological weapons

and would probably develop his first atomic bomb within eighteen months. Most chilling, he had the will to use all his weapons.

President Bush wisely resisted the temptation to take the war into Baghdad. In comparing Saddam to Hitler, Bush had helped to bring on the overwhelming pressure needed to finish the military task in Iraq. Could there be anything less than unconditional surrender with an enemy accused of war crimes and thus not susceptible to negotiations? But Bush recognized the likelihood of the coalition's breakup if he pushed the war into Iraq's capital. He also realized the danger of becoming entangled in street fighting that might not even uncover Saddam, who was hidden, along with his military officers and commanders of

Cease-Fire Talks, March 3, 1991
General H. Norman Schwarzkopf and the commander of Arab ground troops, Saudi Lieutenant General Prince Khalid (on left), meet with the Iraqi commanders (on right), Lieutenant General Mohammed Abdez Rahman al-Dagitistani and Lieutenant General Sabin Abdel-Aziz al-Douri. *(U.S. Army)*

his elite Republican Guard, somewhere deep beneath the city in heavily reinforced bunkers. Most of all, Bush knew that Iraq's destruction would automatically make Iran the chief Islamic power in the region. Had not General Powell told him that "our practical intention was to leave Baghdad enough power to survive as a threat to an Iran that remained bitterly hostile to the United States"? Besides, Bush hoped that Saddam's own soldiers would overthrow him. This did not happen— partly because of videocassettes circulated in the Middle East that showed executed military officers hanging on meat hooks. Saddam held on to power, brutally squelching his opposi- tion at home while defiantly proclaiming vic- tory over his hated imperialist enemy.

The UN success in the Gulf War had im- portant repercussions. Security Council Res- olution 687 sounded as if Iraq had suffered a great defeat. It had to respect Kuwait's bor- der, permit UN peace keepers along the Iraqi borders, and divulge and help to destroy all chemical, biological, and nuclear weaponry. Indeed, the UN inspection teams disposed of more than a hundred Scud missiles along with huge supplies of mustard gas and nerve gas, but they only slowed the production of nu- clear weapons well under way when the war erupted. Although the coalition achieved its

Map 12
Post–Cold War Europe. The end of the Cold War encouraged a greater sense of interdependence among European nations along with their effort to become more independent of the United States. *(Source: author)*

chief objectives of liberating Kuwait and safe-guarding Saudi Arabia, Saddam's regime and country remained intact, providing him with stature in the Arab world as a leader who had warded off the U.S. imperialists. He thus remained a dire threat to his neighbors, adding more stress to the constant turmoil in the Middle East. Furthermore, much of Kuwait lay in ruins and bitterly torn between those Kuwaitis who had fled the country on the Iraqi advance and those who had braved the invasion by remaining behind. In addition, thousands of Palestinians in Kuwait drew the wrath of its people because of the complicity of the Palestine Liberation Organization (PLO) with Saddam. But the Bush adminis-

President Bush and Nelson Mandela
Visit in the Oval Office on June 25, 1990. *(George Bush Library, College Station, Texas)*

tration exploited the UN conquest and deep apprehensions over Saddam to salvage something of potential value: it arranged another round of Middle East peace talks. This time, however, there were two differences: the Israelis agreed to meet with the Arab states, but with the Palestinians (though not the PLO) in attendance as part of Jordan's delegation, and the United States permitted the Soviet Union to participate—a phenomenal turnaround from the past.

The Persian Gulf crisis only temporarily diverted attention from the persistent Arab–Israeli tensions in the Middle East. The region had become a veritable armed camp, thanks to the great majority of weapons that came from the United States itself. Israel's continued refusal to meet with the PLO, combined with its severe military tactics in putting down the *intifada* in Gaza and the West Bank, had alienated Americans and in 1989 drew a

harsh reprimand from the State Department for violating human rights. In addition, Israeli domestic politics had become bitterly divided between Menachem Begin's hard-line Likud Party, which rejected any form of compromise and called for a Greater Israel, and the Labor Party, which supported Secretary of State George Shultz's earlier proposal of giving up occupied land for peace. By the middle of 1990, the chances for a settlement appeared impossible as the more radical wing of the PLO intensified its "holy war" (*jihad*) against Israel and the Likud Party assumed control of the government in Tel Aviv. Israel's new prime minister, Yitzhak Shamir, staunchly proclaimed continued opposition to discussions with the PLO. Then, when Yasir Arafat refused to denounce an aborted terrorist attack on an Israeli beach by one of the PLO's factions, the Bush administration abruptly halted the talks in Tunis. It now hoped that the unity shown in the Gulf War would combine with the widespread fear of Saddam's reckless and brutal behavior to take precedence over ancient Arab–Israeli difficulties and drive both parties to the peace table.

In the Middle East, as in numerous other hot spots in the world, the United States found itself unable to control events. Secretary of State Baker urged the Israelis to negotiate with the PLO and accept, if not a sovereign state, at least its claim to self-government in the Israeli-occupied areas. A Greater Israel was unrealistic, he insisted. Local elections must take place in East Jerusalem, Gaza, and the West Bank. But Shamir rejected any concessions to the PLO, and Israeli–American relations hardened. Yet the Bush administration could do nothing because of both domestic and foreign considerations. Not only did Israel enjoy widespread and effective support in the United States, but it was also the closest ally of the United States in the Middle East.

As Bush left the presidency in 1993, the embittered Middle East stalemate showed few signs of coming to an end. The Cold War was over, which meant that the fear of Russian expansion into the region had greatly diminished. Indeed, the end of this intense international rivalry had the potential of encouraging a move toward peace in the Middle East, largely because the United States provided most of Israel's arms while its chief enemies, Iraq and Syria, received the bulk of their weapons from the now deceased Soviet Union. The Gulf War drove Israel and the United States closer together again, but the wartime rapprochement did not resolve the underlying tensions. The Arab–Israeli–Palestinian problem remained, recently worsened by the arrival in Israel of thousands of Soviet Jewish immigrants, the Israelis' continuing intention to expand settlements and build a Greater Israel, and the Palestinians' desperate conditions in the occupied areas. The most feasible route to peace lay in some sort of settlement worked out by those two parties most actively enjoined in the dispute—Israel and the PLO.

President Clinton: A New Direction in Foreign Policy?

Bush lost his bid for reelection in 1992 to Democratic Governor William Clinton of Arkansas, who sidestepped foreign policy issues and attacked the incumbent's inability to end the nation's economic recession. Despite an 89 percent approval rating following the successful Gulf War, Bush's popularity had plummeted because of the sluggish economy at home and his seeming bewilderment about what remedies to take. While Bush emphasized his victories in the Cold War and in Iraq, Clinton hammered away at diminished economic hopes and an unpromising future for the nation's youth. During the campaign, Clinton tied the failing U.S. economy to the troublesome global situation. The biggest problem was the huge federal deficit, which had fractured the nation's economy and undermined its foreign policy. The trade deficit with Japan alone stood at nearly $50 billion, which crippled the capacity of the United States to invest abroad and thereby generate more jobs at home. Japan had become a chief commercial rival of the United States and an economic and military power in Asia. Perhaps Massachusetts Senator Paul Tsongas, a former Democratic presidential hopeful himself, expressed it best when he declared, "The Cold War's over. Japan won."

After achieving victory with only 43 percent of the popular vote (Bush had 38 percent, and 19 percent went to billionaire Texas businessman H. Ross Perot), President Clinton insisted that the chief impetus to economic recovery at home and abroad was market expansion throughout the world. Reducing his own nation's gigantic budget deficit, he argued, was critical to this overall growth. With these goals in mind, he attended the annual economic summit of 1993, which convened in Tokyo during the summer and brought together the "Group of Seven" leading capitalist nations of Britain, Canada, France, Germany, Italy, Japan, and the United States. There, among other objectives, Clin-

Bill Clinton Inauguration
Clinton takes oath of office as president on January 20, 1993, as his family, Vice President Al Gore, and others watch. *(William J. Clinton Library, Little Rock, Arkansas)*

ton sought a broad commercial agreement with Japan aimed at lowering the U.S. trade deficit. He later participated in talks about global tariff reductions under the auspices of the General Agreement on Tariffs and Trade (GATT), established in 1947 to determine fair trade rules and now with 117 members. Finally, he encouraged the Senate to approve NAFTA worked out by Canada, Mexico, and the United States in December 1992.

Some progress took place toward the establishment of international reciprocity in trade. GATT's member nations agreed to a new commercial arrangement in Geneva during late December 1993. No less important than specific provisions was their decision to drop that unfortunate name—GATT—and replace it in 1995 with the more staid title of World Trade Organization. The new policy reduced tariffs on manufactured goods by an average of 37 percent and encompassed agri-

cultural products for the first time. The United States stood to profit from the total elimination of tariffs in a dozen industries it dominated. In addition, White House pressure had led to the congressional approval of NAFTA in November 1993, offering the hope of building greater commercial ties throughout North America. NAFTA's proponents had argued that it would create 130,000 new American jobs by 1995; instead, NAFTA was responsible for the loss of 125,000 jobs that, fortunately, the robust U.S. economy ameliorated by expanding the country's employment in other areas.

Clinton's policy also worked well in Asia, the location of nearly half of all foreign currency reserves and 40 percent of the world's new markets. In 1993, fifteen national leaders from the Pacific region attended an Asia-Pacific Economic Cooperative (APEC) forum in Seattle that sought to establish a huge

President Bill Clinton
In the Oval Office. *(Library of Congress, Washington, D.C.)*

free-trade zone. The following year, APEC met in Indonesia, where its members agreed to create a free-trading Pacific Rim by 2010. But on the issue of opening Japanese markets to U.S. industries (including auto parts), a final agreement remained elusive until in February 1994 the Clinton administration threatened commercial sanctions against Japan for violating a previous trade arrangement. The Tokyo government agreed to increase its imports of U.S. goods by 85 percent. Furthermore, the two nations negotiated the Japan-American Security Treaty in early 1995 that strengthened their ties and obligated Japan to assume 75 percent of the expense of maintaining at least 100,000 American troops in the Asia–Pacific area.

Clinton early demonstrated a greater awareness than did his predecessor of the interdependence of domestic and foreign problems facing the United States in the post–Cold War era. But this is not to say that he had developed a cohesive strategy in dealing with these world-shaking changes. At a White House policy-making meeting, the new president shook his head with wonderment and confusion. "You know," he moaned after listening to detailed discussions about the international issues facing his administration, "the problem is that in this post–Cold War period, the lines just aren't as clear as they were before." After a pause, a telling response came from James Schlesinger, former defense secretary and now CIA director: "Mr. President, that is your fate. You will just have to get used to dealing with ambiguity."

If the United States had not entered a "brave new world," it certainly confronted what contemporaries have called a "disorderly new world." The president, largely inexperienced in foreign affairs, preferred to leave those matters to subordinates. The result was a strange amalgam of idealism and Wilsonian internationalism that led to a confused and disoriented foreign policy. Only when public opinion demanded his leadership did he shift to a pragmatic "trial-and-error" approach. At the outset of his administration, Clinton prepared for summit meetings in Brussels, Prague, and Moscow that focused on three critical issues: NATO's future and whether the newly independent nations of Eastern Europe should become members, the aftermath of recent elections in Russia and the question of reform, and the continued economic stagnation in Europe. Somehow he had to convince Western Europe that the United States intended to remain involved in Atlantic concerns despite its recent focus on NAFTA and the Pacific Rim.

Most urgent to the new administration was the need to assure East Europeans, once part of the Soviet empire, that Russia under Boris Yeltsin posed no threat to their security. Toward this end, Clinton secured the U.S.-Russian-Ukraine Trilateral Statement and Annex in mid-January 1994, which provided for dismantling all 1,800 long-range nuclear warheads in Ukraine—the third-largest nuclear arsenal in the world. Later that same month, he and Yeltsin signed an agreement requiring the United States and Russia by May 30 to stop targeting their missiles at each other. By January 1997, the United States and Russia had cut more than 20,000 strategically placed warheads (their total as of 1990) to about 7,000; Ukraine and Kazakhstan no longer had nuclear weapons, and neither would Belarus in a short time. The president went farther. On September 25, 1996, he informed the UN General Assembly that the United States would join fifty other nations—including China, France, Russia, and Great Britain—in signing the Comprehensive Test Ban Treaty. Rejoicing over the pact proved premature: India refused to sign until the nations had abolished all existing nuclear weapons. The United States could not agree to such a proposition, nor would it impose sufficient political and economic pressure on the Indian government, given its opposition to free trade and its indecision regarding whether to join the Western alignment. Unlike Bush, however, Clinton had become actively engaged in reshaping the entire East–West relationship.

All this posed a formidable task. Many observers worried that dismantled nuclear weapons might come into the possession of what Washington called "rogue states" such as Cuba, Iran, Iraq, Libya, North Korea, or Syria, all of which threatened democracy. Improved technology now permitted the manufacture of nuclear devices small enough to carry in one hand, making it imperative to keep plutonium and uranium away from terrorists. West Europeans resented the Clinton administration's new emphasis on other sections of the world and began formulating economic and political policies without consulting the United States. But Poland, Czechoslovakia, and Hungary remained concerned about the "security vacuum" stemming from the Soviet collapse and insisted that the Russians were die-hard imperialists and not born-again democrats. Although the United States sympathized with these recently liberated peoples, it could not risk alienating Russia. Any thought of inviting these and other East European states into NATO gave

way to a gradualist process of membership in 1994 called "Partnership for Peace," which rested on limited military cooperation in an effort to avoid provoking the Russians.

The surprising shift from granting immediate NATO membership aroused great resentment in Eastern Europe. The Polish foreign minister angrily dismissed Clinton's program as a "buzz-off project" in which NATO members "ask us to talk and walk and act like a duck." The problem is "that after we've done all that's asked of us, NATO reserves the right to say, 'Well, now we want you to be a chicken instead.'" A spokesman of the Polish Institute of International Affairs in Warsaw renounced the "firm assumption in American policy that reformers will finally win in Russia." "All that is nonsense," stormed a high official in the Czech Defense Ministry. "Yeltsin is not a democrat. He is a Russian feudal lord." Former U.S. Defense Secretary Les Aspin (replaced by William Perry in early February 1994) nonetheless opposed the extension of NATO membership to East European countries, particularly while the United States was in the process of reducing its defense budget. If Poland were allowed into NATO, Aspin warned, "we would be saying that an attack on Poland would be the same as an attack on New York."

NATO continued to be a chief concern of the Clinton administration. The president called that organization the "bedrock" of security; Yeltsin warned that Europe had not yet freed itself of the Cold War and was "in danger of plunging into a cold peace. Why sow the seeds of mistrust?" Ironically, Yeltsin stated, "It is a dangerous delusion to suppose that the destinies of continents and the world community in general can somehow be managed from one single capital." In October 1996, Clinton recommended that in 1999, the fiftieth anniversary of NATO and the tenth anniversary of the destruction of the Berlin Wall, NATO should admit the first of the former members of the Warsaw Pact (disbanded in 1991). "If we fail to seize this historic opportunity to build a new NATO—if we allow the Iron Curtain to be replaced by a veil of influence—we will pay a higher price later." Russia, he urged, should approve NATO's expanded membership as a good-faith effort to "advance the security of everyone." It "[was] not directed against anyone. I know that some in Russia still look at NATO through a Cold War prism, but I ask them to look again. We are building a new NATO just as they are building a new Russia." The decisive factor was both parties' opposition to renewing the Cold War. "We are no longer enemies," Yeltsin had earlier declared, "but partners."

A multilateral approach to foreign policy became crucial as the president faced growing national, ethnic, and religious problems throughout the world that, as in the period before World War I, threatened to pull in outside nations. Regional conflicts became flash points, as the Middle East remained a severely troubled area and Bosnians and Serbs engaged in a genocidal war over control of a tattered and torn pocket of land still known as Yugoslavia. In the south Russian province of Chechnya, an Islamic-led movement for independence caused Yeltsin to use military force in a failing effort to salvage the oil in that area of the Caucasus Mountains and prevent a precedent for similar such actions by other dissidents. The White House had worked closely with the United Nations in winning a war against Iraq during the Bush administration, and it now employed the same strategy in dealing with desperate Haitians seeking refuge in the United States. Economic destitution in Africa remained a major problem, most notably in Somalia, where tribal wars caused such extreme hardship that the United Nations sponsored a massive humanitarian and pacification aid program intended to put down a local warlord and the United States contributed materiel, gunships, and, until the spring of 1994, more than 4,000 combat troops. Apartheid had continued to soften but all too slowly. South Africa's first open elections took place in April 1994, resulting in an overwhelming victory for the African National

Congress that brought in Nelson Mandela as the country's first black president. The U.S. economic embargo on Cuba continued in force, hurting Clinton's efforts to improve relations. Finally, he wanted to resolve the long-time bitter fighting in Northern Ireland.

Given the novelty and magnitude of the foreign problems confronting the United States, the Clinton administration spent much of its first year in office groping its way through these matters. The new president had had little experience in foreign affairs, even though he was a graduate of Georgetown University's prestigious School of Foreign Service; a former staff member of Senator William Fulbright, chair of the Foreign Relations Committee; and a student at Oxford University in England, where he read in Russian and East European history. Clinton's publicly expressed interest in what some have called liberal internationalism, however, had not taken specific form except in general references to spreading democracy and freedom. In the first days of his presidency, he delegated foreign policy making to subordinates, freeing him to concentrate on domestic issues. This kind of standoffish approach could not last in a world undergoing such a profound and sudden transformation. The rapidly changing global situation dictated a flexible U.S. foreign policy that permitted adjustments to constantly changing realities. Yet, as the world stumbled toward a new order, the Clinton administration lacked a comprehensive strategy and proved itself incapable of effective leadership.

Clinton had campaigned on three foreign policy ideas in 1992 that a year later he pulled together in a strategy that became known as "enlargement." His presidency, he had predicted, would have to reshape and modernize the nation's military establishment (including the ending of discrimination against gays, which caused a tremendous uproar); deal with the growing impact of economics in foreign affairs (geoeconomics rather than geopolitics, with the latter's emphasis on military considerations); and encourage the worldwide spread of democracy ("pragmatic neo-Wilsonianism," according to National Security Adviser Anthony Lake). The growth of democratic states, Clinton insisted, ensured international prosperity and security. Enlargement strategy, according to Lake, would "strengthen the community of market democracies," "foster and consolidate new democracies and market economies," "counter the aggression and support the liberalization of states hostile to democracy," and "help democracy and market economies take root in regions of greatest humanitarian reform." The United States felt no idealistic obligation to promote human rights and democracy all over the world. The new policy sought to protect the nation's strategic and economic interests by ridding the post–Cold War era of commercial barriers. World peace would grow out of a free-market economy that rested on law and economic freedom. The new administration intended to emphasize the establishment of economic ties with the emerging democratic states—including Russia. Clinton told Congress that he had put "economic competitiveness at the heart of our foreign policy." He soon created the National Economic Council under Secretary of the Treasury Robert E. Rubin to coordinate this new blend of domestic and foreign economic policies.

Post–Cold War Nationalism: Eastern Europe and the Balkans

The fallout from the end of the Cold War, meanwhile, unleashed deep-rooted forces of nationalism inside several countries, including those in the once-powerful and sprawling Soviet empire, that now threatened to cause international problems. Traditional remedies were no longer available: the shaky economic situation in the United States precluded meaningful assistance to those people seeking change, and the collapse of the Soviet threat to European security greatly reduced NATO's importance. In a critical period that required innovative approaches to a European world no longer burdened by the Cold War, the new president at first reacted haphazardly and often in utter confusion. He initially favored a strong response to a war that broke out in Bosnia and then backed off when receiving no European support. He first advocated the integration of the newly independent nations of Eastern Europe into NATO, but then, in December 1993, he abruptly changed course. In that year, Russia's first democratic election in nearly eight decades brought an ultra-nationalist member of the neofascist Liberal Democratic Party, Vladimir Zhirinovsky, to the lower house of Parliament. His election alarmed many in Eastern Europe that Russia would drop reform efforts at home and become more belligerent abroad, and it caused Clinton to fear that the incorporation of that region's nations into NATO might alienate the Russians by resurrecting Cold War boundaries. The White House therefore stunted NATO's growth, buying time by instituting more steps in the procedure of soliciting membership.

Zhirinovsky's election aroused strong strains of Russian nationalism that sent shock waves throughout Eastern Europe. In August 1991, just after the Gorbachev coup, Zhirinovsky had declared in the Kremlin, "I'll bury radioactive waste along the Lithuanian border and put up powerful fans and blow the stuff across at night. They'll all get radiation sickness. They'll die of it. When they either die out or get down on their knees, I'll stop." His campaign posters in 1993 promised, "I will bring Russia up off her knees." To do this, he demanded the incorporation of Estonia, Latvia, and Lithuania into Russia; the carving up of Poland; the conquest of Finland; and, incredibly, the seizure of Alaska from the United States. Failing to gain satisfaction on these demands could lead to what Zhirinovsky ominously called "new Hiroshimas." Vice President Albert Gore denounced Zhirinovsky's views as "reprehensible and anathema to all freedom-loving people." Clinton refused to see Zhirinovsky during the summit trip to Moscow in 1993 and drew a characteristic verbal tirade. Clinton, Zhirinovsky accused, was a "coward" who should "play his saxophone instead of coming here and meeting with nobodies."

Most observers realized that Zhirinovsky himself posed no threat to world security, but they also recognized that his rise to power signaled the existence of deep unrest inside Russia that Yeltsin must address through reforms. Zhirinovsky's party had fewer than 80 seats in the 450-member lower house, whereas reformers numbered about twice that amount. Clinton saw no reason to expect a "big new dangerous direction in Russian policy." But Ambassador-at-Large Strobe Talbott (a Russian specialist and Clinton's close friend and college classmate at Oxford) considered it necessary to convince Congress that Russia needed more aid rather than less in the election aftermath. He also assured Russia's neighbors that the United States would protect them from this new outburst of Russian nationalism. Talbott insisted that the key to their safety was the continued political and economic reform of Russia.

The most explosive problem in Europe continued to be the Balkans, where Yugoslavia's recent dissolution had led to a civil war in 1991 that reopened a centuries-old struggle between Muslims and Christians in Bosnia and Herzegovina. Yugoslavia after World War I was similar to most other countries in Eastern Europe in that it was a mixed state of diverse nationalities and religions. The populace was primarily Serb (Eastern Orthodox), but it also included significant numbers of Slovenes and Croats (Catholic) along with Bosnians (Muslim). The Serbs headed the national government and armed forces in the capital city of Belgrade and tried in vain to stop the country's disintegration in the post–Cold War period. When the republics of Slovenia and Croatia declared independence in 1991, the European Union (EU) recognized the new nations. The Yugoslav army intervened with force in both areas, setting off bitter fighting that the EU attempted to mediate rather than turn to NATO and invite U.S. participation. All peace efforts failed.

On one side stood the internationally recognized government in Bosnia led by President Alija Izetbegovic, a Muslim; on the other side was Serbia's President Slobodan Milosevic, an outspoken proponent of a "Greater Serbia" free of Islamic fundamentalists. The United Nations admitted both Slovenia and Croatia as member nations and branded Milosevic's Serbian government the aggressor. The Serbs then focused their military assaults on Bosnia-Herzegovina, which also threatened to declare independence. A vicious military campaign ensued, with the Bosnian Serbs pursuing a self-proclaimed policy of "ethnic cleansing" aimed at the majority population of Muslims.

Other nations throughout the world at first only watched these horrifying events unfold in the Balkans. Although Serbia's attacks on Bosnia and Croatia (which were in military alliance) had not endangered the strategic interests of either the United States or Europe, the refusal of outside countries to help Bosnia had the potential of alienating Muslims in friendly Arab states and thereby threatening the West's oil flow. The United Nations announced an arms embargo on all sides in the war that originated out of an attempt to prevent the Russians from helping Serbia. Ironically, however, the Serbian forces already held the military advantage from having received weapons from the Yugoslav army, and the UN action actually augmented that superiority by denying arms to Bosnia. The United Nations also imposed economic sanctions—especially on oil—but half of Serbia's supply came from Russia and China, neither of which favored the oil sanction.

A brief respite in the war soon came, however. In November 1991, a UN Security Council delegation headed by Cyrus Vance, a former secretary of state in the Carter administration, negotiated an uneasy cease-fire between Yugoslavia and Croatia that left the Serbs holding nearly 25 percent of Croatian territory. Soon a UN peace-keeping team comprised primarily of British and French soldiers was en route to the troubled scene. In the following December, the situation sharply deteriorated when Germany ignored Vance's entreaties and extended recognition to Croatia and Slovenia. The remainder of the EU countries did the same, leading the United States to follow suit. Bosnia and Macedonia, the other two self-proclaimed republics, eventually won recognition from the Bush White House as well. Only a shell of Yugoslavia remained. Recognition, the president wishfully asserted, might help to stabilize the Balkans. By no means would he give in to the pressure for a U.S. military intervention that might, he feared, lead to another Vietnam. Nor would Britain or France consider air strikes or any form of stronger action; they realized that the UN peacekeeping forces already in place had become Milosevic's hostages. Yugoslavia, one State Department official asserted, had become a "tar baby" that no one would touch. Bush's greatest fear was that Milosevic would set off a Balkan war by resuming the fighting, this time in Kosovo, a former Yugoslav (now Serb) province heavily populated with Albanians.

The cease-fire quickly crumbled despite several peace efforts, including a partition proposal that sought to divide Bosnia into ten districts under the nominal control of a governing body in Sarajevo. As fighting erupted anew in Bosnia, charges spread of genocide as Serbian forces burned and sacked villages, engaged in mass tortures of non-Serbs in concentration camps, systematically raped Muslim women, and laid a deadly siege on the Bosnian capital of Sarajevo that led to mass starvation. "Like pre-1914 Europe," brooded one French political analyst, "the new world order of George Bush died in Sarajevo." If not dead, the new world order had met its stiffest match: ethnic violence in economically primitive areas has seldom proved subject to economic boycotts or sanctions. And rarely have appeals to compromise been effective when one of the central issues driving that ethnic conflict was nationalism and another was religion—the ancient dispute between Christians and Muslims.

The Clinton administration acted indecisively toward the Balkan crisis. It showed no interest in partition. Not only did such an idea violate the Wilsonian principle of self-determination, but it would also mark a concession to aggression that ignored the chief lesson of Munich. The president must not appear weak. He had already come under attack for his earlier opposition to the Vietnam War and for his appointing advisers characterized as soft on foreign policy issues. *The Economist* of London had declared in December 1992 that the United States under the new president must act as "world cop" by forcefully intervening as the most "humane response" to the Serbs' "systematic nastiness." Clinton, however, could not consider military intervention because Bosnia posed no threat to U.S. interests—a point emphatically made by public opinion polls that showed 70 percent opposition to American involvement. A *New York Times* editorial in February 1993 warned against the "slippery slope" of military involvement: "Is anyone around the Oval Office reading history books?" Yet Clinton had to do something. Former British Prime Minister Margaret Thatcher publicly denounced the West's refusal to adopt stronger measures. "I never thought I would see another holocaust," she said, leaving the implication that her successor, John Major, was repeating the pre–World War II mistakes of Neville Chamberlain. A call for negotiations without the leverage of force, Clinton likewise knew, would not work. Under great pressure from the European governments to support the partition plan, he agreed to do so only if all parties concerned did so first. The Bosnian Serbs rejected the proposal.

President Clinton recommended arming the Muslims, but this idea drew no support from European allies, and the United Nations tried again. It established a 14,000-member peacekeeping force from thirty countries (the first in Europe) to help the more than a million Muslims in the splintered country, most of them gathered in refugee camps euphemistically

called "safe havens" and under UN troop protection. As the casualty lists soared and thousands died of starvation, the Security Council
authorized NATO's military commanders to
approve air strikes against Bosnian Serb forces,
who had laid siege to tens of thousands of Muslims in eastern Bosnia. In the summer of 1993,
the United Nations sent a peacekeeping unit to
the old Yugoslav border on the south to keep
the conflict from spreading into neighboring
Macedonia.

As the Muslims accused the Serbs of genocide, the problems steadily escalated until early
1994, when the United States joined other
NATO countries in warning the Serbs of aerial assaults unless they called off their siege of
Sarajevo. The situation was desperate. In early
January of that year, Bosnian Serbs had declared a cease-fire on the Bosnian capital, only
to resume their barrage shortly thereafter. During the holiday season, both sides violated the
truce, killing more than a hundred civilians in
the process. The commander of the UN peacekeepers in Bosnia resigned in disgust, and a
disgruntled French general bitterly compared
his troops to "goats tied to a stake."

There were no signs of a breakthrough to
peace in what Secretary of State Warren
Christopher called the "problem from hell."
Limited air strikes finally quieted the siege
guns, but the Bosnian Serbs denounced
NATO for intervening on behalf of the Muslims and broke off contact with the United
Nations. In August 1994, Bosnian Serbs
raided a UN weapons depot west of Sarajevo,
carting off a tank, two armored personnel carriers, and an antiaircraft gun. When NATO
planes instantly responded by destroying a
Serb motorized antitank weapon, the speaker
of the Bosnian Serb parliament telephoned
UN officials in Zagreb within two hours of the
theft to assure them of the return of the UN
weapons the next day. In the meantime, Milosevic accused the Bosnian Serbs of "insane political ambitions" and announced a political
and economic break. Although he attributed
this decision to the Bosnian Serbs' refusal to
accept a UN peace plan, it more than likely re-

sulted from the impact of the international
trade embargo on his own country of Serbia.
The Bosnian Serbs' assaults nonetheless continued, drawing more air strikes from NATO
fighter-bombers that provoked the Serbs into
seizing UN peacekeepers as hostages (later released) to embarrass the United Nations and
force an end to the bombing.

In early 1995, several changes made peace
a possibility. A UN withdrawal from Bosnia
seemed imminent, raising talk of a U.S. military intervention ostensibly sent only to protect the UN forces as they pulled out.
Democratic leaders in the United States
warned that Bosnia was eating away at the
presidency, threatening the chances for reelection. The Clinton administration secretly
approved a Croatian proposal to import Iranian weapons, and Congress prohibited the
U.S. Navy from supporting the UN arms
embargo. By August, the better-supplied
Croatian forces had opened a successful assault against the Serbs that regained territorial losses and drew Muslim troop support.
NATO then launched a massive bombing
campaign that, combined with the ongoing
embargo, seriously damaged the Serbian war
effort. But the most important development
was the slaughter engineered by a Serb counteroffensive against UN forces at the safe
havens of Srebrenica and Zepa. World public opinion was furious over the mass killings
in Srebrenica. When the town fell, President
Clinton stormed at his National Security
Council leaders, "I'm getting creamed." Following the European lead, he angrily realized, had led to failure. He had placed the
fate of his presidency in his allies' hands, and
they had acted in their own interests by taking no decisive action. Especially galling was
the snide remark made by French president
Jacques Chirac after a June visit to Washington: the White House, he declared in a
widely publicized quote, was "vacant."

By early September 1995, the chances for
peace had brightened. The president had
called on his advisers to formulate a "comprehensive peace settlement" that rested on

recognition of Bosnia, Croatia, and Yugoslavia, followed by the lifting of economic sanctions after a cease-fire. Popular opposition in the United States to military intervention had lessened, adding teeth to his program. A *Washington Post* editorial in late May 1995 had warned that the "abandonment of Bosnia would rip at the threads of international order." Another Bosnian Serb bombardment of Sarajevo had killed more than thirty people, and NATO had responded with sustained air strikes on military targets. Clinton had put Assistant Secretary of State Richard C. Holbrooke in charge of negotiations, and he warned the White House that the Serb attack and NATO's bombings constituted the "most important test of American leadership since the end of the Cold War . . . not only in Bosnia but in Europe." Unlike the Vietcong, he insisted, the Bosnian Serbs would fold. Belgrade, he argued, would not support them. Milosevic wanted to see the sanctions lifted, the Bosnian Serbs could preserve the lands they had, and the Croatians could safeguard their recent territorial gains. NATO allies were now ready to en-force an agreement, particularly since Clinton assured them of American troop participation in the peace-keeping mission.

On November 21, both sides agreed to a series of U.S.-mediated peace talks at Wright-Patterson Air Force Base near Dayton, Ohio, that resulted in an uneasy settlement of the forty-two-month-long Bosnian conflict. A cease-fire had gone into effect the previous October, about a month after Holbrooke announced the main points of a settlement on September 8. Conditions were right. The Serbs wanted to solidify their gains for Bosnia and to halt the economic sanctions, the Croats sought to guarantee their new state and the security of their people elsewhere, and the Muslims demanded an end to their people's suffering and the establishment of a Bosnian state with strong Muslim representation. Three weeks of negotiations led by Holbrooke produced an agreement to divide Bosnia into two states: one a republic under Bosnian Serb control, the other a Croat–Muslim federation with Sarajevo as capital. Bosnian leaders immediately established a new government led by a three-member presidency, one from each

---

In this cease-fire agreement, the Clinton administration attempted to restore peace to the Balkans.

Dayton Peace Accords, Annex 1A: Agreement on the Military Aspects of the Peace Settlement, November 21, 1995, The Avalon Project at Yale Law School, New Haven, Connecticut, www.yale.edu/lawweb/avalon.

Article I

The United Nations Security Council is invited to adopt a resolution by which it will authorize Member States or regional organizations and arrangements to establish a multinational military Implementation Force (hereinafter "IFOR"). The Parties understand and agree that this Implementation Force may be composed of ground, air and maritime units from NATO and non-NATO nations, deployed to Bosnia and Herzegovina to help ensure compliance with the provisions of this Agreement. . . .

The purposes of these obligations are as follows:

    (a) to establish a durable cessation of hostilities. . . .
    (b) to provide for the support and authorization of the IFOR. . . .
    (c) to establish lasting security and arms control measures. . . .

Article II

The Parties shall comply with the cessation of hostilities begun with the agreement of October 5, 1995 and shall continue to refrain from all offensive operations of any type against each other.

ethnic group and all chosen in a national election. The White House three years earlier had opposed a Bosnian partition but now reversed its position. As a *New York Times* editorial put it on September 9, "The partition plan, imperfect as it is, offers the best hope for ending a war that has done grievous damage to Bosnia's people. It would be better if Bosnia were untouched and intact, but three years of vicious fighting have eliminated that possibility, and the Bosnians themselves are resigned to accepting a good deal less."

On December 14, in France, the presidents of Bosnia, Serbia, and Croatia signed the Paris Peace Accord, which enacted the Dayton agreements. To keep the peace, President Clinton joined Operation Joint Endeavor by pledging 20,000 U.S. ground troops as part of a NATO force of 60,000. The United States, Great Britain, and France would supervise the three zones until the civilian government could take over. America "stood for peace in Bosnia," he proudly declared in his January 23, 1996, State of the Union Address. "Remember the skeletal prisoners, the mass graves, the campaign to rape and torture, the endless lines of refugees, the threat of a spreading war. All these threats, all these horrors have now begun to give way to a promise of peace." Even though critics accused the West of reacting too slowly to the Balkan crisis, its actions had ended a terrible nightmare. In September 1996, elections in Yugoslavia resulted in Serb and Croatian majorities who advocated Bosnia's annexation of their peoples' territories and the establishment of a Muslim ministate around Sarajevo. Muslim president Alija Izetbegovic won enough votes to become chair of the three-member presidency. In the following December, Clinton announced that U.S. forces would stay in Bosnia for an indefinite period.

Peace in the Balkans was short-lived, however. In 1999, violence erupted again when Milosevic ordered an ethnic cleansing of Kosovo, a Serbian province that was comprised primarily of Albanian Muslims but had enjoyed some measure of self-rule. The Kosovo Liberation Army (KLA) had launched a series of assaults on Serbian police in 1996, drawing a severe counteraction. By the spring of 1998, the KLA had intensified its fighting with the aid of additional arms from inside Albania. The situation in Kosovo seemed less complicated than that in Bosnia, but this was not the case. The Serbs constituted nearly a third of Bosnia's people; they were only a small minority in Kosovo. Bosnians spoke the same language; the Serbs and Albanians in Kosovo were distinctly different ethnic groups. Milosevic, who had turned his back on his Serbian allies in Bosnia, had built his nationalist reputation by taking away Kosovo's autonomy during the late 1980s. He and his cohort had been receptive to outside intervention in Bosnia; the Serbian military in Kosovo would oppose such a move, even at the risk of causing a military confrontation with peace-seeking powers. Whereas the violence in Bosnia remained within its boundaries, the intensified fighting in Kosovo threatened to spread into neighboring Albania and Macedonia. Kosovo was not a "second Bosnia," as many Europeans and Americans had surmised. The former U.S. ambassador to Yugoslavia, Warren Zimmermann, offered the most trenchant remark: "Inconceivable though it may seem, Kosovo is . . . a more complex problem than Bosnia."

The West again responded in a haphazard fashion. NATO warned Milosevic to respect Kosovo's sovereignty. The persecutions nonetheless continued, causing NATO's military leaders in March to order the bombing of Serbia's military and communication facilities. This step likewise proved ineffective. The United States reacted as indecisively as it did at the onset of the Bosnian crisis. It denounced the KLA as "terrorists," a charge that might have been accurate but had the unintended impact of encouraging Milosevic to employ military force without fear of Western retaliation. It recommended economic sanctions, only to encounter rigid French and Russian opposition to a measure that had already proved empty in Yugoslavia.

It failed at negotiations—including Clinton's meeting with pacifist Kosovar leader Ibrahim Rugova and Holbrooke's later conference with a KLA leader, effectively legitimizing the organization earlier branded as terrorist. The White House then abruptly reversed its policy and called for military force. The Serbs, meanwhile, continued to kill and rape ethnic Albanians, forcing the KLA into retreat and driving more than 800,000 refugees into the neighboring states of Albania and Macedonia.

Peace finally returned in the summer of 1999. Milosevic called off his brutal assault in June, but only when facing an aerial barrage, an oil embargo, and resistance from all nations around him. He withdrew his Serb forces from Kosovo, allowed the refugees to return home, agreed to a NATO peacekeeping force, and authorized expanded autonomy to Kosovo. The atrocities committed by Milosevic's forces in Kosovo led to indictments against him and his top officers by the International War Crimes Tribunal at The Hague. According to a Western diplomat, Milosevic was "a python, slowly tightening his grip." National elections in September 2000, however, resulted in his overwhelming defeat by Vojislav Kostunica. Milosevic refused to concede, calling for a runoff that ignited student strikes and guaranteed further troubles.

In the spring of 2001, Yugoslav authorities placed Milosevic under arrest, charging him with domestic crimes, but he soon stood trial before a UN court on charges of genocide, war crimes, and crimes against humanity. Before the international tribunal could render a verdict in a trial lasting four years, he was found dead in his cell in March 2006.

Clinton's Balkan policy deserves a mixed verdict. Peace in both Bosnia and Kosovo was his legacy, but had he acted quickly at the beginning of the Bosnian crisis in early 1993, he might have achieved the same cease-fire terms that came in the fall of 1995. Such resolute action might also have prevented the crisis in Kosovo. At the cost of thousands of lives, he had moved only when it became evident that

continued inaction might damage his domestic program and hence his presidency.

The Middle East

In the midst of the Balkan troubles, a faint glimmer of peace appeared in the Middle East in September 1993, when Israel and the PLO agreed to mutual recognition in an agreement hailed by many contemporaries as pathbreaking. On the South Lawn of the White House on September 13, President Clinton presided over an elaborate ceremony that featured a historic handshake between Israeli prime minister Yitzhak Rabin and PLO leader Yasir Arafat, dressed in his olive-drab uniform. "Enough. Enough blood and tears," Rabin had asserted. The "Declaration of Principles on Interim Self-Government Arrangements" marked the culmination of a long process that began during the Yom Kippur War of 1973 and seemingly concluded in Oslo, Norway, where two Israeli professors contacted the PLO and by August 1992 (without U.S. input) hammered out a text. Indeed, the White House had dismissed such talks as unimportant.

The Declaration provided a framework for a comprehensive peace, meaning that success was contingent on subsequent agreements with Israel's bordering countries of Jordan, Lebanon, and Syria. In addition to mutual recognition, the Israelis would withdraw from Gaza and Jericho, but only after receiving security assurances for the 5,000 Israeli settlers in Gaza. Under a Civil Administration of Palestinians, the PLO would control the Gaza Strip and the West Bank, both occupied by Israel since the Six Day War in 1967. Most important, the PLO renounced terrorism, and Arafat promised a repudiation of its charter's call for Israel's destruction. Elections would take place among the nearly 2 million Palestinians on the West Bank and in Gaza, aimed at bringing self-government, first in the town of Jericho on the West Bank and then in Gaza before spreading into every other sector of the West Bank except for East Jerusalem. During a five-year interim period, the Palestinians were to gain autonomy over the lands, and negotiations would begin with the Israelis in 1995 over a final settlement that pointed to the establishment of a Palestinian homeland. The two sides had until December 1993 to implement the September terms.

Why this progress? The PLO could no longer count on Soviet support because of the end of the Cold War. Arafat's ill-advised decision to support Saddam Hussein in the Gulf War had cost the PLO its long-time financial assistance from Iraq's enemy Arab kingdoms. Before these events, however, Arafat's control had come into question when he reacted with restraint to the *intifada*, which had broken out in December 1987 among the West Bank Palestinians in protest against Israeli occupation, and then announced in 1988 the establishment of a Palestinian "authority" in the troubled area, virtually recommending joint governing authority with Israel rather than its elimination. On the other side, Israelis were weary of the long conflict and feared that the *intifada* had won growing support from Palestinian extremists. Peace could bring economic stability in the region, which would profit everyone.

But the much-heralded September agreement in Washington constituted only another step in a long road to peace that lay cluttered with contentious issues. Arafat told reporters that the pact meant the "birth of Palestine" because self-rule provided the nucleus for a Palestinian state with Jerusalem as its capital. "He can forget about it," Rabin emphatically responded. Violence had erupted again—on the day before the agreement. In an incident of September 12 that proved to be the first of many to follow, Palestinian militants attacked Israelis in Gaza City, killing four. Meanwhile, in the occupied West Bank, protests against the accord led to a confrontation in which Israeli soldiers shot and killed two Palestinian youths while wounding eight others.

The December deadline came and passed, with no implementation of the September agreement. Rabin expressed concern about his people's safety and opposed even a token withdrawal of Israeli troops from the Gaza Strip and Jericho. Arafat made new demands, most notably Palestinian control of the border crossings between the autonomous areas and Egypt and Jordan. Border control, he insisted, was a symbolic sign of sovereignty that prevented humiliating interrogations and body searches by Israeli soldiers. But Israel feared that Arafat's hold on these checkpoints would bolster his claim to statehood and allow the infiltration of terrorists. Rabin assured the Knesset (Parliament) in mid-December that "no compromise is possible." In London, Arafat declared, "I haven't given up my dream [of a unified state]. But love cannot be one-sided."

What was the White House position? Clinton hoped to facilitate an Israeli–PLO settlement by first securing agreements with the Arab states of Jordan, Lebanon, and Syria. During his visit to the Middle East the following October 1994, he met with Syria's President Hafez al-Assad in Damascus, vainly attempting to lure him into the peace talks and bring an end to his country's support for international terrorism. Clinton had tried to persuade Syria to enter into a pact with Israel that included Lebanon (Syria's protégé) and would encourage peace along Israel's northern frontier. Since the Six Day War of 1967, Israeli troops had occupied the Golan Heights, a narrow strip of land along northern Israel that Islamic activists used to launch attacks. Rabin and Assad reportedly favored the restoration of the Golan Heights to Syria in exchange for its recognition of Israel, but they took no initiative toward an agreement. In early May 1994, a series of autonomy agreements between Israel and the PLO transferred the administration of Jericho and most of the Gaza Strip to the Palestinians. Under this self-rule agreement, the 5,000 Jewish settlers in the Gaza Strip would remain in their homes, protected by Israeli soldiers and PLO forces. In the following July, the White House canceled Jordan's foreign debt in exchange for its agreement to a treaty with Israel that provided mutual recognition. Jordan's King Hussein and Israel's Prime Minister Rabin also laid the basis for bilateral trade and tourist exchanges by agreeing to adjoining boundaries and dividing water rights and other natural resources. The Clinton administration authorized seed money for aid from Japan, Europe, Scandinavia, and the Gulf Arab states, and it furnished assistance to the new Palestinian communities in the Gaza Strip and Jericho.

But sporadic outbreaks of violence in the Middle East continued to obstruct the erratic move toward a settlement. In late February 1995, trouble broke out on the West Bank when a Jewish extremist shot at least thirty Palestinians while at worship in Hebron and an angry mob beat him to death. The "Hebron massacre" once again drove home the tenuous nature of any Middle East settlement. One Israeli military spokesman observed, "You don't fire warning shots in a combat situation. All Gaza is a combat situation, all the time."

Then, on November 4, a right-wing Israeli student shot and killed Prime Minister Rabin at a peace rally in Tel Aviv, shocking the world and providing another impetus to peace in this battle-scarred land. President Clinton demonstrated his unbroken pursuit of peace by heading a U.S. delegation to Rabin's funeral in Tel Aviv. "Those who practice terror must not succeed," he later declared. "We must root them out, and we will not let them kill the peace." More violence broke out during the Israeli election campaign in the spring of 1996, when Palestinian terrorists in less than two weeks carried out four suicide bombings that killed more than sixty Israelis and wounded more than 200 others. Popular disenchantment with the peace process became clear when the voters narrowly selected a new prime minister, Benjamin Netanyahu, who headed the conservative Likud Party and promised "peace with security" as an unmistakable warning that he would concede nothing to the Arabs without absolute guarantees of Israel's safety. In January 1997, with the

area seething with tension, the White House joined other countries in exerting pressure on Israel to withdraw from Hebron.

This concession had a short-lived impact, however, because of the violent reaction to Netanyahu's call for new Jewish settlements in East Jerusalem, where many Palestinians resided. At a nine-day conference at Camp David, Maryland, in October 1998, Clinton oversaw agreements between Arafat and Netanyahu to withdraw from jointly held areas and release imprisoned Palestinians in exchange for Arafat's assurances (again) of an end to the PLO's demand for Israel's destruction. This was not enough for hard-liners in the Likud Party, however, who turned against Netanyahu and forced a national election in the spring of 1999. He lost to Ehud Barak, who had campaigned for reopened negotiations with the Palestinians. In the summer of 2000, President Clinton attempted to broker a Middle East settlement between the Israelis and the Palestinians, but he secured no treaty by the September deadline. Late that same month, Israeli police killed and wounded a large number of Palestinians in a clash by a holy site in Jerusalem. The violence continued.

Peace in other parts of the Middle East also remained elusive. Saddam Hussein in late 1994 had again shown signs of ordering an invasion of Kuwait, leading the Clinton administration to send a huge military contingent to the Persian Gulf to maintain the peace. Before the World Jewish Congress in April 1995, the president announced his "dual containment" policy, which sought to harness the ambitions of Iraq and Iran. Both countries "harbor terrorists within their borders," he declared. "They establish and support terrorist base camps in other lands. They hunger for nuclear and other weapons of mass destruction. Every day, they put innocent civilians in danger and stir up discord among nations. Our policy toward them is simple: They must be contained." Twice in 1998—in February and November—Clinton dispatched military forces into the Persian Gulf, only to call off attacks at the last minute when Saddam agreed to cooperate with inspection teams. In mid-December, however, Saddam again interfered with the inspection process, leading the president to approve "Operation Desert Fox," an air and missile assault that lasted for four days and again brought an uneasy peace. Critics, however, noted more than a coincidence in the president's resort to force in the midst of the House debate on impeachment over a sex scandal that resulted in an indictment and ultimately ended in a Senate acquittal.

The end of the Cold War had put a different complexion on U.S. interests in the Middle East. Containment and confrontation tactics had proved fruitless. Whereas in the Cold War the United States had used its influence to oppose Soviet expansion in the region while protecting Israel, it realized in the post–Cold War era that an Arab–Israeli conflict could not escalate into a U.S.–Soviet confrontation and thereby lost the sense of urgency in seeking a final settlement. The Oslo agreements had turned the emphasis toward the Palestinians, over whom the United States had little or no leverage, and away from the Arabs, who had been more malleable to its interests. Thus, as the peace focus shifted to the core issue of Palestinian autonomy, the peace process ground nearly to a halt, and White House frustration turned more against the Israelis. This new tension between the United States and Israel received further impetus from the steady decline of U.S. influence in the region after the Gulf War. Indeed, French and Russian resistance to U.S. hegemony in the Middle East had caused some Arab states to inch closer to neutrality. Moreover, the growth of Arab nationalism and Islamic fundamentalism made it prohibitive for Arabs to support the United States in its continuing battle with Saddam, especially in view of Israeli–PLO troubles. In a bizarre reversal of form, Washington began courting Teheran in an effort to exert more pressure on Saddam.

The Arab–Israeli dispute was no longer the exclusive issue in the Middle East. The Soviets had lost their dominance over the Caucasus and Central Asia, meaning that new forms of competition had assumed pivotal importance not only because of the region's rich oil reserves but also because of the fear of nuclear proliferation. What if archenemies Iran and Iraq developed nuclear power? Israel had already acquired such capacity, while both India and Pakistan (age-old enemies) did the same in the spring of 1998. If the end of the Cold War had pushed the Arabs and Israelis closer to a final resolution that included the Palestinians, it had also spawned a host of other regional problems that continued to interfere with the search for a lasting peace.

East Asia and Other Matters

Clinton confronted equally serious problems in East Asia. Realizing this region was fast becoming a commercial Mecca, he sought better trade relations with its leaders. As noted earlier, the United States considered it critical to deal amicably with Japan and in the early summer of 1995 narrowly averted a commercial war by securing a trade agreement and then turning full circle from confrontational policies to economic and political engagement. China, too, presented a problem. Its continued human rights violations and sales of nuclear weapons technology to Pakistan and other nations raised questions about whether the United States should renew its most-favored-nation status with that Communist government. About 40 percent of China's exports entered the United States, resulting in a $30 billion annual commercial surplus. But China refused to yield; instead, it cracked down on citizens who called for democratic changes and jailed Tibetans who demanded independence for their country. In June 1993, however, the Clinton administration extended most-favored-nation commercial rights to Beijing in exchange for China's release of several imprisoned dissidents. The next year, in May, the White House formally separated human rights aspirations from commercial aims, admitting that their linkage had yielded few results and declaring that the old policy of engagement offered greater promise.

Sino–American problems remained. Tensions flared in March 1996 over elections in Taiwan when the Chinese government began an intimidation campaign that included firing three missiles near the island and staging military maneuvers in the Taiwan Strait. Two U.S. carrier task forces headed toward the troubled area. The crisis passed after the White House confirmed its support of "one China" and the Beijing government promised not to help terrorists. Beijing's leaders still claimed Taiwan as part of China and feared that the elections would bring in a new administration that insisted on independence. In February 1997, Deng died, leaving a mixed legacy of human rights abuses, military expansion, and the clampdown on pro-democracy demonstrators at Tiananmen Square along with a massive opening of trade that led to China's economic upswing during the 1990s. Anxious Americans on July 1 joined others throughout the world in watching Hong Kong pass peacefully from British hands to China's. Although Hong Kong's residents totaled only 6 million in comparison with China's 1.2 billion, the former British colony furnished almost 20 percent of China's gross national product and would help the vast country become an even greater force in international affairs. China's new president, Jiang Zemin, visited the United States in October, and in the following year worked with Clinton to ease a crisis between India and Pakistan over nuclear testing. President Clinton reciprocated by traveling to China that same year of 1998, where he expressed the two nations' growing concern over Japan's stumbling economy. The administration's enlargement policy now included China as well as Japan.

In North Korea, the Clinton administration confronted its most dangerous issue when that Communist regime threatened to withdraw from the Non-Proliferation Treaty of 1985 and develop its own nuclear capacity. More serious, North Korea might sell nuclear weapons, which could cause a regional arms race and a major proliferation problem. As tensions soared throughout East Asia, President Clinton reaffirmed the U.S. troop commitment to South Korea during the summer of 1993 and in the following spring made preparations for implanting defensive missiles. The crisis soon passed when former President Jimmy Carter acted as intermediary in persuading Kim Il Sung's North Korean government to halt its nuclear program while talks were under way. Then Kim died in July 1994, leaving the country's leadership to his son Kim Jong Il, who continued the talks in Geneva. The result was a deal in October by which the United States, South Korea, and Japan provided North Korea with nearly $5 billion in energy assistance (including peaceful nuclear reactors), free oil for up to ten years, and diplomatic relations with Washington and Tokyo—all in exchange for its complying with the Nuclear Non-Proliferation Treaty by shutting down its plutonium reprocessing plant and permitting international inspection within eight years (promises made years earlier and broken). Chinese pressure had pushed Kim to relax tensions, primarily out of a desire to diminish the U.S. presence in Asia. Kim also recognized the questionable value in heading a rogue state. In 2000, North Korea and South Korea agreed to end their war that began in June 1950, but their relationship remained uneasy.

Vietnam also posed a major dilemma for the administration as the White House attempted to balance commercial potential with lingering hatreds stemming from America's longest war. In February 1994 the United States lifted its nearly two-decade-long trade embargo on Vietnam and, a little more than a year later, on July 11, 1995, extended diplomatic recognition. The move, argued President Clinton, would triple the trade between the countries to more than $8 billion by the end of the century, facilitate a settlement of the issues of prisoners of war (POWs) and those missing in action (more than 2,200 American soldiers missing in action and still unaccounted for), and, by focusing on economic ties, help put the

U.S.–Vietnam War into the past. To ease the angry fallout of such a move, he appointed as ambassador a former POW in Hanoi for seven years, Pete Peterson. Five years later, in the summer of 2000, the two nations reached a trade agreement permitting generally open commerce for the first time since the end of their war in 1973.

The Clinton administration also tried, with some success, to bring peace to Northern Ireland. It first argued that Sinn Fein, the political voice of the Irish Republican Army (IRA), deserved a seat in the negotiations over the status of Ulster. When the State Department in Washington permitted Sinn Fein leader Gerry Adams to come to the United States, the British government angrily protested that he was a terrorist. Clinton nonetheless invited Adams to the White House in 1995, on St. Patrick's Day. The president's tactics resulted in Adams's attracting American support for his cause and then arranging for the IRA to announce a unilateral cease-fire later that same year. Clinton reciprocated with a visit to Belfast, where he assured a cheering public of U.S. support if the Irish people worked toward peace. The result was a truce agreed to by the British government, the Ulster Defense Association, and the IRA.

Although IRA bombings in London soon broke the truce in April 1996, new talks began in September that culminated twenty-one months later in the Good Friday Peace Accord of April 10, 1998. In Belfast, Northern Ireland, British prime minister Tony Blair and Northern Ireland's prime minister, Bertie Ahern, ended three decades of fighting by approving a peace pact that resulted from a long series of arduous negotiations chaired by former U.S. Senator George Mitchell. To satisfy the Irish unionists, mostly Catholic, who wanted the British province integrated into a united Ireland, and the Irish republicans, mostly Protestant, who wished to continue British rule in Northern Ireland, the British and Irish governments agreed that Northern Ireland would remain within the United Kingdom unless Irish majorities voted for unity. In late May 1998, Irish voters overwhelmingly approved the pact, setting in motion the machinery for implementing the Good Friday Peace Accord. President Clinton encouraged peace with a visit to Northern Ireland in September.

Perhaps the biggest barometer of whether the Clinton administration had taken a new direction in foreign policy was its attitude toward intervention. In Haiti, the White House took an interventionist course when it exerted pressure on strongman Raoul Cédras and his military clique to leave the island after their coup in 1991. With the help of President Carter as intermediary (again), along with General Colin Powell and Senator Sam Nunn, the president achieved Cédras's departure without serious incident. In September 1994, Clinton approved "Operation Uphold Democracy," which authorized U.S. troops to facilitate the peaceful return of ousted President Jean-Bertrand Aristide. The United States and the United Nations then cooperated with the Haitian government in arranging a series of national elections that led to the first democratic change of presidents in that nation's history—the election of René Preval in December 1995. The thirty-nation force had already withdrawn from Haiti in March, leaving the peacekeeping responsibility to the United Nations.

Prospects of a New World Order

As the United States entered the twenty-first century, it became clear that the chief legacy of the Cold War was a distinctly different global order in which no single power was dominant. Franklin D. Roosevelt's vision of a half-century earlier had seemingly emerged: a world order based on the principle of collective security exercised through the United Nations. His World War II aims had finally reached fulfillment with the important position of the United States in international affairs, its resolution of differences with the countries once part of the former Soviet Union, its recognition of China's integral role in a peaceful world, and the collapse of colonial rule. So had the Yalta Declaration on Liberated Europe manifested itself through the democratization of Eastern Europe. The end of the Cold War had brought to a close that long and bitter U.S.–Soviet rivalry in the Security Council, thus allowing the United Nations to become an active guardian of peace.

But the image was considerably different from the reality. The bipolar world of 1945 had rested on military power but had now given way to new power alignments based primarily on economics. The world remained bipolar in terms of nuclear weaponry and delivery mechanisms, but it had divided into three distinct regional blocs. Western Europe had moved toward a union of states by the establishment of the European Common Market in the early 1990s. East Asia was the scene of unparalleled economic growth with Japan leading the way and only the Philippines lagging behind. And third was the bloc taking shape in North America, led by the United States and including Canada, the Caribbean basin, and Mexico. NAFTA had promoted the economic integration of the continent, making it necessary to speak of superblocs rather than superpowers in discussing international leadership. Clinton had made his nation's domestic economy the measure of success, but he had done so only by securing free-trade agreements that created new jobs and strengthened the dollar. Secretary of State Madeleine Albright, Warren Christopher's successor in 1997 following Clinton's reelection in 1996, pointed to one of the most salient facts of the administration: "Thanks to over 200 new market agreements we have created 1.6 million American jobs."

Clinton's foreign policy had a mixed success. He had moved from an idealistic approach that resulted most often in chaos and indecision to a policy based on pragmatism and some sense of strategy built on expanding global trade. He achieved the expansion of NATO to include three East European members by March 1999—Poland, Hungary, and the Czech Republic—and redefined the

meaning of European security while maintaining an active U.S. involvement. The downside, of course, was the disintegration of the "strategic partnership" with Russia that resulted not only from the NATO issue but also from a revived Russian nationalism and a continued reluctance by the West to extend economic assistance. His economic enlargement strategy succeeded in opening new commercial avenues and encouraging economic prosperity at home, but at the cost of near silence on environmental needs in the face of corporate pressure against government regulations. Most telling, the moral stature of the presidency suffered a devastating blow not only from the indecision and backtracking of the administration's foreign policy but also from the personal scandals that rocked the White House.

Free trade had remained Clinton's guide in spreading democracy by integrating the economies of the Pacific Rim, European continent, and Western Hemisphere. "With our help, the forces of reform in Europe's newly free nations have laid the foundations of democracy," the president declared. "We've helped them to develop successful market economies, and now are moving from aid to trade and investment." Martin Walker wrote in *The New Yorker* that "the age of geopolitics has given way to an age of what might be called geo-economics." Clinton's new world order had "abandoned the militarized slogans of the past to the commercial realities of the future." Not only did the United States become the world's military and economic leader, but it also contributed to the global spread of democracy. In the mid-1970s, about 25 percent of the world's independent nations chose their leaders by democratic elections. As the new millennium began, that percentage had doubled. Problems remained in China and Bosnia, the environment was in danger, global terrorism was a recurring threat, and Russian prospects for democracy and economic reforms remained elusive as former Cold Warrior and KGB officer Vladimir Putin succeeded the aged and worn Yeltsin as president in the

George W. Bush Inauguration
Bush takes oath as president on January 20, 2001, as his family and other dignitaries observe the
proceedings. *(Wide World Photos, New York)*

elections of March 2000. The tenets of a free-market democracy had taken hold in several countries, however. In early December 1996, *New York Times* columnist Thomas L. Friedman highlighted the key element in Clinton's enlargement strategy: "No two countries that both have a McDonald's have ever fought a war against each other."

All these problems and more confronted Clinton's successor in the new millennium, President George W. Bush, who narrowly defeated Vice President Al Gore in the hotly contested election of 2000.

Selected Readings

Ambrose, Stephen E., and Douglas G. Brinkley. *Rise to Globalism: American Foreign Policy since 1938.* 8th ed., 1997.

Amos, Deborah. *Lines in the Sand: Desert Storm and the Remaking of the Arab World.* 1992.

Arnson, Cynthia. *Crossroads: Congress, the President, and Central America, 1976–1993.* 1994.

Ash, Timothy G. *In Europe's Name: Germany and the Divided Continent.* 1994.

———. *The Magic Lantern: The Revolution of '89 Witnessed in Warsaw, Budapest, Berlin, and Prague.* 1990.

Aslund, Anders. *Gorbachev's Struggle for Economic Reform: The Soviet Reform Process, 1985–1988.* 1989.

Atkinson, Rick. *Crusade: The Untold Story of the Persian Gulf War.* 1993.

Barnet, Richard J., and John Cavanagh. *Global Dreams: Imperial Corporations and the New World Order.* 1994.

Benedick, Richard E. *Ozone Diplomacy: New Directions in Safeguarding the Planet.* 1998.

Berman, William C. *America's Right Turn: From Nixon to Clinton.* 2nd ed., 1998.

Beschloss, Michael R., and Strobe Talbott. *At the Highest Levels: The Inside Story of the End of the Cold War.* 1993.

Brands, H. W. *The Devil We Knew: Americans and the Cold War.* 1993.

Brown, Archie. *The Gorbachev Factor.* 1996.

Buckley, Kevin. *Panama: The Whole Story.* 1991.

Buckley, Roger. *U.S.-Japan Alliance Diplomacy, 1945–1990.* 1992.

Buckley, Thomas H. "Clinton's Wilsonian Military Interventions: A Critique." In J. Garry Clifford and Theodore A. Wilson, eds., *Presidents, Diplomats, and Other Mortals,* 264–80. 2007.

Burns, James M., and Georgia J. Sorenson. *Dead Center: Clinton-Gore Leadership and the Perils of Moderation.* 1999.

Burrows, William E., and Robert Windrem. *Critical Mass: The Dangerous Race for Superweapons in a Fragmentary World.* 1994.

Bush, George, and Brent Scowcroft. *A World Transformed.* 1998.

Calleo, David P. *Beyond American Hegemony: The Future of the Western Alliance.* 1987.

Chace, James. *The Consequences of the Peace: The New Internationalism and American Foreign Policy.* 1992.

Cheng, Chu-yüang. *Behind the Tiananmen Massacre: Social, Political, and Economic Ferment in China.* 1990.

Clinton, Bill. *My Life.* 2004.

Cohen, Warren I. *America's Failing Empire: U.S. Foreign Relations since the Cold War.* 2005.

———. *America's Response to China: An Interpretive History of Sino-American Relations.* 2000.

Cox, Michael. *U.S. Foreign Policy after the Cold War: Superpower without a Mission?* 1995.

Cronin, James E. *The World the Cold War Made: Order, Chaos, and the Return of History.* 1996.

Dobbs, Michael. *Madeleine Albright: A Twentieth-Century Odyssey.* 1999.

Doder, Dusko, and Louise Branson. *Gorbachev: Heretic in the Kremlin.* 1990.

Drew, Elizabeth. *On the Edge: The Clinton Presidency.* 1994.

Dukes, Paul. *The Last Great Game: USA versus USSR.* 1989.

Ehrman, John. *The Rise of Neoconservatism: Intellectuals and Foreign Affairs, 1945–1994.* 1995.

Evangelista, Matthew. *Unarmed Forces: The Transnational Movement to End the Cold War.* 1999.

Freedman, Lawrence, and Efraim Karsh. *The Gulf Conflict, 1990–1991: Diplomacy and War in the New World Order.* 1993.

Freney, Michael A., and Rebecca S. Hartley. *United Germany and the United States.* 1991.

Friedman, Norman. *Desert Victory: The War for Kuwait.* 1991.

Gaddis, John L. *The Cold War: A New History.* 2005.

———. "The Tragedy of Cold War History." *Diplomatic History* 17 (1993): 1–16.

———. *The United States and the End of the Cold War: Implications, Reconsiderations, Provocations.* 1992.

Garthoff, Raymond L. *The Great Transition: American-Soviet Relations and the End of the Cold War.* 1994.

Gati, Charles. *The Bloc That Failed.* 1990.

Gerner, Deborah J. *One Land, Two Peoples: The Conflict over Palestine.* 1991.

Gittings, John. *China Changes Face: The Road from Revolution, 1949–1989.* 1989.

Gow, James. *Triumph of the Lack of Will: International Diplomacy and the Yugoslav War.* 1997.

Graham, Otis L., Jr. *Losing Time: The Industrial Policy Debate.* 1992.

Graubard, Stephen R. *Mr. Bush's War: Adventures in the Politics of Illusion.* 1992.

Grayson, George W. *The North American Free Trade Agreement: Regional Community and the New World Order.* 1995.

Greenberg, Paul. *No Surprises: Two Decades of Clinton Watching.* 1996.

Greene, John R. *The Presidency of George Bush.* 2000.

Greider, William. *Fortress America: The American Military and the Consequences of Peace.* 1998.

Halberstam, David. *War in a Time of Peace.* 2001.

Hanson, Jim M. *The Decline of the American Empire.* 1993.

Harding, Harry. *A Fragile Relationship: The United States and China since 1972.* 1992.

Haselkorn, Avigdor. *The Continuing Storm: Iraq, Poisonous Weapons and Deterrence.* 1999.

Hiro, Dilip. *Desert Shield to Desert Storm: The Second Gulf War.* 1992.

Hoffmann, Stanley. *World Disorders: Troubled Peace in the Post–Cold War Era.* 1998.

Hogan, Michael J., ed. "The End of the Cold War: A Symposium." *Diplomatic History* 16 (1992): 45–113, 223–318.

———, ed. *The End of the Cold War: Its Meanings and Implications.* 1992.

Holbrooke, Richard. *To End a War.* 1998.

Homer-Dixon, Thomas F. *Environmental Scarcity and Global Security.* 1993.

Hosking, Geoffrey A. *The Awakening of the Soviet Union.* 1991.

Hough, Jerry F. *Democratization and Revolution in the USSR, 1985–1991.* 1997.

Hunter, F. Robert. *The Palestinian Uprising: A War by Other Means.* 1993.

Hyland, William. *Clinton's World: Remaking American Foreign Policy.* 1999.

Kaiser, Robert G. *Why Gorbachev Happened: The Man and His Revolution.* 1991.

Karsh, Efraim, and Inari Rautsi. *Saddam Hussein: A Political Biography.* 1991.

Kaufman, Burton I. *The Arab Middle East and the United States: Inter-Arab Rivalry and Superpower Diplomacy.* 1996.

Kaufmann, William W. *Glasnost, Perestroika, and U.S. Defense Spending.* 1990.

Kennedy, Paul. *The Rise and Fall of the Great Powers: Economic Change and Military Conflict from 1500 to 2000.* 1987.

Kikkink, Kathryn. *Mixed Signals: U.S. Human Rights Policy and Latin America.* 2004.

Kuisel, Richard F. *Seducing the French: The Dilemma of Americanization.* 1993.

LaFeber, Walter. *America, Russia, and the Cold War, 1945–1996.* 8th ed., 1997.

———. *The Clash: A History of U.S.-Japan Relations.* 1997.

Lebow, Richard N., and Janice G. Stein. *We All Lost the Cold War.* 1994.

LeoGrande, William M. *Our Own Backyard: The United States in Central America, 1977–1992.* 1998.

Levering, Ralph B. *The Cold War: A Post-Cold War History.* 1994; rev. ed., 2005.

MacArthur, John R. *Second Front: Censorship and Propaganda in the Gulf War.* 1992.

Maier, Charles S. *Dissolution: The Crisis of Communism and the End of East Germany.* 1997.

Mandelbaum, Michael. *The Dawn of Peace in Europe.* 1996.

Mann, Jim. *About Face: A History of America's Curious Relationship with China from Nixon to Clinton.* 1999.

Marten, Kimberly Z. *Enforcing the Peace: Learning from the Imperial Past.* 2004.

Matthews, Ken. *The Gulf Conflict and International Relations.* 1993.

McMahon, Robert J. *The Limits of Empire: The United States and Southeast Asia since World War II.* 1999.

Melanson, Richard A. *American Foreign Policy since the Vietnam War: The Search for Consensus from Nixon to Clinton.* 2000.

Miller, Judith, and Laurie Mylorie. *Saddam Hussein and the Crisis in the Gulf.* 1990.

Mueller, John E. *Policy and Opinion in the Gulf War.* 1994.

Nau, Henry R. *The Myth of America's Decline: Leading the World Economy into the 1990s.* 1990.

Nesbitt, Francis N. *Race for Sanctions: African Americans against Apartheid, 1946–1994.* 2004.

Oberdorfer, Don. *From the Cold War to a New Era: The United States and the Soviet Union, 1983–1991.* 1998.

———. *The Turn: From the Cold War to a New Era. The United States and the Soviet Union, 1983–1990.* 1991.

Palmer, Michael A. *Guardians of the Gulf: A History of America's Expanding Role in the Persian Gulf.* 1992.

Parmet, Herbert S. *George Bush: The Life of a Lone Star Yankee.* 1997.

Paterson, Thomas G. *On Every Front: The Making and Unmaking of the Cold War.* 1992.

Pérez, Louis A., Jr. *Cuba and the United States: Ties of Singular Intimacy.* 1997.

Prados, John. *Presidents' Secret Wars: CIA Pentagon Covert Operations from World War II through the Persian Gulf.* 1996.

Priest, Dana. *The Mission: Waging War and Keeping Peace with America's Military.* 2003.

Quandt, William B. *Peace Process: American Diplomacy and the Arab-Israeli Conflict since 1967.* 1993.

Raat, W. Dirk. *Mexico and the United States: Ambivalent Vistas.* 1996.

Remnick, David. *Lenin's Tomb: The Last Days of the Soviet Empire.* 1993.

Rieff, David. *At the Point of a Gun: Democratic Dreams and Armed Intervention.* 2005.

Rosecrance, Richard N. *America's Economic Resurgence: A Bold New Strategy.* 1990.

Ruggie, John G. *Winning the Peace: America and World Order in the New Era.* 1996.

Sayigh, Yezid. *Armed Struggle and the Search for State: The Palestinian National Movement, 1949–1993.* 1997.

Schaller, Michael. *Altered States: The United States and Japan since the Occupation.* 1997.

Schoenbaum, David. *The United States and the State of Israel.* 1993.

Schoutz, Lars. *Beneath the United States: A History of U.S. Policy toward Latin America.* 1998.

Scranton, Margaret E. *The Noriega Years: U.S.-Panamanian Relations, 1981–1990.* 1991.

Shacochis, Bob. *The Immaculate Invasion.* 1999.

Sigal, Leon V. *Disarming Strangers: Nuclear Diplomacy with North Korea.* 1998.

Smith, Gaddis. *The Last Years of the Monroe Doctrine, 1945–1993.* 1994.

Smith, Jean Edward. *George Bush's War.* 1992.

Smith, Patrick L. *Japan: A Reinterpretation.* 1997.

Solomon, Robert. *Money on the Move: The Revolution in International Finance since 1980.* 1999.

Spanier, John W., and Steven W. Hook. *American Foreign Policy since World War II.* 14th ed., 1998.

Stares, Paul B. *Global Habit: The Drug Problem in a Borderless World.* 1996.

Steel, Ronald. *Temptations of a Superpower.* 1995.

Stern, Jessica. *The Ultimate Terrorists.* 1999.

Szabo, Stephen F. *The Diplomacy of German Unification.* 1992.

Treverton, Gregory F. *America, Germany, and the Future of Europe.* 1992.

Tucker, Robert W., and David C. Henrickson. *The Imperial Temptation: The New World Order and America's Purpose.* 1992.

Ulam, Adam B. *The Communists: The Story of Power and Lost Illusions, 1948–1991.* 1992.

Van Crefeld, Martin. *Nuclear Proliferation and the Future of Conflict.* 1993.

Weiner, Tim. *Legacy of Ashes: The History of the CIA.* 2007.

Weissman, Stephen R. *A Culture of Deference: Congress's Failure of Leadership in Foreign Policy.* 1995.

Westad, Odd Arne. *The Global Cold War: Third World Interventions and the Making of Our Times.* 2006.

Wittner, Lawrence S. *Toward Nuclear Abolition: A History of the World Nuclear Disarmament Movement, 1971 to the Present.* 2003.

Woodward, Bob. *The Commanders.* 1991.

Woodward, Susan L. *Balkan Tragedy: Chaos and Dissolution after the Cold War.* 1995.

Wyden, Peter. *Wall: The Inside Story of Divided Berlin.* 1989.

Yergin, Daniel. *The Prize: The Epic Quest for Oil, Money, and Power.* 1991.

CHAPTER 10

President George W. Bush and Missionary Diplomacy: 9/11, the Preemptive War with Iraq, and the Global War on Terrorism, 2001–

Regime Change in Iraq

Much like Woodrow Wilson in 1913, George W. Bush came to the presidency in 2001 with little government service and no experience in foreign affairs but with a passion for missionary diplomacy. Also like Wilson, Bush became wartime commander of a universal struggle for freedom that Wilson called a "war to make the world safe for democracy" and that Bush termed a "Global War on Terrorism." Additionally, each figure took office as a minority president, having failed to win a popular majority. Finally, both presidents advocated an interventionist foreign policy that at first appeared simple but ultimately developed into complicated and dangerous entanglements.

Two events have defined the Bush presidency: 9/11, or the terrorist attacks on the United States on September 11, 2001 by al-Qaeda, a Muslim extremist network trained in Afghanistan, and the March 2003 invasion of Iraq, stemming primarily from the belief that Saddam Hussein had weapons of mass destruction (WMD) but also as retaliation for his alleged complicity with al-Qaeda's leader, Saudi-born Osama bin Laden, in 9/11. Thus did the Iraqi conflict become an integral part

of the war on terrorism. When coalition forces led by Americans invaded Iraq in "Operation Iraqi Freedom" (OIF), the United States engaged in its first preemptive war.

Whether the administration manipulated the evidence, carefully selected only those items necessary to justify the Iraq War, or was so set on retribution that it saw only what it wanted to see, the Bush White House rushed into action based on suspicions and suppositions rather than hard evidence. It did not explore every avenue of diplomacy, pursued a plan heavily flawed in strategy and tactics, and failed to foresee the mammoth problems of occupation. The president intended to follow the path of his predecessor Bill Clinton in seeking regime change in Iraq, but unlike Clinton, Bush chose war over containment in a nation-building program aimed at creating a democratic government whose principles would extend beyond Iraqi borders and bring peace to the Middle East.

The roots of the Iraqi invasion lay in what the Bush administration regarded as the failure in the Gulf War to follow the expulsion of Iraq from Kuwait with the installation of a new government in Baghdad. Encouraged by White House rhetoric, Iraqi military forces in Basra launched a rebellion in March 1991 eagerly joined by urban Shiites. But the American military did not come to their aid. Saddam unleashed his legions on the Shiites in the south, and some weeks later, when the Kurds in the north rebelled, he turned on them with a vengeance. Upward of 20,000 Shiites perished, along with many thousands of Kurds who were gassed by Saddam's forces or fled into Turkey and died from exposure in the mountains. Most important, the bloody outcome generated a visceral Iraqi hatred for Americans who had left him in power. As an army reserve major in intelligence and expert on the Middle East remarked, "I don't think you can understand OIF without understanding the end of the '91 war, especially the distrust of Americans."

The highest-ranking member of the elder Bush administration favoring U.S. troop assistance to the Shiites in the spring of 1991 was Paul Wolfowitz, the undersecretary of defense. However, Wolfowitz could not dent the formidable resistance that came from his superior, Secretary of Defense Richard Cheney, along with others, including the president, Chair of the Joint Chiefs Colin Powell, National Security Adviser Brent Scowcroft, and the field commander in the Gulf War, General H. Norman Schwarzkopf. The president, Cheney, and Schwarzkopf were particularly vocal in their opposition. The occupation of Iraq, Bush senior declared, would have violated the UN mandate and "destroyed the precedent of international response to aggression that we hoped to establish. Had we gone the invasion route, the United States could conceivably still be an occupying power in a bitterly hostile land." Over ABC's *This Week* television show shortly after the Gulf War, Cheney asserted, "I think for us to get American military personnel involved in a civil war inside Iraq would literally be a quagmire." Schwarzkopf concurred. "I am certain that had we taken all of Iraq, we would have been like the dinosaur in the tar pit—we would still be there."

Saddam, meanwhile, solidified his control at home by maintaining the facade of strength without challenging the West. Although disposing of his chemical and biological supplies, he blocked UN attempts to confirm this action in an effort to terrorize his people and his neighbors. A senior military adviser suspected that Saddam sought to avoid antagonizing the United States and chose *not* to fire on American aircraft enforcing no-fly zones and periodically dropping bombs and missiles onto military and intelligence targets. "To my mind, it was carefully calibrated to show defiance, but not to provoke us." Saddam "was doing enough to show his people he was confronting the mighty United States, but not more than that."

By early 1998, numerous Republicans called for a regime change in Baghdad. Containment, they insisted, did not help the Iraqi people; rather, it permitted Saddam to crack down on domestic protest. He also ordered the UN inspection teams out of Iraq, which aroused suspicions that he was replenishing his WMD. Wolfowitz and others, including former Secretary of Defense Donald Rumsfeld, argued that diplomacy had failed. Before a congressional hearing in late 1998, Wolfowitz asserted that "I think a weakened, fragmented, chaotic Iraq . . . is more dangerous in the long run than a contained Saddam is now." In December's *New Republic* magazine, he insisted that "toppling Saddam is the only outcome that can satisfy the vital U.S. interest in a stable and secure Gulf region."

General Anthony Zinni, head of U.S. Central Command, or CentCom (comprised of over twenty-five countries in the Middle East and Southwest Asia), countered that the containment policy had pushed Saddam to the edge of collapse. American intelligence confirmed this conclusion, citing intercepts among his military leaders that revealed fear of his demise. Arab allies agreed that the regime was about to fall and asked Zinni what the United States intended to do in the post-Saddam period. "Do you guys have a plan?" What about the certain mass exodus of refugees into surrounding countries, with all the accompanying economic problems? Who would neutralize Iran? "You tip this guy over, you could create a bigger problem for us than we have now. So, what are you going to do about it?"

Wolfowitz angered Zinni by suggesting that American troops establish a safe haven in southern Iraq from which Saddam's opponents could operate. Wolfowitz, the general believed, had listened to Iraqi exile leader Ahmed Chalabi, who wanted an "enclave" from which his followers with U.S. military assistance would overthrow Saddam. Zinni thought this a "ridiculous" idea that could lead to an extensive U.S. military involvement and an enormous loss of life. But Wolfowitz's independent approach typified a growing trend. Despite Zinni's position as senior commander, he repeatedly encountered congressional staffers and retired generals who developed war plans that could "lead us into a mess" and "piecemeal us into a fight."

Opposition to Wolfowitz's call for U.S. military involvement in Iraq came from more than Zinni. An article in the winter 1998–1999 issue of *Foreign Affairs* magazine supported the general's position, its three writers coming from highly respected national security institutions—the Rand Corporation, the National Defense University, and the Council on Foreign Relations. Saddam would not fall that easily, they argued. Wolfowitz and other supporters of this "Rollback Fantasy" were wrong. For the United States to drop containment "would be a terrible mistake that could easily lead to thousands of unnecessary deaths."

Wolfowitz considered freedom indivisible and warned that Americans must implant democracy in Iraq to safeguard their own security. Based on his diplomatic experiences in South Korea and the Philippines during the 1970s and 1980s, he believed any people capable of becoming democratic. In Wilsonian rhetoric, Wolfowitz sermonized, "I think democracy is a universal idea. And I think letting people rule themselves happens to be something that serves Americans and America's interests."

President Bush and 9/11

In the presidential campaign of 2000, the Republicans sent mixed signals on their military orientation while seemingly supporting the status quo in Iraq. They promised to restore the stature of the military that had taken so many blows during the Clinton administration, with Cheney promising in his vice-presidential nomination acceptance speech that "help is on the way." Both Bush and Cheney criticized Clinton for relying too much on the military, and in the first television debate with Democratic candidate Al Gore, Bush blasted him for advocating nation building. Eight days later, Bush took a different course, declaring that "our troops ought to be used to help overthrow a dictator . . . when it's in our best interests." Cheney, however, repeated his defense of the Gulf War decision not to invade Baghdad. On NBC's *Meet the Press*, he insisted that the United States must not act as "an imperialist power, willy-nilly moving into capitals in that part of the world, taking down governments."

Despite Wolfowitz's call for a forceful regime change in Iraq, the newly elected Bush administration initially continued the containment policy. In February 2001, Secretary of State Colin Powell toured the Middle East and recommended against any alteration of policy. Wolfowitz sharply disagreed. Leaving his deanship at the Johns Hopkins School of Advanced International Studies, he became deputy defense secretary, where during his confirmation hearings he urged an immediate removal of Saddam. The Middle East "would be a safer place, Iraq would be a much more successful country, and the American national interest would benefit greatly." But he was among only a few who demanded an instant change. National Security Adviser Condoleezza Rice emphasized that the administration would follow Powell's lead in trying to improve containment through "smart sanctions" based on striking most goods and services from the trade embargo while stepping up efforts to close the country's borders and isolate Saddam from the outside world.

President Bush at "Ground Zero" in New York, September 14, 2001
Three days after 9/11, President Bush stood in the ashes resulting from the terrorist attack and pledged to meet the calls for justice from across the country. Rescue workers cheered and chanted "USA, USA." (*White House*)

But everything changed on the morning of September 11, 2001, when for the first time since the War of 1812, the United States came under foreign attack. Nineteen al-Qaeda terrorists working out of Afghanistan hijacked four U.S. commercial planes and steered two of them into the twin towers of the World Trade Center in New York City and a third into the Pentagon in Washington. The fourth, commandeered by its passengers as it headed toward the White House, crash-landed in a western Pennsylvania field, killing everyone on board. More than 3,000 died and countless others were injured in the combined assaults, with the victims coming from more than eighty countries. "We're at war," remarked the president. In what became known as the Bush Doctrine, he told Americans over national television that evening, "We will make no distinction between the terrorists

who committed these acts and those who harbor them."

Making 9/11 worse for the White House was the realization that it had virtually ignored numerous warnings of a terrorist assault. Richard Clarke, the chair of the National Security Council's Counterterrorism Security Group under Clinton and now advising the new president, told the investigatory 9/11 Commission that before the assault "al Qaeda threats and other terrorist threats" had run into "the tens of thousands—probably hundreds of thousands." In one scenario, the Federal Aviation Administration warned of a possible "suicide hijacking operation." Clarke alerted the new administration about al-Qaeda's capabilities and the probable presence of sleeper cells inside the United States. The CIA, he asserted, sent the president forty-four warnings between the inauguration and 9/11 of an al-Qaeda attack on the United States. By the mid-summer of 2001, a CIA representative told the Counterterrorism Security Group that al-Qaeda intended to launch a "spectacular" attack. "The system was blinking red," CIA Director George Tenet insisted, adding in late July that the situation could not "get any worse." "It's my sixth sense," he told Clarke, "but I feel it coming. This is going to be the big one."

But Wolfowitz's cold reception to a briefing on terrorism a week after the inauguration helped set the tone for the administration. "Well, I just don't understand why we are beginning by talking about this one man bin Laden." When Clarke tried to explain the threat to the United States, Wolfowitz brushed him aside without looking in his direction by commenting that "there are others that do as well, at least as much. Iraqi terrorism for example." Clarke was dumbfounded. "I am unaware of any Iraqi-sponsored terrorism directed at the United States, Paul, since 1993, and I think FBI and CIA concur in that judgment, right, John?" CIA Deputy Director John McLaughlin agreed. "Yes, that is right, Dick. We have no evidence of any active Iraqi terrorist threat against the U.S." Wolfowitz finally turned toward Clarke. "You give bin Laden too much credit. He could not do all these things like the 1993 attack on New York, not without a state sponsor. Just because FBI and CIA have failed to find the linkages does not mean they don't exist."

In the administration's defense, the domestic warnings were vague in comparison to the specifics relating to foreign threats about which it was better prepared. As the bipartisan *911 Commission Report* of 2006 put it, the domestic agencies "did not have direction, and did not have a plan to institute. The borders were not hardened. Transportation systems were not fortified. Electronic surveillance was not targeted against a domestic threat. State and local law enforcement were not marshaled to augment the FBI's efforts. The public was not warned." Furthermore, the various agencies involved did not pool their information,

"sometimes inadvertently or because of legal misunderstandings." At times, materials "were lost across the divide separating the foreign and domestic agencies of the government." The agencies were "like a set of specialists in a hospital, each ordering tests, looking for symptoms, and prescribing medications. What is missing is the attending physician who makes sure they work as a team."

But the *911 Commission Report* also indicted the CIA's Counterterrorism Center (CTC) for failing to employ methods developed since Pearl Harbor in dealing with surprise attacks. Four basic features characterize such preparation: "(1) think about how surprise attacks might be launched; (2) identify telltale indicators connected to the most dangerous possibilities; (3) where feasible, collect intelligence on these indicators; and (4) adopt defenses to deflect the most dangerous possibilities or at least trigger an earlier warning." The CTC did not consider the possibility of terrorists using an aircraft as a weapon, even though suicidal attacks had become a major tactic in the Middle East. Nor did it look for indicators such as terrorists who had engaged in flight training or purchased flight simulators.

Most chilling, according to the *911 Commission Report*, was Clarke's admission that "his policy advice, even if it had been accepted immediately and turned into action, would not have prevented 9/11."

President Bush had to deal with a devastating terrorist attack that had traumatized the nation and led Wolfowitz and the head of the Defense Policy Board, Richard Perle, to demand war with Iraq as al-Qaeda's state sponsor. "The idea that we could live with another twenty years of stagnation in the Middle East that breeds terrorism is just unacceptable," Wolfowitz told the *Jerusalem Post*. To a group in New York, he asserted, "We cannot go back to business as usual. We cannot think that this problem of Islamic extremist-based terrorism is going to leave us alone." Perle angrily declared that "Iraq has to pay a price for what happened yesterday. They bear responsibility."

To resolve the terrorist threat, the 9/11 Commission proposed a global approach.
Recommendations of *The 9/11 Commission Report*, July 22, 2004, 363, 367, 374, 376, 379–80, 383, 385, 387, 389, 396, 399–400, The Avalon Project at Yale Law School, New Haven, Connecticut, www.yale.edu/lawweb/avalon.

WHAT TO DO? A GLOBAL STRATEGY

The present transnational danger is Islamist terrorism. What is needed is a broad political-military strategy that rests on a firm tripod of policies to

- attack terrorists and their organizations,
- prevent the continued growth of Islamist terrorism, and
- protect against and prepare for terrorist attacks.

ATTACK TERRORISTS AND THEIR ORGANIZATIONS

The U.S. government must identify and prioritize actual or potential terrorist sanctuaries. For each, it should have a realistic strategy to keep possible terrorists insecure and on the run, using all elements of national power. We should reach out, listen to, and work with other countries that can help. . . .

PREVENT THE CONTINUED GROWTH OF ISLAMIST TERRORISM

The U.S. government must define what the message is, what it stands for. We should offer an example of moral leadership in the world, committed to treat people humanely, abide by the rule of law, and be generous and caring to our neighbors. . . .

The United States should engage other nations in developing a comprehensive coalition strategy against Islamist terrorism . . . .

The United States should engage its friends to develop a common coalition approach toward the detention and humane treatment of captured terrorists. . . .

PROTECT AGAINST AND PREPARE FOR TERRORIST ATTACKS

Targeting travel is at least as powerful a weapon against terrorists as targeting their money. . . .

The U.S. border security system should be integrated into a larger network of screening points that includes our transportation system and access to vital facilities. . . .

The Department of Homeland Security, properly supported by the Congress, should complete, as quickly as possible, a biometric entry-exit screening system, including a single system for speeding qualified travelers. . . .

Homeland security assistance should be based strictly on an assessment of risks and vulnerabilities. Now, in 2004, Washington, D.C., and New York City are certainly at the top of any such list. . . .

HOW TO DO IT? A DIFFERENT WAY OF ORGANIZING THE GOVERNMENT

As presently configured, the national security institutions of the U.S. government are still the institutions constructed to win the Cold War. The United States confronts a very different world today. Instead of facing a few very dangerous adversaries, the United States confronts a number of less visible challenges that surpass the boundaries of traditional nation-states and call for quick, imaginative, and agile responses. . . .

Those attacks showed, emphatically, that ways of doing business rooted in a different era are just not good enough. Americans should not settle for incremental, ad hoc adjustments to a system designed generations ago for a world that no longer exists.

(continues)

We recommend significant changes in the organization of the government. . . .

The United States has the resources and the people. The government should combine them more effectively, achieving unity of effort. We offer five major recommendations to do that:

—unifying strategic intelligence and operational planning against Islamist terrorists across the foreign-domestic divide with a National Counterterrorism Center;

—unifying the intelligence community with a new National Intelligence Director;

—unifying the many participants in the counterterrorism effort and their knowledge in a network-based information sharing system that transcends traditional governmental boundaries;

—unifying and strengthening congressional oversight to improve quality and accountability; and

—strengthening the FBI and homeland defenders.

Four days after 9/11, the president met with his national security team at Camp David to devise a response that soon developed into a debate over whether Iraq had colluded with al-Qaeda and should be the first target of an attack. The day following 9/11, President Bush had pondered the possibility of Iraq's having a hand in the disaster. "See if Saddam did this," he instructed Clarke. "See if he's linked in any way." That same day, Donald Rumsfeld, again secretary of defense, argued that the terrorist attacks had provided an "opportunity" to hit Iraq at the same time as bin Laden. But at the presidential retreat only Wolfowitz advocated such a response. Cheney warned that "if we go after Saddam Hussein, we lose our rightful place as good guy." Powell likewise saw no connection between Saddam and 9/11. Our allies' support would not continue if we attacked Iraq. "They'll view it as bait and switch—it's not what they signed up to do."

But 9/11 had marked a turning point in the president's thinking that led him to approve the destruction of the Islamic fundamentalist Taliban regime in Afghanistan for harboring al-Qaeda, but as the initial thrust of a worldwide campaign against terror that would ultimately focus on Iraq. Two years later, Bush told Bob Woodward, the longtime reporter and editor of the *Washington Post*, that "September the 11th obviously changed my thinking a lot about my responsibility as president." Events of that day, he noted in a puzzling revelation, had "made the security of the American people the priority . . . a sacred duty for the president." The assault on the United States had demonstrated "Saddam Hussein's capacity to create harm" and made "all his terrible features . . . much more threatening. Keeping Saddam in a box seemed less and less feasible to me." He was a "madman" who "had used weapons of mass destruction" and had destabilized "the neighborhood" by invading Iran and Kuwait. Bush told Rice at the meeting that the first target was Afghanistan. "We won't do Iraq now. We're putting Iraq off. But eventually we'll have to return to that question."

Less than a week after the 9/11 attacks, President Bush warned the nation of the global terrorist threat. "Tonight," he declared in an address before Congress, "we are a country awakened to danger." Al-Qaeda had been responsible for 9/11, the embassy bombings of 1998 in Kenya and Tanzania (12 Americans among 257 dead), and the 2000 assault on the U.S.S. *Cole* at port in Yemen (17 sailors killed). The administration had told Taliban leaders to "hand over the terrorists, or they will share in their fate." The U.S. objective was not Islam. "Our enemy is a radical network of terrorists, and every government that supports them." The world's leaders had a choice. "Every nation, in every region, now has a decision to make: Either you are with us, or you are with the terrorists." The "war on terror begins with al

At the Texas Ranch
L–R: National Security Adviser Condoleezza Rice, Vice President Richard Cheney, President George W. Bush, Secretary of Defense Donald Rumsfeld, and Chair of the Joint Chiefs of Staff, Air Force General Richard Myers. (*Jeff Mitchell/Reuters/Corbis*)

Qaeda, but does not end there. It will not end until every terrorist group of global reach has been found, stopped, and defeated."

In November 2001, President Bush launched "Operation Enduring Freedom," a military campaign in Afghanistan comprised of U.S. Special Forces, CIA operatives, coalition troops, and Afghan militias, all supported by U.S. aircraft. Despite alarm that the Afghan involvement would result in a quagmire similar to that in Vietnam, nothing of the sort happened. The combined forces quickly

Architects and Practitioners of America's Strategy in Iraq
L–R: Deputy Defense Secretary Paul Wolfowitz, Secretary of Defense Donald Rumsfeld, and Air Force General Richard Myers, Chair of the Joint Chiefs of Staff. (*Jason Reed/Reuters/Corbis*)

seized control over half the country and liberated the capital of Kabul, forcing Taliban and al-Qaeda legions to flee south toward Pakistan's mountainous frontier.

The White House was ebullient, best expressed by a heady Rumsfeld as he jockeyed with the press. With the head of Central Command, Army General Tommy Franks, at his side, the defense secretary bragged that the enemy was on the run. "How much of it frankly is a surprise?" asked a reporter. "I think that what was taking place in the earlier phases was exactly as planned," Rumsfeld smugly replied. "It looked like nothing was happening. Indeed, it looked like we were in a—all together now—QUAGMIRE!"

By late November, the administration realized it was engaged in a new kind of war, and the vice president devised a measuring stick for determining the appropriate U.S. response that became known as the Cheney Doctrine. At a lengthy session in the White House Situation Room, he set the bar surprisingly low in justifying a military solution. Tenet had just summarized the actions of the Ummah Tameer-e-Nau ("Islamic revival") in Afghanistan, Pakistan, and Saudi Arabia, when Cheney emerged from his quietude to say in a low voice as if speaking to himself, "We have

The Fighting in Afghanistan
Soldiers from the 561st Military Police
Company patrol the rugged and desolate Nijrab
region of Afghanistan in late October 2006.
(Photo courtesy of U.S. Army. Credit Sergeant
First Class Dexter D. Clouden)

to deal with this new type of threat in a way
we haven't yet defined. . . . I'm frankly not
sure how we engage. We're going to have to
look at it in a completely different way." Pausing for emphasis, Cheney declared, "If there's
a one percent chance that Pakistani scientists
are helping al Qaeda build or develop a nuclear weapon, we have to treat it as a certainty
in terms of our response." Silence again before he finished with these words: "It's not
about our analysis, or finding a preponderance of evidence. It's about our response."

The Cheney Doctrine revolutionized the
U.S. approach to military measures by no
longer tying decisions to either facts or intelligence analysis. Evidence lost nearly all rele-
vance, replaced by suspicions and impressions
that condoned instant action based on im-
pulse rather than proof. And in the case of a
faith-based president such as Bush, the
chances for immediate and hard-line correc-
tives dramatically heightened as the world
took on black-and-white hues with no gray in
between. If there was the slightest chance—
even a 1 percent chance—that an enemy could
secure WMD, the United States must take
military action. When everyone present con-

curred, Rice instructed Tenet to formulate the
new approach. "Sorry," she said. "There's no
second option." Cheney solemnly added,
"You'll represent the President. Your words
will be his."

So sharply had the administration's mood
risen from the depths of 9/11 to the euphoric
heights of the Afghan operation that in that
same month of November, it directed the
Pentagon to begin war planning in Iraq. General Franks scurried back and forth between
Washington and his headquarters in Tampa,
planning an invasion that suddenly got caught
in the crosshairs of the military and the defense secretary over whether to continue the
Afghan assault or expand the fighting into
Iraq—a decision that would determine the
number of troops needed. General Jack
Keane, second in command, argued for maintaining the focus on capturing bin Laden in
Tora Bora, that intricate network of Afghan
caves along the Pakistani border; Franks
wanted more troops than presently under consideration for an invasion of Iraq. Rumsfeld favored an assault on Iraq that relied on speed
and thus required fewer troops than previous
war plans had suggested. Franks went with
Rumsfeld.

Central Command thus worked under the
pressure of following the invasion of
Afghanistan with a larger thrust into Iraq.
Greatly expanded responsibilities taxed the
military's effort to deal with both matters at
the same time. His staff exhausted, Franks
nonetheless pushed his subordinates over the
course of the next year into crafting what was
at best a halfway plan—one detailing the tactics for overthrowing the Baghdad regime
without indicating how to restore order and
form a new government.

In their war planning, Franks's strategists
shelved the recommendations of General
Zinni, who had years earlier thought 350,000
troops were needed to take Iraq. The new
plan encompassed a much smaller and quicker
force based on "precision weapons," explained
one officer. Franks intended that a single

heavy division lead the assault, supported by the 101st Airborne's helicopters along with lighter aid—drawn from the 82nd Airborne and a few marine and British units.

Toward Preemptive War

In his first State of the Union Address in January 2002, President Bush introduced a new strategy that he pronounced as policy less than six months later—the preemptive strike. Representative Ike Skelton of Missouri, senior Democrat on the House Armed Services Committee, termed the speech "a declaration of war" on the three rogue states of Iraq, Iran, and North Korea. "States like these and their terrorist allies," Bush alleged, "constitute an axis of evil, arming to threaten the peace of the world. We'll be deliberate; yet time is not on our side. I will not wait on events while dangers gather. I will not stand by as peril draws closer and closer. The United States will not permit the world's most dangerous regimes to threaten us with the world's most destructive weapons." The following June, before the U.S. Military Academy at West Point, he broke with American military tradition by asserting that the United States could fire the first shot if threatened. "We must take the battle to the enemy, disrupt his plans, and confront the worst threats before they emerge. If we wait for threats to fully materialize, we will have waited too long."

Many U.S. military leaders appeared baffled by the imminent invasion of Iraq. Saddam might use WMD, American troops would mire down in urban fighting, postwar occupation would prove astronomically costly in blood and treasure, and the effort would undercut the drive against al-Qaeda. "What in the hell are we doing?" asked several senior officers. "Why Iraq? Why now?"

Republican Brent Scowcroft, former national security adviser to President George H. W. Bush and friend of the family, likewise warned against a war in Iraq. On CBS's *Face the Nation*, he predicted that an invasion "could turn the whole region into a cauldron, and thus destroy the war on terrorism." Soon afterward, he wrote an editorial titled "Don't Attack Saddam" for the *Wall Street Journal*. "We will all be better off when he is gone," Scowcroft admitted, but in an argument supported by Henry Kissinger, James Baker, and numerous senior military officers, he found "scant evidence to tie Saddam to terrorist organizations, and even less to the Sept. 11 attacks." Furthermore, there "is little evidence to indicate that the United States itself is an object of his aggression." A "military campaign very likely would have to be followed by a large-scale, long-term military occupation."

But the Bush administration had taken a new direction that even Powell could not deter. Rather than regard Middle East stability as the essence of peace, as his father's White House had done, the new president turned that policy on its head. Bush sided with Wolfowitz and Cheney in arguing that stability provided the quickest route to terrorism because it was conducive to Saddam-like regimes that led to weak economies and an angry populace. Major changes were needed in Iraq and throughout the region that destroyed the hotbeds of terrorist recruitment and fostered democracy. Powell and Rice had spent a long evening with the president in early August 2002, first with dinner and afterward with Powell urging him not to war on Iraq. "You are going to be the proud owner of twenty-five million people. You will own all their hopes, aspirations and problems. You'll own it all. . . . It's going to suck the oxygen out of everything. . . . *This will become the first term*." Iraq has never been democratic, emphasized Powell. "So you need to understand that this is not going to be a walk in the woods. It's nice to say we can do it unilaterally, except you can't. If you think it's just a matter of picking up the phone and blowing a whistle and it goes—no, you need allies."

Bush had patiently listened for the most part before finally asking, "What should I do? What else can I do?"

Powell posed an alternative to war. "You can still make a pitch for a coalition or U.N. action to do what needs to be done." Most countries would go along. "If you take it to the U.N., you've got to recognize that they might be able to solve it. In which case there's no war. That could mean a solution that is not as clean as just going in and taking the guy out. The international cover could also result in a different outcome."

The occasionally tense conversation did not change the president's stand. Bush later remarked that "my job is to secure America. And I also believe that freedom is something people long for. And that if given a chance, the Iraqis over time would seize the moment." Powell's responsibility was tactics. "My job is to be strategic. Basically what he was saying was, was that if in fact Saddam is toppled by military [invasion], we better have a strong understanding about what it's going to take to rebuild Iraq." Powell strongly supported working through the United Nations; others in the administration doubted that the United Nations could do the job. The next day, General Franks ordered his subordinates to plan a fast-paced war as the president retired to his Texas ranch for a month's vacation.

The administration's campaign for war intensified in late August, when at the Veterans of Foreign Wars' national meeting in Nashville, Vice President Cheney stifled the debate over a preemptive war by declaring that Saddam had WMD. His regime "has in fact been very busy enhancing its capabilities in the field of chemical and biological agents, and they continue to pursue the nuclear program they began so many years ago. . . . Many of us are convinced that Saddam Hussein will acquire nuclear weapons fairly soon." Nothing had halted this process, including UN inspections and the Desert Fox campaign. "Simply stated, there is no doubt that Saddam Hussein now has weapons of mass destruction" and that "he is amassing them to use against our friends, against our allies, and against us."

General Zinni was on the stage that day to receive an award and was stunned by the vice president's assertion about WMD. "In my time at CentCom, I watched the intelligence and never—not once—did it say, 'He has WMD.'" Although retired, Zinni still had top-secret access to intelligence and saw nothing to support Cheney's allegation. "It was never there, never there."

Cheney's speech nonetheless made the charge seem irrefutable. Rumsfeld repeated the claim to Pentagon leaders, and so did intelligence officials assume it true. As one senior figure noted, "When the vice president stood up and said 'We are sure'—well, who are we to argue? With all the compartmentalization, there's a good chance that a guy that senior has seen stuff you haven't."

The war's proponents within the administration meanwhile attacked the CIA for not supporting an assault on Iraq. Patrick Lang in the Office of Special Plans criticized the agency and other intelligence experts for failing to see the danger. "You don't understand your own data," he complained. "We know that Saddam is evil and deceptive, and if you see this piece of data, to say just because it is not well supported it's not true is to be politically naïve." Perle claimed that his own analysts had uncovered evidence of WMD. "Within a very short period of time, they began to find links that nobody else had previously understood or recorded in a useful way. They [noticed] things that nobody else had noticed. It was there all along, it simply hadn't been noticed . . . because the CIA and DIA [Defense Intelligence Agency] were not looking." The excuses raised by the intelligence community were "really quite pathetic." He acidly concluded, "Let me be blunt about this: The level of competence on past performance of the Central Intelligence Agency, in this area, is appalling."

More than one contemporary accused Perle and others in the administration of "stovepiping" or cherry-picking intelligence to find items supporting a view already adopted. According to Greg Thielmann of the State Department's Bureau of Intelligence and Research, those calling for war "were cherry-picking the information that we provided to use whatever pieces of it that fit their overall interpretation. Worse than that, they were dropping qualifiers and distorting some of the information that we provided to make it seem even more alarmist and dangerous than the information that we were giving them." Marine General Gregory Newbold, head of operations on the Joint Staff, agreed, declaring that "they cherry-picked obscure, unconfirmed information to reinforce their own philosophies and ideologies."

To win congressional authorization for an invasion of Iraq, the president on the morning of September 4, 2002, met with eighteen legislative leaders and then with Democratic Representative Ike Skelton on an individual basis. Later that afternoon, Skelton sent the president a note warning of the myriad problems involved in an occupation. According to Prussian military theorist Karl von Clausewitz, Skelton declared, the first rule of war was "not to take the first step without considering the last." And the master of strategy, Sun Tzu, cautioned, "To win victory is easy; to preserve its fruits, difficult." Skelton reflected the thinking of numerous Middle East specialists along with army strategists when he asserted, "I have no doubt that our military would decisively defeat Iraq's forces and remove Saddam. But like the proverbial dog chasing the car down the road, we must consider what we would do after we caught it."

The only White House reaction came from one of its liaisons with Congress, Daniel Keniry, who haughtily told Skelton, "Well, Congressman, we really don't need your vote. We've got the votes."

The administration then took its case to allies and the American people. At Camp David three days later, President Bush, with his closest ally, British Prime Minister Tony Blair, standing beside him, declared that Saddam had WMD. On Tim Russert's *Meet the Press* television show of the following day,

Cheney asserted that Saddam was trying "through his illicit procurement network, to acquire the equipment he needs to be able to enrich uranium" for nuclear use. Skeptics have not "seen all the intelligence that we have seen." That same day, the administration formed the White House Iraq Group to "educate the public" about Saddam's threat, and Rice that evening on CNN's *Late Edition* issued a chilling warning. "The problem here is that there will always be some uncertainty about how quickly [Saddam] can acquire nuclear weapons. But we don't want the smoking gun to be a mushroom cloud."

The increased likelihood of war seemingly convinced Saddam, but even his change in position failed to stop the White House move toward a preemptive war. On September 16, the Iraqi government agreed to the UN inspectors' return "without conditions," but the next day the Bush administration ignored this diplomatic triumph and formalized its call for the preemption strategy. In a thirty-one-page document titled "The National Security Strategy of the United States of America," the new approach became clear: "We cannot let our enemies strike first. The overlap between states that sponsor terror and those that pursue WMD compels us to action. . . . To forestall or prevent such hostile acts by our adversaries, the United States will, if necessary, act pre-emptively."

Anglo-American forces had already begun preemptive action against Iraq. *Nation* magazine in that same month of September reported air assaults on Iraqi command and communication networks, the Revolutionary Guard, and other defensive facilities. Most ambitious was a major joint bombardment by a hundred planes out of Kuwait, including U.S. F-15 Strike Eagles and British Tornado ground-assault planes. Their purpose: disable Saddam's air defense system in the west and clear the way for Special Forces helicopters operating out of Jordan.

On October 2, after a congressional request for evidence of Iraq's WMD, the White House provided a National Intelligence Estimate (NIE) by the CIA that clinched the case for war. This ninety-two-page study, titled "Iraq's Continuing Programs for Weapons of Mass Destruction," stated that "Baghdad has chemical and biological weapons" and was "reconstituting its nuclear program." Iraq, the study alleged, has begun "vigorously trying to procure uranium ore and yellowcake [pure uranium capable of processing for use in nuclear weapons]" in Niger, Somalia, and Congo. Most alarming, Iraq and Niger "reportedly were still working out arrangements for this deal, which could be up to 500 tons of yellowcake." Indeed, "We judge that we are seeing only a portion of Iraq's WMD efforts."

The story that Iraq and Niger had struck a deal over uranium had circulated within the intelligence community for three years without winning credibility. Rumors of such an arrangement were fueled by a January 2001 break-in into the Niger embassy in Rome in which the only items stolen, curiously enough, were letterhead stationery and official seals—both necessary to forge documents. Shortly after 9/11, CIA officials received a dossier containing documents alleging that Niger had agreed to send tons of uranium to Iraq. The State Department thought the so-called proof highly questionable, although Tenet later claimed that the CIA had uncovered additional though "fragmentary evidence" of Iraq's efforts to buy uranium in this period.

Notwithstanding the lack of conclusive evidence, the charge repeatedly appeared, clearly driven by those making a case for war. In early February 2002, the CIA issued a new report that included an alleged "verbatim text" of a deal between Iraq and Niger. State Department analysts were skeptical, but within a week the vice president received "a finished intelligence product" from the Defense Intelligence Agency asserting that Iraq's ambassador to the Vatican had traveled to Niger in 1999 and agreed to purchase 500 tons of uranium for what "probably" was a nuclear weapons program. "What about this?" Cheney asked

the CIA briefer, who passed the request to the agency's clandestine division, the Directorate of Operations. The question then went to the Counterproliferation Division, where CIA operative Valerie Plame responded in a memo that "my husband has good relations with both the PM [prime minister] and the former Minister of Mines (not to mention lots of French contacts), both of whom could possibly shed light on this sort of activity."

In a matter of days, Plame's husband, Joseph Wilson, took on the assignment, albeit with considerable skepticism. Wilson was a former ambassador to Gabon in Africa, a deputy chief of mission at the U.S. embassy in Baghdad during the first Bush presidency, and an adviser on African policy on the National Security Council in the Clinton administration. He was not a novice in the world of intelligence and was dubious about this "unverified intelligence report." After arriving in Niger in late February, he returned to Washington a few days later to tell the CIA that he found no evidence for the charge and that any documents supporting this allegation had to be forgeries.

The NIE's assertions were suspect, as its own admissions demonstrated. It could not confirm an actual Iraqi procurement, and the State Department considered the claims "highly dubious." A month earlier, the British had released a white paper alleging that Iraq had sought "significant quantities of uranium from Africa," but they cited no hard evidence. To acquire such a huge amount meant that Iraq must purchase one-sixth of the uranium produced in Niger in a year while concealing both the transaction and the loading process from the French, German, Spanish, Japanese, and Nigerian consortium that operated the mines as well as the International Atomic Energy Agency that monitored the consortium. Perhaps the most telling question came from Air Force Lieutenant Colonel Karen Kwiatkowski then assigned to the Pentagon: "If Saddam wanted to make nuclear bombs, why would he want unprocessed ore when the best thing to do would be to get processed stuff in the Congo?"

The NIE was riddled with uncertainties that went virtually unnoticed or unread in the urgency of the time. Without specifically declaring that Saddam *had* WMD, the document noted reports that Iraq had secretly procured the ingredients necessary for such production. In a statement belying the opening assertion that Iraq *had* biological weapons, the NIE declared that "we judge Iraq has some lethal and incapacitating BW [biological warfare] agents and is capable of quickly producing and weaponizing a variety of such agents." The NIE asserted with "moderate confidence" that "Iraq does not yet have a nuclear weapon or sufficient material to make one but is likely to have a weapon by 2007 to 2009." Another sentence deep inside the text cast doubt on an alliance between Iraq and al-Qaeda: "We have no specific intelligence information that Saddam's regime has directed attacks against U.S. territory." Not only did the NIE express "low confidence" in its own findings, but the State Department intelligence bureau wrote an eleven-page rebuttal, concluding that the report had failed to make a "compelling case" for Iraq's having "an integrated and comprehensive approach to acquire nuclear weapons."

Despite its many qualifiers, the NIE convinced the White House and Congress that Saddam had WMD and had provided a staging ground for al-Qaeda. Did this constitute the 1 percent minimum of certainty stipulated by the Cheney Doctrine? The White House thought so. The NIE moved the president and Rumsfeld firmly into the Cheney–Wolfowitz camp, leaving Powell and other skeptics decidedly weakened. Furthermore, Tenet affirmed the presence of WMD, and Cheney darkly warned that the administration must not again look unprepared as with 9/11. "The president," according to a general having close contact with Rumsfeld, "became convinced that [going to war] was the right

thing to do." When some senators expressed concern about giving the president a blank check for invasion, his chief lobbyist on Capitol Hill, Nicholas Calio, warned, "Today's the day—we resolve all differences today or we're going without you." That same day, the president gathered a number of legislators around him in the Rose Garden to announce in a news conference that they had reached a bipartisan agreement that "will show to friend and enemy alike the resolve of the United States" to stand up against Saddam as "a student of Stalin."

In early October, President Bush took his war campaign to Cincinnati, where he emphasized the threat posed by Iraq's WMD. In an earlier draft of the speech, the new national security adviser, Stephen Hadley, had asked the CIA to approve the insertion of the Niger charge by claiming that Saddam "has been caught attempting to purchase up to 500 metric tons of this material." But the CIA immediately faxed a memo calling the claim unproven and telling Hadley to take out the sentence. When Hadley's aides only altered the draft without changing its substance, Tenet stepped in and quashed the subject, telling Hadley that the "reporting was weak" and that the "president should not be a fact witness on this issue." Bush nonetheless asserted that Saddam "is moving ever closer to developing a nuclear weapon." The president then repeated Rice's much-publicized warning. "If we know Saddam Hussein has dangerous weapons today—and we do—does it make any sense for the world to . . . wait for the final proof, the smoking gun that could come in the form of a mushroom cloud?"

In an action reminiscent of the 1964 Gulf of Tonkin Resolution, Congress on October 11, 2002, overwhelmingly approved military action against Iraq. The president's war resolution easily passed both houses of Congress, with 77 of the 100 senators voting in favor and 296 of the 435 House members doing the same. Congress thus authorized the president to "use the armed forces of the United

States as he determines to be necessary and appropriate in order to defend the national security of the United States against the continuing threat posed by Iraq."

Three days earlier, the administration had briefed nearly fifty senators on the NIE and arranged for copies of the full study to sit in two heavily guarded vaults on Capitol Hill, ready for perusal. Nearly every congressional member chose to read only its five-page executive summary. Indeed, neither the president nor Rice had read the entire document.

The congressional vote was so predictable that only a single reporter attended the House debate and neither the House nor the Senate had as many as 10 percent of its members present. As one long-time observer noted, "Usually, when there are few people around, it means that they don't like what's happening but don't feel they can do anything about it." Dana Milbank noted in the *Washington Post* that "the outcome—lopsided support for Bush's resolution—was preordained." Helping the president's case was his reminder of the Cuban missile crisis of forty years earlier when the Soviet Union had implanted offensive missiles on the island and raised the specter of nuclear war. For full effect, Bush quoted President Kennedy in declaring that "we no longer live in a world where only the actual firing of weapons represents a sufficient challenge to a nation's security to constitute maximum peril." Politics, too, played a role in the decision. Midterm elections were nigh, and Democrats remembered that those who had opposed the Gulf War had fared badly in the next three presidential elections. Voting for the new resolution might restore their credibility as guardians of national security.

Yet the Democrats were not united on the measure. The majority of party members in the House voted against it, but in the Senate they assented twenty-nine to twenty-one. Senator Edward Kennedy of Massachusetts argued against the resolution, insisting that the White House had not presented "a convincing case that we face such an imminent threat to our national security that a unilateral, preemptive American strike and an immediate war are necessary." The president's call for preemptive war befitted a "21st century American imperialism that no other nation can or should accept." But his Massachusetts colleague John Kerry disagreed, saying he would vote for forcefully disarming Saddam because "a deadly arsenal of weapons of mass destruction in his hands is a threat, and a grave threat, to our security." Kerry hedged his vote, however, by declaring his expectation that the president would "fulfill the commitments he has made to the American people in recent days—to work with the United Nations Security Council to adopt a new resolution . . . and to act with allies at our side if we have to disarm Saddam Hussein by force."

Another party member was not so circumspect. My fellow Democrats "were intimidated," complained West Virginia Senator Robert Byrd in the august chamber. "There is no debate, no discussion, no attempt to lay out for the nation the pros and cons of this particular war. We stand passively mute . . . paralyzed by our own uncertainty, seemingly studded by the sheer turmoil of events." The Senate was "rushing to vote on whether to declare war on Iraq without pausing to ask why," he charged. "Why is war being dealt with not as a last resort but as a first resort?"

Most everyone expected no major obstacles in the invasion and considered the occupation their greatest concern. At the Marine Corps birthday dinner in November, General Zinni as guest speaker warned that "if you guys don't go through the enemy in six weeks, we'll disown you. But then the hard work begins. . . . We have lit a fuse, and we don't know what's at the other end—a nuke, a hand grenade, or a dud?" A week later, seventy experts on national security and the Middle East gathered at the National Defense University in Washington to warn against totally disarming the Iraqi army in the postwar period because of the need to restore domestic security. And in early December, a bevy of specialists in numerous fields attended a two-day conference in the Pentagon and likewise recommended retaining the Iraqi army along with carefully selected government figures to deal with postwar problems. Only with experienced military and domestic leaders can the occupation result in a rebuilt Iraq. General Schwarzkopf agreed. "I would hope that we have in place the adequate resources to become an army of occupation, because you're going to walk into chaos."

Final Road to War

The administration's certainty of a connection between al-Qaeda and Iraq meanwhile ran afoul of a December 2002 report by the "Joint Inquiry" on *Intelligence Community Activities before and after the Terrorist Attacks of September 11, 2001*. Al-Qaeda, the findings emphasized, did not fit the standard mold of state-sponsored terrorism of the 1980s; rather, its network of followers crossed national lines, operated in a decentralized fashion, and did not depend on outside assistance. This new brand of terrorist "became radicalized in Germany, held meetings in Malaysia, and received funds channeled through the United Arab Emirates." It sought recruits, financial support, meeting places, and safe haven in a number of countries, including Yemen, Malaysia, Germany, Saudi Arabia, Afghanistan, Indonesia, Egypt, the United Arab Emirates, the United Kingdom, Pakistan, Spain, Bosnia, Chechnya, Morocco, Thailand, the Philippines, Dubai, Belgium, the Czech Republic, Switzerland, and the United States. Noticeably absent from the list was Iraq.

Controversy has also risen over an Oval Office discussion on the Saturday morning of December 21 that focused on whether Iraq had WMD. According to a story in the *Washington Post* and later in Bob Woodward's two works on this period, *Plan of Attack* and *State of Denial*, Tenet presented the case for WMD to the president and a host of advisers that included CIA Deputy Director John McLaughlin,

Cheney, Rice, and White House Chief of Staff Andy Card. When the charts, graphs, photos, and intercepts failed to convince the president, he derisively asked Tenet, "I've been told all this intelligence about having WMD and this is the best we've got?" Tenet suddenly sat forward in the couch and with his arms held high declared, "It's a slam dunk case!" Bush pushed harder. "George, how confident are you?" Again he assured the president, "Don't worry, it's a slam dunk!" Such conviction did not typify Tenet's usual flair for understatement, which made his dramatic assertion all the more credible. Cheney was convinced—as was the president, who emphasized that Tenet's confidence "was very important."

Tenet, however, has vehemently rejected this story. In his own account of the period, *At the Center of the Storm*, he expressed regret over his choice of words, but he insists that they referred to the ease with which he could make a better case to the public for Saddam's having WMD and *not* for presenting an ironclad case for war with Iraq. The White House needed a justification for war; it had never engaged in a "serious debate" about whether Saddam posed an imminent threat to the United States or if containment might have been better than an invasion. All discussions in 2002 had focused on *how* to go to war and never on *why*. Indeed, he believes that someone at the meeting purposely twisted the exchange and leaked it to the press in an effort to blame the CIA for the war decision. If events did not take their predicted course, the administration could refuse to accept responsibility and send the message: "Don't blame us. George Tenet and the CIA got us into this mess."

It is too early to offer conclusions about an issue that goes to the heart of the administration's defense of the war, but one can note several inconsistencies on the part of the White House. On the one side, it criticized the CIA for failing to warn the president of an imminent terrorist attack that climaxed on 9/11, and on the other side, it praised the CIA for the "slam dunk" reference as the final proof for Saddam's having WMD and hence the critical factor in the decision for war. Some critics have dismissed Tenet's book as self-serving and denounced him for not speaking out more strongly against the coming war. Yet the record shows that months before 9/11 he specifically alerted the administration of the al-Qaeda threat—a warning that went unheeded. In addition, he had insisted there was no link between Iraq and al-Qaeda. Finally, and most important, the White House had moved toward war months before the December 2002 meeting, meaning that Tenet's assurance, regardless of its intention, played no role in that decision. In the fall of 2006, Tenet notes, Cheney twice told *Meet the Press* that the "slam dunk" reference provided the basis for going to war. "I remember watching and thinking, 'As if you needed me to say "slam dunk" to convince you to go to war with Iraq.'"

Whatever the truth regarding this strange occurrence in the Oval Office, President Bush, in his second State of the Union Address on January 28, 2003, focused on the charges that Saddam had WMD and, ignoring the Joint Inquiry's negative findings about state-sponsored terrorism, emphasized an Iraqi–al-Qaeda connection. Certain weapons the United Nations had been unable to find, he declared—including 25,000 liters of anthrax, enough botulinum toxin to put "millions of people to death by respiratory failure," other nerve gases, and, finally, mobile labs working on additional biological weapons. At one point, he insisted that "Saddam Hussein aids and protects terrorists, including members of al-Qaeda."

But the most striking part of the president's address came in sixteen words affirming Iraq's intention to build nuclear weapons: "The British government has learned that Saddam Hussein recently sought significant quantities of uranium from Africa."

Thus, despite the lack of evidence for this charge, the president had resurrected it in a national forum by citing the unsubstantiated British claim. Indeed, after the NIE contro-

versy in the previous October, the National Intelligence Council, overseer of fifteen agencies in the American intelligence community, stated two months after that "the Niger story was baseless and should be laid to rest." But even though the Council's findings went to the president, they did not steer him away from sending a report to Congress on January 20, 2003, referring to Iraq's efforts "to acquire uranium and the means to enrich it" and eight days later including the charge in his State of the Union Address. His reference to a uranium purchase was no "smoking gun," of course, but combined with the certainties expressed by Tenet, Cheney, and Rumsfeld, the case seemed conclusive that Saddam intended to raise the East–West encounter to a

President Bush Delivers State of Union Address, January 28, 2003
With Vice President Cheney seated behind him, President Bush accuses Saddam Hussein of having weapons of mass destruction. *(White House)*

nuclear level. Tenet had cut the Niger passage from the October speech in Cincinnati for lack of convincing evidence, and the British had never corroborated their charge. But this time, Tenet admitted that he did not review the address beforehand, and Hadley claimed to have forgotten the CIA's warning. The most conclusive statement for WMD, it appeared, had stemmed from a pair of careless mistakes.

Dispute has developed over whether these were *calculated* mistakes. "It is inconceivable to me that George Tenet didn't read that speech," remarked Milt Bearden, a former CIA station chief in a number of countries that included Nigeria. "At that point, he was effectively no longer D.C.I. [director of central intelligence]" but "part of the cabal, and no longer able to carry an honest message." A close associate of Tenet's, however, considered it "absurd" to call him part of a "cabal" and insisted that he "was unaware of attempts to put the Niger information in the State of the Union speech." Had he known, "he would have vigorously tried to have it removed."

The truth remains impossible to discern, but the insertion of the Niger charge hardly seems to have been an accident. Tenet claims to have been so exhausted that he told his staff to screen the speech. If so, this is negligence of duty. But given the hot nature of this issue—the so-called evidence providing support for an invasion—it is difficult to believe that Hadley *forgot* Tenet's directive against including the accusation in the president's October 2002 speech in Cincinnati. Purposeful or not, the claim fed the fear that Saddam had WMD capped by a growing nuclear potential.

About a week later, on February 5, the administration took its greatest stride toward war with Iraq by sending Powell to make its case before the United Nations. The secretary of state had remained skeptical to the last moment about Iraq's having WMD. He knew that Saddam had used such weapons in the 1980s and hid them in the following decade. If he had destroyed his chemical and biological weapons as alleged, why did he force the UN inspectors to leave Iraq in 1998? Powell

found it difficult to disagree with Cheney, who asked, "Why in the world would [Saddam] subject himself for all those years to U.N. sanctions and forgo an estimated $100 billion in oil revenue? It makes no sense!"

So in good conscience, Powell went before the world to indict the Iraqi regime for having WMD. "My colleagues," he declared in his opening, "every statement I make today is backed up by sources, solid sources." With Tenet seated directly behind him and in the camera's eye to enhance credibility, Powell stood before viewers as one of the most respected figures in America, a major leader in the Gulf War, and a man of unquestioned integrity. With his hands clasped on the podium before him, he prepared to have a conversation with millions of Americans.

"I cannot tell you everything that we know, but what I can share with you, when combined with what all of us have learned over the years, is deeply troubling. What you will see is an accumulation of facts and disturbing patterns of behavior." Wielding a pack of slides and other visual materials, he referred to eyewitness accounts confirming that "a missile brigade outside Baghdad was disbursing rocket launchers and warheads containing biological warfare agents to various locations." Satellite photos and further intelligence revealed that the Iraqis had relocated a great mass of materials close to chemical and biological weapons plants just before UN inspectors arrived. "We don't know what Iraq was moving, but the inspectors already knew about these sites, so Iraq knew that they would be coming. We must ask ourselves: Why would Iraq suddenly move equipment of this nature before inspections if they were anxious to demonstrate what they had or did not have?"

Powell then turned to "the potentially much more sinister nexus between Iraq and the al Qaeda network." Many have argued against this proposition, insisting that "Saddam Hussein's secular tyranny and al Qaeda's religious tyranny do not mix." But this argument is not comforting. "Ambition and hatred are enough to bring Iraq and al Qaeda together."

The United States could hesitate no longer. "We know that Saddam Hussein is determined to keep his weapons of mass destruction; he's determined to make more. Should we take the risk that he will not someday use these weapons at a time and a place and in a manner of his choosing, at a time when the world is in a much weaker position to respond? The United States will not and cannot run that risk to the American people."

In seventy-six minutes, Powell had presented a compelling case for war.

Yet, even as he spoke, several experts realized that the evidence, though unknown to him, belied his assertions. The bipartisan Senate Select Committee on Intelligence concluded that much of the information furnished by the CIA "was overstated, misleading, or incorrect." Indeed, Powell had drawn heavily from the NIE of October 2002, which had *not* proved the presence of WMD. His argument rested largely on Saddam's attempt to secure aluminum tubes for enriching uranium, yet the State Department two days before the speech had disproved that claim. Furthermore, Powell's charge regarding biological weapons depended primarily on the report of a defector code-named Curveball, who had no credibility.

But some contemporaries insisted that the Bush administration had already decided on war, which made the evidence irrelevant. A senior CIA officer noted, "Let's keep in mind the fact that this war's going to happen regardless of what Curveball said or didn't say, and that the Powers That Be probably aren't terribly interested in whether Curveball knows what he's talking about." A Joint Staff officer deeply involved in the war planning understood how the evidence did not matter. "If we find weapons, that means Saddam is cheating and that means we go to war." And yet, "if we don't find weapons, that means Saddam is cheating, because he is hiding them." This was of no concern, however, in that it was *Powell* who had made the accusation. "If he believes it, I believe it, because I put a lot of stock in what he says. And I figure that people above me had information I didn't have access to."

Powell had rallied support from most of the American press. Liberal news columnist Mary McGrory from the *Washington Post* did not trust either Cheney or Wolfowitz, but she believed Powell. "I can only say that he persuaded me, and I was as tough as France to convince." Although not yet ready for war, she now believed "it might be the only way to stop a fiend." Editorials across the country sang his praise, with the *Denver Post* characterizing the speech as a high-noon presentation with "Marshal Dillon facing down a gunslinger in Dodge City." Maureen Dowd in the *New York Times* nonetheless remained skeptical. "The case was less persuasive than the presenter," she wrote. "And it was not clear why the presenter had jumped to the warlike side." But her caution did little to stem the popular tide.

Barely discernible within the accolades for Powell's speech were troublesome signs from America's allies. French President Jacques Chirac told Bush, "I do not share your spirit for why we need war." Chirac soon issued a joint public statement with Russian leader Vladimir Putin and German Chancellor Gerhard Schroeder declaring their support for reopening weapons inspections. "Nothing today justifies war. Russia, Germany and France are determined to ensure that everything possible is done to disarm Iraq peacefully."

Powell had grown impatient with the continued calls for inspections as the avenue to disarmament. The previous November, a UN resolution required Saddam to permit weapons inspectors to return after the four-year absence. But Powell assured the Security Council that "these are all tricks that are being played on us." Disarmament through the UN resolution was a simple task if Iraq were sincere. "It isn't brain surgery!" As for the French recommendation, "More inspectors—sorry. It's not the answer." Powell did not want war. "Force should be a last resort . . . but it must be a resort."

A short time after Powell's speech, Rumsfeld attended a security conference in Munich and had an on-stage confrontation with German foreign minister Joschka Fischer, who remained skeptical about the need for war. The defense secretary seemed puzzled. "It is difficult to believe there still could be questions in the minds of reasonable people open to the facts before them." Saddam "wasn't 'in the box'" and "has not been contained." His weapons programs "are maturing every day. . . . Diplomacy has been exhausted, almost." Fischer repeatedly asked "Why now?" Turning to the American delegation, he remarked in English, "Excuse me, I am not convinced." The United States was about to take on too much. "You're going to have to occupy Iraq for years and years. The idea that democracy will suddenly blossom is something that I can't share. . . . Are Americans ready for this?"

Bush continued to push for war despite his allies' flagging resolve. The White House had considered February 15 the day for the war's beginning, but his chief allies, British Prime Minister Tony Blair (referred to as "Bush's poodle" by a critical British press), Australian Prime Minister John Howard, and Spanish President José María Aznar, were facing resistance at home. Bush had no choice but to tell Rumsfeld, "Slow down your troop movements."

President Bush meanwhile signed a secret National Security Presidential Directive, NSPD-24, which set up an "Iraq Postwar Planning Office" inside the Defense Department to deal with the occupation. Heading the new Office for Reconstruction and Humanitarian Affairs in Baghdad was retired three-star General Jay Garner, who in late February warned the president and others in the White House Situation Room that the occupation forces were too small in number and that he must have at his disposal 200,000 to 300,000 Iraqi soldiers in the postwar era. Wolfowitz, however, called this figure "wildly" exaggerated and thought around 30,000 troops would suffice for the few months needed after the invasion. "I am reasonably certain that they will greet us as liberators, and that will help us keep requirements down."

A few days afterward, Wolfowitz defended the administration's case before a largely receptive audience of 300 Iraqi exiles from the Detroit area in Michigan. As he stood before a crowd on its feet cheering his forthcoming address, he opened with words that fitted nicely with those on the huge banner overhead: "Saddam Must Go." The Koran, Wolfowitz declared, teaches that "surely God does not change the condition of the people until they change their condition." At least one Shiite in the audience remained skeptical about American assurances. Not only did the United States support Saddam in the 1980s, but its military forces pulled out after the Gulf War to leave him to slaughter hordes of fellow Shiites in 1991. "Why should we here, with all due respect, trust or believe" the Bush administration's promises? Wolfowitz emphasized that "one of the most powerful military forces ever assembled" now stood ready to finish the job started years earlier. "If we commit those forces, we're not going to commit them for anything less than a free and democratic Iraq." To the *Detroit News* afterward, he insisted that "once that happens . . . you're going to find Iraqis out cheering American troops." There would be no conflict among the Kurds, Shiites, and Sunnis. "I think the ethnic differences in Iraq are there but they're exaggerated."

A four-star general later commented that the policymakers making these decisions ignored the military's advice. "The people around the president were so, frankly, intellectually arrogant. They *knew* that postwar Iraq would be easy and would be a catalyst for change in the Middle East." They rejected advice. "These are educated men, they are smart men. But they are not wise men."

Although the Pentagon insisted it had a postwar plan, many contemporaries said there was no plan because it seemed unnecessary. Army Lieutenant General Joseph Kellogg from the Joint Staff declared, "I was there for all the planning, all the execution. I saw it all." But he never saw a plan for Phase IV—the post-Saddam era. "There was no real plan. The thought was, you didn't need it. The assumption was that everything would be fine after the war, that they'd be happy they got rid of Saddam." Also from the Joint Staff, Army Colonel Gregory Gardner settled into his new position with U.S. occupation headquarters and saw no need for a plan. "Politically, we'd made a decision that we'd turn it over to the Iraqis in June." So why have a Phase IV plan? Iraqi security forces would change allegiances and work with the Americans in the occupation, other nations would drop their opposition to the war and help the U.S. military, and a new government would suddenly appear, permitting a "quick handoff to Iraqi interim administration with UN mandate." A Rand Corporation report noted the dominant view—"the task would not be difficult."

Coming on the heels of the highly successful Gulf War, the strategists estimated the fighting to last as few as seven days and no more than thirty. The entire venture hinged on the "shock and awe" of military firepower.

In the final moments of peace, the White House emphasized that its major objective was to find Saddam's WMD. At a lush breakfast in a Washington hotel in early March, the Joint Chiefs' chair, Air Force General Richard Myers, met with the press and expressed support for Powell's allegations made before the United Nations. "There are things you can't reveal because then your sources and methods are compromised, and in some cases, people get hurt." Although no one knew where the WMD were, the Iraqis would reveal the locations once the American troops had entered their country. "They're playing a giant shell game right now. That shell game, with forces on the ground, would come to a halt." Then the "people will come forward and say, 'Here's where this is, here's where that is.'" Rumsfeld agreed. In an interview with the Arabic satellite television news channel Al Jazeera, the defense secretary repeated that the war was "about weapons of mass destruction." President Bush drove home the point: "Intelligence gathered by this and other governments leaves no doubt that the Iraq regime continues to possess and conceal some of the most lethal weapons ever devised."

The previous December 2002, Wolfowitz had attempted to alleviate all doubt about whether the invading troops would recognize WMD if they saw them. In a private meeting with NATO ambassadors, he declared, "It's like the judge said about pornography. I can't define it, but I will know it when I see it."

Operation Iraqi Freedom

On the evening of March 17, President Bush announced to Americans that the clock was winding down toward the invasion. In what he termed an "ultimatum speech" and not a "declaration of war speech," he warned that "Saddam Hussein and his sons must leave Iraq within forty-eight hours. Their refusal to do so will result in military conflict, commenced at a time of our choosing."

Two days later, in the White House Situation Room, President Bush informed the National Security Council that Saddam had not met the terms of the ultimatum and that the invasion would begin. "Do you have any last comments, recommendations or thoughts?" No one had anything to say, and the president turned to his video connection with Franks at Prince Sultan Air Base in Saudi Arabia. "The rules of engagement and command and control are in place," Franks declared. "The force is ready to go, Mr. President." Bush responded, "For the peace of the world and the benefit and freedom of the Iraqi people, I hereby give the order to execute Operation Iraqi Freedom. May God bless the troops."

At that point, the president left for the Oval Office and, not stopping there, went through its door for an outside walk during which he prayed for the troops. Returning to his office, he phoned the coalition leaders to assert, "We're launching!"

The first harbinger of trouble came in the opening assault on March 20 (March 19 Washington time)—a rain of cruise missiles and bunker-busting bombs on Dora Farm along the Tigris River in southern Baghdad's outer rim, where CIA intelligence had determined the location of Saddam and his family. Whether or not he was in the thick palm grove, the venture came up empty.

A second sign of concern came with the actual invasion. The following dawn of March 21, the ground assault began with 145,000 troops, a force less than half the size recommended by General Zinni in his long-since-filed Desert Crossing plan. Accompanying them were an equally small contingent of 247 army tanks along with other fighting vehicles. Facing the invasion force was a formidable Iraqi defense of 400,000 troops, 4,000 tanks and other armored vehicles, Republican Guard divisions and the Special Republican Guard that safeguarded Baghdad, and a brutal paramilitary band led by Saddam's son Uday and known as the *Fedayeen Saddam*. En route, the coalition force became victims of the weather when a giant sandstorm combined with a torrent of rain to unleash what one officer called "a tornado of mud" that for three days grounded the helicopters and almost sank the troops in muck.

Almost as soon as the invasion force rolled out of Kuwait toward Baghdad, it was clear that, as one U.S. commander noted, "the enemy we're fighting is different from the one we'd war-gamed against." Instead of the promised welcome by the Iraqi citizenry, the troops encountered an angry populace, some armed with AK-47 rifles, rocket-launched grenades, and mortars. "For the first, but not the last time," according to the army's history of the war, "well-armed paramilitary forces, indistinguishable, except for their weapons, from civilians, attacked." Some days later, a suicide car bombing killed four American soldiers in Najaf. "We were absolutely convinced, in a lot of ways, that [Saddam] was going to capitulate with all these southern forces," claimed General James Thorman in operations. "We were told that by the CIA. We were told that by . . . intel reports, in the assessment. And that isn't what happened. We had to fight our way through every town."

On the third day of the invasion, the U.S. Army's 507th Maintenance Company, a sup-

port unit of thirty-three soldiers, lost its way and was ambushed deep behind enemy lines in Nasiriyah to the southeast of Baghdad. With no troop guides at critical points, the unit made a wrong turn while following a long convoy. An inquiry afterward noted that the unit "was not trained to be in the situation they were in, was not equipped to be there, [had] no GPS [Global Positioning System or satellite-guided navigation system], no radios, no training on crew-served weapons, only one crew-served weapon in there, [and] no night vision" apparatus. Marines saved ten soldiers from capture or death, but eleven died, a dozen were wounded, and six were captured, including Private Jessica Lynch. A week later, Americans liberated her in a daring venture, making her the first prisoner of war rescued since World War II. This debacle starkly underlined the need for a larger invasion force and the lack of preparation and proper equipment for what was emerging as unconventional warfare.

These revelations led to a furious debate in Washington's highest military circles over troop size but, curiously, *not* over the nature of the war itself. Gulf War commanders related their experiences in 1991, warning that present numbers were grossly insufficient both in the attack and for the occupation afterward. General Myers bristled under the assault from commanders senior to him. "My view of those reports—and since I don't know who you're quoting, who the individuals are—is that they're bogus," the Joint Chiefs chair hotly asserted in the Pentagon. "I don't know how they get started, and I don't know how they've been perpetuated, but it's not been by responsible members of the team that put this all together. They either weren't there, or they don't know, or," in an implicit question of their loyalty, "they're working another agenda, and I don't know what that agenda might be." Apparently thinking no one should criticize leadership in wartime, he declared, "It is not helpful to have those kind of comments come out when we've got troops in combat, because first of all, they're false, they're absolutely wrong, they bear no resemblance to the truth, and it's just, it's just harmful to our troops that are out there fighting very bravely, very courageously."

Despite the early setbacks, the coalition forces took Saddam International Airport on April 3 and two days later stormed into Baghdad. After what one commander called "eight hours of continuous fighting" in the initial run, the conflagration went into a second drive on April 7 that found them in Saddam's palace area in the city's center and thinking the regime had collapsed and so, seemingly, had the war.

But Rumsfeld and Franks had confused strategy with tactics, meaning that the mere capture of the enemy's capital did not signify an end to a war that was becoming more of a battle with irregulars than Iraqi troops. Their plan appeared disarmingly simple: exploit America's technical superiority in winning the war quickly and with few men. No better example was there than the battle for Baghdad. In invading the city, the forces quickly cut through opposing troop lines, convinced that the Iraqis could not adjust to having the enemy front and back. These tactics worked on the battlefront, but in a striking similarity to what happened in Vietnam, Rumsfeld and Franks failed to realize that strategy called for Iraq's political transformation, indicating that the battle was not the end but, rather, a means toward that end.

This truth became increasingly elusive as two images in particular left the impression of a triumphant end of the war. The first was the inexplicable optimism expressed by Iraqi's information minister, Mohammed Saeed Sahhaf, who boasted to the press of imminent Iraqi victory even as the rapidly uncoiling cordon of American troops wrapped itself around the capital. Saddam's forces were pushing the invaders back into the desert and to their deaths, he announced at an April 7 news conference that seemed surreal in its elegant setting inside the Palestine Hotel. As cameras revealed the marines trudging on to the capital and the army erecting camp at the city's airport, Sahhaf proclaimed, "There is not any American presence or troops in the heart of the capital, at all." Saddam's soldiers "gave them a great lesson that history will not forget." A day later,

he repeated the theme, telling news correspondents that American soldiers were "going to surrender or be burned in their tanks." Furthermore, he darkly added, "I can say, and I am responsible for what I am saying, that they have started to commit suicide under the walls of Baghdad. We will encourage them to commit more suicides quickly." His last public appearance was on April 8, when he told the press that the Americans "are going to surrender or be burned in their tanks. They will surrender, it is they who will surrender."

"Baghdad Bob," as he became known to pundits, perhaps believed what he was saying—that "authentic sources, many authentic sources" had assured him the Iraqi military had turned the tide by a brilliant counterattack that would lead to victory. But so fearful were Iraqis of relaying bad news to their leaders that they either cast a favorable slant on the most untoward events or outright lied in the face of contrary evidence. Or, perhaps, they were simply guilty of buffoonery.

The second image that implanted victory in the minds of the president and other Americans was the fall of Saddam's statue in Baghdad square at the hands of an angry Iraqi populace helped by U.S. Marines on April 9. Embedded military historian Rick Atkinson remarked that the days afterward were "as good as it got, the high-water mark of the invasion." President Bush's popularity soared after the capture of Baghdad.

But rumblings of trouble had already appeared. Veteran army officers declared they could "lose the peace" if they failed to restore the city to normal—and quickly. Otherwise, one declared, "the gunmen will start appearing and taking shots at [the] U.S. military. Then the suicide bombers will appear." Another said, "I suspect that serious people somewhere—probably hiding out in Syria—are planning the counterattack." Intelligence officers likewise expressed concern. "It is premature to be doing victory laps," a senior Middle East specialist asserted. "The hard part is going to be the occupation. The Israelis won in six days—but have been fighting ever since—for thirty years."

In military terms, the coalition forces had successfully completed their campaign in 26 days and with only 161 dead. But as one officer in the Central Command noted, "We designed success in negative terms—getting rid of the regime, instead of establishing a democratic regime."

President Bush interpreted the *military* outcome of the fighting as a major success and a near end to the war. Boarding a four-seat navy jet, he set out for the U.S.S. *Abraham Lincoln*, an aircraft carrier lying off the southern California coast. After 2 fly-bys with the president piloting at one point, the S-3B Viking made a "tailhook" landing at 150 miles per hour and came to a stop in less than 400 feet. Shucking his green flight suit and white helmet, Bush stood before television cameras in suit and tie to announce that the war had approached its climax. In the background just above his head in full television view hung a sweeping banner on the tower saying "Mission Accomplished."

"Major combat operations in Iraq have ended," he proclaimed in this orchestrated photo-op. "In the battle of Iraq, the United States and our allies have prevailed." Work remained. Reestablishing order would be dangerous. The hunt for Saddam and his henchmen would continue. "We've begun the search for hidden chemical and biological weapons and already know of hundreds of sites that will be investigated." The implantation of democracy would take time. "The battle of Iraq is one victory in a war on terror" that began with the 9/11 attack on the United States. Speaking to U.S. military forces, he declared, "Because of you, our nation is more secure. Because of you, the tyrant has fallen, and Iraq is free."

The Occupation and a New Kind of War

President Bush's allusion to the war's end proved premature. Great numbers of Iraqis, fueled by years of Saddam's oppressive rule, unleashed their anger in weeks of looting and vandalism in Baghdad as the outnumbered oc-cupation forces stood by, under no orders to restore security. "Stuff happens!" Rumsfeld testily declared at a Pentagon briefing on April 11. "But in terms of what's going on in that country, it is a fundamental misunderstanding to see those images over, and over, and over again of some boy walking out with a vase and say, 'Oh, my goodness, you didn't have a plan.' That's nonsense. They know what they're doing, and they're doing a terrific job. And it's untidy, and freedom's untidy, and free people are free to make mistakes and commit crimes and do bad things. They're also free to live their lives and do wonderful things, and that's what's going to happen here." As his rhetoric rang hollow, the Iraqi people's confidence in Americans plummeted when their troops did nothing to establish order and provide security.

The occupation continued to flounder as the search for WMD came up empty and the roots of an insurgency began to appear. The soldiers discovered huge supplies of conventional weapons in bunkers across the country, but commanders refused to approve their destruction out of fear that the storage places might contain poison gas and other WMD. Moving on in the hunt, they left the dumps guarded by the few soldiers they could spare, and insurgents encountered little resistance in carting off tons of weapons. It soon became clear that the small size of the occupation troops had another unexpected impact: Iraq's borders lay open, allowing free passage of *jihadis* (supporters of holy war) in and out of Syria to the west.

In mid-May, the White House made a change in policy when it appointed L. Paul "Jerry" Bremer head of a UN-created Coalition Provisional Authority (CPA). A retired diplomat and expert in terrorism, he became the chief civilian administrator in Iraq with the responsibility of supervising the "reconstruction process" and building new "institutions and governing structures." No one declared that the CPA would supersede the Office for Reconstruction and Humanitarian Affairs, nor did anyone say that Bremer would replace Garner. But the president, Rumsfeld, and Powell had all interviewed Bremer for the position and made clear their concern about maintaining control over the timing of a new government. Indeed, before Bremer became CPA administrator, Douglas Feith, as head of the Pentagon's Office of Special Plans, informed him of the need to prohibit leaders of Saddam's Ba'ath Party from holding government positions.

Bremer arrived with a team of advisers almost two months before Garner's scheduled departure from Baghdad and immediately put him in an awkward position. Garner had just agreed to the establishment of an interim Iraqi advisory team comprised of Kurds, Shiites, and Sunnis—all to involve the Iraqis in the formation of a provisional government. Two days later, he learned that Bremer was en route to Baghdad. Garner realized this arrangement could not work. "Bremer didn't want my advice. . . . He's a hardworking guy, twenty hours a day. But he cut me out the first day, didn't have me to any of his meetings." Garner knew Bremer was freezing him out of the proceedings. "You can't have the guy who used to be in charge and the guy who's now in charge there, because you divide the loyalties of the people. So the best thing for me is just to step out of here." On the third day he was there, I said, 'Jerry, I'm going home.' We just didn't get along."

Garner remained long enough to sharply differ with Bremer over policy. First, Bremer emphasized his intention to deny government participation to about 50,000 members of Saddam's Ba'ath Party. "Hell," the general warned Bremer, "you won't be able to run anything if you go this deep." Bremer refused to change course and, indeed, the next day declared his plan to dismantle the entire Iraqi military and internal security force. "We have always made plans to bring the army back," Garner protested. "Well, the plans have changed," Bremer retorted. He then informed the Iraqi advisory team that "one thing you need to realize is you're not the government. We are. And we're in charge."

On May 16, Bremer issued the order barring Saddam's supporters from public service and soon directed the confiscation of the party's assets and property. Occupation staff members "went nuts," declared an army officer. The order "just cleaned out the ministries. The guys said, 'We can't run our ministries now.'" Bremer ignored one expert who argued that Iraq "was not the first totalitarian system we had engaged with, not the first one-party state that we had worked with, and that there was absolutely no experience in any country that said that being a member of the dominant political party meant you were a bad guy." Bremer insisted in his order that "the Ba'athist ideology, which had been responsible for so many of the human-rights abuses and mistreatment of the people in the country over the last forty years, had to be extirpated finally and completely from society, much as the American government decided to completely extirpate Nazism from Germany at the end of the Second World War." The order effectively undermined all hope of restoring the infrastructure so vital to a functioning country.

A week later, Bremer continued his effort to "eradicate Saddamism" in Iraq by disbanding its army, thereby eliminating the sole source of national unity and intensifying anti-American feeling. This order meant the dissolution of 385,000 members of the Iraqi military, 285,000 police and security forces of the Ministry of the Interior, and 50,000 guardians of the president. Furthermore, it removed thousands of leading Iraqis from the pension lists and, according to a specialist on the Ba'athist Party, "created a vast pool of humiliated, antagonized, and politicized men." More than that, great numbers of them had weapons they carried home. A high-ranking military officer warned Bremer, "You guys just blindsided Centcom." On that day, he asserted, "we snatched defeat from the jaws of victory and created an insurgency."

Bremer's two actions within a week injected a greater impetus into a growing insurgency. The dissembling of the Ba'ath Party and the army alienated more than 500,000 Iraqis and destroyed two major institutions that might have crossed sectarian and ethnic boundaries and united the country. Army Colonel Alan King at Central Command noted the instant reaction in Baghdad's streets. "The insurgency went crazy. May was the turning point" for the coalition's involvement. When Bremer "disbanded the military, and announced we were occupiers—that was it. Every moderate, every person that had leaned toward us, was furious. One Iraqi who had saved my life in an ambush said to me, 'I can't be your friend anymore.'" Former members of the Iraqi army angrily joined the demonstrations, with one officer telling the Reuters news agency in a quotation circulated throughout the Central Command, "All of us will become suicide bombers." Another told Arab news, "The only thing left for me is to blow myself up in the face of tyrants."

Garner had meanwhile returned home in June and, after a couple of weeks stewing over Bremer's decisions, expressed his concerns to Rumsfeld. "We've made three tragic decisions," Garner declared. "Really?" Rumsfeld responded. "Three terrible mistakes," emphasized Garner: banning the Ba'ath Party from the government, dismissing the Iraqi advisory group, and, most important, dismantling the army. Many thousands of angry, unemployed, and armed Iraqis now threatened the occupation. "There's still time to rectify this," he declared. "There's still time to turn it around." With a glazed look, Rumsfeld asserted that "I don't think there is anything we can do, because we are where we are." But he agreed to accompany Garner to the Oval Office, where the general had his chance to repeat his fears but, perhaps overwhelmed by the setting and wanting to please the president, highlighted only the successes in Iraq. "Oh, that's good," declared Bush. As Garner walked out, the president clapped him on the back and asked, "Hey Jay, you want to do Iran?" "Sir, the boys and I talked about that and we want to hold out for Cuba. We think the rum and the cigars are a little better. . . . The women are prettier." Bush saw the humor. "You got it. You got Cuba." In all the banter, Garner did not mention his worries about Bremer's policies and left the president convinced the program was going well.

War Enters a New Phase

As the fighting expanded, reporters asked Rumsfeld in late June whether the coalition was fighting a guerrilla war. "I don't know that I would use the word," the defense secretary responded. There was "no question" that the trouble came from thugs and "leftover remnants of the Saddam Hussein regime." In a Pentagon briefing just days later, CNN's Jamie McIntyre pushed the growing issue. "Can you tell us why you're so reluctant to say that what's going on in Iraq now is a guerrilla war?" Rumsfeld replied, "I guess the reason I don't use the phrase 'guerrilla war' is because there isn't one." McIntyre read aloud the Defense Department's definition of guerrilla war: "military and paramilitary operations conducted in enemy-held or hostile territory by irregular ground indigenous forces." Looking at Rumsfeld, McIntyre declared, "This seems to fit a lot of what's going on in Iraq." "It really doesn't," Rumsfeld noted.

The concern over definitions constituted more than a matter of semantics, for the type of struggle going on provided a barometer of the coalition's performance and determined what tactics to use. If the war were with Saddam's loyalists, its architects had overthrown the regime and were now in the mopping-up process. If a guerrilla war, the occupation forces had alienated the national populace by replacing Saddam as the country's chief enemy. American combat units trained in conventional warfare meanwhile continued these tactics because that was what they knew best. "You know the old saying," a senior intelligence officer declared, "'If all you have is a hammer, everything looks like a nail.'"

After thirty-six years of service, Franks retired at the peak of his career in early July following the invasion, and his second in command, Army Lieutenant General John Abizaid, replaced him. Abizaid promptly broke with the administration by admitting to a guerrilla war in Iraq that required American soldiers to stay there for a long time. His independent stance was not out of character.

Holding a master's degree in Middle Eastern studies from Harvard, he spoke Arabic and was a Lebanese known by his West Point classmates as "an Arabian Vince Lombardi." In the Pentagon after a discussion with Rumsfeld, Abizaid surprised reporters by disagreeing with his superior's denial that they were fighting a guerrilla war. We "are conducting what I would describe as a classical guerrilla-type campaign against us."

The administration sustained another blow that same summer of 2003 when the alleged Iraqi–Niger deal over uranium surfaced again and fed growing suspicion that the White House had tailored the evidence to justify the war. Walter Pincus published a front-page story in the *Washington Post* asserting that the CIA had sent a "retired U.S. ambassador" to Africa early in 2002 to investigate the Niger claim. The unnamed former diplomat, as noted earlier, was Joseph Wilson, who on July 6 followed Pincus's story with an op-ed piece in the *New York Times* titled "What I Didn't Find in Africa." After his visit to Niger in February 2002, Wilson found it "highly doubtful" that there had been a deal because the uranium industry had "too much oversight" to permit such an acquisition. His opening set the tone of the 1,452-word essay: "Did the Bush administration manipulate intelligence about Saddam Hussein's weapons programs to justify an invasion of Iraq? Based on my experience with the administration in the months leading up to the war, I have little choice but to conclude that some of the intelligence related to Iraq's nuclear weapons program was twisted to exaggerate the Iraqi threat." If so, "we went to war under false pretenses."

As fate would have it, the presidential entourage was visiting Africa when the story broke, and Rice immediately telephoned Tenet in the middle of the night, seeking the chronology of events. Tenet, as noted, had not read the president's January 2003 speech beforehand and opted to protect him by accepting "shared responsibility" with the White House. Throughout the morning hours, he and his staff at Langley crafted a public statement that they first ran by Karl Rove and his aides at the White House. "The CIA," Tenet wrote, "approved the President's State of the Union address before it was delivered . . . I was responsible for the approval process in my Agency . . . the President had every reason to believe that the text presented to him was sound. These sixteen words should never have been included in the text written for the President."

But when the press asked Rice whether the CIA had approved the speech, she simply responded that "the CIA cleared the speech in its entirety." To Tenet's surprise, she made no reference to the White House sharing responsibility. "Now, I can tell you," she continued, "if the CIA, the Director of Central Intelligence, had said, take this out of the speech, it would have been gone, without question." Had we known "what we now know, that some of the Niger documents were apparently forged, we wouldn't have put this in the President's speech—but that's knowing what we know now."

Tenet's acceptance of blame proved too much for his colleagues in the CIA, who were furious over Rice's accusations and thought the administration had misled Americans into war. "White House Points at CIA over Iraq Uranium Charge," declared the Reuters news agency. Senator Pat Roberts, a confidant of the vice president, criticized the CIA's "sloppy handling of the issue" and accused it of a "campaign of press leaks" intended to "discredit the president." The yellowcake reference in the State of the Union Address "wasn't an accident," insisted Milt Bearden, a former CIA station chief in a number of countries that included Nigeria. "This wasn't fifteen monkeys in a room with typewriters." Melvin Goodman, another longtime CIA veteran, asserted that "they needed this to go to war. It serves no other purpose."

Colonel Larry Wilkerson, Powell's former chief of staff in the State Department, declared that hawkish neoconservatives "were just relentless" in making this charge. "You would take it out and they would stick it back in. That was their favorite bureaucratic technique—ruthless relentlessness." They would "stick that baby in there forty-seven times and on the forty-seventh time it will stay. At every level of the decision-making process you had to have your ax out, ready to chop their fingers off. Sooner or later you would miss one and it would get in there."

About a week later, conservative news analyst Robert Novak responded to Wilson's piece with an article in the *Washington Post* that raised ethical and legal questions by going beyond the Niger issue and thereby culminated in a highly publicized court case. Novak asserted that "two senior administration officials" had revealed Wilson's wife as Valerie Plame, a CIA "operative on weapons of mass destruction" who had arranged his visit to Niger. Many observers thought the public identification of a covert CIA operative a crime. Indeed, the Justice Department opened a criminal inquiry into how Plame's identity became known to the press and whether the action had illegally unmasked a secret agent. The investigation uncovered the source—Lewis "Scooter" Libby, presidential assistant and chief of staff and, most striking, national security adviser to the vice president. The court found him guilty of perjury for having lied about leaking information in a verdict that many critics thought had made him a scapegoat for crimes committed by higher officials in the Bush administration.

Making matters worse for the White House, the war took a new and more violent direction that autumn of 2003. In early August, a car bomb blew up outside the Jordanian embassy in Baghdad that left eleven dead and more than fifty injured. Less than two weeks later, insurgents drove a cement truck filled with explosives into the outer wall of UN headquarters in eastern Baghdad, killing twenty-two—including the Brazilian chief of the mission—and wounding seventy. The United Nations frantically reduced its staff from 800 to 15, which meant that U.S. leaders no longer had UN mediators to maintain communication with Shiites who refused to talk directly with Americans. Furthermore,

that explosion followed by another one a month afterward led to the withdrawal of a number of international organizations. "That was a brilliant campaign," asserted a marine specialist in counterinsurgency assigned to the CPA's training program. "They hit the UN, the Red Cross, the Jordanian embassy, and the Iraqi police. And we were calling them 'dead-enders'? Who do you think is disorganized at that point?" The senior army commander, Lieutenant General Ricardo Sanchez, noted that the insurgents were trying to undermine the coalition by attacking U.S. and Iraqi security forces, political leaders, and the various foreign elements in the country. Their objective was to isolate the United States.

The insurgents soon escalated the violence by using an improvised explosive device (IED). The most lethal weapon in this expanded warfare was a low-cost and highly effective remote-controlled roadside bomb, which required no telltale wiring apparatus and, hidden beneath rocks or trash in the streets or inside dead dogs, proved the greatest threat to American forces. Particularly vulnerable were the Humvees, which had insufficient armor for protection. Soon the insurgents attached IEDs to light poles or tree branches and leaves, which meant that explosions hit soldiers manning the guns on the outside of the vehicles along with those on the inside as the force struck the area above the armor-protected doors and blew windows inward. And if the bomb failed to kill, its percussion badly damaged the skull. "This was penetrating trauma to the nth degree," noted a surgeon from the United States. "It was massive. The tissue destruction was like nothing I'd ever seen before. . . . Imagine shards of metal going everywhere. . . . Add the percussion from the blast. Then put someone inside a Bradley fighting vehicle and add fire to it and burning flesh. A person inhales and [suffers] inhalation injury."

In late October, the Muslim holy month of Ramadan opened with the insurgency launching its first full-fledged offensive. Especially shocking were the fatality figures—the highest the Americans sustained since the spring—and

Humvee
Soldiers from the 10th Mountain Division patrol Baghdad on foot and in their Humvee, March 14, 2006.
(Photo Courtesy of U.S. Army. Credit Senior Airman Desiree N. Palacios)

the rocket assault on the Rasheed Hotel, the CPA headquarters inside the highly protected Green Zone and where Wolfowitz had lodged for a brief visit. The insurgents launched six rockets on the hotel, probably aimed at him, but he escaped uninjured while the missiles killed an army officer one story down. Much as the Vietcong had destroyed the notion of territorial sanctity by invading U.S. embassy grounds in Saigon in 1968, so did the insurgents' rockets end the illusion of safety inside the Green Zone. Within a few days, casualty figures showed that more Americans had died in combat after May 1, when President Bush proclaimed an end to the war, than in the spring invasion that had begun the war.

"We got him!" proudly proclaimed Bremer to reporters on December 14, throwing a ray of light onto a steadily darkening situation. Operation Red Dawn had climaxed after thirty-eight weeks with Saddam's capture in an orchard ten miles southeast of Tikrit and close to his birthplace of Auja. Pulled out of a hole beneath a prayer rug thrown over a Styrofoam lid, he surrendered without resistance to a contingent of Special Operations troops and infantry. "This is a great day in your history," Bremer declared to Iraqis. "With the arrest of Saddam Hussein, there is a new opportunity for members of the former regime, whether military or civilian, to end their bitter opposition. Let them come forward now in a spirit of reconciliation and hope, lay down their arms, and join you, their fellow citizens, in the task of building the new Iraq."

American military leaders were likewise exuberant. General Sanchez told the press, "The former regime elements we have been combating have been brought to their knees. Capturing Saddam was a major operational and psychological defeat for the enemy." The insurgency was now "a fractured, sporadic threat, with the leadership destabilized, finances interdicted, and no hope of the Ba'athists' return to power." The reconstruction program had progressed to the point that "within six months you're going to see some normalcy. I really believe that." Another American commander exclaimed that Saddam's capture "will have a tremendous negative impact on the Ba'athist insurgency" as former members of the regime "melt away and begin to reintegrate into normal society." An army officer confidently asserted, "I think this puts a nail in the coffin of hopes that the Ba'ath Party could ever regain control of Iraq. There is no longer any central figure around whom such a movement could coalesce."

Saddam's capture had actually raised false hopes for peace. According to a senior officer, "we missed an incredible opportunity to bring the Sunnis into the fold during that December-January time frame. A lot of infrastructure spending and a push to reach out to religious and tribal leaders could potentially have changed the course of the war." Shaking his head, he declared, "That was the great missed opportunity." But he and other coalition leaders had failed to grasp the thrust of a war that no longer revolved around Saddam but on a deep native hostility toward all outsiders. Rather than breaking the back of the insurgency, the end of Saddam opened the way for his opponents to turn on the Americans and their allies with the objective of forcing them out of the homeland. "We are not fighting for Saddam," said one religious student in Fallujah. "We are fighting for our country, for our honor, for Islam."

By the end of 2003, U.S. forces were mired down in a protracted ground war that the Army War College called a major blunder. In a publication carrying the imprimatur of its Strategic Studies Institute, historian Jeffrey Record insisted that the White House had gotten involved in a war it did not have to fight and, in so doing, turned attention from a war in Afghanistan it had to fight. "The result has been an unnecessary preventive war of choice against a deterred Iraq that has created a new front in the Middle East for Islamic terrorism and diverted attention and resources away from securing the American homeland against further assault by an undeterrable al Qaeda. The war against Iraq was not integral to the GWOT [Global War on Terrorism] but rather a detour from it."

The war escalated again in April 2004 when a series of atrocities led to a marine assault on the city of Fallujah in western Iraq. The insurgents had captured, beaten, and dismembered four American contractors and left their bodies hanging from a bridge, where a mob tore them down and, with news cameras rolling, threw them into a pile of burning tires. The White House angrily demanded retaliation. Marine Major General James Mattis was on the scene, however, and warned that the enemy *wanted* that reaction. "Let's find out who did this, and get them; this is a city of three hundred thousand in which a few hundred people did something." Sending in a marine division would lead to widespread destruction and further alienate the people. But his warnings went unheeded. The marines on April 5 launched a major offensive code-named Operation Vigilant Resolve, which focused on Fallujah but soon spread into Ramadi near the center of the country and into Baghdad to the south. The insurgents countered with rocket-propelled grenades and roadside bombs in ambushes along the roads leading into Fallujah, threatening to cut off the marines from their supplies.

Then, just as suddenly as the marines had launched the assault on Fallujah, they called a cease-fire on April 9, under orders from either the White House or Bremer. Mattis was infuriated. As one marine general complained, "It was like going in half-assed and then run-

Urban Fighting in Baghdad
An Iraqi National Police officer and soldiers from the First Armored Division search a building for
terrorists and weapons in the Iraqi capital, September 19, 2006. *(Photo courtesy of U.S. Army.
Credit Air Force Master Sergeant Jonathan Doti)*

ning away." No one had considered the consequences. "It was the same as the way they
went to war, and the same way that Bremer
operated." The White House expressed concern that continuing the assault would destroy
the coalition, and Bremer explained that the
attack threatened to undermine Iraqis' support for Americans. The marines were infuriated. "Our job was not to be emotional," one
officer cynically observed. "Our job was to
put lipstick on that pig as best we could."

President Bush triumphantly proclaimed on
April 28 that "most of Fallujah is returning to
normal," but the truth was that the city belonged to the insurgents. The marine operation had not led to the capture of those who

killed the contractors, nor had it quashed the
terrorists and established law and order. Instead, according to a marine commander leading the fighting, "we turned the city over to
the Fallujah Brigade—which was made up of
people we'd been fighting against." The CIA
and the marines had apparently devised this
face-saving measure, which another marine officer ridiculed as "hiring the inmates to run
the asylum." An Iraqi insurgency expert at the
U.S. Naval War College pronounced Fallujah
"a political victory for the insurgents. The
United States had backed down, and, more
important, had negotiated with the enemy. It
also was a military victory: the insurgents had
fought the Americans to a standstill." Or, in

the words of an insurgent, "we won." A Special Forces veteran recalled that "I looked Iraqis in the eye, and they were thinking, 'We can get rid of these guys.' That was the day we lost the initiative. The Iraqis realized that they could kick our ass."

As the coalition disintegrated in the face of widened fighting, Washington remained remarkably upbeat. Increasing numbers of allies became disenchanted with their involvement (as Powell had warned), insisting that their sole task was peacekeeping. As one CPA official complained, "Except for the Brits, they weren't there to fight. The Dutch did good patrols, on foot. The Italians only patrolled by vehicle. . . . The Japanese didn't patrol at all." In fairness to the coalition forces, fighting was never part of the arrangement. "We came for Phase IV—security and stabilization operations," said a Polish paratrooper. "All of a sudden, against our will, we find ourselves in the combat zone." By 2005, Spain's 1,300 troops had left Iraq, followed by those of Honduras, the Dominican Republic, Nicaragua, the Philippines, Hungary, the Netherlands, and Ukraine. Also announcing departure plans were Poland, Bulgaria, and Italy. Even though thirty-one countries on the coalition list remained in Iraq as late as the fall of 2004, their contribution totaled only 24,000 troops. Yet, Joint Chiefs Chair Myers typified Washington's attitude when he told the press in mid-April 2004 that the spring fighting was "a symptom of the success we're having here in Iraq."

The official optimism also ran counter to a marked change in Americans' outlook toward the war. In May 2004, for the first time in the war, a majority of Americans—51 percent of those polled—expressed dissatisfaction with how the war was going, even though 53 percent wanted the troops to remain until Iraq had a sound government. Later that month, the majority of Americans responding to a *Washington Post*/ABC poll saw no purpose in continuing the war. "I have seen this movie," remarked General Zinni. "It was called Vietnam."

The White House nonetheless claimed major progress, with Bremer in late June declaring his task complete and turning over the Iraqi government to Prime Minister Ayad Allawi on an interim basis. During a NATO meeting in Turkey, Condoleezza Rice slipped a note to President Bush: "Iraq is sovereign." At the bottom of the note, he scribbled, "Let freedom reign!" Bremer had already left the country, with no fanfare during the secret change of government and none at the Baghdad airport. "He left Iraq in such an appropriate way, running out of town," snidely remarked a Special Forces officer.

Shortly after Bremer's departure, Army Lieutenant General George Casey replaced Sanchez as senior U.S. commander and, recognizing the new direction of the war, introduced a counterinsurgency plan. Casey had secured the assistance of an expert in counterinsurgency warfare—Professor Kalev Sepp at the Naval Postgraduate School, a retired Special Forces officer with a doctorate in history from Harvard who had advised the Salvadoran army on dealing with insurgents. Sepp called for clearing, holding, and expanding safe areas; isolating the insurgents from the people and stopping their avenues of entry and escape by closing Iraq's borders; offering an amnesty and rehabilitation program; selecting a strong leader to unify the civilian and military effort; working with and circulating among the Iraqi people to establish trust; removing the emphasis from killing and capturing the enemy in huge roundup operations; and putting the Iraqi security forces in the front of the struggle, with the U.S. military as backup.

But before Casey could institute the new tactics, a scandal broke in August over prisoner abuses at Saddam's old prison at Abu Ghraib just west of Baghdad. Shortly after its opening a year earlier, stories had spread of torture used to extract information. The following January 2004, General Sanchez authorized a secret investigation into the charges, which in March confirmed "systemic and illegal" abuse of prisoners and led to a reprimand and a demotion of the officer in charge. But in late April, CBS television's *60 Minutes II* released photographs of the abuses, and *New Yorker* magazine posted on its website a lengthy story by investigative journalist Seymour Hersh, along with photographs and testimonies from military investigations. Responsibility for the prison camp rested with the secretary of defense.

Rumsfeld twice offered to resign; both times the president refused to accept the resignation and praised his work despite further embarrassing inquiries into the treatment of prisoners of war (POWs). Rumsfeld asked former Secretary of Defense James Schlesinger to head an independent panel to examine the allegations and determine their causes. Before the press in August, Schlesinger characterized Abu Ghraib as "a kind of animal house on the night shift." The officers in charge, his report concluded, were "directly responsible," but Rumsfeld and other Pentagon civilian leaders, along with General Sanchez and others at CentCom, bore responsibility as well. Their vaguely worded interrogation policies had fostered an atmosphere in which "the existence of confusing and inconsistent interrogation technique policies contributed to the belief that additional interrogation techniques were condoned." That same month, three army generals heading another investigation found twenty-three soldiers and four private contractors guilty of abuses.

Especially damning were revelations of similar behavior at Guantanamo. Its treatment of prisoners had drawn praise for its humanity, but this argument fell flat when in December the public learned that the FBI had been aware of abuses in the naval base detention center as early as 2002. Since its opening in January of that year, the prison at Guantanamo had held, without charges or attorney privileges, about 550 men suspected of having connections with either Afghanistan's Taliban regime or al-Qaeda. Photographs and other evidence showed torture and humiliation, denial of toilet use, excessively cold temperatures in the cells, a prisoner gagged with duct tape, others isolated in cells flooded with light, beatings with sledgehammer handles, use of unmuzzled dogs, stripped Iraqi prisoners in compromising sexual positions, and

at least one death of an Iraqi general resulting from interrogation.

Despite these allegations, the Pentagon concluded that after twelve investigations, it found no pattern of abuses in Afghanistan, Iraq, and Cuba and attributed the violations to a few.

To the Present

President Bush won reelection in November over Democrat John Kerry, a celebrated Vietnam war hero who, in a poorly run campaign, found great difficulty criticizing a war he had voted for in Congress. Despite the Democrats' claims to a failing war, the president remained convinced that he had a popular mandate to stay the course.

Casey got his first real test of leadership just after President Bush's reelection, when American forces prepared to destroy all insurgent safe havens—and especially the biggest one at Fallujah. Second Fallujah, as the battle became known in Washington, included Iraqi units and demonstrated a greater degree of military and political preparation along with a much larger attack force than the April encounter. For 10 days, 6,500 marines, 1,500 army forces, and 2,000 Iraqi troops pounded the city, with 2,500 navy personnel taking on various support tasks or working as medics or doctors. One account noted that "the fighting was intense, close and personal, the likes of which has been experienced on just a few occasions since the battle of Hué City in the Vietnam War."

When Fallujah finally fell, more than a thousand insurgents had died in the carnage while most of the others had fled before the battle began. American casualties numbered 479, including 54 dead, and Iraqis suffered 51 casualties, among them 8 dead. The mop-up afterward, however, proved more stressful than the attack. "It was exhausting, dangerous work," observed a former Pentagon official then embedded with the marines. "Walking down narrow, dust-clogged alleys behind growling tanks, barely able to hear the shouts of the fire team and squad leaders, hurling grenades in windows, slapping C-4 to door fronts, ducking from the blast, waiting for the dust to clear a bit, then bursting in, a stack of four or six Marines with rifles and pistols, firing and blasting from room to room." The onslaught—artillery, mortar shells, and bombs—destroyed 2,000 buildings and badly damaged 10,000 more.

To some, the outcome of Second Fallujah confirmed the effectiveness of sheer firepower; to others, the so-called victory came freighted with warning signs. Marines thought it a major success, one high officer declaring that they had "broken the back of the insurgency" by eliminating "this safe haven" and putting the insurgents "on the run." Their harsh methods, according to another marine officer, involved "individual Marines with small arms going from house to house, killing. We may not want to say that, but that's what it is about." One colonel was not so sure. "What's the impact on a ten-year-old kid when he goes back and sees his neighborhood destroyed? And what is he going to do when he is eighteen years old?" According to another officer, "The Battle of Fallujah was not a defeat. But we cannot afford many more victories like it."

Powell realized he no longer could support the war and on November 12 resigned as secretary of state. Bush moved quickly to replace him, asking Rice to move over to the State Department. The heavy burden Powell carried was a devastating loss of credibility attributable to his UN speech of February 2003. "I'm the one who made the television moment," he told the London *Daily Telegraph* following his resignation. "I was mightily disappointed when the sourcing of it all became very suspect and everything started to fall apart. The problem was stockpiles. None have been found. I don't think any will be found. . . . I will forever be known as the one who made the case."

Opposition to the war, meanwhile, intensified. Some senior advisers surprised the president by reporting that the war was not going well. One told him in November that "we weren't winning, and he was shocked." Con-

gressman John Murtha, a highly decorated marine veteran in Vietnam, introduced a resolution that same month calling for removing the troops from Iraq as soon as possible. A marine officer quoted in *Atlantic Monthly* warned, "We can lose in Iraq and destroy our Army, or we can just lose."

Shortly afterward, Army Colonel Derek Harvey warned of a long war. An intelligence specialist on Iraq, he held a doctorate in Islamic studies and won an audience with the president after presenting his gloomy findings to CIA and National Security Council officers. The insurgency, Harvey asserted, was "robust, it's well led, it's diverse. Absent some sort of reconciliation it's going to go on, and that risks a civil war." They rely heavily on Syria and others outside Iraq. The real problem, however, rests *inside* Iraq. At the heart of the insurgency was "the old Sunni oligarchy using religious nationalism as a motivating force. That's it in a nutshell."

Bush found this pessimism difficult to believe even after a special mission he sent to Iraq reached similar conclusions. Retired Army General Gary Luck returned in February 2005, declaring that security had dropped more than reported, the insurgency had grown, the Iraqi training program was inadequate, and American intelligence was poor. The president nonetheless retained his public optimism. Some weeks after this dire news, he awarded the Presidential Medal of Freedom to Franks, Bremer, and Tenet for making "our country more secure."

Rumsfeld likewise remained optimistic despite open discontent among U.S. troops. In a December 2004 meeting with National Guard units in Kuwait about to deploy to Iraq, the defense secretary was momentarily taken aback by the negativism expressed by the soldiers. "Our vehicles are not armored," complained a mechanic from Tennessee. "We're digging pieces of rusted scrap metal and compromised ballistic glass that's already been shot up . . . picking the best out of this scrap to put on our vehicles to take into combat. We do not have proper . . . vehicles to

Map 13
War in Iraq. Major battles of the Iraq War that began in March 2003. *(Source: author)*

carry with us north." The soldier's buddies broke out with applause, but Rumsfeld appeared unmoved. "As you know," he remarked, "you go to war with the Army you have. They're not the Army you might want or wish to have at a later time." That cold response deepened the resentment. When the questions persisted and the soldiers began mumbling to one another, he appealed to his age as a reason for having no suitable reply. "Settle down. Hell, I'm an old man and it's early in the morning."

Nor did Wolfowitz waver. Recent events in Iraq, he told the Senate Armed Services Committee in early 2005, upheld his position. "The secret security forces of the former regime—best analogized, I think, to the Gestapo and the SS of the Nazi regime—are now allied with new terrorists drawn from across the region. Like their Ba'athist allies, these new terrorists are ideologically opposed to democracy and fearful of what the success of freedom in this important Arab country will mean for them." By April, he had left the Pentagon to become, like McNamara following the Vietnam War, president of the World Bank. Wolfowitz harbored no misgivings about the war. "Three years is a very short time into this," he later declared. "War is a tough business. This has been a tough war. The early stages were much easier than we feared they would be, and the subsequent stages were much tougher than people anticipated."

In early May 2005, the administration's troubles intensified when the *Sunday Times* of London published the "Downing Street Memo." Written by a British official in the summer of 2002, it reported to Prime Minister Tony Blair that the White House had already decided to attack Iraq even though realizing it had sparse evidence of direct threats to the United States and needed to weave together a case for war. Sir Richard Dearlove, the chief of British intelligence MI-6, had met with Bush administration officials in late July and went home convinced that the White House had undergone "a perceptible shift in attitude" and considered military action "inevitable." President Bush sought Saddam's removal, based on "the conjunction of terrorism and WMD." Dearlove recommended contributing up to 40,000 British troops to the invasion even while noting that the "intelligence and facts were being fixed around the policy" and that Washington had engaged in "little discussion" of the postwar period. Blair agreed that the Bush administration's case was weak but thought it could justify military measures if the United Nations requested the inspectors' return and Saddam rejected the idea.

The American people's doubts about the war became clear in November 2006, when the Democrats emerged triumphant in the congressional elections. The results tipped the power balance in Congress in their favor and heightened pressure from the victors aligned with a few Republicans to phase down American involvement in the war as the first step toward ultimate withdrawal. The day following the elections, Rumsfeld resigned, replaced by a former CIA director and then president of Texas A&M University, Robert Gates.

The growing pressure for change received further impetus in early December, when the Iraq Study Group, a ten-member bipartisan panel appointed by Congress to investigate the Iraq War, made its recommendations. Headed by James Baker, a Republican and former secretary of state under the first President Bush, and Lee Hamilton, a Democrat and former U.S. representative, the advisers called for a phased withdrawal of American combat forces aimed at having them out by early 2008, a dialogue with Syria and Iran intended to internationalize the effort to stabilize Iraq and the Middle East, and new initiatives aimed at resolving the Israeli–Palestinian dispute. Baker warned that he and his colleagues had no "magic bullet" to settle the Iraq War. But the administration must focus on more than a military solution. It must seek "the active and constructive engagement of all governments that have an interest in avoiding chaos in Iraq." Hamilton concurred. "The task ahead of us is daunting . . . but it is not, by any means, lost."

The report encountered instant opposition. President Bush met with Tony Blair in a news conference the same day of its release and, for the first time, admitted to the need for a "new approach" to a "bad" situation in Iraq. He could not accept all recommendations but would seriously consider them. Three other studies would arrive on his desk in the near future—from the Pentagon, the State Department, and the National Security Council—and he intended to made decisions based on all four sets of recommendations. He would talk with Iran and Syria on only two conditions: Iran must halt its nuclear efforts, and Syria must stop helping the opposition groups in Lebanon, support its government of Prime Minister Fouad Siniora, and extend economic assistance to Iraq. Republican senator and former POW in Vietnam, John McCain, questioned the panel's military advice, and fellow Republican Senator Susan Collins of Maine joined Democratic Senator Joe Lieberman from Connecticut in criticizing the call for discussions with Iran. Iraqi President Jalai Talabani termed the conclusions "very dangerous" to his country's sovereignty and declared, "As a whole, I reject this report." Other critics simply dismissed the panel as the "Iraq Surrender Group."

By the fall of 2005, former Joint Chiefs Chair General Myers seemed confused about the war. He had just completed testimony before Congress that focused on his achievements in Iraq, but McCain was not convinced. "Things have not gone as we had planned or expected, nor as we were told by you, General Myers." The general abruptly changed his position by asserting that he had never been confident in the operation. In a statement that belied his well-known public pronouncements while heading the military effort as well as his remarks made just moments before in this congressional hearing, he declared that "I don't think this committee or the American public has ever heard me say that things are going very well in Iraq."

Ironically, as the public perception of the war became increasingly skeptical, Casey appeared to make progress with his counterinsurgency plan. The American troop level reached 159,000 by the end of the year as he turned first to Baghdad, then to an insurgent safe haven at Tall Afar in the northwest to close the Syrian border, and finally in the fall to the settled areas along the Euphrates valley between Baghdad and the border. The objective: clear and hold areas, which necessitated more American soldiers to clear and more Iraqis to hold. The insurgency had nonetheless heightened in ferocity as it developed napalmlike bombs fitted with propane and other weapons powerful enough to destroy armored vehicles. But the soldiers' emphasis was now on preparing the Iraqi security forces for taking over the operations and on engaging with the people to build trust.

"We are finally getting around to doing the right things," remarked an army reserve officer to a companion over coffee in a Baghdad hotel in the Green Zone. "I think we're getting better, I do." But, he pondered, "is it too little, too late?"

By the summer of 2008, the debate over the war had become embittered, particularly because the Bush administration had not justified its two chief reasons for going to war: to find WMD in Iraq and to establish its link to al-Qaeda. The focus on Saddam had seriously undercut the war on terrorism and, according to the CIA, made Iraq rather than Afghanistan the new "magnet for international terrorist camps." Bin Laden remained uncaught, even though Saddam was dead, hanged on December 29, 2006, after a highly publicized international trial. The U.S. claim to legitimacy in waging this preemptive war stood on shaky grounds with coalition members and had seriously hurt American credibility throughout the world. As David Kay asked over CNN, "How many people are going to believe us when we say, 'It's a slam dunk'—to use George Tenet's phrase—'Iran has nuclear weapons'? The answer is going to be, 'You said that before.'"

The president had meanwhile elevated his wartime objective of liberating Iraq from repression to nation building. In the language of Vietnam and the Cold War for which he had so roundly criticized Gore in the 2000 election, Bush sought to construct a democratic model in the global "struggle between good and evil." In his second inaugural address of January 20, 2005, he declared it "the policy of the United States to seek and support the growth of democratic movements and institutions in every nation and culture, with the ultimate goal of ending tyranny in the world." Cheney concurred. "The hopes of the civilized world ride with us."

Despite the president's May 2003 claim that the invasion "made our country more secure," the evidence shows that it destabilized the Middle East and *intensified* the threat to American and world security. More than 4,000 members of the U.S. military have died since the war began in March 2003, and the United States has spent in excess of $200 billion, only to see Iraq sink into sectarian violence that could lead to a civil war between two well-armed groups, the pro-Iranian Shiites in the national police and the anti-Iranian Sunnis in the army. The invasion stirred up a cauldron of trouble that had simmered for years and appeared ready to spread beyond national borders and develop into a high-stakes contest for Middle East oil. "We have lit multiple fuses" in the region that will cause "multiple explosions," lamented a marine specialist in counterinsurgency. "I'm thinking our grandkids could easily be there."

As Powell had warned, Iran has benefited from the Iraq War by seeking to build a nuclear capacity that, from the American perspective, poses a regional and perhaps global threat to peace. President Bush's verbal assaults on Iran have unnerved many who fear another preemptive strike. Zbigniew Brzezinski, national security adviser to President Jimmy Carter, warned that making war on Iran would be an even greater blunder than the one on Iraq. "I think of war with Iran as the ending of America's present role in the world," he declared in a *Washington Post* interview. "Iraq may have been a preview of that, but it's still redeemable if we get out fast. In a war with Iran, we'll get dragged down for twenty or thirty years. The world will condemn us. We will lose our position in the world." For decades, Iran and Iraq have balanced off each other, but the American assaults on both Afghanistan and Iraq have hurt Iran's two greatest enemies and made it, according to former CIA official Milt Bearden, "the biggest beneficiary of the war in Iraq."

Vice President Cheney nonetheless picked up the tempo against critics and drew a sharp Democratic retort. When congressional members voted for a nonbinding resolution against the president's call for troop and funding increases, he accused them of following "an antiwar strategy that's been called slow bleed; they're not supporting the troops, they are un-

dermining them." The discussion of withdrawal tells "the enemy to watch the clock and wait us out." Democratic House Speaker Nancy Pelosi immediately criticized the White House for continuing "an open-ended commitment in Iraq while brushing aside the advice of military leaders and the bipartisan Iraq Study Group, all of whom argue that the war in Iraq cannot be resolved militarily but only through diplomatic, economic and political means."

On March 19, 2007, the fourth anniversary of the war's beginning, President Bush appeared over national television, no longer ebullient as in the halcyon May 2003 days of "Mission Accomplished." Now, in the face of growing difficulties, he soberly declared that the war in Iraq "*can* be won."

Later that same month, the debate over the war heated up when Congress passed a resolution aimed at removing all American troops in 2008 and the president called for a troop "surge." Bush denounced the congressional action, calling it interference with the war effort and warning that he would veto the measure. Cheney told a Republican fund-raising group in Birmingham, Alabama, "When members of Congress speak not of victory but of time limits, deadlines, or other arbitrary measures, they're telling the enemy to simply watch the clock and wait us out. It's time the self-appointed strategists on Capitol Hill understood a very simple concept. You cannot win a war if you tell the enemy when you're going to quit," he declared to a standing ovation. The president would veto the legislation and he had enough supporters in Congress to sustain the veto. "And so it is pointless for the Democrats to continue pursuing this legislation."

House Majority Leader Steny Hoyer, a Democrat from Maryland, responded that "it is not 'pointless' for the Congress to heed the will of the American people; however, it is pointless for this Administration to continue with its failing stay-the-course strategy." Howard Dean, the chair of the Democratic National Committee, asserted that "Democrats will not be lectured to, nor have our patriotism questioned by an administration that sent our troops off to war without the proper life-saving equipment, a clear plan for success or the quality care they deserve when they return home."

In May 2007, the president vetoed the congressional bill, and Congress could not amass enough votes for an override. The president then secured his troop surge. After a while, violence dropped in Iraq, but the war drummed on.

As of this writing, in the summer of 2008, the volatile situation in the Middle East remains the chief preoccupation of the Bush administration and still shows no signs of significant improvement. Five years of war have led to 33,000 U.S. military casualties, including 4,000 dead, along with untold thousands of Iraqi deaths, including Security Forces and civilians. The president has called for a peace plan by the end of the year but, according to critics, unwisely refuses to approve all-inclusive negotiations because, he believes, such a move would signal appeasement of the enemy. The war in Iraq has continued without an end in sight and hence with no discernible timetable for a meaningful withdrawal of American forces. The war on terrorism has not abated, continuing to mount casualty rates on all sides and fueled by intermittent warnings of new al-Qaeda attacks.

In late May, a new book appeared by a Bush insider that heated the public debate over the issues that have dogged the Bush administration, and in particular the war in Iraq. Scott McClellan, longtime friend of the president and his press secretary from mid-2003 through spring 2006, published an explosive memoir that shot to the top of the bestseller list even before its official release. Titled *What Happened: Inside the White House and Washington's Culture of Deception*, it accused the president and his tight circle of advisers of deceiving Americans about a number of matters, including the reasons for going to war with Iraq. A major breaking point for McClellan was the Valerie Plame controversy. After receiving orders to assure the press that White House aides Karl Rove and Lewis Libby had not leaked the CIA operative's identity, he learned from a criminal investigation that they had been responsible and that he had been misled. Indeed, McClellan thought Vice President Cheney was "possibly" involved as well. But the shocker was the president's admission to McClellan that he had leaked information on the October 2002 National Intelligence Estimate that discredited Plame's husband, Joseph Wilson, for accusing the White House of misleading the country into war with Iraq.

The invasion of Iraq, McClellan knew at the time, was a "serious strategic blunder." The United States must wage war only when necessary, he declared, "and the Iraq war was not necessary." The White House atmosphere, McClellan wrote, was "insular, secretive, and combative," its principals always acting with one eye on the political campaign and creating a "culture of deception." The president and his advisers knew that "the American people would almost certainly not support a war launched primarily for the ambitious purpose of transforming the Middle East." So he approved "a strategy for selling the war that was less than candid and honest." Its underlying rationale lay in "a philosophy of coercive democracy, a belief that Iraq was ripe for conversion from a dictatorship into a beacon of liberty through the use of force, and a conviction that this could be achieved at nominal cost." Thus would the Iraqi people "welcome and embrace freedom." To undercut criticism of what McClellan called a "carefully orchestrated campaign to shape and manipulate sources of public approval" for war in the spring of 2003, the president had leaked portions of the NIE report erroneously declaring that Iraq had weapons of mass destruction.

Not surprisingly, McClellan came under immediate attack. His detractors accused him of betrayal and wondered why he waited until the midst of an election campaign to publish his charges. Some charged him with merely wanting to sell books; others thought him lashing back for being forced to resign; still others claimed the administration fell victim to faulty intelligence. The present press secretary, Dana Perino, expressed sympathy for McClellan. "For those of us who fully supported him, before, during, and after he was press secretary, we are puzzled. It is sad. This is not the Scott we knew." Rove characterized McClellan's writings as that of a "left-wing blogger," and claimed he should have expressed his "moral qualms" earlier. The president refused to respond to McClellan's accusations, derisively saying he had "more pressing matters than to spend time commenting on books by former staffers."

Yet support for many of McClellan's charges came with the June release of a Senate Intelligence Committee report accusing the president and vice president of misleading the nation into war. The evidence compiled by the bipartisan group was signed by ten members, including two Republicans, but came with the strong dissent of five other Republicans; yet it concluded that intelligence findings did not find either a connection between al-Qaeda and Saddam Hussein or the existence of weapons of mass destruction in Iraq. "In making the case for war," argued the committee chair, Democratic Senator Jay Rockefeller of West Virginia, "the administration repeatedly presented intelligence as fact when in reality it was unsubstantiated, contradicted, or even non-existent." The White House relied on "flawed evidence" in convincing the American people that the Iraqi threat was greater than it was. "Sadly, the Bush administration led the nation into war under false pretenses."

Most ominous on this pre-November presidential election eve is the onset of what numerous observers have called a new Cold War—a burgeoning U.S. contest with Iran in league with Syria and terrorist groups Hamas and Hezbollah. As secretary of state, Colin Powell had warned the president before the U.S. invasion of Iraq that to disable that country would upset the delicate balance in the Middle East and invite Iran to fill the power vacuum. The Republican candidate for the presidency, John McCain from Arizona, has followed the Bush approach of wanting to stay the course in Iraq and refusing to negotiate with the enemy, claiming that to engage in talks signaled appeasement. Democratic candidate Barack Obama of Illinois, however, has offered to discuss the matter with any group, arguing that the appeasement of the 1930s came from giving in to Hitler's demands, not from meeting with him. Having voted against the invasion of Iraq, Obama has advocated a phased withdrawal from a war he considers a major mistake. These problems and more await the new president in 2009.

Selected Readings

Allawi, Ali A. *The Occupation of Iraq: Winning the War, Losing the Peace.* 2007.

Anderson, Terry H. "George W. Bush, Dick Cheney, and the Origins of the Iraq War." In J. Garry Clifford and Theodore A. Wilson, eds., *Presidents, Diplomats, and Other Mortals*, 231–49. 2007.

Baker, James A., III, and Lee H. Hamilton. *The Iraq Study Group Report: The Way Forward—A New Approach.* 2006.

Bamford, James. *A Pretext for War: 9/11, Iraq, and the Abuse of America's Intelligence Agencies.* 2004.

Blix, Hans. *Disarming Iraq.* 2004.

Bose, Meena. "Comment: Defining U.S. Foreign Policy in the Post-9/11 World." *Diplomatic History*, 26 (2002): 619–26.

Bremer, Paul, III. *My Year in Iraq: The Struggle to Build a Future of Hope.* 2005.

Brigham, Robert K. *Is Iraq Another Vietnam?* 2006.

Brzezinski, Zbigniew. *Second Chance: Three Presidents and the Crisis of American Superpower.* 2007.

Bush, George H.W., and Brent Scowcroft. *A World Transformed.* 1998.

Byrd, Robert C. *Losing America: Confronting a Reckless and Arrogant Presidency.* 2004.

Clarke, Richard A. *Against All Enemies: Inside America's War on Terror.* 2004.

Cohen, Warren I. *America's Falling Empire: U.S. Foreign Relations since the Cold War.* 2005.

Everest, Larry. *Oil, Power, and Empire: Iraq and the U.S. Global Order.* 2004.

Gaddis, John L. *Surprise, Security, and the American Experience.* 2004.

Gardner, Lloyd C., and Marilyn B. Young, eds. *Iraq and the Lessons of Vietnam, or, How Not to Learn from the Past.* 2007.

Gordon, Michael R., and Bernard E. Trainor. *Cobra II: The Inside Story of the Invasion and Occupation of Iraq.* 2006.

Keegan, John. *The Iraq War.* 2005.

Lowry, Richard S. *Marines in the Garden of Eden: The True Story of Seven Bloody Days in Iraq.* 2006.

May, Ernest R. *The 9/11 Commission Report with Related Documents.* 2007.

McClellan, Scott. *What Happened: Inside the Bush White House and Washington's Culture of Deception.* 2008.

Offner, Arnold A. "Harry S. Truman, George W. Bush, and the Perils of Regime Change." In J. Garry Clifford and Theodore A. Wilson, eds., *Presidents, Diplomats, and Other Mortals*, 281–304. 2007.

Packer, George. *The Assassins' Gate: America in Iraq.* 2005.

Pillar, Paul R. "Intelligence, Policy, and the War in Iraq." *Foreign Affairs* 85 (March/April 2006): 15–27.

Pollock, Kenneth M. *The Persian Puzzle: The Conflict between Iran and America.* 2004.

Powers, Thomas. "The Vanishing Case for War." *New York Review of Books* 50 (December 4, 2003): 1–12 (Internet copy).

Prados, John. *Hoodwinked: The Documents That Reveal How Bush Sold Us a War.* 2004.

Prestowitz, Clyde. *Rogue Nation: American Unilateralism and the Failure of Good Intentions.* 2003.

Ricks, Thomas E. *Fiasco: The American Military Adventure in Iraq.* 2006.

Risen, James. *State of War: The Secret History of the CIA and the Bush Administration.* 2006.

Suskind, Ron. *The One Percent Doctrine: Deep Inside America's Pursuit of Its Enemies Since 9/11.* 2006.

———. *The Price of Loyalty: George W. Bush, the White House, and the Education of Paul O'Neill.* 2004.

Tenet, George J. *At the Center of the Storm: My Years at the CIA.* 2007.

The 9/11 Commission Report: Final Report of the National Commission on Terrorist Attacks Upon the United States. 2004.

Unger, Craig. "The War They Wanted, the Lies They Needed." *Vanity Fair* (July 2006): 93–97, 149–56.

Weiner, Tim. *Legacy of Ashes: The History of the CIA.* 2007.

Wilson, Joseph C. *The Politics of Truth: Inside the Lies That Led to War and Betrayed My Wife's CIA Identity.* 2004.

Woodward, Bob. *Plan of Attack.* 2004.

———. *State of Denial.* 2006.

Wright, Lawrence. *The Looming Tower: Al-Qaeda and the Road to 9/11.* 2006.

INDEX

ABOUT THE AUTHOR

Howard Jones received a Ph.D. from Indiana University and taught at the University of Nebraska before coming to the University of Alabama in 1974. He is now Research Professor of History. A recipient of both the John F. Burnum Distinguished Faculty Award for teaching and research and the Blackmon-Moody Outstanding Professor Award, he teaches courses in American foreign relations and the U.S.–Vietnam War.

He is the author or editor of more than a dozen books, including *To the Webster-Ashburton Treaty: A Study in Anglo-American Relations, 1783–1843* (1977)—recipient of the Phi Alpha Theta Book Award and nominated for the Pulitzer Prize and the Stuart L. Bernath Book Award; *Mutiny on the Amistad: The Saga of a Slave Revolt and Its Impact on American Abolition, Law, and Diplomacy* (1987, revised 1997)—used in writing the screenplay for Steven Spielberg's movie *Amistad* and a selection of the Book-of-the-Month Club, the History Book Club, and the Quality Paperbacks Book Club; *"A New Kind of War": America's Global Strategy and the Truman Doctrine in Greece* (1989)—nominated for the Harry S. Truman Book Award and for the Phi Alpha Theta Book Award; with Randall B. Woods, *Dawning of the Cold War: The United States' Quest for Order* (1991)—nominated for the Warren F. Kuehl Award and for the George Louis Beer Prize; *Union in Peril: The Crisis over British Intervention in the Civil War* (1992)—a History Book Club Selection and winner of the Phi Alpha Theta Book Award; with Donald A. Rakestraw, *Prologue to Manifest Destiny: Anglo-American Relations in the 1840s* (1997)—recognized by *Choice* magazine as one of the "Outstanding Academic Books" for 1997; *Abraham Lincoln and a New Birth of Freedom: The Union and Slavery in the Diplomacy of the Civil War* (1999)—nominated for the Lincoln Prize and the Bancroft Prize; and *Death of a Generation: How the Assassinations of Diem and JFK Prolonged the Vietnam War* (2003)—recognized by *Choice* magazine as one of the "Outstanding Academic Books" for 2003. He has published articles in several journals, including one in the *Journal of American History* that was the centerpiece of a forum and titled "Cinqué of the *Amistad* a Slave Trader? Perpetuating a Myth." He has just published a book titled *The Bay of Pigs* and is presently working on a study of Union and Confederate diplomacy during the Civil War.